SITE DETAILS

Warning and Disclaimer

Acknowledgments

This book is a combination effort of LANDCADD, Inc. and VERSEN-LANDSCAPE ARCHITECTURE. Significant contributions to this publication were made by Wanda K. Huh, Ken Mathis and Frank Weiss. Their efforts are deeply appreciated.

Trademarks

Some of the details provided in this book are manufacturer specific. These include:

- Irrigation details by Weathermatic
- Stamped paving patterns by Bomanite
- Site furniture by AlphaPrecast

SITE DETAILS

Gregory W. Jameson, ASLA
Michael A. Versen, ASLA

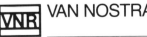

VNR VAN NOSTRAND REINHOLD
New York

Library of Congress Catalog Card Number 88-32963

ISBN 0-914886-46-0

Printed in the United States of America

Van Nostrand Reinhold
115 Fifth Avenue
New York, New York 10003

Van Nostrand Reinhold International Company Limited
11 New Fetter Lane
London EC4P 4EE, England

Van Nostrand Reinhold
480 La Trobe Street
Melbourne, Victoria 3000, Australia

Macmillan of Canada
Division of Canada Publishing Corporation
164 Commander Boulevard
Agincourt, Ontario M1S 3C7, Canada

16 15 14 13 12 11 10 9 8 7 6 5 4 3 2 1

Library of Congress Cataloging in Publication Data

Jameson, Gregory W., 1957-
Site details.

Chiefly ill.
1. Building sites--Planning--Data Processing.
2. Architecture--Details--Data Processing. 3. Computer-aided design. I. Versen, Michael A., 1947- II. Title.
NA2728.J36 1989 720'.28'40285 88-32963
ISBN 0-914886-46-0

CONTENTS

INTRODUCTION

Construction detailing in the design/engineering profession is changing through the use of computers. Computer generated drawings have improved to the point of surpassing the quality and drawing process of hand drawn work. The flexibility in modifying work and ease of information transferral between disciplines is moving all levels of professional practice toward a CAD system.

This book illustrates site construction details in a consistent and uniform drawing format of line types and lettering styles. This concept is to provide the user with a unified system of hundreds of construction details.

These construction details cover a wide range of topics for site planning, engineering and landscape architectural design. They are arranged alphabetically by topic. They were plotted on a Hewlett-Packard Laser Jet Series II printer at a resolution of 300 dots per inch. Each detail is presented at a scale that can be used as is, or is easily enlarged or reduced for use with a variety of projects and drawings. While this material is copyrighted, we encourage the use of these details.

This collection of drawings represent work produced by experienced landscape architects utilizing a LANDCADD/AutoCAD system. This work was produced for LANDCADD by the authors as an integrated part of the LANDCADD site planning and design software system. LANDCADD, the USA's leading site planning software system offers these details on diskette in either .DWG or .DXF format. As computer generated drawings, the details can be easily modified and re-plotted for an unlimited variety of alternatives.

Happy detailing!

Arbors

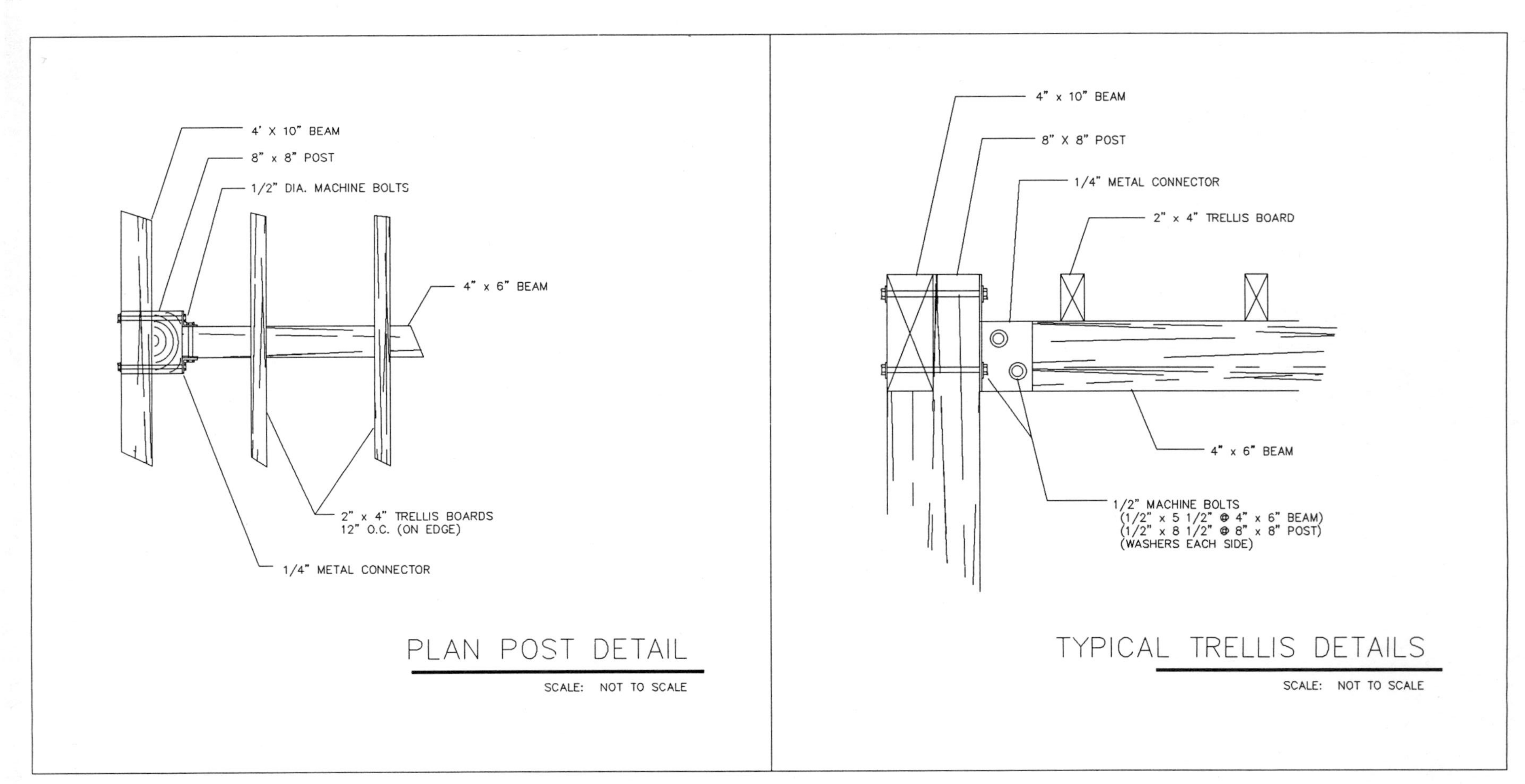

4' X 10" BEAM
8" x 8" POST
1/2" DIA. MACHINE BOLTS
4" x 6" BEAM
2" x 4" TRELLIS BOARDS
12" O.C. (ON EDGE)
1/4" METAL CONNECTOR
PLAN POST DETAIL
SCALE: NOT TO SCALE
4" x 10" BEAM
8" X 8" POST
1/4" METAL CONNECTOR
2" x 4" TRELLIS BOARD
4" x 6" BEAM
1/2" MACHINE BOLTS
(1/2" x 5 1/2" ⊕ 4" x 6" BEAM)
(1/2" x 8 1/2" ⊕ 8" x 8" POST)
(WASHERS EACH SIDE)
TYPICAL TRELLIS DETAILS
SCALE: NOT TO SCALE

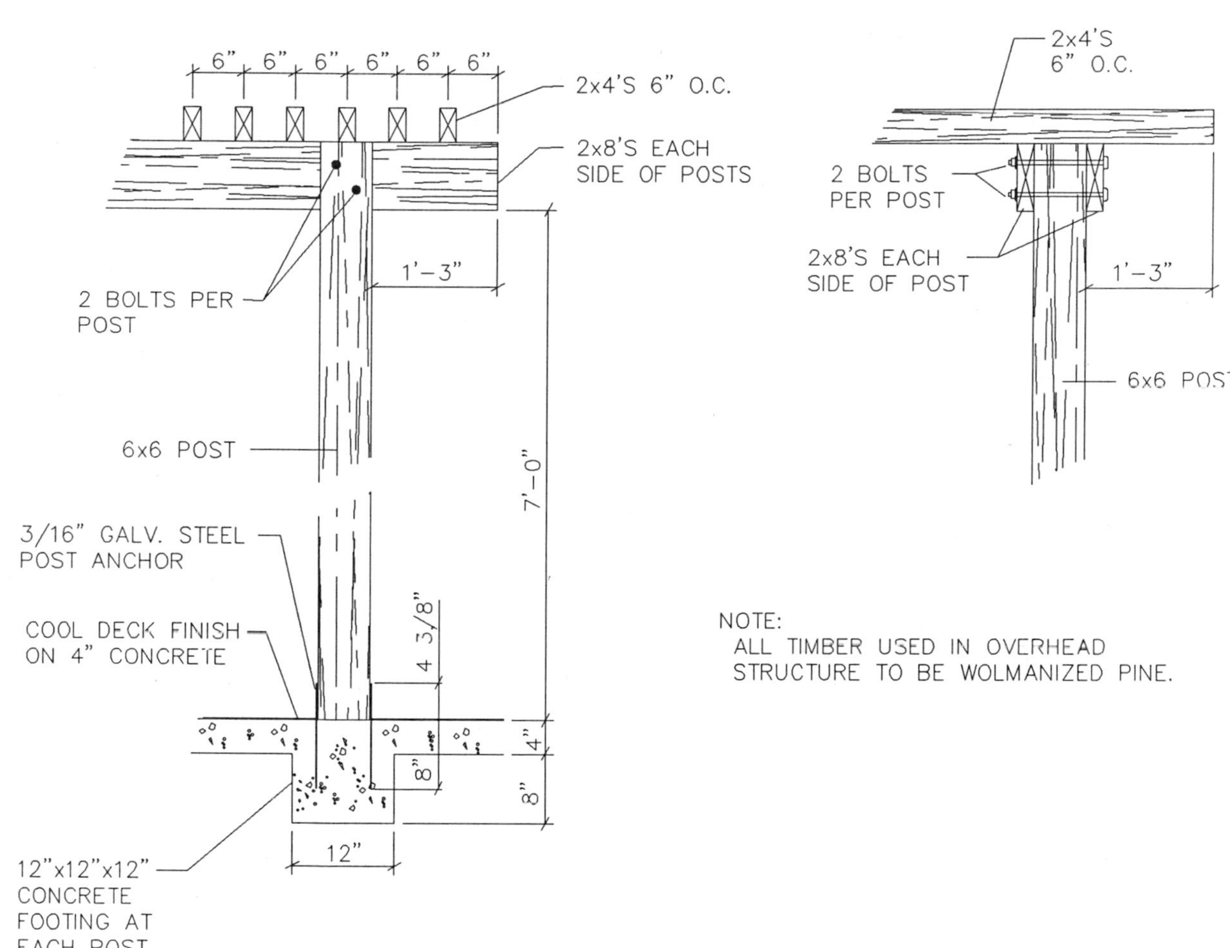
6"
6"
6"
6"
6"
6"
2x4'S 6" O.C.
2x8'S EACH SIDE OF POSTS
2 BOLTS PER POST
1'–3"
6x6 POST
7'–0"
3/16" GALV. STEEL POST ANCHOR
COOL DECK FINISH ON 4" CONCRETE
4 3/8"
4"
8"
8"
12"
12"x12"x12" CONCRETE FOOTING AT EACH POST
2x4'S 6" O.C.
2 BOLTS PER POST
2x8'S EACH SIDE OF POST
1'–3"
6x6 POST

NOTE:
ALL TIMBER USED IN OVERHEAD STRUCTURE TO BE WOLMANIZED PINE.

OVERHEAD STRUCTURE

SCALE: NOT TO SCALE

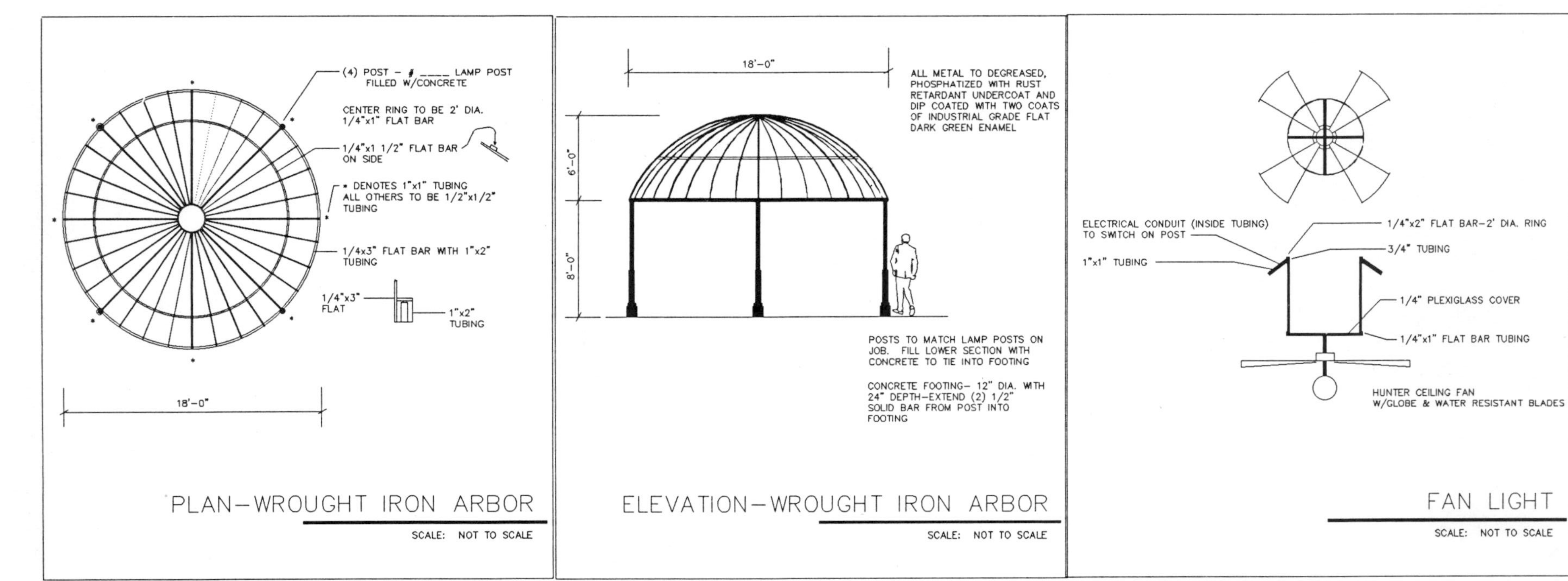
(4) POST - # ____ LAMP POST FILLED W/CONCRETE
CENTER RING TO BE 2' DIA. 1/4"x1" FLAT BAR
1/4"x1 1/2" FLAT BAR ON SIDE
* DENOTES 1"x1" TUBING ALL OTHERS TO BE 1/2"x1/2" TUBING
1/4x3" FLAT BAR WITH 1"x2" TUBING
1/4"x3" FLAT
1"x2" TUBING
18'-0"
PLAN-WROUGHT IRON ARBOR
SCALE: NOT TO SCALE
18'-0"
6'-0"
8'-0"
ALL METAL TO DEGREASED, PHOSPHATIZED WITH RUST RETARDANT UNDERCOAT AND DIP COATED WITH TWO COATS OF INDUSTRIAL GRADE FLAT DARK GREEN ENAMEL
POSTS TO MATCH LAMP POSTS ON JOB. FILL LOWER SECTION WITH CONCRETE TO TIE INTO FOOTING
CONCRETE FOOTING- 12" DIA. WITH 24" DEPTH-EXTEND (2) 1/2" SOLID BAR FROM POST INTO FOOTING
ELEVATION-WROUGHT IRON ARBOR
SCALE: NOT TO SCALE
ELECTRICAL CONDUIT (INSIDE TUBING) TO SWITCH ON POST
1"x1" TUBING
1/4"x2" FLAT BAR-2' DIA. RING
3/4" TUBING
1/4" PLEXIGLASS COVER
1/4"x1" FLAT BAR TUBING
HUNTER CEILING FAN W/GLOBE & WATER RESISTANT BLADES
FAN LIGHT
SCALE: NOT TO SCALE

Curbs & Bumper Stops

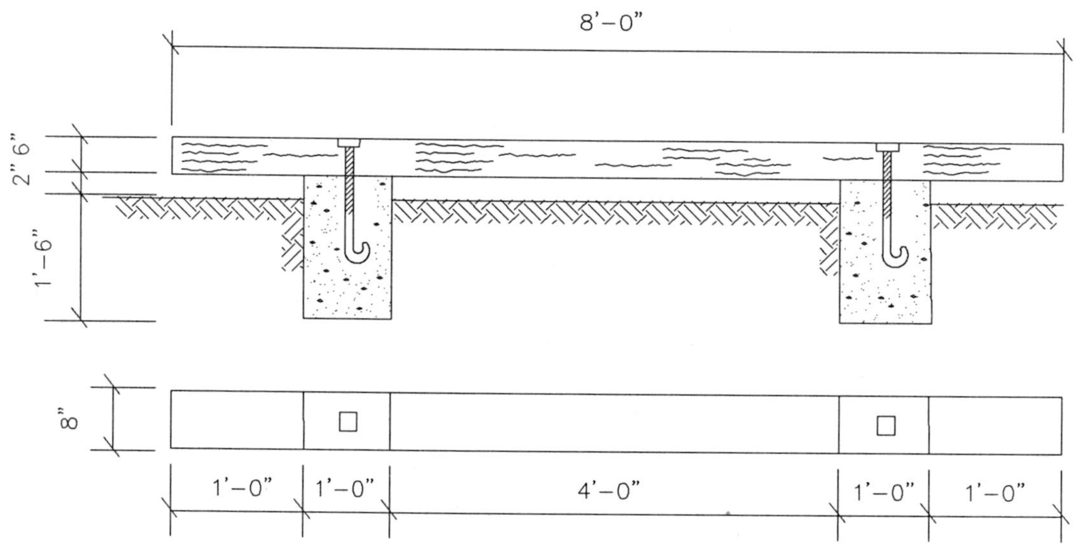
NEW CREOSOTED TREATED RAILROAD TIE
BOLTED W/THREADED 3/4" REINF. RODS
W/WASHERS TO CONCRETE BASE.
8'-0"
2" 6"
1'-6"
8"
1'-0"
1'-0"
4'-0"
1'-0"
1'-0"

RAILROAD TIE BUMPER STOP

SCALE: NOT TO SCALE

BRICK PAVERS TO MATCH EXISTING
BRICK PAVEMENT ON SITE.
USE 1/4" MORTAR JOINTS

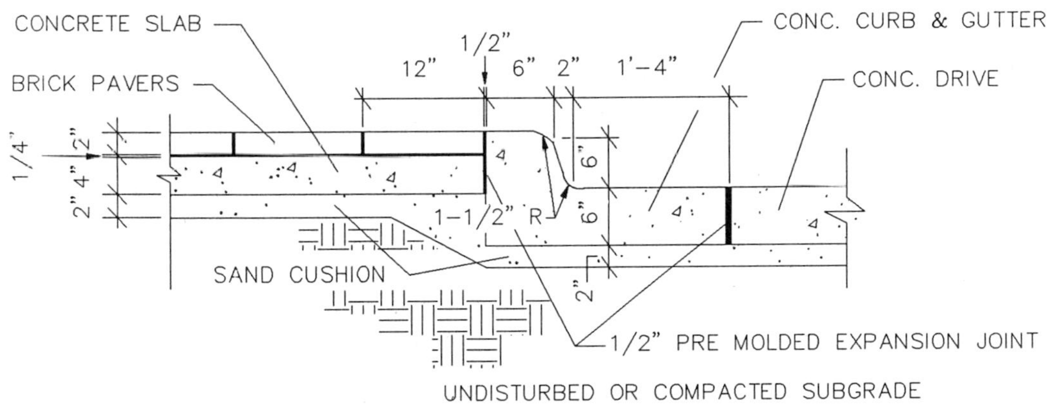

CONCRETE SLAB
BRICK PAVERS
CONC. CURB & GUTTER
CONC. DRIVE
1/2"
12"
6"
2"
1'-4"
1/4"
2"
4"
2"
6"
6"
1-1/2" R
2"
SAND CUSHION
1/2" PRE MOLDED EXPANSION JOINT
UNDISTURBED OR COMPACTED SUBGRADE

BRICK TO CURB SECTION

SCALE: NOT TO SCALE

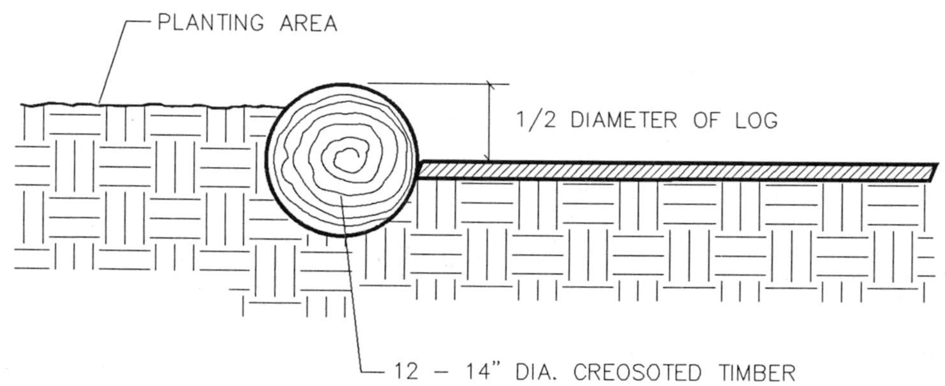
PLANTING AREA
1/2 DIAMETER OF LOG
12 – 14" DIA. CREOSOTED TIMBER

PARKING AREA DIVIDERS

SCALE: NOT TO SCALE

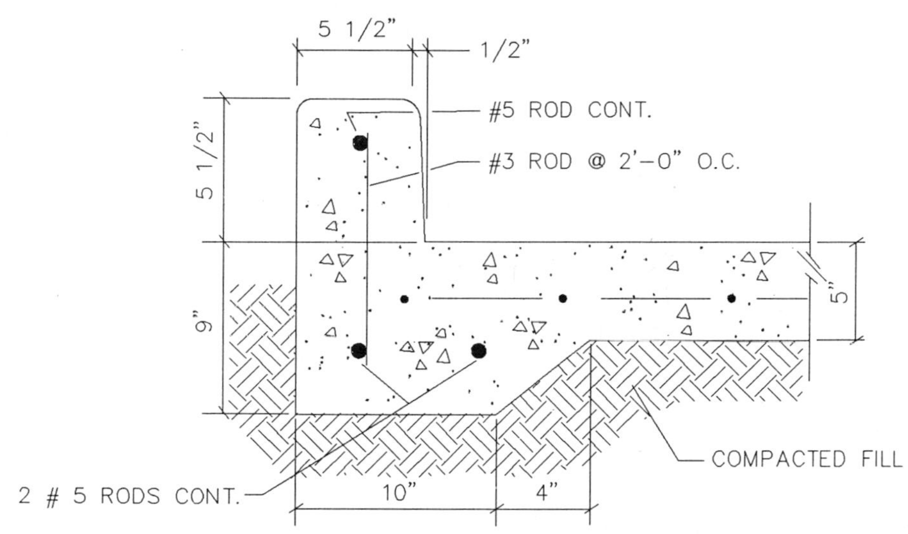
5 1/2"
1/2"
#5 ROD CONT.
#3 ROD @ 2'-0" O.C.
5 1/2"
9"
5"
COMPACTED FILL
2 # 5 RODS CONT.
10"
4"

CURB DETAIL AT CONCRETE DRIVE

SCALE: NOT TO SCALE

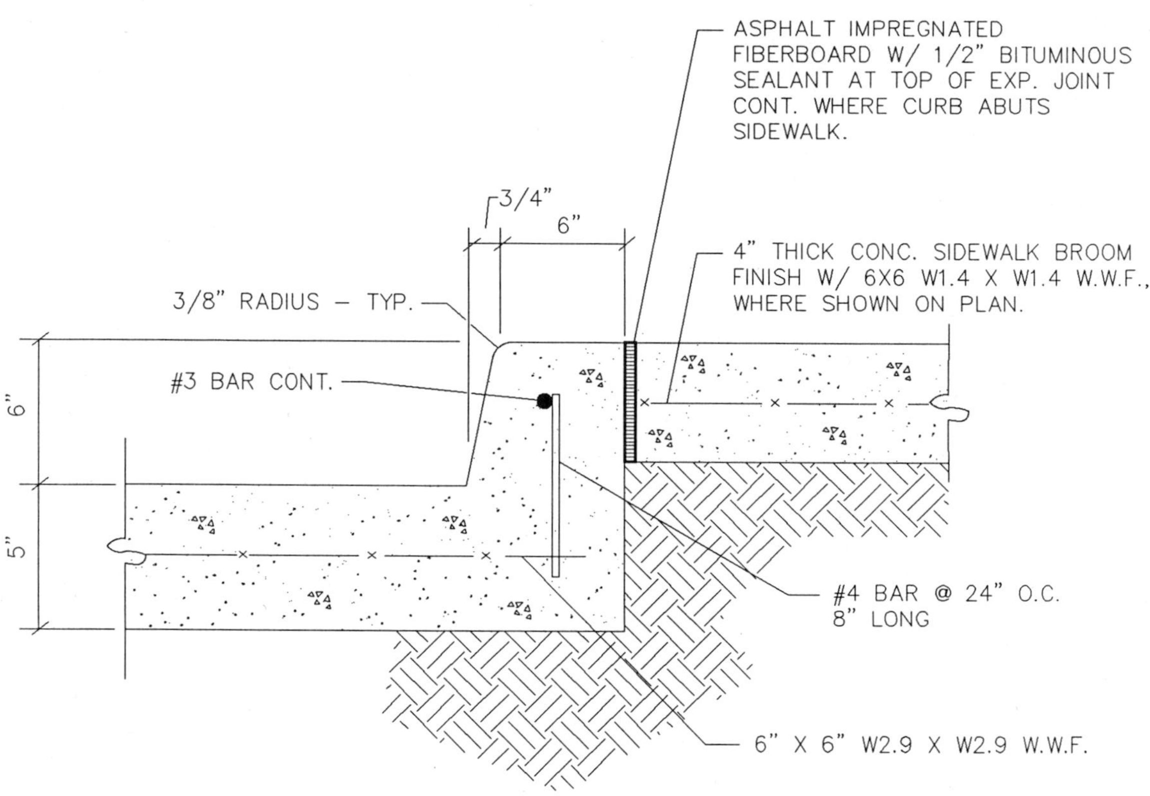
ASPHALT IMPREGNATED FIBERBOARD W/ 1/2" BITUMINOUS SEALANT AT TOP OF EXP. JOINT CONT. WHERE CURB ABUTS SIDEWALK.
3/4"
6"
3/8" RADIUS – TYP.
4" THICK CONC. SIDEWALK BROOM FINISH W/ 6X6 W1.4 X W1.4 W.W.F., WHERE SHOWN ON PLAN.
#3 BAR CONT.
6"
5"
#4 BAR @ 24" O.C. 8" LONG
6" X 6" W2.9 X W2.9 W.W.F.

CONCRETE CURB @ WALK

SCALE: NOT TO SCALE

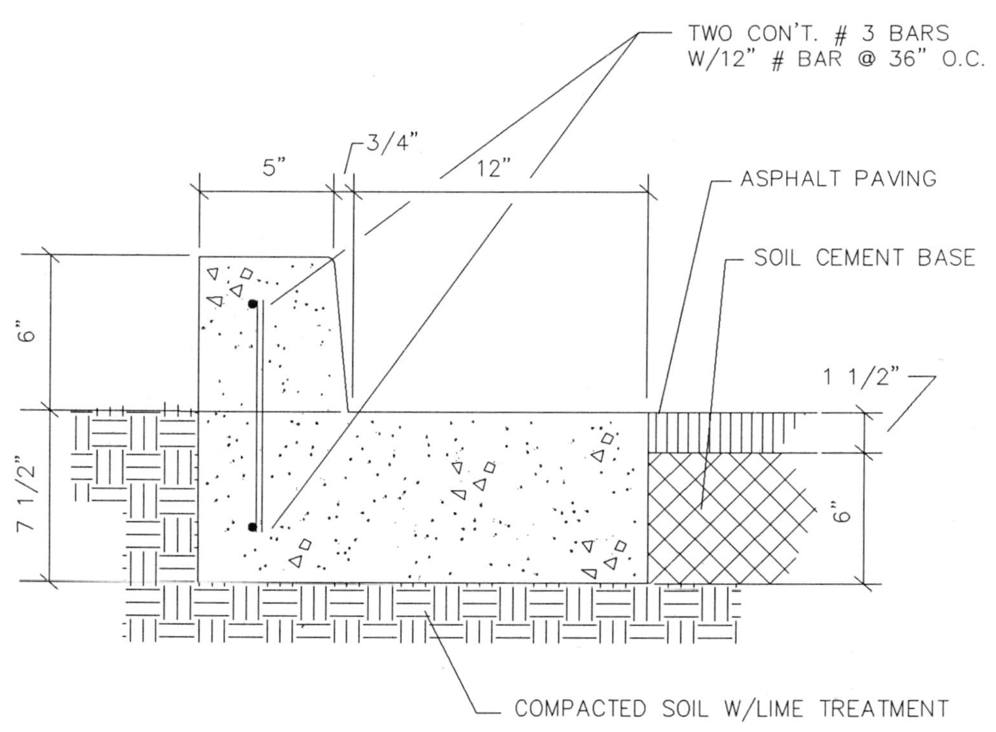
TWO CON'T. # 3 BARS
W/12" # BAR @ 36" O.C.
3/4"
5"
12"
ASPHALT PAVING
SOIL CEMENT BASE
6"
1 1/2"
7 1/2"
6"
COMPACTED SOIL W/LIME TREATMENT

CURB @ ASPHALT

SCALE: NOT TO SCALE

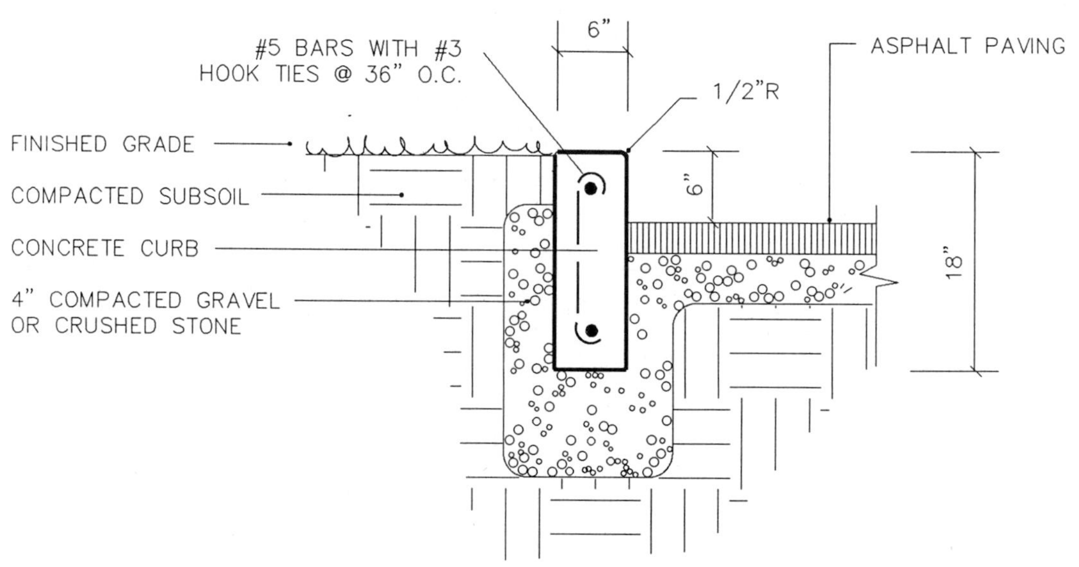
#5 BARS WITH #3
HOOK TIES @ 36" O.C.
6"
ASPHALT PAVING
1/2"R
FINISHED GRADE
COMPACTED SUBSOIL
CONCRETE CURB
4" COMPACTED GRAVEL
OR CRUSHED STONE
6"
18"

CONCRETE CURB

SCALE: NOT TO SCALE

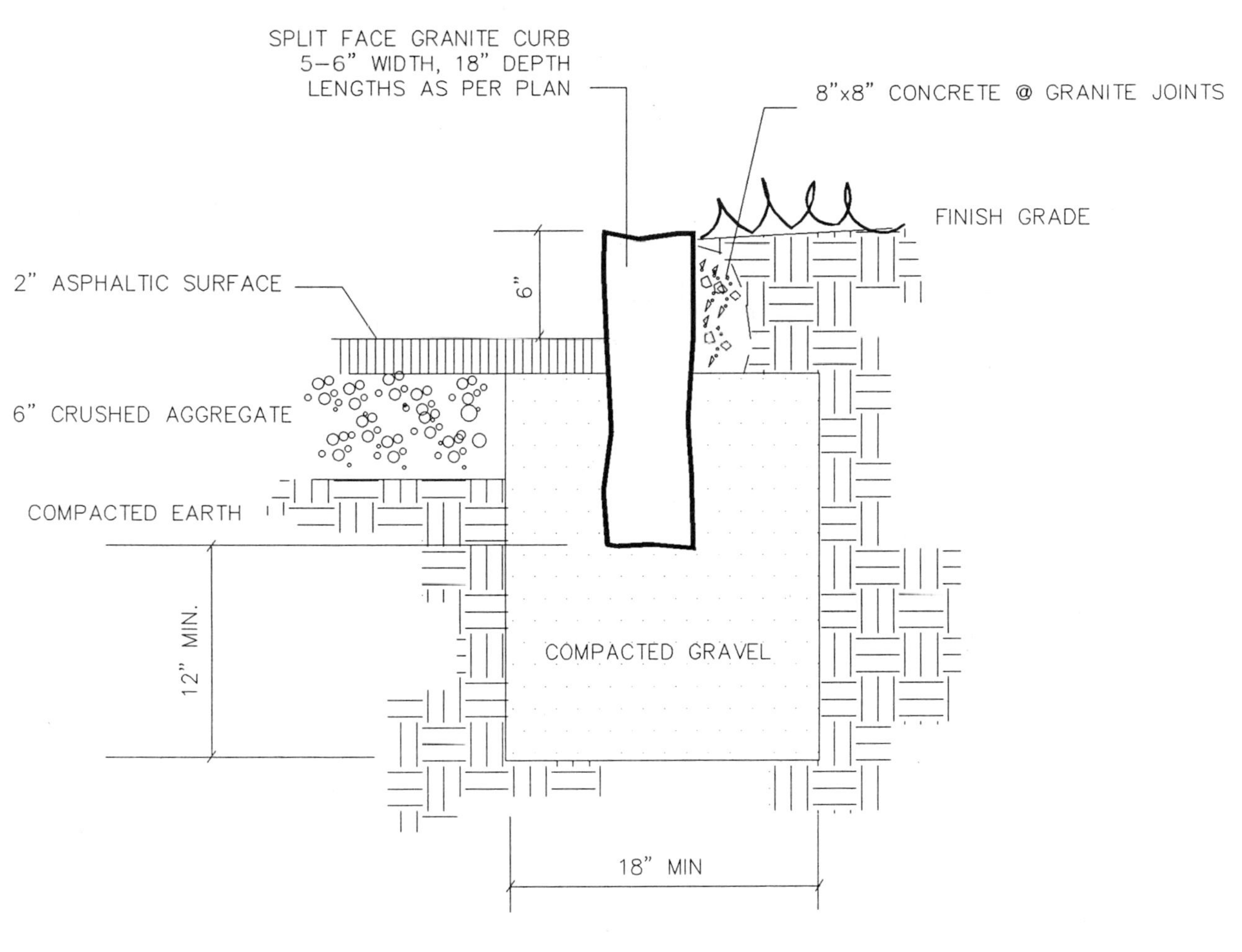
SPLIT FACE GRANITE CURB
5–6" WIDTH, 18" DEPTH
LENGTHS AS PER PLAN
8"x8" CONCRETE @ GRANITE JOINTS
FINISH GRADE
2" ASPHALTIC SURFACE
6"
6" CRUSHED AGGREGATE
COMPACTED EARTH
12" MIN.
COMPACTED GRAVEL
18" MIN

GRANITE CURB @ ASPHALT WALK

SCALE: NOT TO SCALE

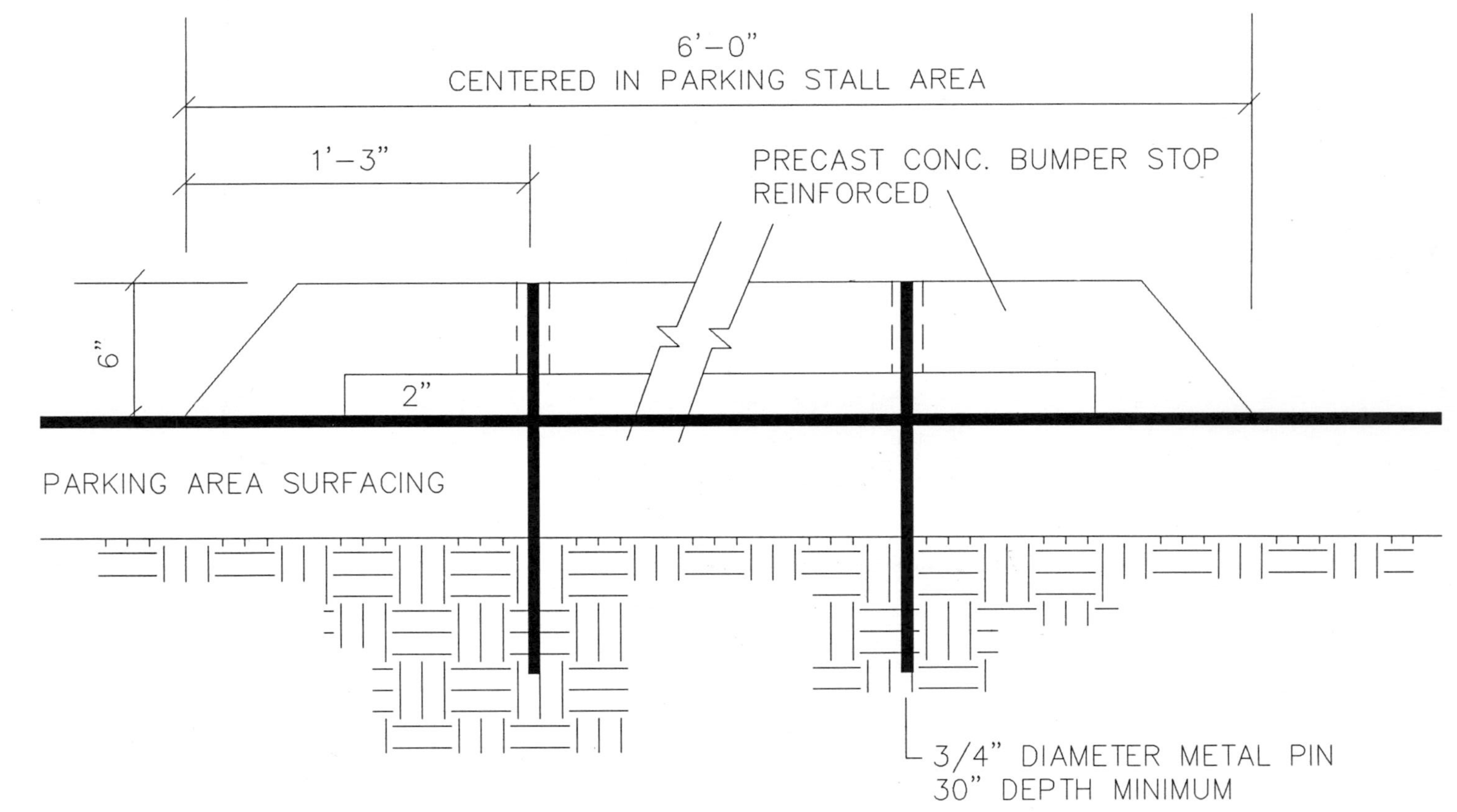
6'–0"
CENTERED IN PARKING STALL AREA
1'–3"
PRECAST CONC. BUMPER STOP
REINFORCED
6"
2"
PARKING AREA SURFACING
3/4" DIAMETER METAL PIN
30" DEPTH MINIMUM

PRECAST CONCRETE BUMPER STOP

SCALE: NOT TO SCALE

Decks & Bridges

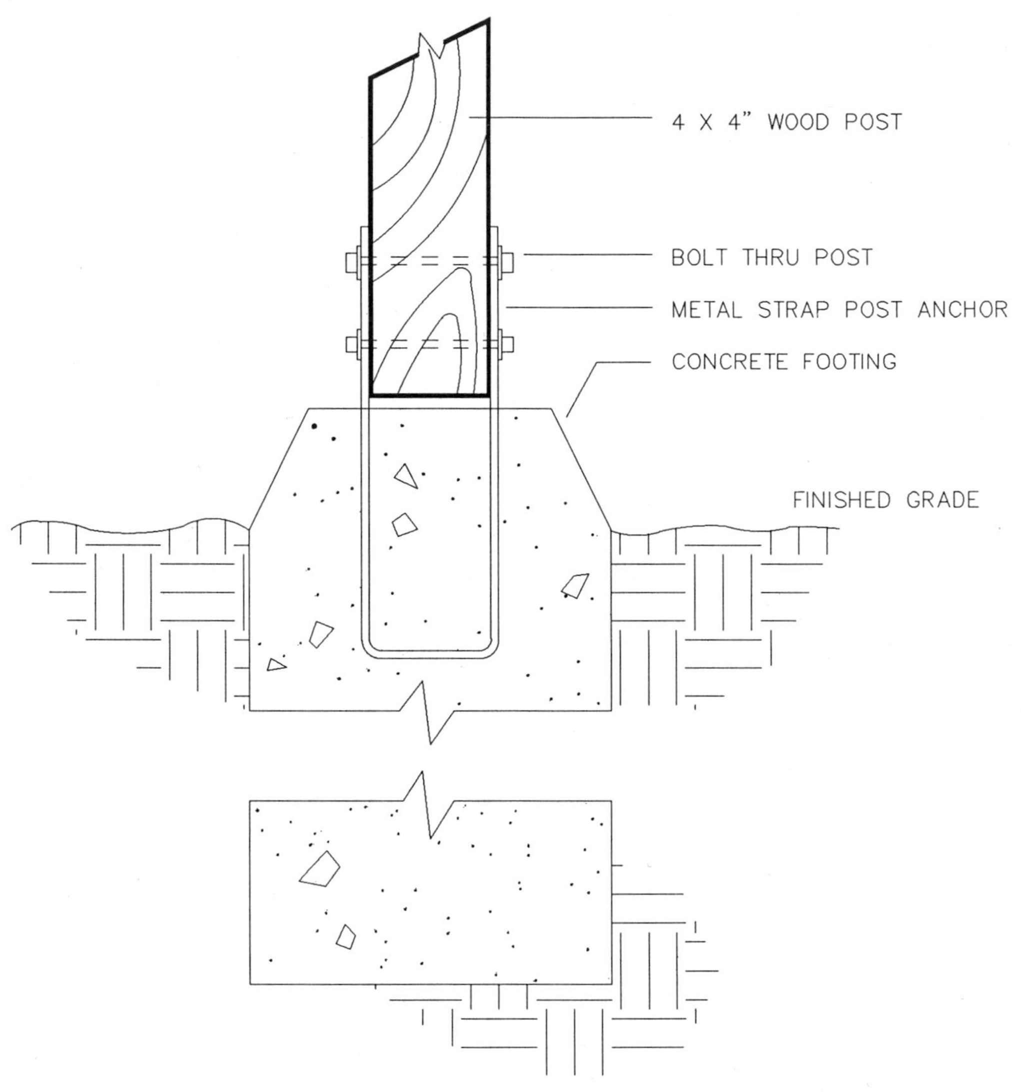

4 X 4" WOOD POST
BOLT THRU POST
METAL STRAP POST ANCHOR
CONCRETE FOOTING
FINISHED GRADE

POST TO FOOTING W/ SADDLE ANCHOR

SCALE: NOT TO SCALE

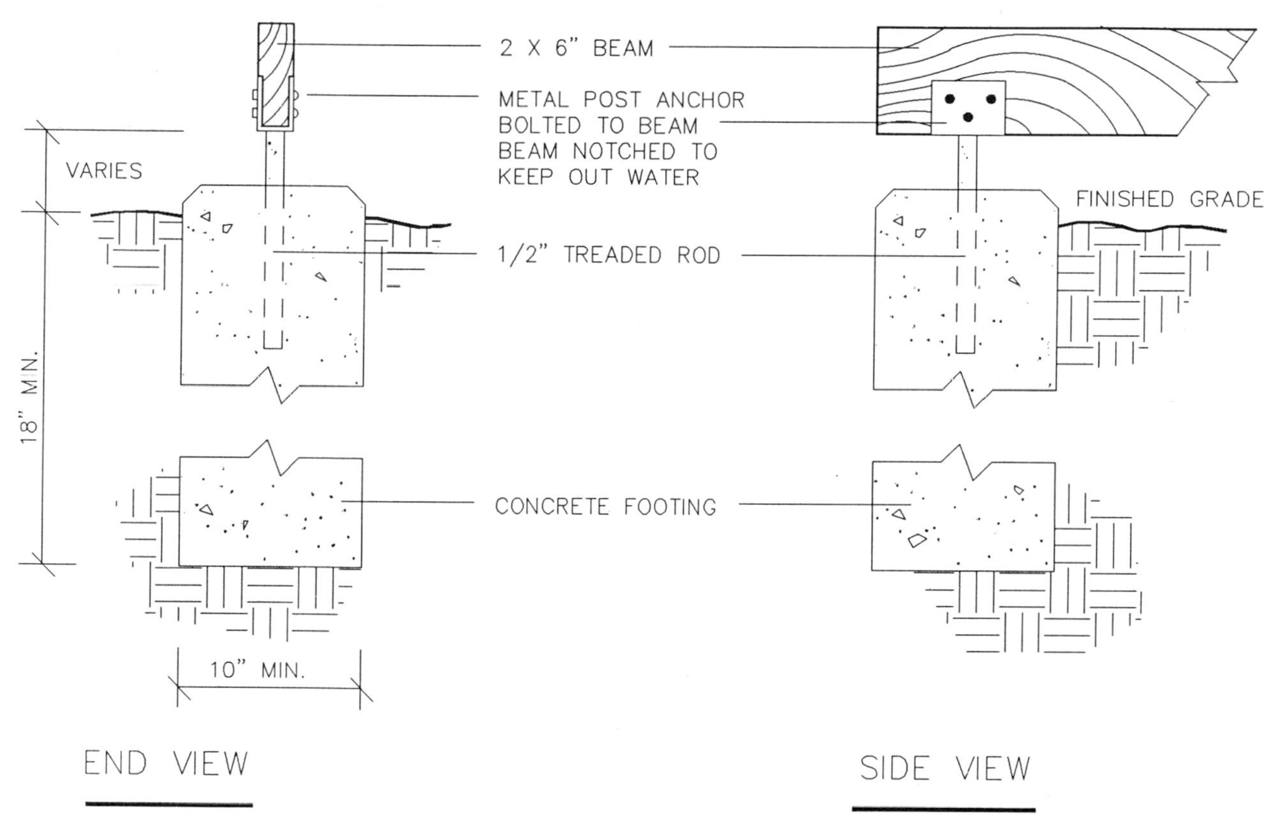
2 X 6" BEAM
METAL POST ANCHOR
BOLTED TO BEAM
BEAM NOTCHED TO
KEEP OUT WATER
VARIES
FINISHED GRADE
1/2" TREADED ROD
18" MIN.
CONCRETE FOOTING
10" MIN.
END VIEW
SIDE VIEW

BEAM TO FOOTING W/ METAL POST ANCHOR

SCALE: NOT TO SCALE

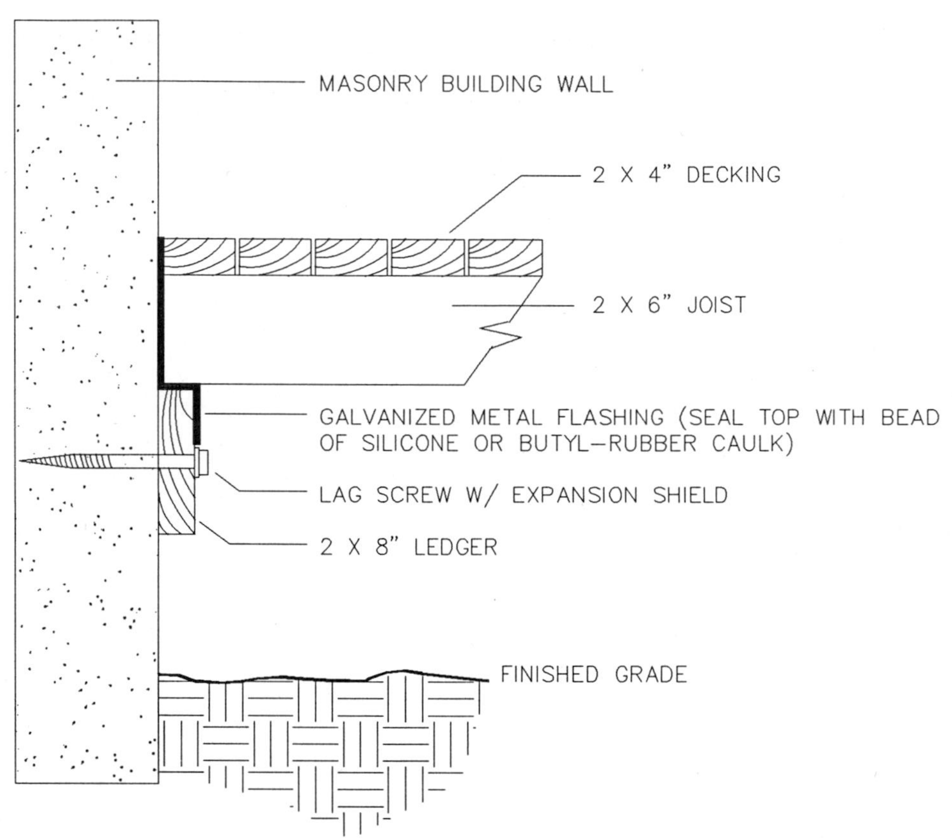
MASONRY BUILDING WALL
2 X 4" DECKING
2 X 6" JOIST
GALVANIZED METAL FLASHING (SEAL TOP WITH BEAD OF SILICONE OR BUTYL-RUBBER CAULK)
LAG SCREW W/ EXPANSION SHIELD
2 X 8" LEDGER
FINISHED GRADE

LEDGER TO MASONRY WALL

SCALE: NOT TO SCALE

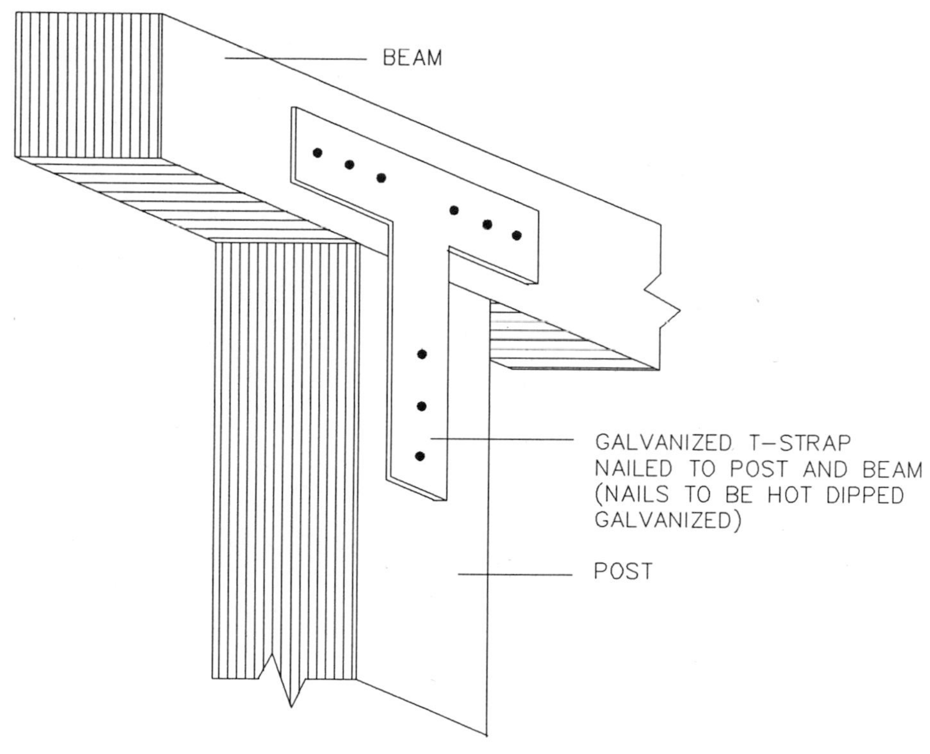
BEAM
GALVANIZED T-STRAP
NAILED TO POST AND BEAM
(NAILS TO BE HOT DIPPED
GALVANIZED)
POST

T-STRAP POST TO BEAM CONNECTION

SCALE: NOT TO SCALE

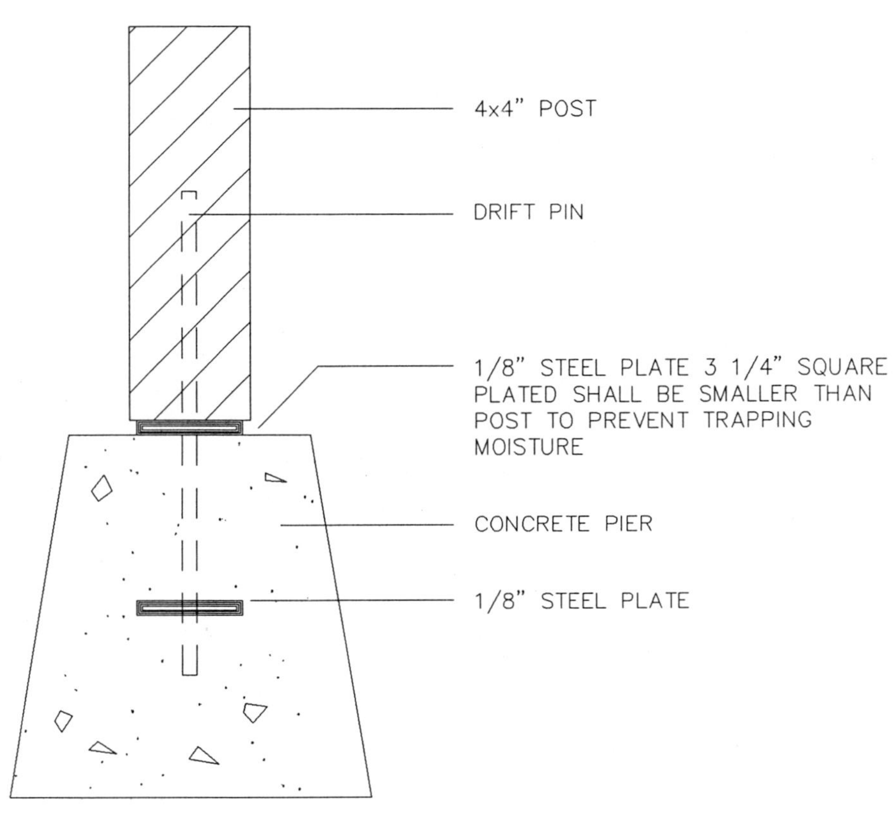
4x4" POST
DRIFT PIN
1/8" STEEL PLATE 3 1/4" SQUARE
PLATED SHALL BE SMALLER THAN
POST TO PREVENT TRAPPING
MOISTURE
CONCRETE PIER
1/8" STEEL PLATE

POST TO CONCRETE PIER W/ DRIFT PIN

SCALE: NOT TO SCALE

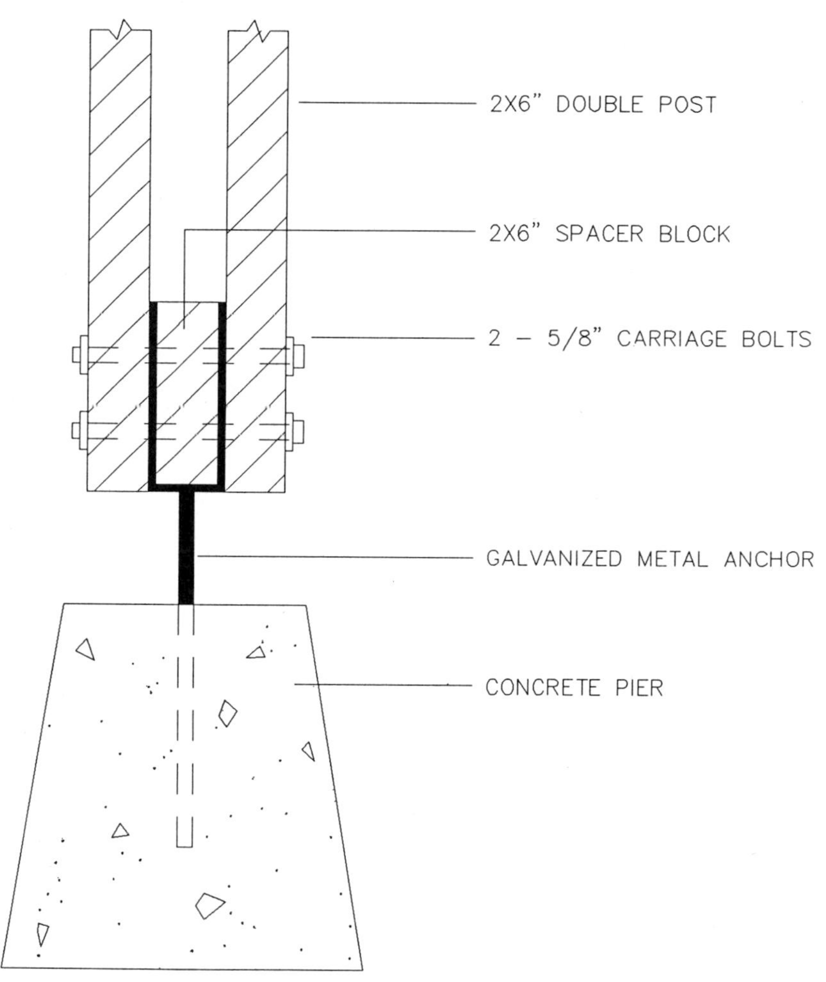
2X6" DOUBLE POST
2X6" SPACER BLOCK
2 – 5/8" CARRIAGE BOLTS
GALVANIZED METAL ANCHOR
CONCRETE PIER

DOUBLE POST ANCHOR

SCALE. NOT TO SCALE

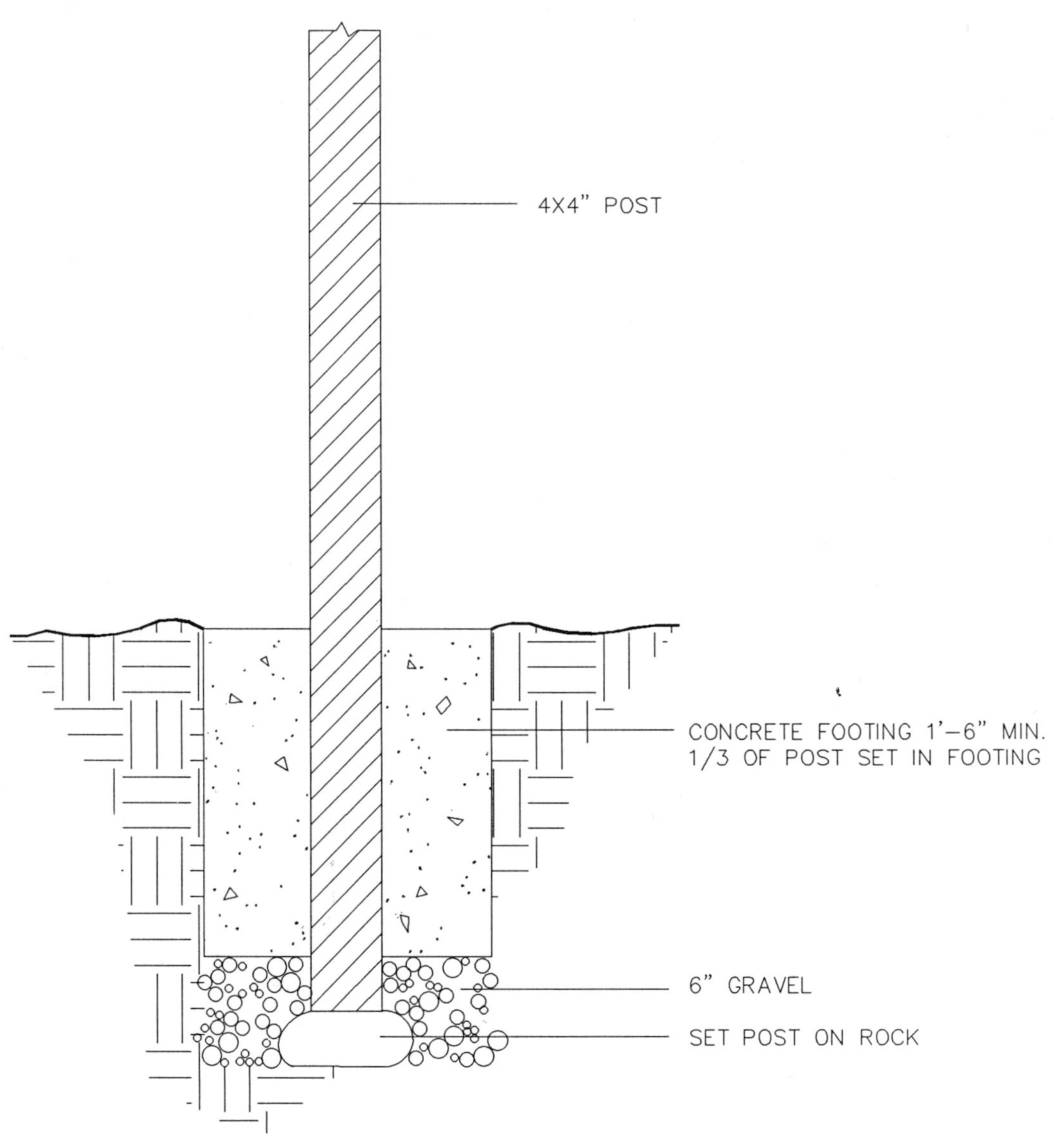
4X4" POST
CONCRETE FOOTING 1'–6" MIN.
1/3 OF POST SET IN FOOTING
6" GRAVEL
SET POST ON ROCK

POST IN CONCRETE FOOTING

SCALE: NOT TO SCALE

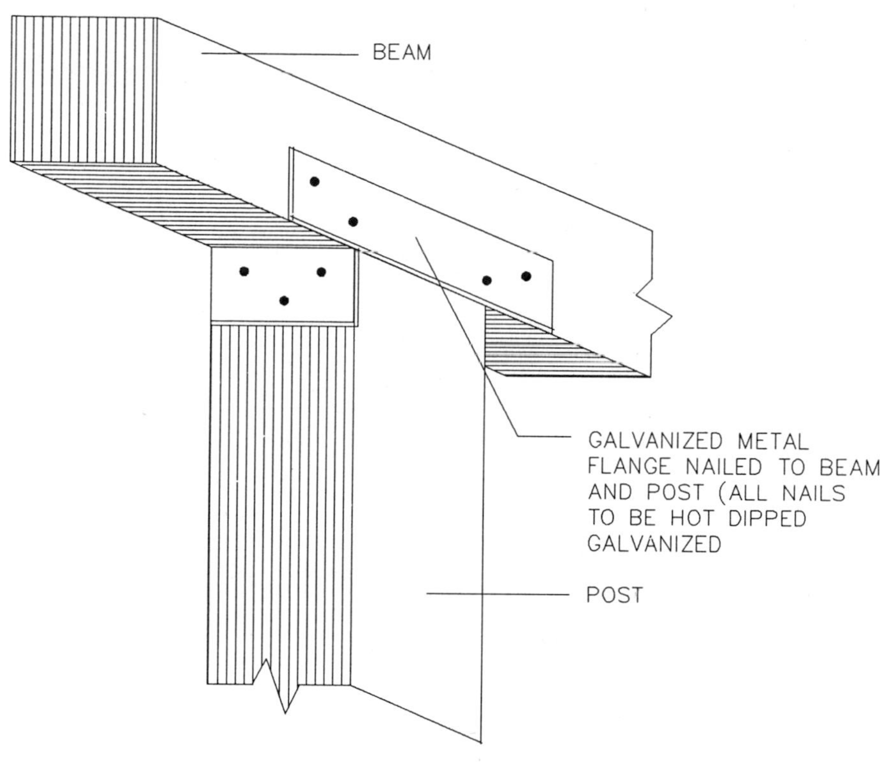
BEAM
GALVANIZED METAL
FLANGE NAILED TO BEAM
AND POST (ALL NAILS
TO BE HOT DIPPED
GALVANIZED
POST

METAL FLANGE POST TO BEAM CONNECTION

SCALE: NOT TO SCALE

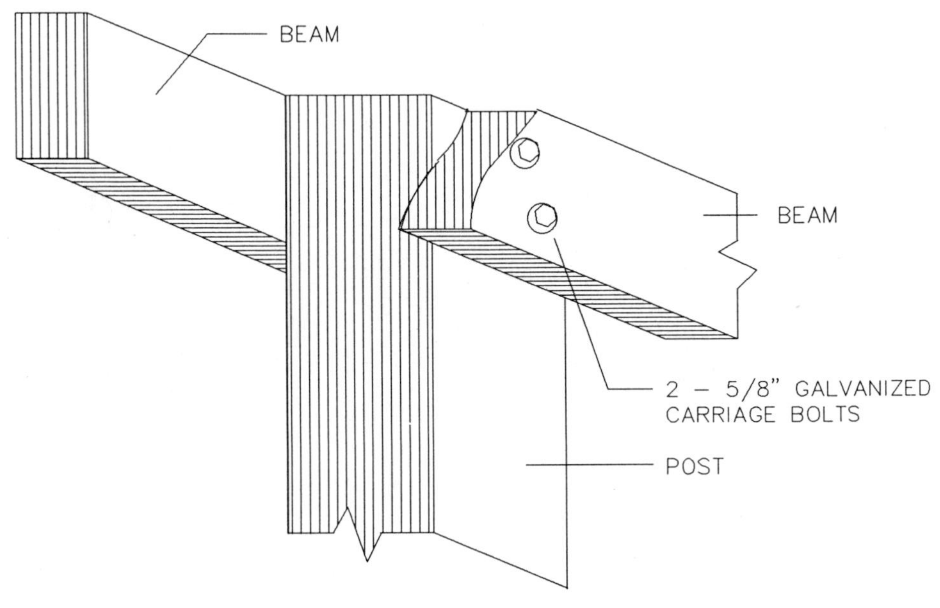
BEAM
BEAM
2 – 5/8" GALVANIZED
CARRIAGE BOLTS
POST

DOUBLE BEAM BOLTED TO POST

SCALE: NOT TO SCALE

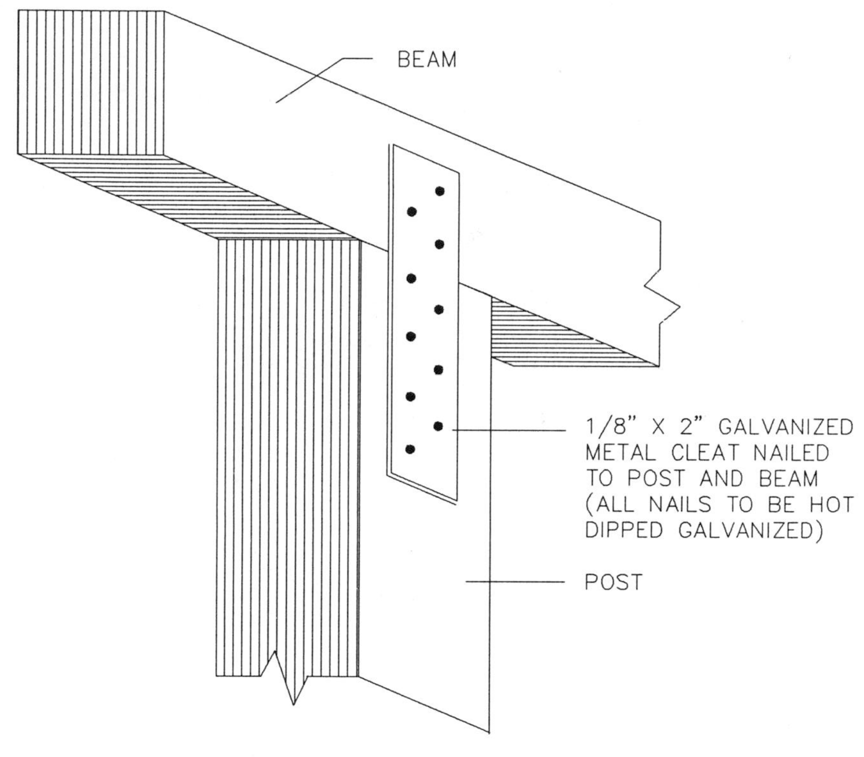
BEAM
1/8" X 2" GALVANIZED
METAL CLEAT NAILED
TO POST AND BEAM
(ALL NAILS TO BE HOT
DIPPED GALVANIZED)
POST

METAL CLEAT
POST TO BEAM CONNECTION

SCALE: NOT TO SCALE

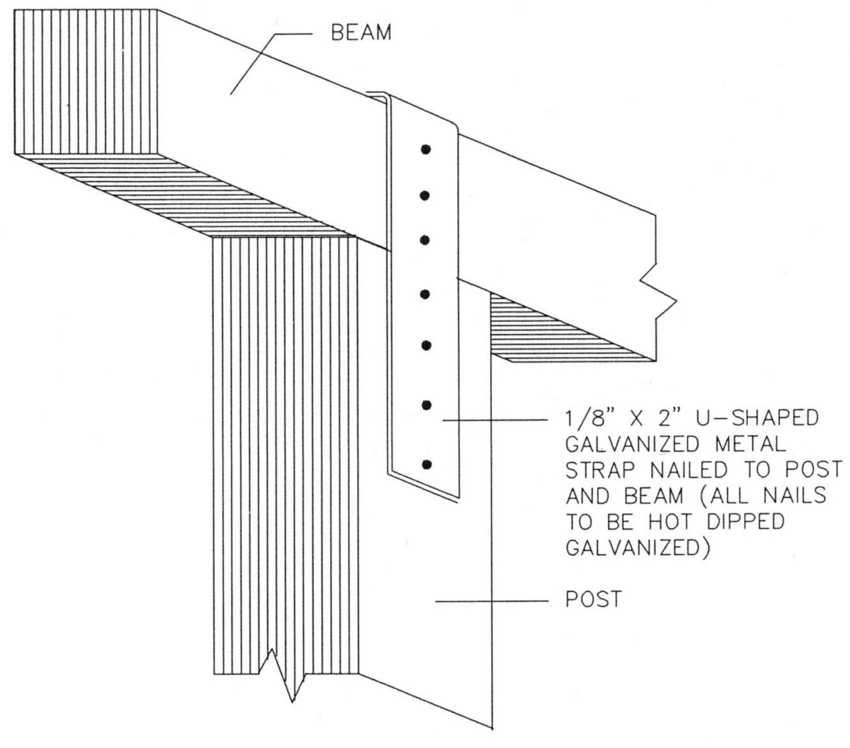
BEAM
1/8" X 2" U-SHAPED
GALVANIZED METAL
STRAP NAILED TO POST
AND BEAM (ALL NAILS
TO BE HOT DIPPED
GALVANIZED)
POST

METAL STRAPPING POST TO BEAM CONNECTION

SCALE: NOT TO SCALE

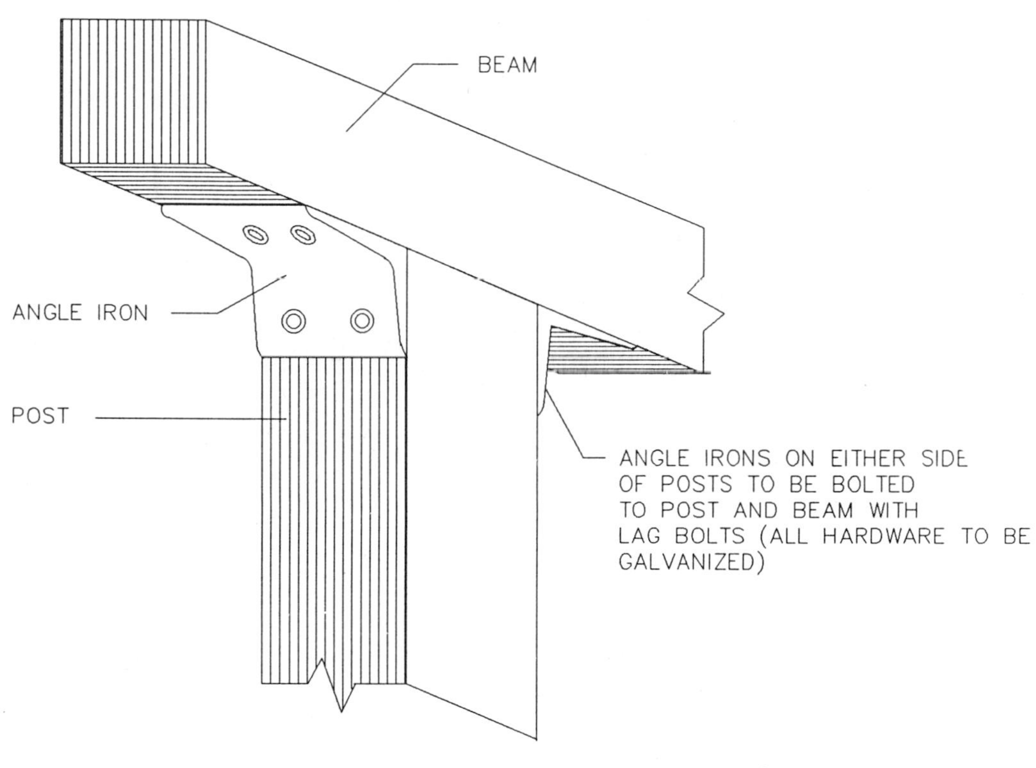
BEAM
ANGLE IRON
POST
ANGLE IRONS ON EITHER SIDE
OF POSTS TO BE BOLTED
TO POST AND BEAM WITH
LAG BOLTS (ALL HARDWARE TO BE
GALVANIZED)

ANGLE IRONS
POST TO BEAM CONNECTION

SCALE: NOT TO SCALE

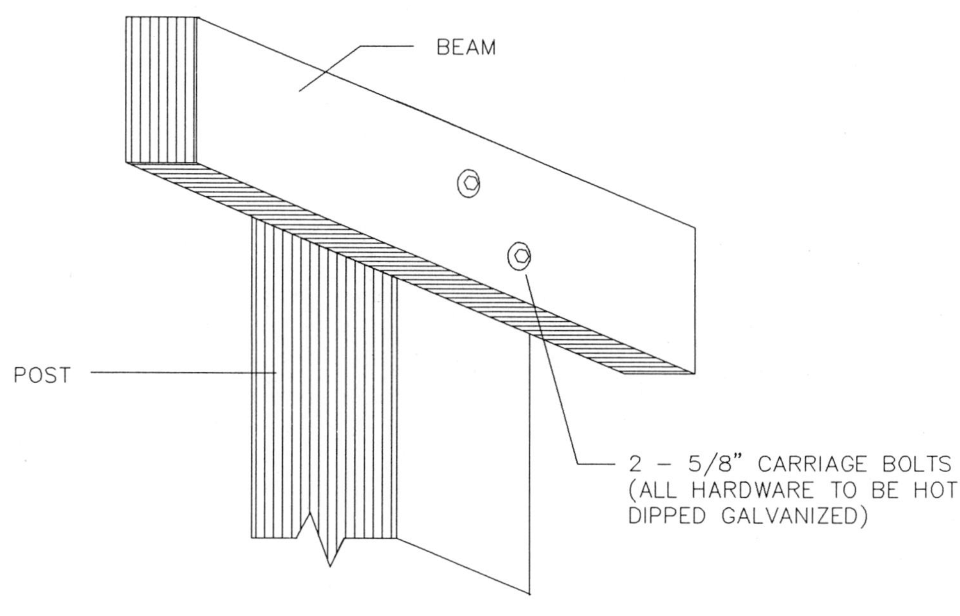
BEAM
POST
2 – 5/8" CARRIAGE BOLTS
(ALL HARDWARE TO BE HOT
DIPPED GALVANIZED)

SINGLE BEAM BOLTED TO POST

SCALE: NOT TO SCALE

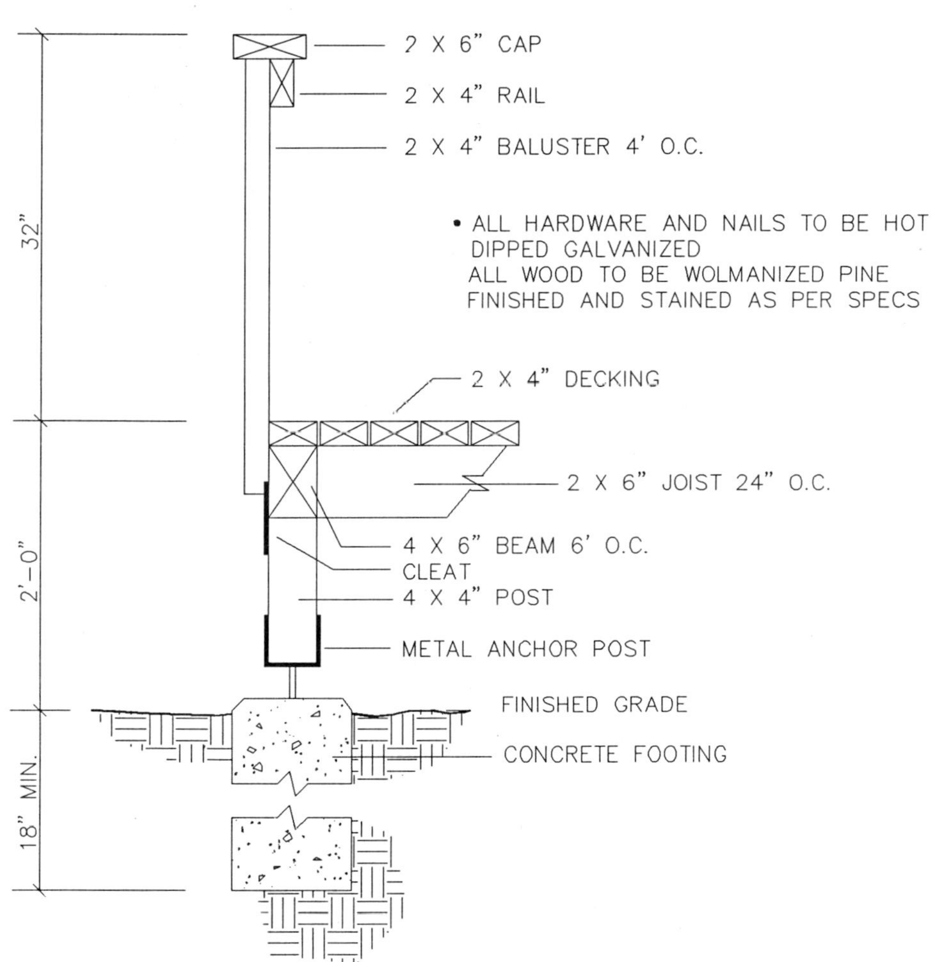
2 X 6" CAP
2 X 4" RAIL
2 X 4" BALUSTER 4' O.C.
• ALL HARDWARE AND NAILS TO BE HOT DIPPED GALVANIZED
ALL WOOD TO BE WOLMANIZED PINE FINISHED AND STAINED AS PER SPECS
2 X 4" DECKING
2 X 6" JOIST 24" O.C.
4 X 6" BEAM 6' O.C.
CLEAT
4 X 4" POST
METAL ANCHOR POST
FINISHED GRADE
CONCRETE FOOTING
32"
2'-0"
18" MIN.

RAIL TO DECK CONNECTION

SCALE: NOT TO SCALE

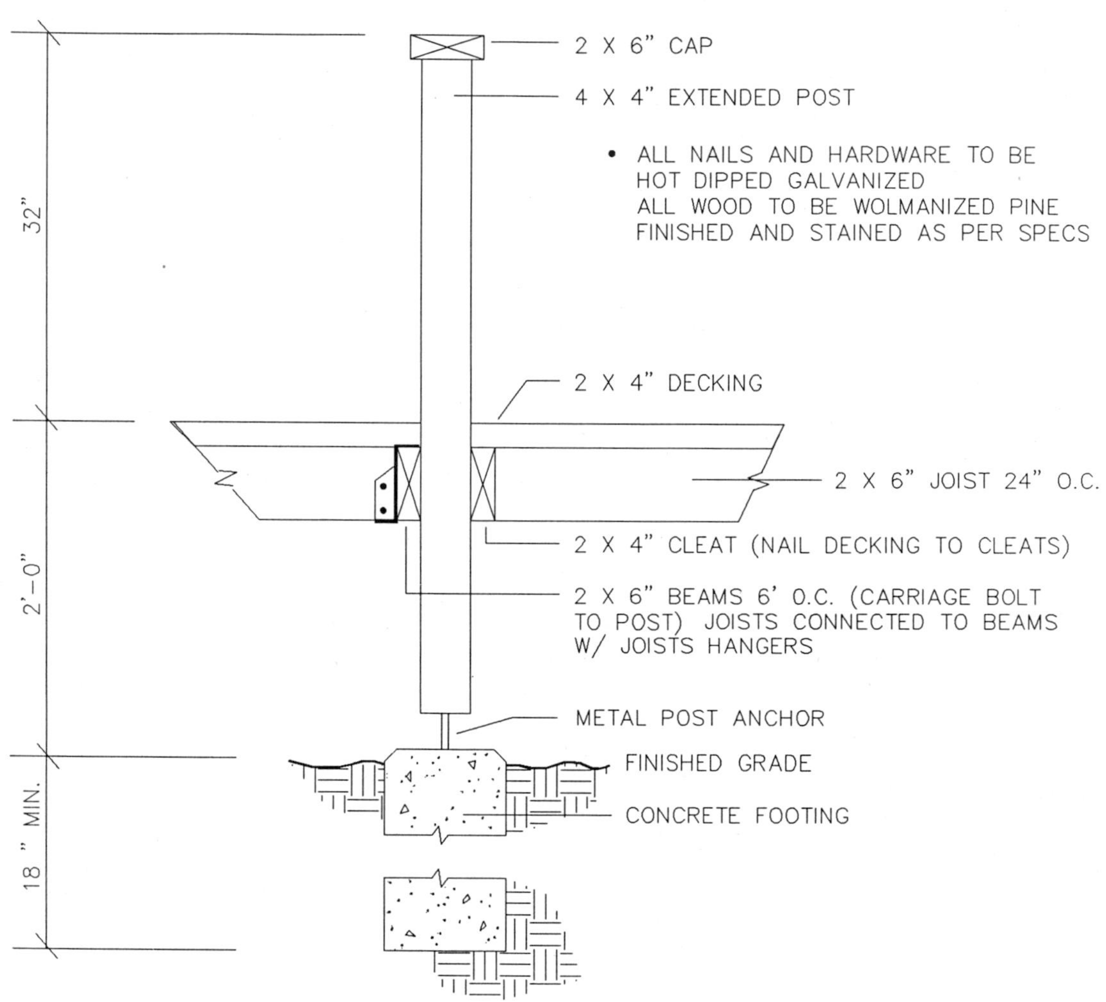
2 X 6" CAP
4 X 4" EXTENDED POST
• ALL NAILS AND HARDWARE TO BE HOT DIPPED GALVANIZED
ALL WOOD TO BE WOLMANIZED PINE FINISHED AND STAINED AS PER SPECS
32"
2 X 4" DECKING
2 X 6" JOIST 24" O.C.
2 X 4" CLEAT (NAIL DECKING TO CLEATS)
2'-0"
2 X 6" BEAMS 6' O.C. (CARRIAGE BOLT TO POST) JOISTS CONNECTED TO BEAMS W/ JOISTS HANGERS
METAL POST ANCHOR
FINISHED GRADE
CONCRETE FOOTING
18 " MIN.

DECK W/ EXTENDED POST RAIL

SCALE: NOT TO SCALE

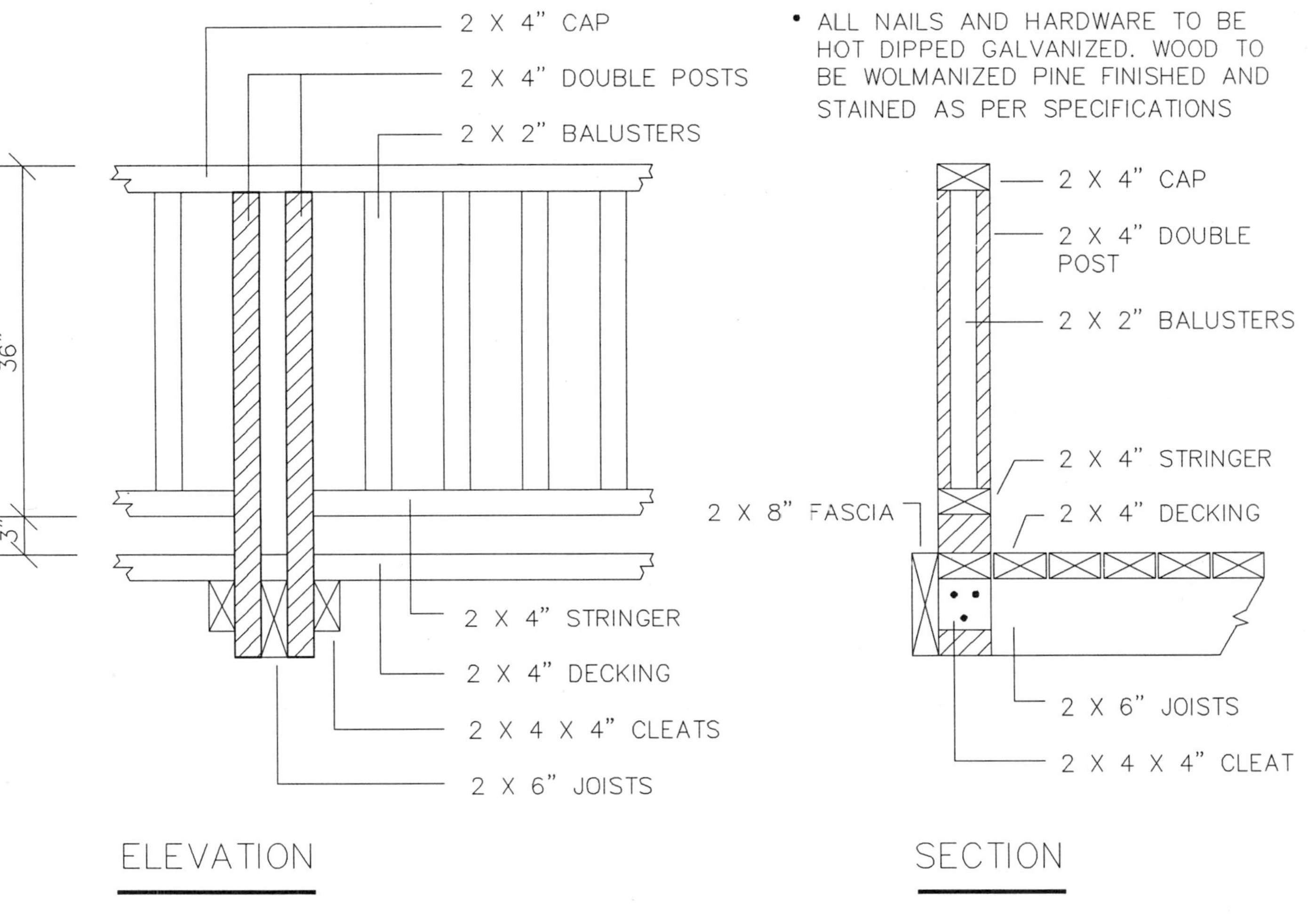
2 X 4" CAP
2 X 4" DOUBLE POSTS
2 X 2" BALUSTERS
36"
3"
2 X 4" STRINGER
2 X 4" DECKING
2 X 4 X 4" CLEATS
2 X 6" JOISTS
ELEVATION
• ALL NAILS AND HARDWARE TO BE HOT DIPPED GALVANIZED. WOOD TO BE WOLMANIZED PINE FINISHED AND STAINED AS PER SPECIFICATIONS
2 X 4" CAP
2 X 4" DOUBLE POST
2 X 2" BALUSTERS
2 X 4" STRINGER
2 X 8" FASCIA
2 X 4" DECKING
2 X 6" JOISTS
2 X 4 X 4" CLEAT
SECTION

BUILT—UP POST AND DECK CONNECTION

SCALE: NOT TO SCALE

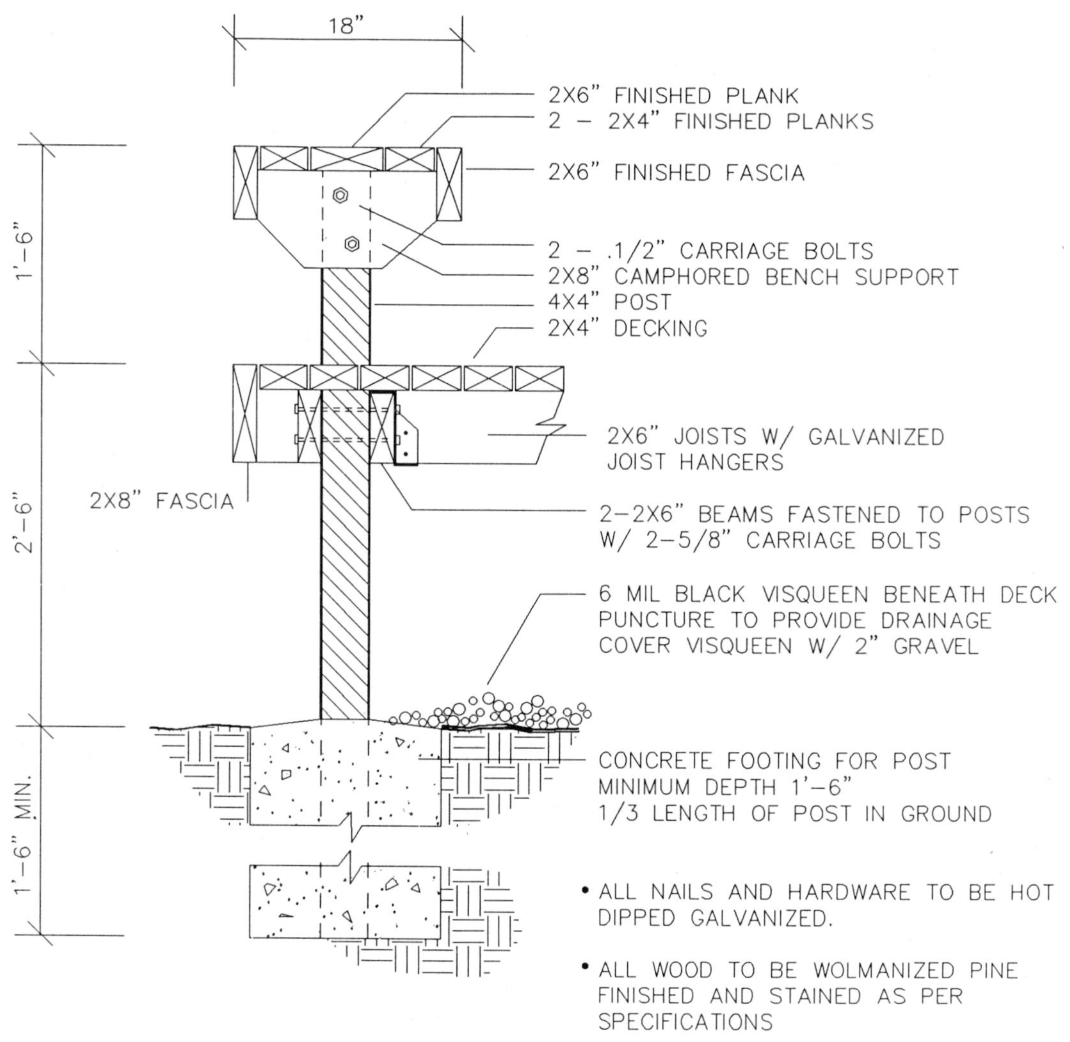
18"
1'-6"
2'-6"
1'-6" MIN.
2X6" FINISHED PLANK
2 – 2X4" FINISHED PLANKS
2X6" FINISHED FASCIA
2 – .1/2" CARRIAGE BOLTS
2X8" CAMPHORED BENCH SUPPORT
4X4" POST
2X4" DECKING
2X6" JOISTS W/ GALVANIZED JOIST HANGERS
2X8" FASCIA
2-2X6" BEAMS FASTENED TO POSTS W/ 2-5/8" CARRIAGE BOLTS
6 MIL BLACK VISQUEEN BENEATH DECK PUNCTURE TO PROVIDE DRAINAGE COVER VISQUEEN W/ 2" GRAVEL
CONCRETE FOOTING FOR POST MINIMUM DEPTH 1'-6" 1/3 LENGTH OF POST IN GROUND

- ALL NAILS AND HARDWARE TO BE HOT DIPPED GALVANIZED.
- ALL WOOD TO BE WOLMANIZED PINE FINISHED AND STAINED AS PER SPECIFICATIONS

BENCH AND WOOD DECK

SCALE: NOT TO SCALE

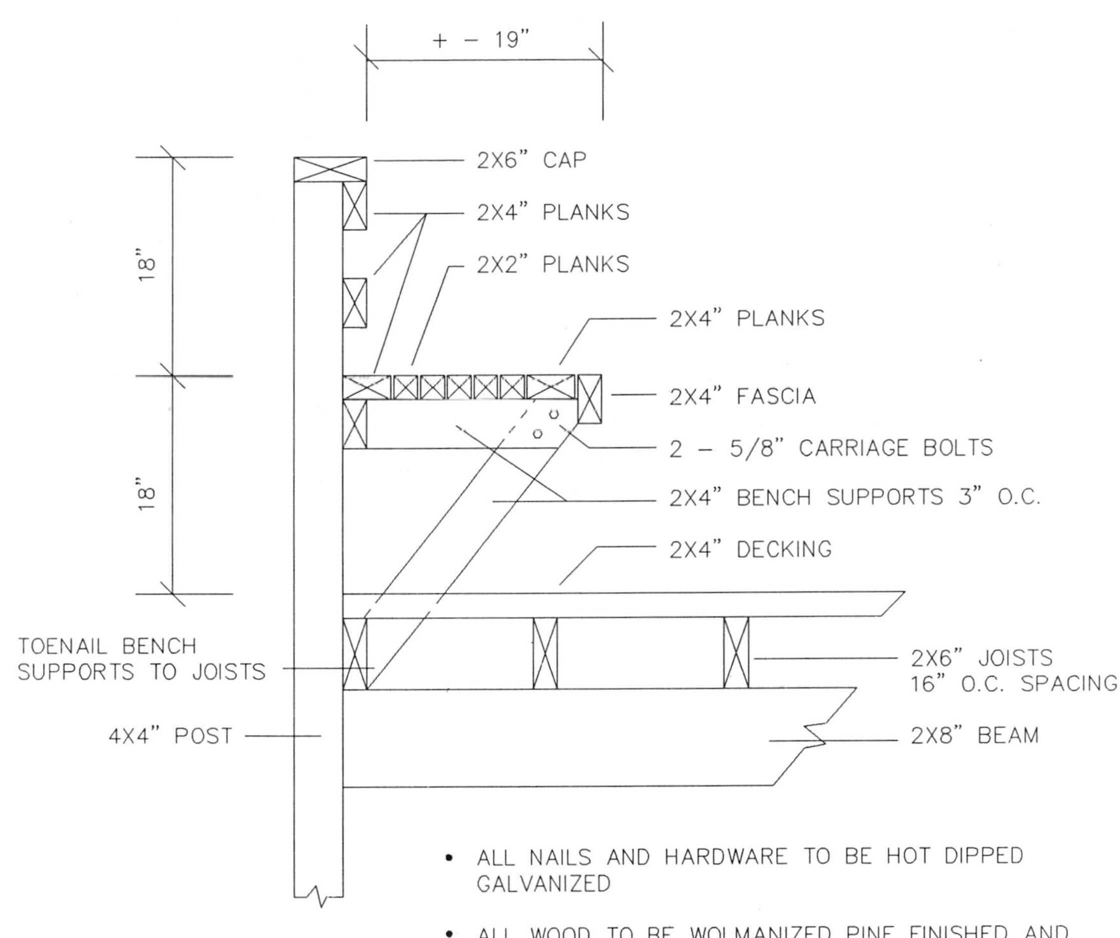
+ - 19"
2X6" CAP
2X4" PLANKS
2X2" PLANKS
18"
2X4" PLANKS
2X4" FASCIA
2 - 5/8" CARRIAGE BOLTS
18"
2X4" BENCH SUPPORTS 3" O.C.
2X4" DECKING
TOENAIL BENCH
SUPPORTS TO JOISTS
2X6" JOISTS
16" O.C. SPACING
4X4" POST
2X8" BEAM

- ALL NAILS AND HARDWARE TO BE HOT DIPPED GALVANIZED
- ALL WOOD TO BE WOLMANIZED PINE FINISHED AND STAINED AS PER SPECIFICATION

BENCH TO RAILING CONNECTION

SCALE: NOT TO SCALE

Drainage

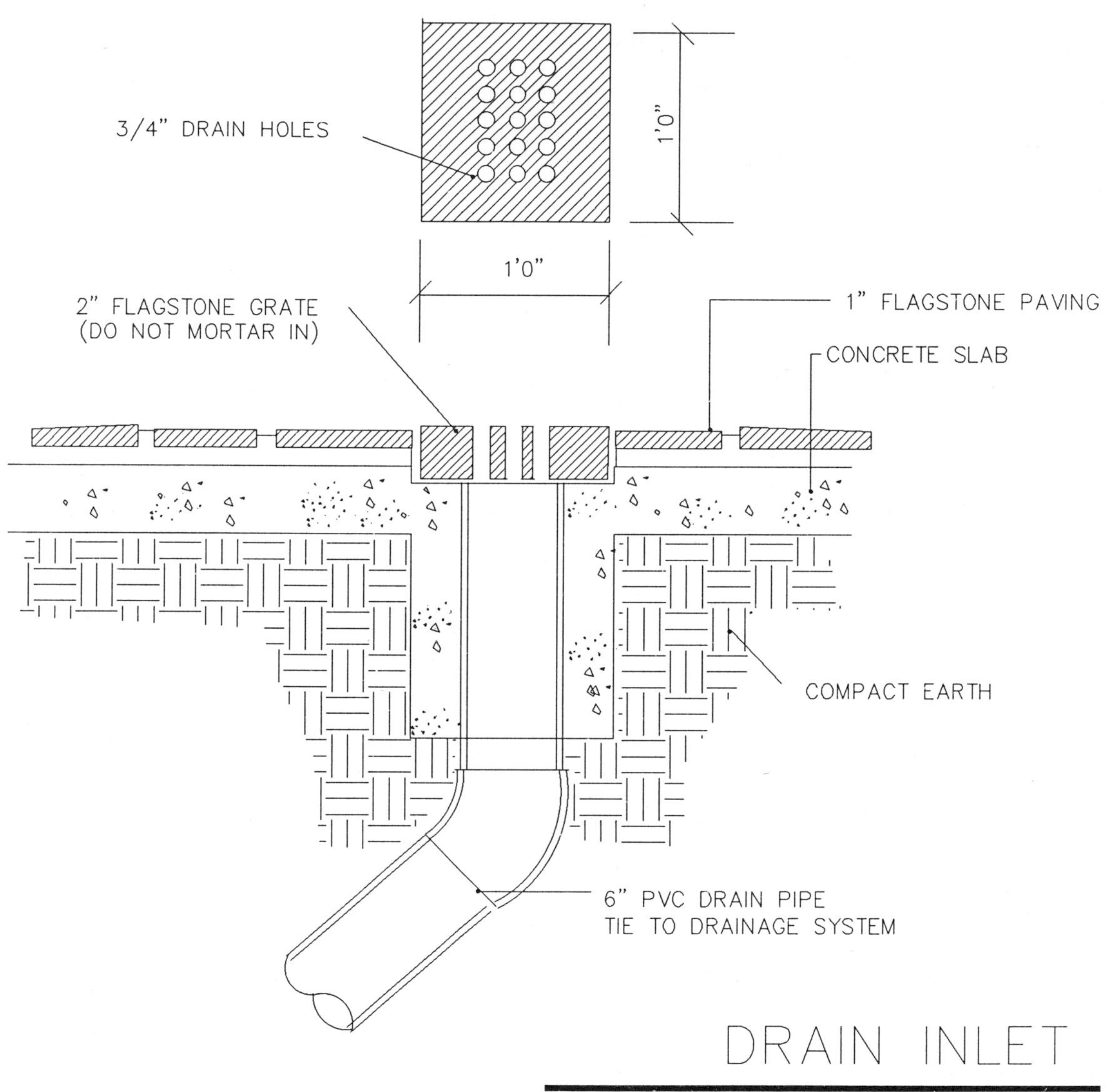
3/4" DRAIN HOLES
1'0"
1'0"
2" FLAGSTONE GRATE
(DO NOT MORTAR IN)
1" FLAGSTONE PAVING
CONCRETE SLAB
COMPACT EARTH
6" PVC DRAIN PIPE
TIE TO DRAINAGE SYSTEM

DRAIN INLET

SCALE: NOT TO SCALE

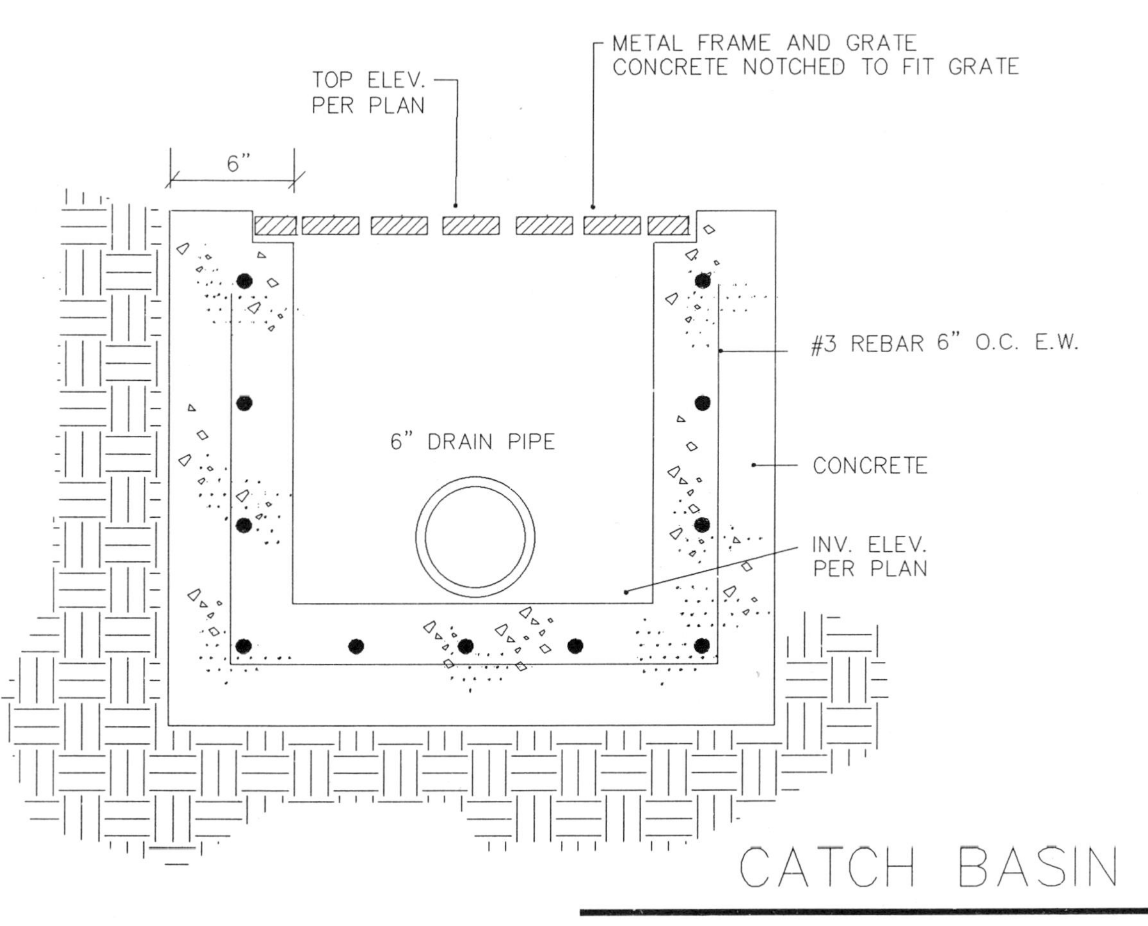
METAL FRAME AND GRATE
CONCRETE NOTCHED TO FIT GRATE
TOP ELEV.
PER PLAN
6"
#3 REBAR 6" O.C. E.W.
6" DRAIN PIPE
CONCRETE
INV. ELEV.
PER PLAN

CATCH BASIN

SCALE: NOT TO SCALE

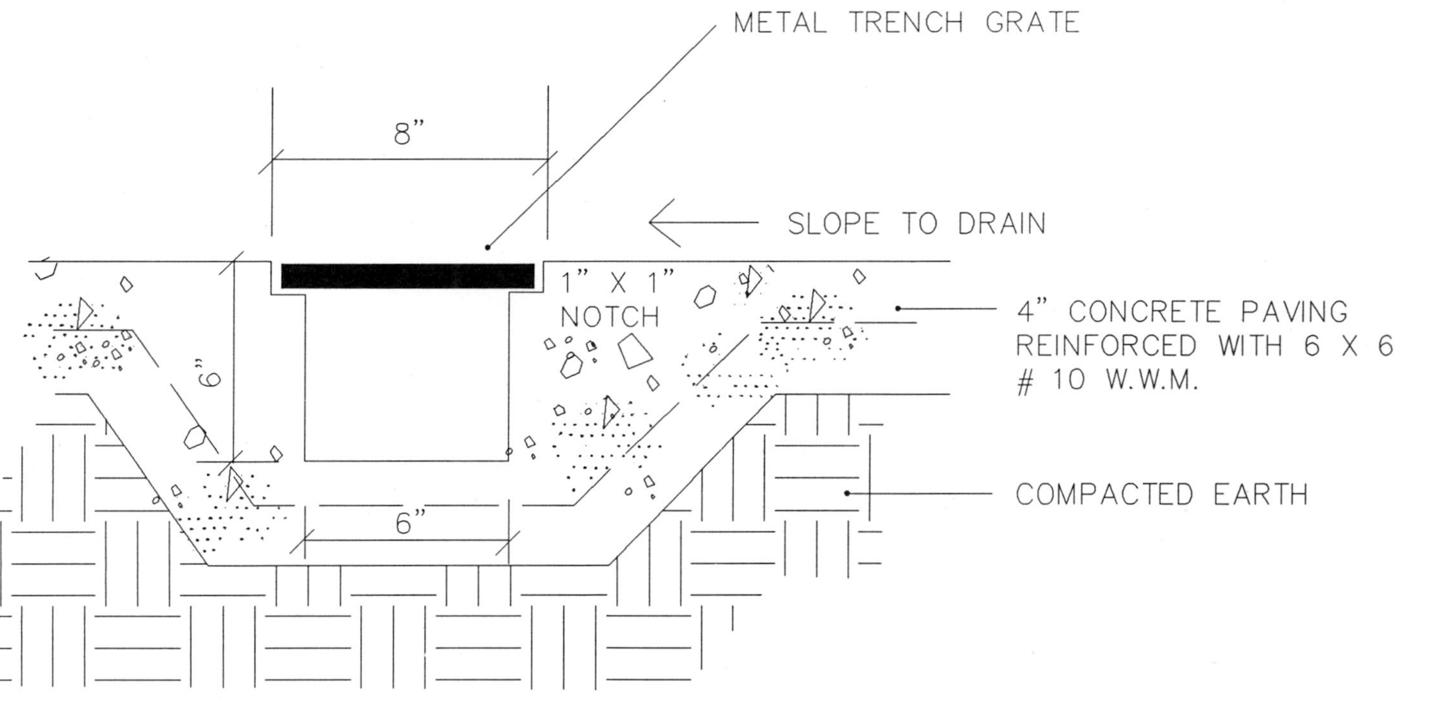
METAL TRENCH GRATE
8"
SLOPE TO DRAIN
1" X 1" NOTCH
4" CONCRETE PAVING
REINFORCED WITH 6 X 6
10 W.W.M.
COMPACTED EARTH
6"
6"
* SLOPE BOTTOM OF TRENCH DRAIN
TO TIE IN WITH EXISTING DRAINAGE

TRENCH DRAIN

SCALE: NOT TO SCALE

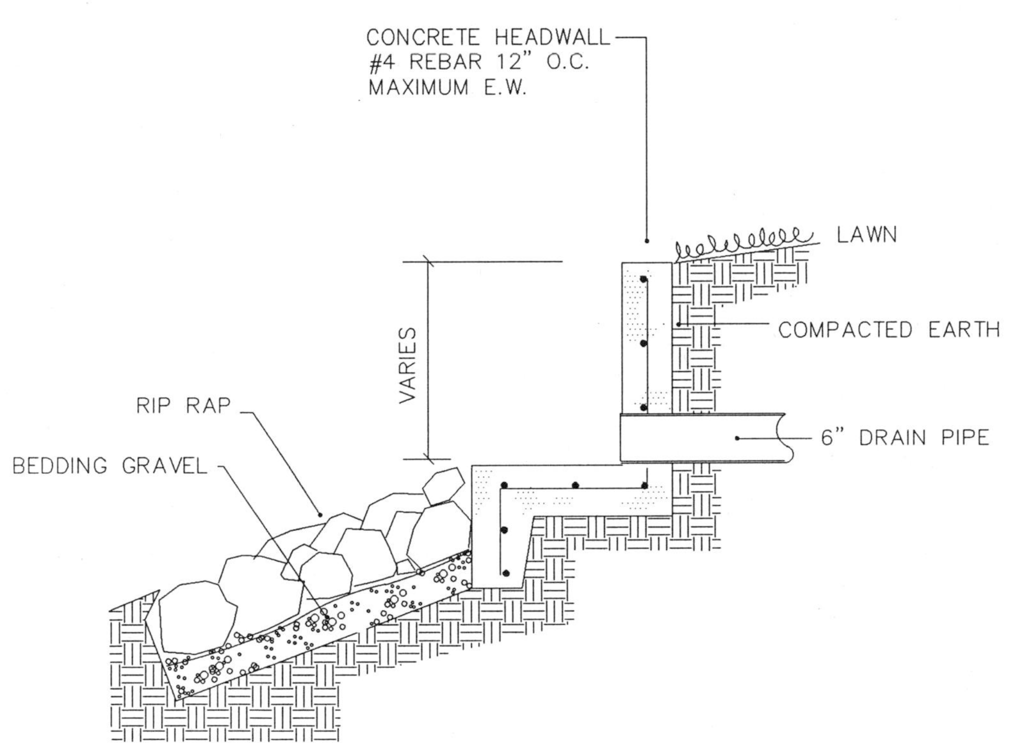
CONCRETE HEADWALL
#4 REBAR 12" O.C.
MAXIMUM E.W.
LAWN
COMPACTED EARTH
VARIES
RIP RAP
BEDDING GRAVEL
6" DRAIN PIPE

OUTFALL HEADWALL

SCALE: NOT TO SCALE

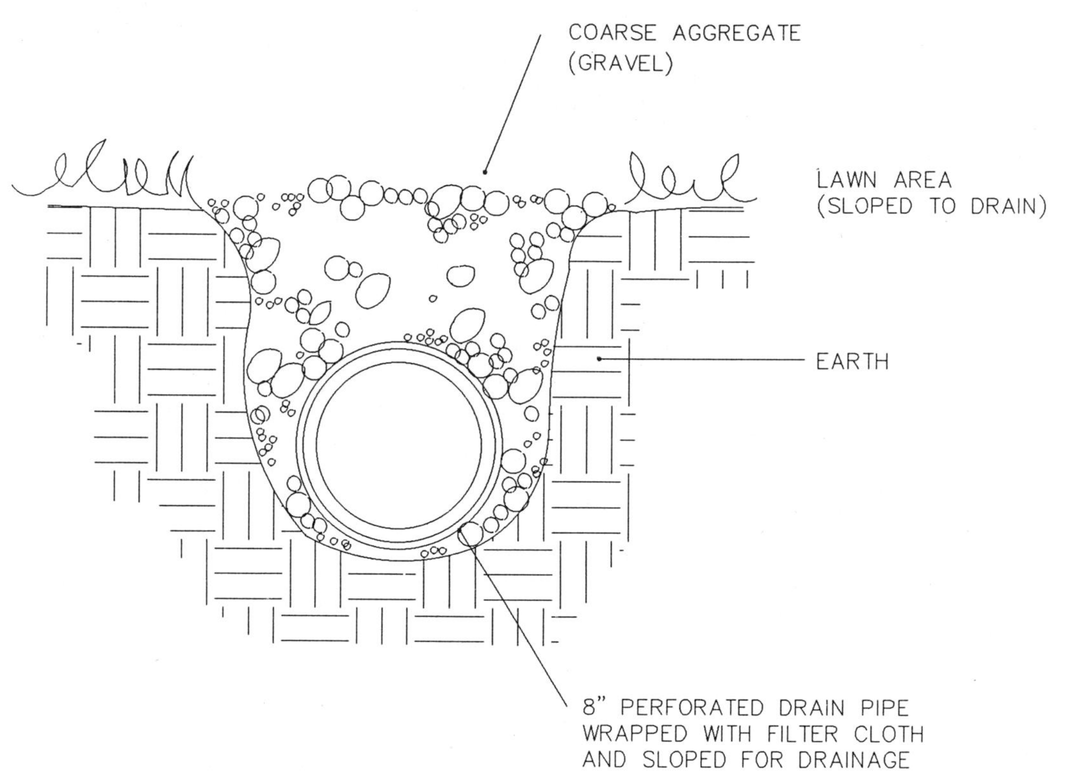
COARSE AGGREGATE
(GRAVEL)
LAWN AREA
(SLOPED TO DRAIN)
EARTH
8" PERFORATED DRAIN PIPE
WRAPPED WITH FILTER CLOTH
AND SLOPED FOR DRAINAGE

FRENCH DRAIN

SCALE: NOT TO SCALE

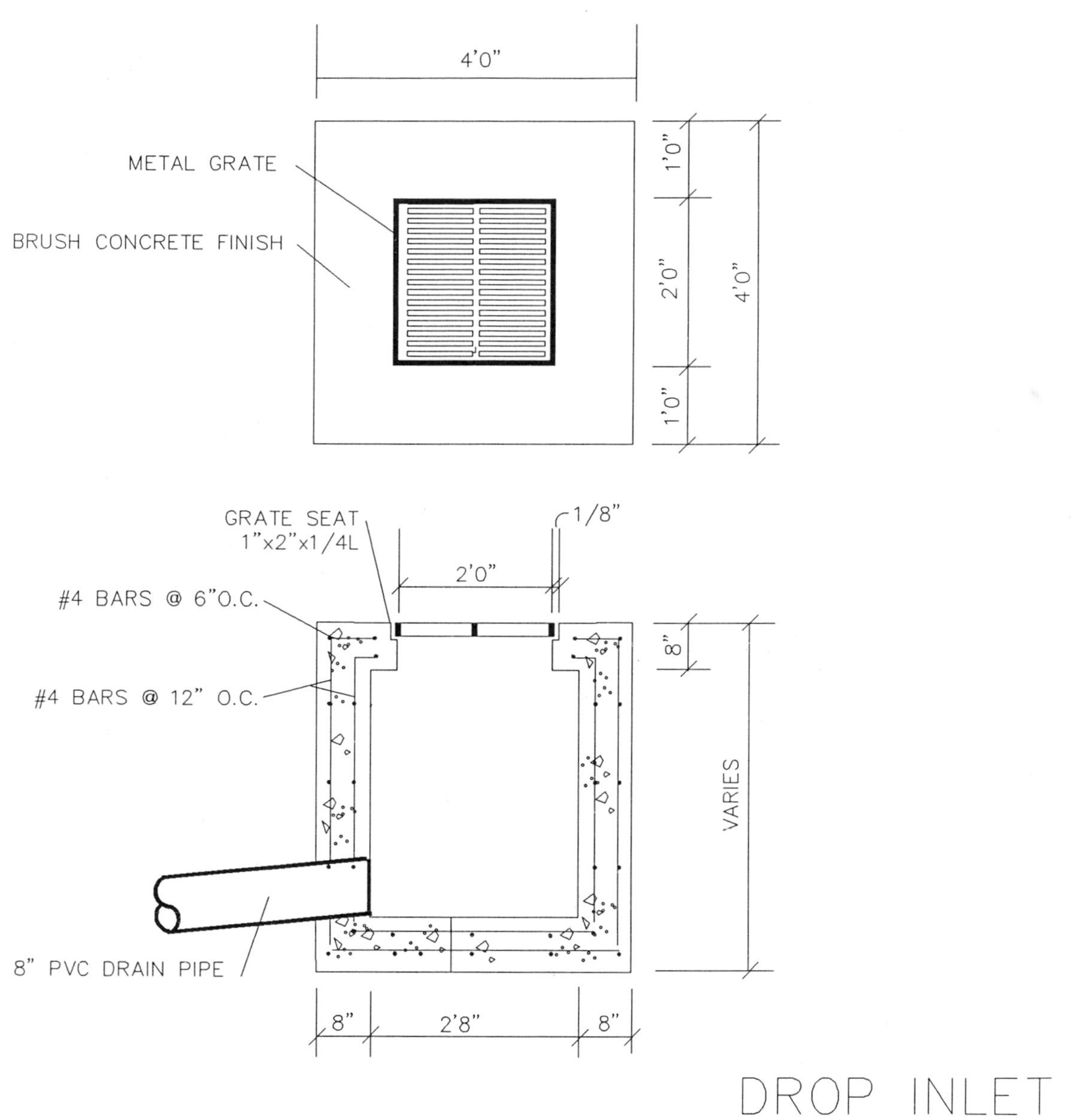
4'0"
METAL GRATE
BRUSH CONCRETE FINISH
1'0"
2'0"
4'0"
1'0"
GRATE SEAT
1"x2"x1/4L
1/8"
2'0"
#4 BARS @ 6"O.C.
#4 BARS @ 12" O.C.
8"
VARIES
8" PVC DRAIN PIPE
8"
2'8"
8"

DROP INLET

SCALE: NOT TO SCALE

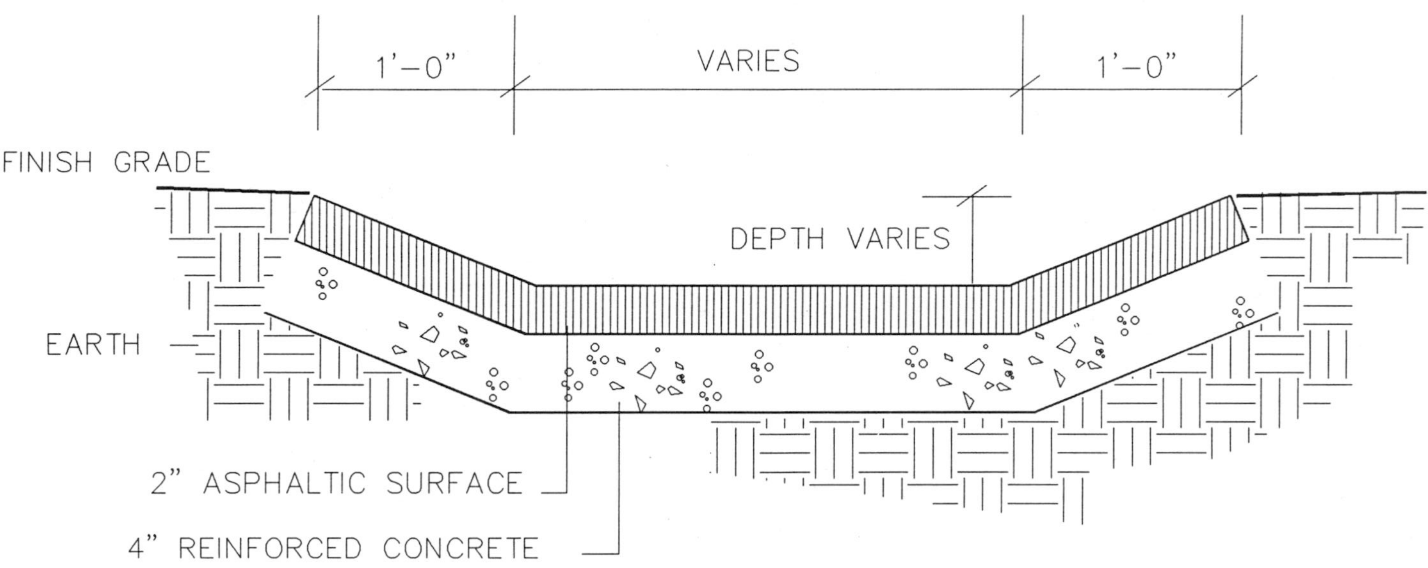
1'–0"
VARIES
1'–0"
FINISH GRADE
DEPTH VARIES
EARTH
2" ASPHALTIC SURFACE
4" REINFORCED CONCRETE

BITUMINOUS CONCRETE SWALE –1

SCALE: NOT TO SCALE

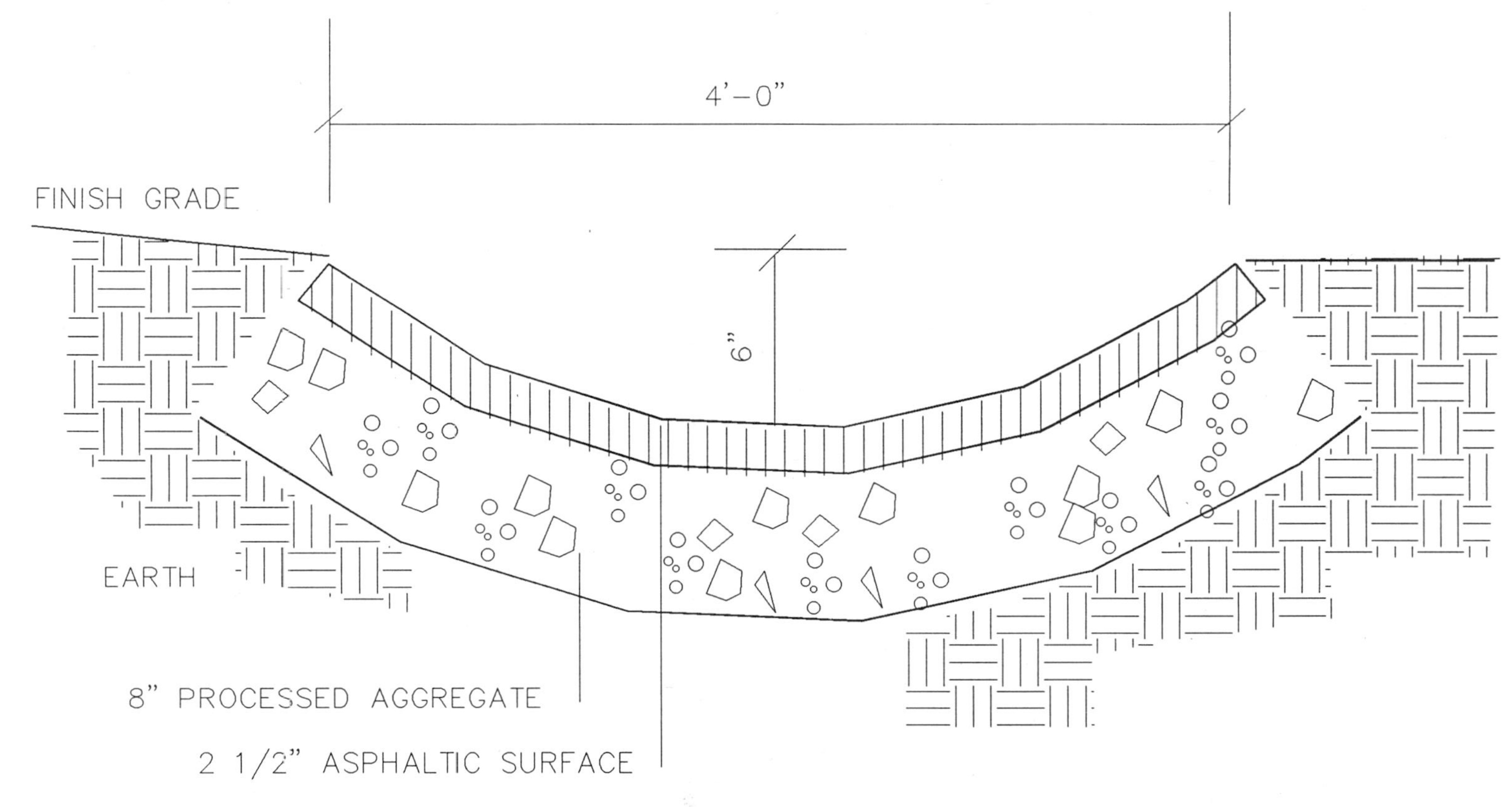
4'–0"
FINISH GRADE
6"
EARTH
8" PROCESSED AGGREGATE
2 1/2" ASPHALTIC SURFACE

BITUMINOUS CONCRETE SWALE –2

SCALE: NOT TO SCALE

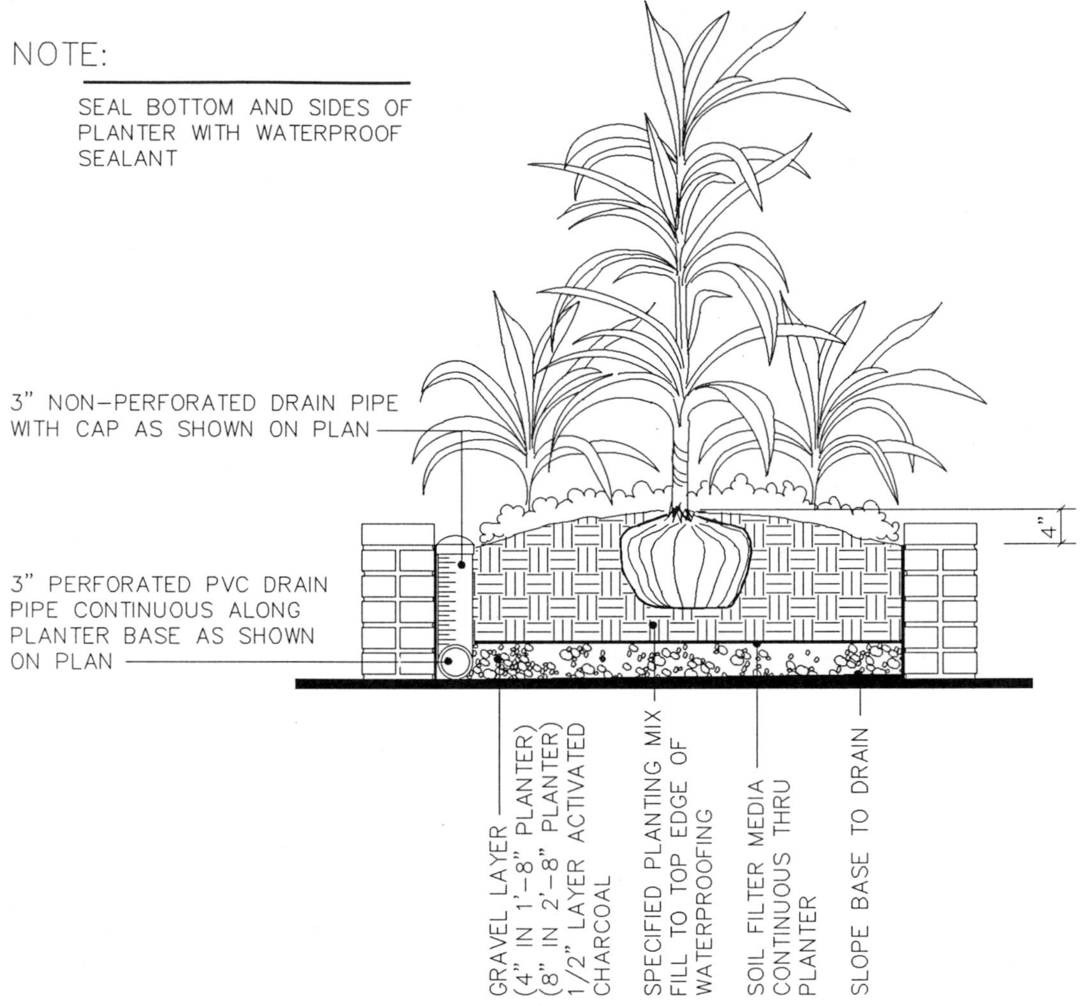

NOTE:
SEAL BOTTOM AND SIDES OF
PLANTER WITH WATERPROOF
SEALANT
3" NON–PERFORATED DRAIN PIPE
WITH CAP AS SHOWN ON PLAN
3" PERFORATED PVC DRAIN
PIPE CONTINUOUS ALONG
PLANTER BASE AS SHOWN
ON PLAN
4"
GRAVEL LAYER
(4" IN 1'–8" PLANTER)
(8" IN 2'–8" PLANTER)
1/2" LAYER ACTIVATED
CHARCOAL
SPECIFIED PLANTING MIX
FILL TO TOP EDGE OF
WATERPROOFING
SOIL FILTER MEDIA
CONTINUOUS THRU
PLANTER
SLOPE BASE TO DRAIN

INTERIOR PLANTING / DRAINAGE

SCALE: NOT TO SCALE

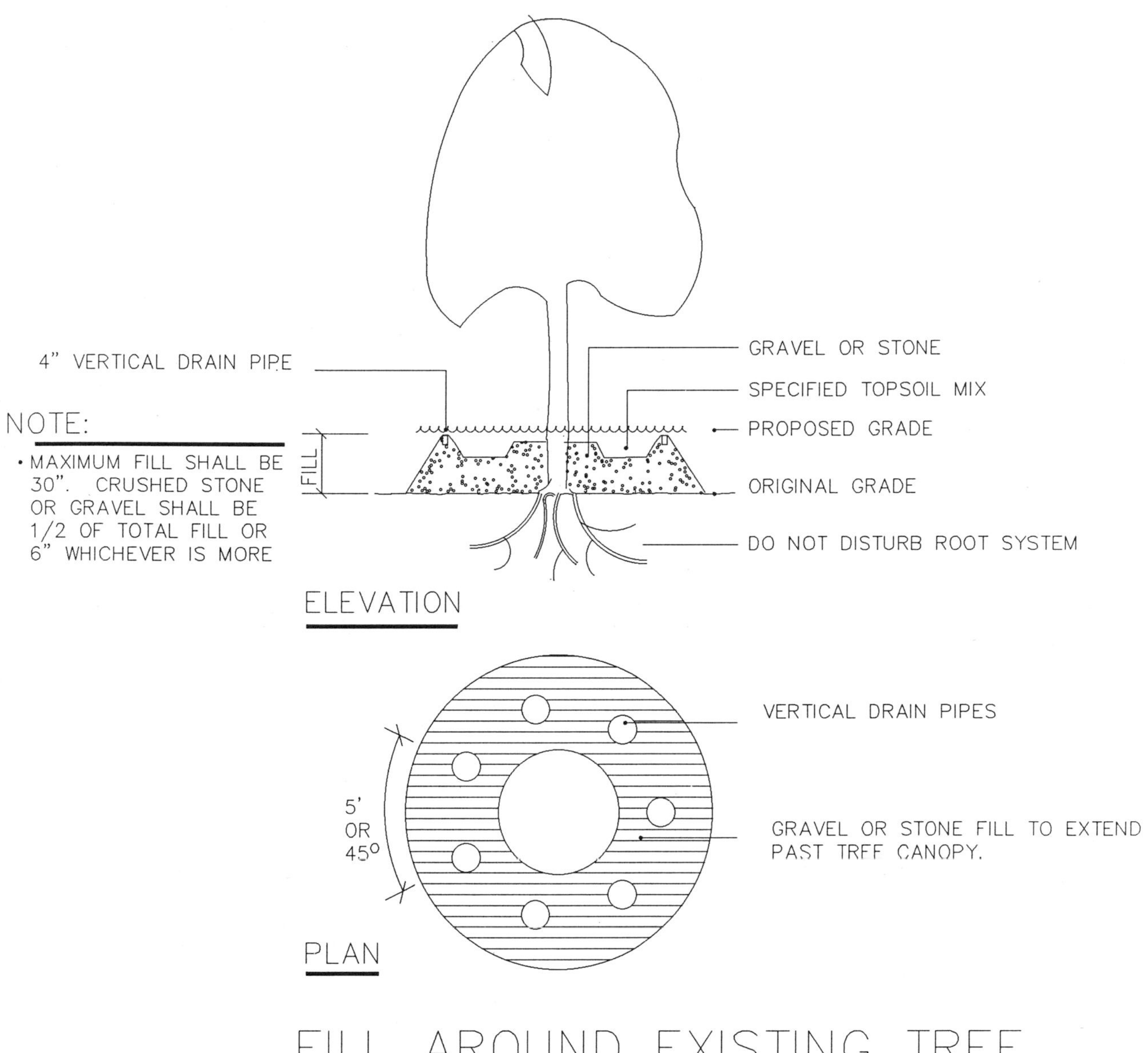
4" VERTICAL DRAIN PIPE
NOTE:
• MAXIMUM FILL SHALL BE 30". CRUSHED STONE OR GRAVEL SHALL BE 1/2 OF TOTAL FILL OR 6" WHICHEVER IS MORE
FILL
GRAVEL OR STONE
SPECIFIED TOPSOIL MIX
PROPOSED GRADE
ORIGINAL GRADE
DO NOT DISTURB ROOT SYSTEM
ELEVATION
VERTICAL DRAIN PIPES
5' OR 45°
GRAVEL OR STONE FILL TO EXTEND PAST TREE CANOPY.
PLAN

FILL AROUND EXISTING TREE

SCALE: NOT TO SCALE

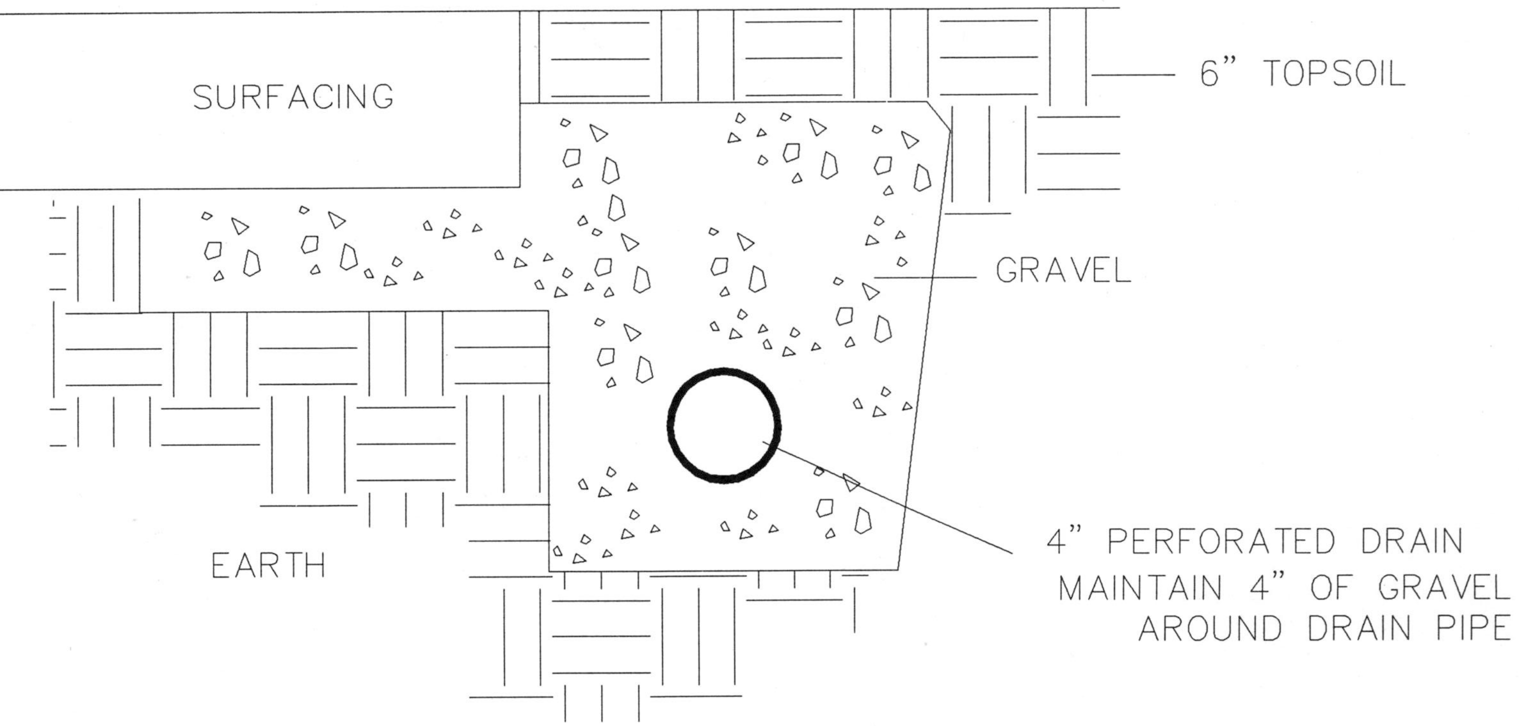
6" TOPSOIL
SURFACING
GRAVEL
EARTH
4" PERFORATED DRAIN
MAINTAIN 4" OF GRAVEL
AROUND DRAIN PIPE

PERIMETER DRAIN

SCALE: NOT TO SCALE

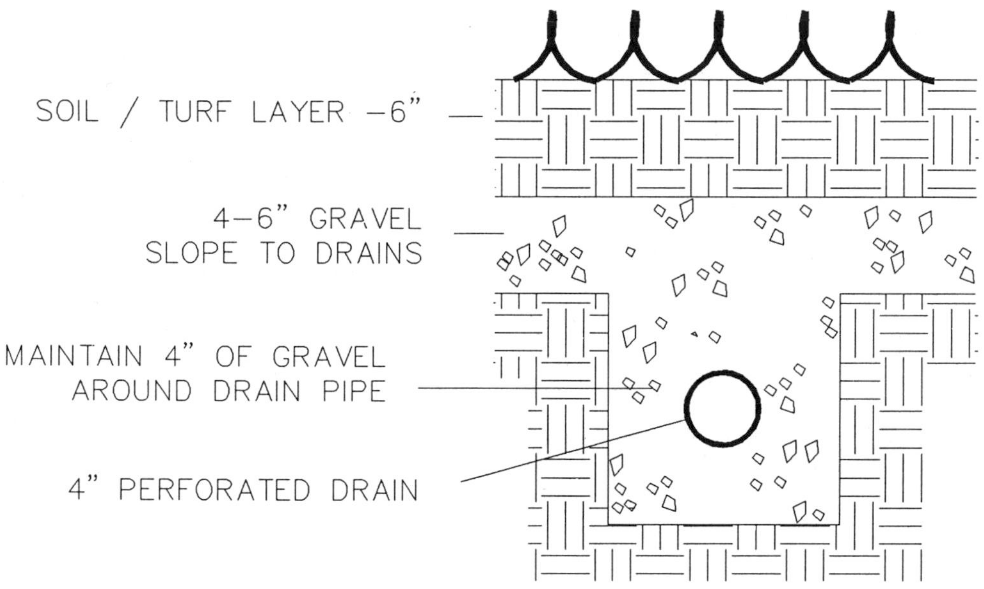
SOIL / TURF LAYER -6"
4-6" GRAVEL
SLOPE TO DRAINS
MAINTAIN 4" OF GRAVEL
AROUND DRAIN PIPE
4" PERFORATED DRAIN

* SEE PLAN FOR DRAIN SPACING

SUBSOIL DRAIN

SCALE: NOT TO SCALE

Erosion Control & Soil Stabilization

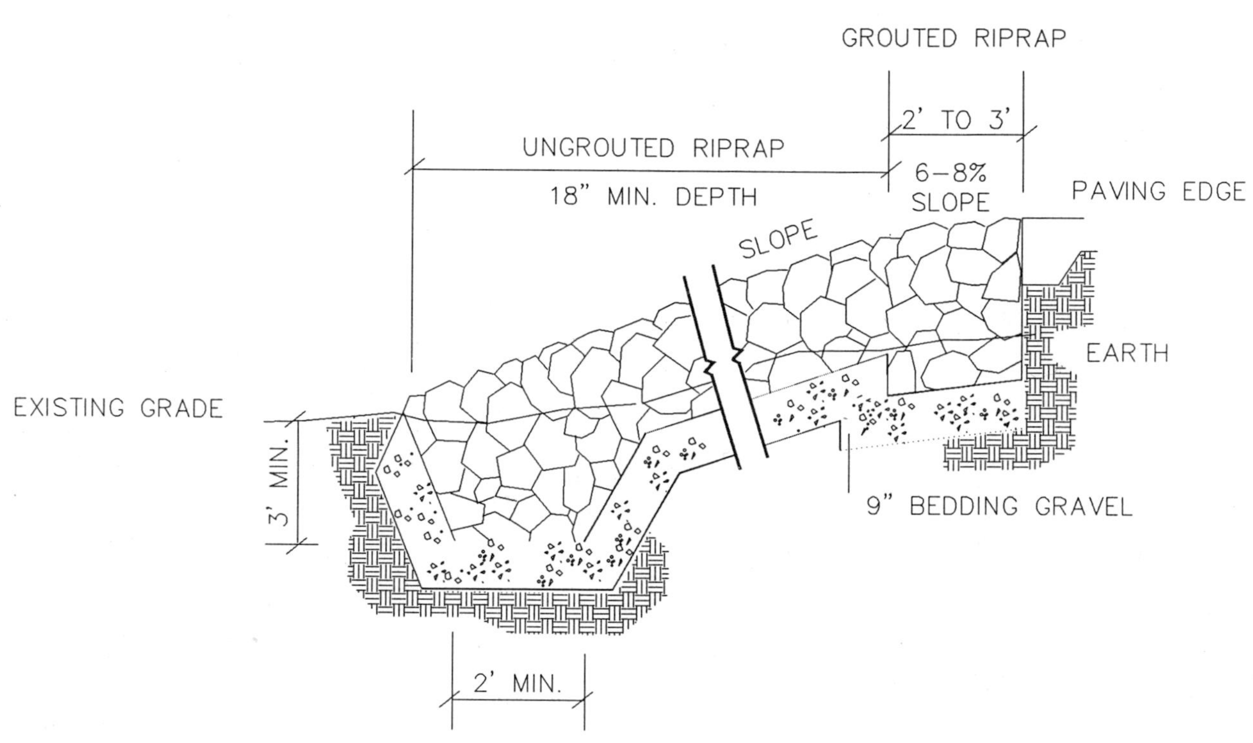
GROUTED RIPRAP
2' TO 3'
UNGROUTED RIPRAP
18" MIN. DEPTH
6–8%
SLOPE
PAVING EDGE
SLOPE
EARTH
EXISTING GRADE
3' MIN.
9" BEDDING GRAVEL
2' MIN.

RIPRAP SLOPE

SCALE: NOT TO SCALE

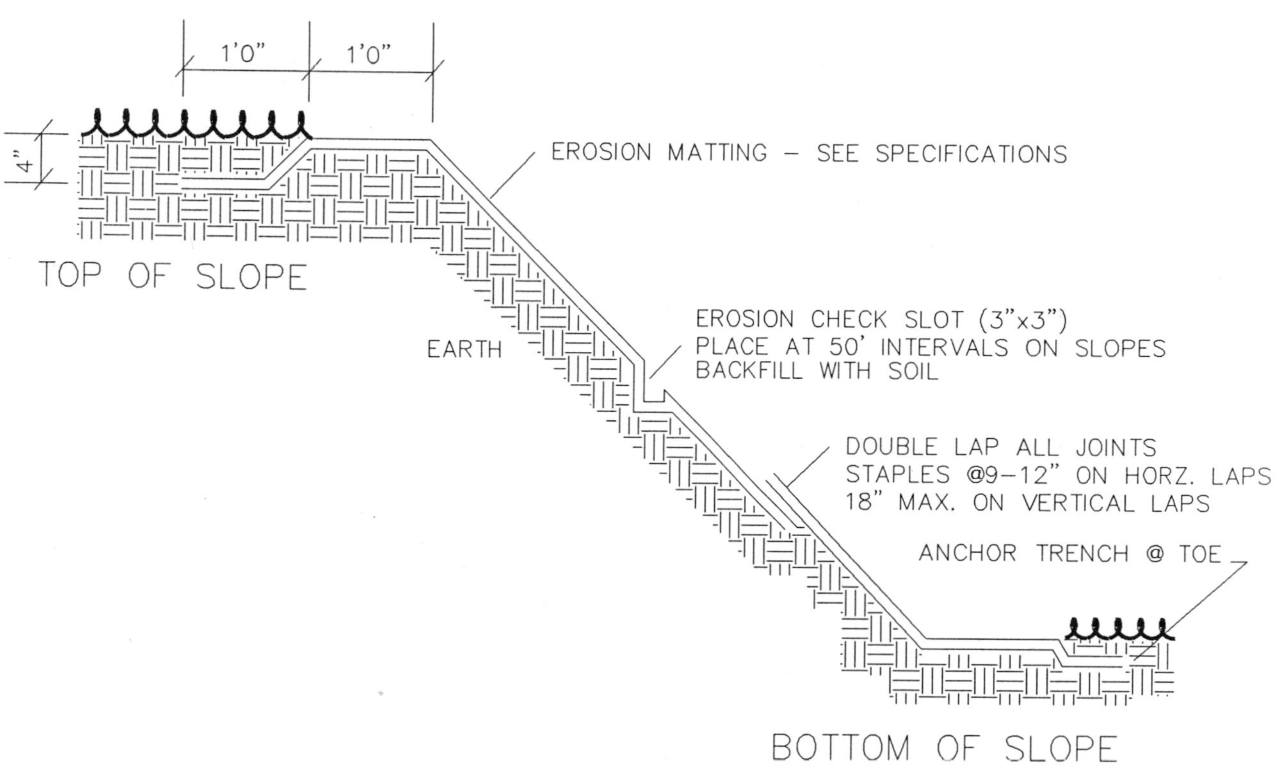
1'0"
1'0"
4"
EROSION MATTING – SEE SPECIFICATIONS
TOP OF SLOPE
EARTH
EROSION CHECK SLOT (3"x3")
PLACE AT 50' INTERVALS ON SLOPES
BACKFILL WITH SOIL
DOUBLE LAP ALL JOINTS
STAPLES @9–12" ON HORZ. LAPS
18" MAX. ON VERTICAL LAPS
ANCHOR TRENCH @ TOE
BOTTOM OF SLOPE

EROSION MATTING

SCALE: NOT TO SCALE

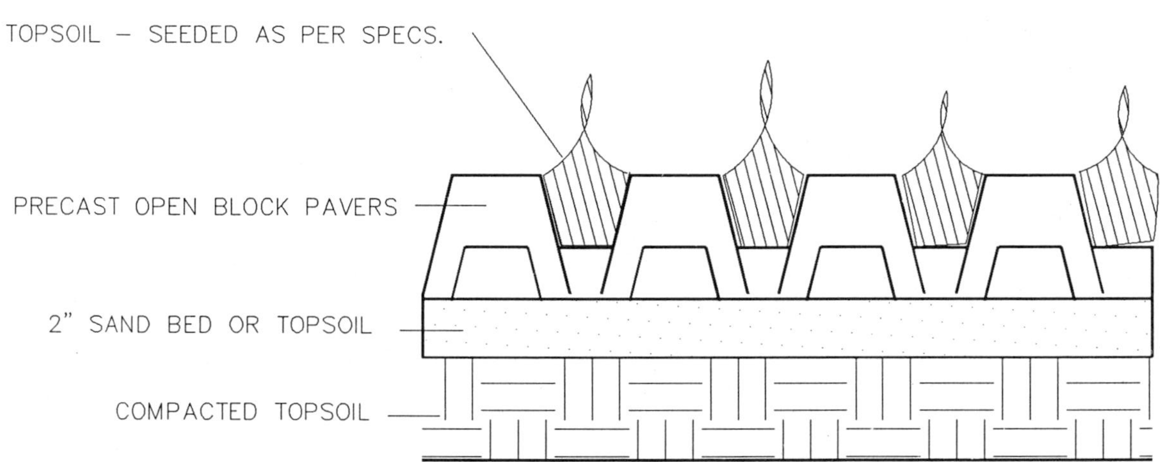
TOPSOIL – SEEDED AS PER SPECS.
PRECAST OPEN BLOCK PAVERS
2" SAND BED OR TOPSOIL
COMPACTED TOPSOIL

OPEN BLOCK PAVERS

SCALE: NOT TO SCALE

Fences

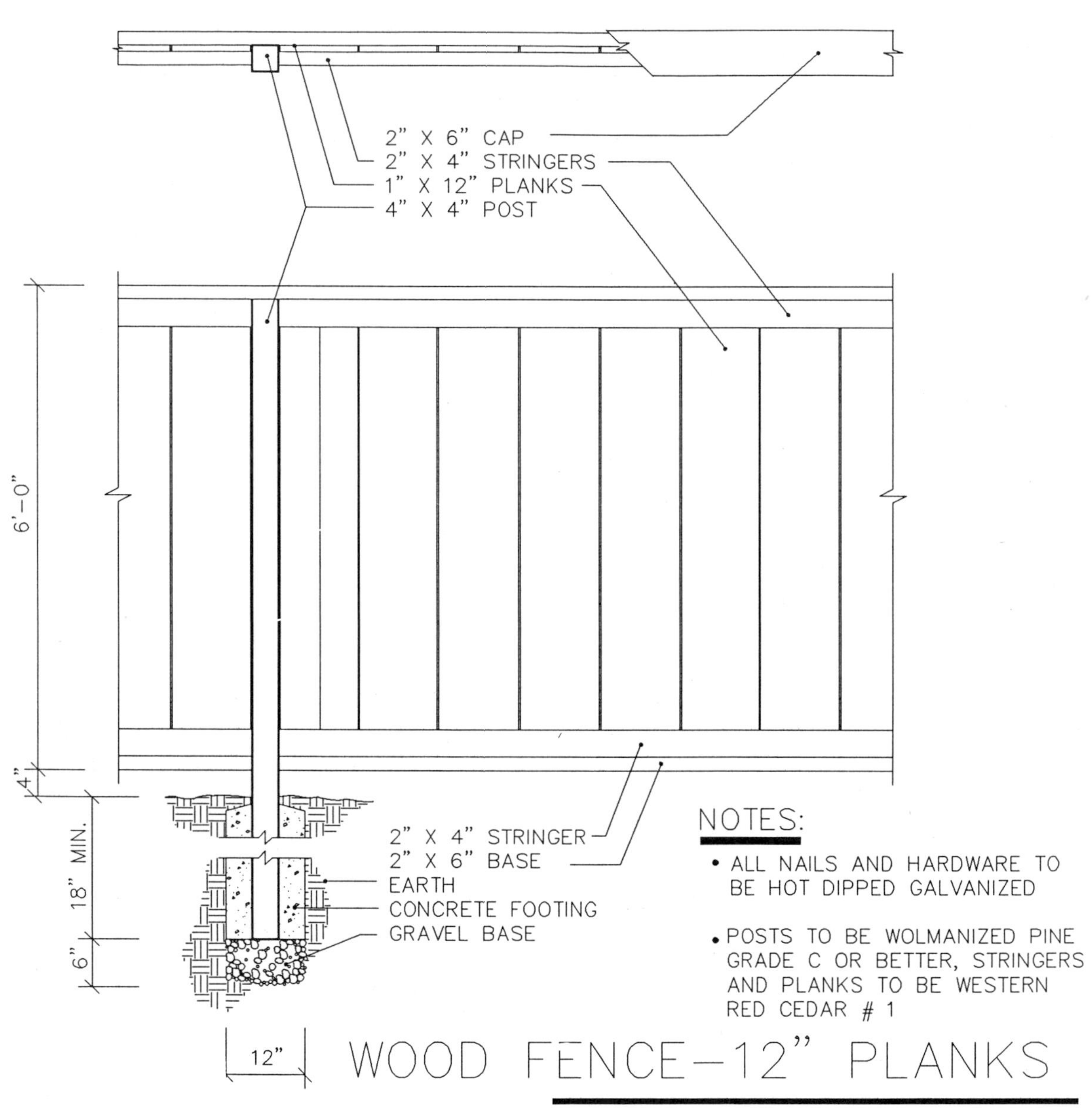
2" X 6" CAP
2" X 4" STRINGERS
1" X 12" PLANKS
4" X 4" POST
6'-0"
4"
18" MIN.
6"
2" X 4" STRINGER
2" X 6" BASE
EARTH
CONCRETE FOOTING
GRAVEL BASE
12"

NOTES:

- ALL NAILS AND HARDWARE TO BE HOT DIPPED GALVANIZED
- POSTS TO BE WOLMANIZED PINE GRADE C OR BETTER, STRINGERS AND PLANKS TO BE WESTERN RED CEDAR # 1

WOOD FENCE–12" PLANKS

SCALE: NOT TO SCALE

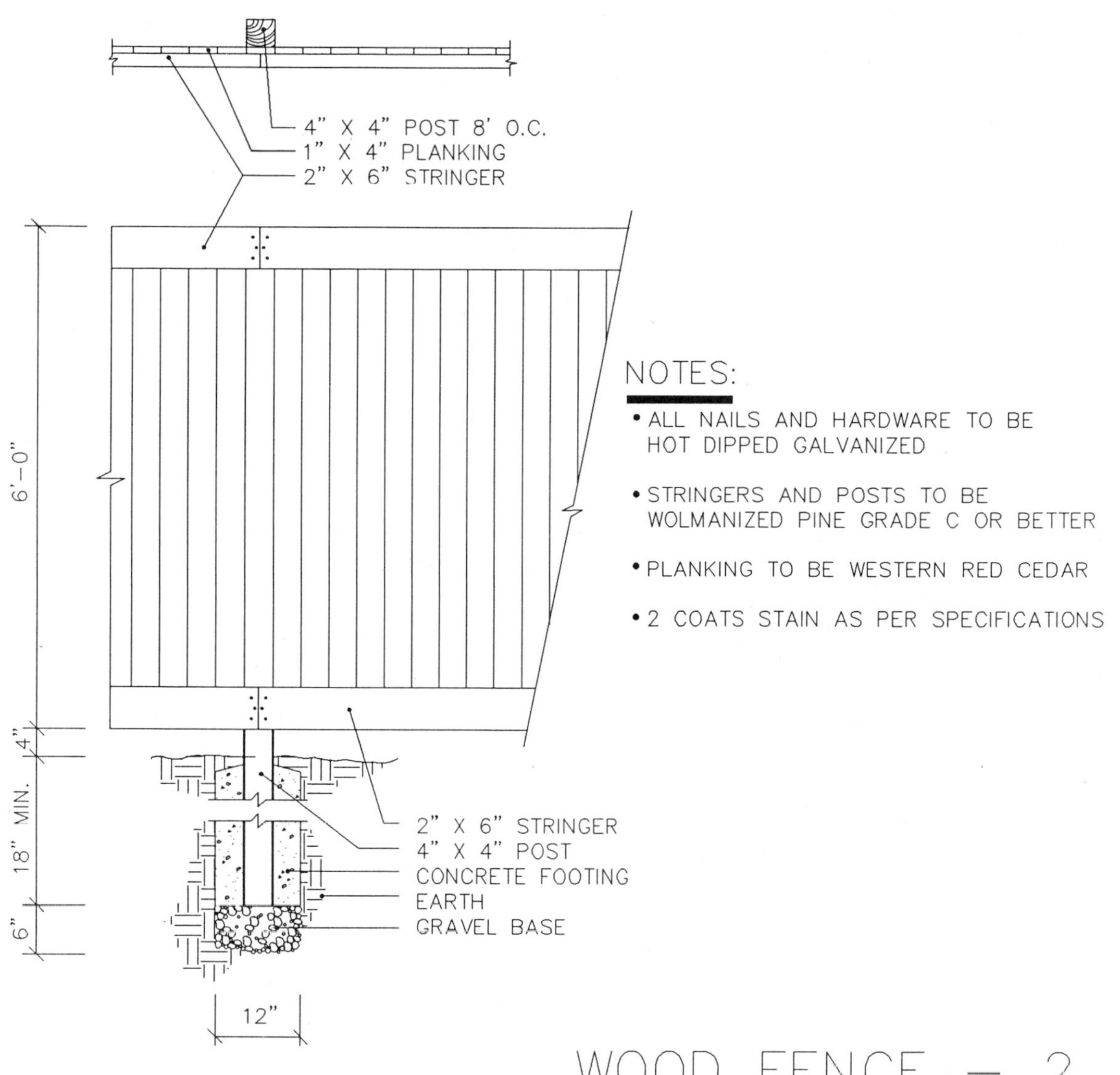
4" X 4" POST 8' O.C.
1" X 4" PLANKING
2" X 6" STRINGER
6'-0"
4"
18" MIN.
6"
NOTES:
• ALL NAILS AND HARDWARE TO BE HOT DIPPED GALVANIZED
• STRINGERS AND POSTS TO BE WOLMANIZED PINE GRADE C OR BETTER
• PLANKING TO BE WESTERN RED CEDAR
• 2 COATS STAIN AS PER SPECIFICATIONS
2" X 6" STRINGER
4" X 4" POST
CONCRETE FOOTING
EARTH
GRAVEL BASE
12"

WOOD FENCE – 2

SCALE: NOT TO SCALE

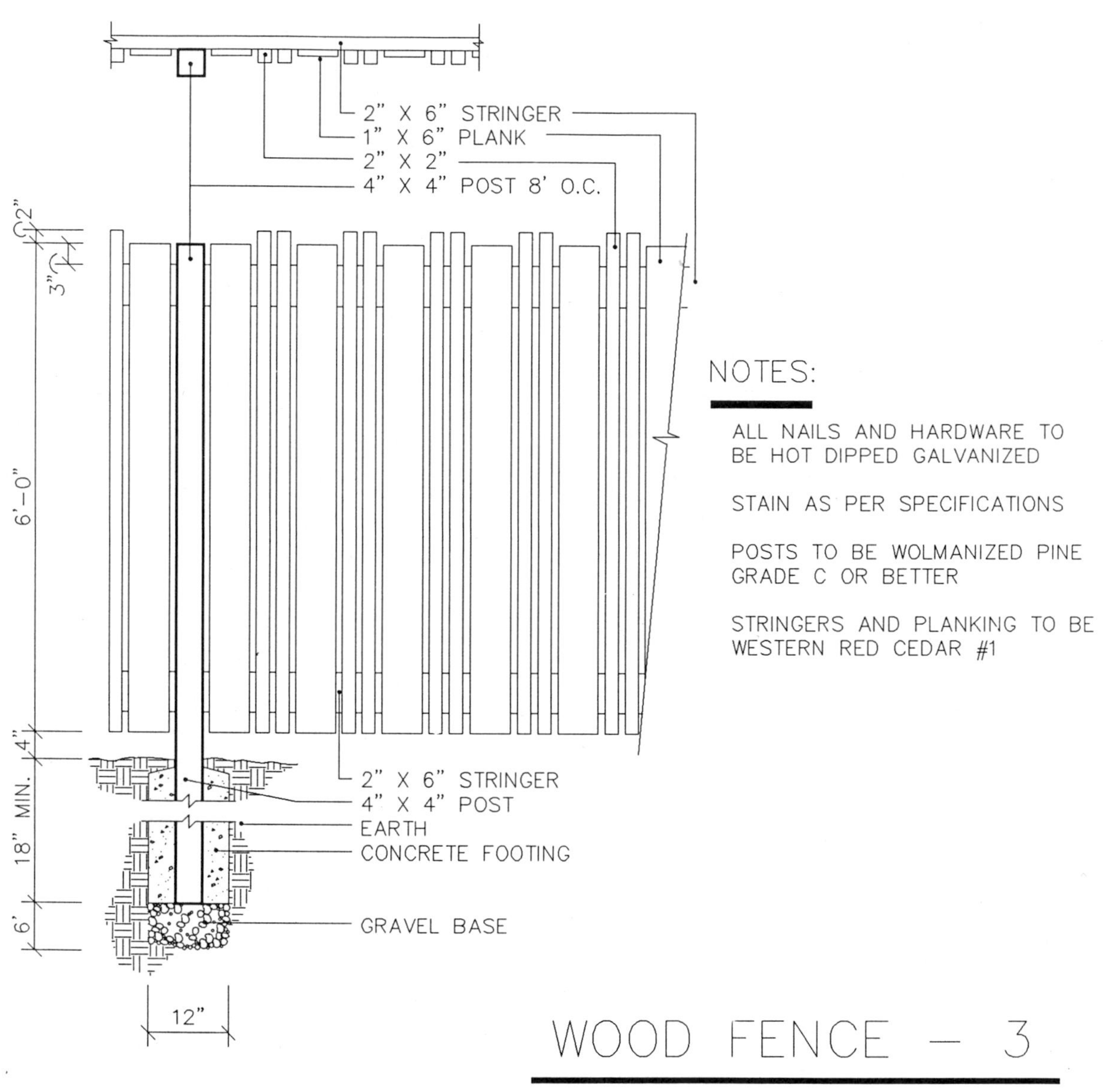
2" X 6" STRINGER
1" X 6" PLANK
2" X 2"
4" X 4" POST 8' O.C.
2"
3"
6'–0"
4"
18" MIN.
6'
2" X 6" STRINGER
4" X 4" POST
EARTH
CONCRETE FOOTING
GRAVEL BASE
12"

NOTES:

ALL NAILS AND HARDWARE TO BE HOT DIPPED GALVANIZED

STAIN AS PER SPECIFICATIONS

POSTS TO BE WOLMANIZED PINE GRADE C OR BETTER

STRINGERS AND PLANKING TO BE WESTERN RED CEDAR #1

WOOD FENCE – 3

SCALE: NOT TO SCALE

NOTES:

- ALL NAILS AND HARDWARE TO BE HOT DIPPED GALVANIZED
- WIRE MESH TO BE GALVANIZED AND FASTENED TO STRINGERS WITH 3/4" U STAPLES
- POSTS AND STRINGERS TO BE WOLMANIZED PINE GRADE C OR BETTER
- STAIN WOOD AS PER SPECIFICATIONS

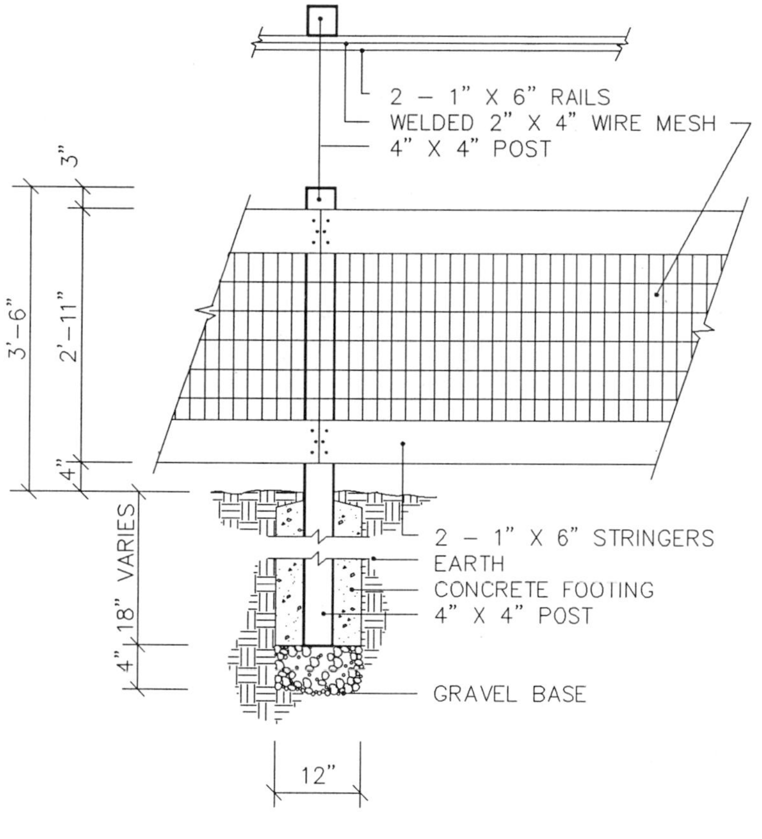

2 – 1" X 6" RAILS
WELDED 2" X 4" WIRE MESH
4" X 4" POST
3"
3'-6"
2'-11"
4"
2 – 1" X 6" STRINGERS
EARTH
CONCRETE FOOTING
4" X 4" POST
18" VARIES
4"
GRAVEL BASE
12"

WIRE AND WOOD FENCE

SCALE: NOT TO SCALE

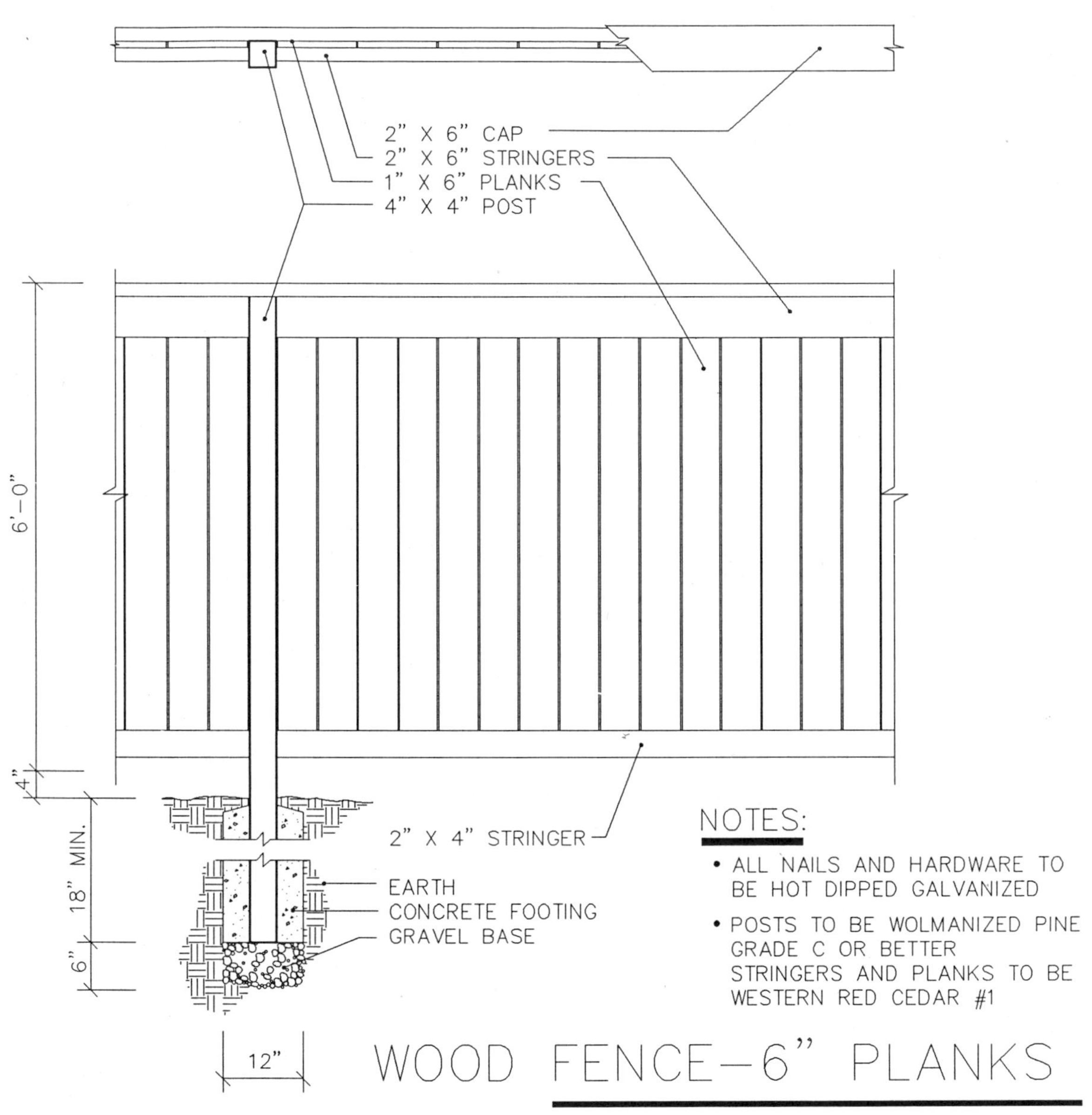

2" X 6" CAP
2" X 6" STRINGERS
1" X 6" PLANKS
4" X 4" POST
6'-0"
4"
18" MIN.
6"
2" X 4" STRINGER
EARTH
CONCRETE FOOTING
GRAVEL BASE
12"

NOTES:

- ALL NAILS AND HARDWARE TO BE HOT DIPPED GALVANIZED
- POSTS TO BE WOLMANIZED PINE GRADE C OR BETTER STRINGERS AND PLANKS TO BE WESTERN RED CEDAR #1

WOOD FENCE–6" PLANKS

SCALE: NOT TO SCALE

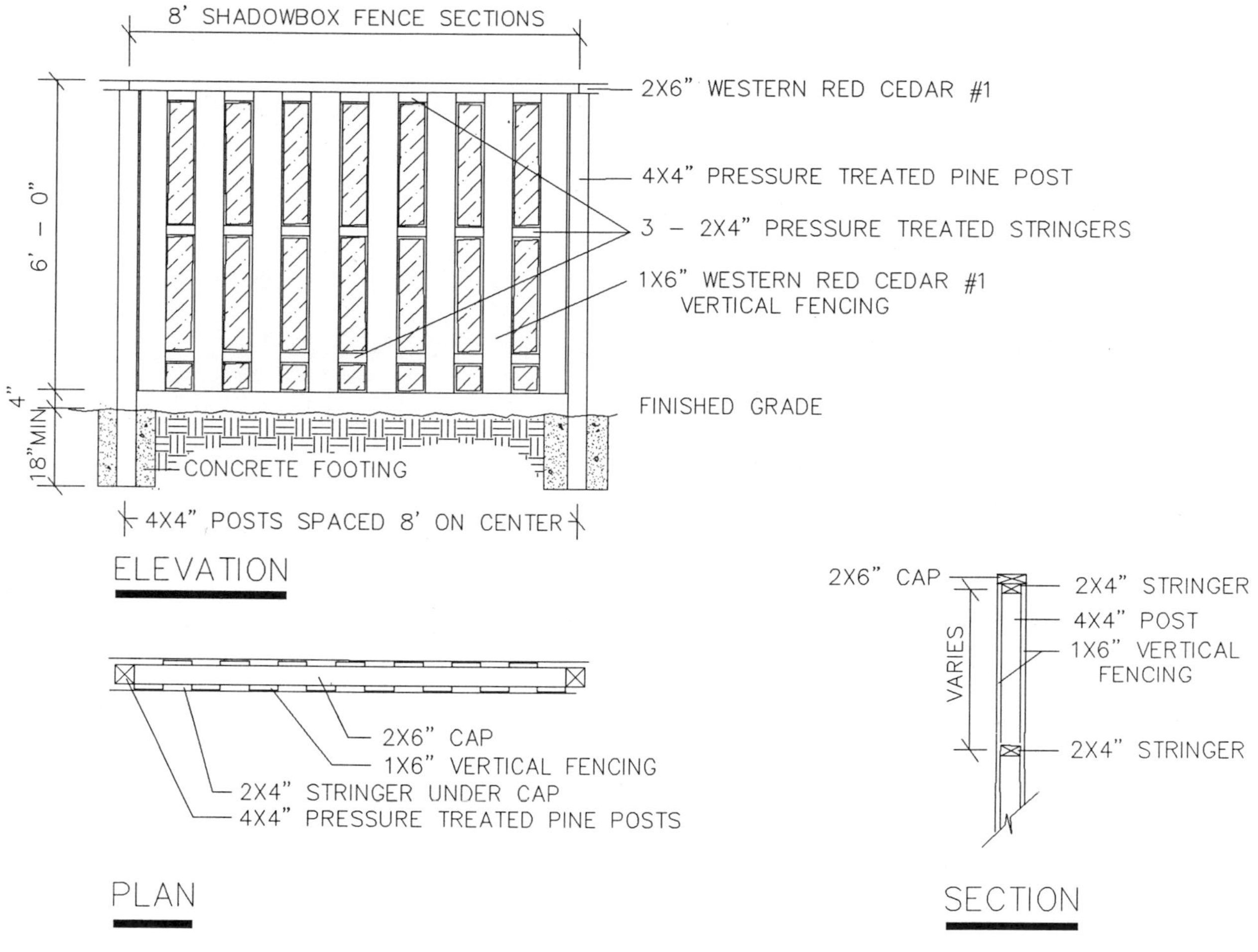

8' SHADOWBOX FENCE SECTIONS
2X6" WESTERN RED CEDAR #1
4X4" PRESSURE TREATED PINE POST
3 – 2X4" PRESSURE TREATED STRINGERS
1X6" WESTERN RED CEDAR #1
VERTICAL FENCING
6' – 0"
4"
18"MIN
FINISHED GRADE
CONCRETE FOOTING
4X4" POSTS SPACED 8' ON CENTER
ELEVATION
2X6" CAP
1X6" VERTICAL FENCING
2X4" STRINGER UNDER CAP
4X4" PRESSURE TREATED PINE POSTS
PLAN
2X6" CAP
2X4" STRINGER
4X4" POST
1X6" VERTICAL
FENCING
VARIES
2X4" STRINGER
SECTION

SHADOWBOX FENCE

SCALE: NOT TO SCALE

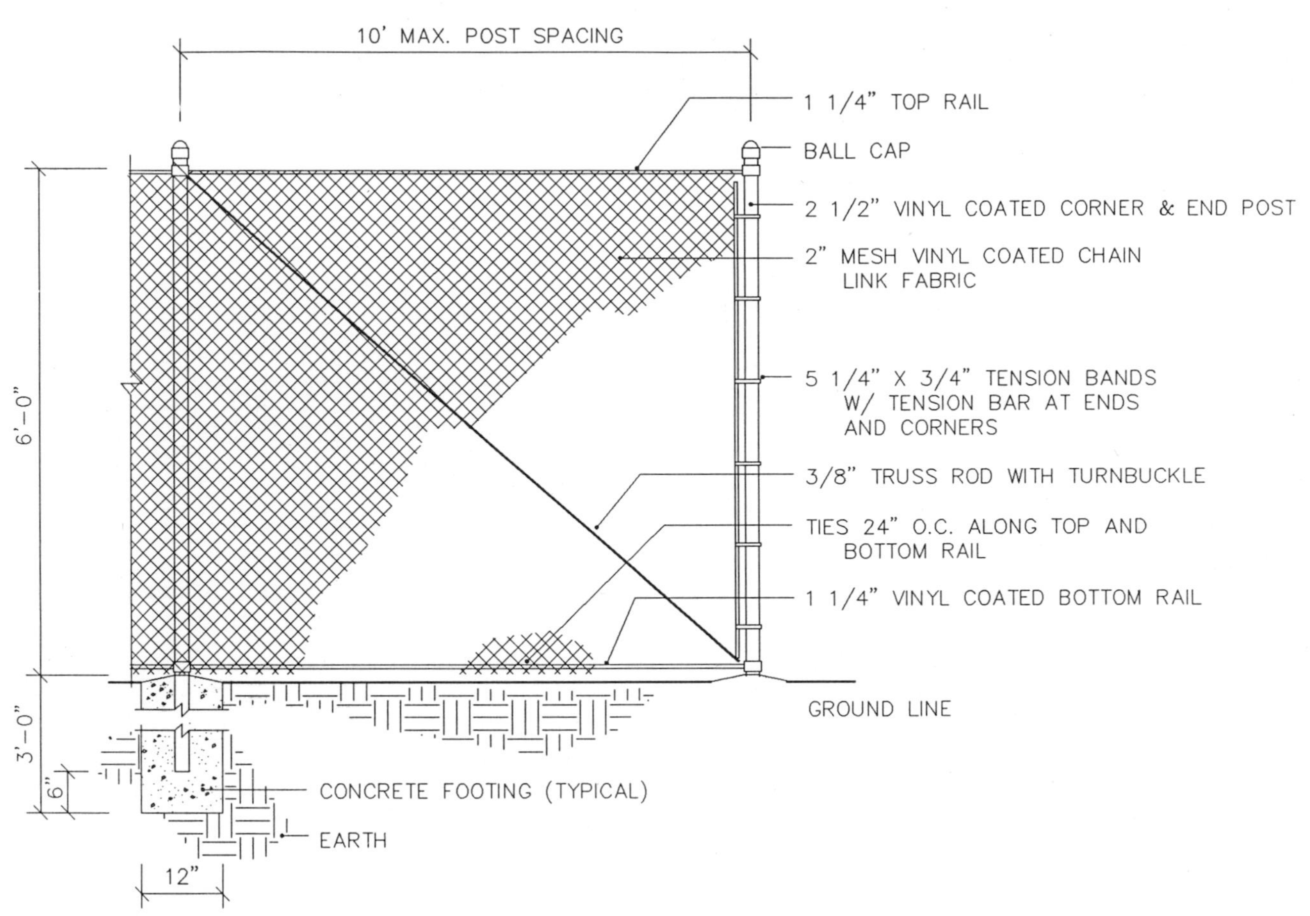

10' MAX. POST SPACING
1 1/4" TOP RAIL
BALL CAP
2 1/2" VINYL COATED CORNER & END POST
2" MESH VINYL COATED CHAIN LINK FABRIC
5 1/4" X 3/4" TENSION BANDS W/ TENSION BAR AT ENDS AND CORNERS
3/8" TRUSS ROD WITH TURNBUCKLE
TIES 24" O.C. ALONG TOP AND BOTTOM RAIL
1 1/4" VINYL COATED BOTTOM RAIL
GROUND LINE
6'-0"
3'-0"
6"
CONCRETE FOOTING (TYPICAL)
EARTH
12"

VINYL CLAD CHAIN LINK FENCE

SCALE: NOT TO SCALE

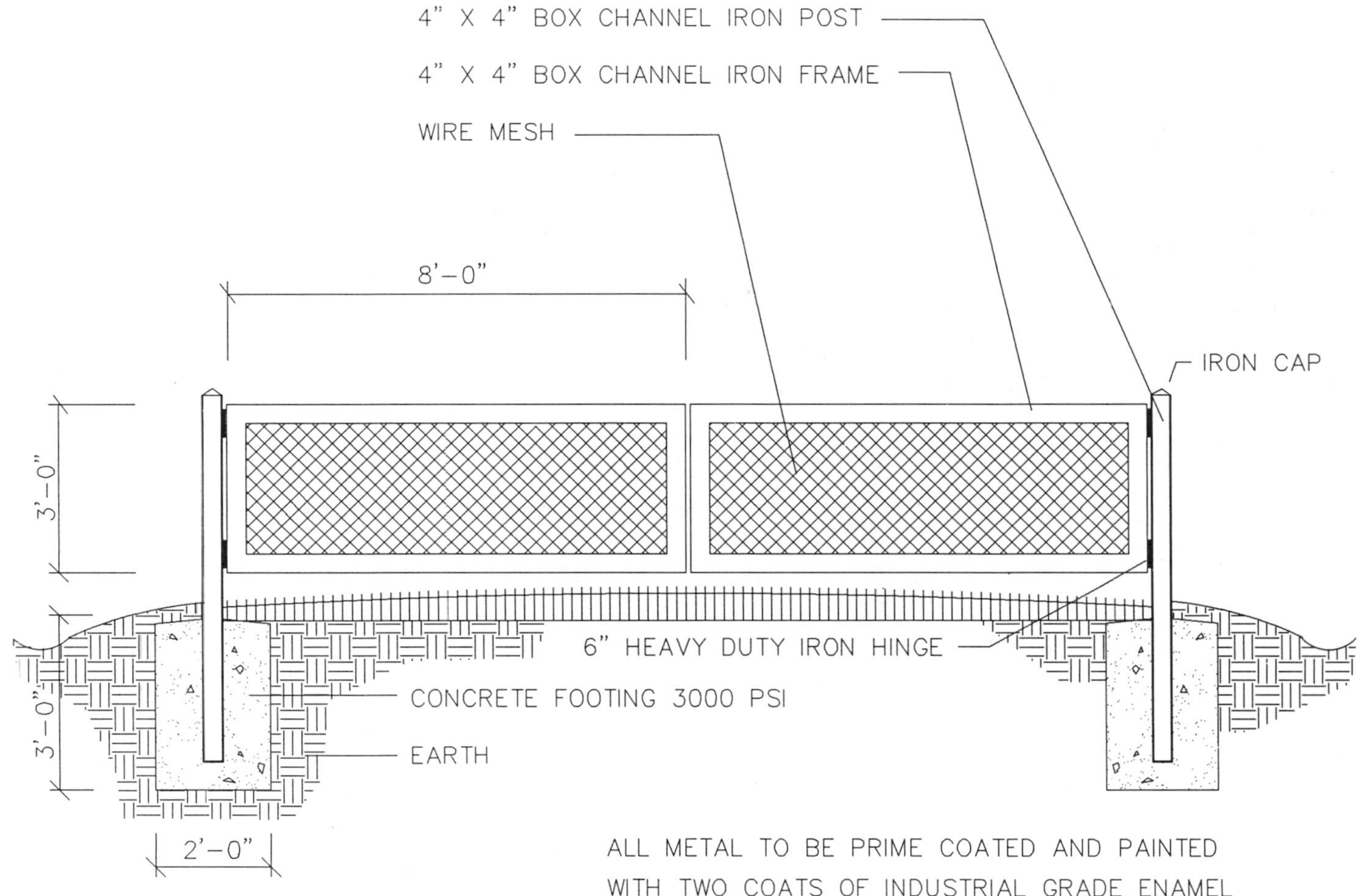
4" X 4" BOX CHANNEL IRON POST
4" X 4" BOX CHANNEL IRON FRAME
WIRE MESH
8'-0"
IRON CAP
3'-0"
6" HEAVY DUTY IRON HINGE
CONCRETE FOOTING 3000 PSI
EARTH
3'-0"
2'-0"
ALL METAL TO BE PRIME COATED AND PAINTED
WITH TWO COATS OF INDUSTRIAL GRADE ENAMEL
IRON AND MESH ENTRY GATE
SCALE: NOT TO SCALE

NOTES:

- ALL METAL TO BE DEGREASED, PHOSPHATIZED WITH RUST RETARDANT UNDERCOAT AND DIP COATED WITH TWO COATS OF INDUSTRIAL GRADE FLAT BLACK ENAMEL.

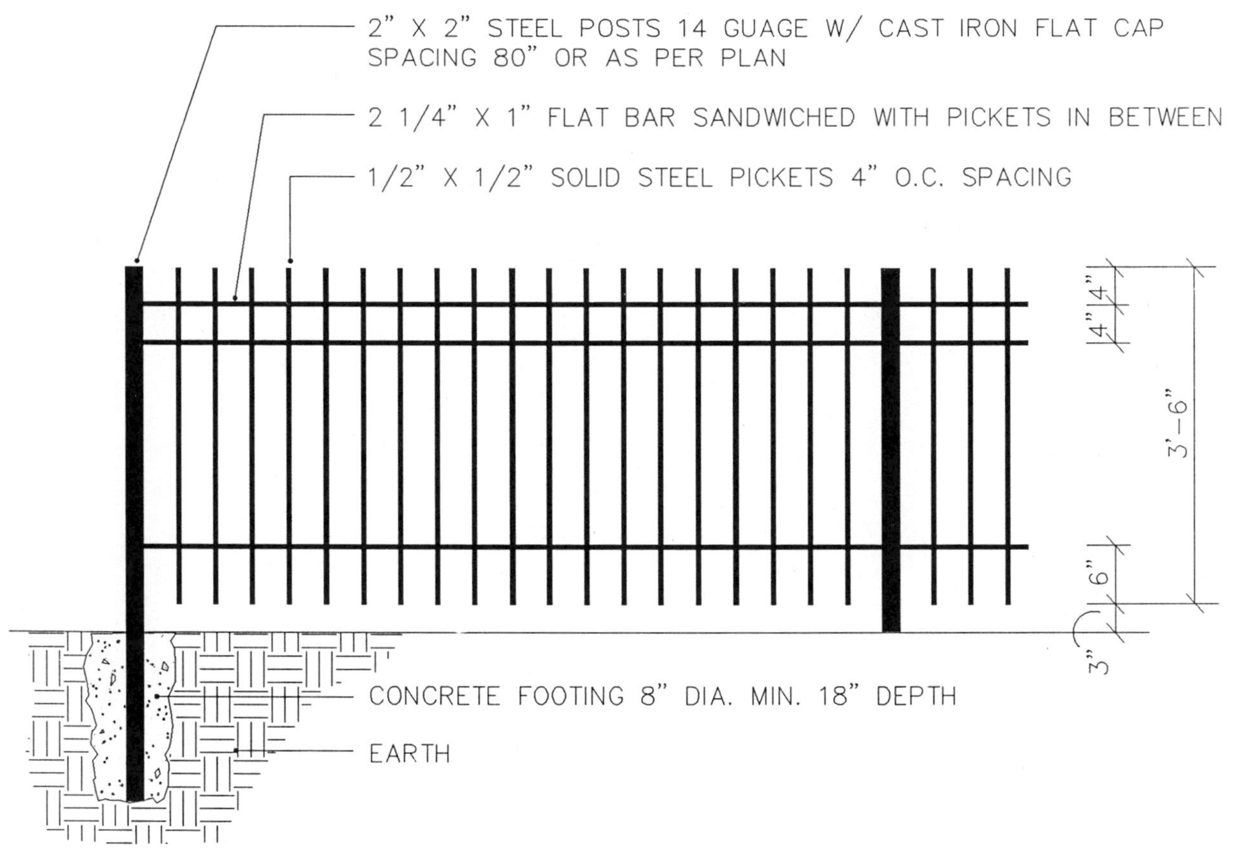

2" X 2" STEEL POSTS 14 GUAGE W/ CAST IRON FLAT CAP
SPACING 80" OR AS PER PLAN
2 1/4" X 1" FLAT BAR SANDWICHED WITH PICKETS IN BETWEEN
1/2" X 1/2" SOLID STEEL PICKETS 4" O.C. SPACING
4"
4"
3'-6"
6"
3"
CONCRETE FOOTING 8" DIA. MIN. 18" DEPTH
EARTH

WROUGHT IRON FENCE

SCALE: NOT TO SCALE

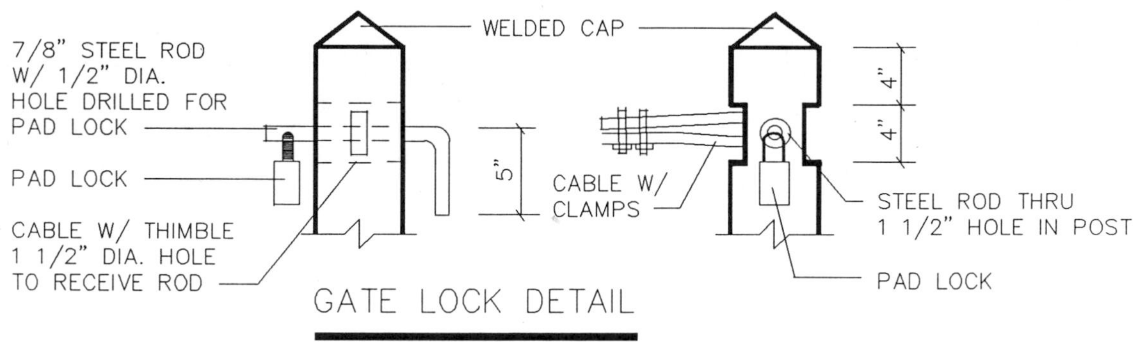
7/8" STEEL ROD W/ 1/2" DIA. HOLE DRILLED FOR PAD LOCK
PAD LOCK
CABLE W/ THIMBLE 1 1/2" DIA. HOLE TO RECEIVE ROD
WELDED CAP
5"
CABLE W/ CLAMPS
4"
4"
STEEL ROD THRU 1 1/2" HOLE IN POST
PAD LOCK

GATE LOCK DETAIL

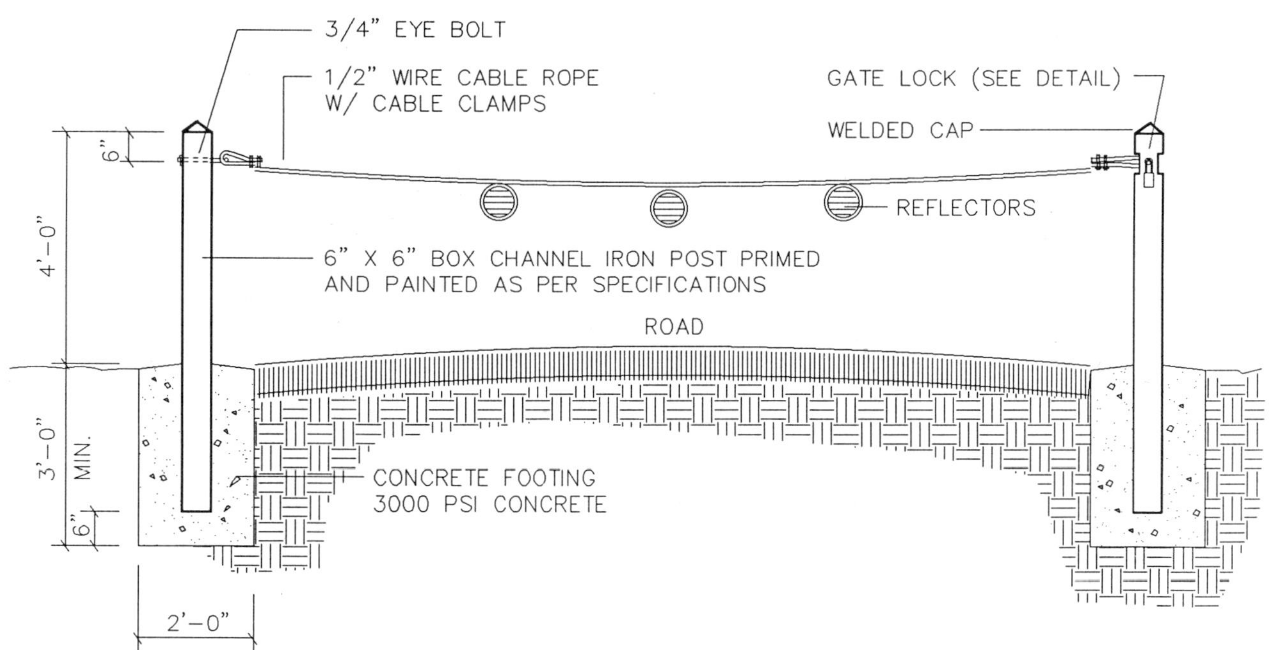
3/4" EYE BOLT
1/2" WIRE CABLE ROPE W/ CABLE CLAMPS
GATE LOCK (SEE DETAIL)
WELDED CAP
REFLECTORS
6" X 6" BOX CHANNEL IRON POST PRIMED AND PAINTED AS PER SPECIFICATIONS
ROAD
CONCRETE FOOTING 3000 PSI CONCRETE
6"
4'–0"
3'–0" MIN.
6"
2'–0"

WIRE CABLE GATE

SCALE: NOT TO SCALE

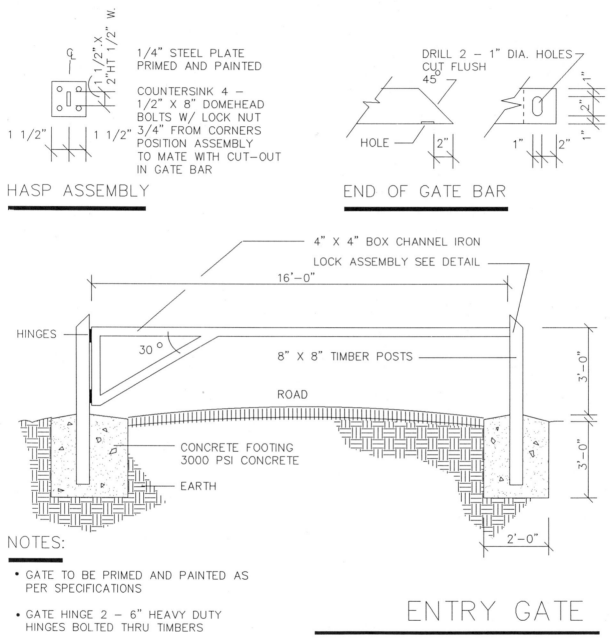

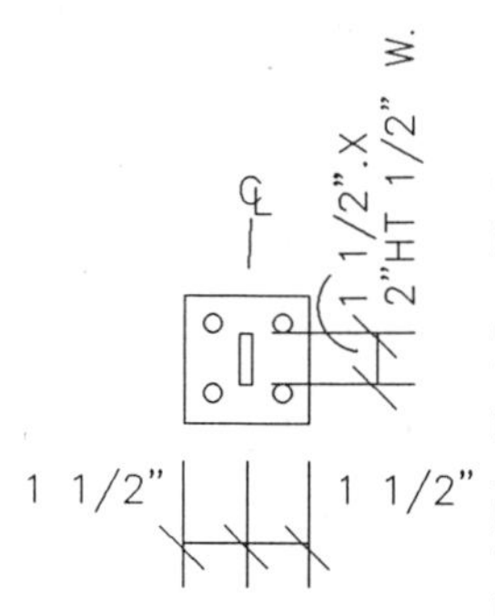

℄
1 1/2" X 2"HT 1/2" W.
1 1/2"
1 1/2"

1/4" STEEL PLATE PRIMED AND PAINTED

COUNTERSINK 4 – 1/2" X 8" DOMEHEAD BOLTS W/ LOCK NUT 3/4" FROM CORNERS POSITION ASSEMBLY TO MATE WITH CUT–OUT IN GATE BAR

HASP ASSEMBLY

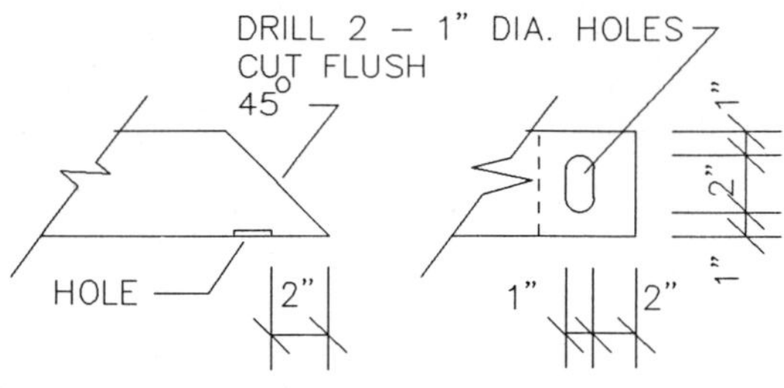

DRILL 2 – 1" DIA. HOLES
CUT FLUSH
45°
HOLE
2"
1"
2"
1"
2"
1"

END OF GATE BAR

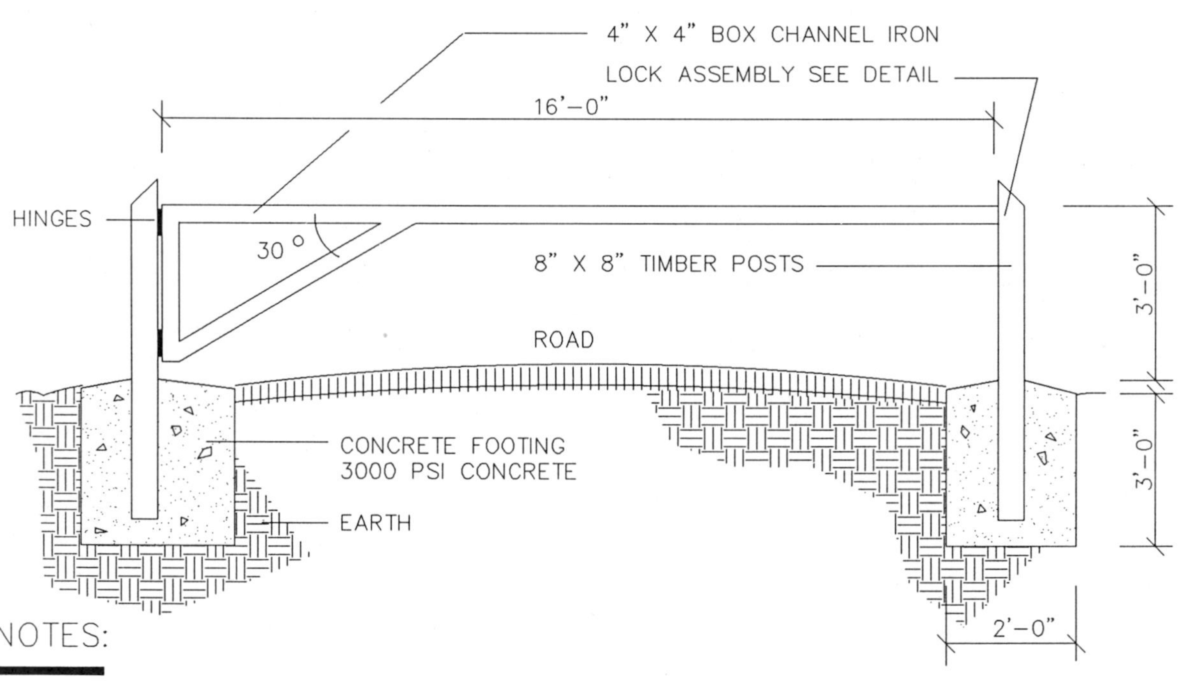

4" X 4" BOX CHANNEL IRON
LOCK ASSEMBLY SEE DETAIL
16'–0"
HINGES
30°
8" X 8" TIMBER POSTS
ROAD
3'–0"
3'–0"
CONCRETE FOOTING
3000 PSI CONCRETE
EARTH
2'–0"

NOTES:

- GATE TO BE PRIMED AND PAINTED AS PER SPECIFICATIONS
- GATE HINGE 2 – 6" HEAVY DUTY HINGES BOLTED THRU TIMBERS

ENTRY GATE

SCALE: NOT TO SCALE

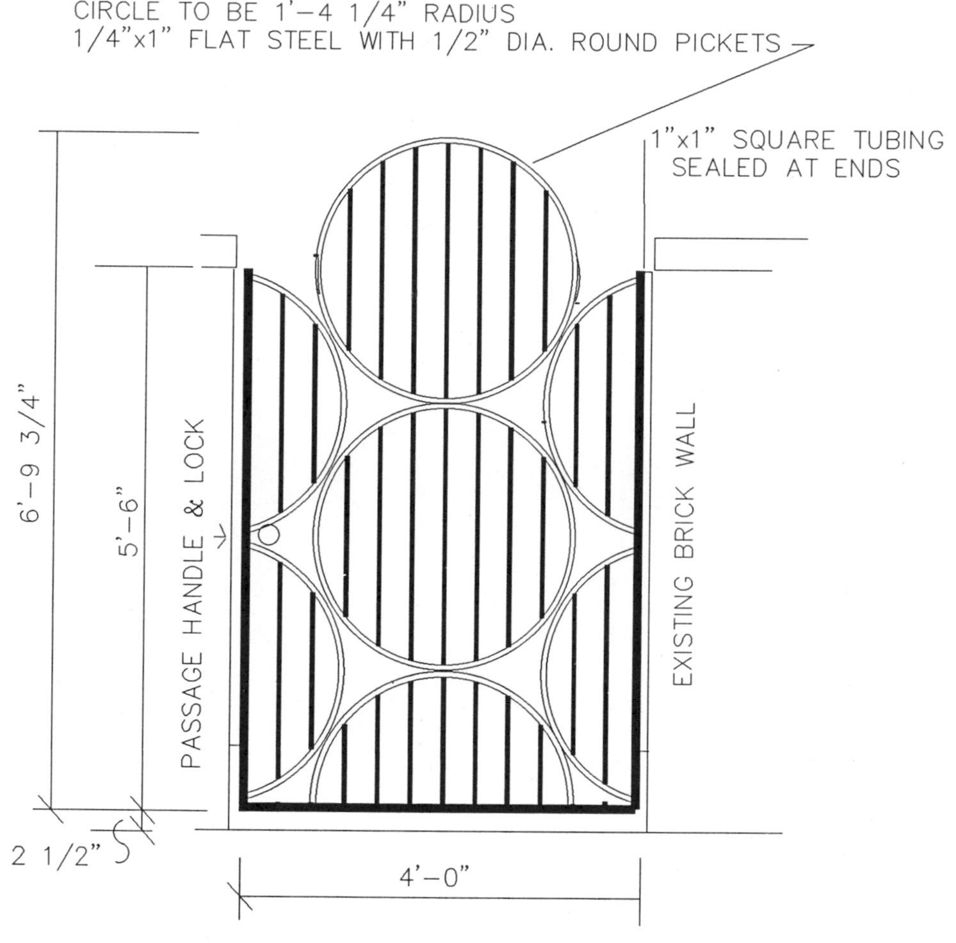

CIRCLE TO BE 1'–4 1/4" RADIUS
1/4"x1" FLAT STEEL WITH 1/2" DIA. ROUND PICKETS
1"x1" SQUARE TUBING
SEALED AT ENDS
6'–9 3/4"
5'–6"
PASSAGE HANDLE & LOCK
EXISTING BRICK WALL
2 1/2"
4'–0"

ALL METAL TO BE DEGREASED, PHOSPHATIZED
WITH RUST RETARDANT UNDERCOAT
AND DIP COATED WITH TWO COATS
OF INDUSTRIAL GRADE BLUE (COLOR SELECTED BY LANDSCAPE ARCHITECT)

DECORATIVE IRON GATE

SCALE: NOT TO SCALE

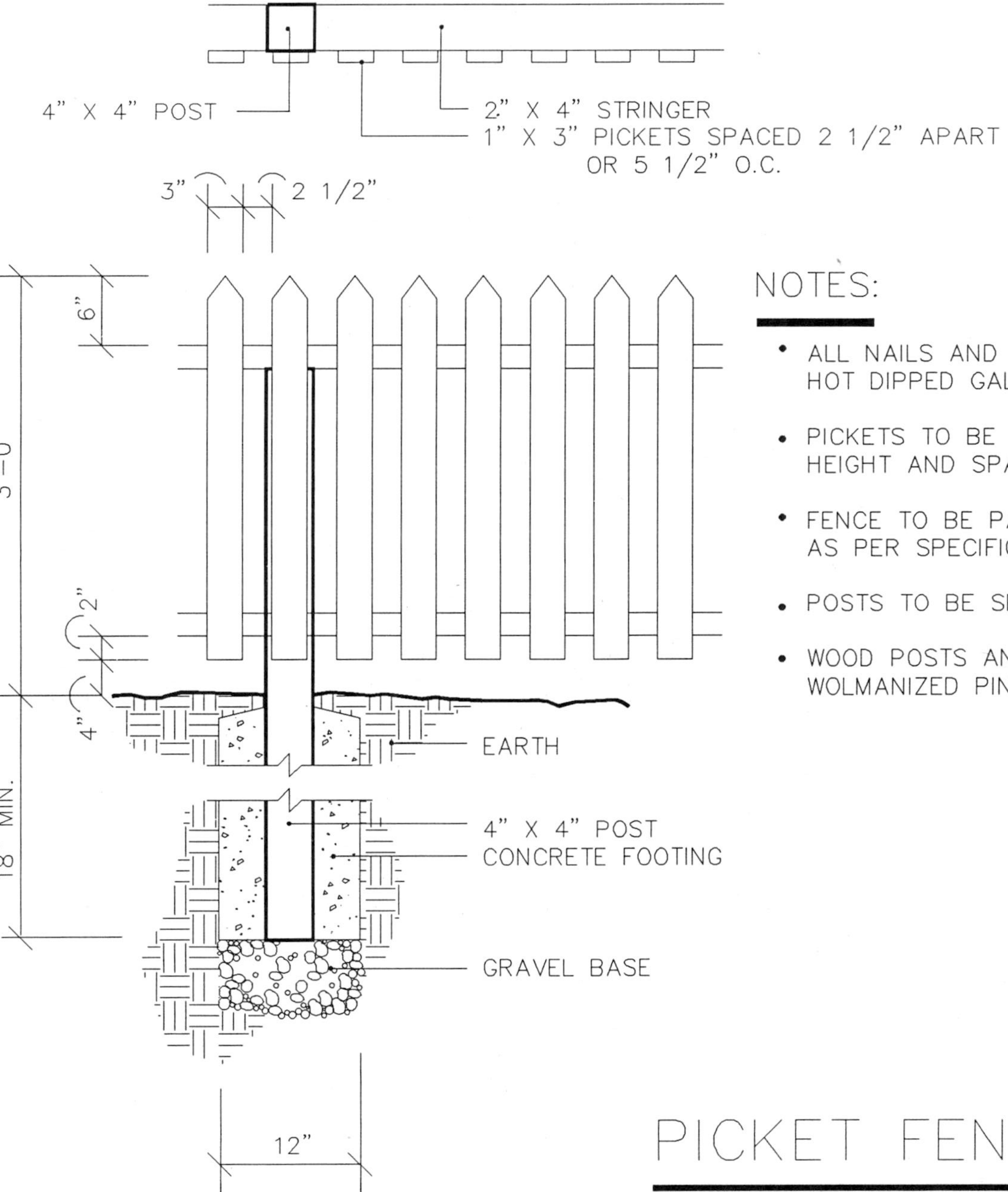
4" X 4" POST
2" X 4" STRINGER
1" X 3" PICKETS SPACED 2 1/2" APART
OR 5 1/2" O.C.
3"
2 1/2"
6"
3'–0"
2"
4"
18" MIN.
EARTH
4" X 4" POST
CONCRETE FOOTING
GRAVEL BASE
12"

NOTES:

- ALL NAILS AND HARDWARE TO BE HOT DIPPED GALVANIZED
- PICKETS TO BE HUNG WITH UNIFORM HEIGHT AND SPACING.
- FENCE TO BE PAINTED OR STAINED AS PER SPECIFICATIONS
- POSTS TO BE SPACED 6" O.C.
- WOOD POSTS AND STRINGERS TO BE WOLMANIZED PINE GRADE C OR BETTER

PICKET FENCE – 1

SCALE: NOT TO SCALE

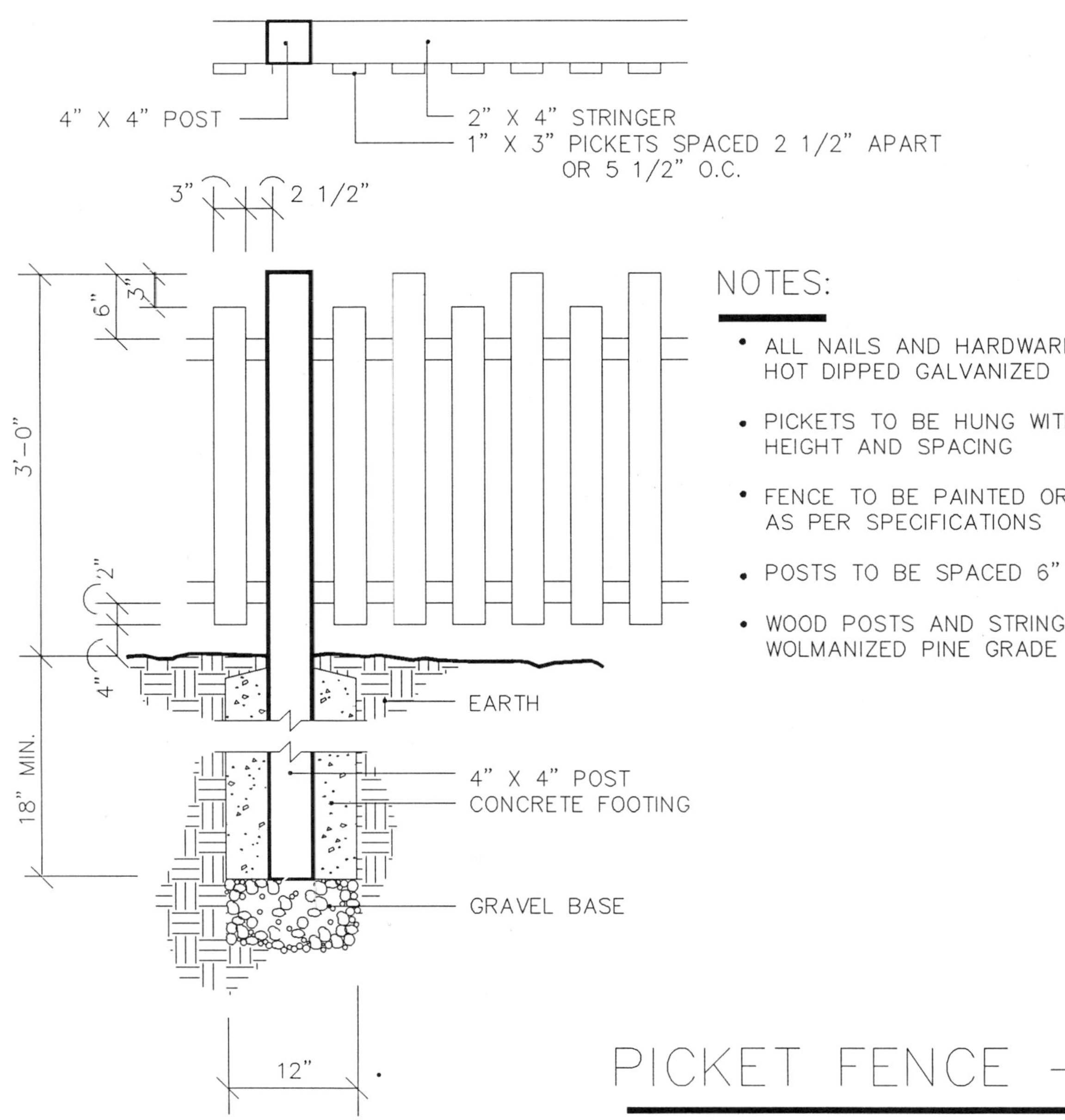
4" X 4" POST
2" X 4" STRINGER
1" X 3" PICKETS SPACED 2 1/2" APART
OR 5 1/2" O.C.
3"
2 1/2"
6"
3"
3'–0"
2"
4"
18" MIN.
EARTH
4" X 4" POST
CONCRETE FOOTING
GRAVEL BASE
12"

NOTES:

- ALL NAILS AND HARDWARE TO BE HOT DIPPED GALVANIZED
- PICKETS TO BE HUNG WITH UNIFORM HEIGHT AND SPACING
- FENCE TO BE PAINTED OR STAINED AS PER SPECIFICATIONS
- POSTS TO BE SPACED 6" O.C.
- WOOD POSTS AND STRINGERS TO BE WOLMANIZED PINE GRADE C OR BETTER

PICKET FENCE – 2

SCALE: NOT TO SCALE

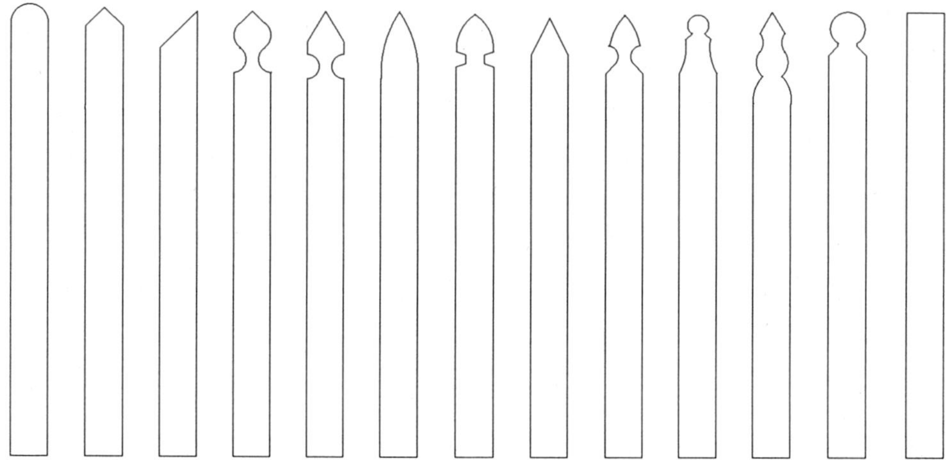

PICKETS

POSTS

PICKET AND POST STYLES

SCALE: NOT TO SCALE

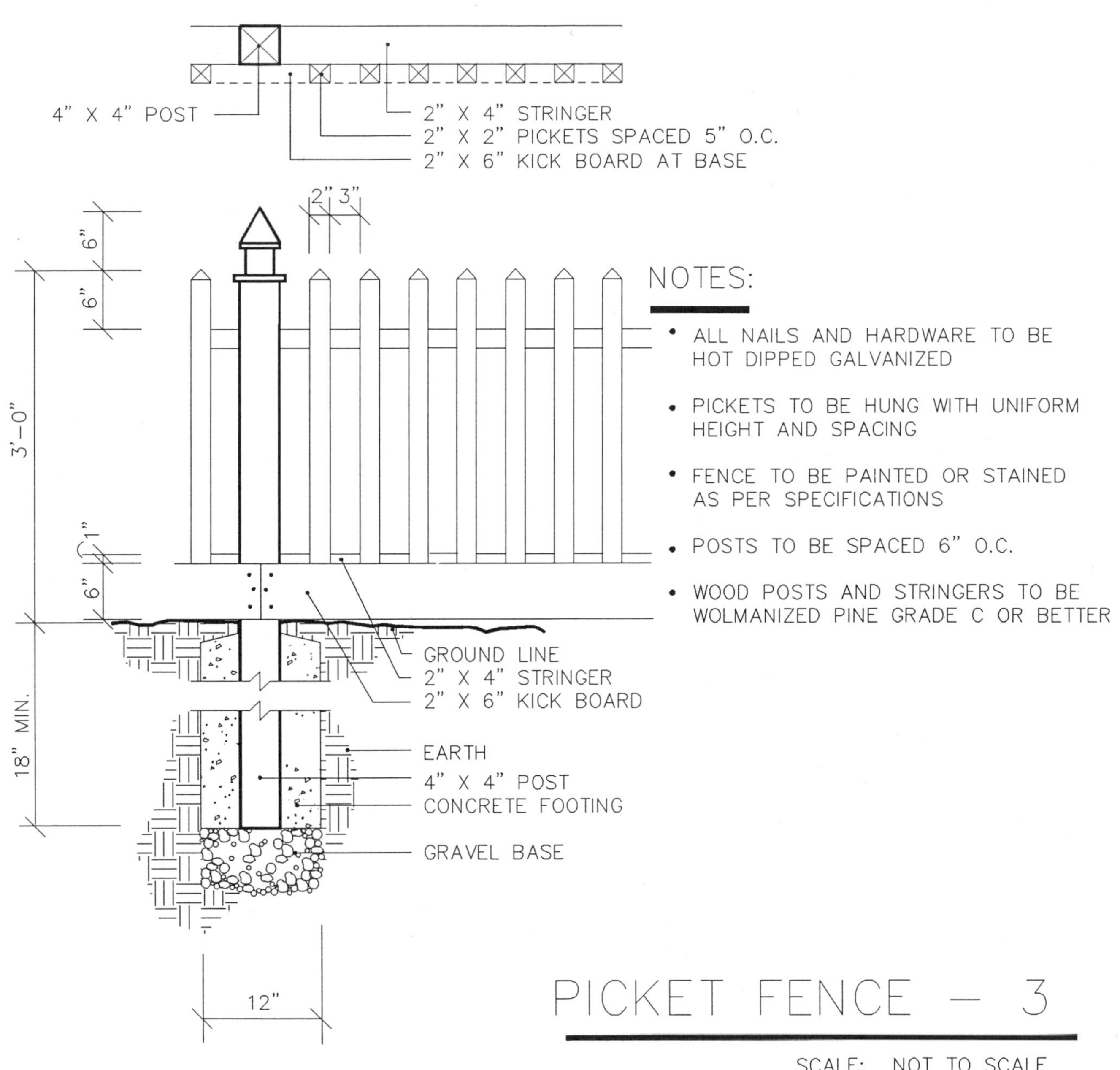
4" X 4" POST
2" X 4" STRINGER
2" X 2" PICKETS SPACED 5" O.C.
2" X 6" KICK BOARD AT BASE
2"
3"
6"
6"
3'-0"
1"
6"
18" MIN.
12"
NOTES:
• ALL NAILS AND HARDWARE TO BE HOT DIPPED GALVANIZED
• PICKETS TO BE HUNG WITH UNIFORM HEIGHT AND SPACING
• FENCE TO BE PAINTED OR STAINED AS PER SPECIFICATIONS
• POSTS TO BE SPACED 6" O.C.
• WOOD POSTS AND STRINGERS TO BE WOLMANIZED PINE GRADE C OR BETTER
GROUND LINE
2" X 4" STRINGER
2" X 6" KICK BOARD
EARTH
4" X 4" POST
CONCRETE FOOTING
GRAVEL BASE
PICKET FENCE – 3
SCALE: NOT TO SCALE

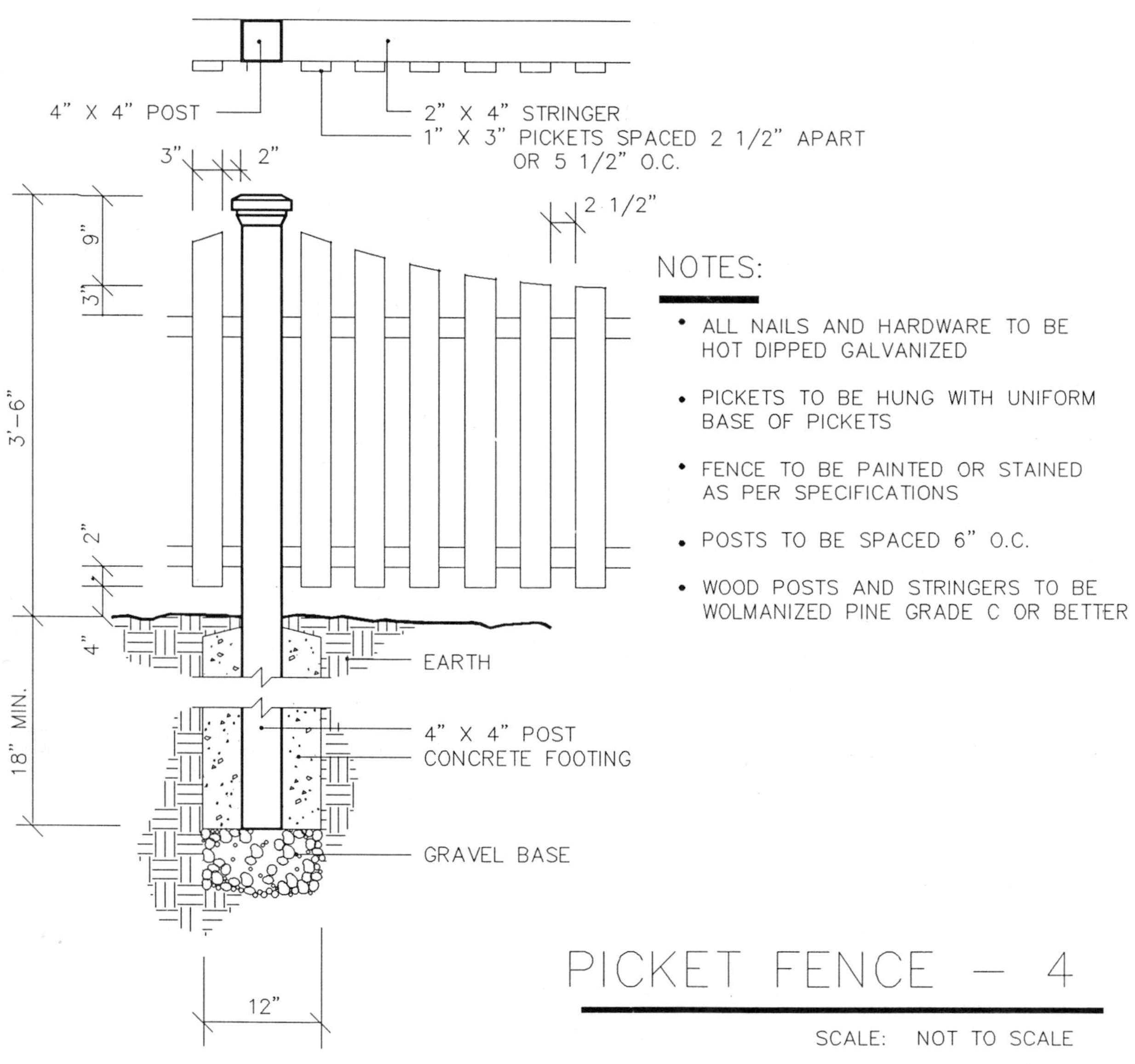
4" X 4" POST
2" X 4" STRINGER
1" X 3" PICKETS SPACED 2 1/2" APART
OR 5 1/2" O.C.
3"
2"
2 1/2"
9"
3"
3'-6"
2"
4"
18" MIN.
EARTH
4" X 4" POST
CONCRETE FOOTING
GRAVEL BASE
12"
NOTES:
ALL NAILS AND HARDWARE TO BE HOT DIPPED GALVANIZED
PICKETS TO BE HUNG WITH UNIFORM BASE OF PICKETS
FENCE TO BE PAINTED OR STAINED AS PER SPECIFICATIONS
POSTS TO BE SPACED 6" O.C.
WOOD POSTS AND STRINGERS TO BE WOLMANIZED PINE GRADE C OR BETTER

PICKET FENCE — 4

SCALE: NOT TO SCALE

Fountains & Pools

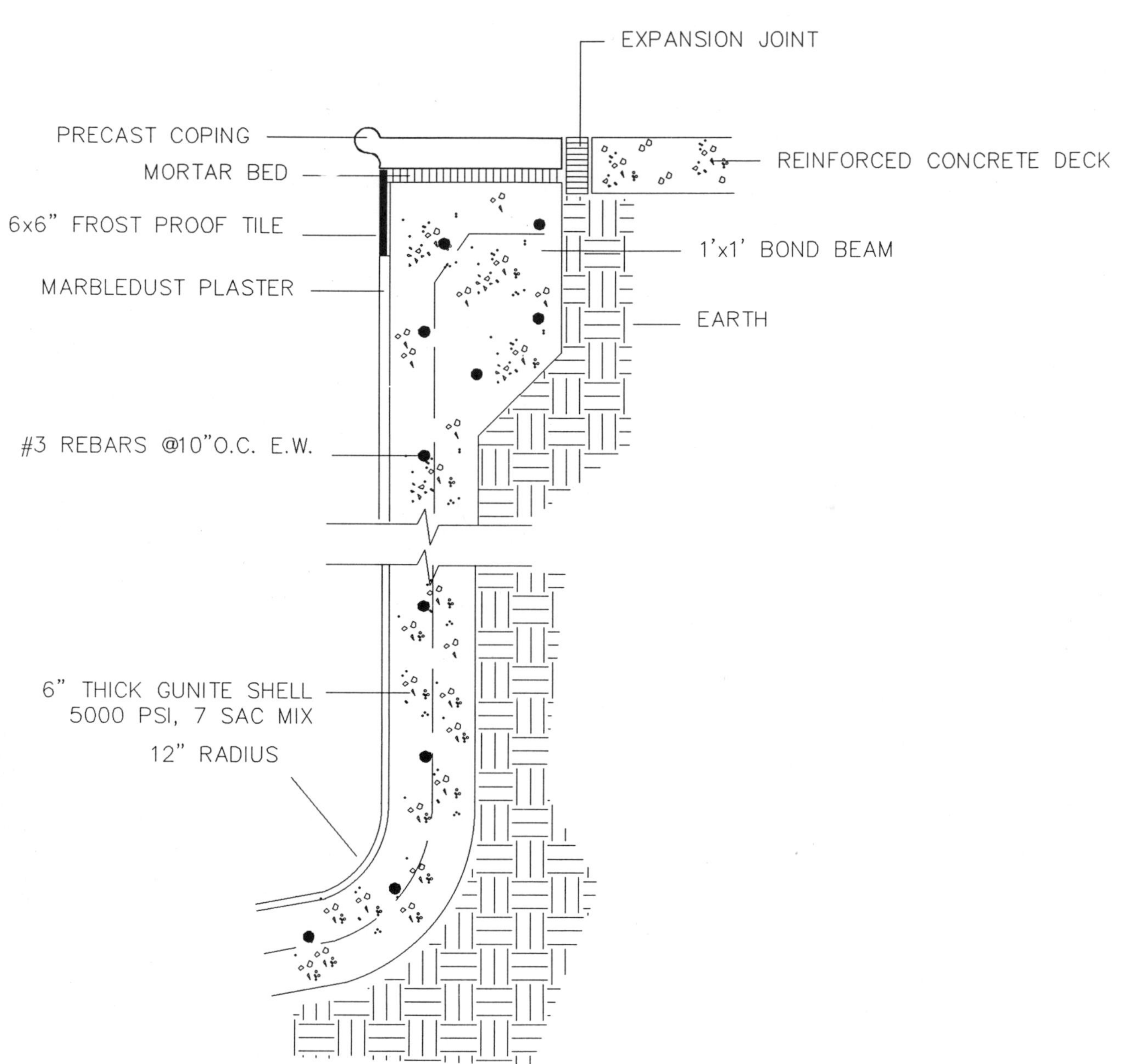
EXPANSION JOINT
PRECAST COPING
MORTAR BED
REINFORCED CONCRETE DECK
6x6" FROST PROOF TILE
1'x1' BOND BEAM
MARBLEDUST PLASTER
EARTH
#3 REBARS @10"O.C. E.W.
6" THICK GUNITE SHELL
5000 PSI, 7 SAC MIX
12" RADIUS

POOL WALL SECTION

SCALE: NOT TO SCALE

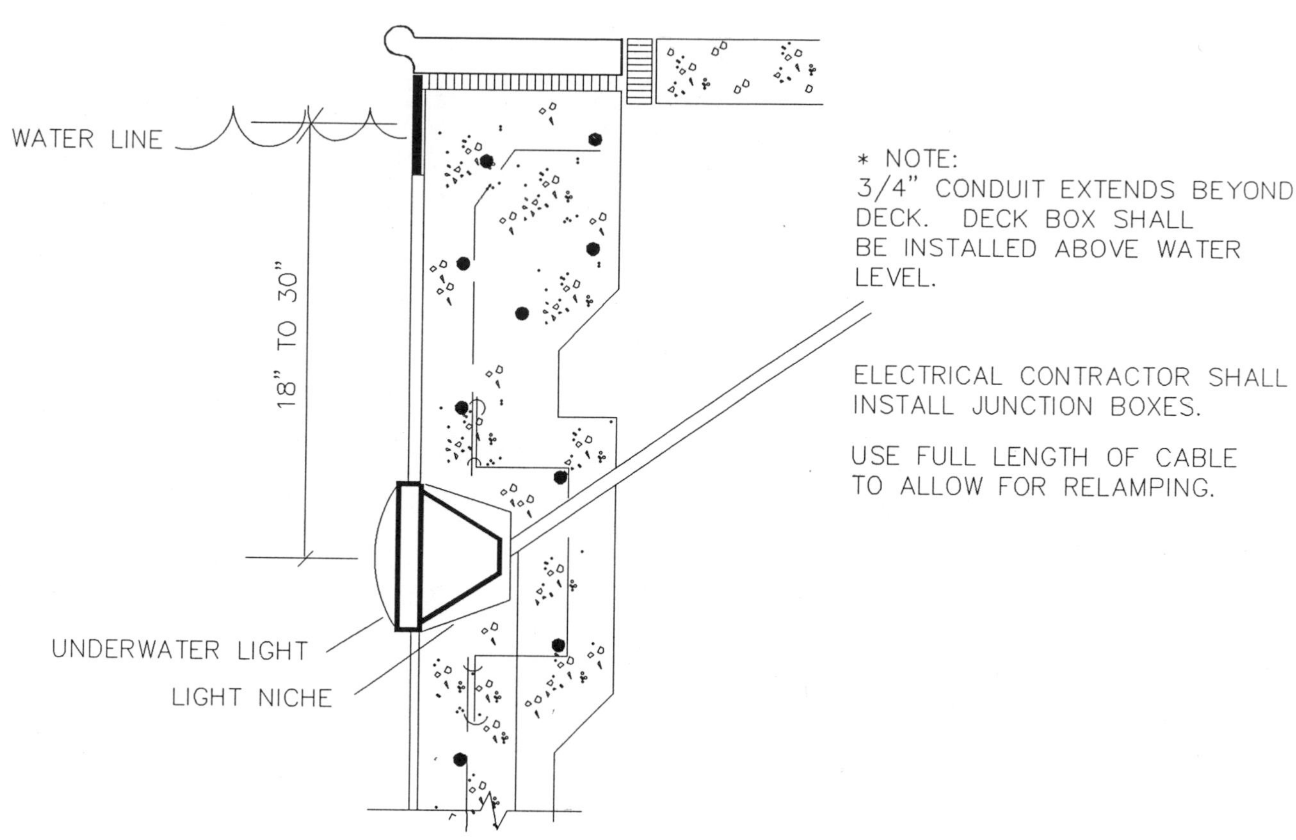
WATER LINE
18" TO 30"
UNDERWATER LIGHT
LIGHT NICHE
* NOTE:
3/4" CONDUIT EXTENDS BEYOND
DECK. DECK BOX SHALL
BE INSTALLED ABOVE WATER
LEVEL.
ELECTRICAL CONTRACTOR SHALL
INSTALL JUNCTION BOXES.
USE FULL LENGTH OF CABLE
TO ALLOW FOR RELAMPING.

POOL WALL LIGHT

SCALE: NOT TO SCALE

NOTE:

- ALL CONCRETE TO BE 4800 P.S.I. RATED
- INTERIOR OF FOUNTAIN TO HAVE 2 COATS OF PLASTER 5/8" MAX. PAINT WITH 2 COATS BLACK EPOXY PAINT
- RECIRCULATING FOUNTAIN KIT MODEL # AS PER SPECIFICATIONS
- USE PUMP TO DRAIN FOUNTAIN

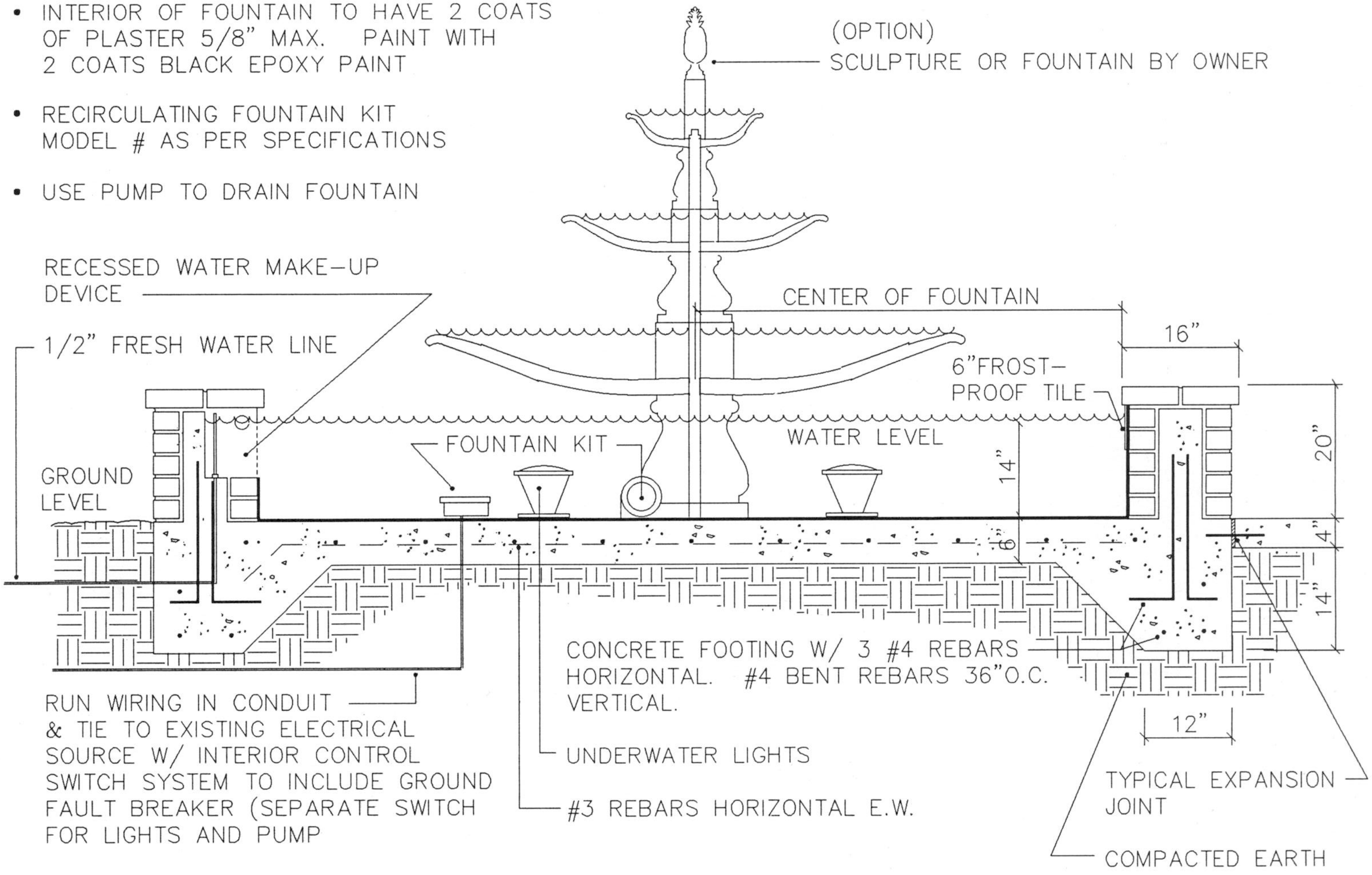

(OPTION)
SCULPTURE OR FOUNTAIN BY OWNER

RECESSED WATER MAKE-UP DEVICE

1/2" FRESH WATER LINE

CENTER OF FOUNTAIN

16"

6"FROST-PROOF TILE

WATER LEVEL

FOUNTAIN KIT

14"

20"

GROUND LEVEL

6"

4"

14"

CONCRETE FOOTING W/ 3 #4 REBARS HORIZONTAL. #4 BENT REBARS 36"O.C. VERTICAL.

12"

RUN WIRING IN CONDUIT & TIE TO EXISTING ELECTRICAL SOURCE W/ INTERIOR CONTROL SWITCH SYSTEM TO INCLUDE GROUND FAULT BREAKER (SEPARATE SWITCH FOR LIGHTS AND PUMP

UNDERWATER LIGHTS

#3 REBARS HORIZONTAL E.W.

TYPICAL EXPANSION JOINT

COMPACTED EARTH

RAISED BRICK FOUNTAIN

SCALE: NOT TO SCALE

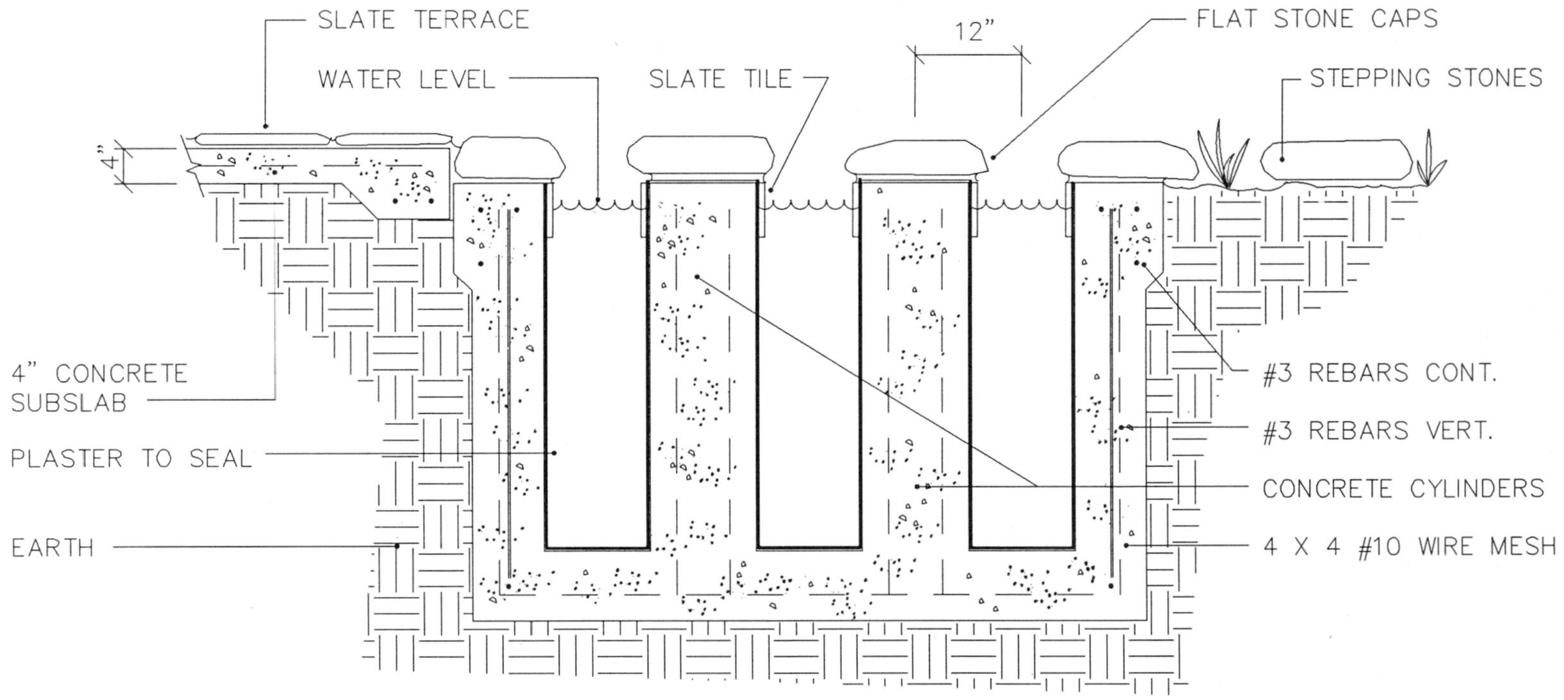

SLATE TERRACE
WATER LEVEL
SLATE TILE
12"
FLAT STONE CAPS
STEPPING STONES
4"
4" CONCRETE SUBSLAB
PLASTER TO SEAL
EARTH
#3 REBARS CONT.
#3 REBARS VERT.
CONCRETE CYLINDERS
4 X 4 #10 WIRE MESH

POOL STEPPING STONES

SCALE: NOT TO SCALE

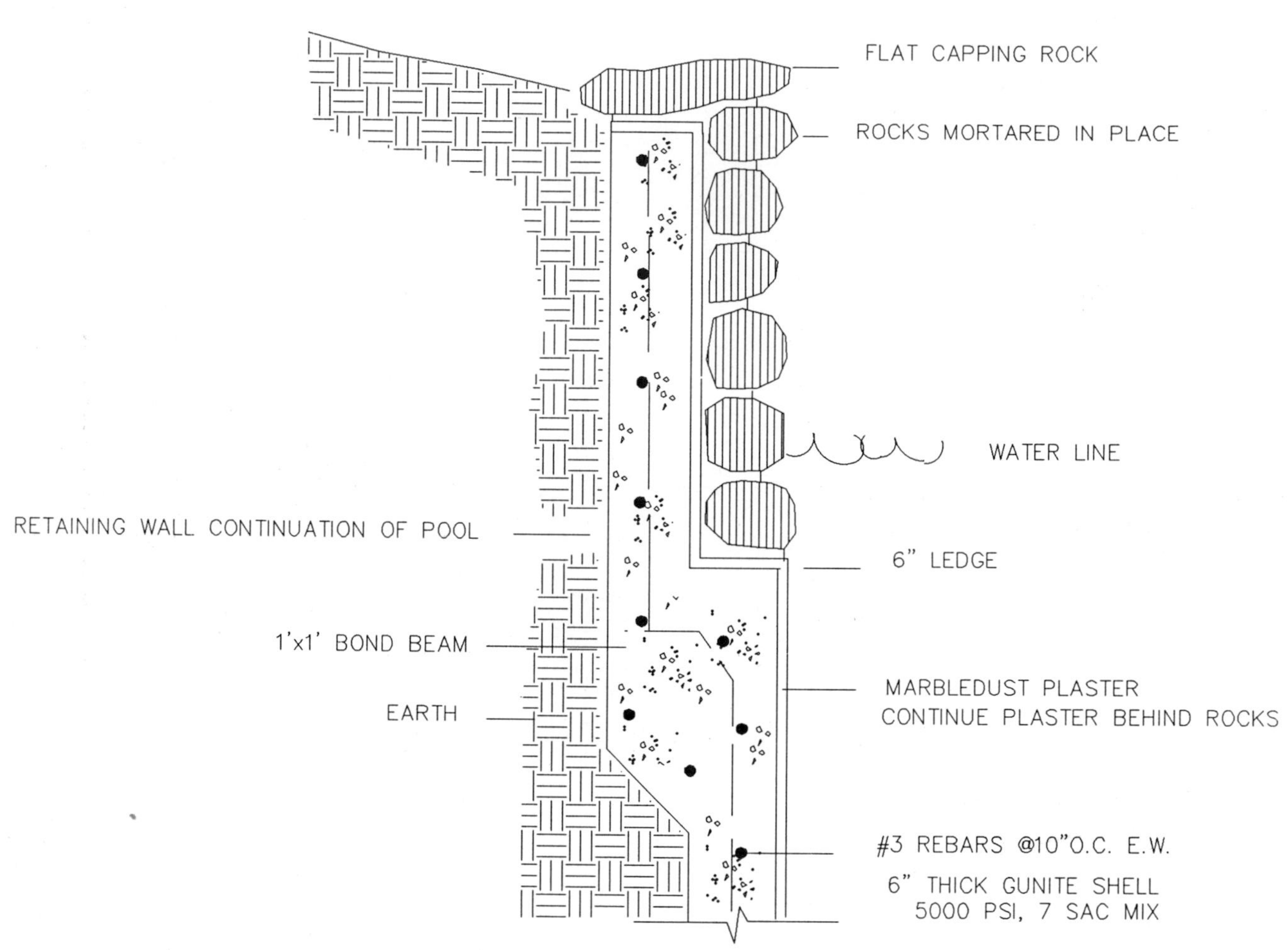
FLAT CAPPING ROCK
ROCKS MORTARED IN PLACE
WATER LINE
RETAINING WALL CONTINUATION OF POOL
6" LEDGE
1'x1' BOND BEAM
MARBLEDUST PLASTER
CONTINUE PLASTER BEHIND ROCKS
EARTH
#3 REBARS @10"O.C. E.W.
6" THICK GUNITE SHELL
5000 PSI, 7 SAC MIX

ROCK POOL WALL

SCALE: NOT TO SCALE

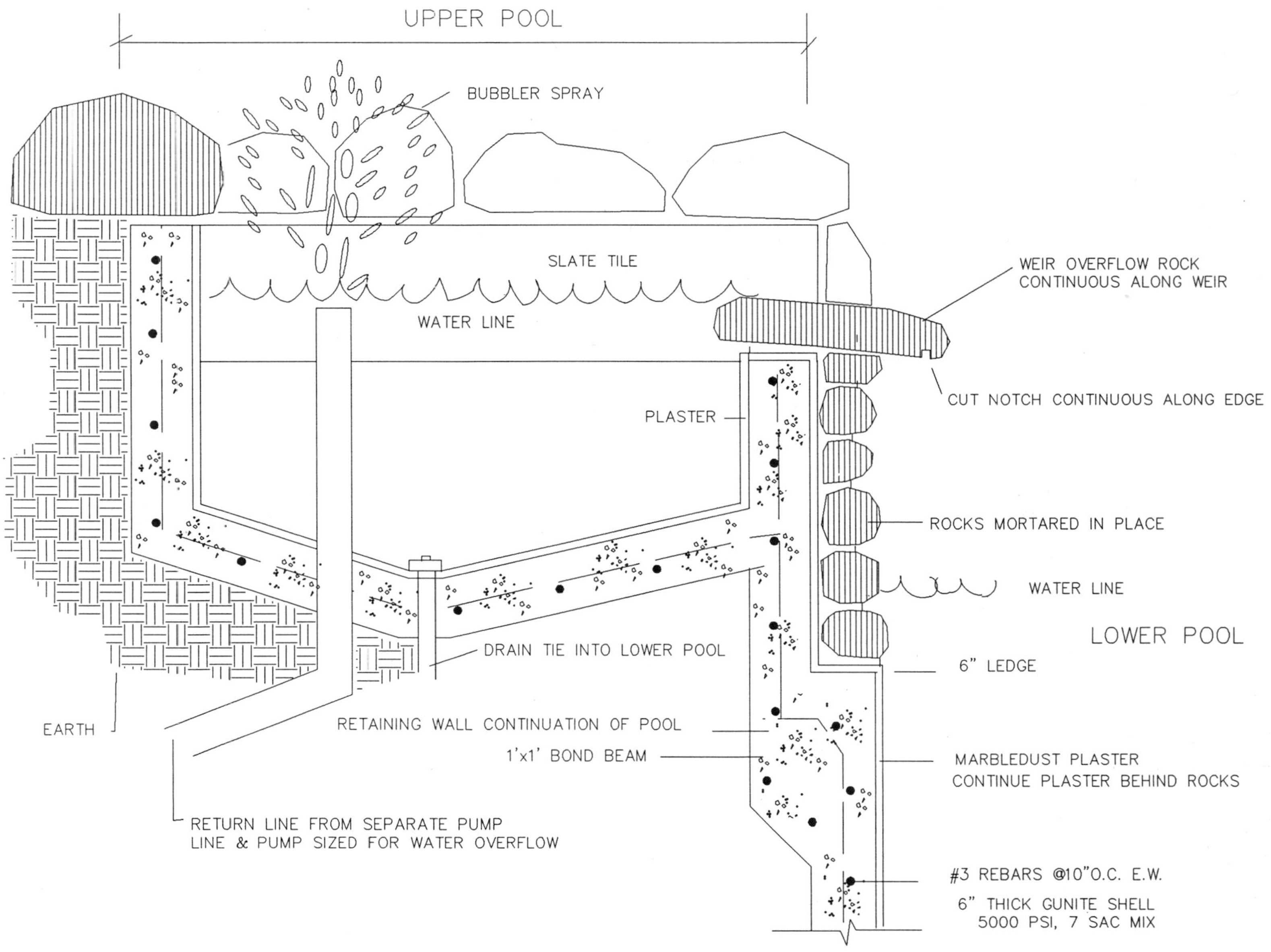

UPPER POOL

BUBBLER SPRAY

SLATE TILE

WATER LINE

WEIR OVERFLOW ROCK
CONTINUOUS ALONG WEIR

CUT NOTCH CONTINUOUS ALONG EDGE

PLASTER

ROCKS MORTARED IN PLACE

WATER LINE

LOWER POOL

6" LEDGE

DRAIN TIE INTO LOWER POOL

EARTH

RETAINING WALL CONTINUATION OF POOL

1'x1' BOND BEAM

MARBLEDUST PLASTER
CONTINUE PLASTER BEHIND ROCKS

RETURN LINE FROM SEPARATE PUMP
LINE & PUMP SIZED FOR WATER OVERFLOW

#3 REBARS @10"O.C. E.W.

6" THICK GUNITE SHELL
5000 PSI, 7 SAC MIX

ROCK FOUNTAIN / WATERFALL

SCALE: NOT TO SCALE

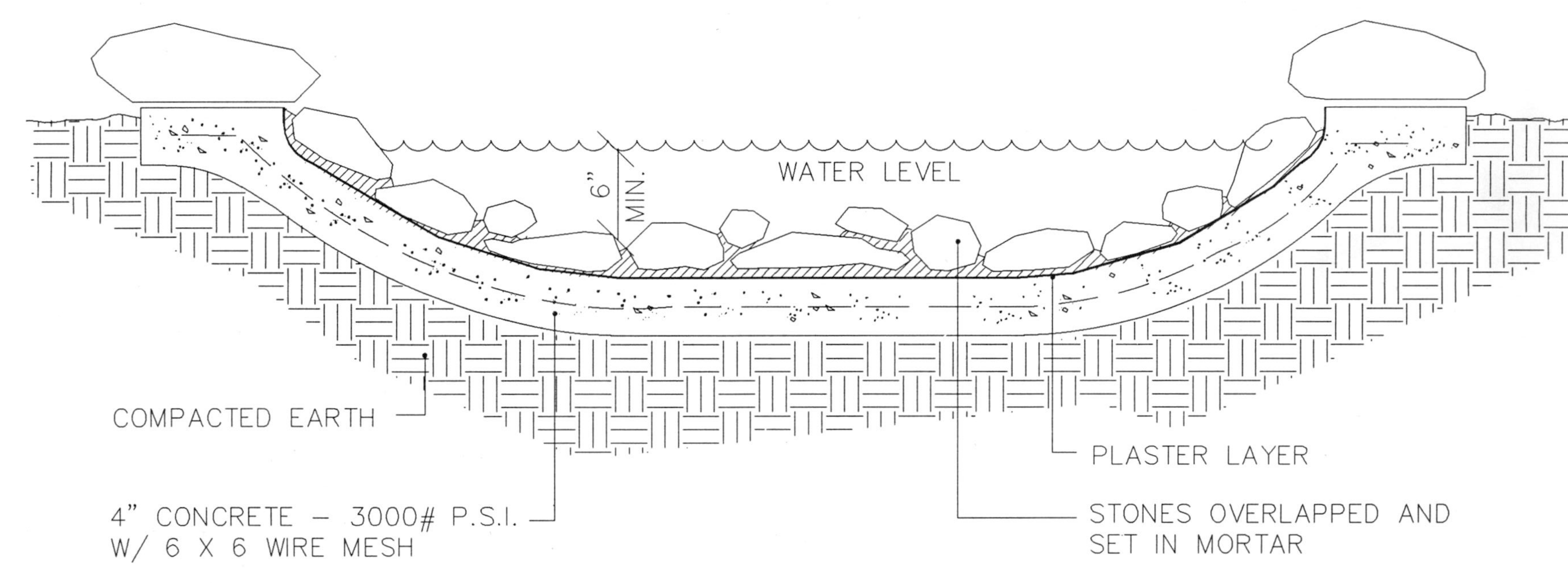

WATER LEVEL
6" MIN.
COMPACTED EARTH
PLASTER LAYER
4" CONCRETE – 3000# P.S.I.
W/ 6 X 6 WIRE MESH
STONES OVERLAPPED AND
SET IN MORTAR

NOTE:

DEPTH AND WIDTH AS PER PLAN

STREAM BED SECTION

SCALE: NOT TO SCALE

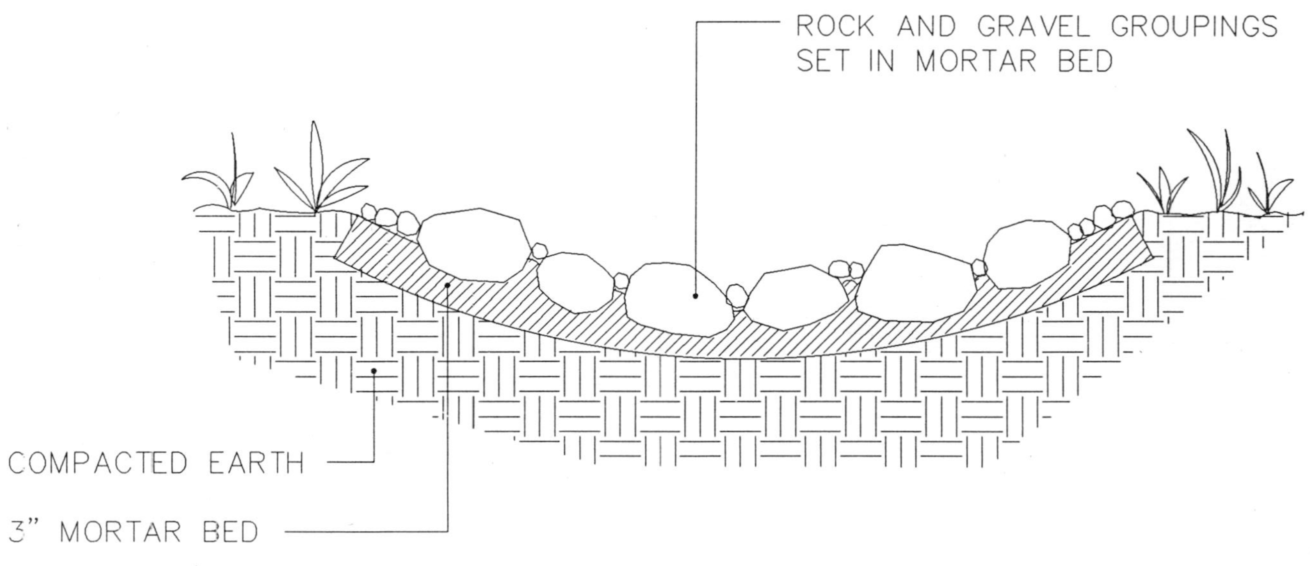

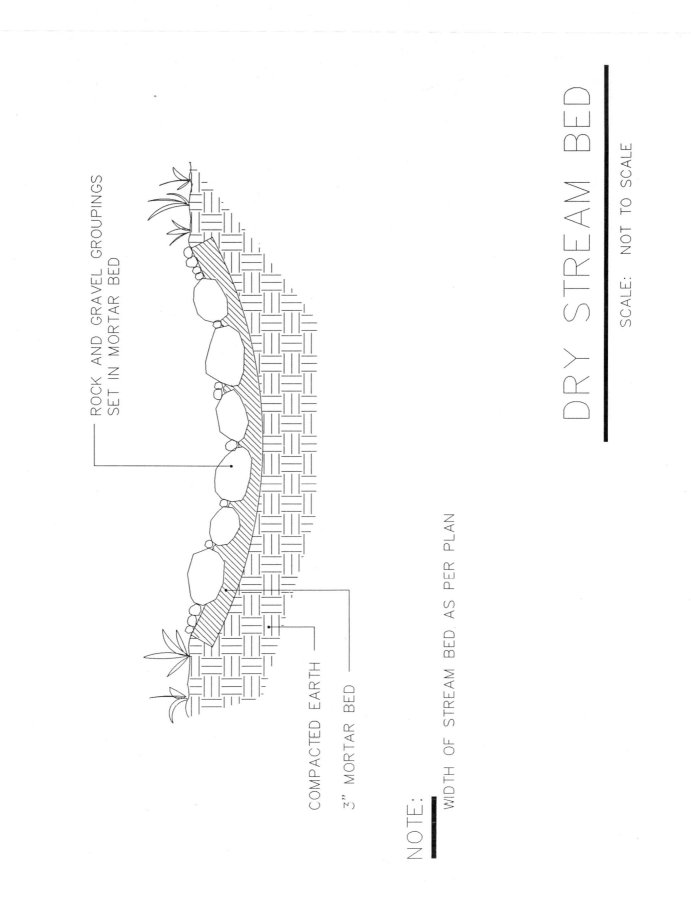

ROCK AND GRAVEL GROUPINGS
SET IN MORTAR BED

COMPACTED EARTH

3" MORTAR BED

NOTE:

WIDTH OF STREAM BED AS PER PLAN

DRY STREAM BED

SCALE: NOT TO SCALE

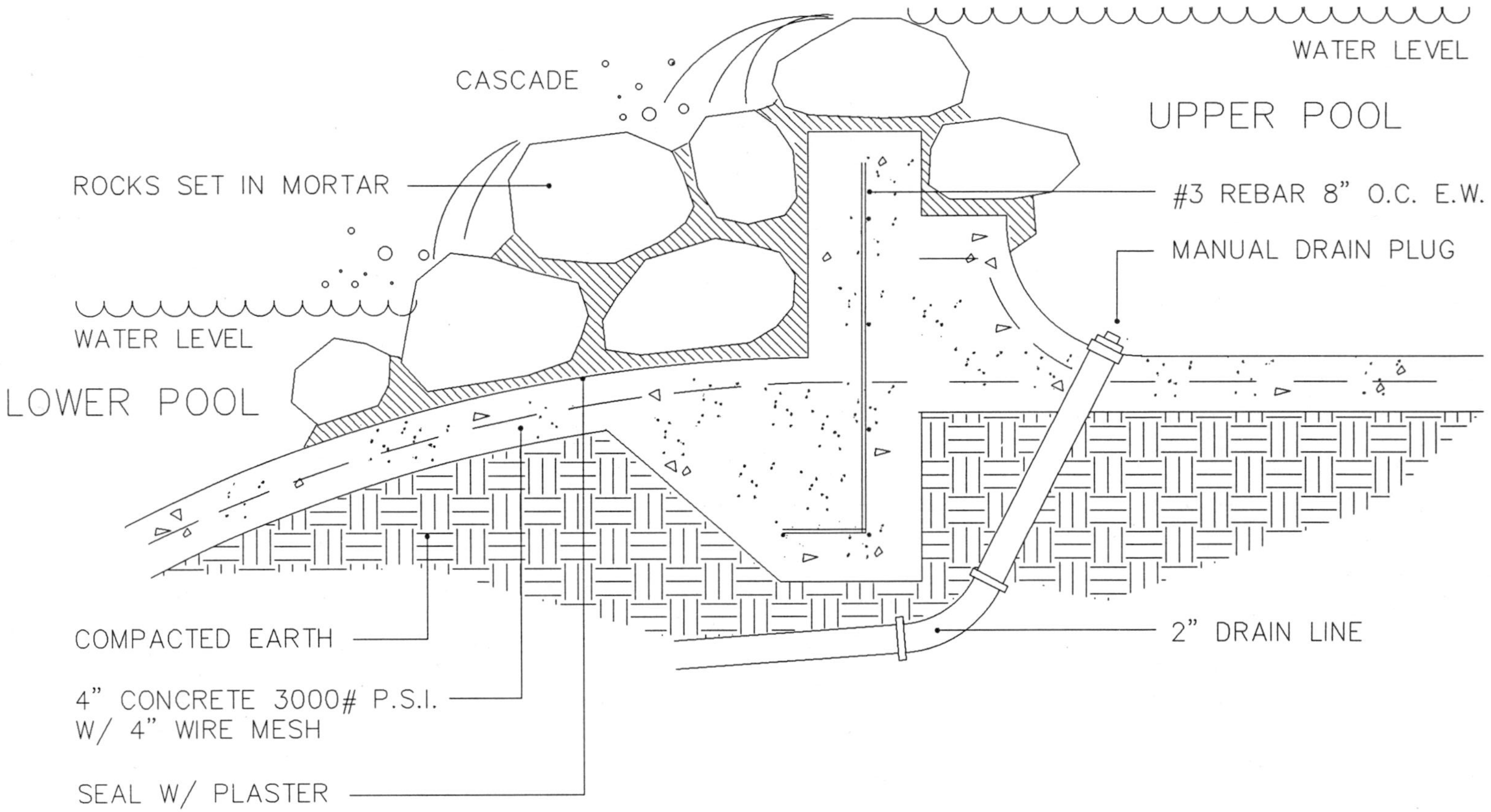

WATER LEVEL
CASCADE
UPPER POOL
ROCKS SET IN MORTAR
#3 REBAR 8" O.C. E.W.
MANUAL DRAIN PLUG
WATER LEVEL
LOWER POOL
COMPACTED EARTH
2" DRAIN LINE
4" CONCRETE 3000# P.S.I.
W/ 4" WIRE MESH
SEAL W/ PLASTER

STREAM CASCADE

SCALE: NOT TO SCALE

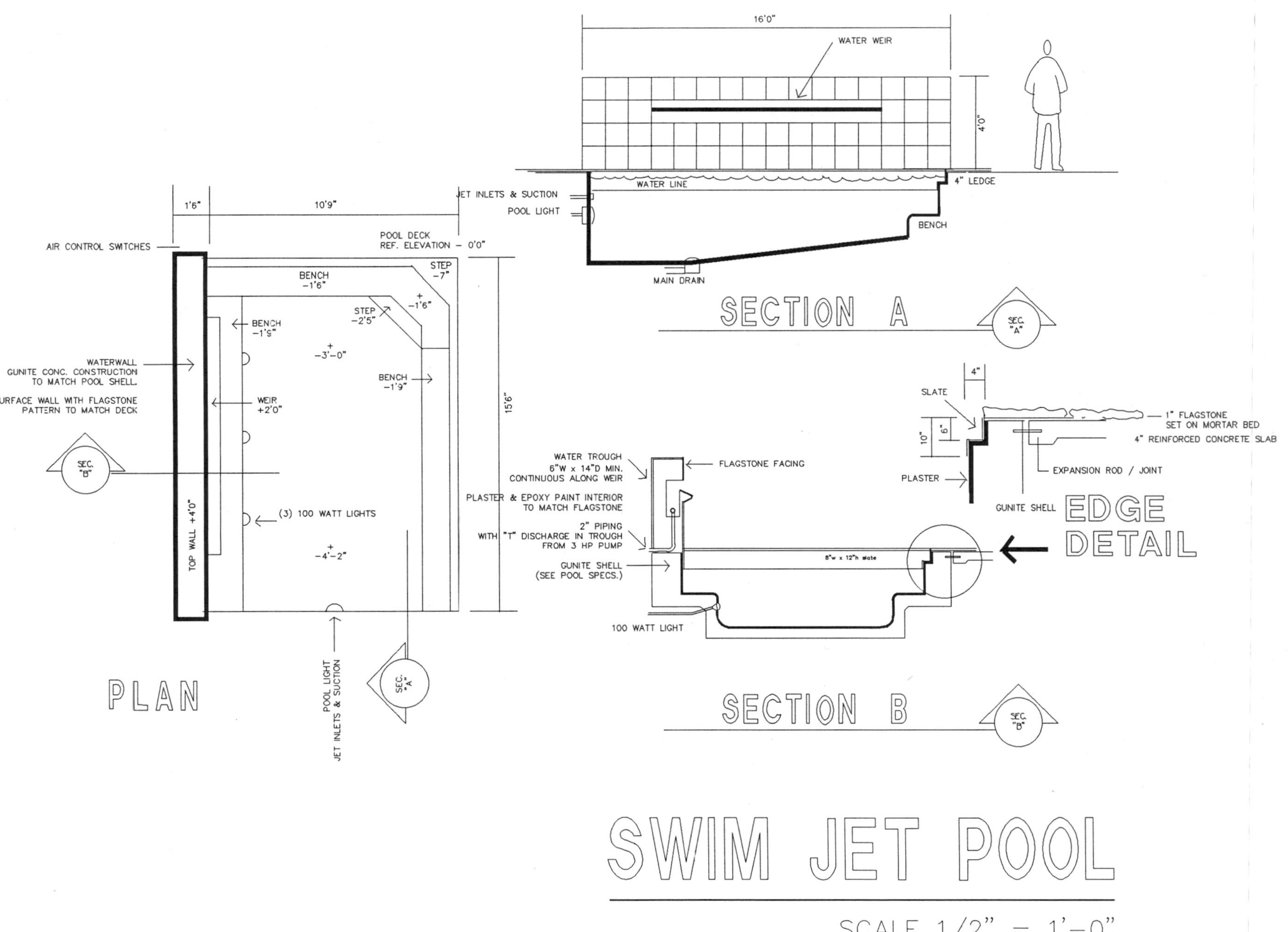
16'0"
WATER WEIR
4'0"
4" LEDGE
WATER LINE
JET INLETS & SUCTION
POOL LIGHT
BENCH
MAIN DRAIN
SECTION A
SEC. "A"
1'6"
10'9"
AIR CONTROL SWITCHES
POOL DECK REF. ELEVATION – 0'0"
BENCH –1'6"
STEP –7"
+ –1'6"
STEP –2'5"
BENCH –1'9"
+ –3'–0"
BENCH –1'9"
WATERWALL GUNITE CONC. CONSTRUCTION TO MATCH POOL SHELL
SURFACE WALL WITH FLAGSTONE PATTERN TO MATCH DECK
WEIR +2'0"
15'6"
SEC. "B"
(3) 100 WATT LIGHTS
TOP WALL +4'0"
+ –4'–2"
PLAN
POOL LIGHT JET INLETS & SUCTION
SEC. "A"
4"
SLATE
10"
6"
1" FLAGSTONE SET ON MORTAR BED
4" REINFORCED CONCRETE SLAB
EXPANSION ROD / JOINT
PLASTER
GUNITE SHELL
EDGE DETAIL
WATER TROUGH 6"W x 14"D MIN. CONTINUOUS ALONG WEIR
FLAGSTONE FACING
PLASTER & EPOXY PAINT INTERIOR TO MATCH FLAGSTONE
2" PIPING WITH "T" DISCHARGE IN TROUGH FROM 3 HP PUMP
GUNITE SHELL (SEE POOL SPECS.)
100 WATT LIGHT
SECTION B
SEC. "B"
SWIM JET POOL
SCALE 1/2" = 1'–0"

Site Design for the Handicapped

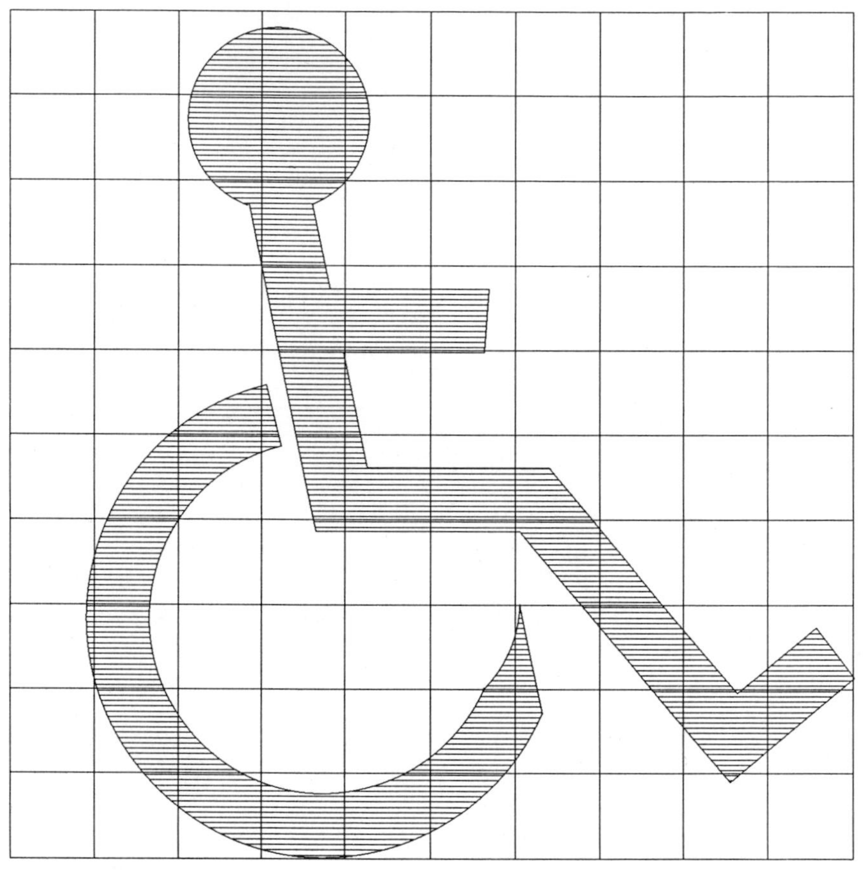

GRID FOR LAYOUT ONLY
ONE SQUARE EQUALS 4"x 4"

HANDICAPPED SIGN

SCALE: NOT TO SCALE

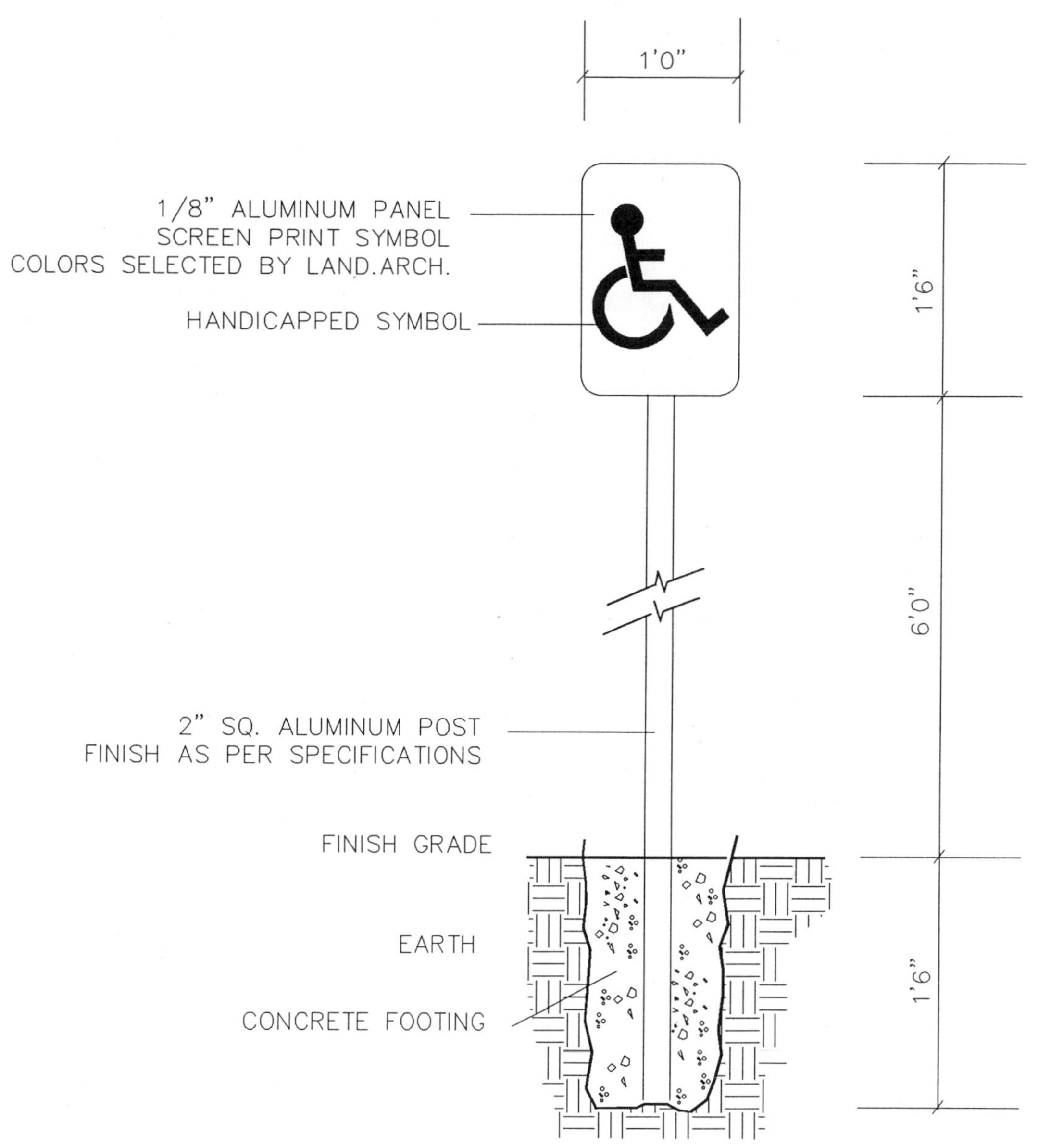
1'0"
1/8" ALUMINUM PANEL
SCREEN PRINT SYMBOL
COLORS SELECTED BY LAND.ARCH.
HANDICAPPED SYMBOL
1'6"
6'0"
2" SQ. ALUMINUM POST
FINISH AS PER SPECIFICATIONS
FINISH GRADE
EARTH
CONCRETE FOOTING
1'6"

HANDICAPPED PARKING SIGN

SCALE: NOT TO SCALE

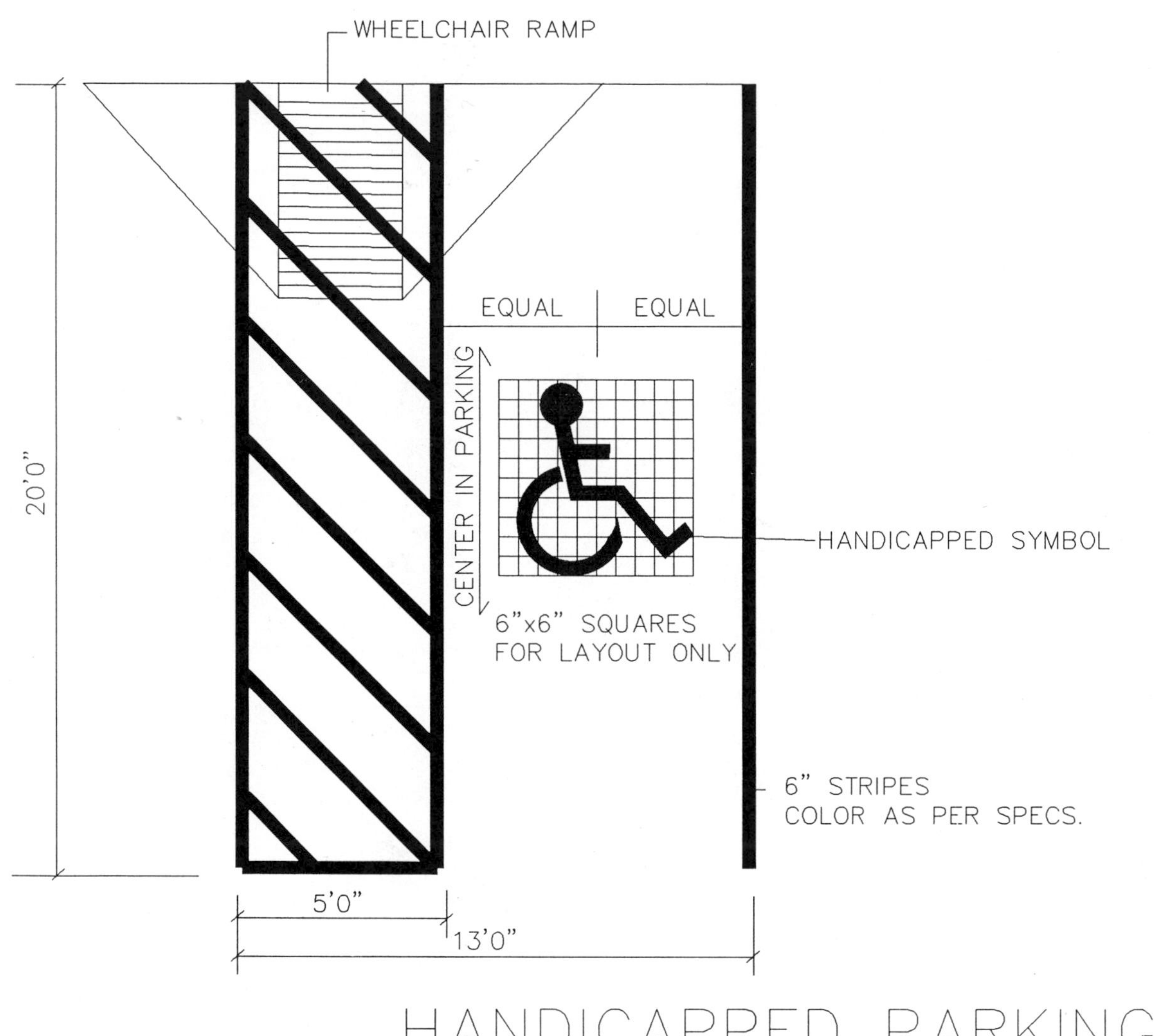
WHEELCHAIR RAMP
EQUAL
EQUAL
CENTER IN PARKING
6"x6" SQUARES
FOR LAYOUT ONLY
HANDICAPPED SYMBOL
20'0"
6" STRIPES
COLOR AS PER SPECS.
5'0"
13'0"

HANDICAPPED PARKING

SCALE: NOT TO SCALE

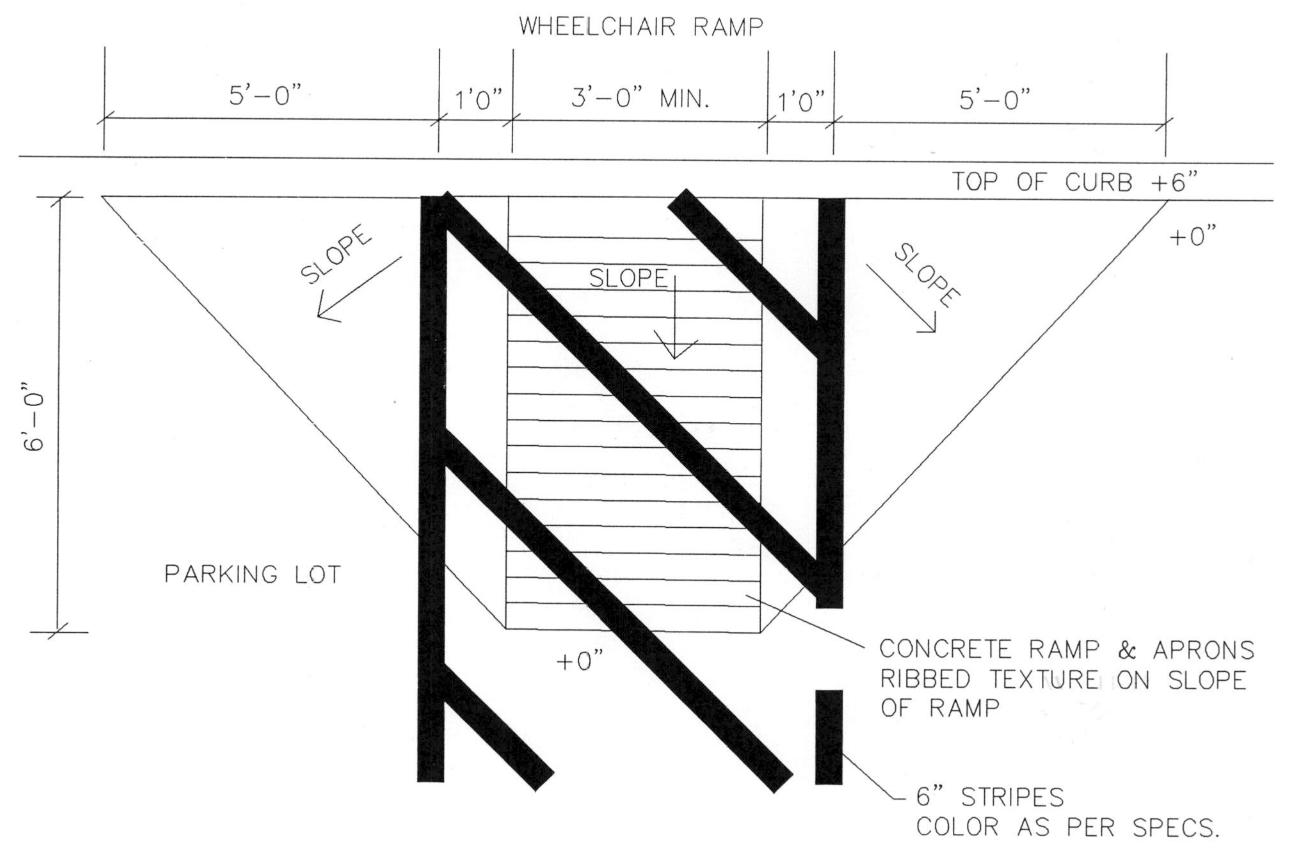

WHEELCHAIR RAMP
5'-0"
1'0"
3'-0" MIN.
1'0"
5'-0"
TOP OF CURB +6"
+0"
SLOPE
SLOPE
SLOPE
6'-0"
PARKING LOT
+0"
CONCRETE RAMP & APRONS
RIBBED TEXTURE ON SLOPE
OF RAMP
6" STRIPES
COLOR AS PER SPECS.

WHEELCHAIR RAMP

SCALE: NOT TO SCALE

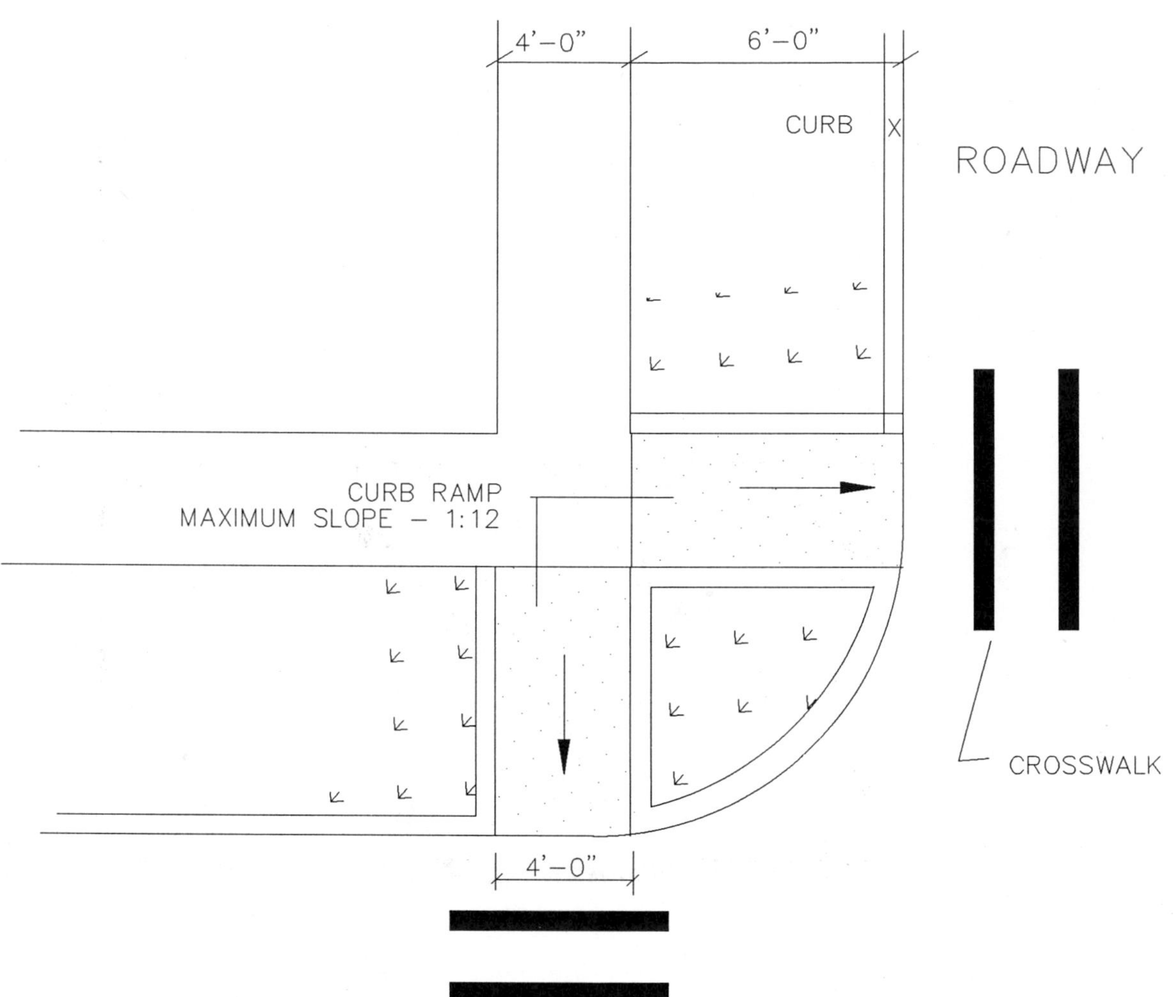

4'–0"
6'–0"
CURB
X
ROADWAY
CURB RAMP
MAXIMUM SLOPE – 1:12
CROSSWALK
4'–0"

CORNER SIDEWALK RAMPS

SCALE: NOT TO SCALE

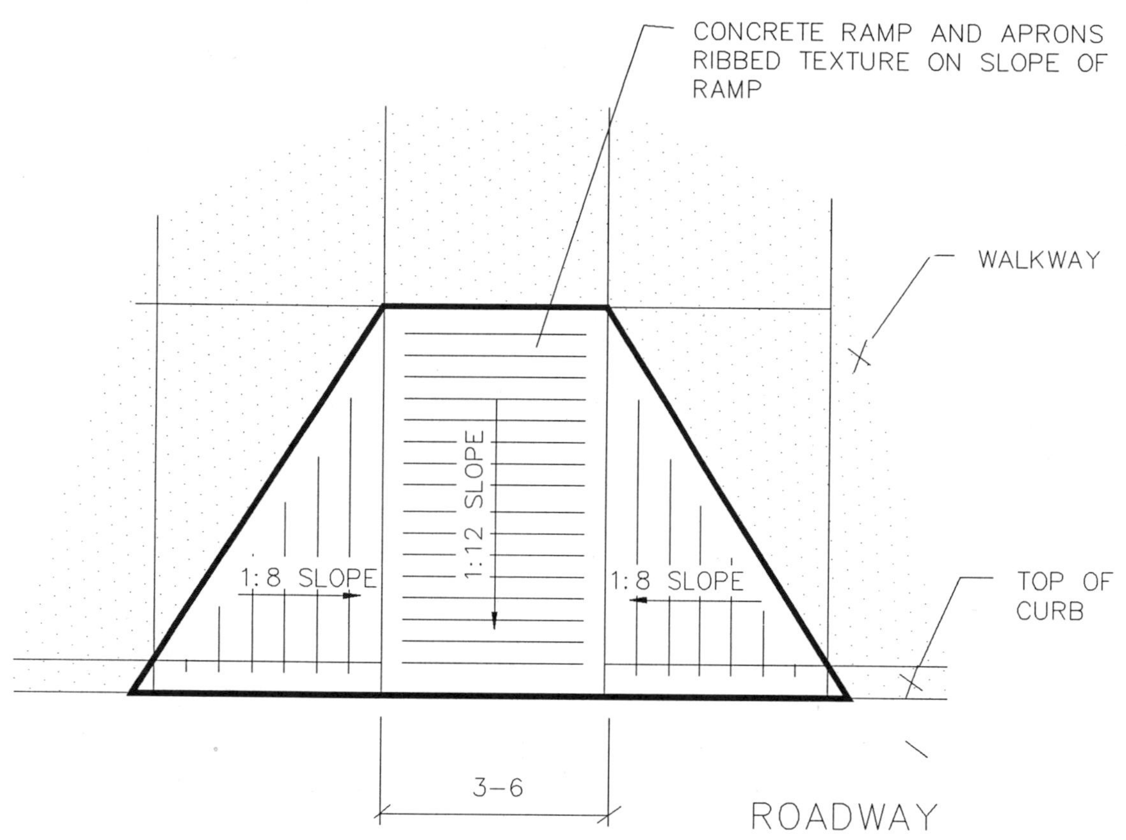
CONCRETE RAMP AND APRONS
RIBBED TEXTURE ON SLOPE OF
RAMP
WALKWAY
1:12 SLOPE
1:8 SLOPE
1:8 SLOPE
TOP OF
CURB
3-6
ROADWAY

CURB RAMP — 1

SCALE: NOT TO SCALE

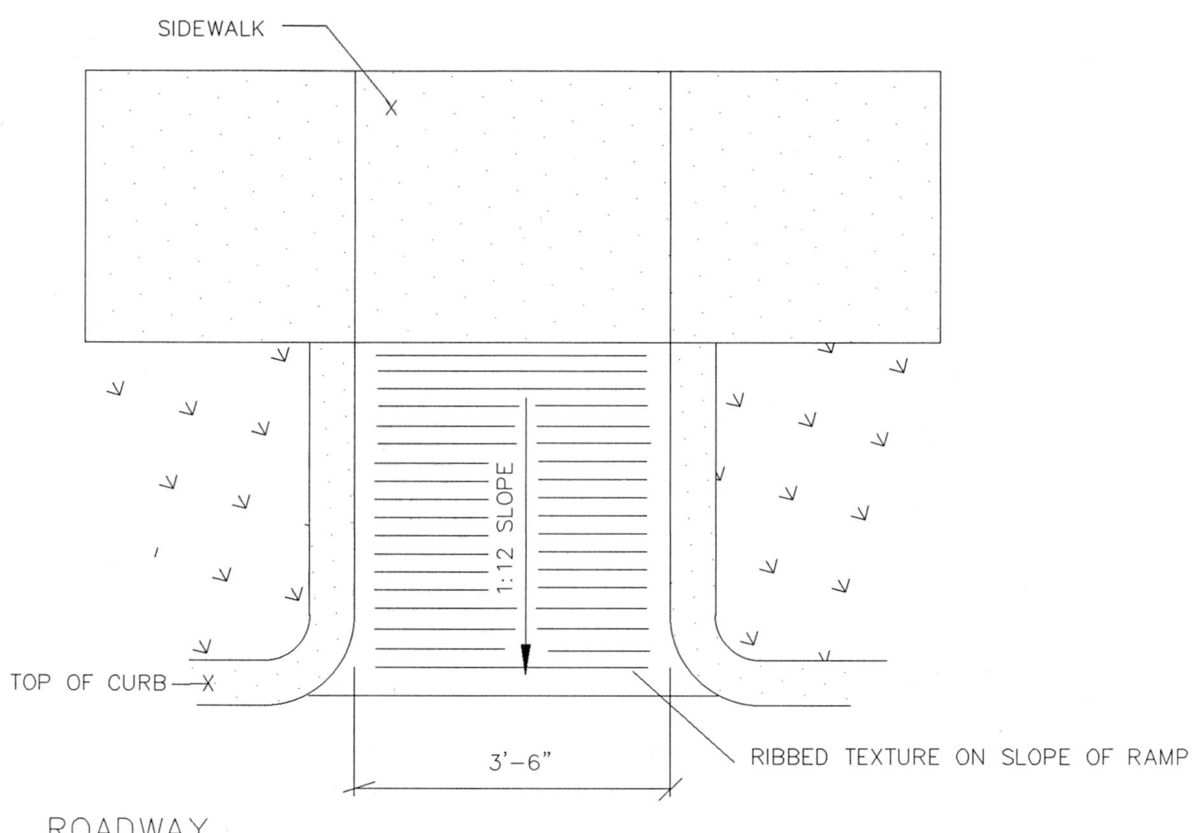

SIDEWALK
1:12 SLOPE
TOP OF CURB
3'–6"
RIBBED TEXTURE ON SLOPE OF RAMP
ROADWAY

CURB RAMP – 2

SCALE: NOT TO SCALE

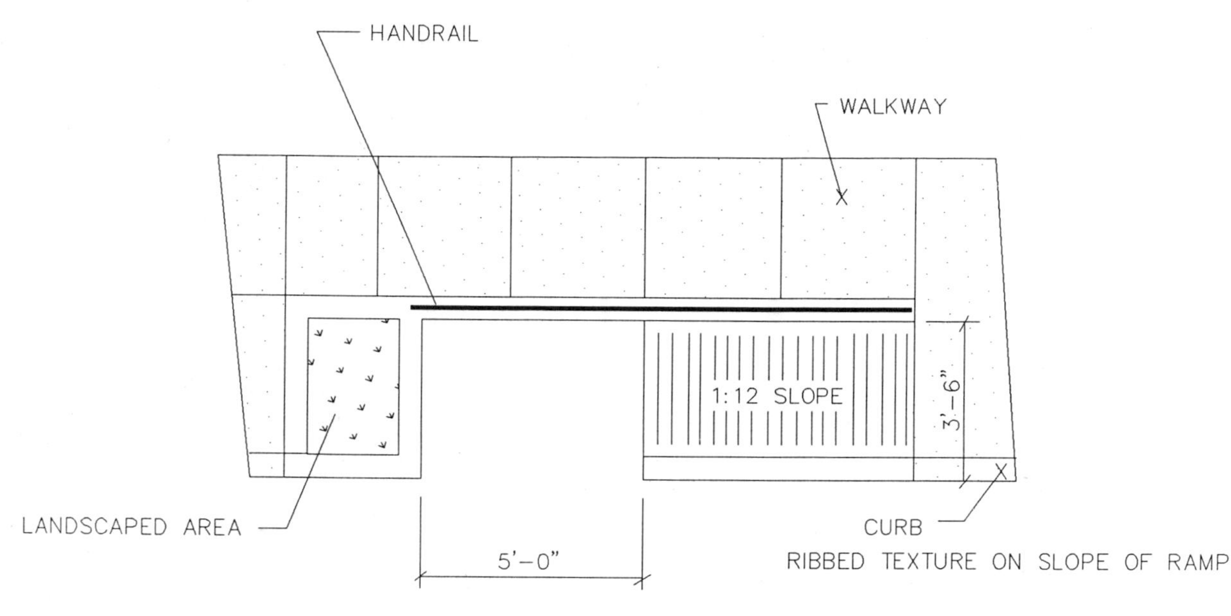
HANDRAIL
WALKWAY
1:12 SLOPE
3'–6"
LANDSCAPED AREA
CURB
5'–0"
RIBBED TEXTURE ON SLOPE OF RAMP
ROADWAY

CURB RAMP – 3

SCALE: NOT TO SCALE

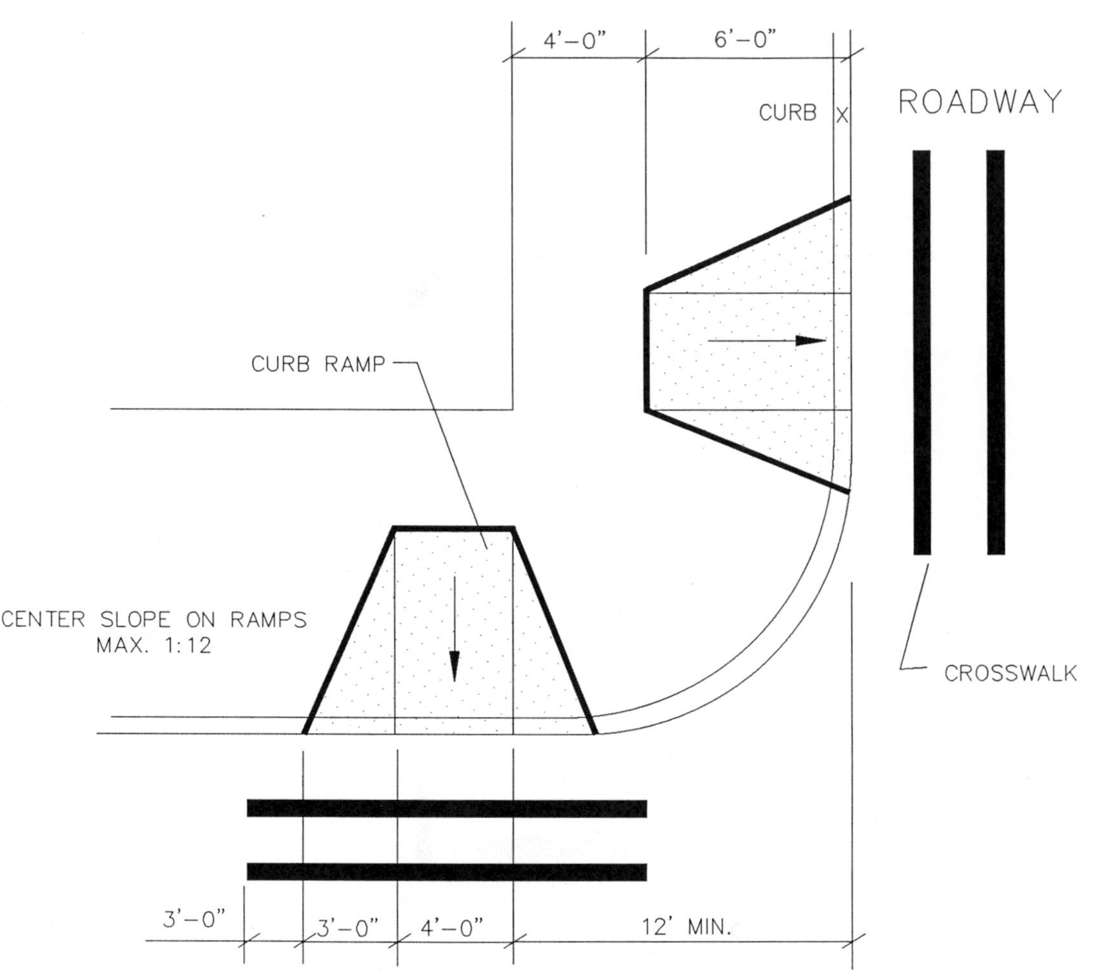
4'–0"
6'–0"
CURB
X
ROADWAY
CURB RAMP
CENTER SLOPE ON RAMPS
MAX. 1:12
CROSSWALK
3'–0"
3'–0"
4'–0"
12' MIN.

CORNER RAMPS – 90 DEGREES

SCALE: NOT TO SCALE

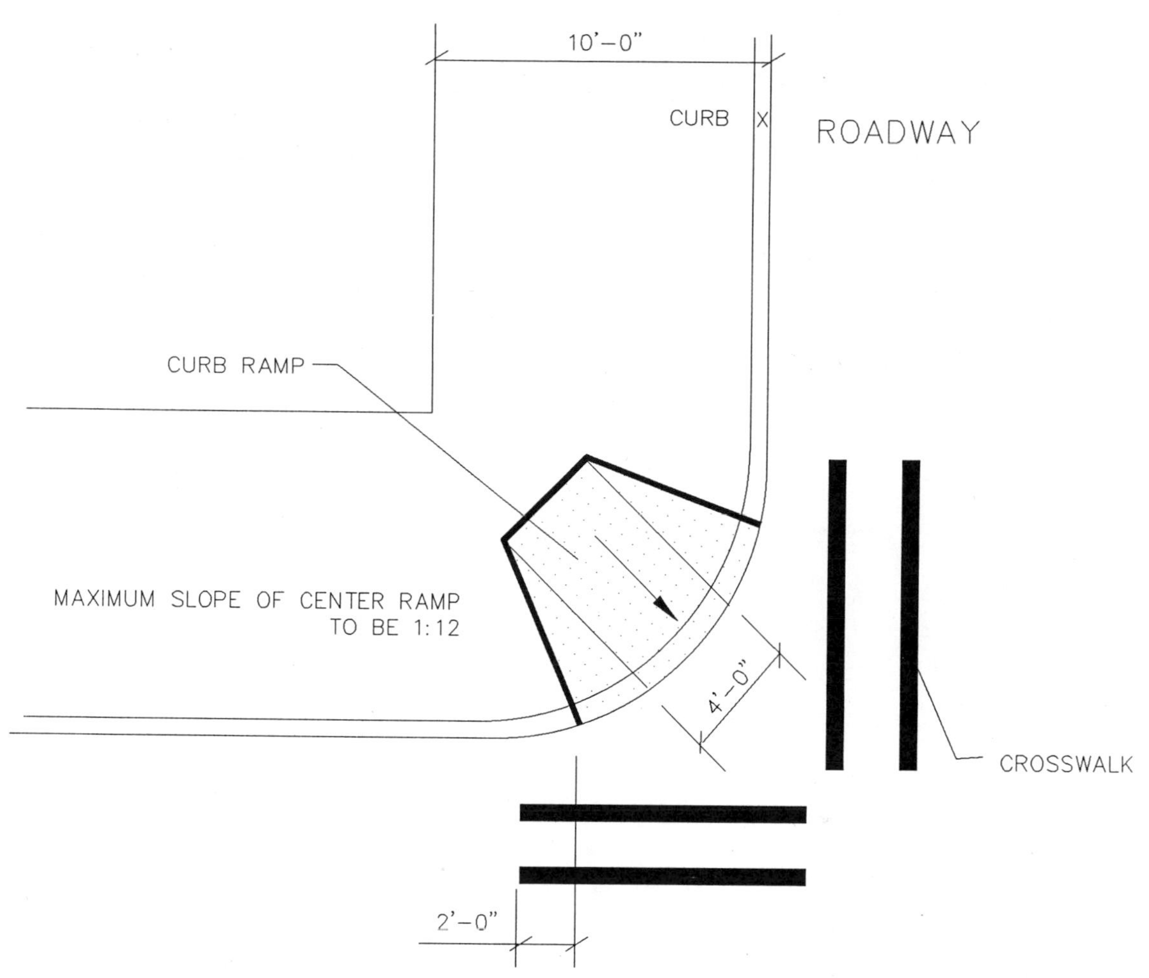
10'–0"
CURB
ROADWAY
CURB RAMP
MAXIMUM SLOPE OF CENTER RAMP
TO BE 1:12
4'–0"
CROSSWALK
2'–0"

CORNER RAMP

SCALE: NOT TO SCALE

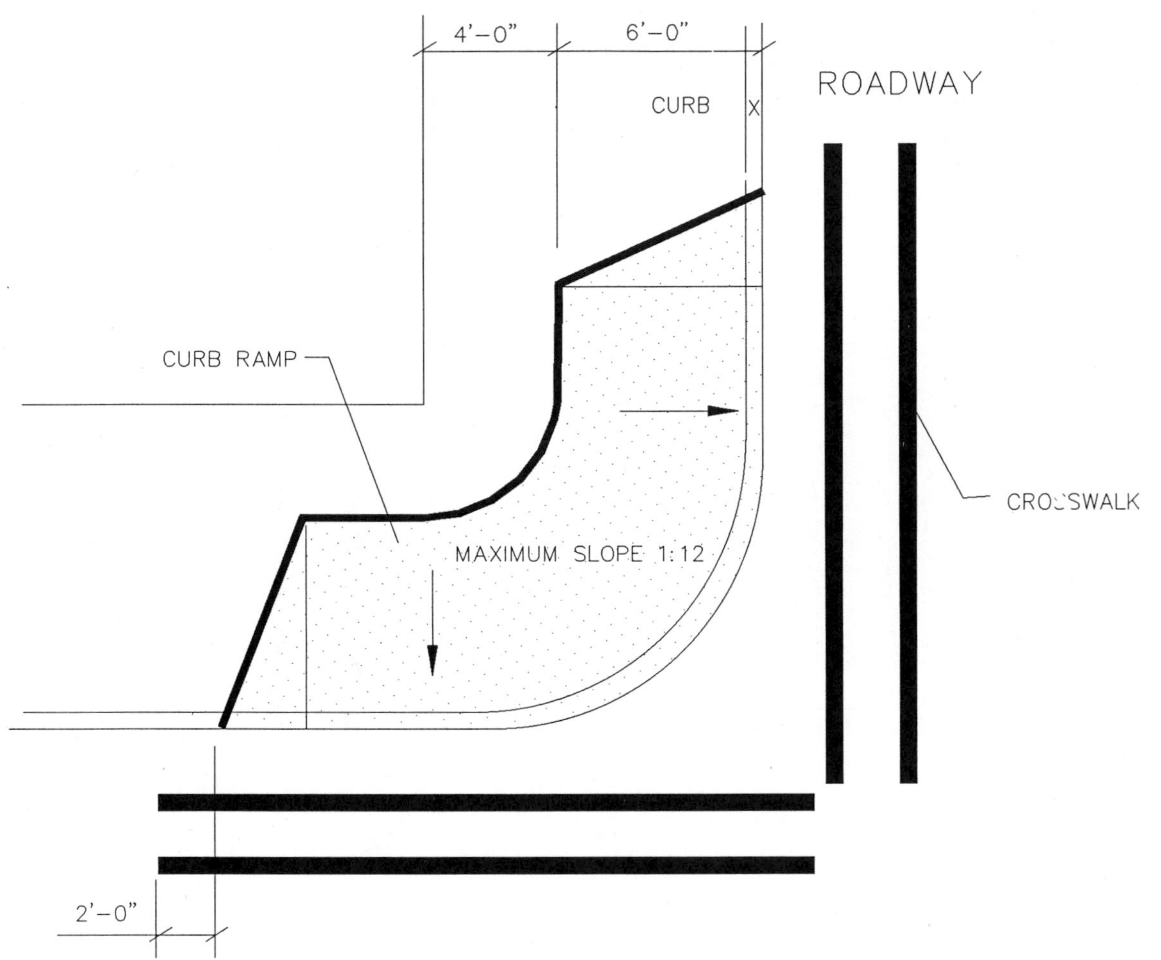
4'–0"
6'–0"
CURB
X
ROADWAY
CURB RAMP
MAXIMUM SLOPE 1:12
CROSSWALK
2'–0"

WIDE CORNER RAMP

SCALE: NOT TO SCALE

Irrigation

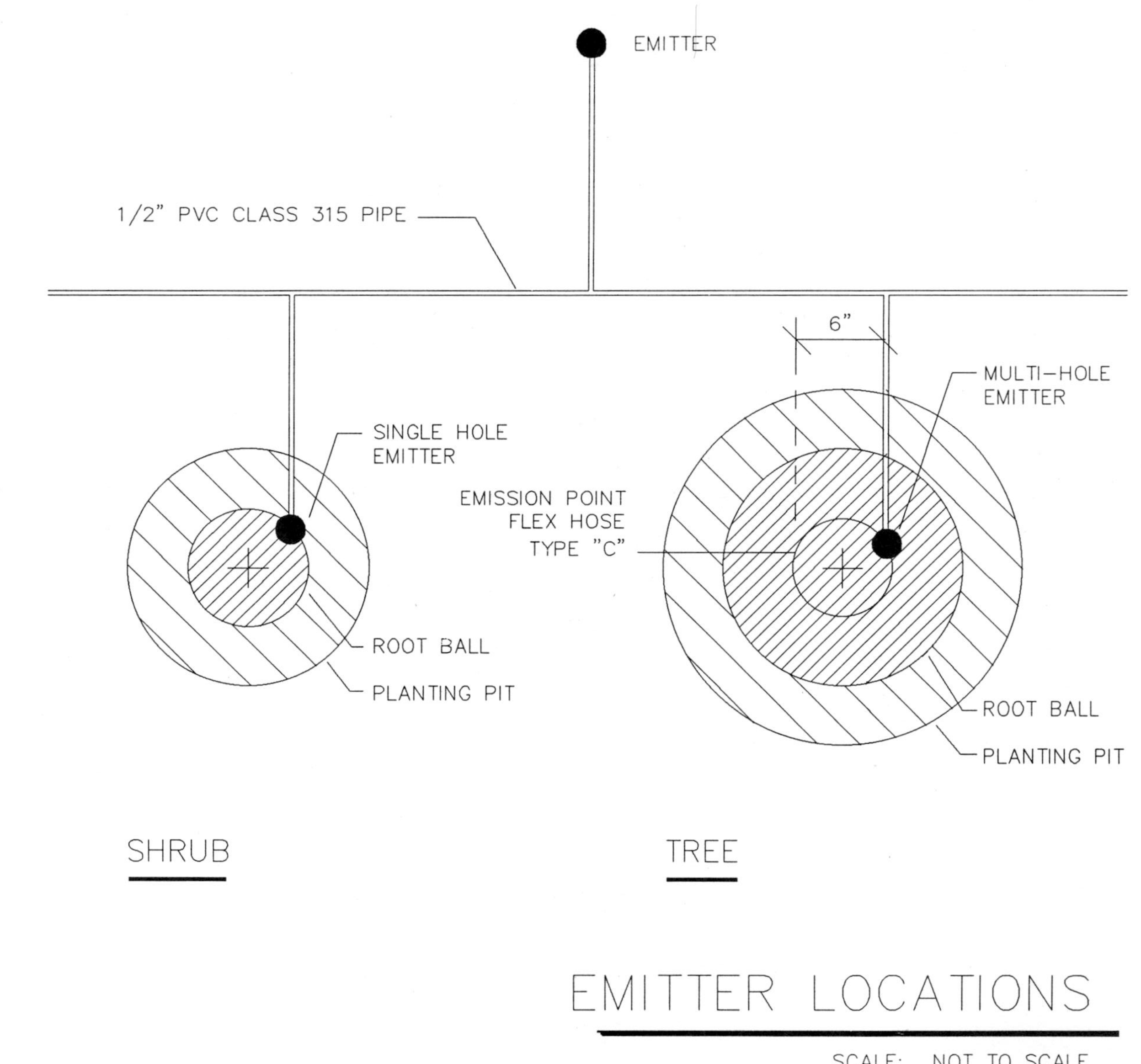
EMITTER
1/2" PVC CLASS 315 PIPE
6"
MULTI-HOLE
EMITTER
SINGLE HOLE
EMITTER
EMISSION POINT
FLEX HOSE
TYPE "C"
ROOT BALL
PLANTING PIT
ROOT BALL
PLANTING PIT
SHRUB
TREE
EMITTER LOCATIONS
SCALE: NOT TO SCALE

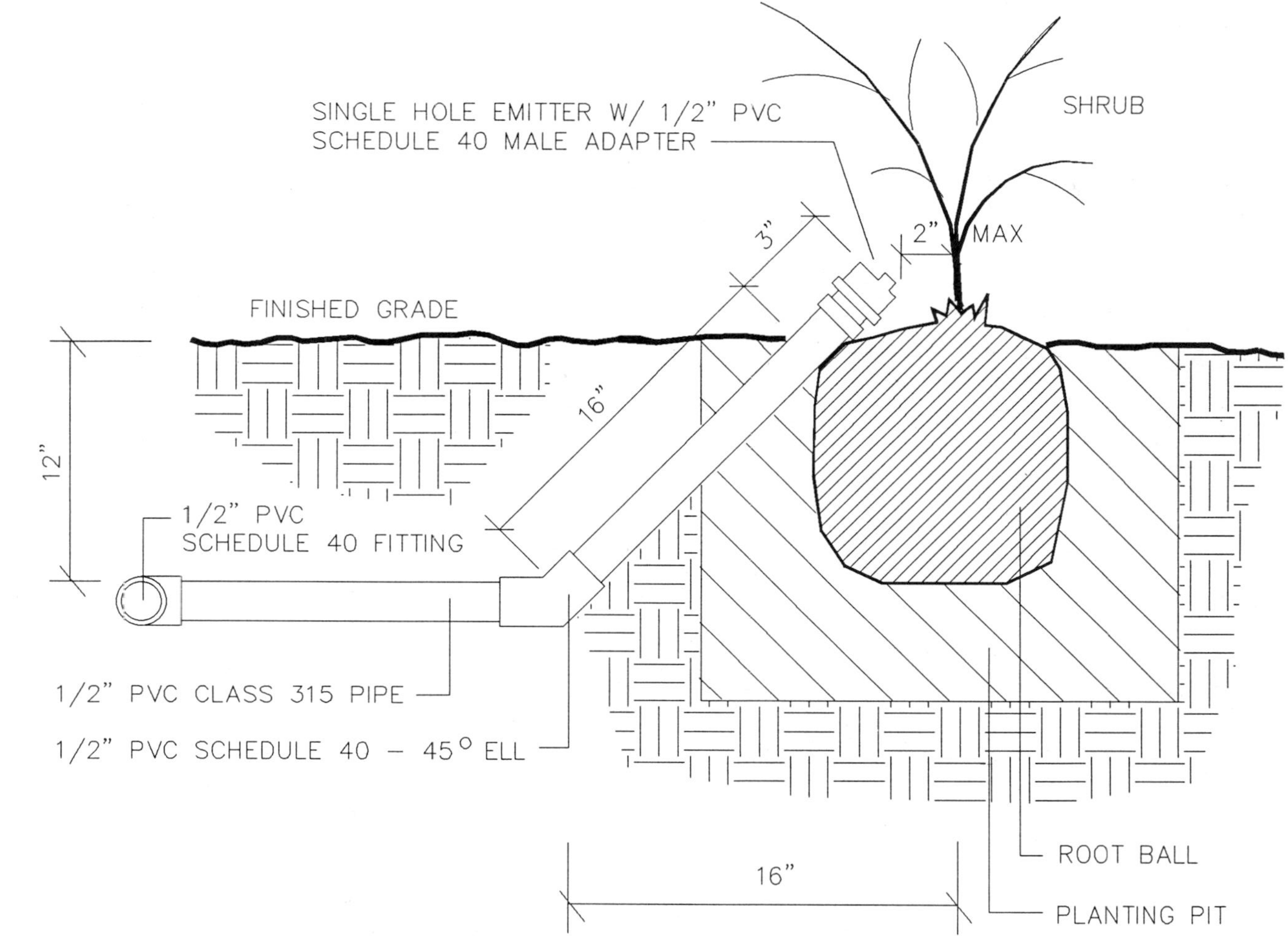
SINGLE HOLE EMITTER W/ 1/2" PVC
SCHEDULE 40 MALE ADAPTER
SHRUB
3"
2"
MAX
FINISHED GRADE
16"
12"
1/2" PVC
SCHEDULE 40 FITTING
1/2" PVC CLASS 315 PIPE
1/2" PVC SCHEDULE 40 – 45° ELL
ROOT BALL
16"
PLANTING PIT

SINGLE OUTLET EMITTER

SCALE: NOT TO SCALE

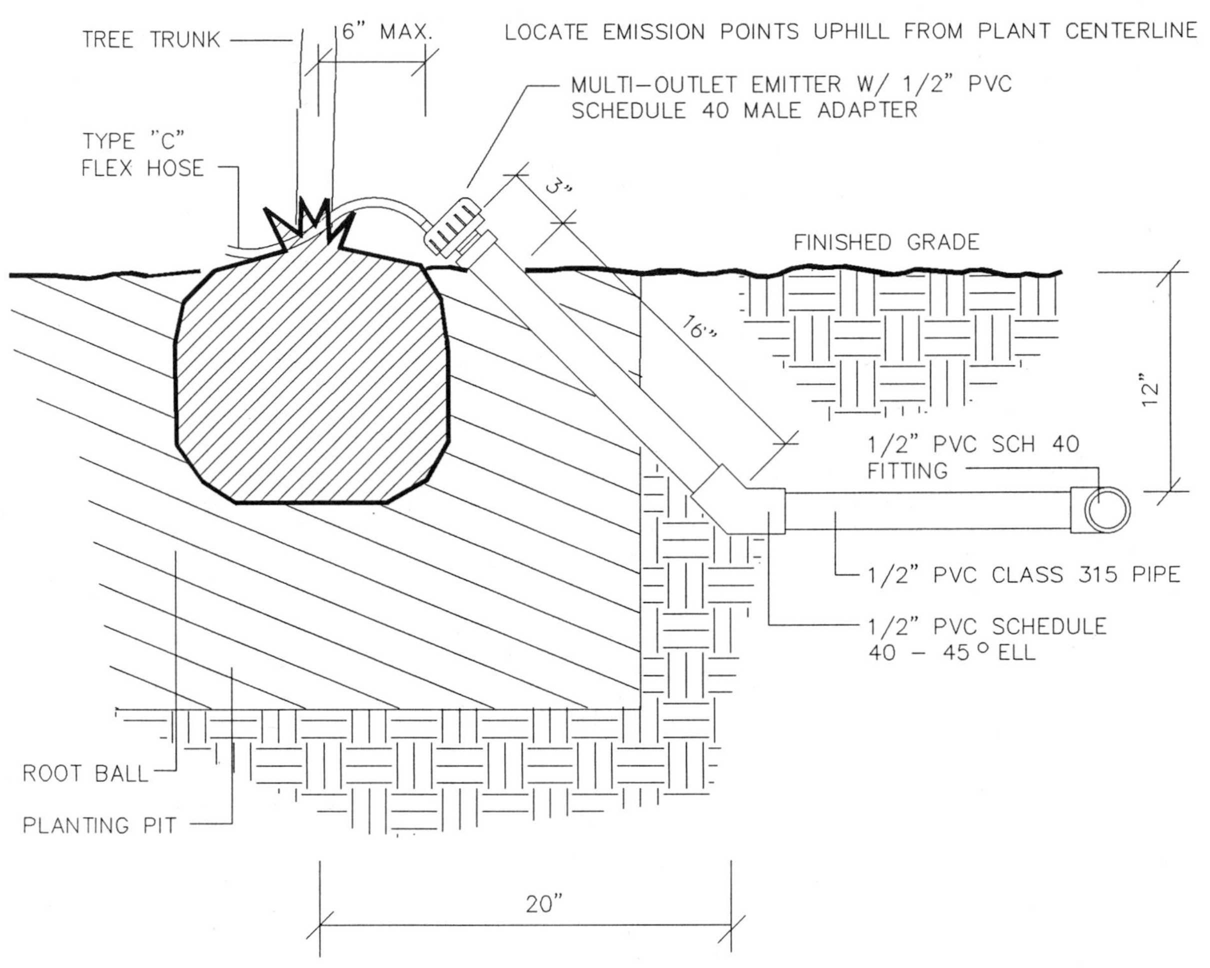

TREE TRUNK
6" MAX.
LOCATE EMISSION POINTS UPHILL FROM PLANT CENTERLINE
MULTI-OUTLET EMITTER W/ 1/2" PVC
SCHEDULE 40 MALE ADAPTER
TYPE "C"
FLEX HOSE
3"
FINISHED GRADE
16"
12"
1/2" PVC SCH 40
FITTING
1/2" PVC CLASS 315 PIPE
1/2" PVC SCHEDULE
40 – 45° ELL
ROOT BALL
PLANTING PIT
20"

MULTI–OUTLET EMITTER

SCALE: NOT TO SCALE

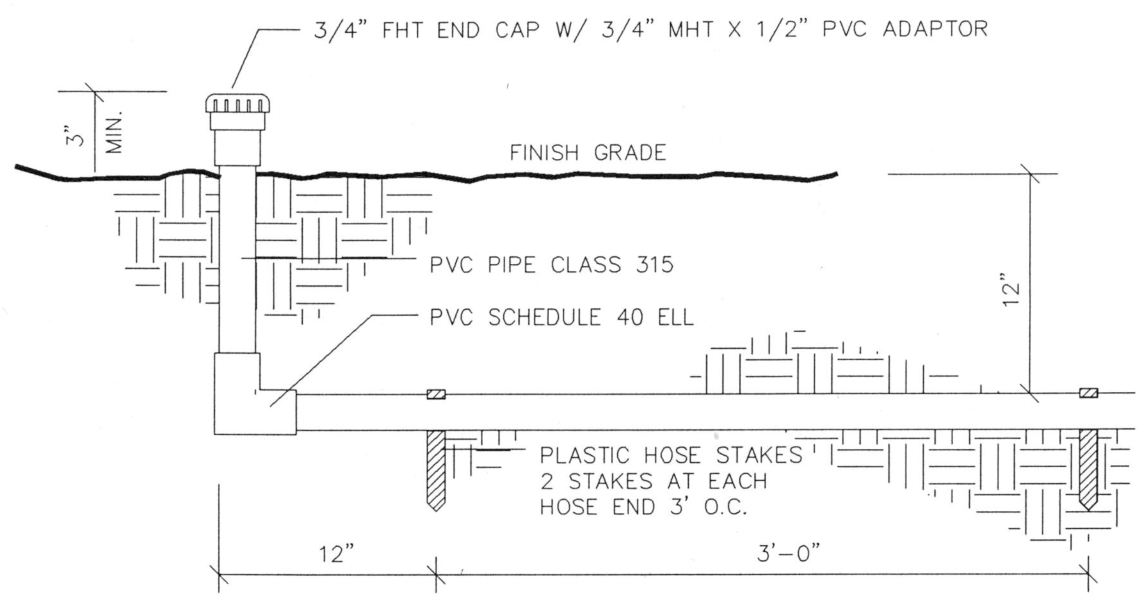
3/4" FHT END CAP W/ 3/4" MHT X 1/2" PVC ADAPTOR
3"
MIN.
FINISH GRADE
PVC PIPE CLASS 315
PVC SCHEDULE 40 ELL
12"
PLASTIC HOSE STAKES
2 STAKES AT EACH
HOSE END 3' O.C.
12"
3'-0"

STAKING DETAIL AND HOSE END FLUSH DEVICE

SCALE: NOT TO SCALE

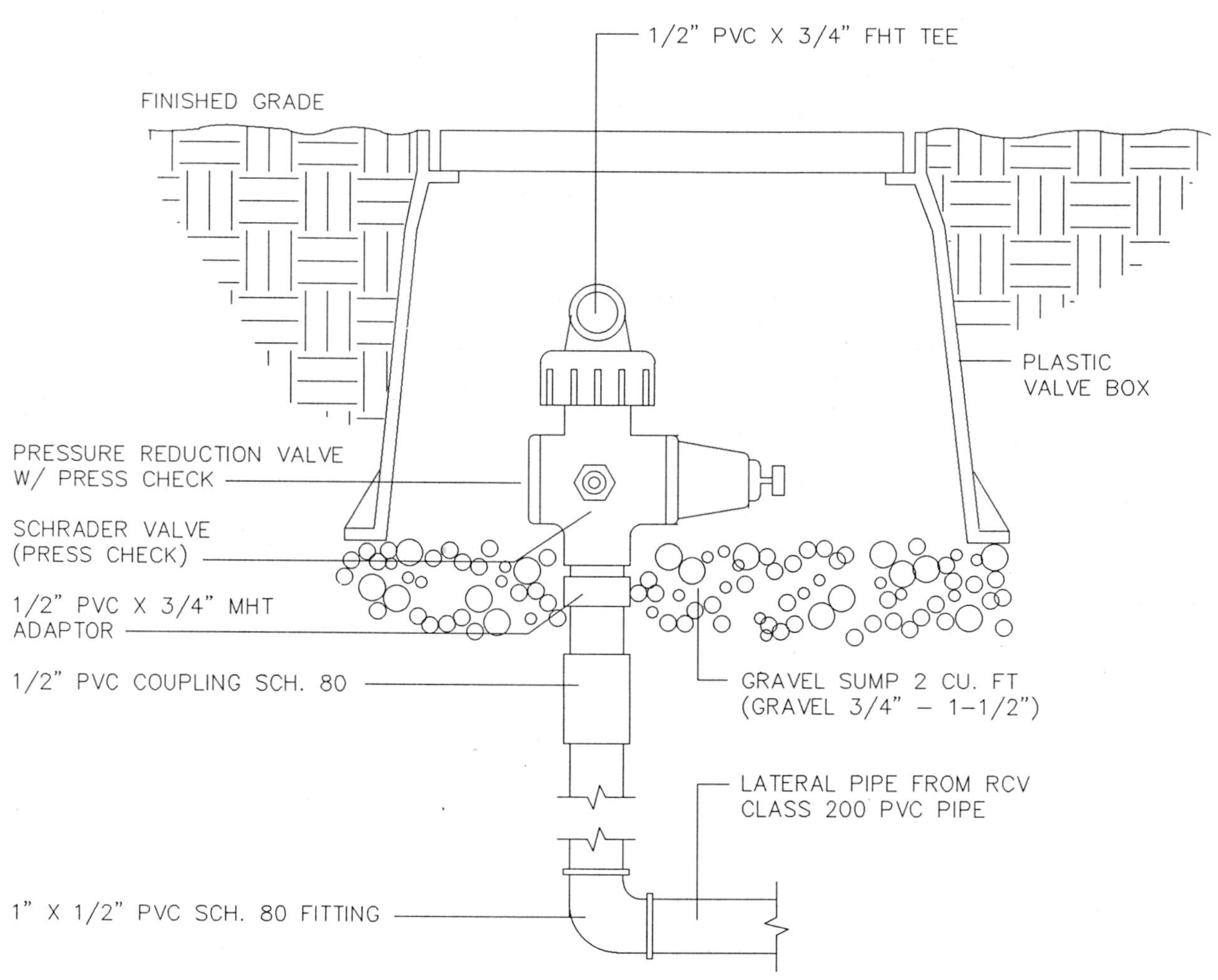
1/2" PVC X 3/4" FHT TEE
FINISHED GRADE
PLASTIC VALVE BOX
PRESSURE REDUCTION VALVE W/ PRESS CHECK
SCHRADER VALVE (PRESS CHECK)
1/2" PVC X 3/4" MHT ADAPTOR
1/2" PVC COUPLING SCH. 80
GRAVEL SUMP 2 CU. FT (GRAVEL 3/4" – 1-1/2")
LATERAL PIPE FROM RCV CLASS 200 PVC PIPE
1" X 1/2" PVC SCH. 80 FITTING

PRESSURE REDUCTION RISER

SCALE: NOT TO SCALE

WATER METER
CONTROLLER
BACKFLOW PREVENTOR
FILTER
PRESSURE REGULATOR
VALVE ID BOX
REMOTE CONTROL VALVE
MANUAL VALVE
GATE VALVE
Q.C.
QUICK COUPLING VALVE
FLUSH VALVE
DRAIN VALVE
PUMP
MAIN LINE
LATERAL PIPE OR EMITTER MAIN
SLEEVE
DRIP LINE
360 DEG. TURF HEAD
270 DEG. TURF HEAD
225 DEG. TURF HEAD
180 DEG. TURF HEAD
135 DEG. TURF HEAD
90 DEG. TURF HEAD
ADJUSTABLE TURF HEAD
PART CIRCLE TURF HEAD
CENTER STRIP TURF HEAD
END STRIP TURF HEAD
SIDE STRIP TURF HEAD
6 GPH EMITTER
5 GPH EMITTER
3 GPH EMITTER
2 GPH EMITTER
.5 GPH EMITER
BUBBLER

IRRIGATION SYMBOLS

SCALE: NOT TO SCALE

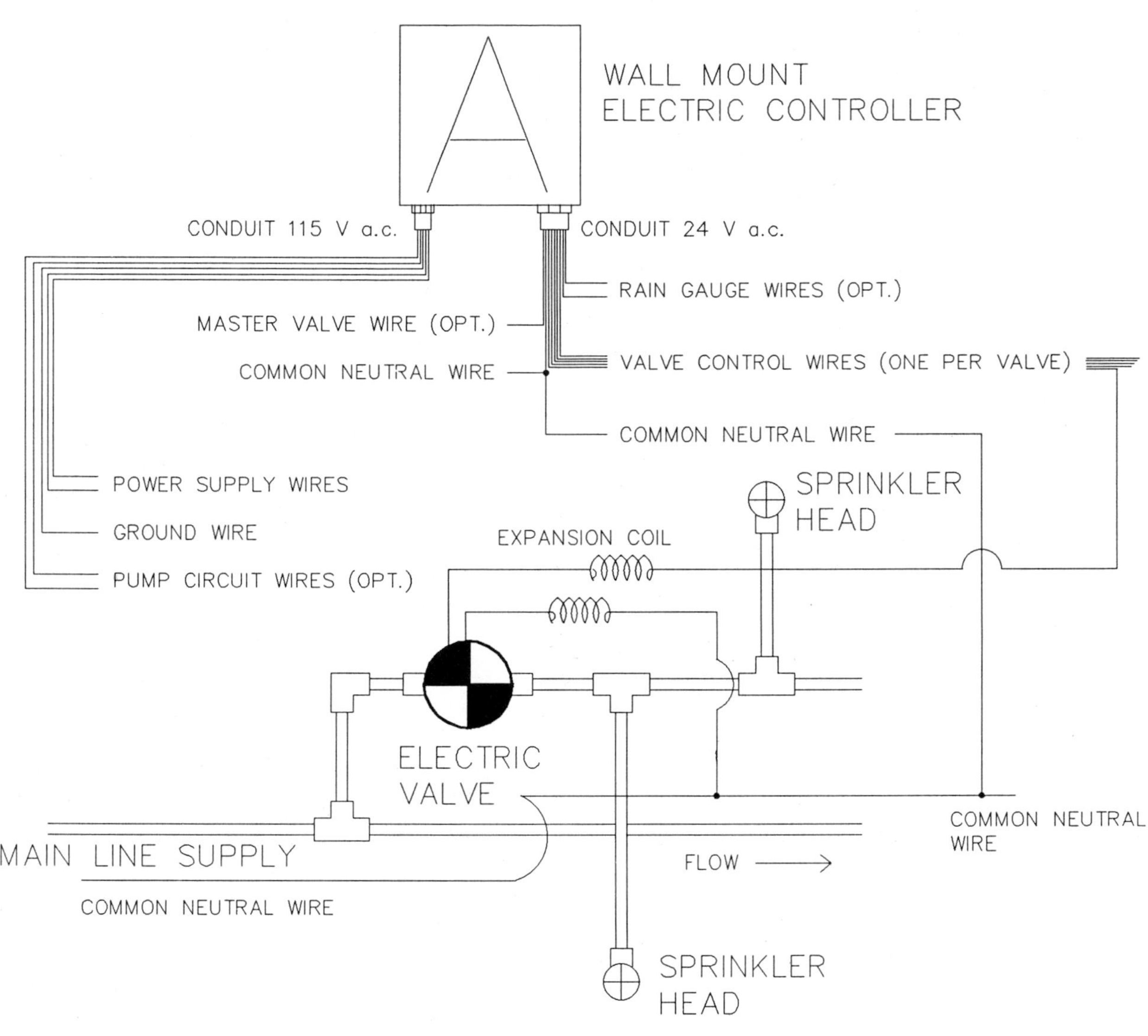
WALL MOUNT
ELECTRIC CONTROLLER
CONDUIT 115 V a.c.
CONDUIT 24 V a.c.
RAIN GAUGE WIRES (OPT.)
MASTER VALVE WIRE (OPT.)
COMMON NEUTRAL WIRE
VALVE CONTROL WIRES (ONE PER VALVE)
COMMON NEUTRAL WIRE
POWER SUPPLY WIRES
GROUND WIRE
PUMP CIRCUIT WIRES (OPT.)
SPRINKLER HEAD
EXPANSION COIL
ELECTRIC VALVE
MAIN LINE SUPPLY
COMMON NEUTRAL WIRE
FLOW
COMMON NEUTRAL WIRE
SPRINKLER HEAD

DIAGRAM — ELECTRIC CONTROLLER WIRING CONNECTION

SCALE: NOT TO SCALE

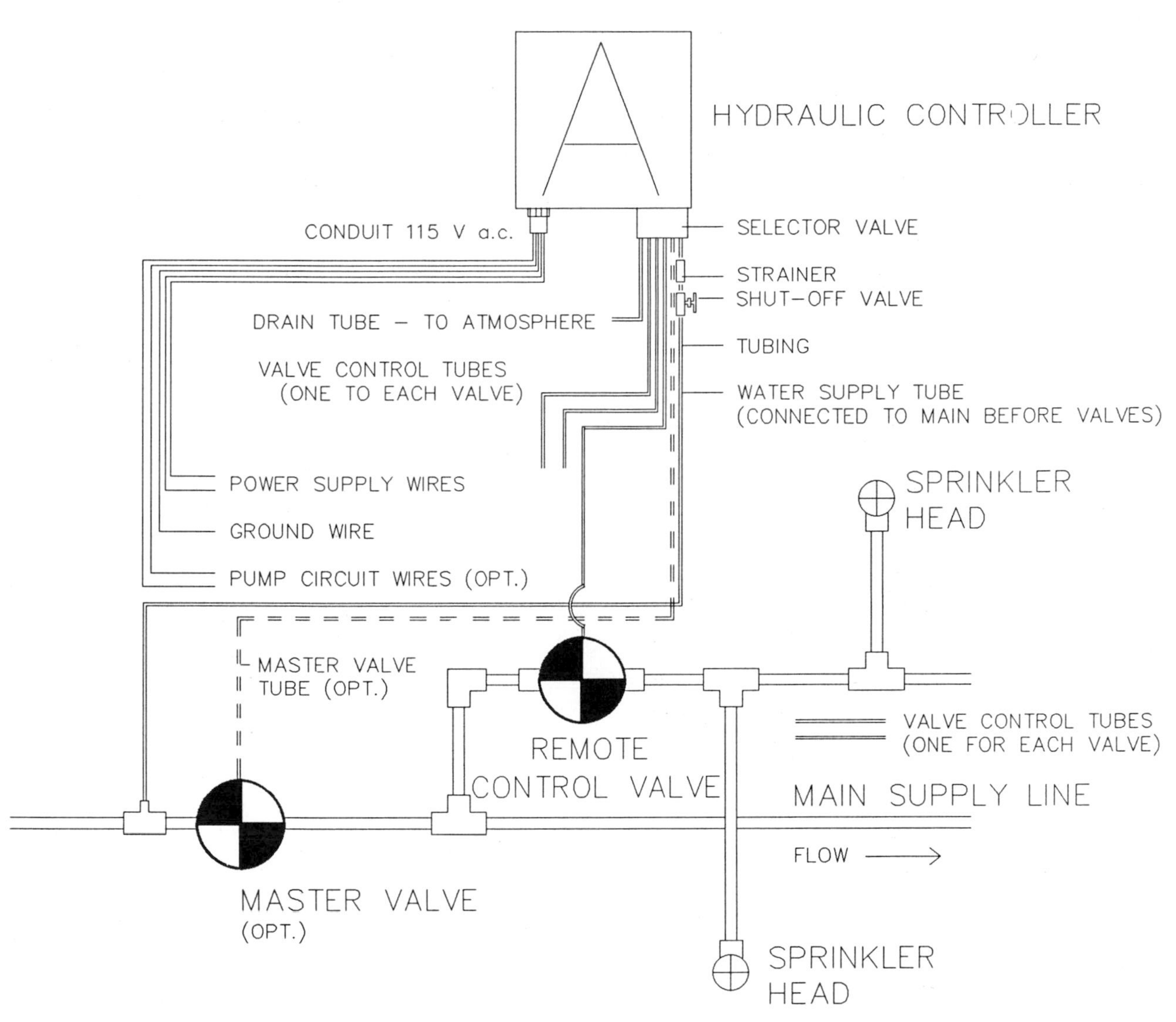
HYDRAULIC CONTROLLER
CONDUIT 115 V a.c.
SELECTOR VALVE
STRAINER
SHUT-OFF VALVE
DRAIN TUBE – TO ATMOSPHERE
TUBING
VALVE CONTROL TUBES
(ONE TO EACH VALVE)
WATER SUPPLY TUBE
(CONNECTED TO MAIN BEFORE VALVES)
SPRINKLER HEAD
POWER SUPPLY WIRES
GROUND WIRE
PUMP CIRCUIT WIRES (OPT.)
MASTER VALVE
TUBE (OPT.)
REMOTE
CONTROL VALVE
VALVE CONTROL TUBES
(ONE FOR EACH VALVE)
MAIN SUPPLY LINE
FLOW
MASTER VALVE
(OPT.)
SPRINKLER
HEAD

DIAGRAM – HYDRAULIC CONTROLLER
TUBING INSTALLATION

SCALE: NOT TO SCALE

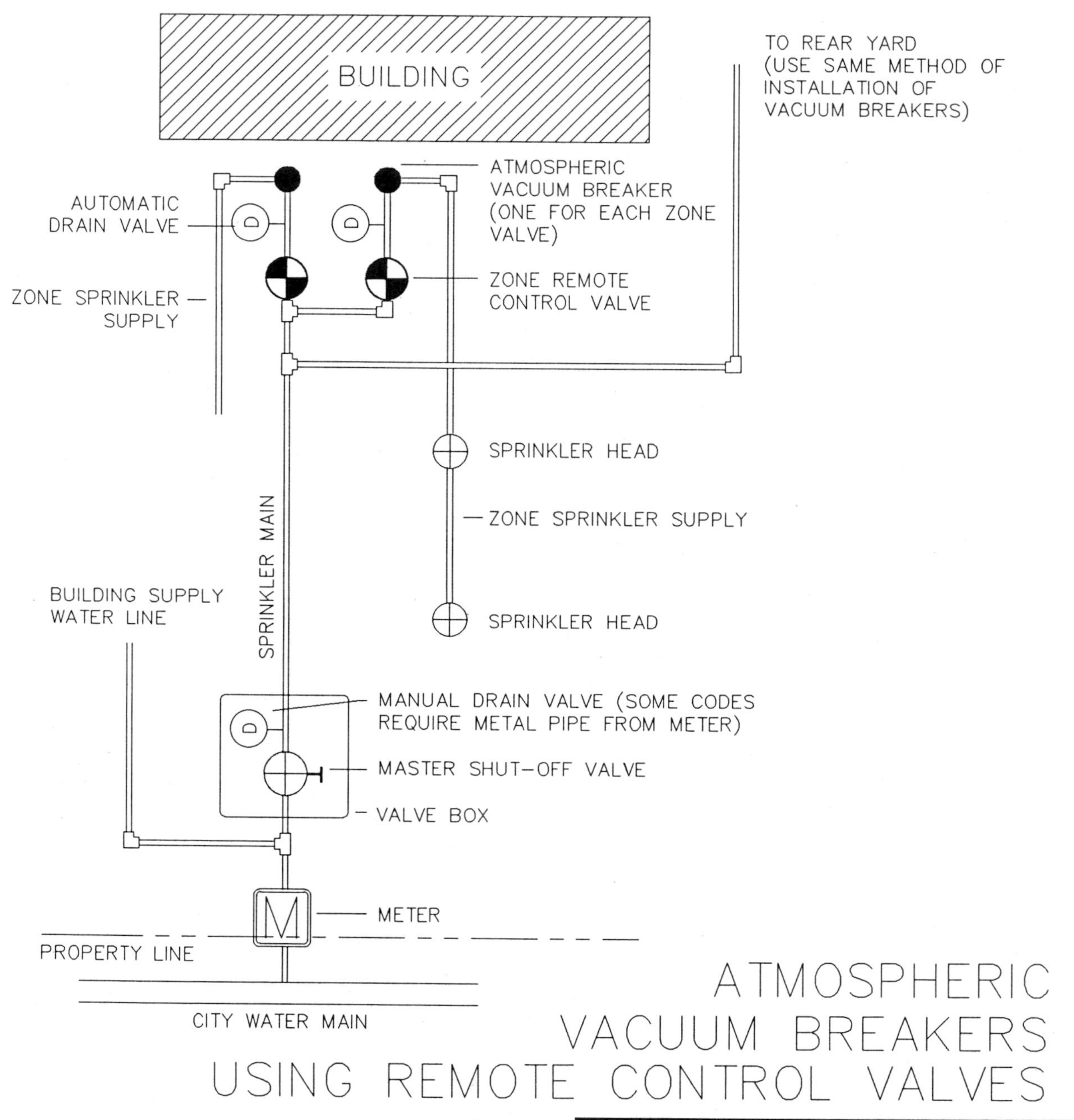
BUILDING
TO REAR YARD
(USE SAME METHOD OF
INSTALLATION OF
VACUUM BREAKERS)
ATMOSPHERIC
VACUUM BREAKER
(ONE FOR EACH ZONE
VALVE)
AUTOMATIC
DRAIN VALVE
D
D
ZONE REMOTE
CONTROL VALVE
ZONE SPRINKLER
SUPPLY
SPRINKLER HEAD
ZONE SPRINKLER SUPPLY
SPRINKLER MAIN
BUILDING SUPPLY
WATER LINE
SPRINKLER HEAD
MANUAL DRAIN VALVE (SOME CODES
REQUIRE METAL PIPE FROM METER)
D
MASTER SHUT-OFF VALVE
VALVE BOX
M
METER
PROPERTY LINE
CITY WATER MAIN

ATMOSPHERIC VACUUM BREAKERS USING REMOTE CONTROL VALVES

SCALE: NOT TO SCALE

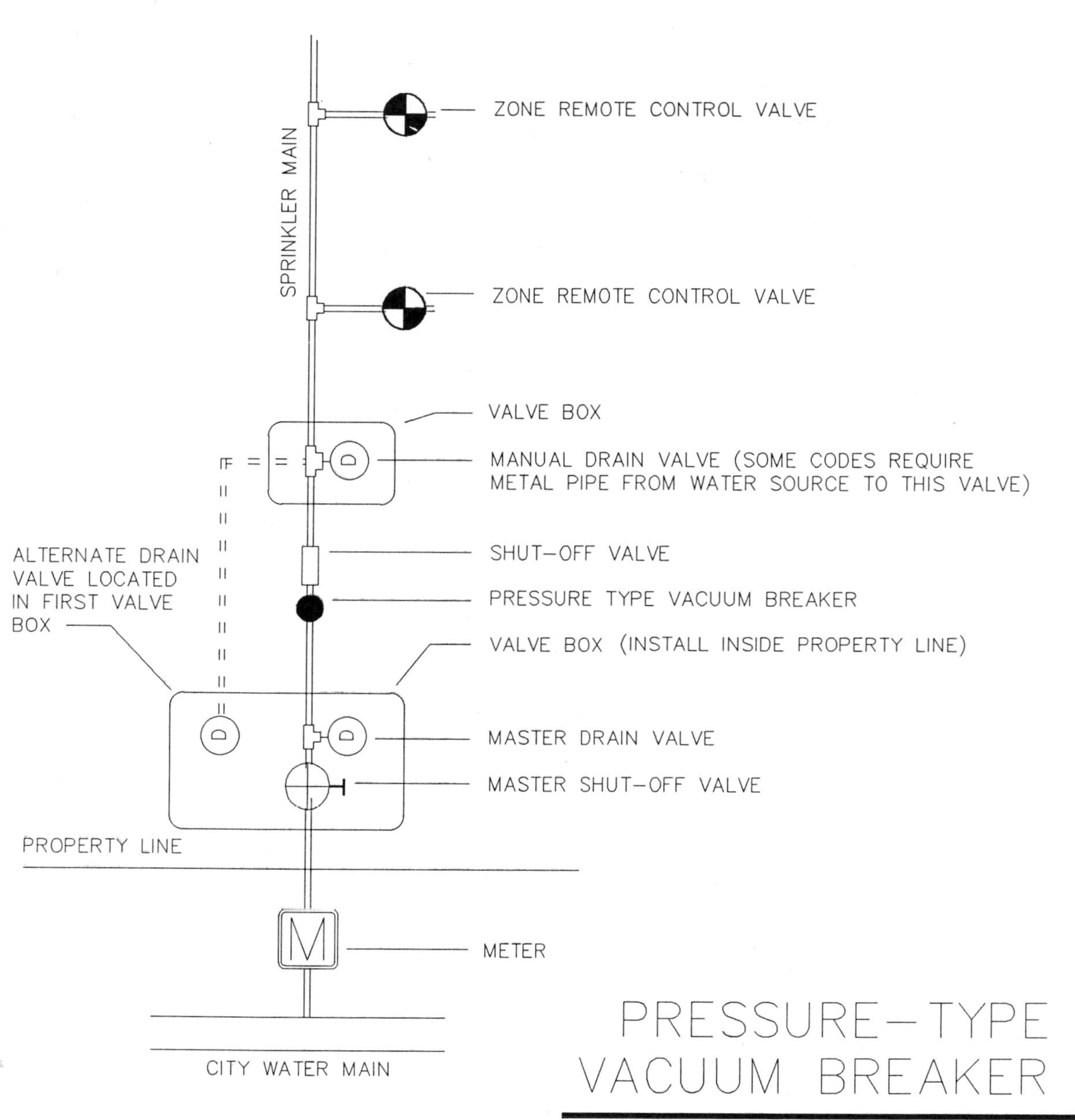
ZONE REMOTE CONTROL VALVE
SPRINKLER MAIN
ZONE REMOTE CONTROL VALVE
VALVE BOX
MANUAL DRAIN VALVE (SOME CODES REQUIRE METAL PIPE FROM WATER SOURCE TO THIS VALVE)
ALTERNATE DRAIN VALVE LOCATED IN FIRST VALVE BOX
SHUT–OFF VALVE
PRESSURE TYPE VACUUM BREAKER
VALVE BOX (INSTALL INSIDE PROPERTY LINE)
D
D
D
MASTER DRAIN VALVE
MASTER SHUT–OFF VALVE
PROPERTY LINE
M
METER
CITY WATER MAIN

PRESSURE–TYPE VACUUM BREAKER

SCALE: NOT TO SCALE

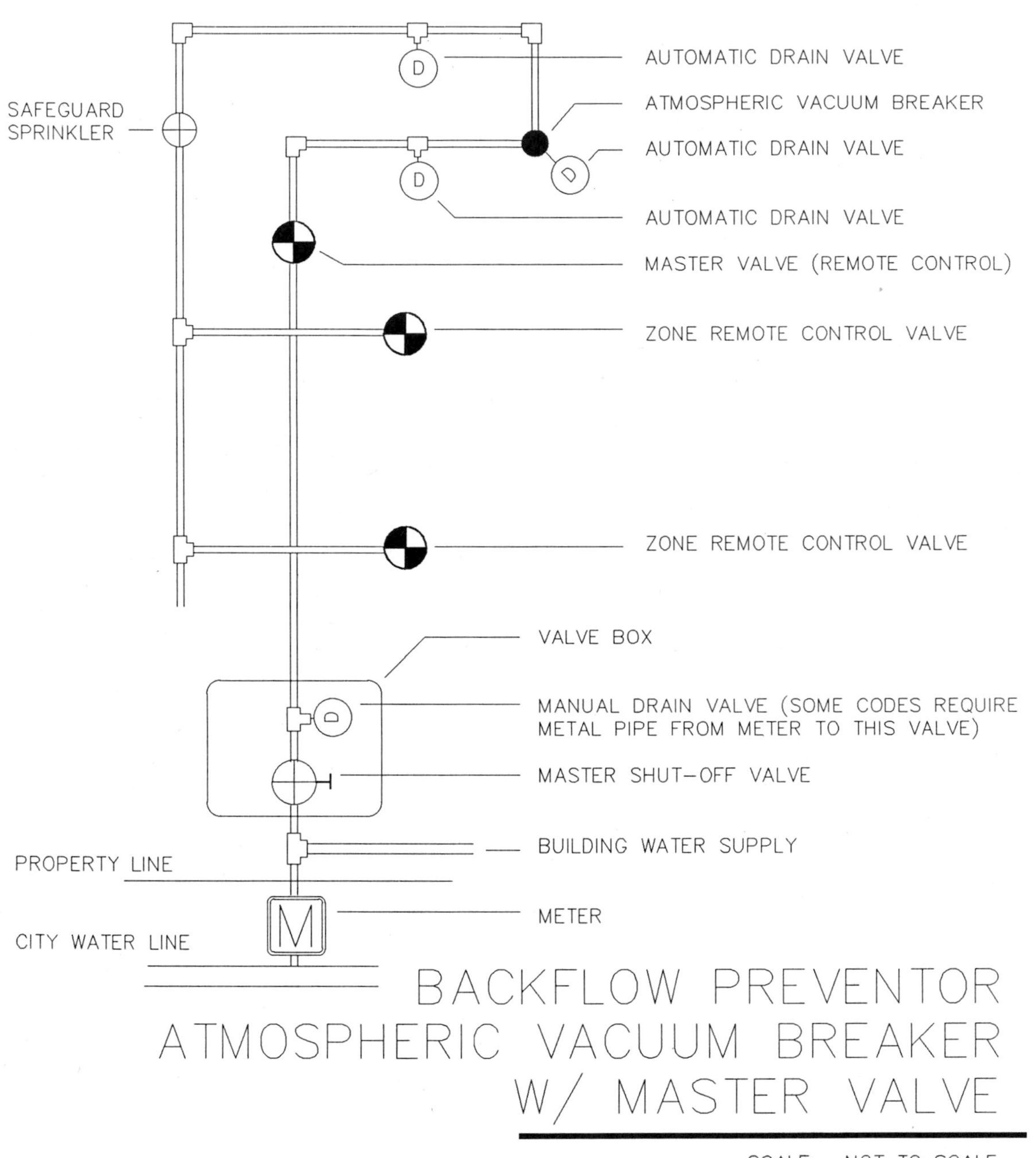
AUTOMATIC DRAIN VALVE
ATMOSPHERIC VACUUM BREAKER
SAFEGUARD SPRINKLER
AUTOMATIC DRAIN VALVE
AUTOMATIC DRAIN VALVE
MASTER VALVE (REMOTE CONTROL)
ZONE REMOTE CONTROL VALVE
ZONE REMOTE CONTROL VALVE
VALVE BOX
MANUAL DRAIN VALVE (SOME CODES REQUIRE METAL PIPE FROM METER TO THIS VALVE)
MASTER SHUT-OFF VALVE
BUILDING WATER SUPPLY
PROPERTY LINE
METER
CITY WATER LINE
D
M

BACKFLOW PREVENTOR ATMOSPHERIC VACUUM BREAKER W/ MASTER VALVE

SCALE: NOT TO SCALE

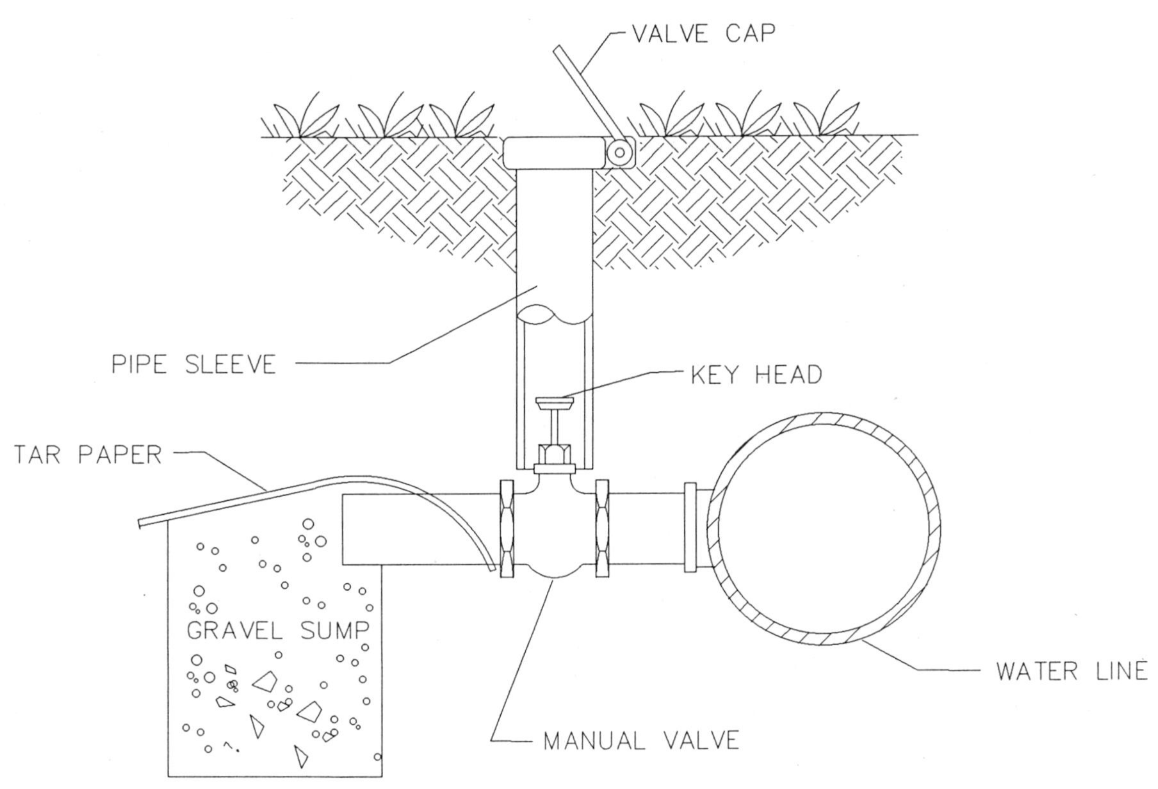
VALVE CAP
PIPE SLEEVE
KEY HEAD
TAR PAPER
GRAVEL SUMP
WATER LINE
MANUAL VALVE

INSTALLATION OF MANUAL DRAIN

SCALE: NOT TO SCALE

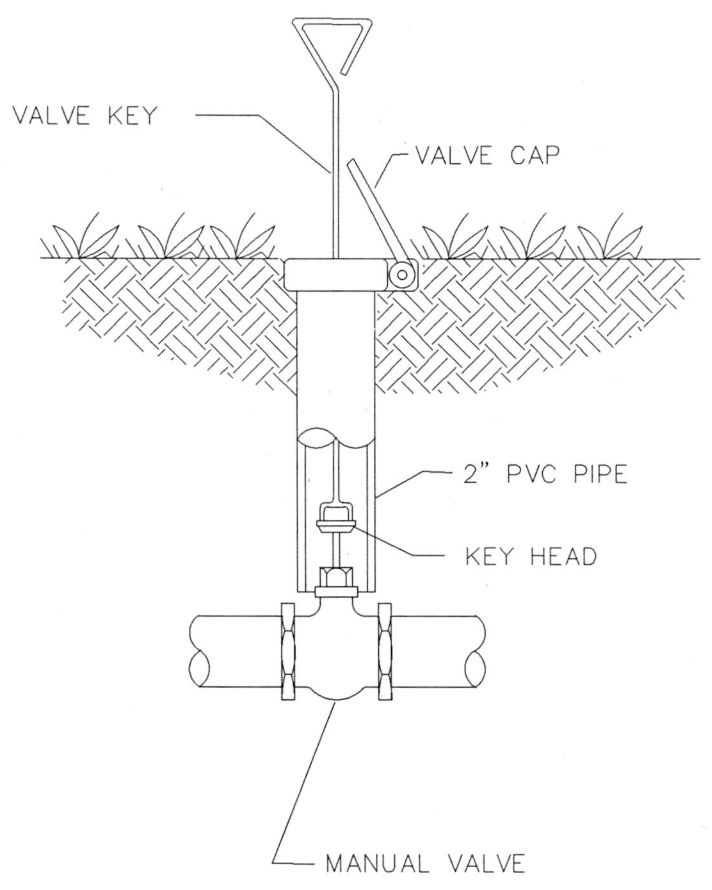
VALVE KEY
VALVE CAP
2" PVC PIPE
KEY HEAD
MANUAL VALVE

VALVE CAP AND SLEEVE INSTALLATION

SCALE: NOT TO SCALE

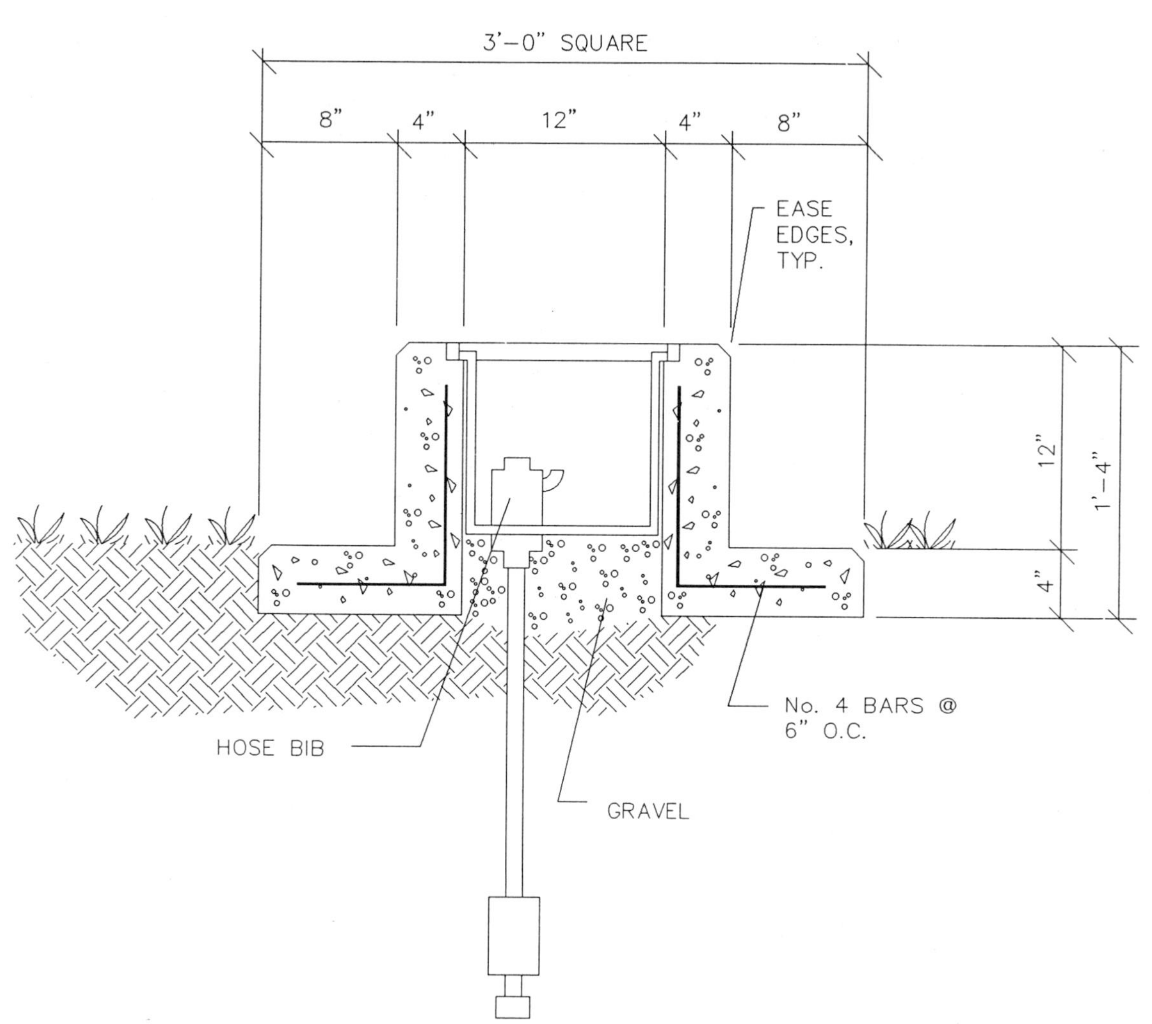
3'–0" SQUARE
8"
4"
12"
4"
8"
EASE
EDGES,
TYP.
12"
1'–4"
4"
No. 4 BARS @
6" O.C.
HOSE BIB
GRAVEL

YARD HYDRANT BOX

SCALE: NOT TO SCALE

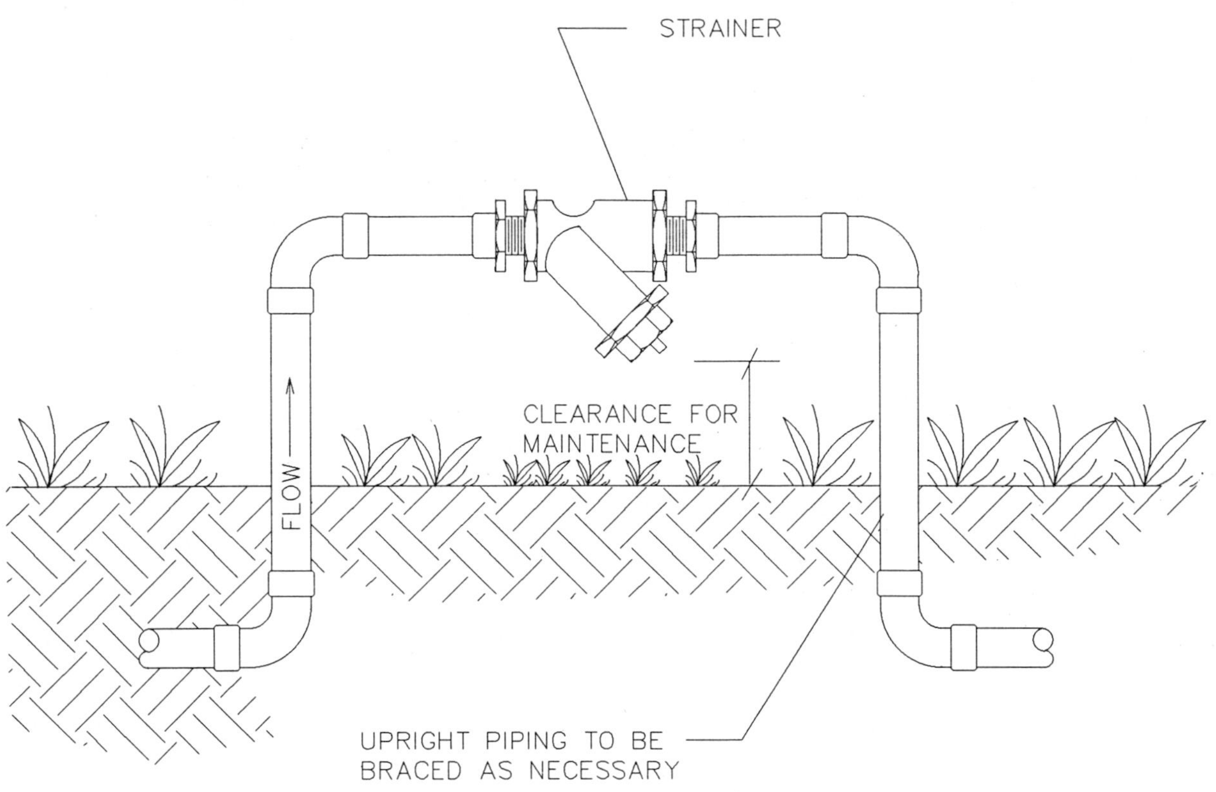
STRAINER
FLOW
CLEARANCE FOR
MAINTENANCE
UPRIGHT PIPING TO BE
BRACED AS NECESSARY

STRAINER INSTALLATION

SCALE: NOT TO SCALE

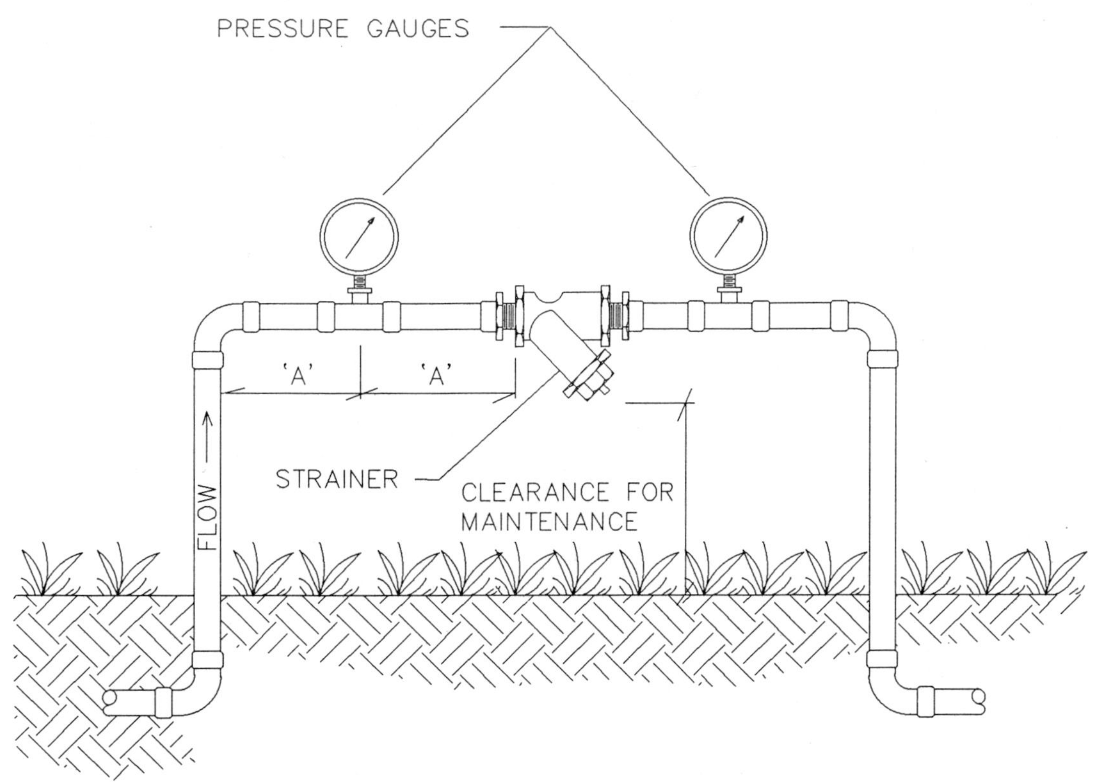
PRESSURE GAUGES
'A'
'A'
FLOW
STRAINER
CLEARANCE FOR
MAINTENANCE

'A' GREATER THAN 6 TIMES PIPE DIAMETER

STRAINER WITH PRESSURE GAUGES

SCALE: NOT TO SCALE

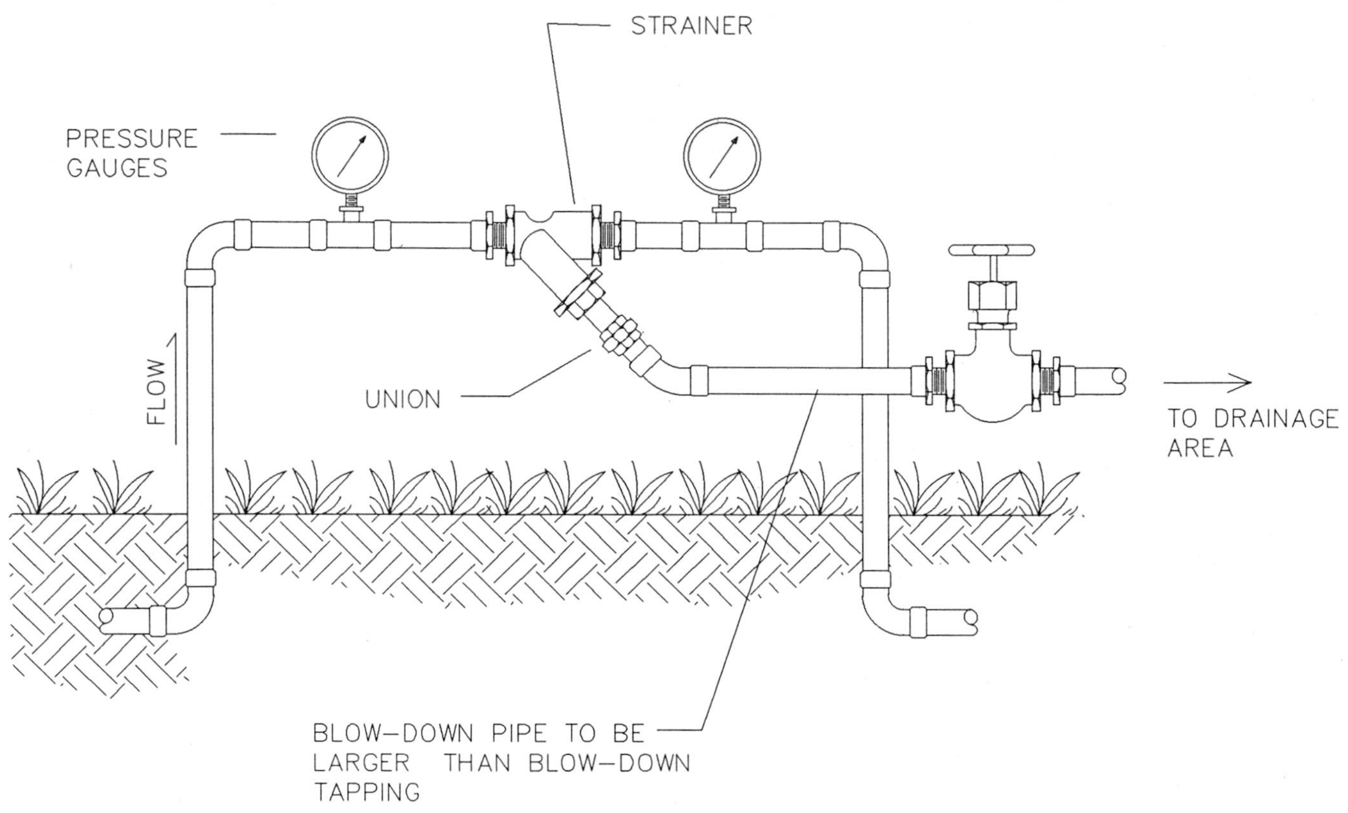
STRAINER
PRESSURE
GAUGES
FLOW
UNION
TO DRAINAGE
AREA
BLOW-DOWN PIPE TO BE
LARGER THAN BLOW-DOWN
TAPPING

"Y" STRAINER FOR CLEANING

SCALE: NOT TO SCALE

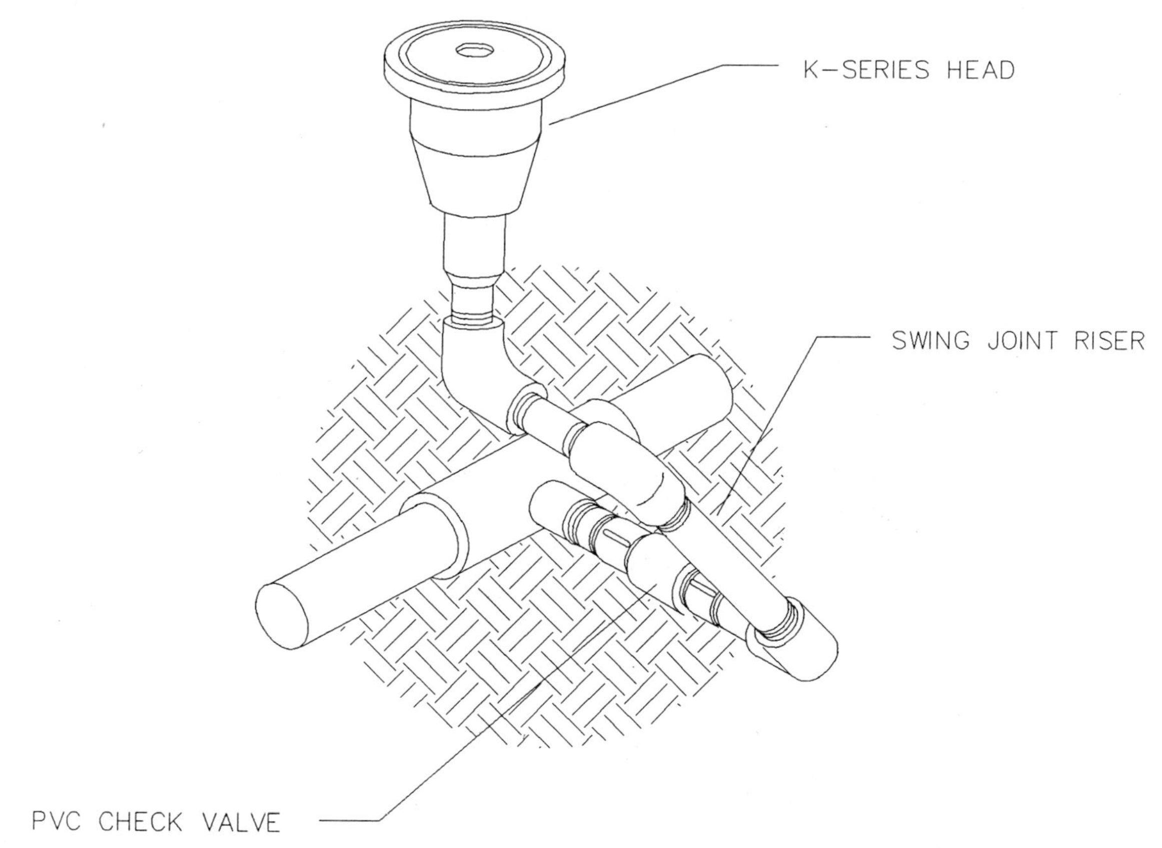
K–SERIES HEAD
SWING JOINT RISER
PVC CHECK VALVE

TYPICAL INSTALLATION OF PVC CHECK VALVE UNDER–HEAD

SCALE: NOT TO SCALE

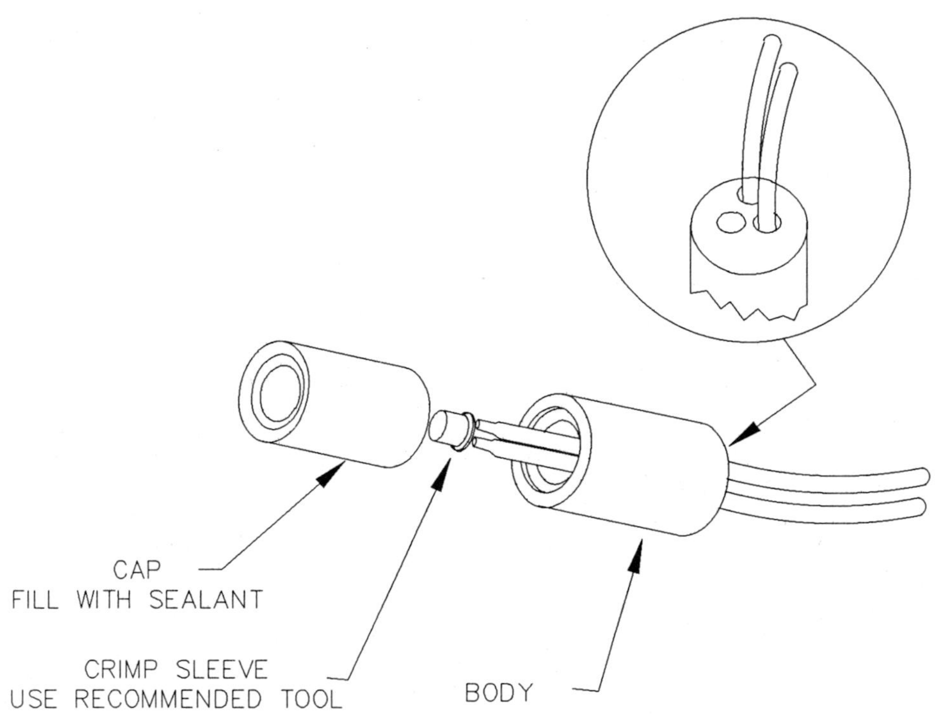
CAP
FILL WITH SEALANT
CRIMP SLEEVE
USE RECOMMENDED TOOL
BODY

TYPICAL WIRE CONNECTION

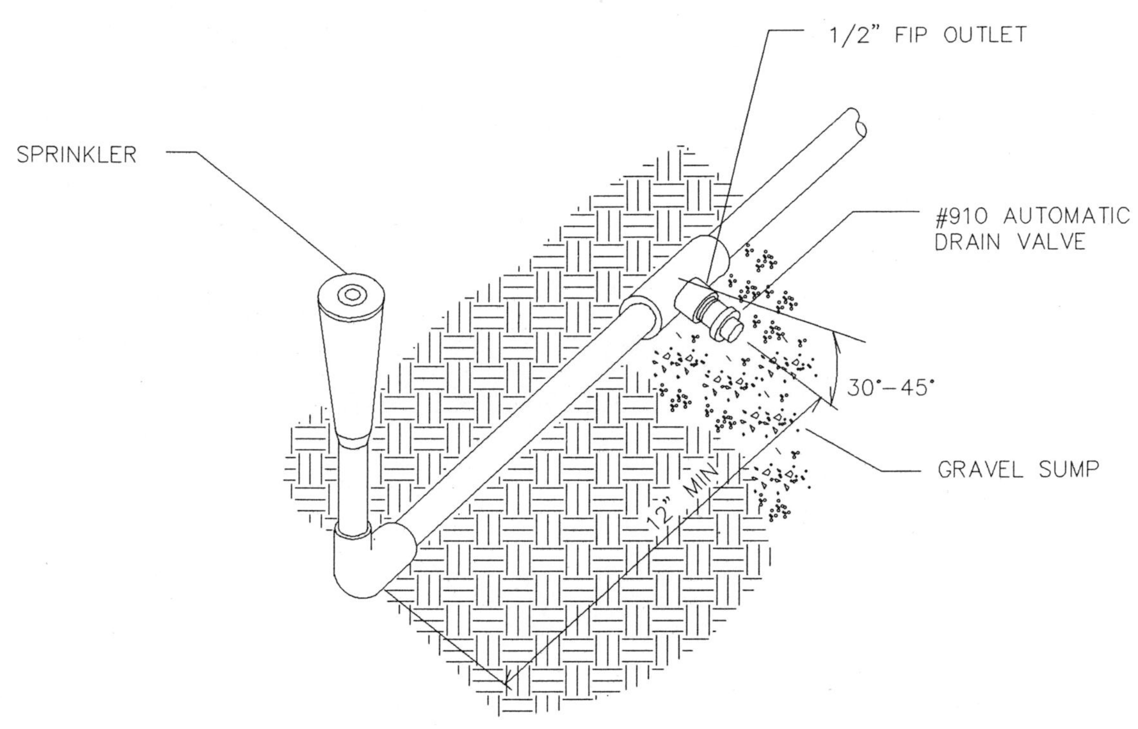
1/2" FIP OUTLET
SPRINKLER
#910 AUTOMATIC
DRAIN VALVE
30°-45°
GRAVEL SUMP
12" MIN

TYPICAL INSTALLATION OF #910 AUTOMATIC DRAIN VALVE

SCALE: NOT TO SCALE

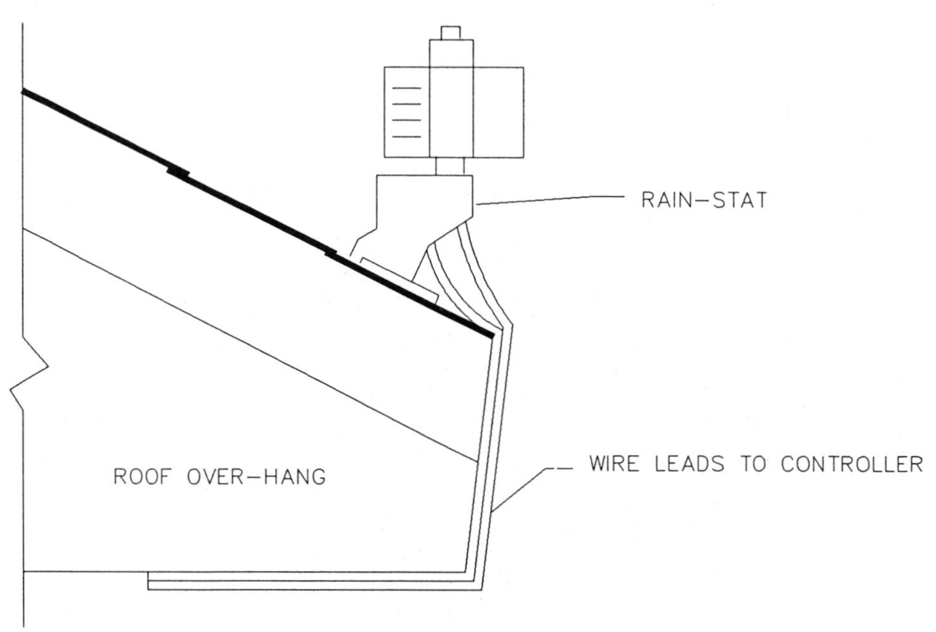
RAIN-STAT
ROOF OVER-HANG
WIRE LEADS TO CONTROLLER

RAIN-STAT, TYPICAL INSTALLATION

SCALE: NOT TO SCALE

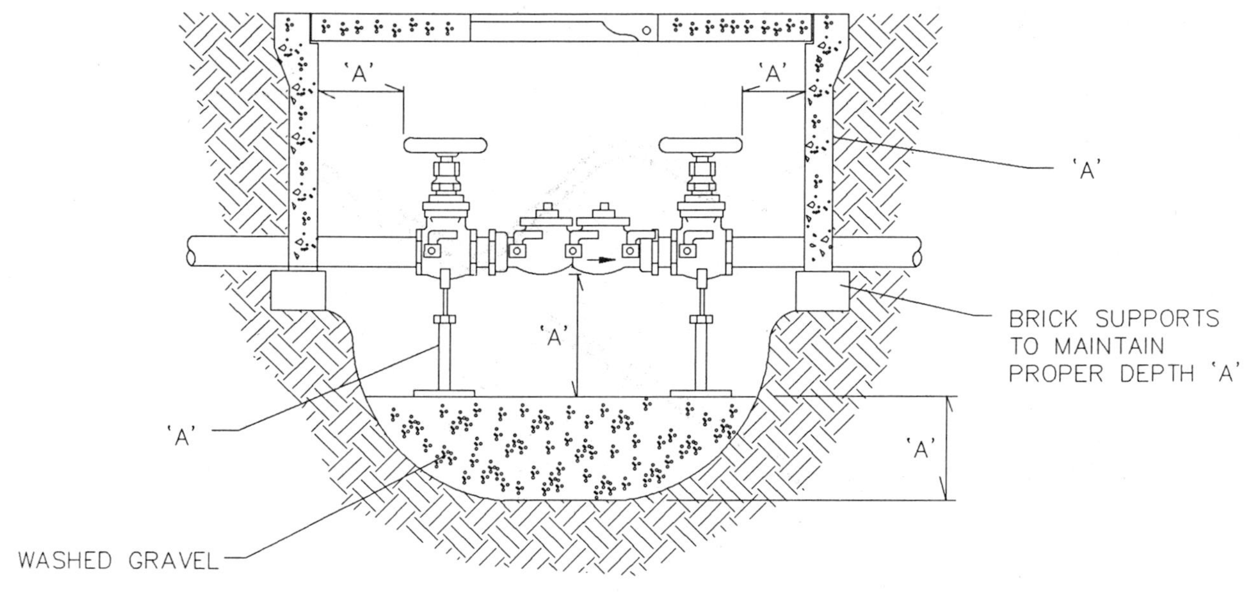
'A'
'A'
'A'
'A'
BRICK SUPPORTS
TO MAINTAIN
PROPER DEPTH 'A'
'A'
'A'
WASHED GRAVEL

'A' AS PER LOCAL CODE

TYPICAL INSTALLATION DOUBLE CHECK VALVE ASSEMBLY

SCALE: NOT TO SCALE

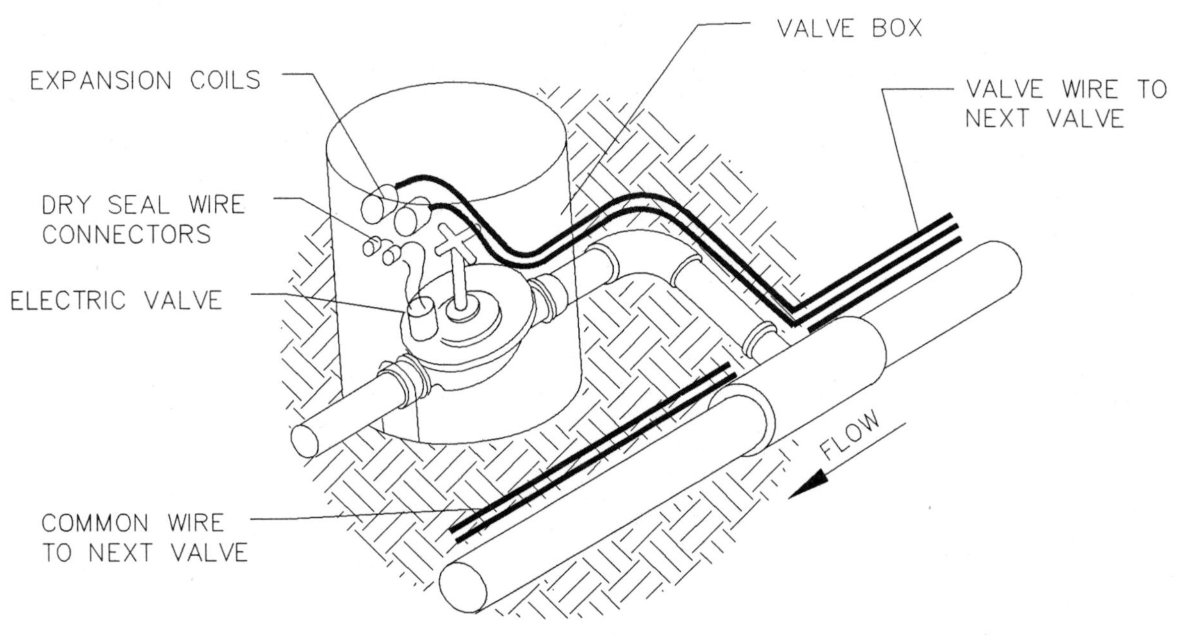
VALVE BOX
EXPANSION COILS
VALVE WIRE TO
NEXT VALVE
DRY SEAL WIRE
CONNECTORS
ELECTRIC VALVE
FLOW
COMMON WIRE
TO NEXT VALVE

TYPICAL INSTALLATION OF ELECTRIC VALVE, VALVE BOX

SCALE: NOT TO SCALE

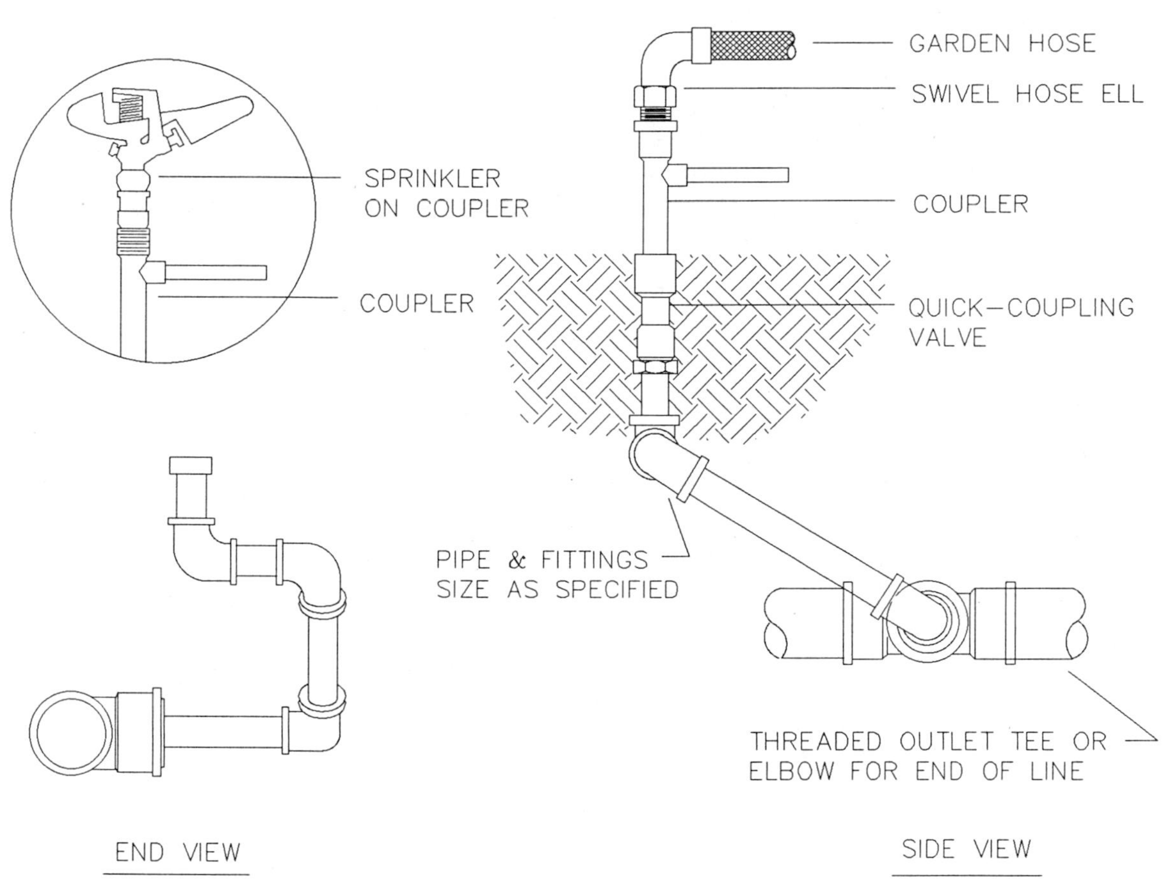
GARDEN HOSE
SWIVEL HOSE ELL
SPRINKLER ON COUPLER
COUPLER
COUPLER
QUICK–COUPLING VALVE
PIPE & FITTINGS SIZE AS SPECIFIED
THREADED OUTLET TEE OR ELBOW FOR END OF LINE
END VIEW
SIDE VIEW

TYPICAL EXAMPLE OF QUICK–COUPLING VALVE ON SWING JOINT RISER

SCALE: NOT TO SCALE

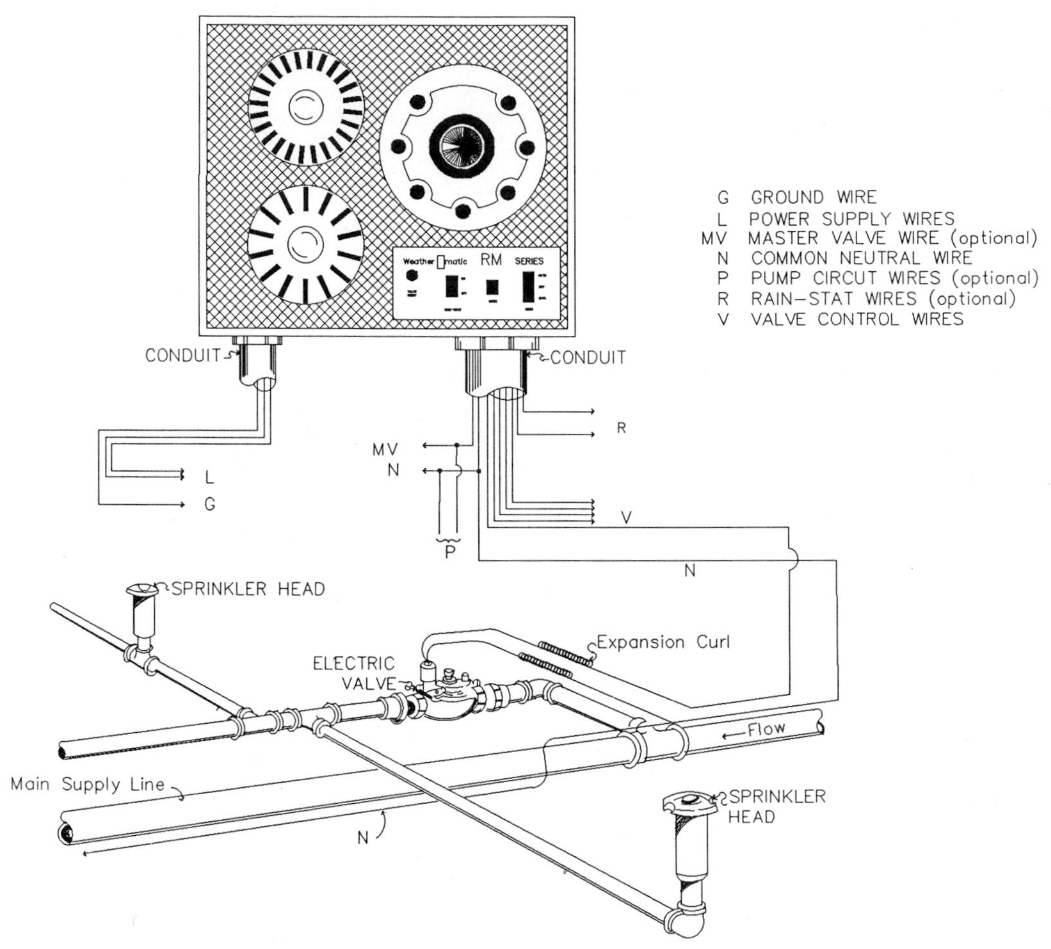
RM
SERIES
G GROUND WIRE
L POWER SUPPLY WIRES
MV MASTER VALVE WIRE (optional)
N COMMON NEUTRAL WIRE
P PUMP CIRCUT WIRES (optional)
R RAIN-STAT WIRES (optional)
V VALVE CONTROL WIRES
CONDUIT
CONDUIT
R
MV
N
L
G
V
P
N
SPRINKLER HEAD
Expansion Curl
ELECTRIC
VALVE
Flow
Main Supply Line
N
SPRINKLER
HEAD

TYPICAL INSTALLATION OF RM CONTROL & VALVES

SCALE: NOT TO SCALE

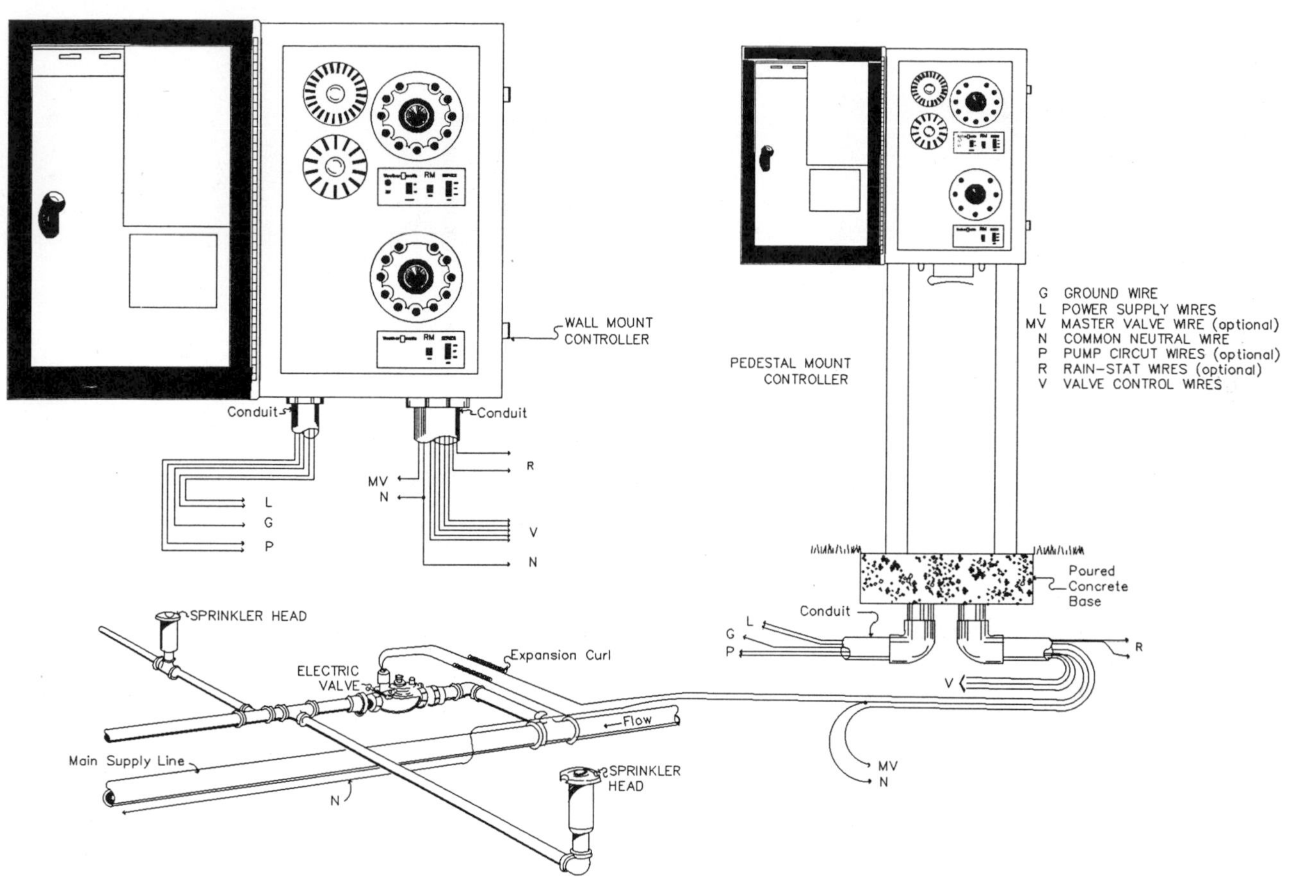

WALL MOUNT CONTROLLER
Conduit
Conduit
L
G
P
MV
N
R
V
N
PEDESTAL MOUNT CONTROLLER
G GROUND WIRE
L POWER SUPPLY WIRES
MV MASTER VALVE WIRE (optional)
N COMMON NEUTRAL WIRE
P PUMP CIRCUT WIRES (optional)
R RAIN-STAT WIRES (optional)
V VALVE CONTROL WIRES
Poured Concrete Base
Conduit
SPRINKLER HEAD
Expansion Curl
ELECTRIC VALVE
Flow
Main Supply Line
N
SPRINKLER HEAD
MV
N

TYPICAL INSTALLATION OF RM 18/22 CONTROLLFR & VALVES

SCALE: NOT TO SCALE

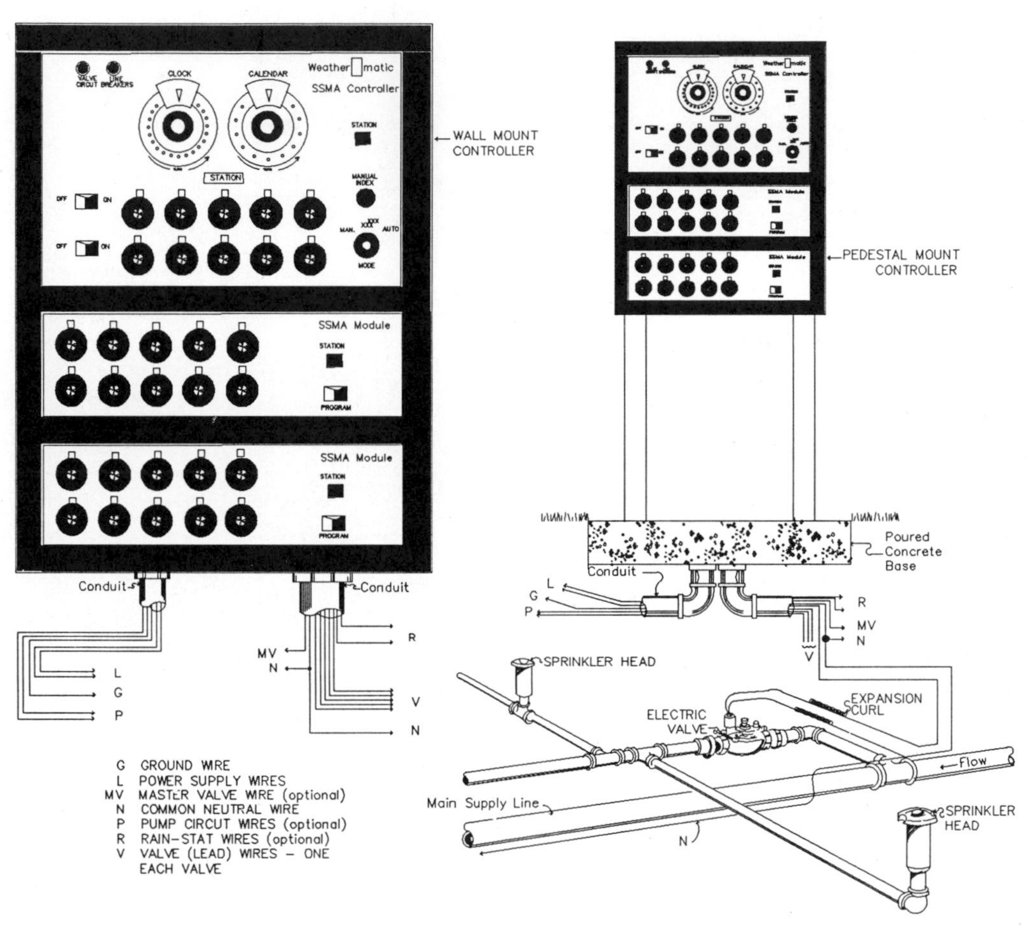
Weather matic
SSMA Controller
CLOCK
CALENDAR
STATION
MANUAL INDEX
MAN.
AUTO
MODE
OFF
ON
SSMA Module
STATION
PROGRAM
WALL MOUNT CONTROLLER
PEDESTAL MOUNT CONTROLLER
Conduit
L
G
P
MV
N
R
V
Poured Concrete Base
SPRINKLER HEAD
ELECTRIC VALVE
EXPANSION CURL
Flow
Main Supply Line
G GROUND WIRE
L POWER SUPPLY WIRES
MV MASTER VALVE WIRE (optional)
N COMMON NEUTRAL WIRE
P PUMP CIRCUT WIRES (optional)
R RAIN-STAT WIRES (optional)
V VALVE (LEAD) WIRES – ONE EACH VALVE

TYPICAL INSTALLATION OF SSMA CONTROLLER & VALVES

SCALE: NOT TO SCALE

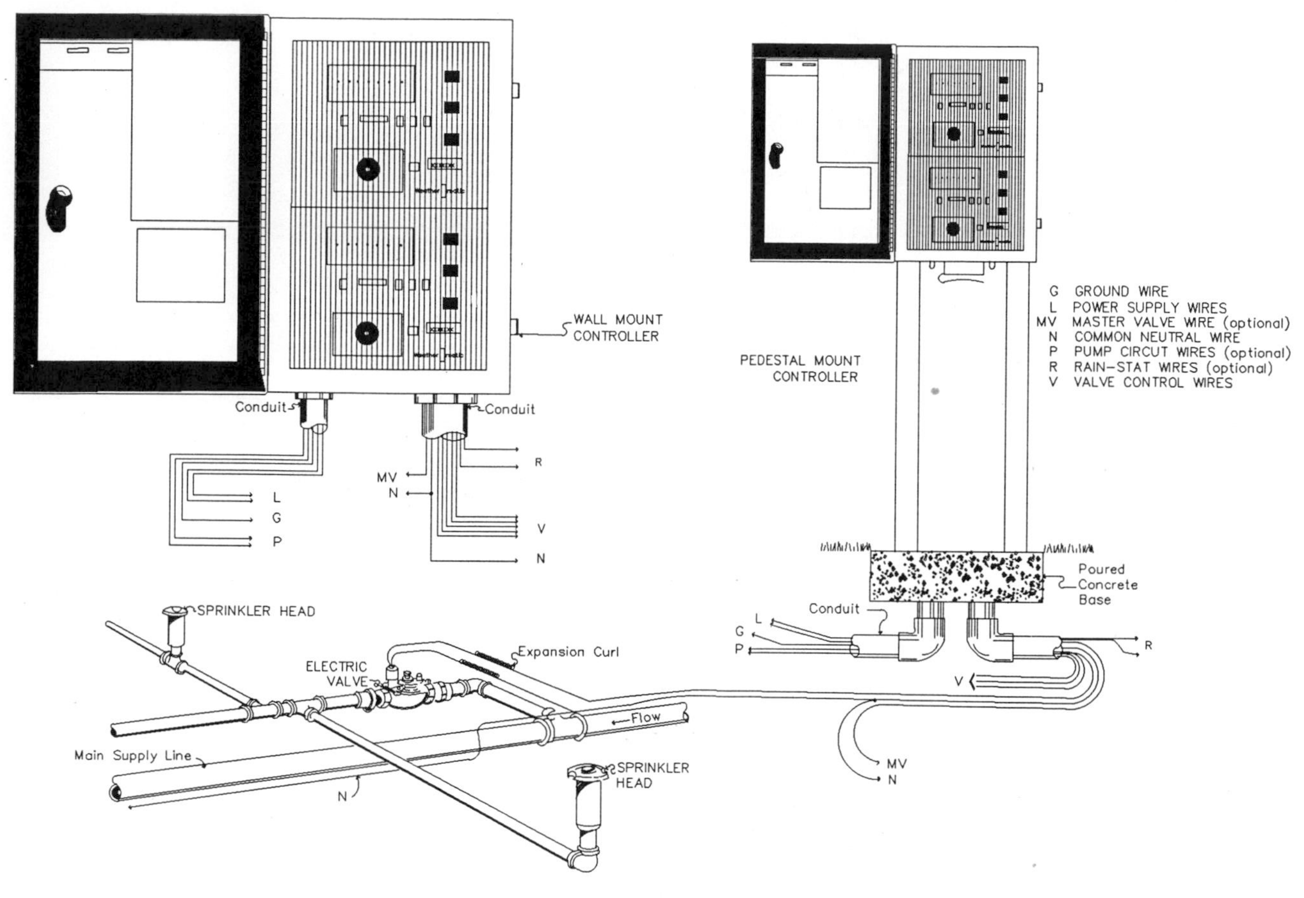
WALL MOUNT
CONTROLLER
Conduit
Conduit
R
MV
N
L
G
P
V
N
PEDESTAL MOUNT
CONTROLLER
G GROUND WIRE
L POWER SUPPLY WIRES
MV MASTER VALVE WIRE (optional)
N COMMON NEUTRAL WIRE
P PUMP CIRCUT WIRES (optional)
R RAIN-STAT WIRES (optional)
V VALVE CONTROL WIRES
Poured
Concrete
Base
Conduit
SPRINKLER HEAD
Expansion Curl
ELECTRIC
VALVE
Flow
Main Supply Line
SPRINKLER
HEAD
MV
N

TYPICAL INSTALLATION OF MARK CONTROLLER & VALVES

SCALE: NOT TO SCALE

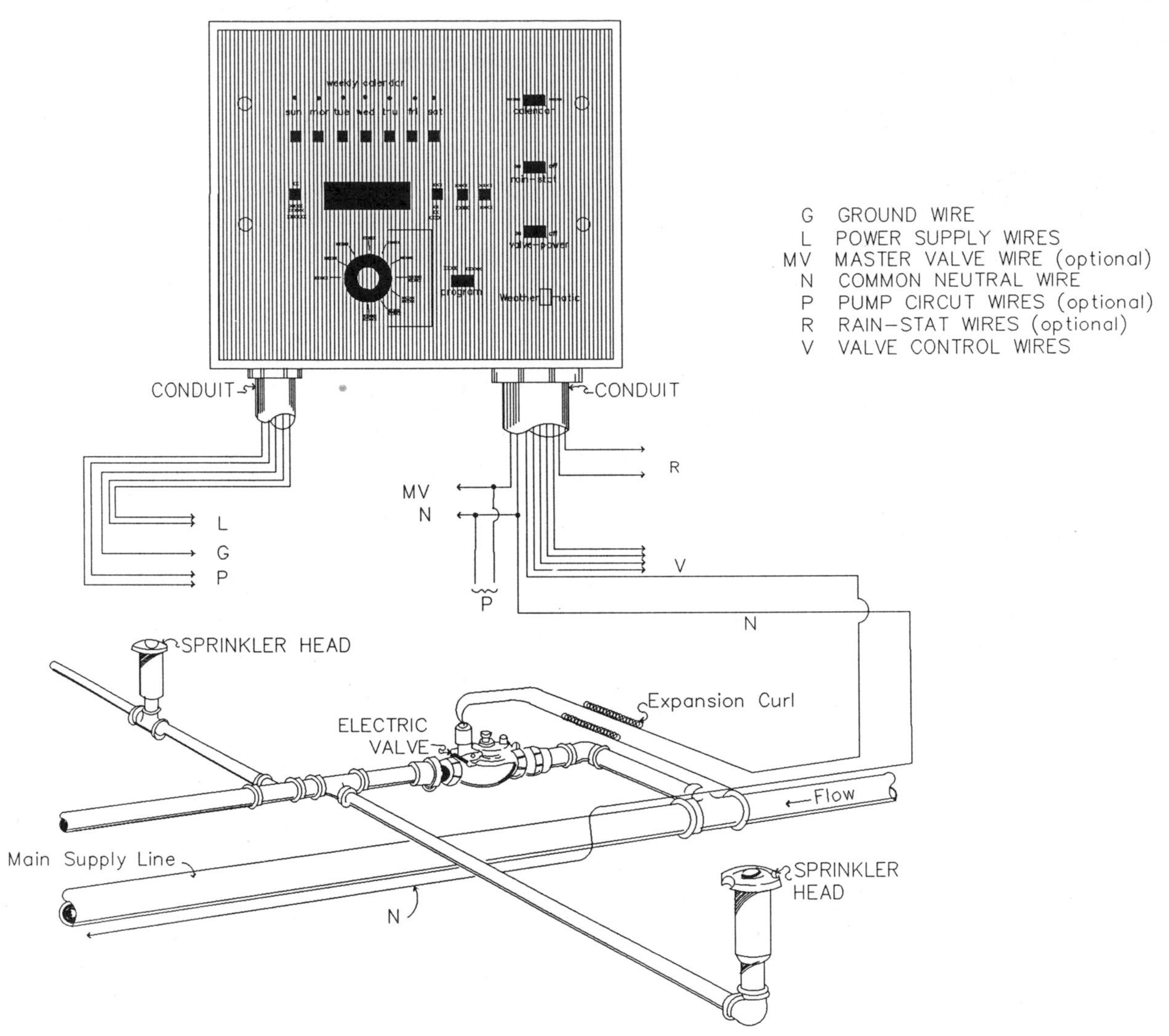

weekly calendar
sun
mon
tue
wed
thu
fri
sat
calendar
rain-stat
valve-power
program
Weather
G GROUND WIRE
L POWER SUPPLY WIRES
MV MASTER VALVE WIRE (optional)
N COMMON NEUTRAL WIRE
P PUMP CIRCUT WIRES (optional)
R RAIN-STAT WIRES (optional)
V VALVE CONTROL WIRES
CONDUIT
CONDUIT
R
MV
N
L
G
P
V
P
N
SPRINKLER HEAD
Expansion Curl
ELECTRIC VALVE
Flow
Main Supply Line
SPRINKLER HEAD
N

TYPICAL INSTALLATION OF MARK SERIES CONTROLLERS

SCALE: NOT TO SCALE

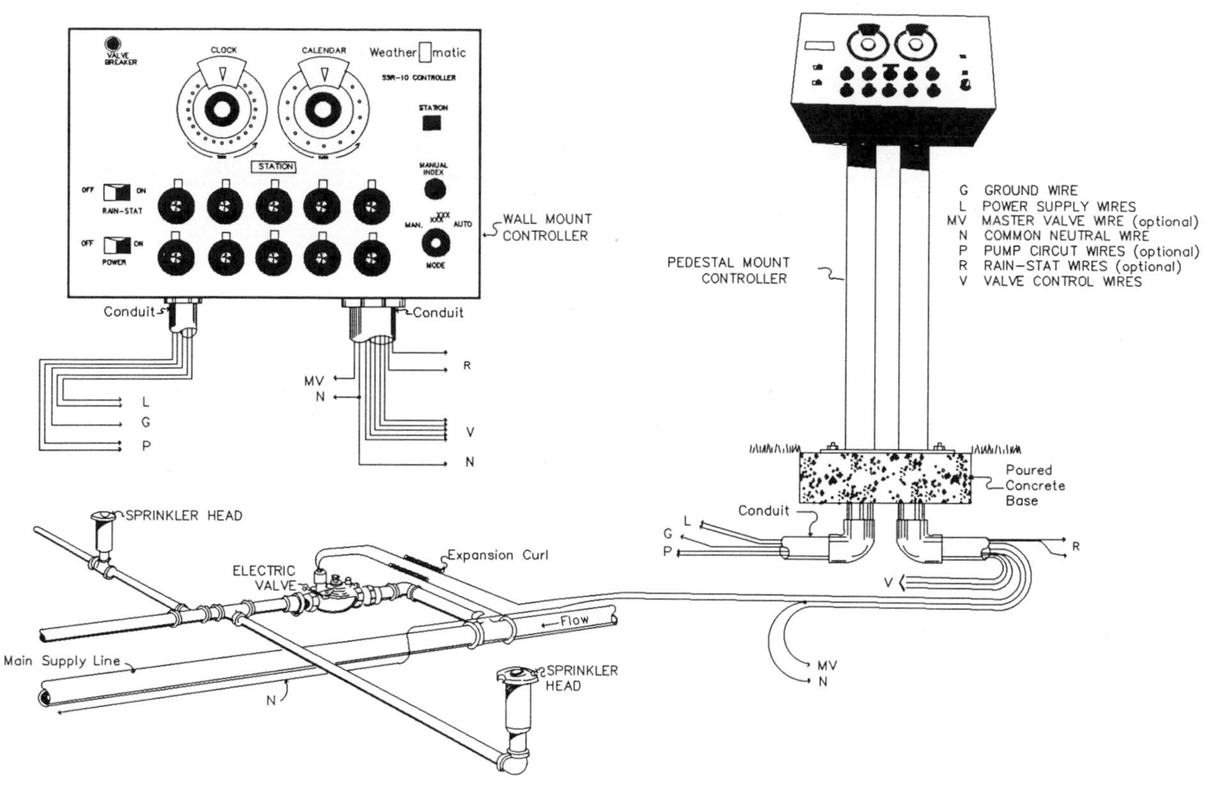
VALVE BREAKER
CLOCK
CALENDAR
Weather matic
SSR-10 CONTROLLER
STATION
MANUAL INDEX
OFF ON
RAIN-STAT
OFF ON
POWER
MAN. XXX AUTO
MODE
WALL MOUNT CONTROLLER
Conduit
Conduit
L
G
P
MV
N
R
V
N
PEDESTAL MOUNT CONTROLLER
G GROUND WIRE
L POWER SUPPLY WIRES
MV MASTER VALVE WIRE (optional)
N COMMON NEUTRAL WIRE
P PUMP CIRCUT WIRES (optional)
R RAIN-STAT WIRES (optional)
V VALVE CONTROL WIRES
Poured Concrete Base
Conduit
L
G
P
R
V
MV
N
SPRINKLER HEAD
Expansion Curl
ELECTRIC VALVE
Flow
Main Supply Line
N
SPRINKLER HEAD

TYPICAL INSTALLATION OF SSR-10 CONTROLLER & VALVES

SCALE: NOT TO SCALE

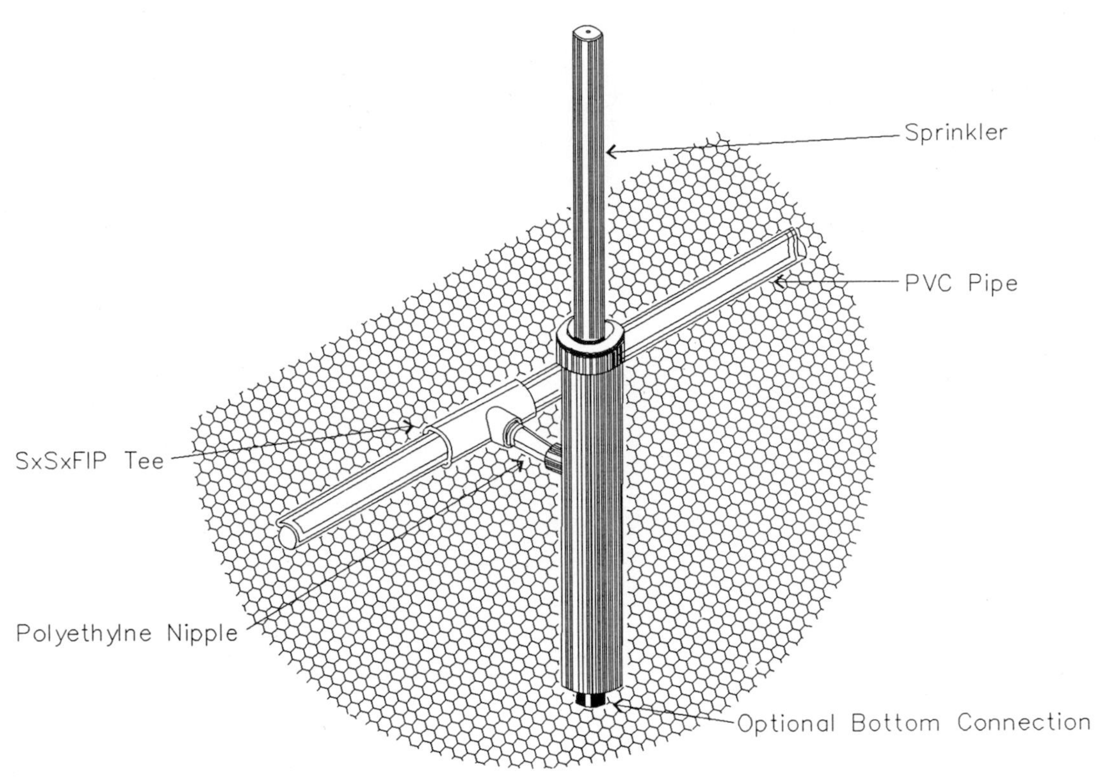
Sprinkler
PVC Pipe
SxSxFIP Tee
Polyethylne Nipple
Optional Bottom Connection

TYPICAL INSTALLATION OF 36P/37P
HIGH-POP SHRUB SPRAY HEADS

SCALE: NOT TO SCALE

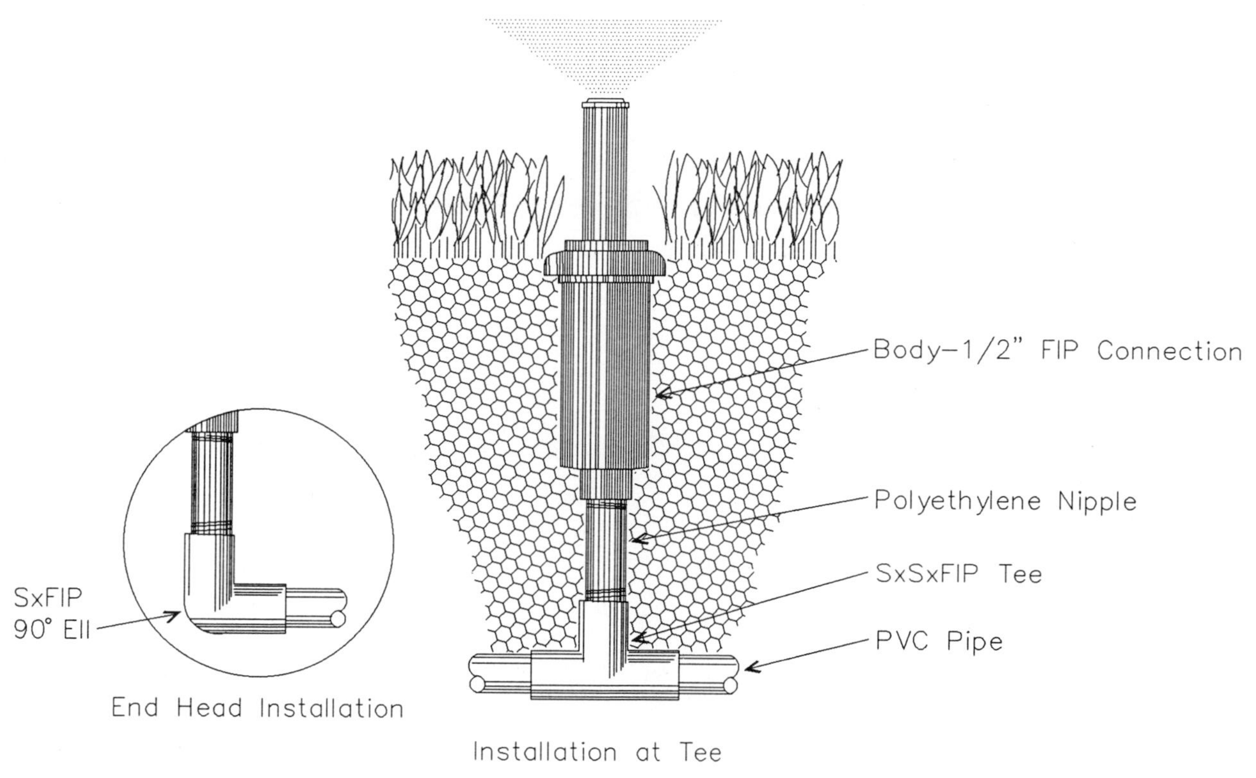
Body–1/2" FIP Connection
Polyethylene Nipple
SxSxFIP Tee
PVC Pipe
SxFIP
90° Ell
End Head Installation
Installation at Tee

TYPICAL INSTALLATION OF HIGH–POP SPRAY HEAD

SCALE: NOT TO SCALE

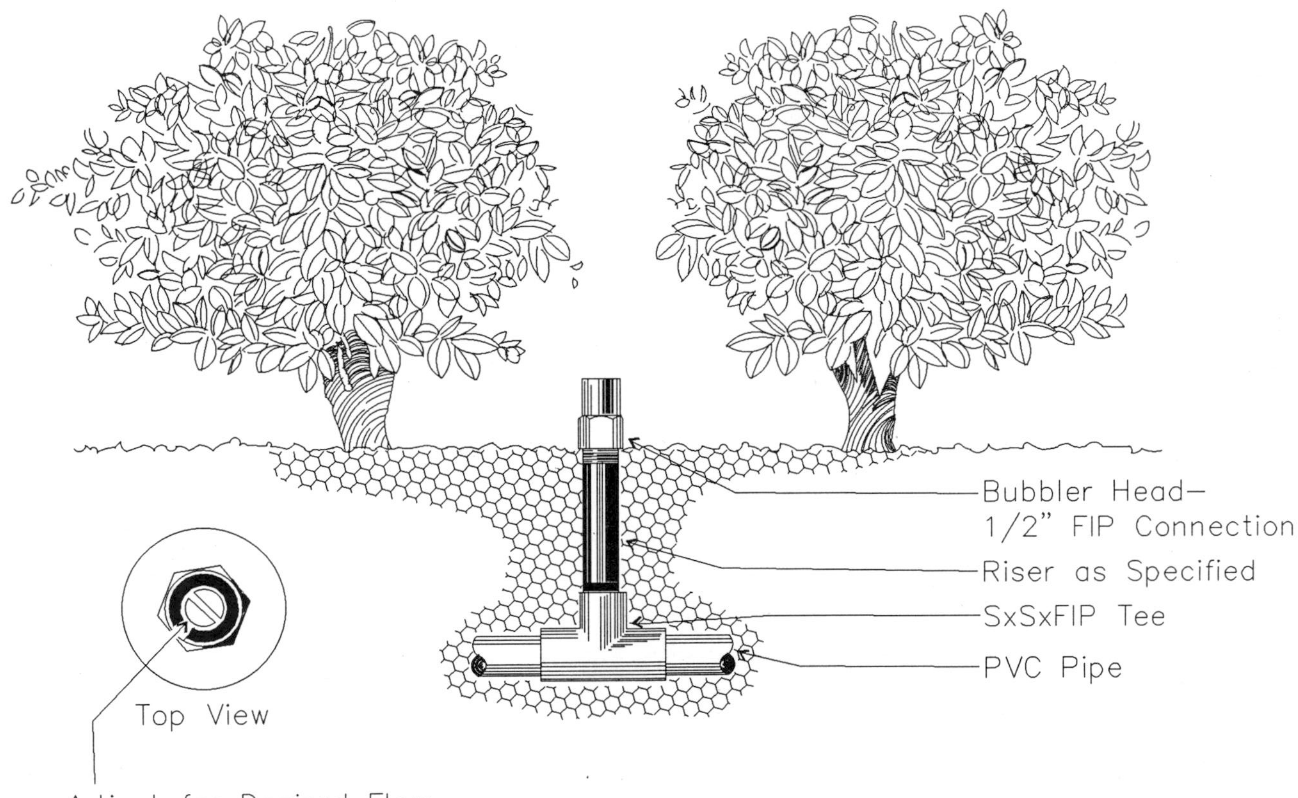
Bubbler Head—
1/2" FIP Connection
Riser as Specified
SxSxFIP Tee
PVC Pipe
Top View
Adjust for Desired Flow

TYPICAL INSTALLATION OF
BUBBLER HEAD

SCALE: NOT TO SCALE

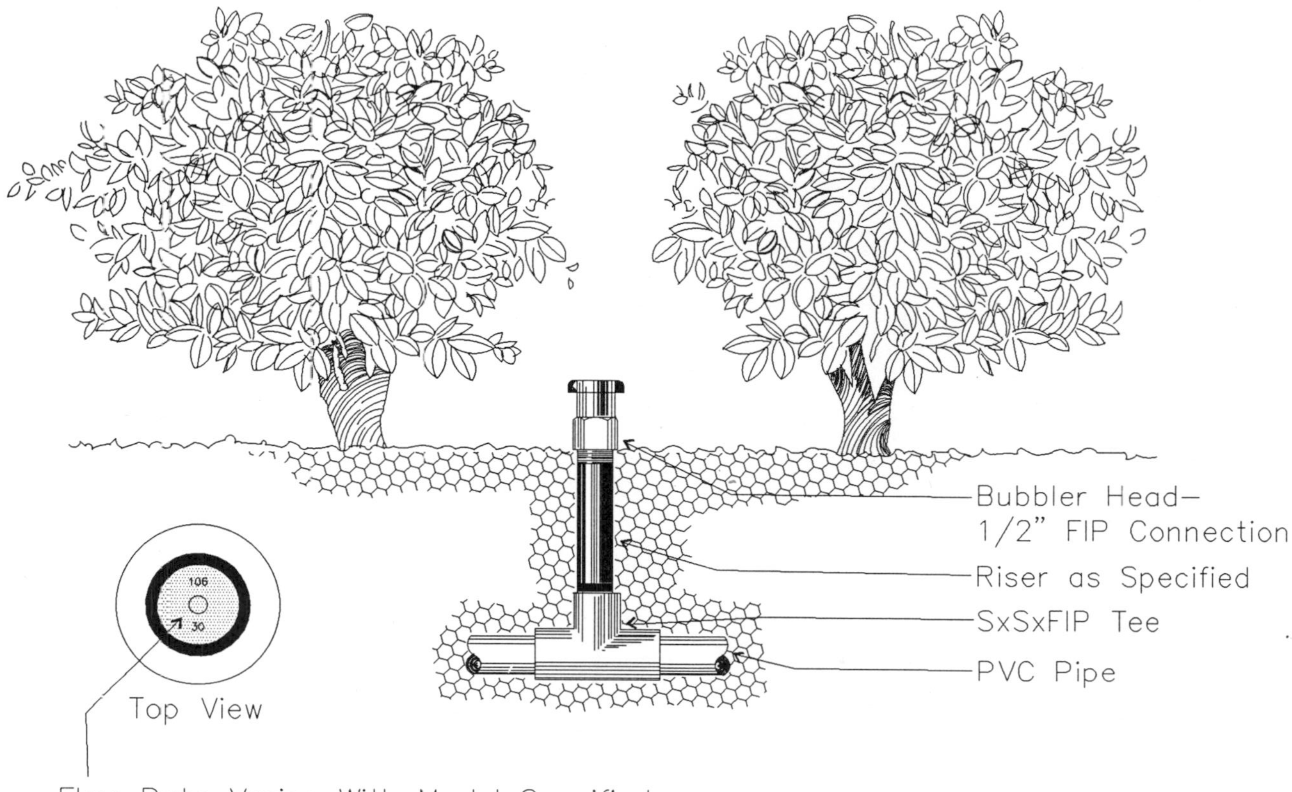
Bubbler Head—
1/2" FIP Connection
Riser as Specified
SxSxFIP Tee
PVC Pipe
106
30
Top View
Flow Rate Varies With Model Specified

TYPICAL INSTALLATION OF PRESSURE COMPENSATING BUBBLER

SCALE: NOT TO SCALE

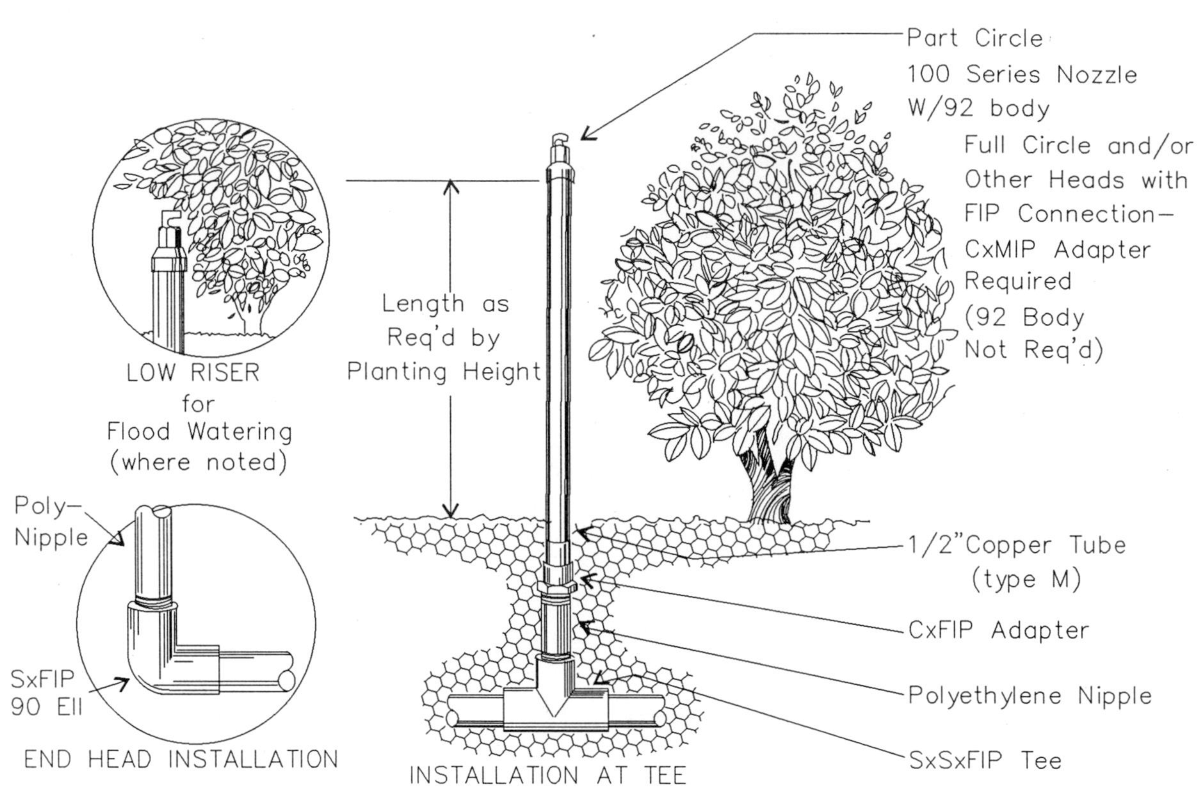
Part Circle
100 Series Nozzle
W/92 body
Full Circle and/or
Other Heads with
FIP Connection–
CxMIP Adapter
Required
(92 Body
Not Req'd)
Length as
Req'd by
Planting Height
LOW RISER
for
Flood Watering
(where noted)
Poly–
Nipple
SxFIP
90 Ell
END HEAD INSTALLATION
INSTALLATION AT TEE
1/2"Copper Tube
(type M)
CxFIP Adapter
Polyethylene Nipple
SxSxFIP Tee

TYPICAL INSTALLATION OF SHRUB HEAD ON COPPER RISER

SCALE: NOT TO SCALE

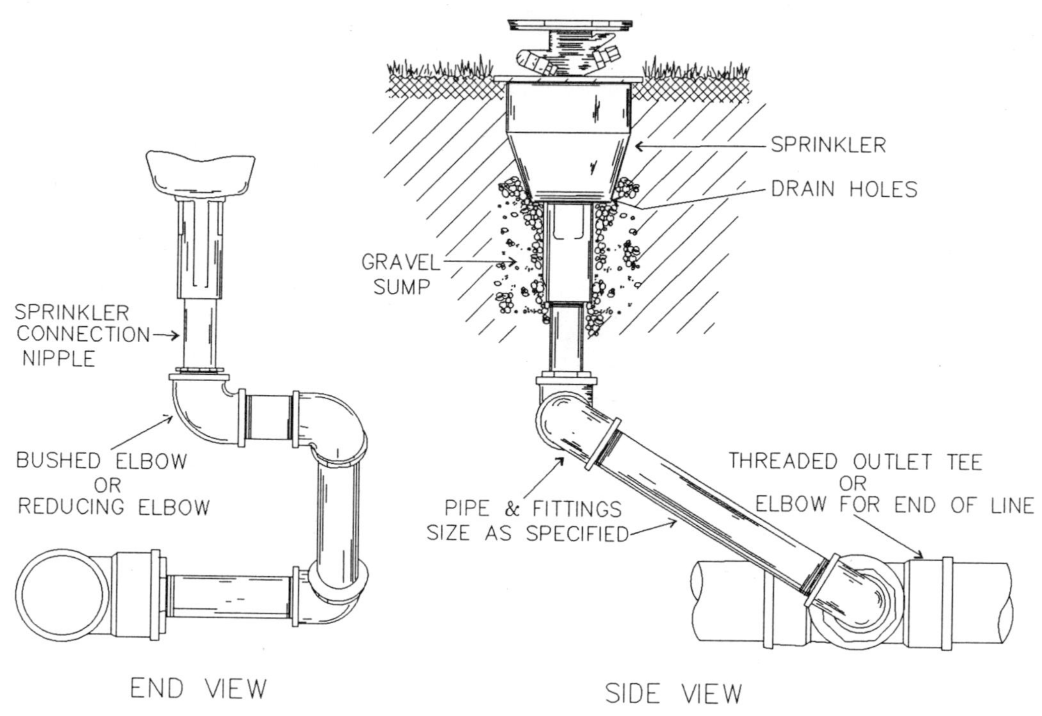
SPRINKLER
DRAIN HOLES
GRAVEL SUMP
SPRINKLER CONNECTION NIPPLE
BUSHED ELBOW OR REDUCING ELBOW
THREADED OUTLET TEE OR ELBOW FOR END OF LINE
PIPE & FITTINGS SIZE AS SPECIFIED
END VIEW
SIDE VIEW

TYPICAL INSTALLATION OF "K" SERIES ROTARY SPRINKLER ON SWING-JOINT RISER

SCALE: NOT TO SCALE

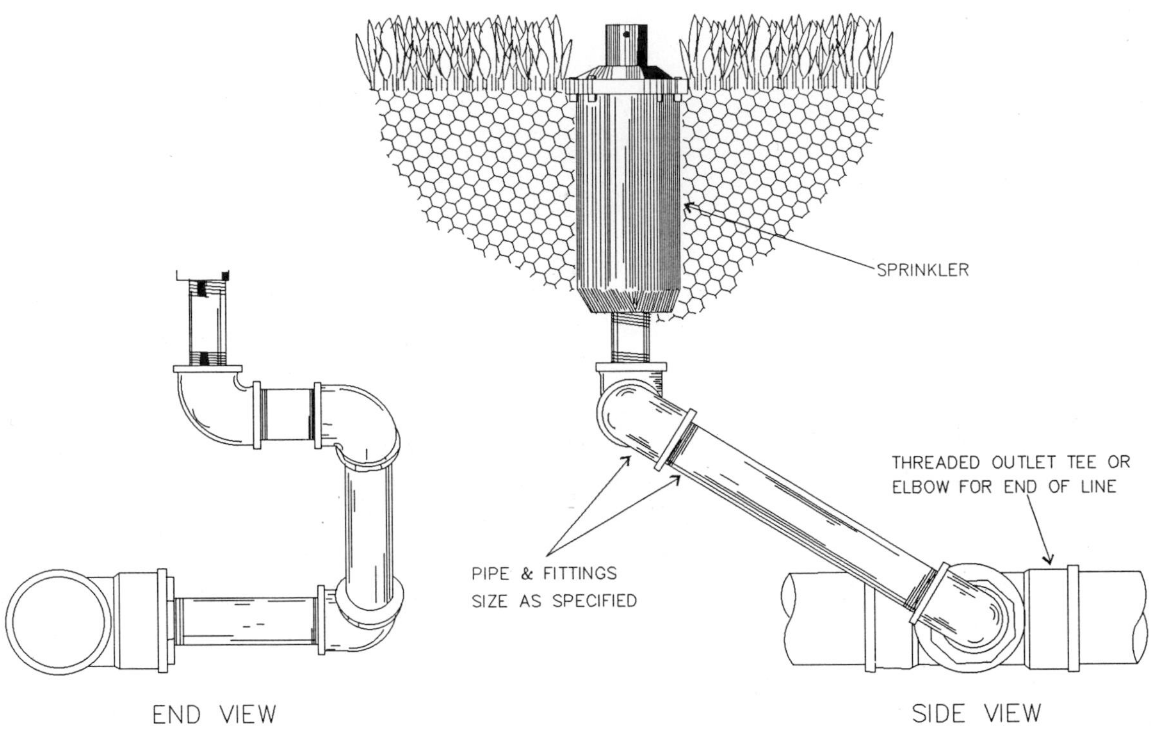
SPRINKLER
THREADED OUTLET TEE OR
ELBOW FOR END OF LINE
PIPE & FITTINGS
SIZE AS SPECIFIED
END VIEW
SIDE VIEW

TYPICAL INSTALLATION OF "G" SERIES ROTARY SPRINKLER ON SWING-JOINT RISER

SCALE: NOT TO SCALE

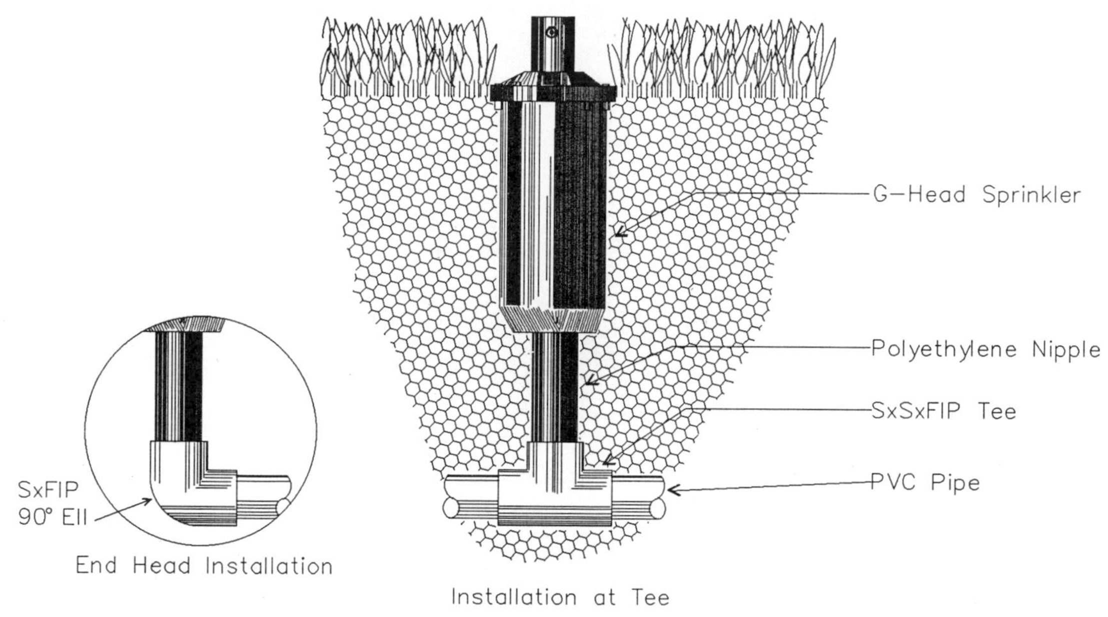
G–Head Sprinkler
Polyethylene Nipple
SxSxFIP Tee
PVC Pipe
SxFIP
90° Ell
End Head Installation
Installation at Tee

TYPICAL INSTALLATION OF G–HEAD ON FLEXIBLE RISER

SCALE: NOT TO SCALE

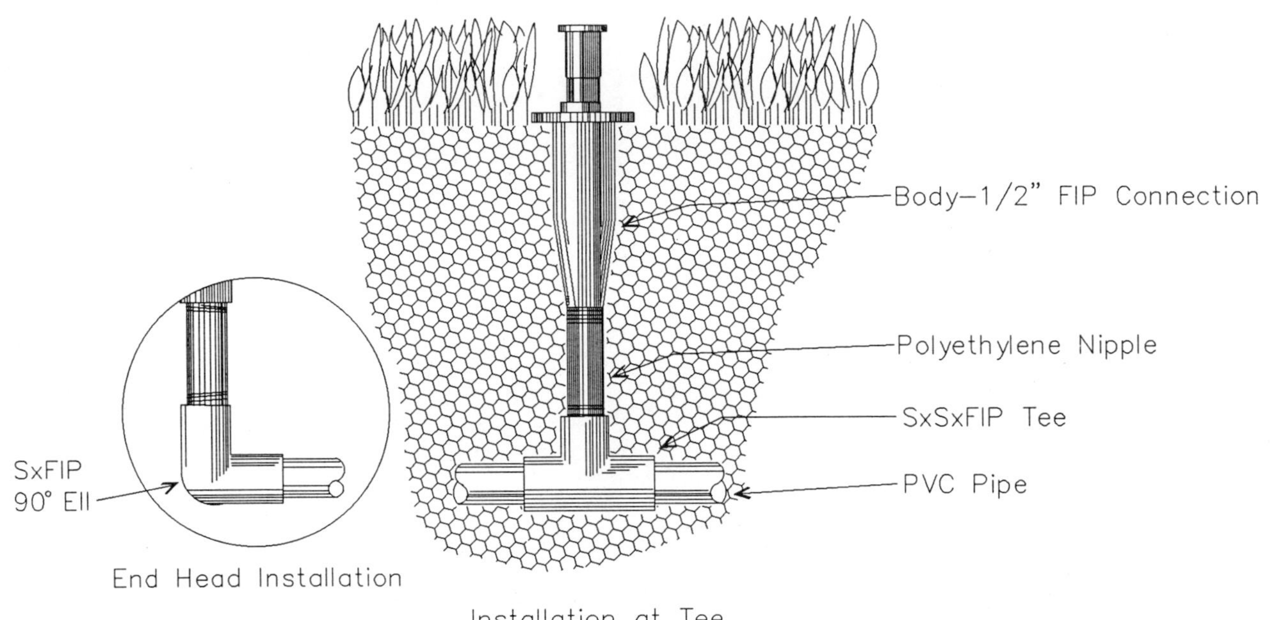
Body–1/2" FIP Connection
Polyethylene Nipple
SxSxFIP Tee
PVC Pipe
SxFIP
90° Ell
End Head Installation
Installation at Tee

TYPICAL INSTALLATION OF LAWN HEAD

SCALE: NOT TO SCALE

Lighting

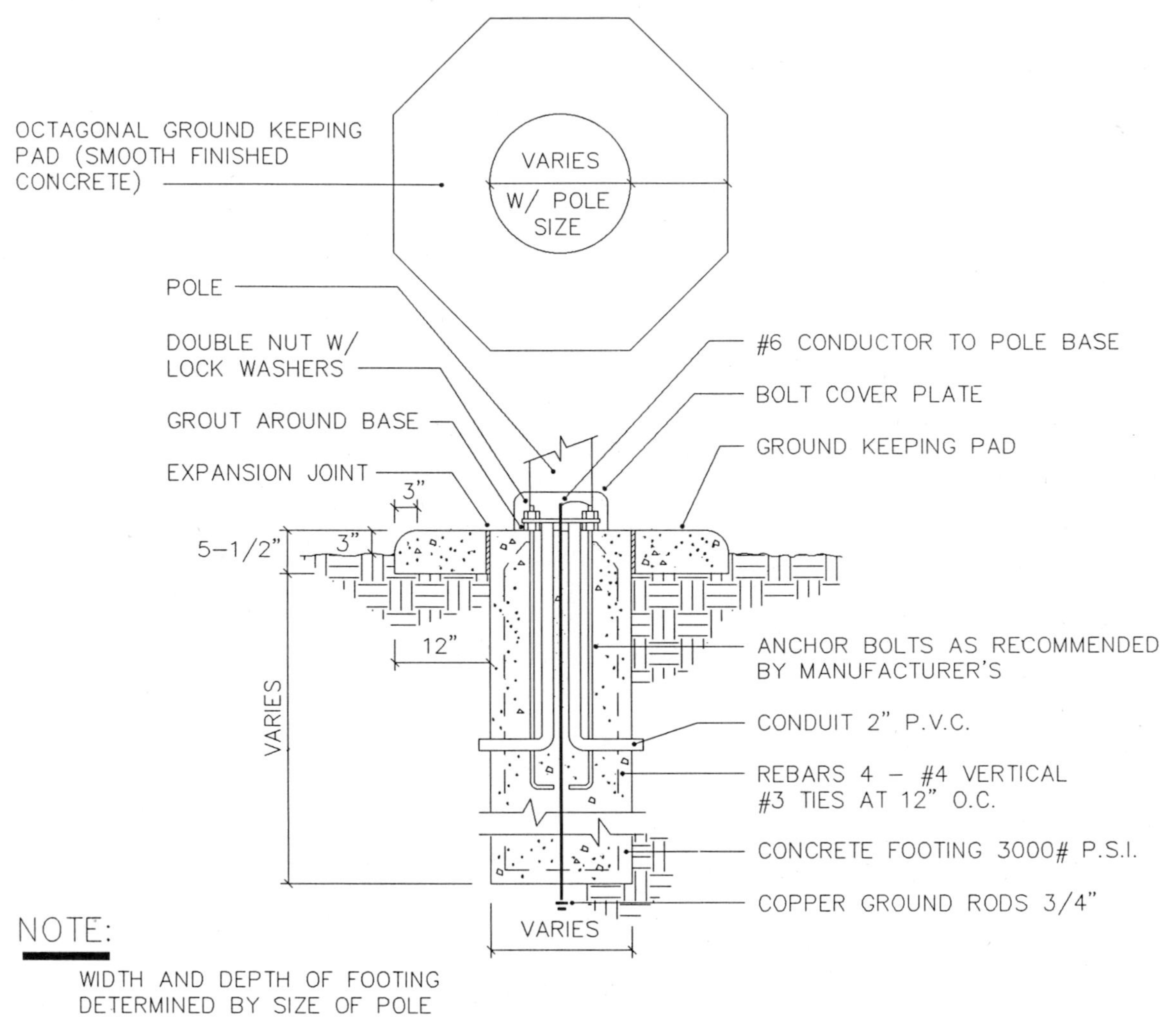

OCTAGONAL GROUND KEEPING PAD (SMOOTH FINISHED CONCRETE)
VARIES W/ POLE SIZE
POLE
DOUBLE NUT W/ LOCK WASHERS
GROUT AROUND BASE
EXPANSION JOINT
#6 CONDUCTOR TO POLE BASE
BOLT COVER PLATE
GROUND KEEPING PAD
3"
5-1/2"
3"
12"
VARIES
ANCHOR BOLTS AS RECOMMENDED BY MANUFACTURER'S
CONDUIT 2" P.V.C.
REBARS 4 – #4 VERTICAL #3 TIES AT 12" O.C.
CONCRETE FOOTING 3000# P.S.I.
COPPER GROUND RODS 3/4"
VARIES

NOTE:

WIDTH AND DEPTH OF FOOTING DETERMINED BY SIZE OF POLE

LIGHT POLE FOOTING

SCALE: NOT TO SCALE

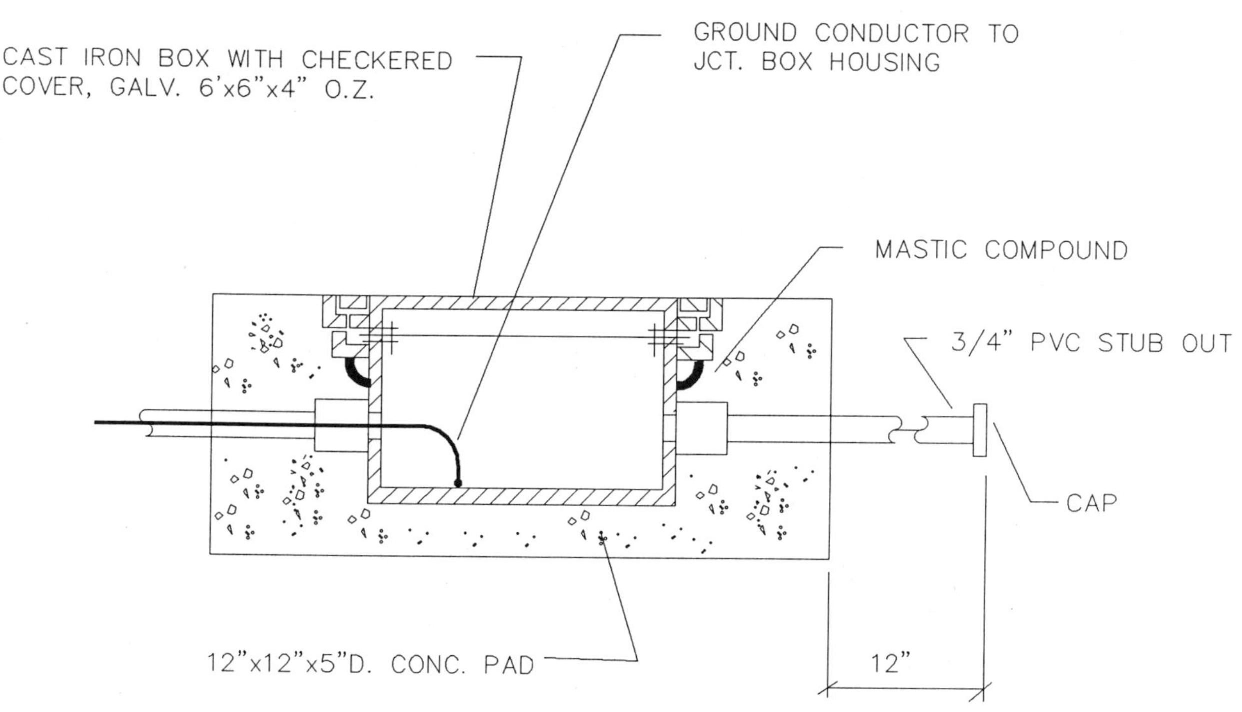
CAST IRON BOX WITH CHECKERED
COVER, GALV. 6'x6"x4" O.Z.
GROUND CONDUCTOR TO
JCT. BOX HOUSING
MASTIC COMPOUND
3/4" PVC STUB OUT
CAP
12"x12"x5"D. CONC. PAD
12"

LIGHTING JUNCTION BOX

SCALE: NOT TO SCALE

AERIAL LIGHTING

POLE

STREET LIGHT & BRACKET

AREA LIGHT

TRANSFORMER

PRIMARY CIRCUIT

SECONDARY CIRCUIT

DOWN GUY

HEAD GUY

SIDEWALK GUY

UNDERGROUND ELECTRICAL

M MANHOLE

H HANDHOLE

TM TRANSFORMER–MANHOLE OR VAULT

TP TRANSFORMER PAD

UNDERGROUND DIRECT BURIAL CABLE

UNDERGROUND DUCT LINE

STREET LIGHT STANDARD FED FROM UNDERGROUND CIRCUIT

CIRCUITS, PANELS & MISC.

DISTRIBUTION PANEL

POWER PANEL

WIRING, CONCEALED IN WALL OR CEILING

WIRING CONCEALED IN FLOOR

WIRING EXPOSED

HOME RUN TO PANEL BOARD

FEEDERS

WIRING TURNED UP

WIRING TURNED DOWN

G GENERATOR

M MOTOR

I INSTRUMENT (SPECIFY)

T TRANSFORMER

CONTROLLER

EXTERNALLY OPERATED DISCONNECT SWITCH

ELECTRICAL SYMBOLS – 1

SCALE: NOT TO SCALE

RECEPTACLE OUTLETS

- SINGLE RECEPTACLE OUTLET
- DUPLEX RECEPTACLE OUTLET
- TRIPLEX RECEPTACLE OUTLET
- QUADRUPLEX RECEPTACLE OUTLET
- DUPLEX RECEPTACLE OUTLET–SPLIT WIRED
- TRIPLEX RECEPTACLE OUTLET–SPLIT WIRED
- SINGLE SPECIAL–PURPOSE RECEPTACLE OUTLET
- DUPLEX SPECIAL–PURPOSE RECEPTACLE OUTLET
- DW SPECIAL PURPOSE CONNECTION
- X" MULTI–OUTLET ASSEMBLY
- F FAN HANGER RECEPTACLE
- FLOOR SINGLE RECEPTACLE OUTLET
- FLOOR DUPLEX RECEPTI\ACLE OUTLET
- FLOOR SPECIAL PURPOSE OUTLET
- FLOOR TELEPHONE OUTLET–PUBLIC
- FLOOR TELEPHONE OUTLET–PRIVATE

SWITCH OUTLETS

S	SINGLE POLE SWITCH
S_{2}	DOUBLE POLE SWITCH
S_{3}	THREE WAY SWITCH
S_{4}	FOUR WAY SWITCH
S_{D}	AUTOMATIC DOOR SWITCH
S_{K}	KEY OPERATED SWITCH
S_{P}	SWITCH AND PILOT LAMP
S_{CB}	CIRCUIT BREAKER
S_{WCB}	WEATHERPROOF CIRCUIT BREAKER
S_{MC}	MOMENTARY CONTACT SWITCH
S_{RC}	REMOTE CONTROL SWITCH
S_{WP}	WEATHERPROOF SWITCH
S_{F}	FUSED SWITCH
S_{WF}	WEATHERPROOF FUSED SWITCH
S_{L}	SWITCH–LOW VOLTAGE
S_{LM}	MASTER SWITCH–LOW VOLTAGE
S_{T}	TIME SWITCH
(S)	CEILING PULL SWITCH
$\ominus_{S}$	SWITCH & SINGLE RECEPTACLE
$\ominus_{S}$	SWITCH & DOUBLE RECEPTACLE

ELECTRICAL SYMBOLS – 2

SCALE: NOT TO SCALE

LIGHTING OUTLETS

SURFACE INCANDESCENT

RECESS INCANDESCENT

BLANKED OUTLET

DROP CORD

ELECTRICAL OUTLET

JUNCTION BOX

OUTLET CONTROLLED BY LOW VOLTAGE SWITCHING RELAY IN OUTLET BOX

SIGNALING SYSTEMS

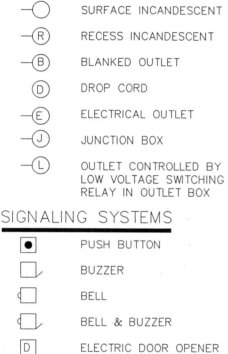

PUSH BUTTON

BUZZER

BELL

BELL & BUZZER

ELECTRIC DOOR OPENER

RADIO OUTLET

TELEVISION OUTLET

THERMOSTAT

SYSTEMS SYMBOLS

PAGING SYSTEM DEVICE

FIRE ALARM SYSTEM DEVICE

ELECTRICAL CLOCK SYSTEM DEVICE

PUBLIC TELEPHONE SYSTEM DEVICE

PRIVATE TELEPHONE SYSTEM DEVICE

WATCHMAN SYSTEM DEVICE

SOUND SYSTEM

OTHER SIGNAL SYSTEM DEVICES

ELECTRICAL SYMBOLS — 3

SCALE: NOT TO SCALE

Paving

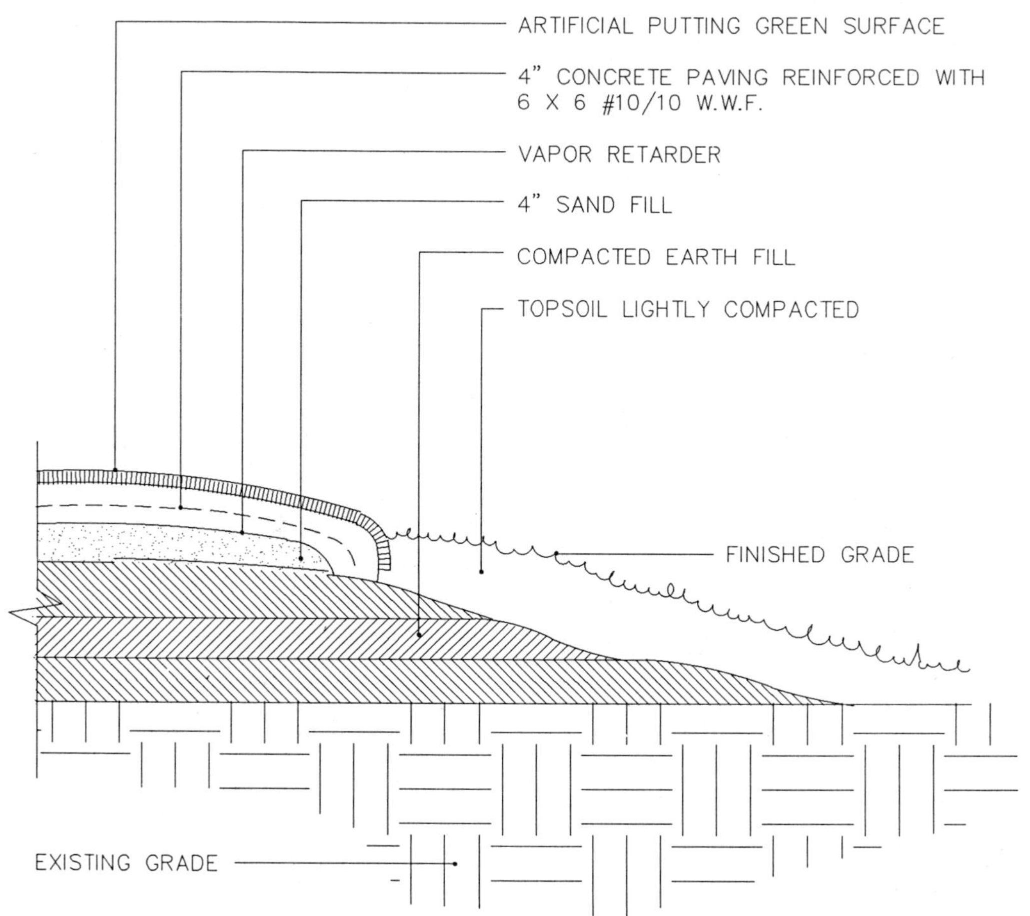
ARTIFICIAL PUTTING GREEN SURFACE
4" CONCRETE PAVING REINFORCED WITH
6 X 6 #10/10 W.W.F.
VAPOR RETARDER
4" SAND FILL
COMPACTED EARTH FILL
TOPSOIL LIGHTLY COMPACTED
FINISHED GRADE
EXISTING GRADE

ARTIFICIAL PUTTING GREEN SURFACE

SCALE: NOT TO SCALE

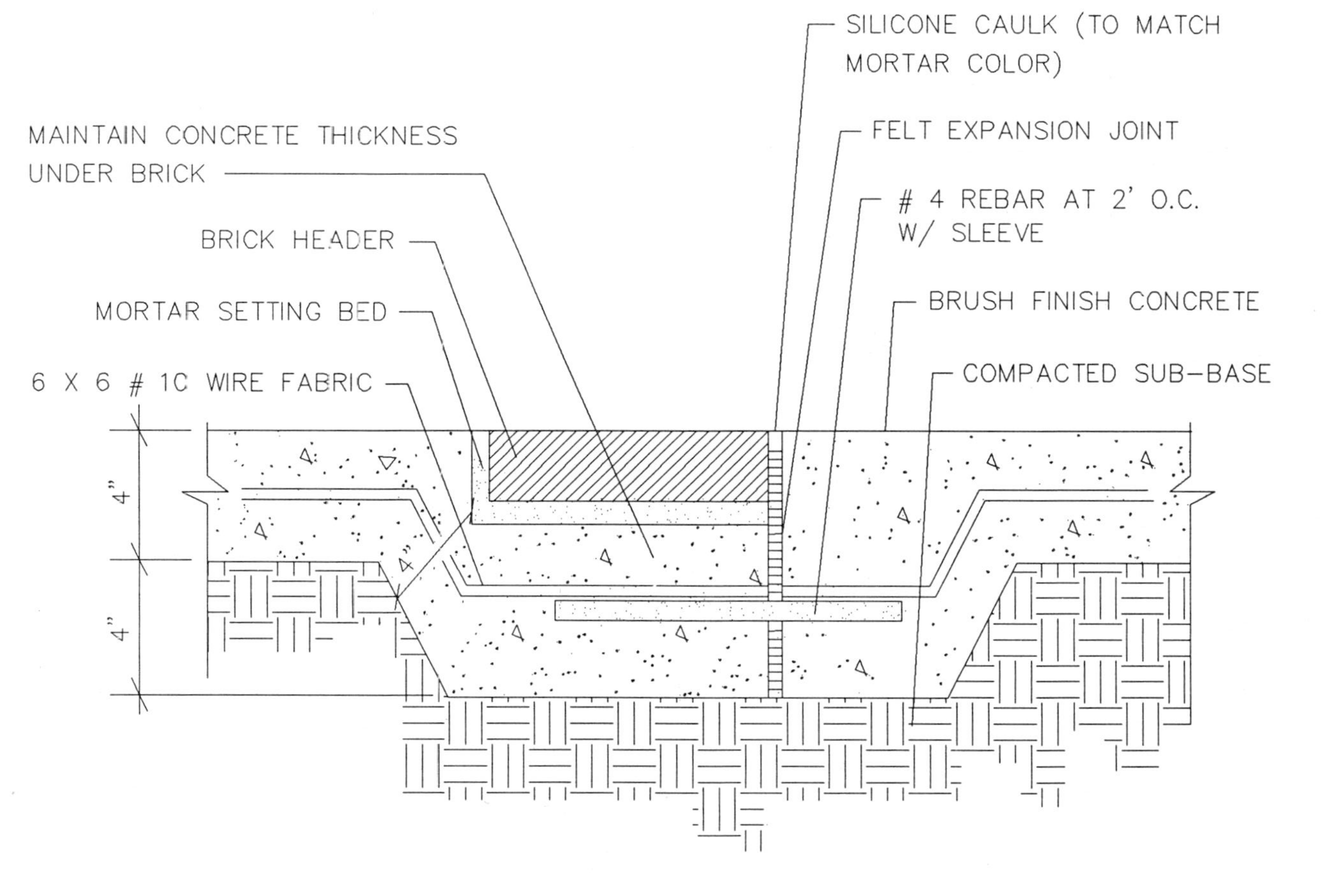
SILICONE CAULK (TO MATCH
MORTAR COLOR)
FELT EXPANSION JOINT
4 REBAR AT 2' O.C.
W/ SLEEVE
BRUSH FINISH CONCRETE
COMPACTED SUB-BASE
MAINTAIN CONCRETE THICKNESS
UNDER BRICK
BRICK HEADER
MORTAR SETTING BED
6 X 6 # 1C WIRE FABRIC
4"
4"
4"

BRICK EXPANSION JOINT

SCALE: NOT TO SCALE

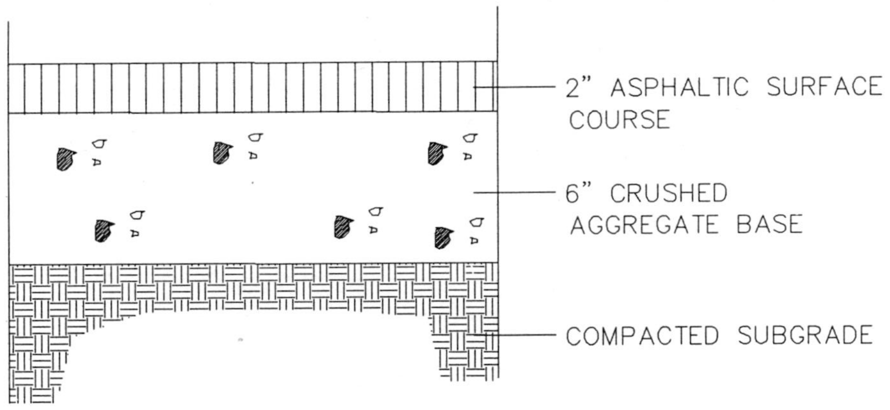

2" ASPHALTIC SURFACE COURSE

6" CRUSHED AGGREGATE BASE

COMPACTED SUBGRADE

ASPHALTIC CONCRETE WALKS, RAMPS & TERRACES

SCALE: NOT TO SCALE

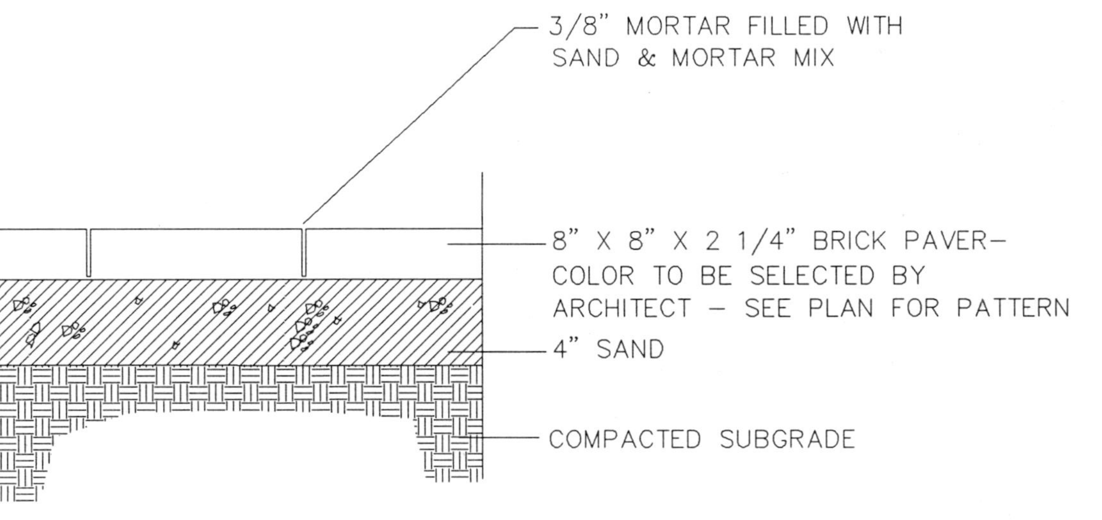
3/8" MORTAR FILLED WITH
SAND & MORTAR MIX
8" X 8" X 2 1/4" BRICK PAVER–
COLOR TO BE SELECTED BY
ARCHITECT – SEE PLAN FOR PATTERN
4" SAND
COMPACTED SUBGRADE

BRICK PAVERS ON SAND

SCALE: NOT TO SCALE

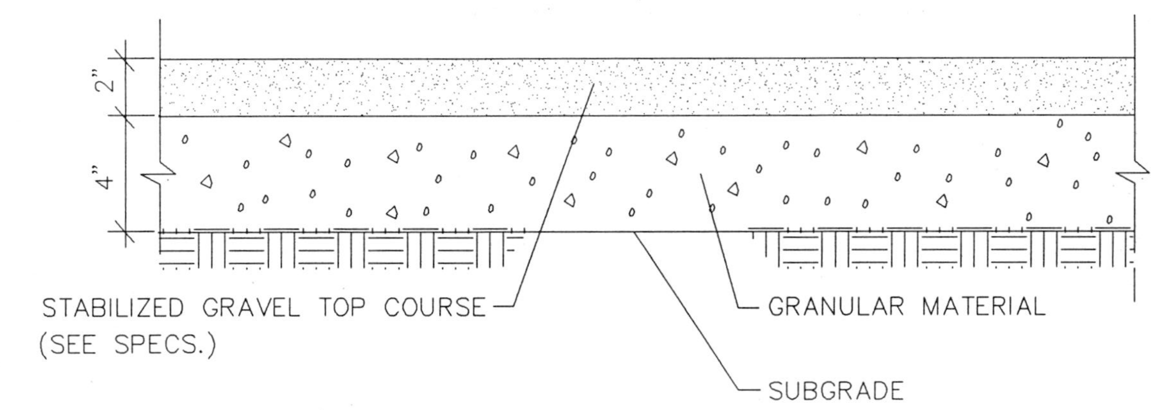
2"
4"
STABILIZED GRAVEL TOP COURSE
(SEE SPECS.)
GRANULAR MATERIAL
SUBGRADE

STABILIZED GRAVEL

SCALE: NOT TO SCALE

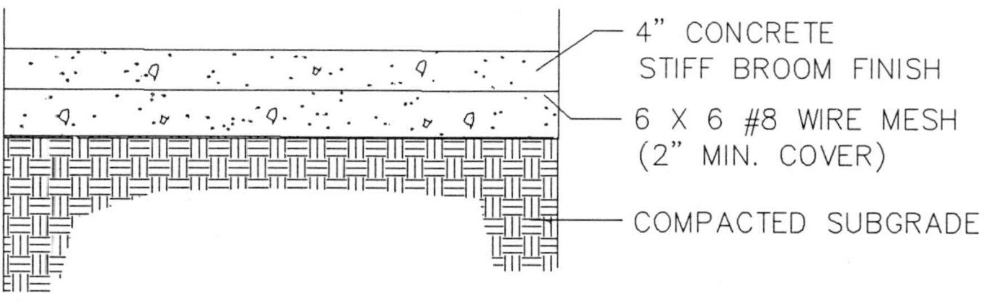
4" CONCRETE
STIFF BROOM FINISH
6 X 6 #8 WIRE MESH
(2" MIN. COVER)
COMPACTED SUBGRADE

CONCRETE PAVEMENT

SCALE: NOT TO SCALE

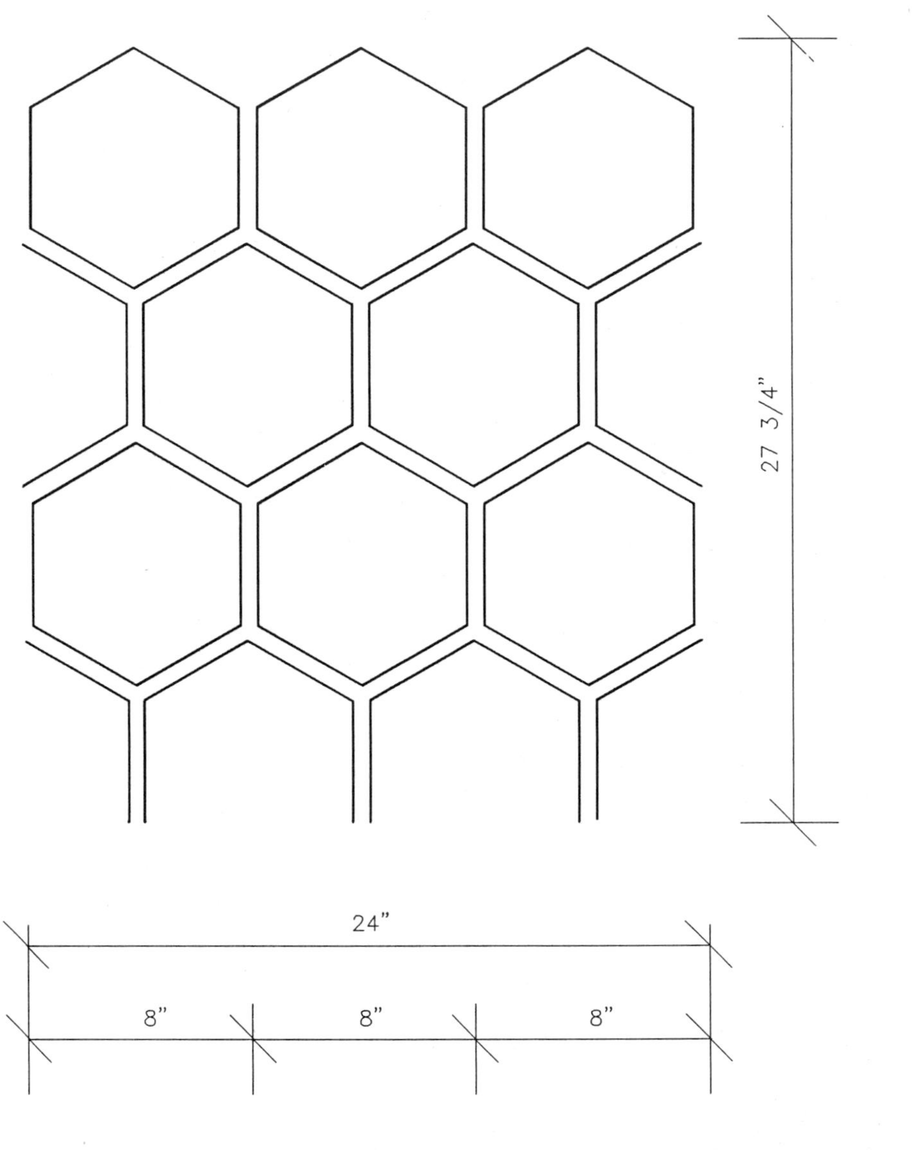
27 3/4"

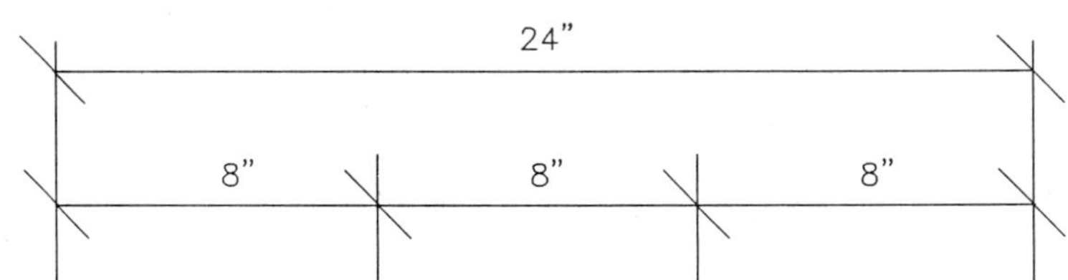
24"
8"
8"
8"

8" HEX TILE – BOMANITE

SCALE: NOT TO SCALE

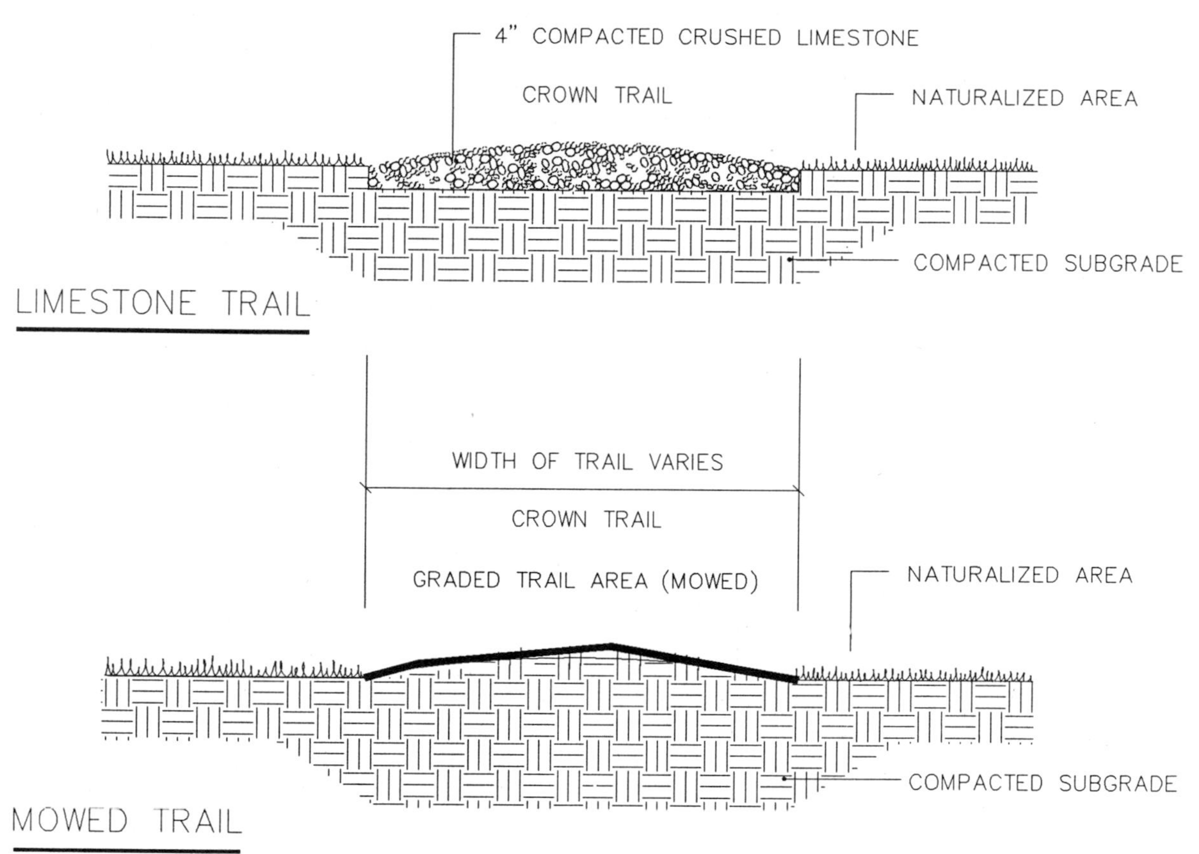
4" COMPACTED CRUSHED LIMESTONE
CROWN TRAIL
NATURALIZED AREA
COMPACTED SUBGRADE
LIMESTONE TRAIL
WIDTH OF TRAIL VARIES
CROWN TRAIL
GRADED TRAIL AREA (MOWED)
NATURALIZED AREA
COMPACTED SUBGRADE
MOWED TRAIL

FITNESS TRAIL SURFACING

SCALE: NOT TO SCALE

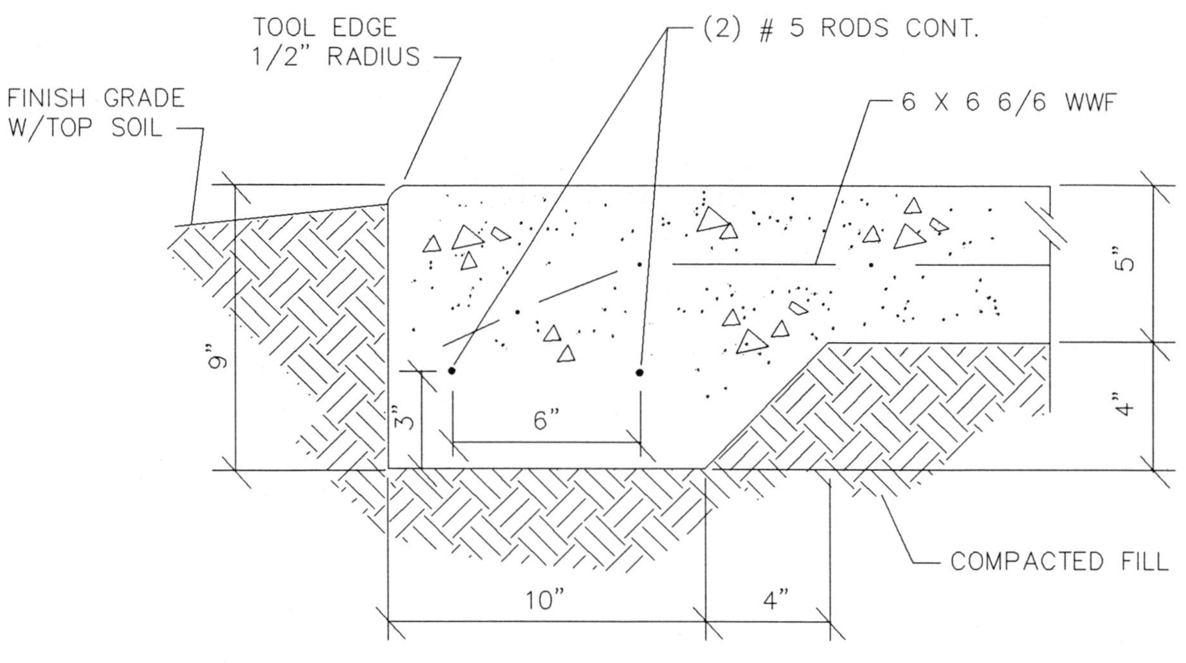
TOOL EDGE
1/2" RADIUS
(2) # 5 RODS CONT.
FINISH GRADE
W/TOP SOIL
6 X 6 6/6 WWF
5"
9"
3"
6"
4"
COMPACTED FILL
10"
4"

EDGE OF CONCRETE DRIVE

SCALE: NOT TO SCALE

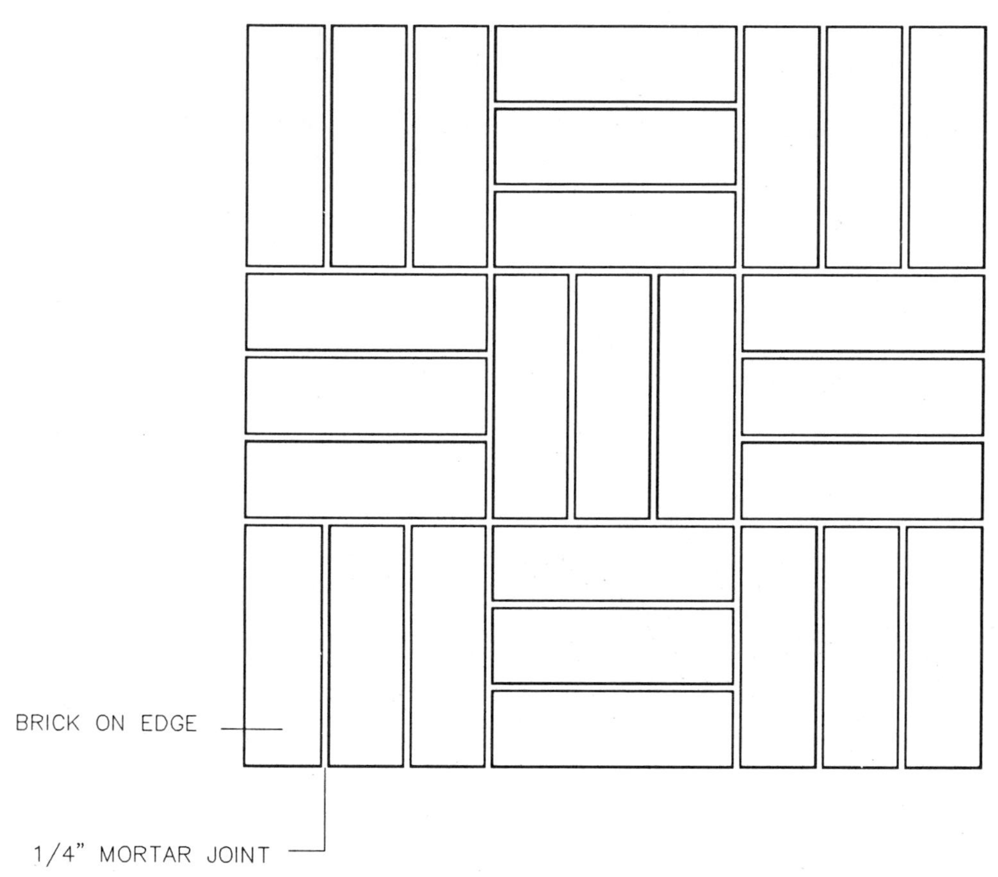
BRICK ON EDGE
1/4" MORTAR JOINT

BASKET WEAVE BRICK – ON EDGE

SCALE: NOT TO SCALE

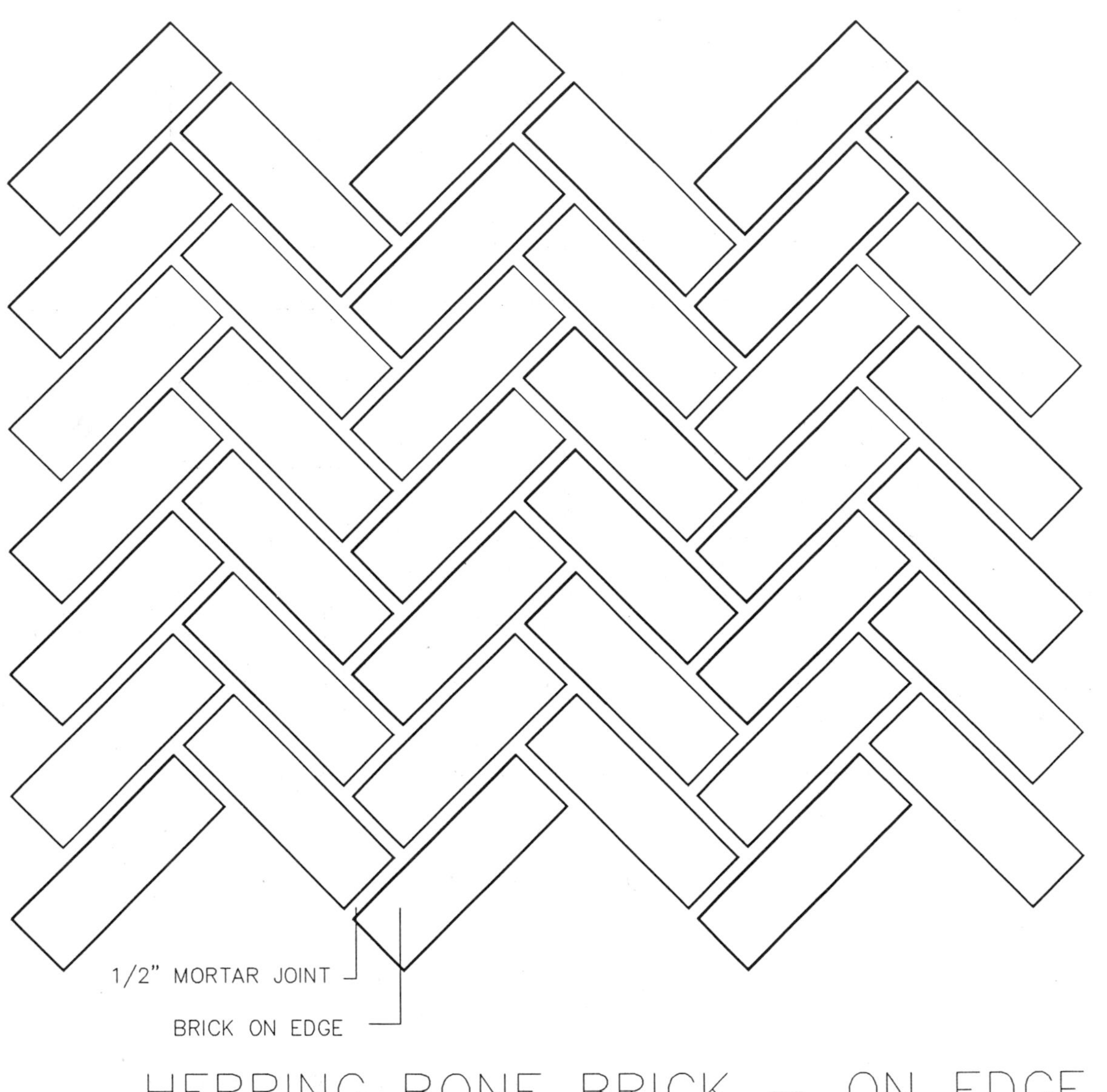
1/2" MORTAR JOINT
BRICK ON EDGE

HERRING BONE BRICK – ON EDGE

SCALE: NOT TO SCALE

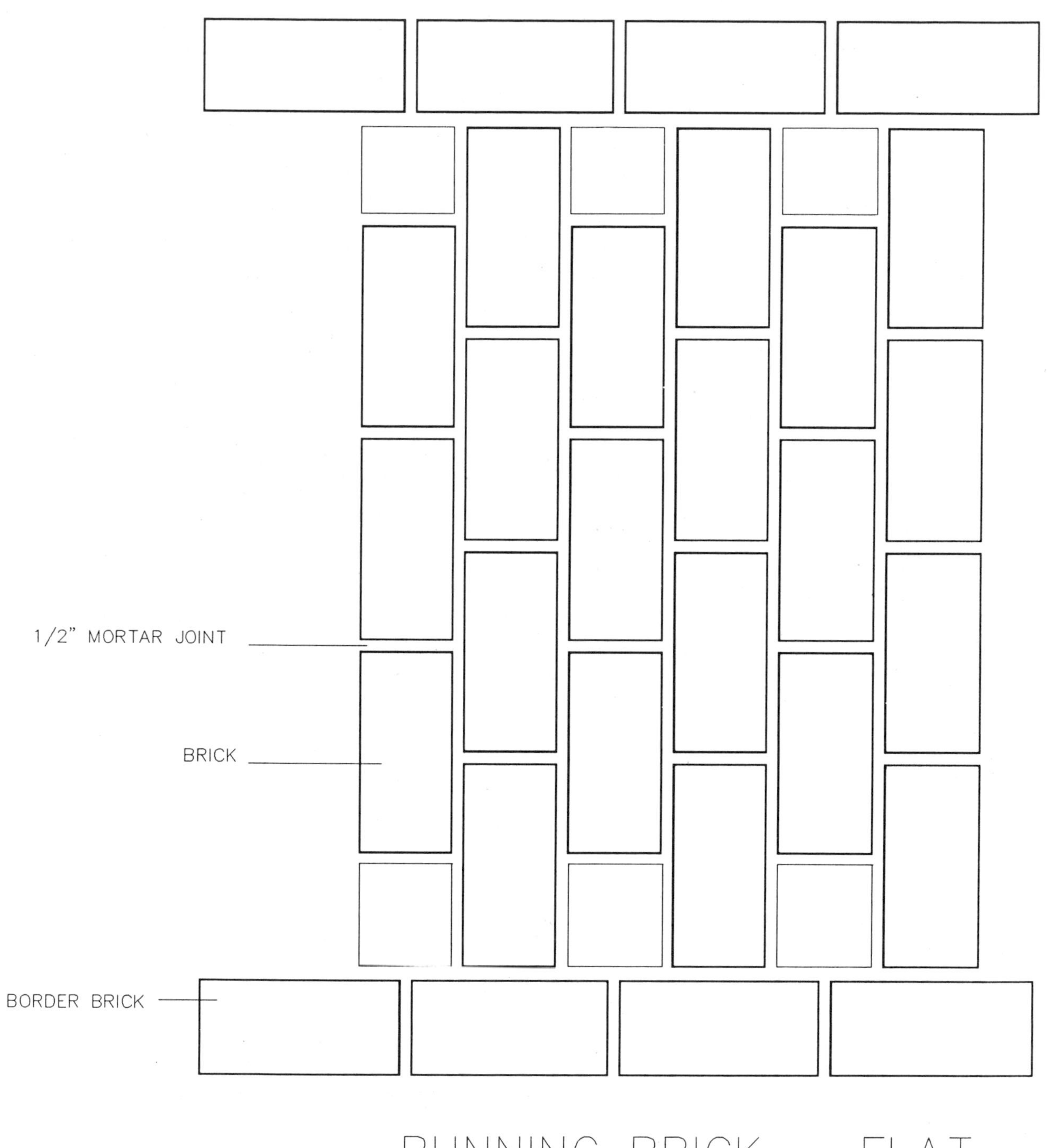
1/2" MORTAR JOINT
BRICK
BORDER BRICK

RUNNING BRICK – FLAT

SCALE: NOT TO SCALE

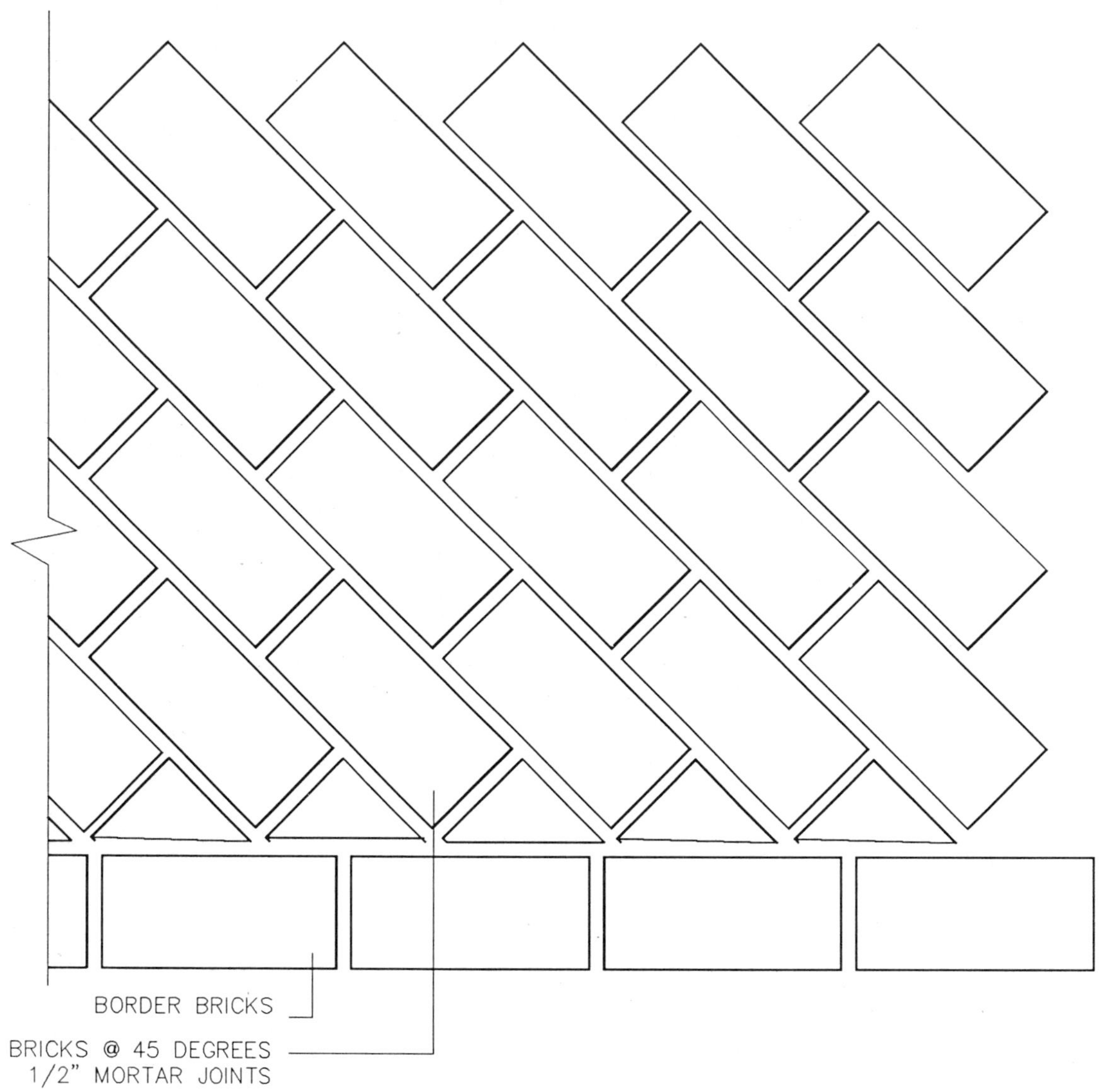
BORDER BRICKS
BRICKS @ 45 DEGREES
1/2" MORTAR JOINTS

DIAGONAL BRICK — FLAT

SCALE: NOT TO SCALE

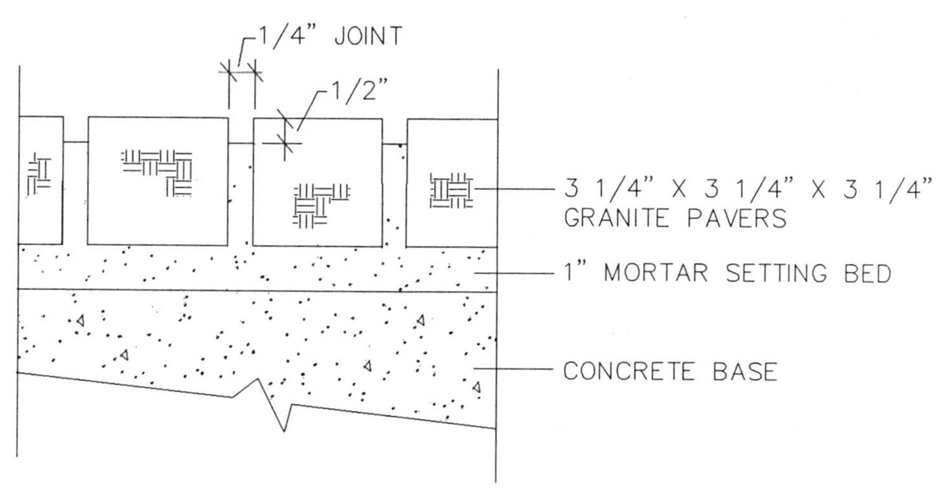
1/4" JOINT
1/2"
3 1/4" X 3 1/4" X 3 1/4"
GRANITE PAVERS
1" MORTAR SETTING BED
CONCRETE BASE

GRANITE PAVERS

SCALE: NOT TO SCALE

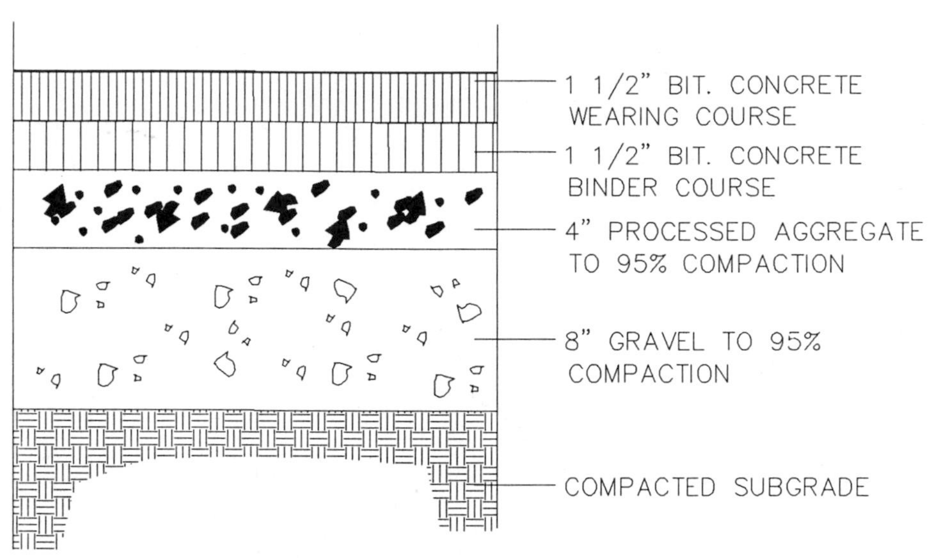
1 1/2" BIT. CONCRETE
WEARING COURSE
1 1/2" BIT. CONCRETE
BINDER COURSE
4" PROCESSED AGGREGATE
TO 95% COMPACTION
8" GRAVEL TO 95%
COMPACTION
COMPACTED SUBGRADE

BITUMINOUS CONCRETE DRIVES & PARKING

SCALE: NOT TO SCALE

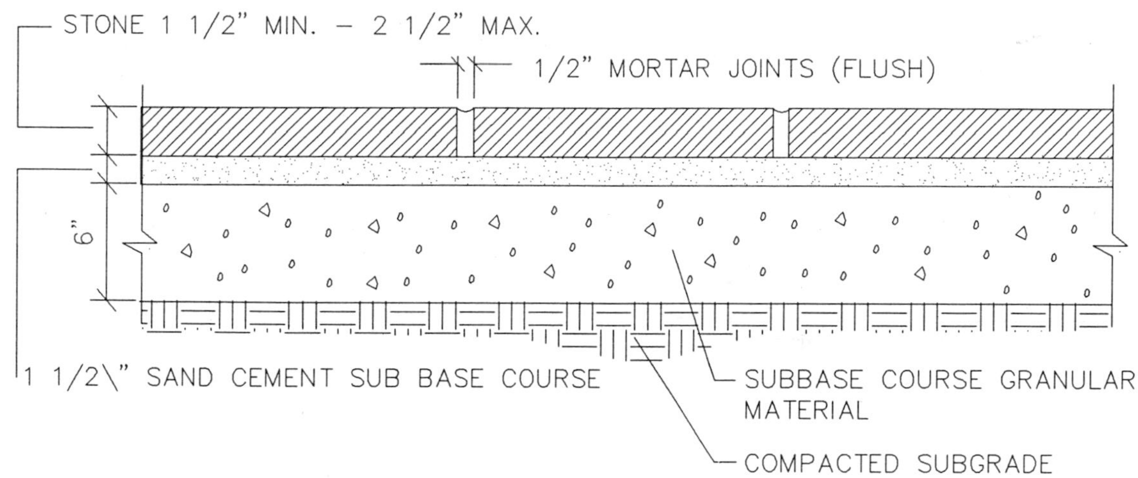
STONE 1 1/2" MIN. – 2 1/2" MAX.
1/2" MORTAR JOINTS (FLUSH)
6"
1 1/2\" SAND CEMENT SUB BASE COURSE
SUBBASE COURSE GRANULAR MATERIAL
COMPACTED SUBGRADE

STONE PAVEMENT

SCALE: NOT TO SCALE

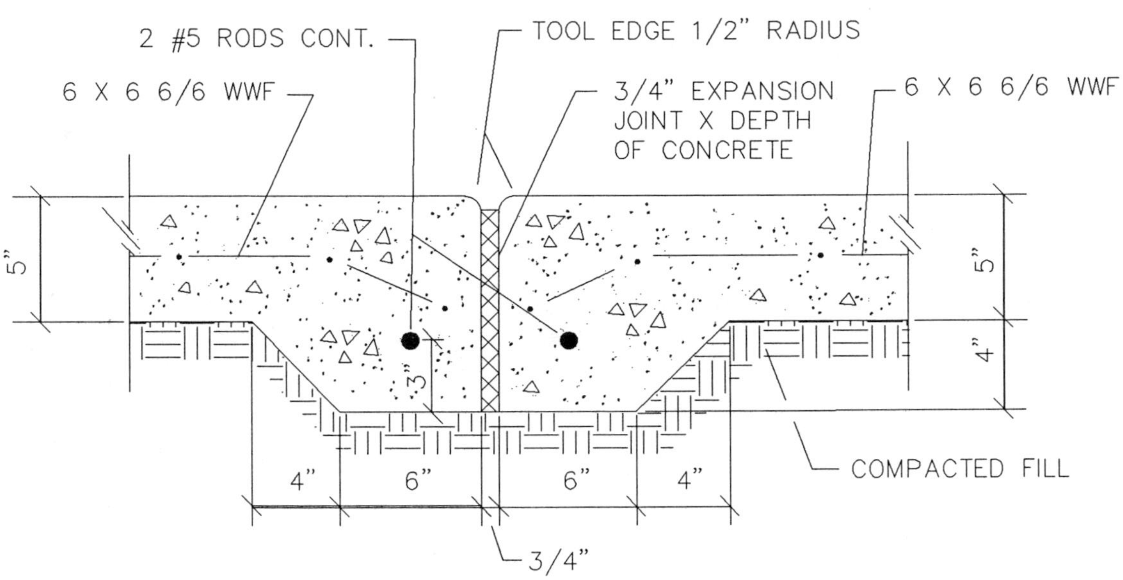
2 #5 RODS CONT.
TOOL EDGE 1/2" RADIUS
6 X 6 6/6 WWF
3/4" EXPANSION
JOINT X DEPTH
OF CONCRETE
6 X 6 6/6 WWF
5"
5"
4"
3"
COMPACTED FILL
4"
6"
6"
4"
3/4"

EXPANSION IN CONCRETE DRIVE

SCALE: NOT TO SCALE

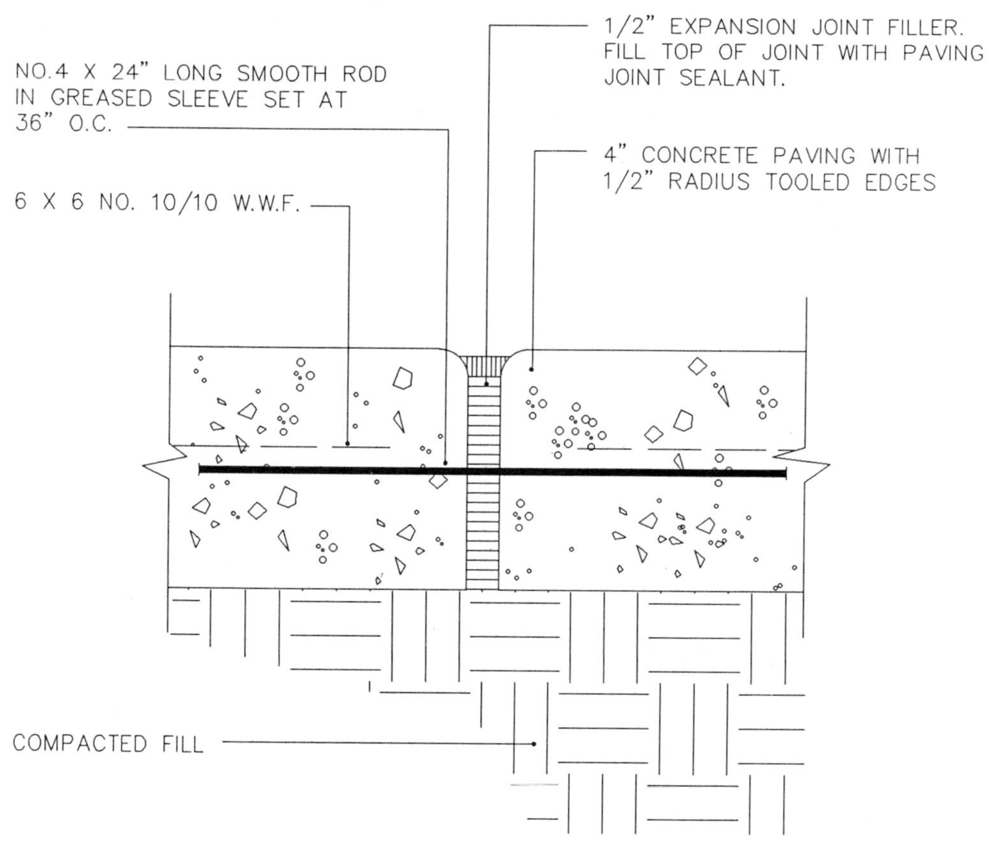
1/2" EXPANSION JOINT FILLER. FILL TOP OF JOINT WITH PAVING JOINT SEALANT.
NO.4 X 24" LONG SMOOTH ROD IN GREASED SLEEVE SET AT 36" O.C.
4" CONCRETE PAVING WITH 1/2" RADIUS TOOLED EDGES
6 X 6 NO. 10/10 W.W.F.
COMPACTED FILL

EXPANSION JOINT

SCALE: NOT TO SCALE

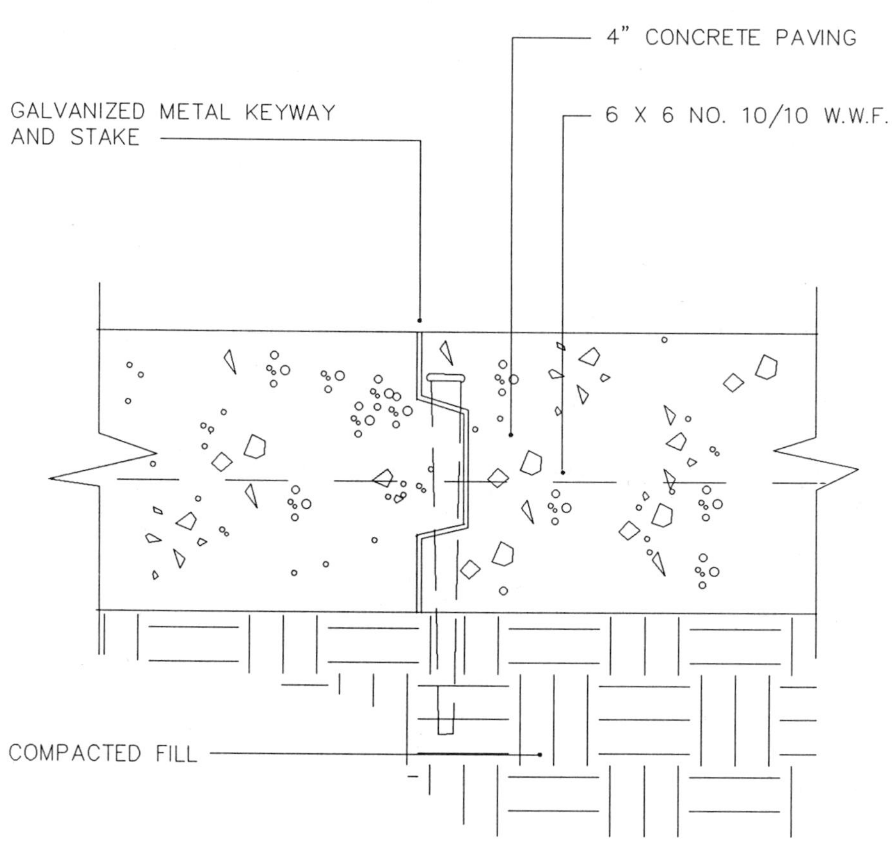
4" CONCRETE PAVING
GALVANIZED METAL KEYWAY
AND STAKE
6 X 6 NO. 10/10 W.W.F.
COMPACTED FILL

CONSTRUCTION JOINT

SCALE: NOT TO SCALE

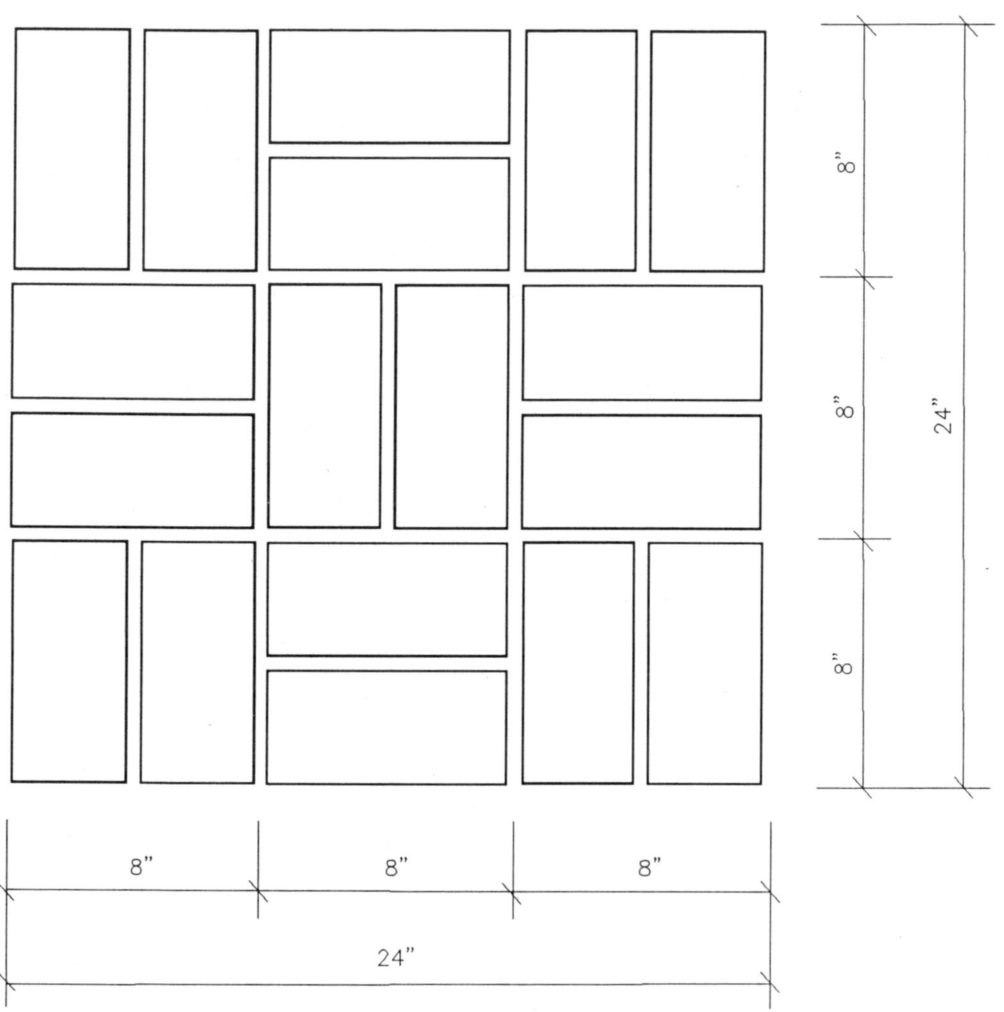
8"
8"
8"
24"
8"
8"
8"
24"

BASKETWEAVE BRICK – BOMANITE

SCALE: NOT TO SCALE

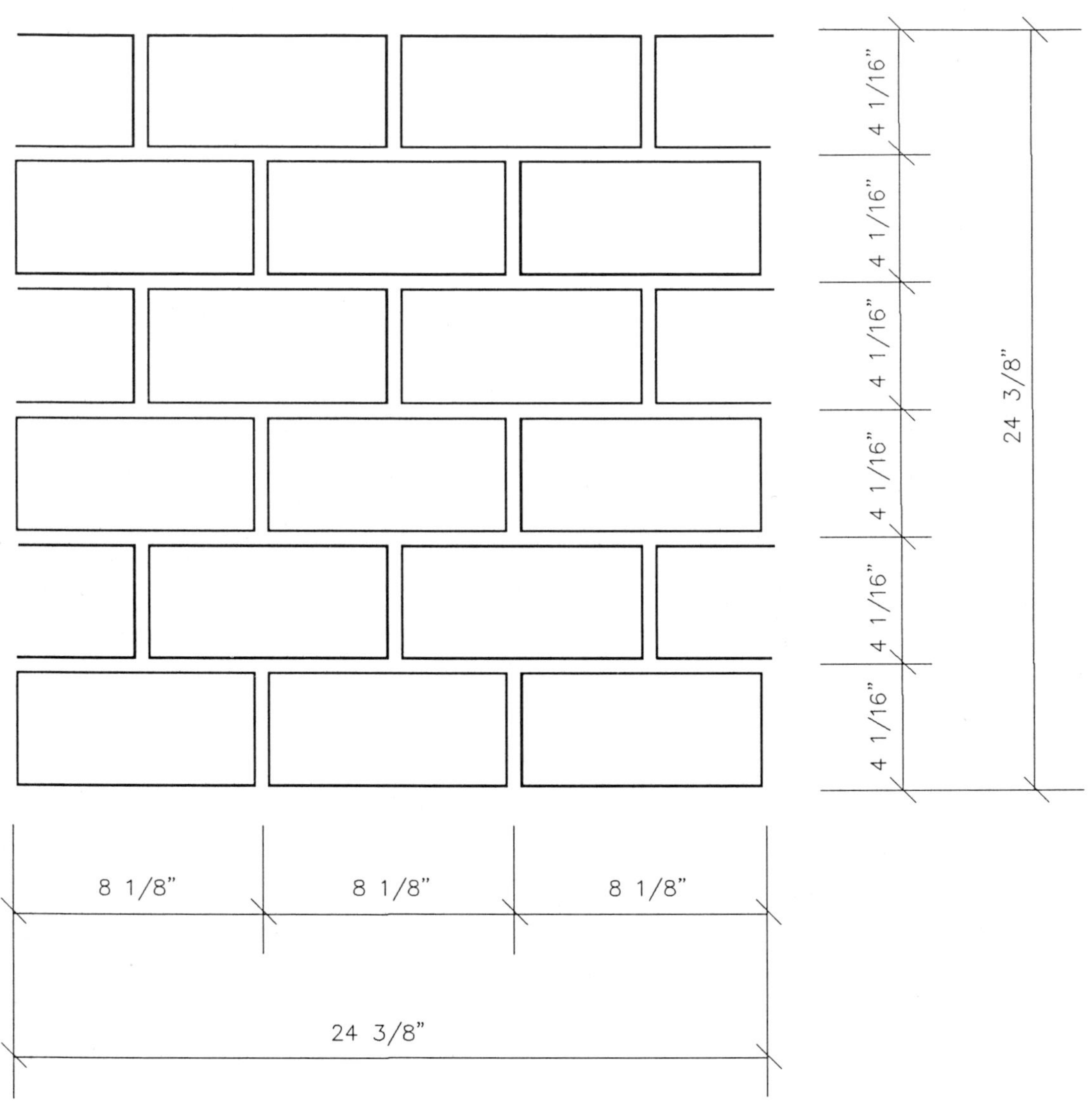
4 1/16"
4 1/16"
4 1/16"
4 1/16"
4 1/16"
4 1/16"
24 3/8"
8 1/8"
8 1/8"
8 1/8"
24 3/8"

RUNNING BOND BRICK – BOMANITE

SCALE: NOT TO SCALE

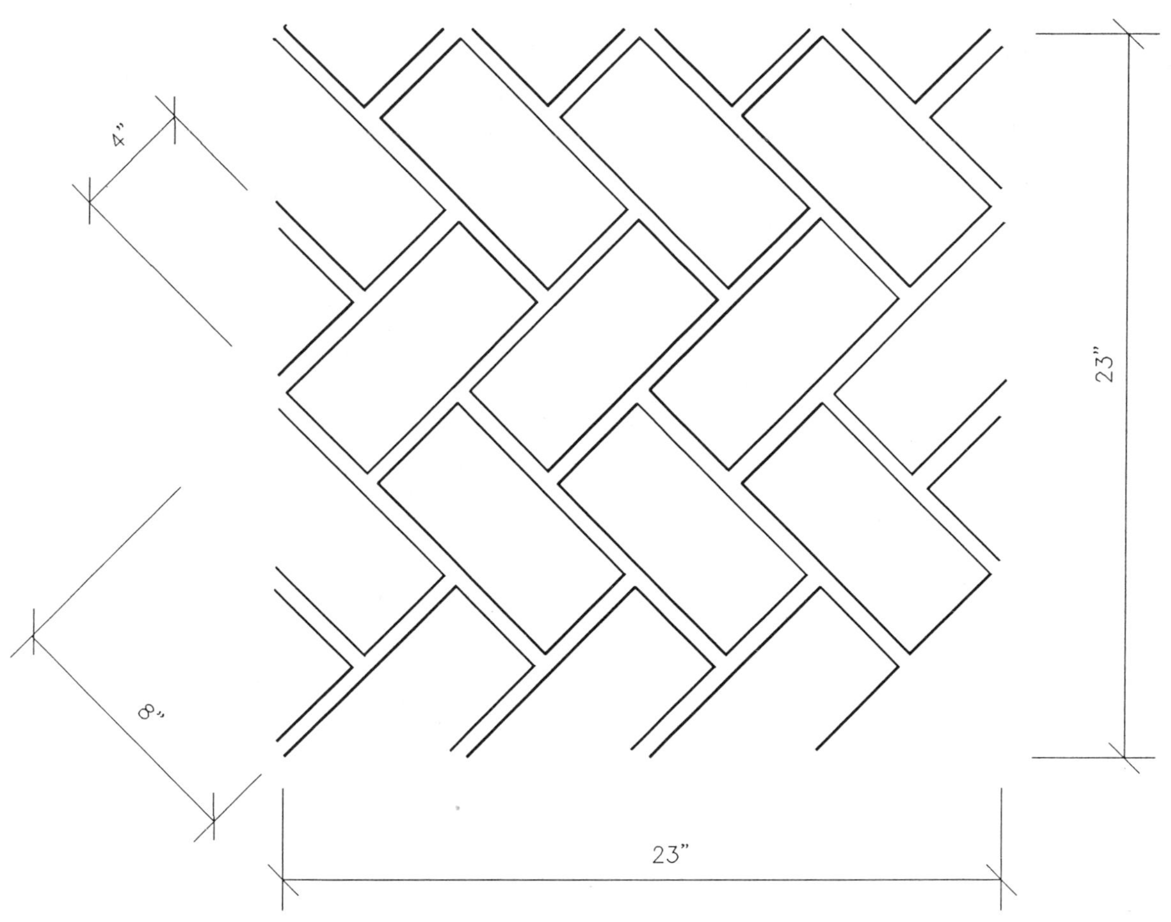
4"
8"
23"
23"

HERRINGBONE BRICK – BOMANITE

SCALE: NOT TO SCALE

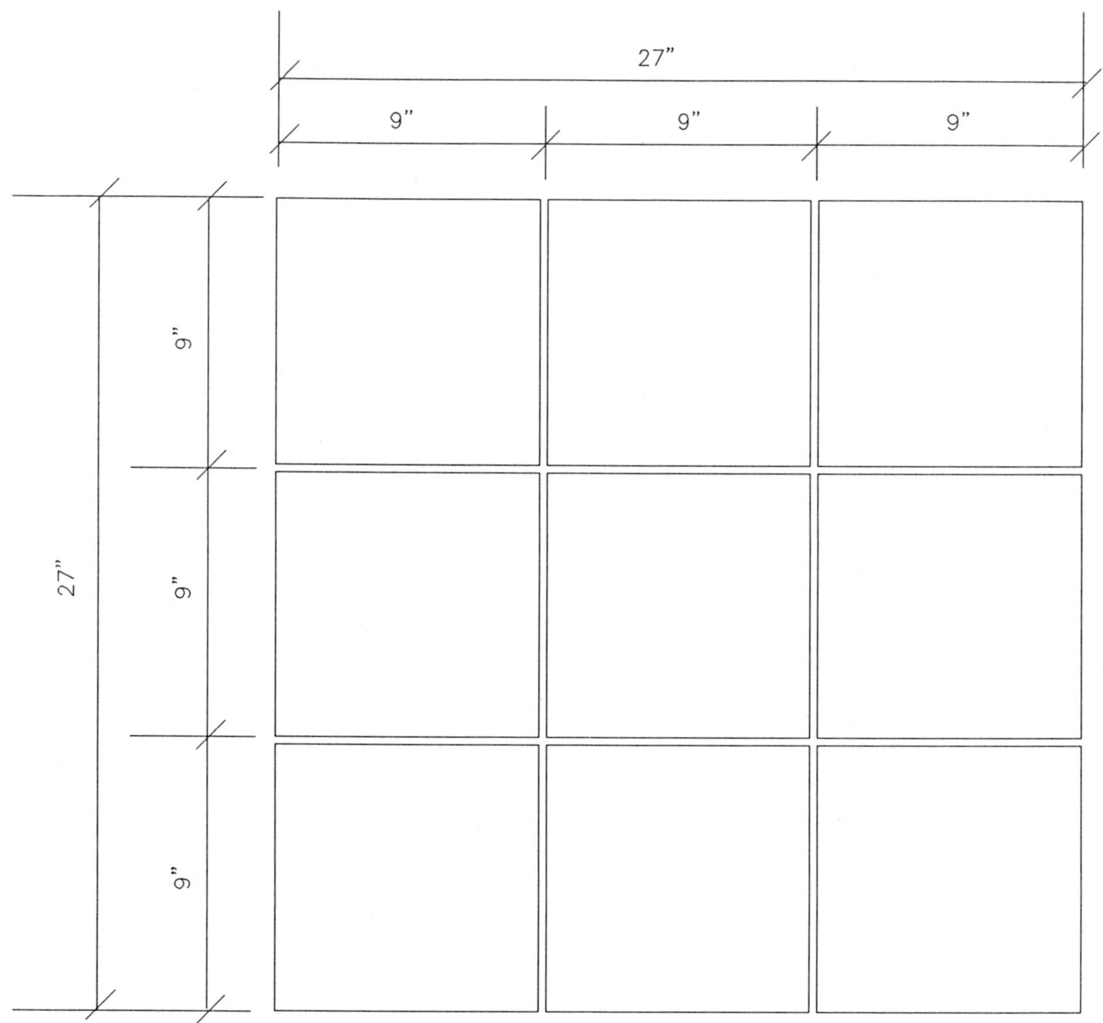
27"
9"
9"
9"
27"
9"
9"
9"

9" X 9" TILE – BOMANITE

SCALE: NOT TO SCALE

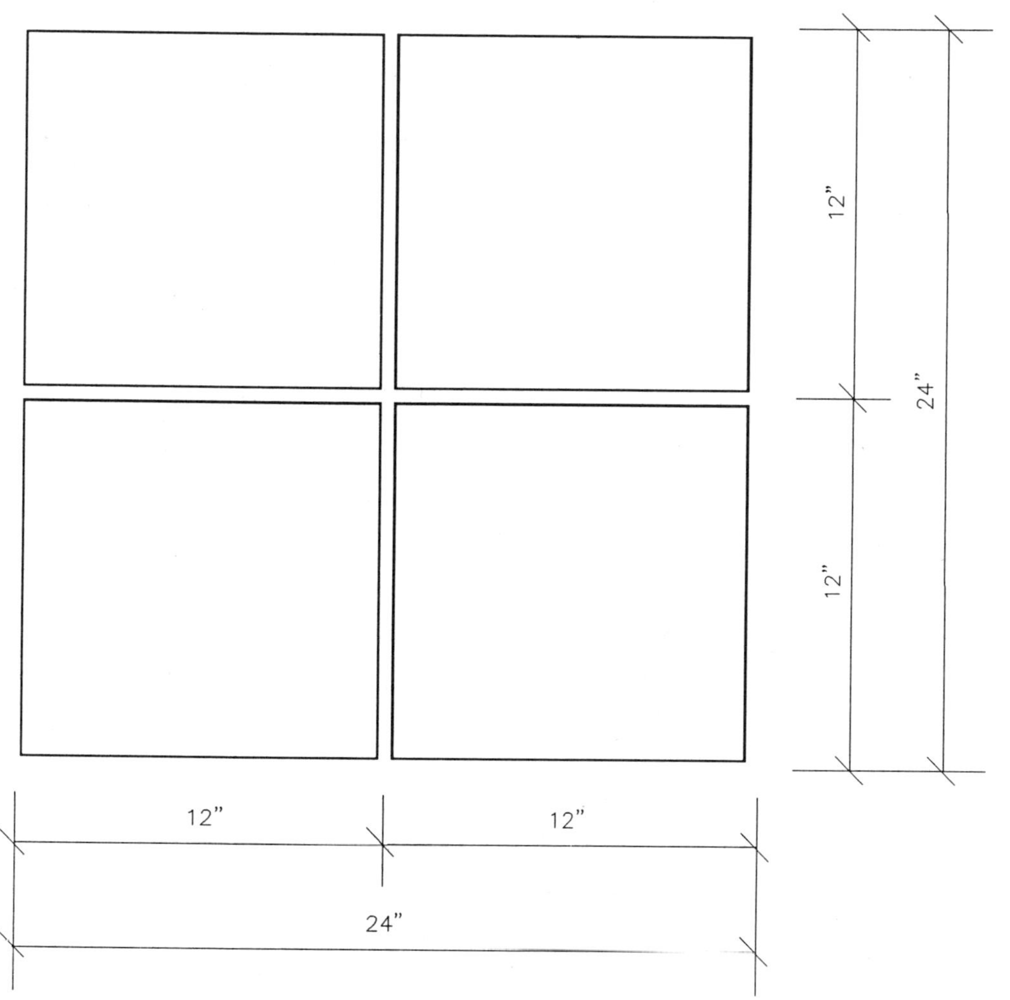
12"
12"
12"
12"
24"
24"

12" X 12" TILE – BOMANITE

SCALE: NOT TO SCALE

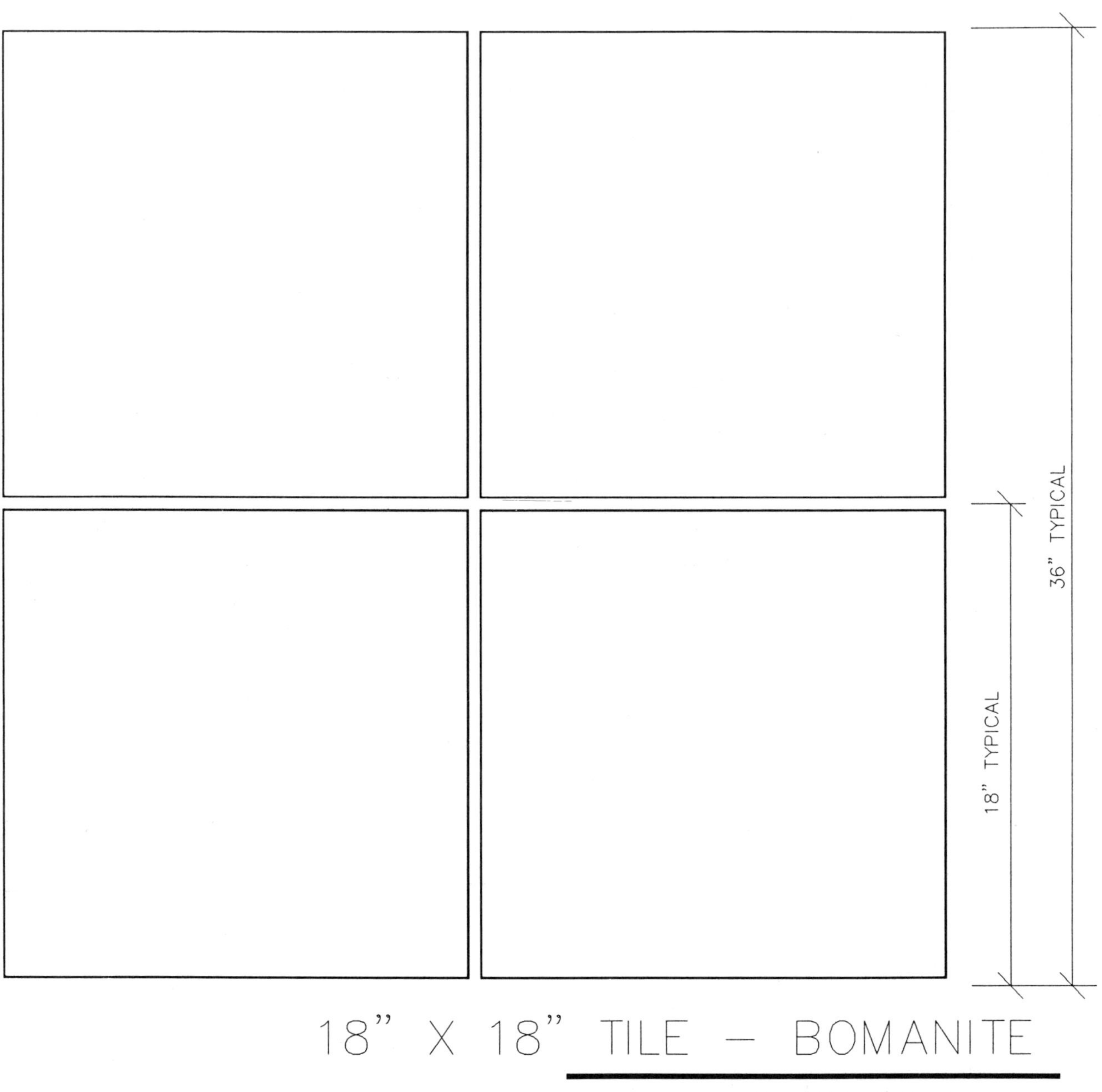
36" TYPICAL
18" TYPICAL

18" X 18" TILE – BOMANITE

SCALE: NOT TO SCALE

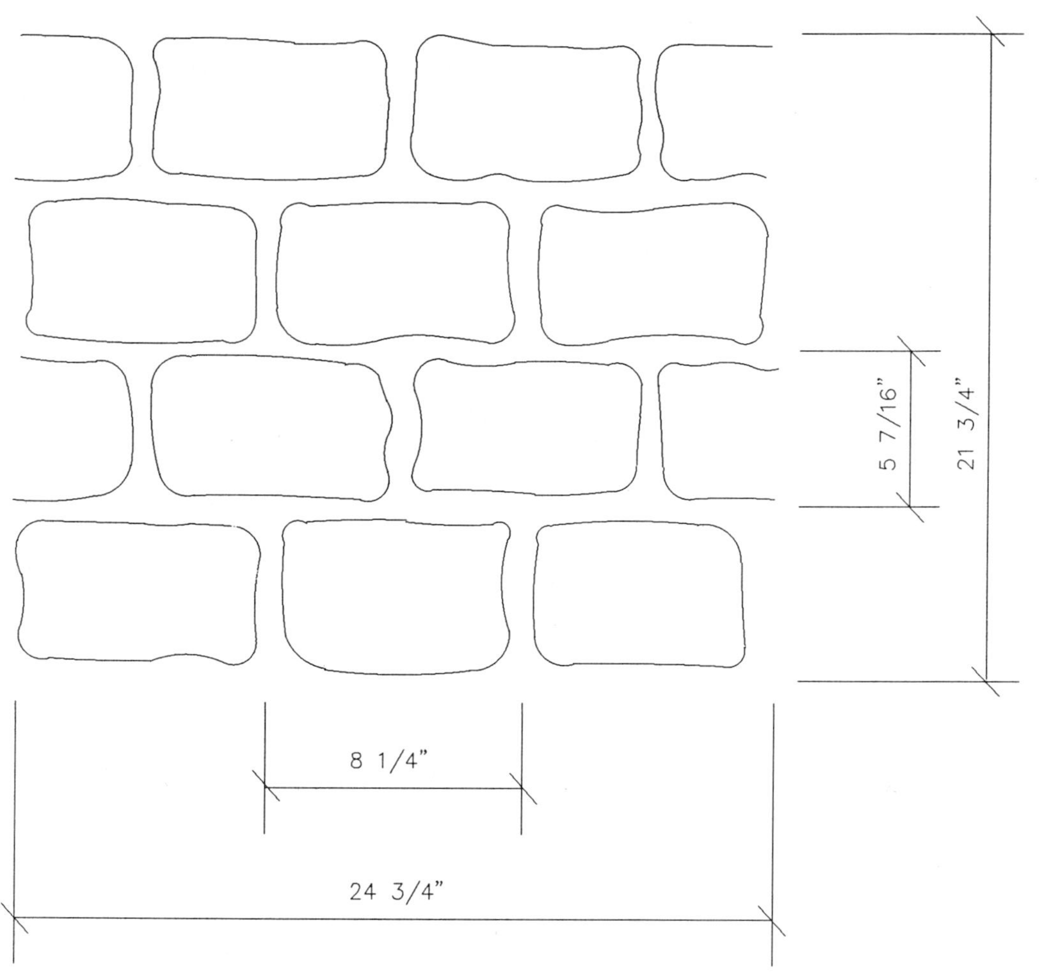
5 7/16"
21 3/4"
8 1/4"
24 3/4"

RUNNING BOND
COBBLESTONE – BOMANITE

SCALE: NOT TO SCALE

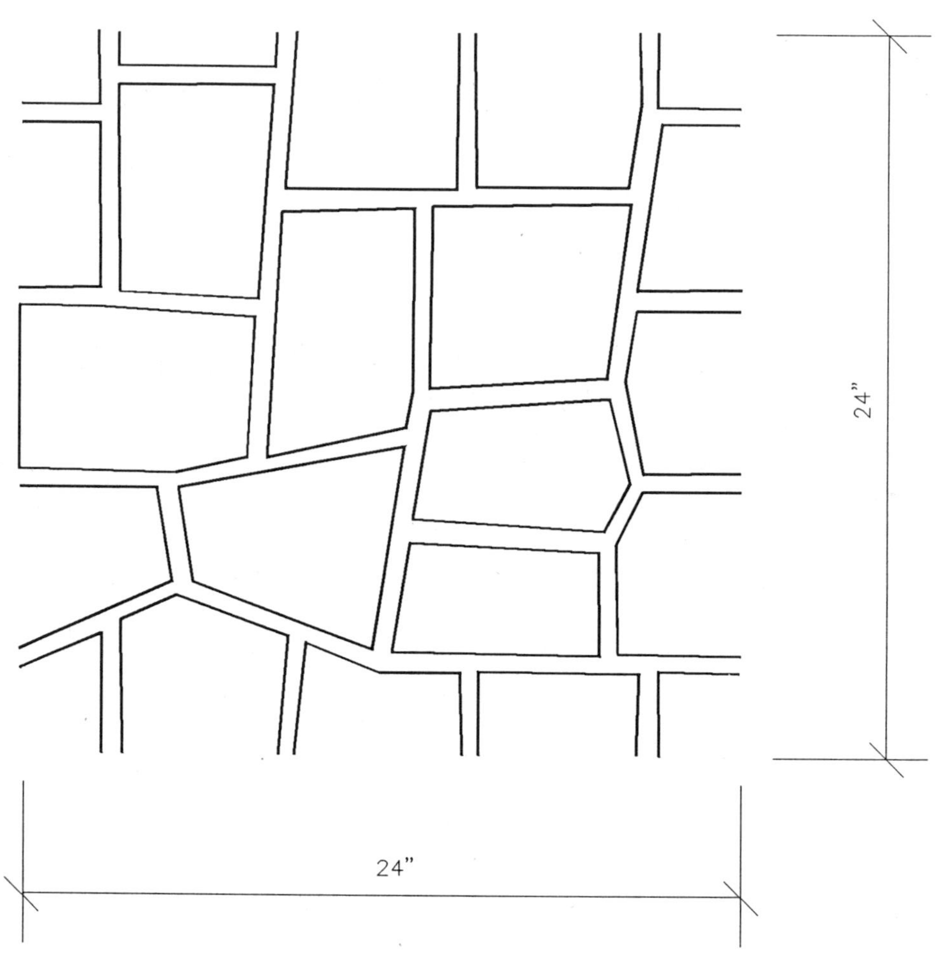
24"
24"

FLAGSTONE – BOMANITE

SCALE: NOT TO SCALE

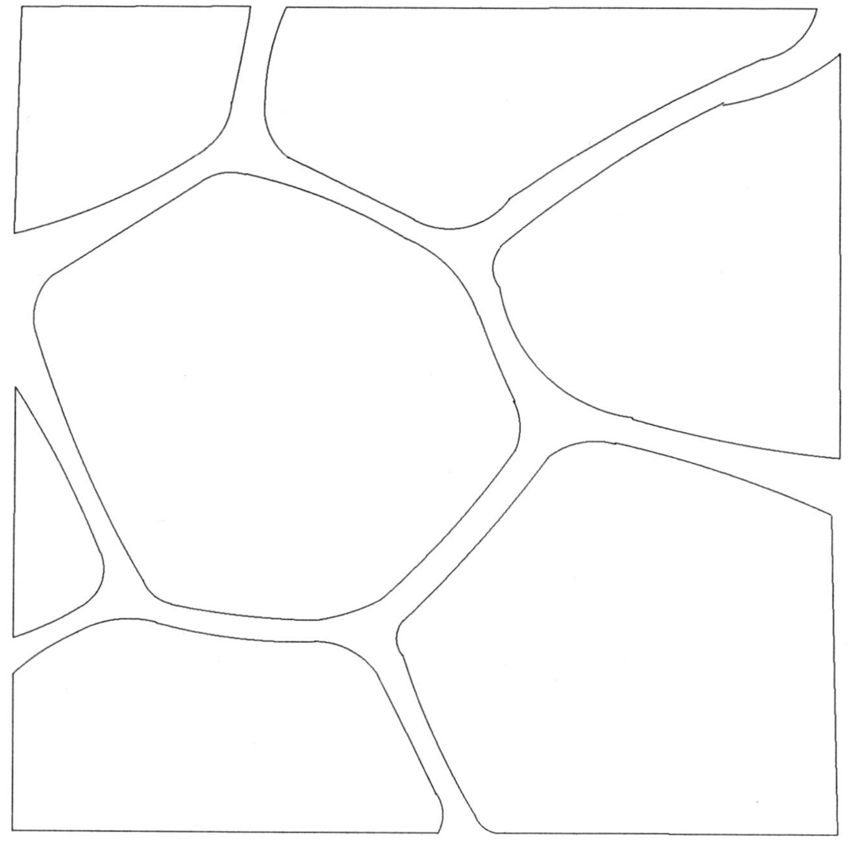

RANDOM STONE – BOMANITE

SCALE: NOT TO SCALE

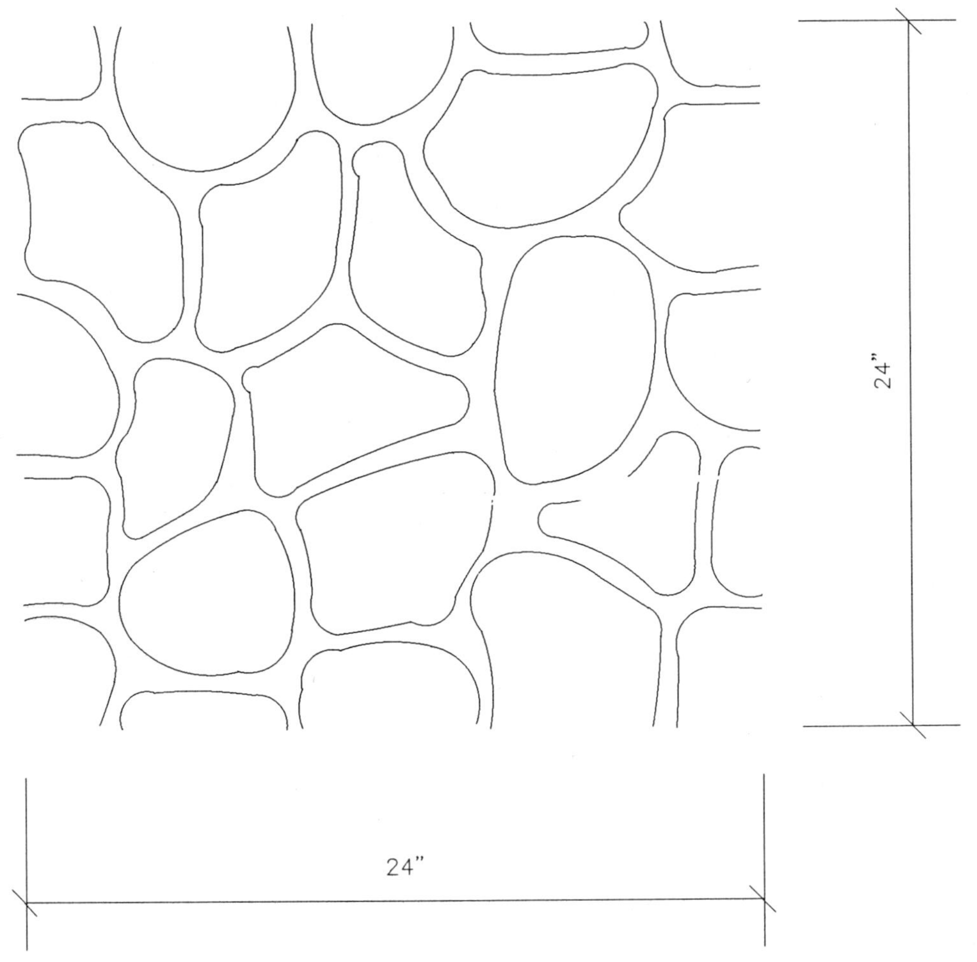
24"
24"

4" TO 6" RIVER ROCK – BOMANITE

SCALE: NOT TO SCALE

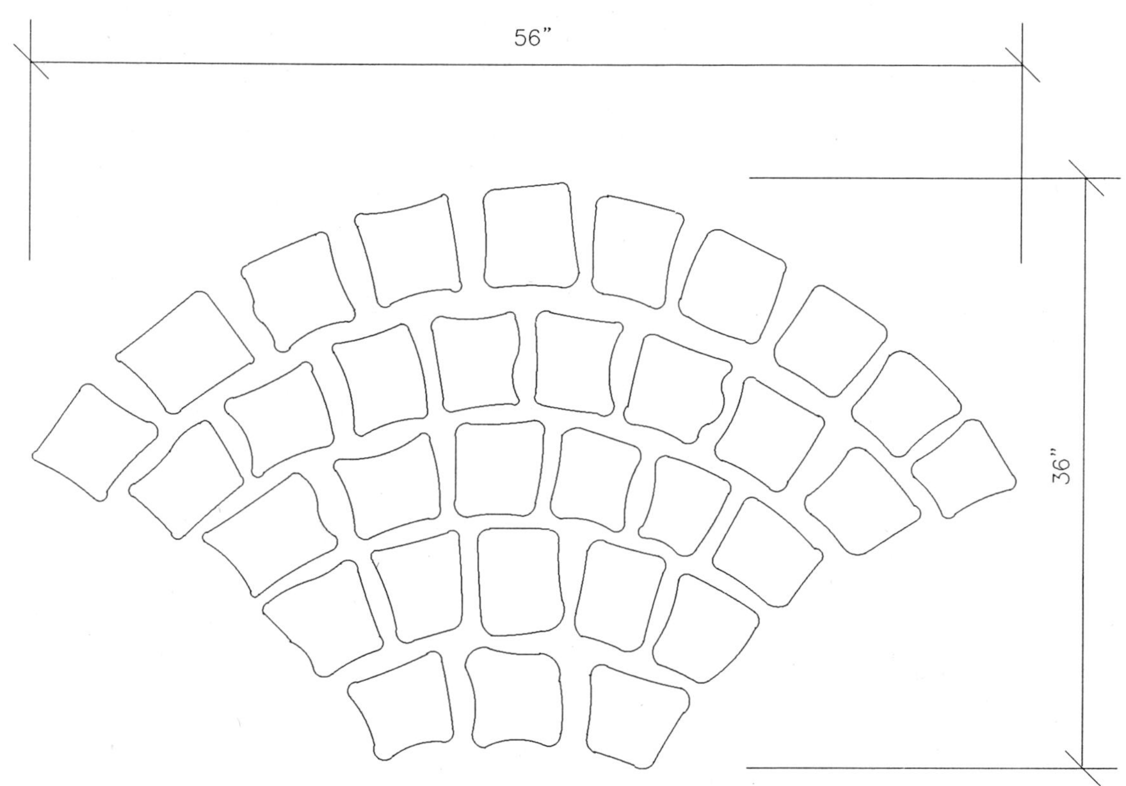
56"
36"

FISHSCALE COBBLESTONE – BOMANITE

SCALE: NOT TO SCALE

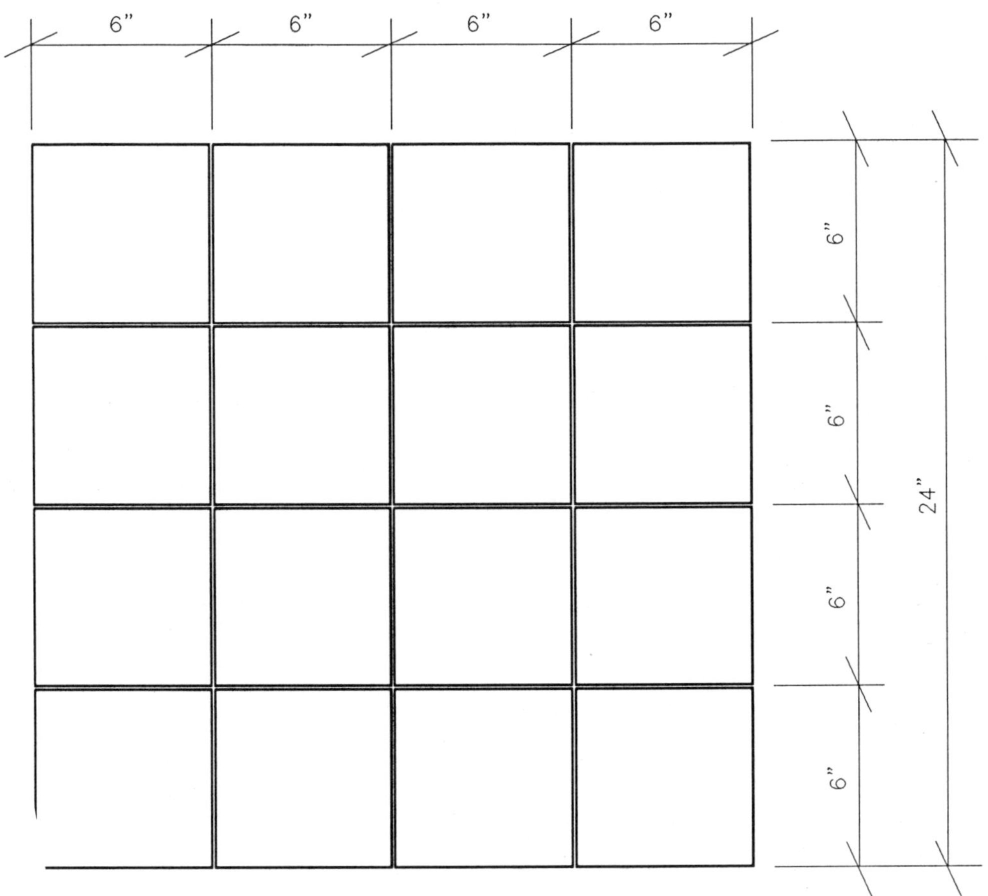

6"
6"
6"
6"
6"
6"
6"
6"
24"

6" x 6" TILE – BOMANITE

SCALE: NOT TO SCALE

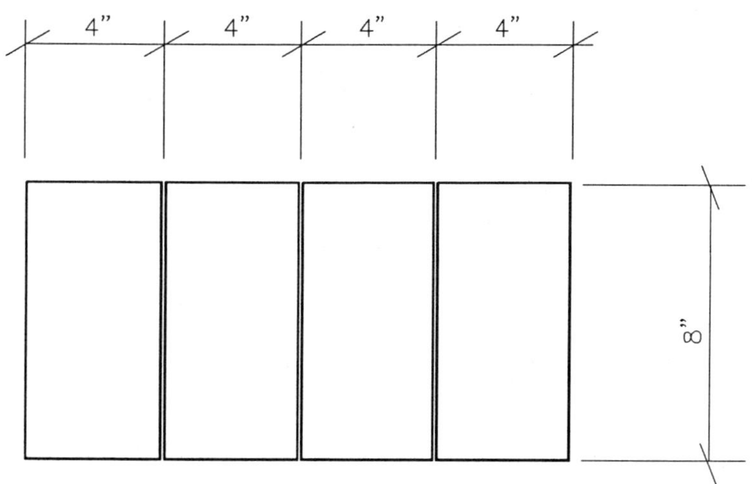
4"
4"
4"
4"
8"

BOMANITE

4" x 8" SOLDIER COURSE BRICK

SCALE: NOT TO SCALE

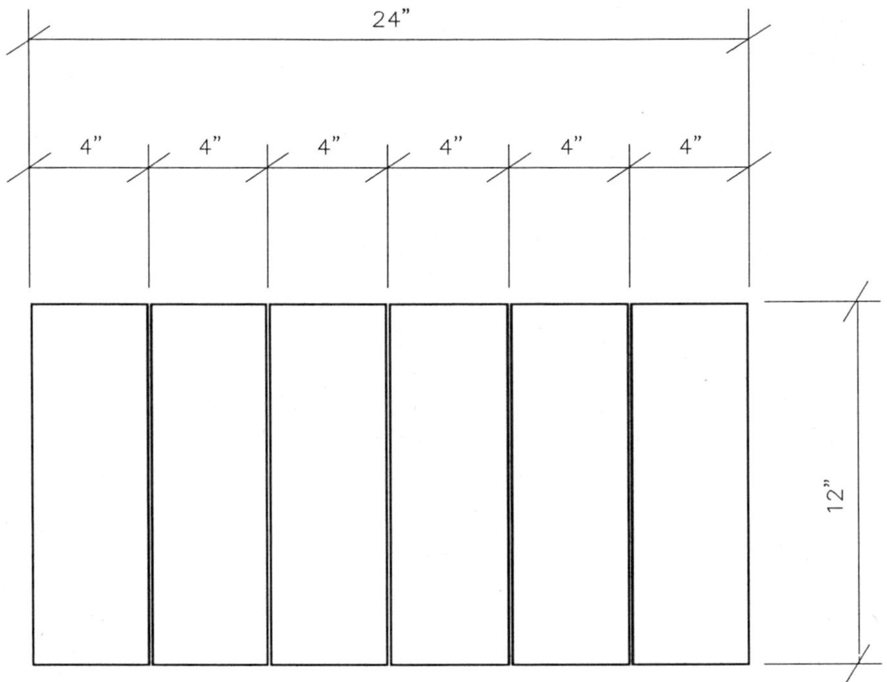
24"
4"
4"
4"
4"
4"
4"
12"

BOMANITE

4" x 12" SOLDIER COURSE BRICK

SCALE: NOT TO SCALE

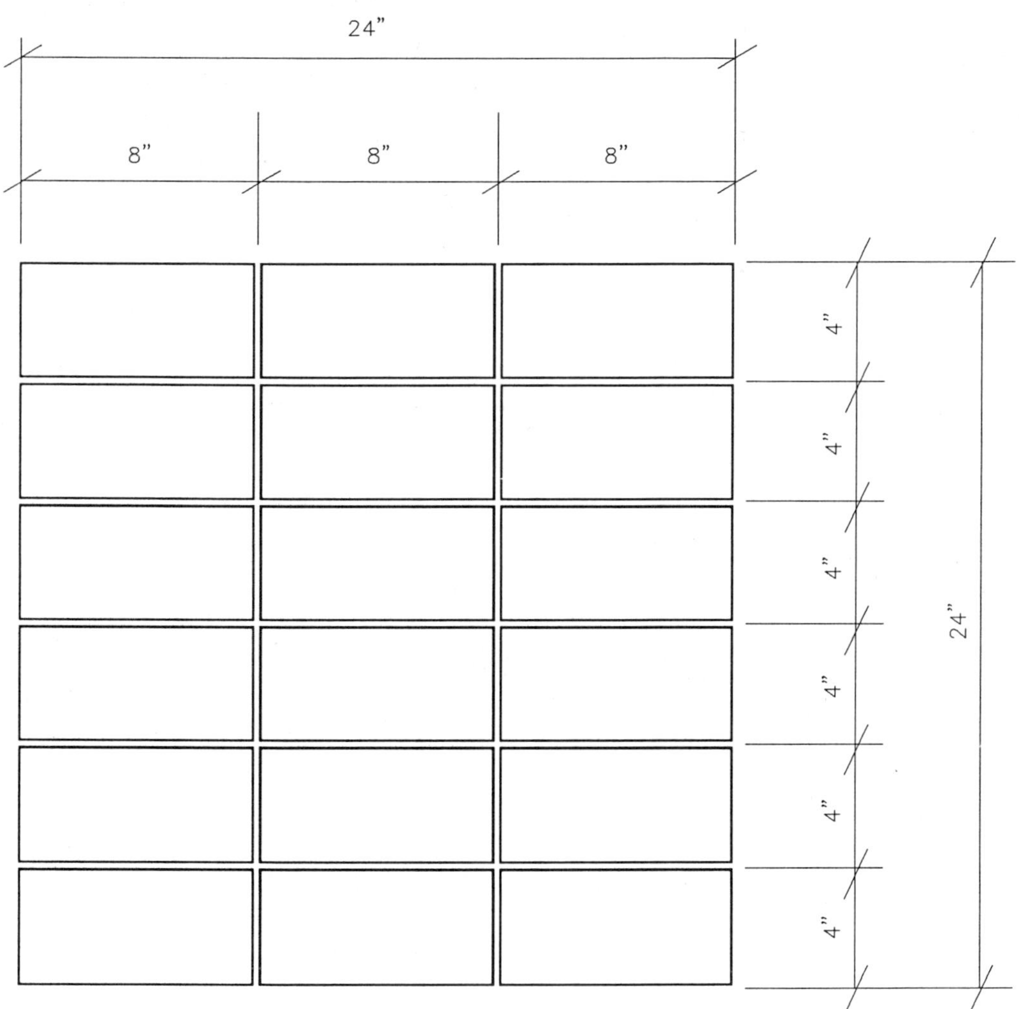
24"
8"
8"
8"
4"
4"
4"
4"
4"
4"
24"

STACKED BOND BRICK – BOMANITE

SCALE: NOT TO SCALE

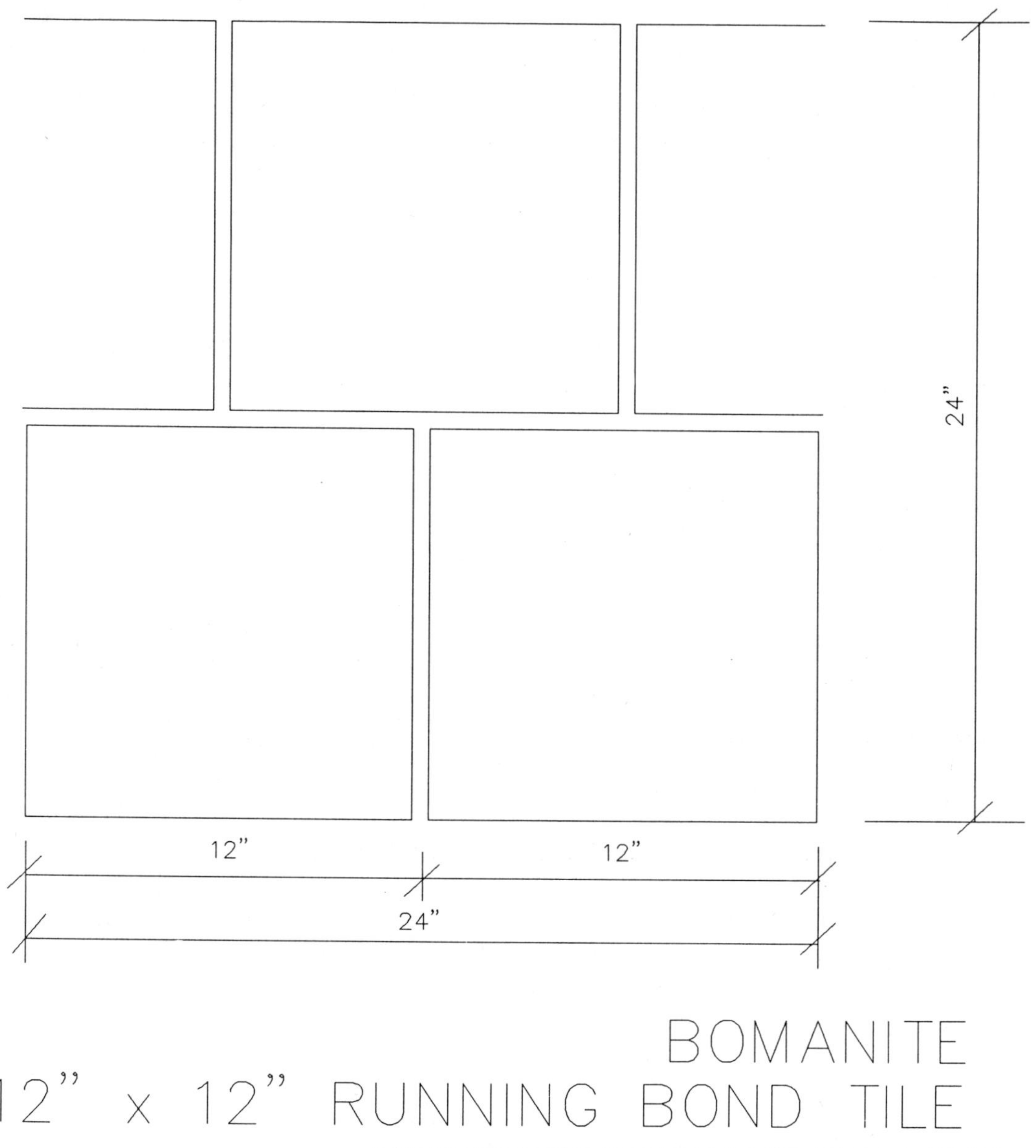
12"
12"
24"
24"

BOMANITE
12" x 12" RUNNING BOND TILE

SCALE: NOT TO SCALE

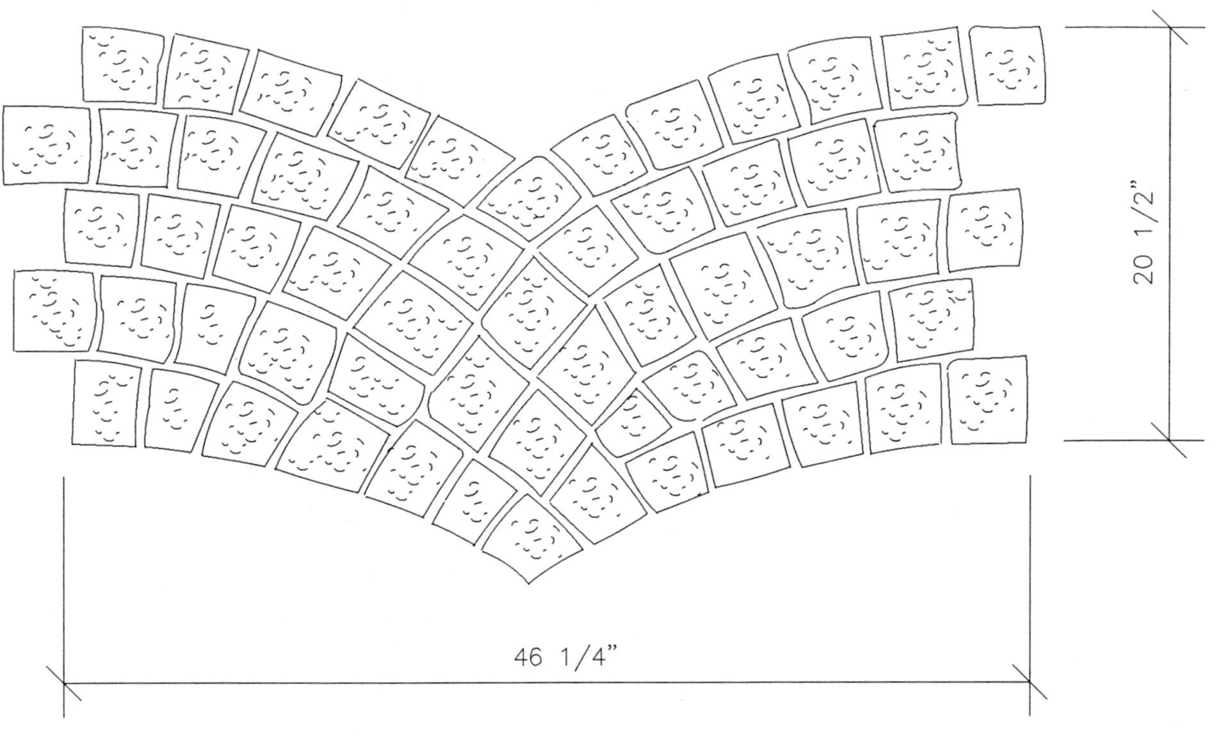
20 1/2"
46 1/4"

FISHSCALE
GRANITE SETTS – BOMACRON

SCALE: NOT TO SCALE

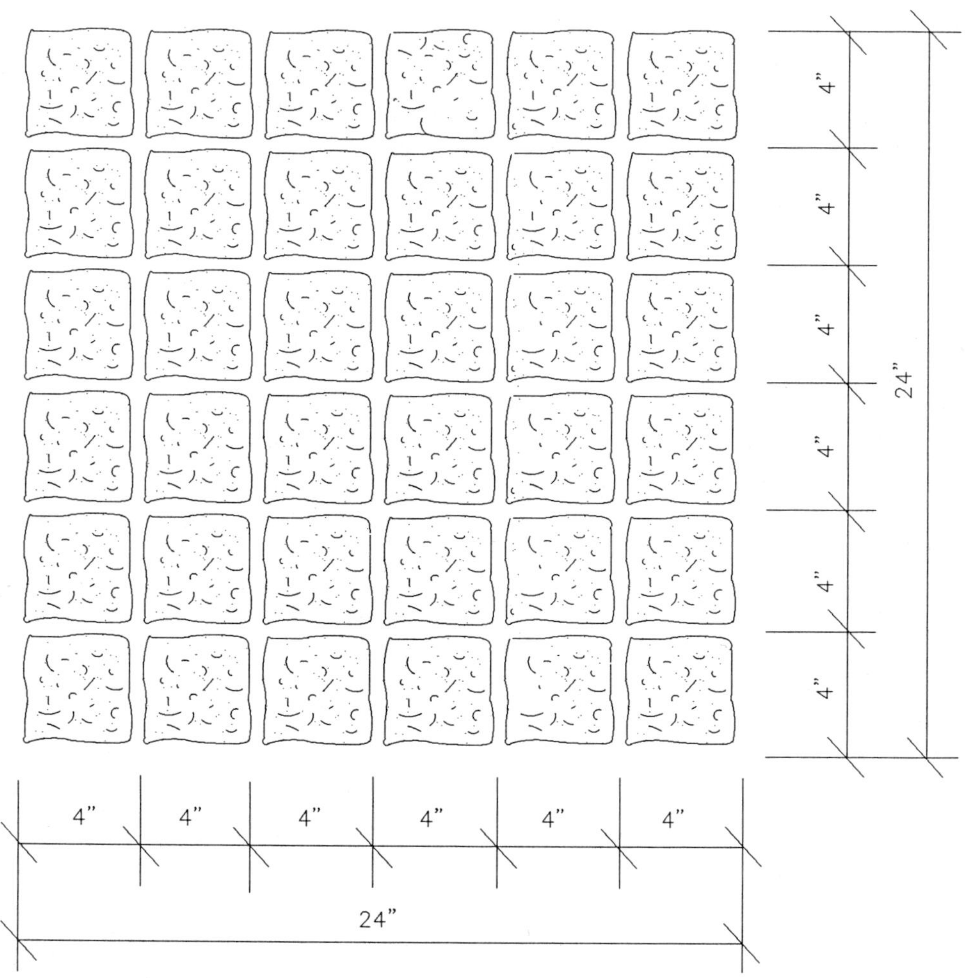
4"
4"
4"
4"
4"
4"
24"
4"
4"
4"
4"
4"
4"
24"

STACKED BOND
GRANITE SETTS — BOMACRON

SCALE: NOT TO SCALE

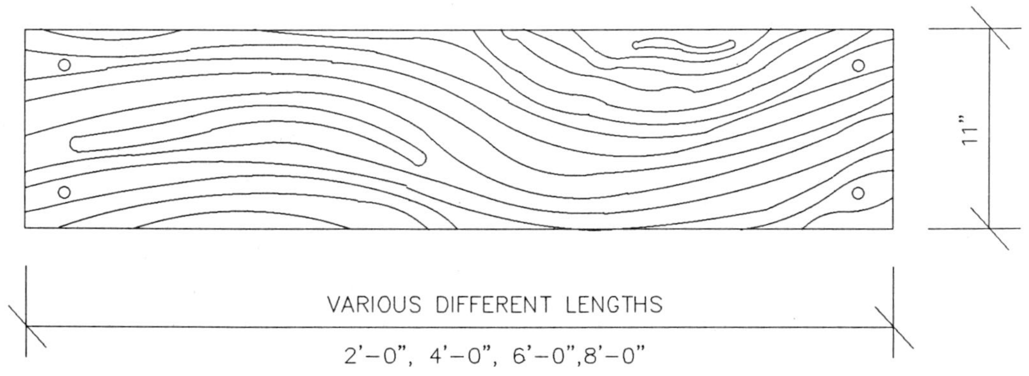
11"
VARIOUS DIFFERENT LENGTHS
2'-0", 4'-0", 6'-0",8'-0"

BOARDWALK – BOMACRON

SCALE: NOT TO SCALE

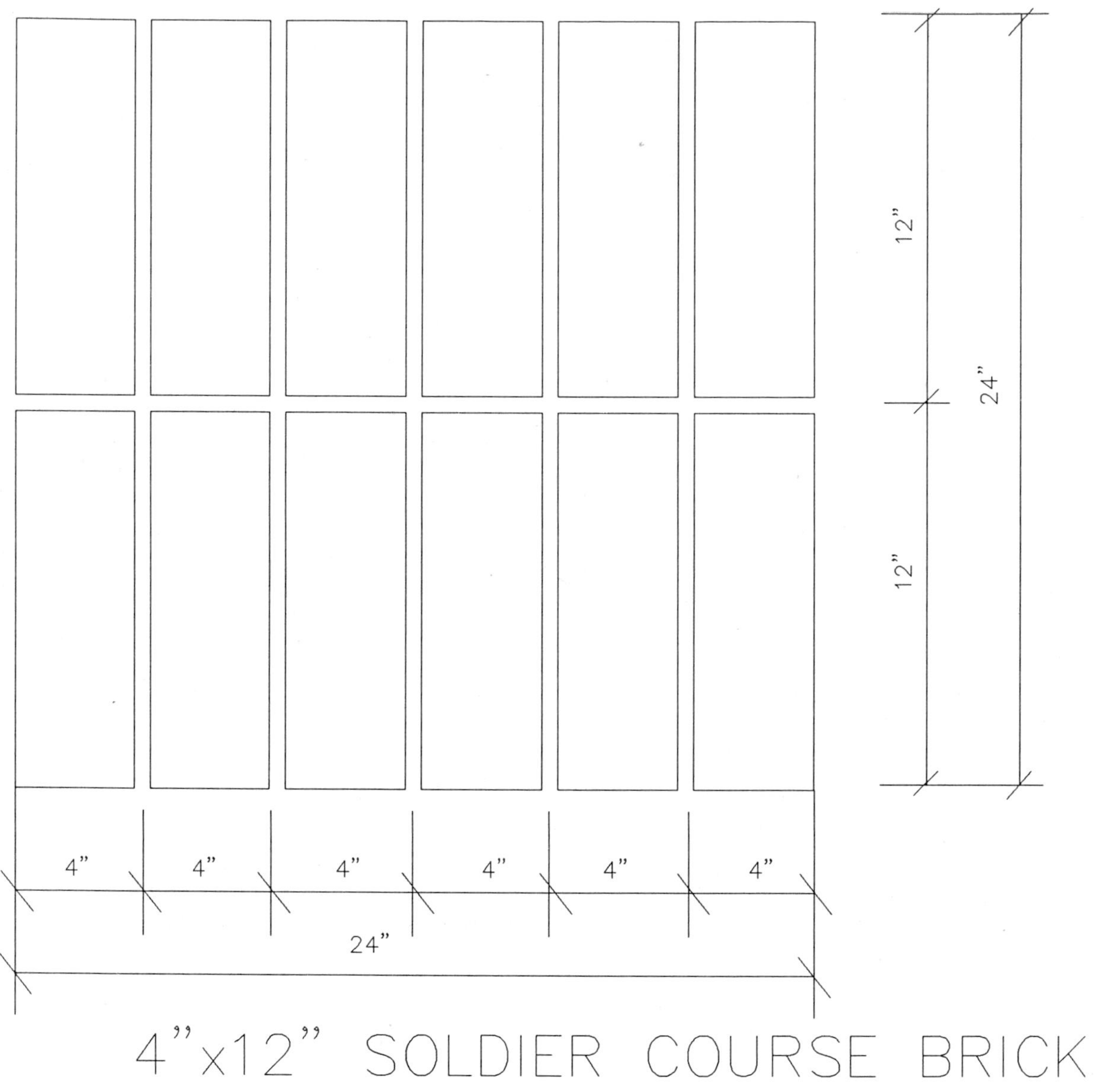
12"
24"
12"
4"
4"
4"
4"
4"
4"
24"

4"x12" SOLDIER COURSE BRICK
DOUBLE ROW – BOMANITE

SCALE: NOT TO SCALE

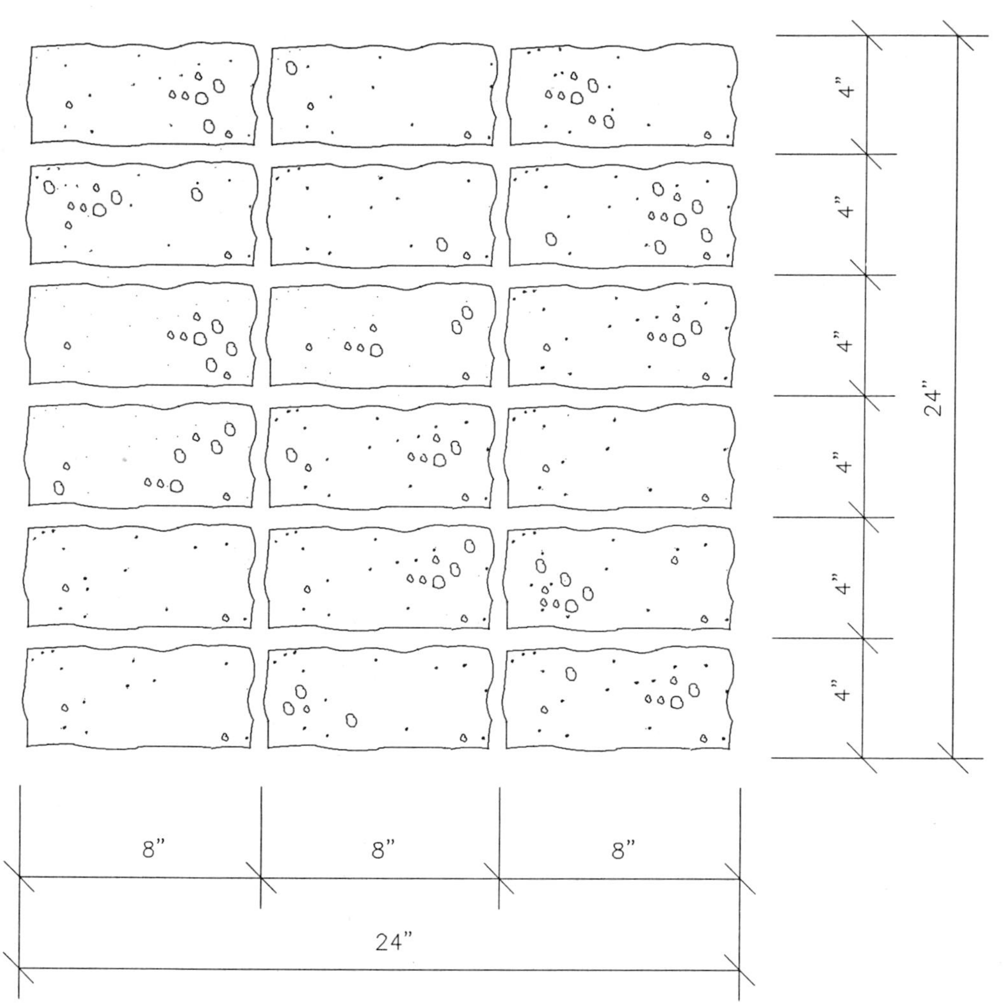
4"
4"
4"
4"
4"
4"
24"
8"
8"
8"
24"

STACKED BOND
USED BRICK – BOMACRON

SCALE: NOT TO SCALE

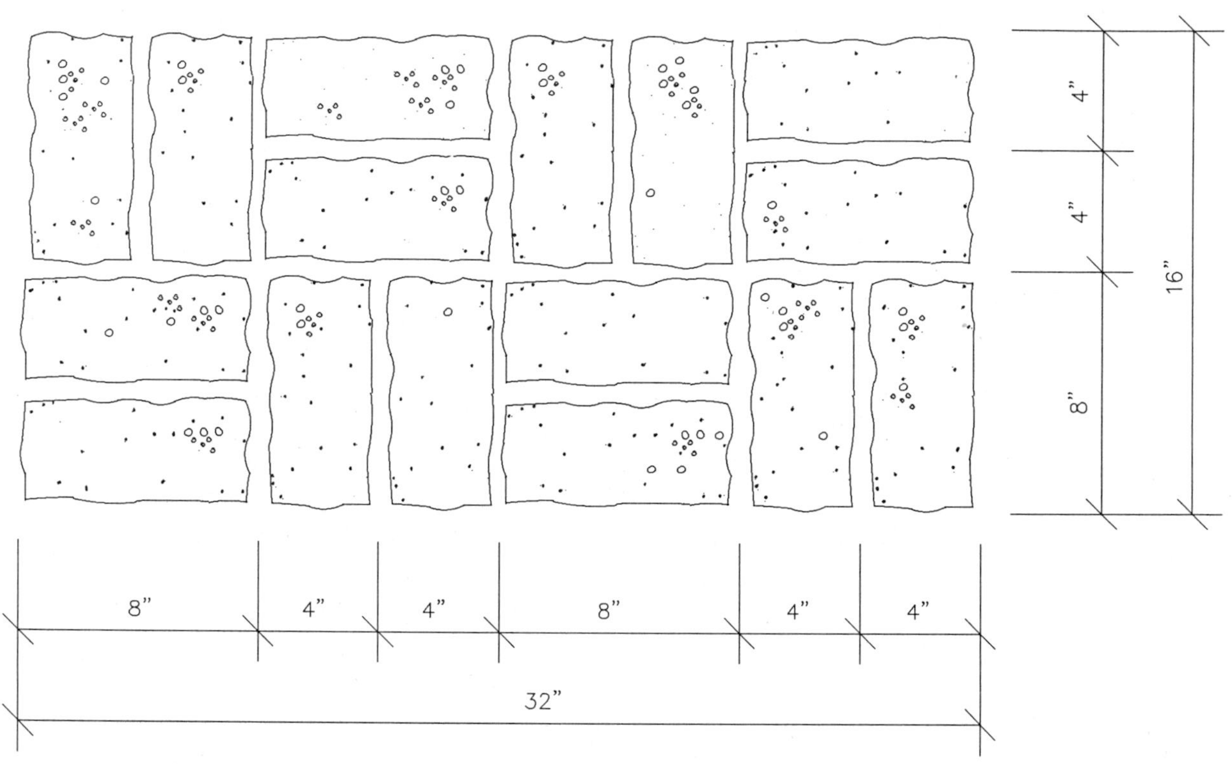
4"
4"
8"
16"
8"
4"
4"
8"
4"
4"
32"

BASKETWEAVE
USED BRICK – BOMACRON

SCALE: NOT TO SCALE

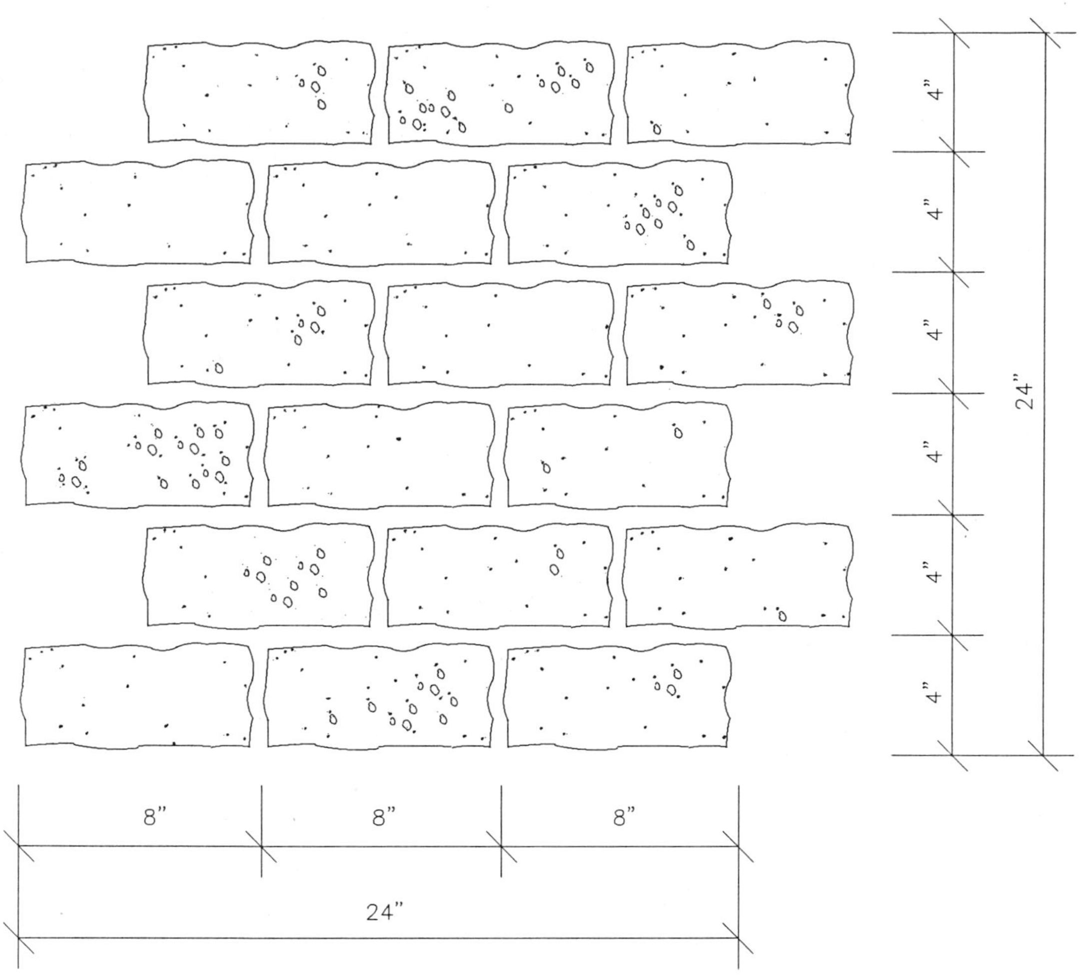
4"
4"
4"
4"
4"
4"
24"
8"
8"
8"
24"

RUNNING BOND
USED BRICK – BOMACRON

SCALE: NOT TO SCALE

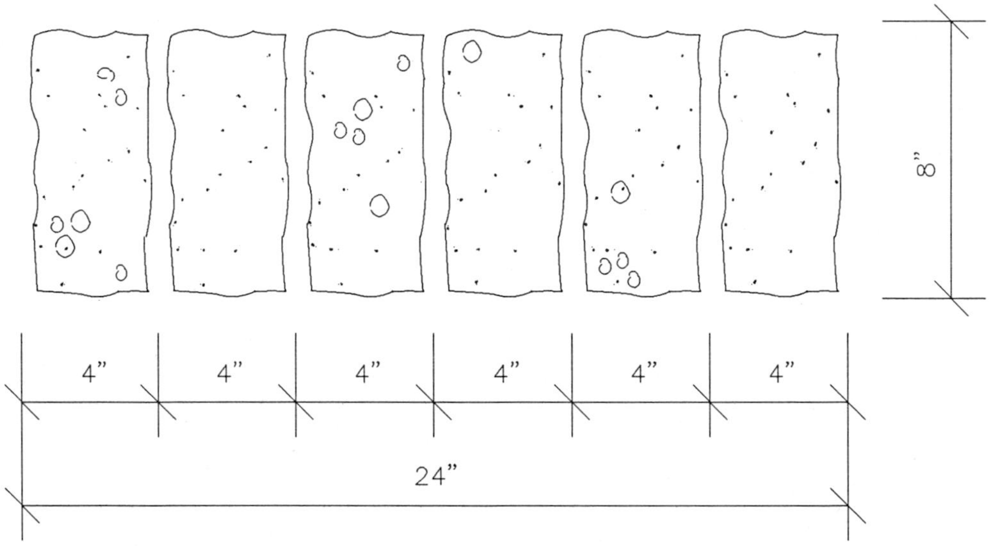
8"
4"
4"
4"
4"
4"
4"
24"

SOLDIER COURSE
USED BRICK – BOMACRON

SCALE: NOT TO SCALE

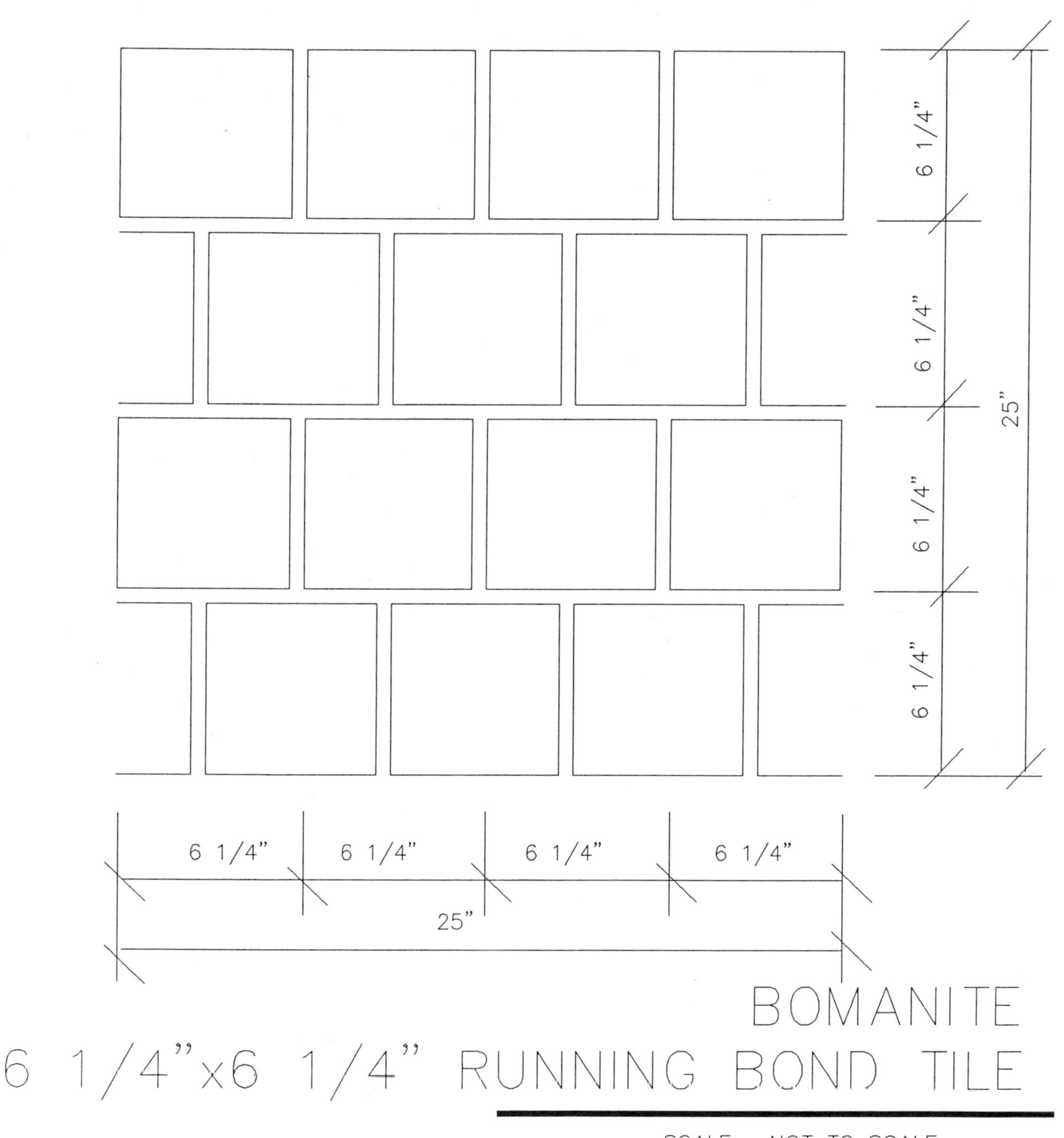

6 1/4"
6 1/4"
6 1/4"
6 1/4"
25"
6 1/4"
6 1/4"
6 1/4"
6 1/4"
25"

BOMANITE
6 1/4"x6 1/4" RUNNING BOND TILE

SCALE: NOT TO SCALE

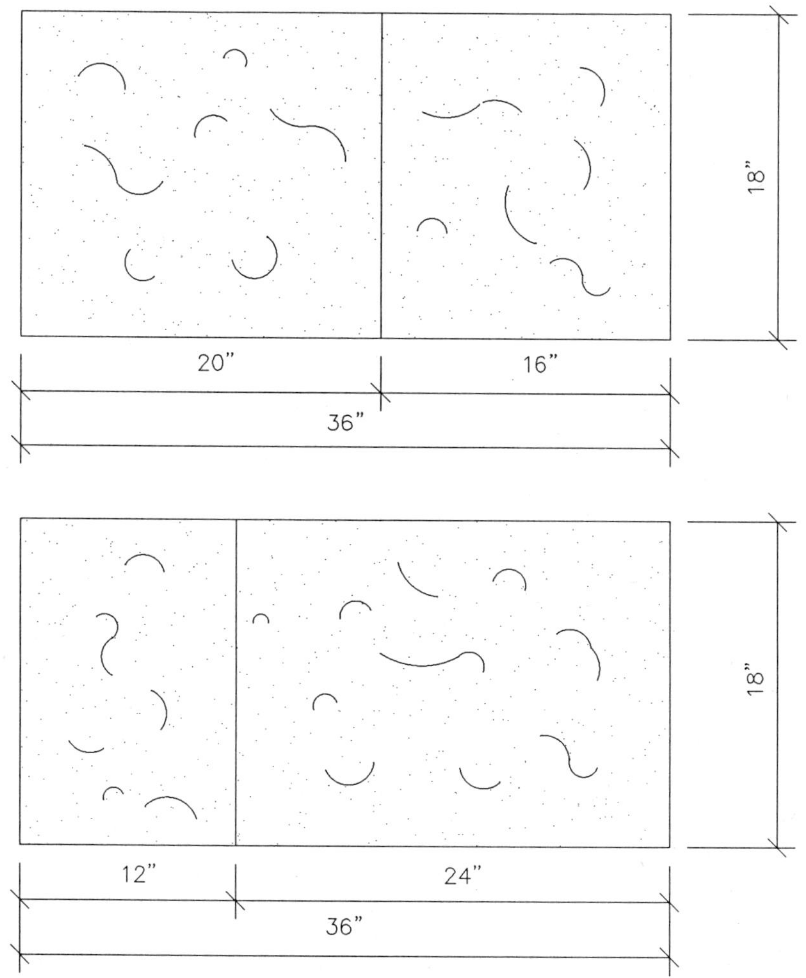
20"
16"
36"
18"
12"
24"
36"
18"

ENGLISH SIDEWALK
SLATE – BOMACRON

SCALE: NOT TO SCALE

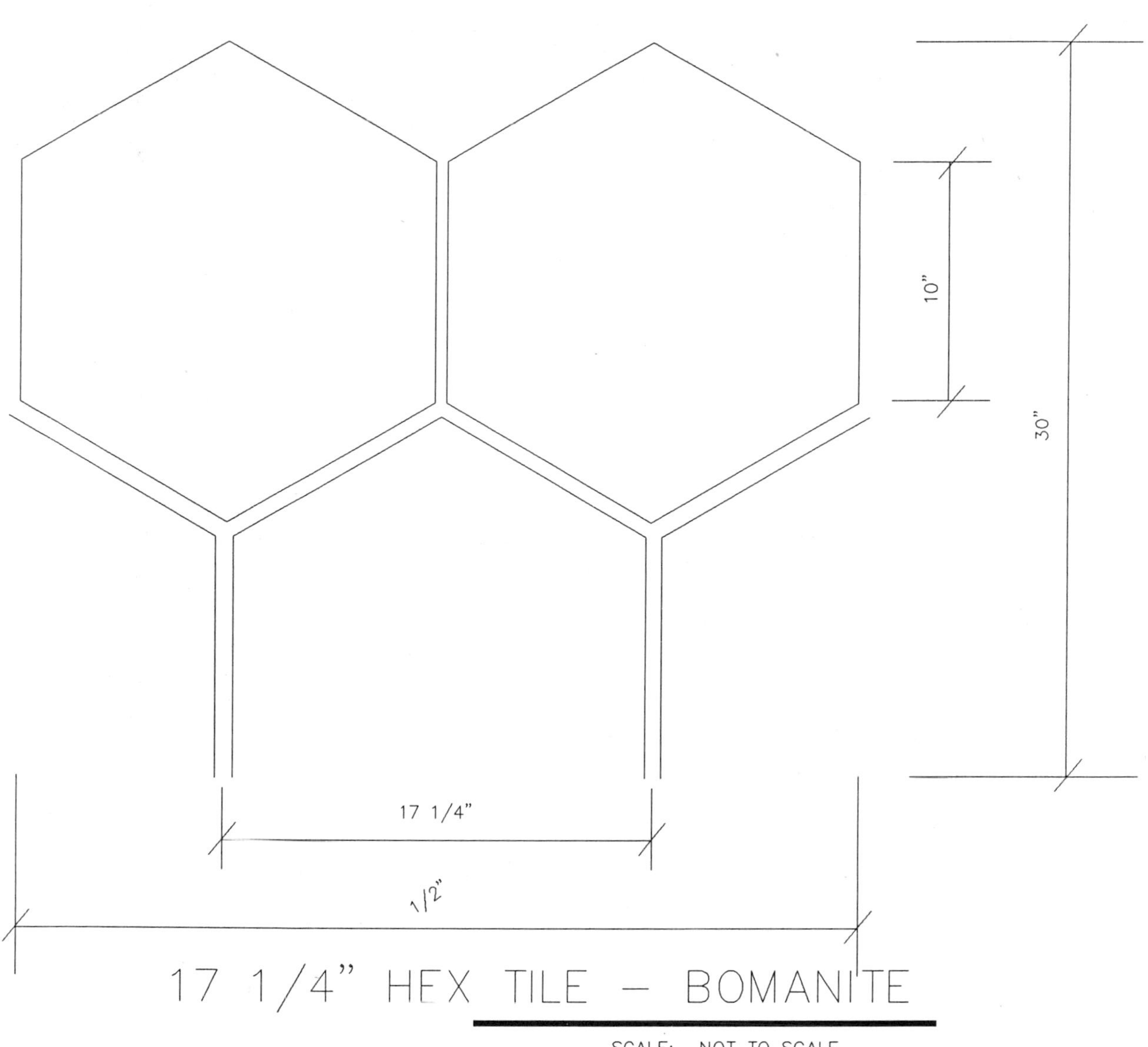
10"
30"
17 1/4"
1/2"

17 1/4" HEX TILE – BOMANITE

SCALE: NOT TO SCALE

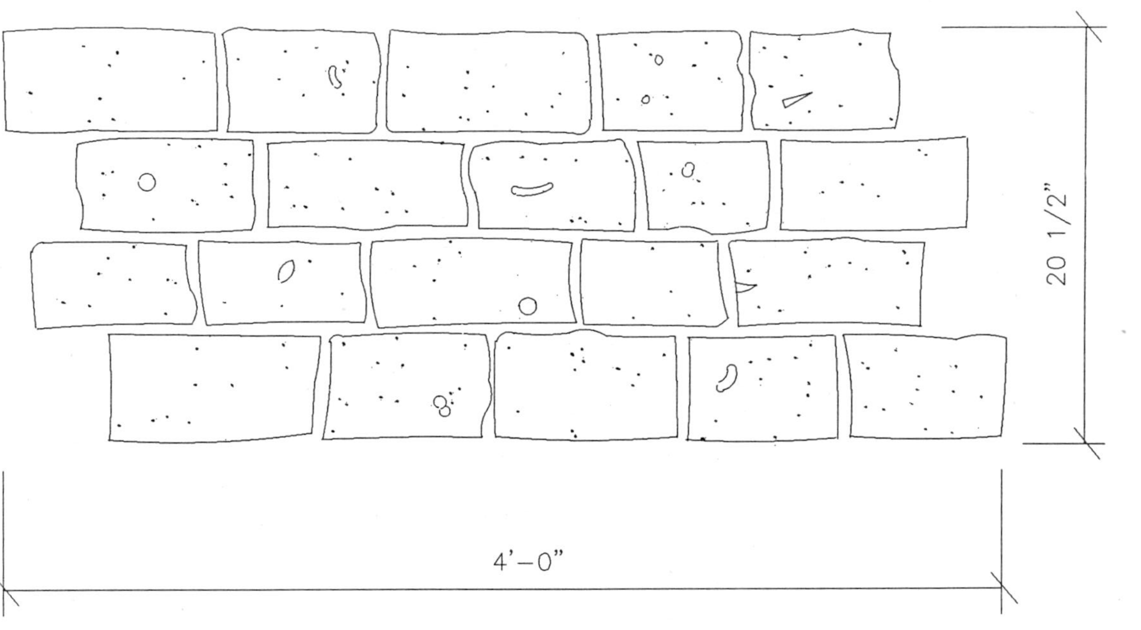
20 1/2"
4'-0"

RUNNING BOND
BELGIAN BLOCK — BOMACRON

SCALE: NOT TO SCALE

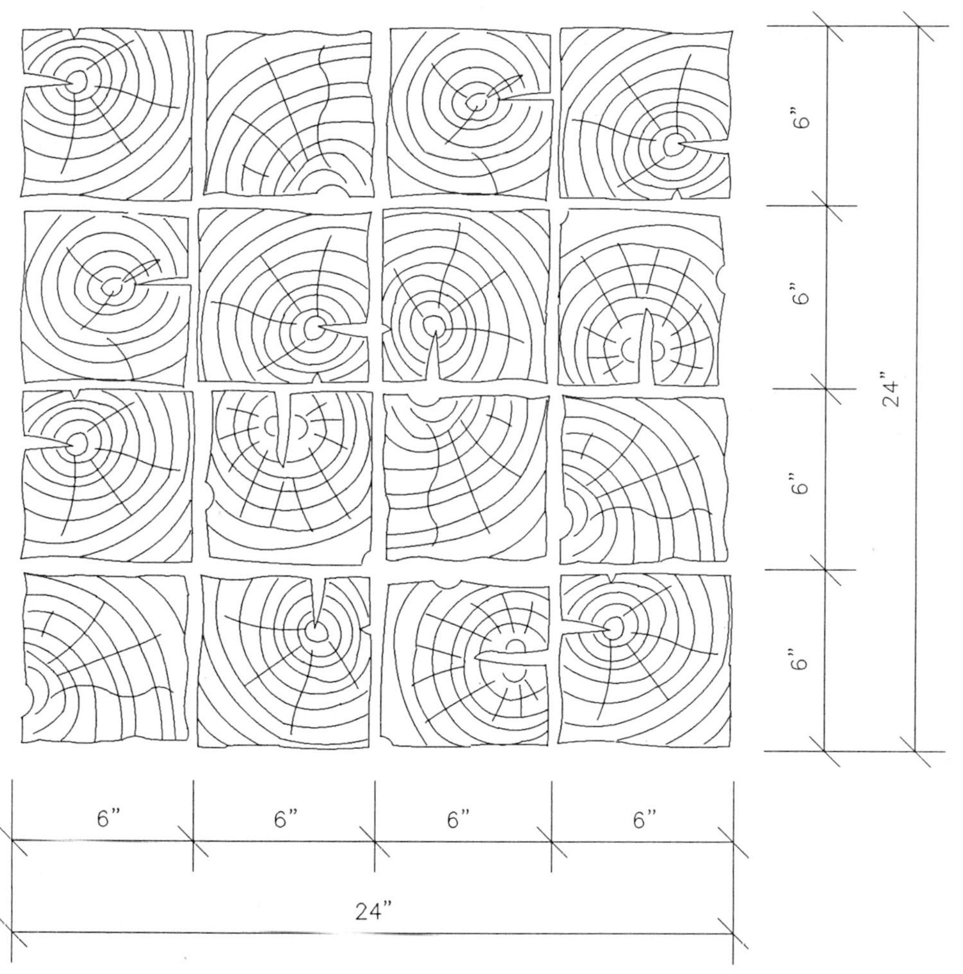
6"
6"
6"
6"
24"
6"
6"
6"
6"
24"

STACKED BOND
WOOD BLOCK – BOMACRON

SCALE: NOT TO SCALE

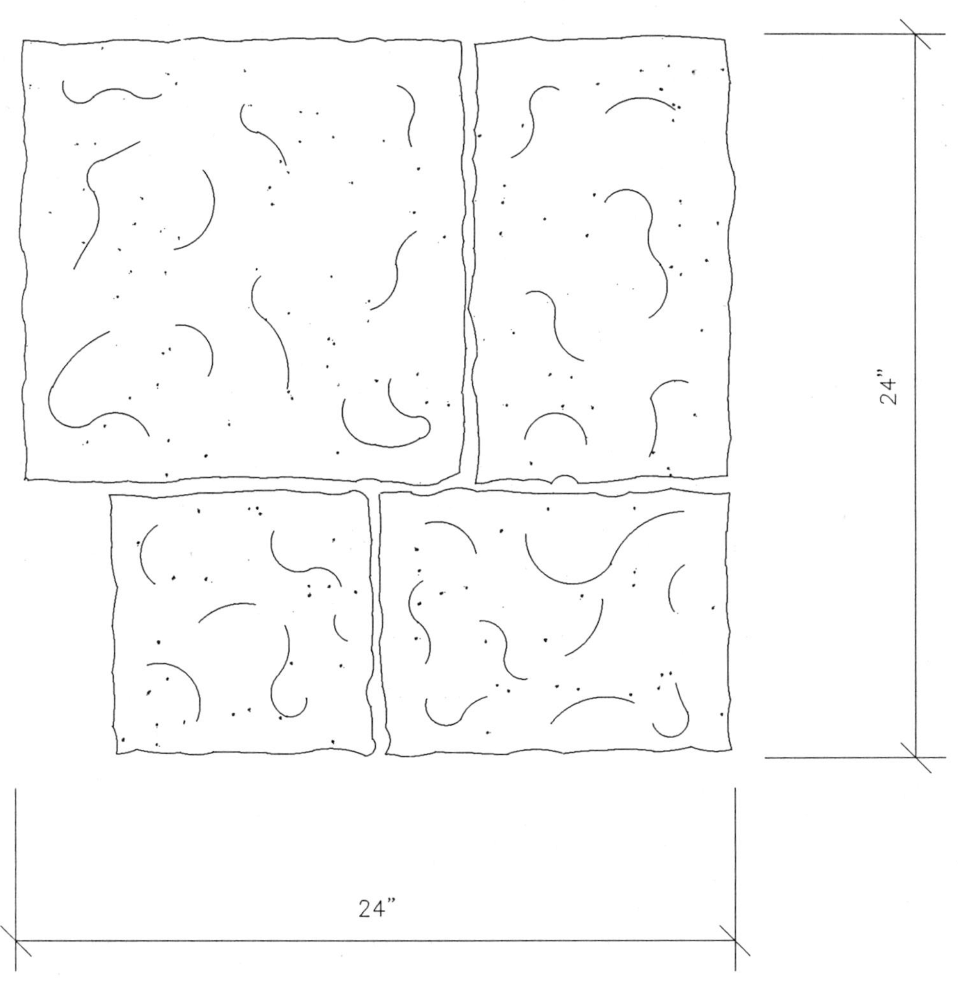
24"
24"

ASHLAR SLATE – BOMACRON

SCALE: NOT TO SCALE

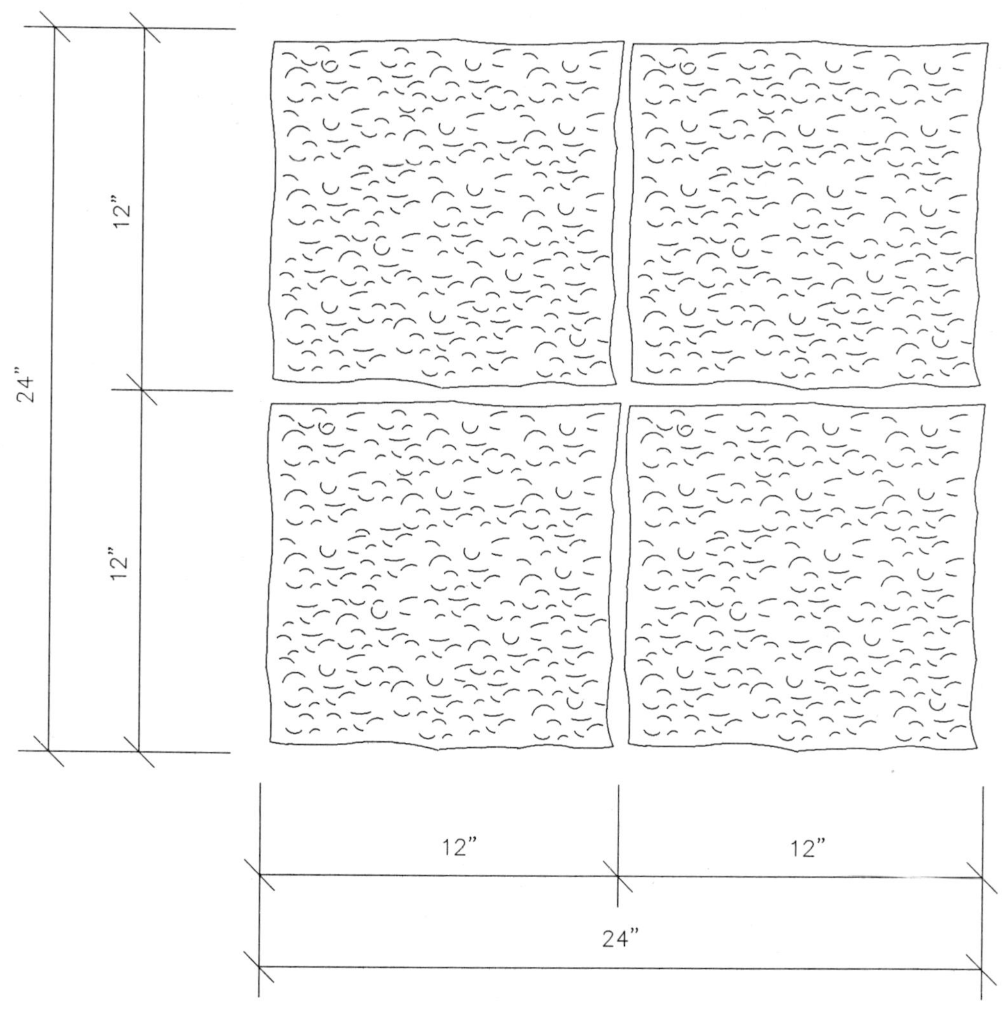
12"
12"
24"
12"
12"
24"

12" X 12" GRANITE – BOMACRON

SCALE: NOT TO SCALE

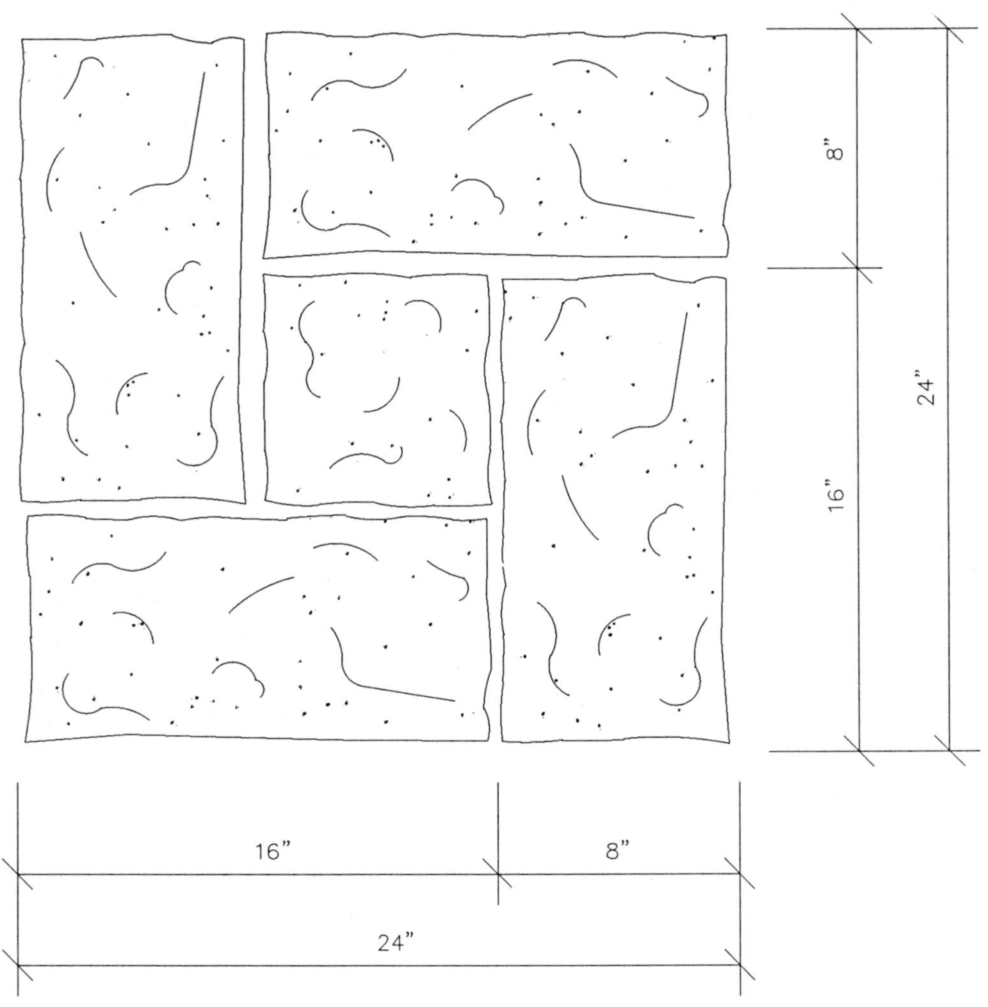
8"
16"
24"
16"
8"
24"

8" X 16" RIVERSIDE SLATE – BOMACRON

SCALE: NOT TO SCALE

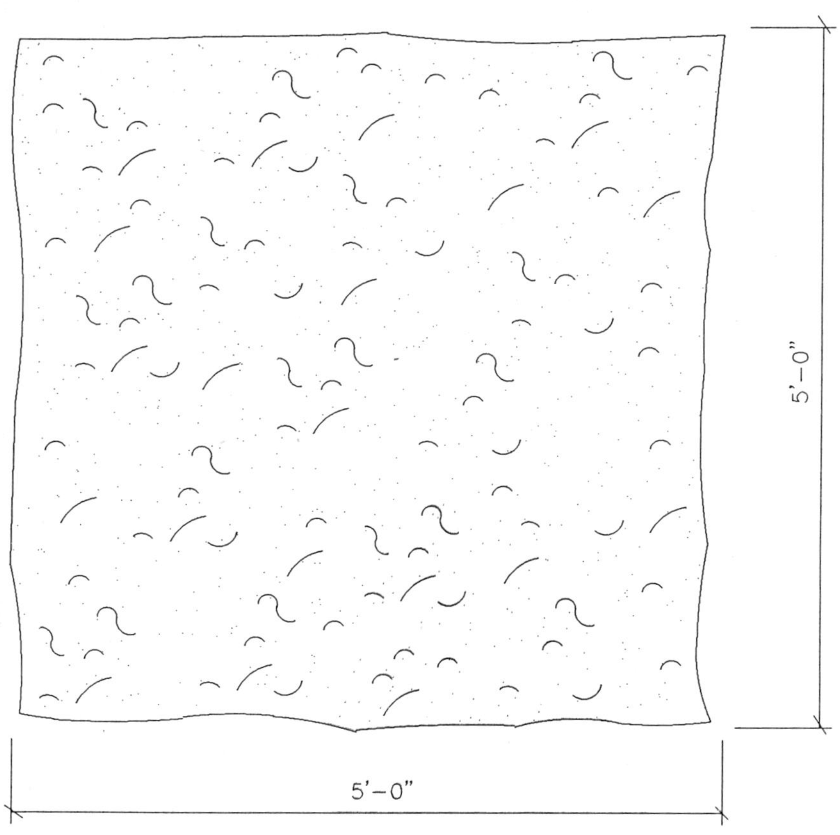
5'–0"
5'–0"

5'–0" X 5'–0" SLATE – BOMACRON

SCALE: NOT TO SCALE

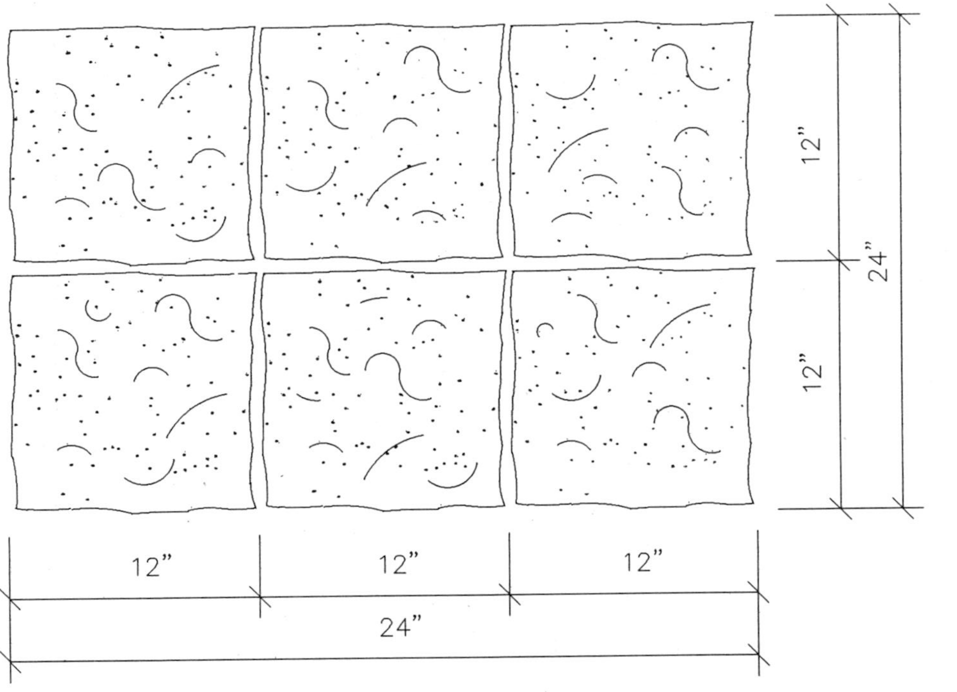
12"
12"
12"
24"
12"
12"
24"

12" X 12" SLATE – BOMACRON

SCALE: NOT TO SCALE

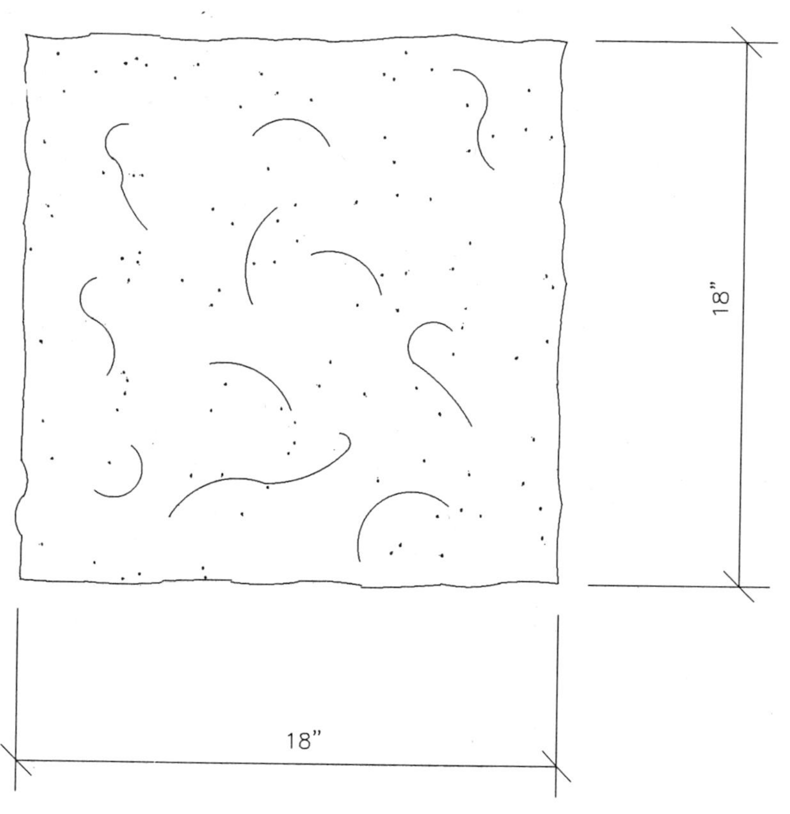
18"
18"

18' X 18" SLATE – BOMACRON

SCALE: NOT TO SCALE

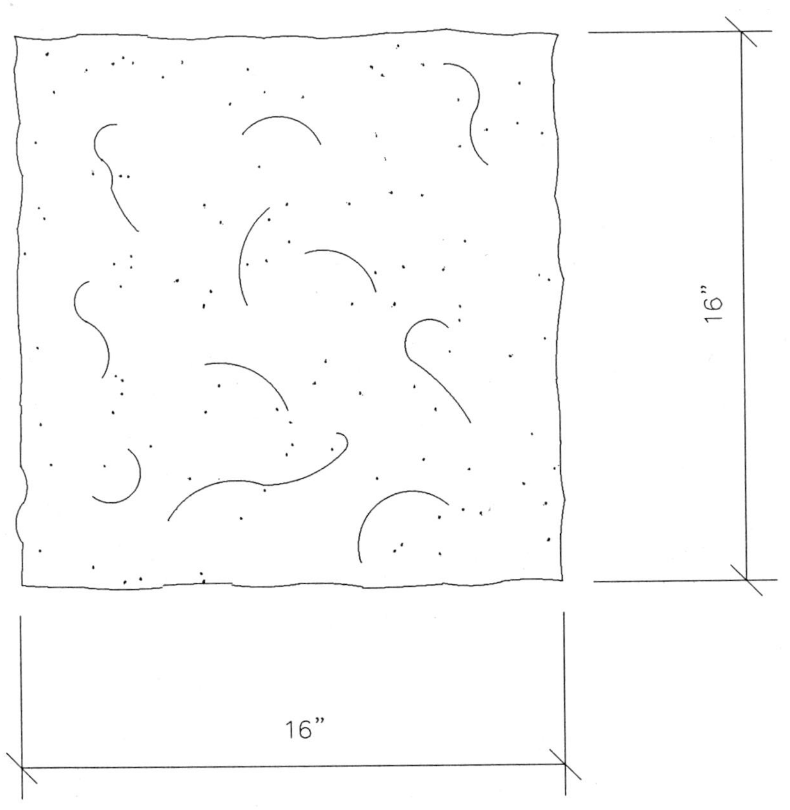
16"
16"

16' X 16" SLATE – BOMACRON

SCALE: NOT TO SCALE

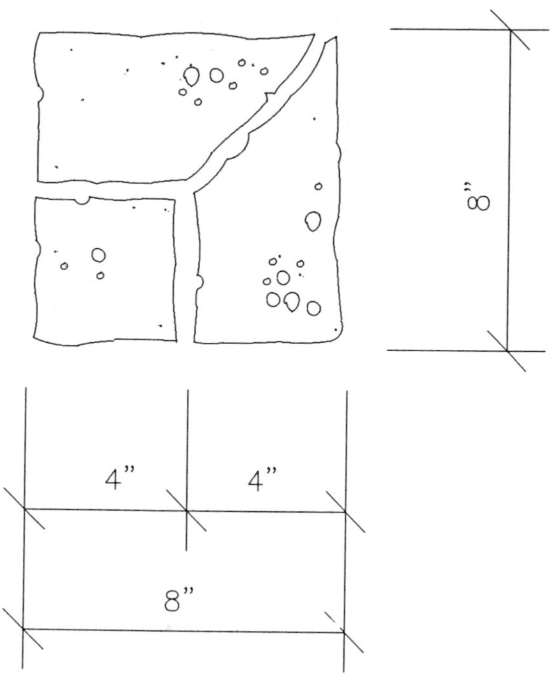
8"
4"
4"
8"

SOLDIER COURSE CORNER
USED BRICK – BOMACRON

SCALE: NOT TO SCALE

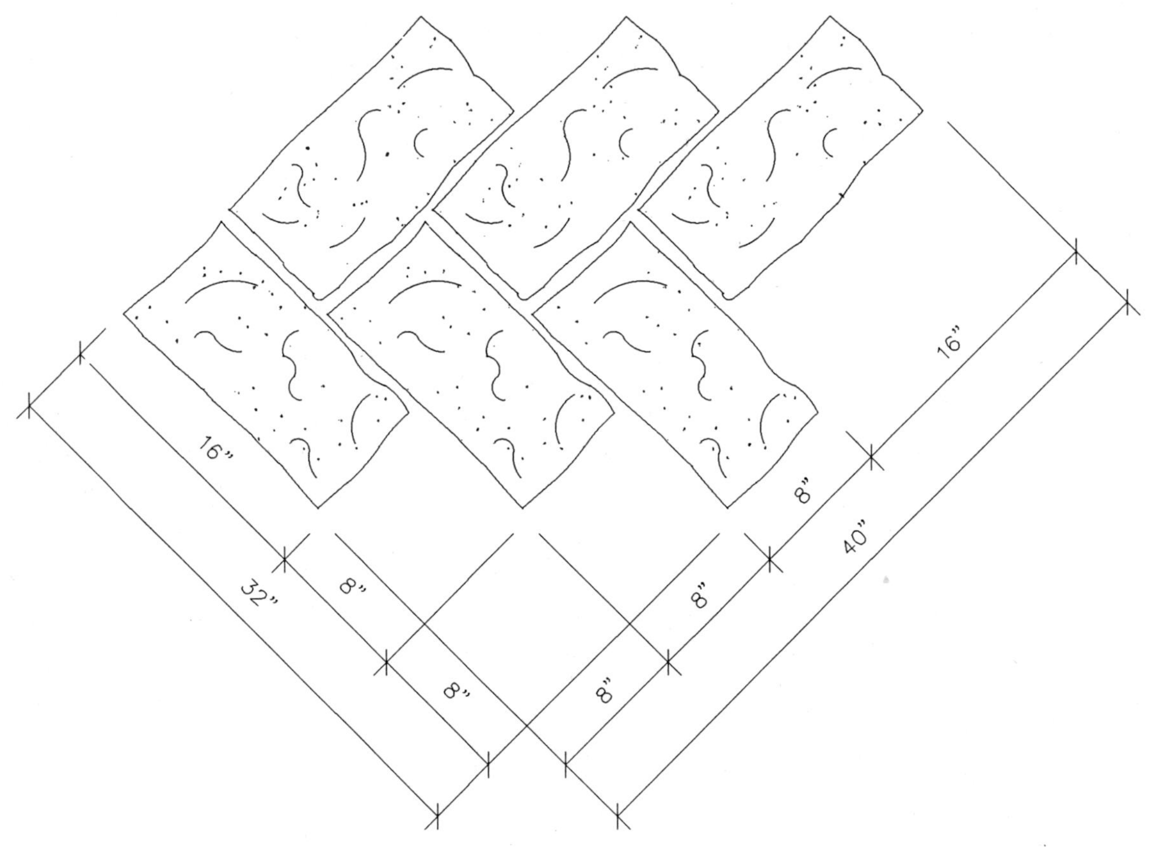
16"
32"
8"
8"
8"
8"
8"
16"
40"

8" X 16" HERRINGBONE SLATE – BOMACRON

SCALE: NOT TO SCALE

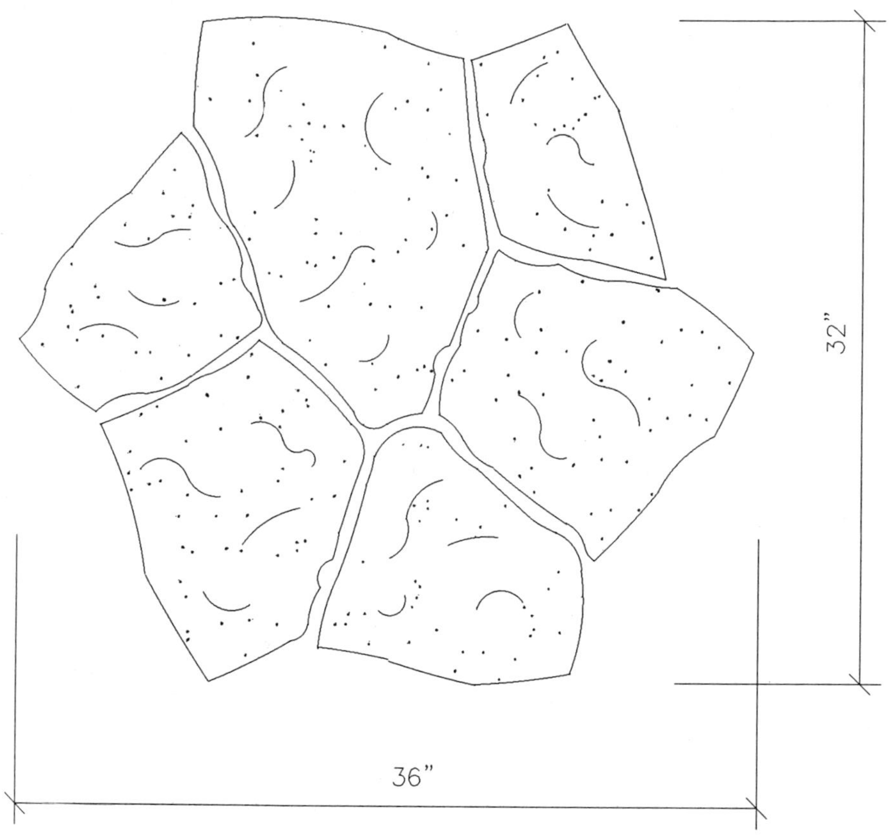
32"
36"

CANYON STONE – BOMACRON

SCALE: NOT TO SCALE

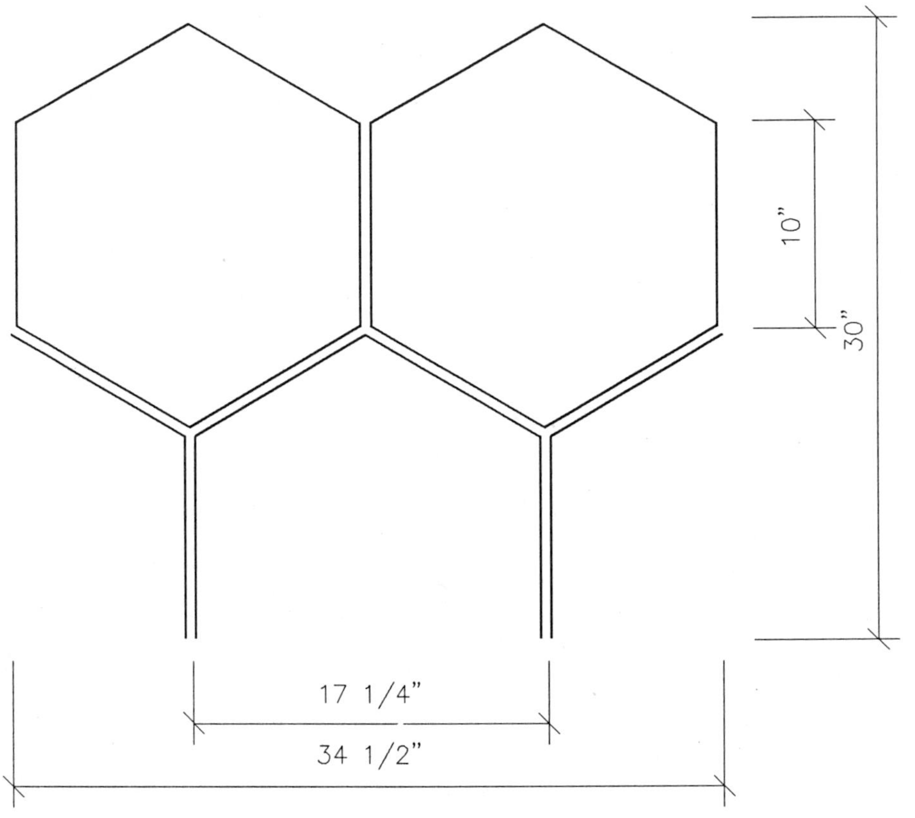
10"
30"
17 1/4"
34 1/2"

17 1/4" HEX TILE – BOMANITE

SCALE: NOT TO SCALE

Playground Equipment

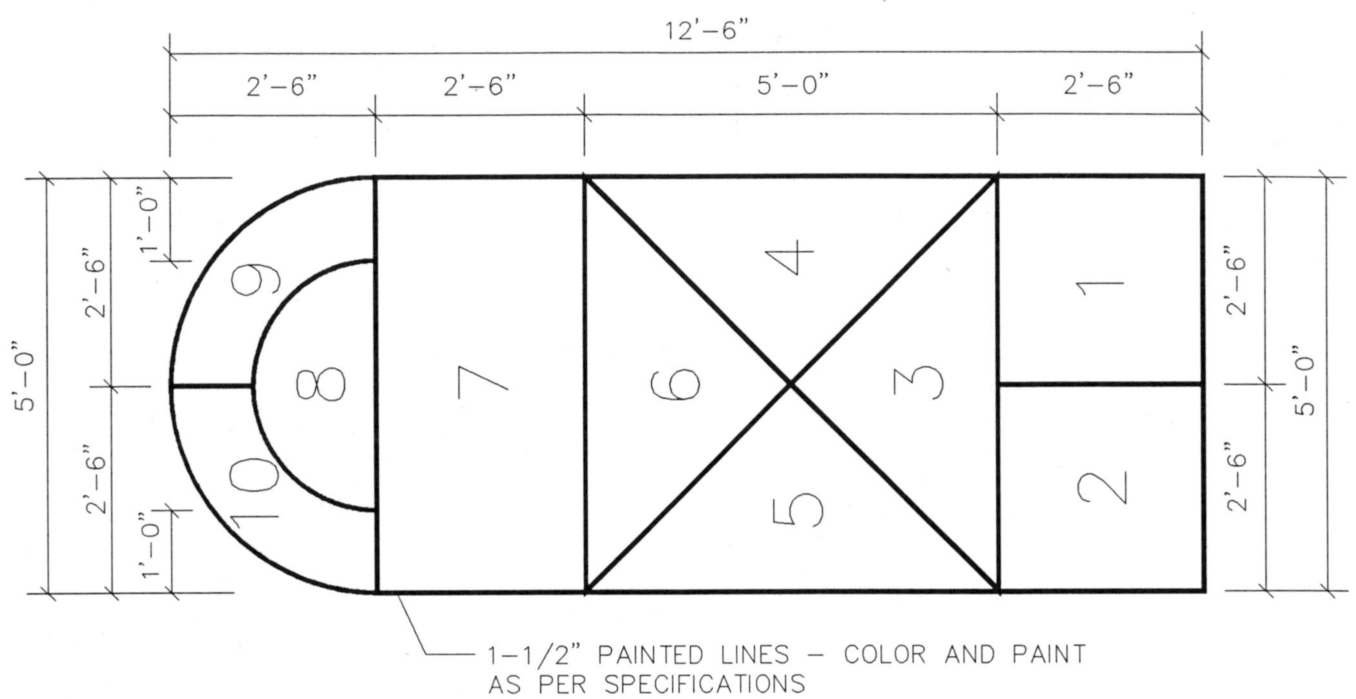
12'-6"
2'-6"
2'-6"
5'-0"
2'-6"
5'-0"
2'-6"
2'-6"
1'-0"
1'-0"
1
2
3
4
5
6
7
8
9
10
2'-6"
2'-6"
5'-0"
1-1/2" PAINTED LINES - COLOR AND PAINT
AS PER SPECIFICATIONS

HOPSCOTCH

SCALE: NOT TO SCALE

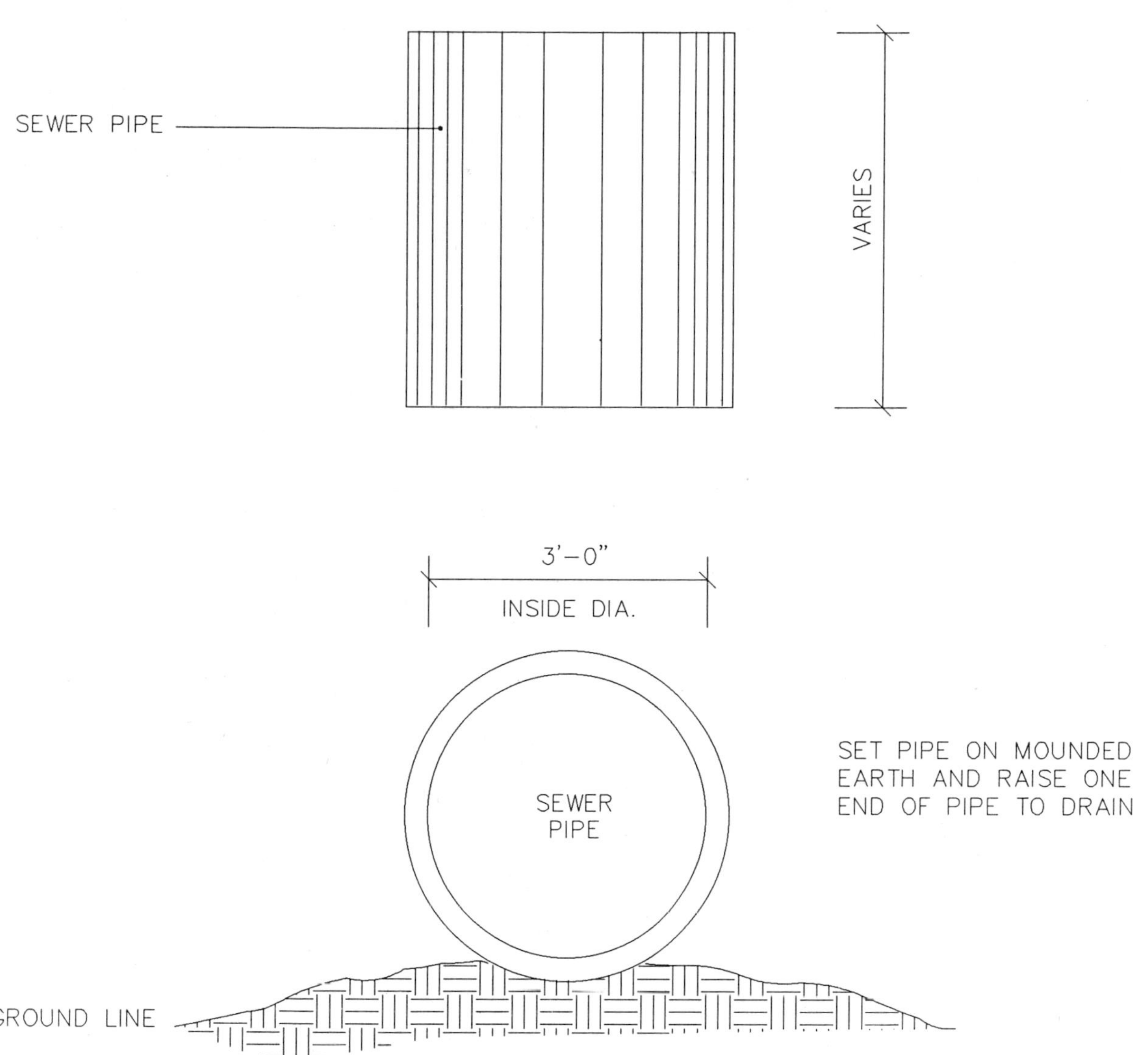
SEWER PIPE
VARIES
3'–0"
INSIDE DIA.
SEWER
PIPE
SET PIPE ON MOUNDED
EARTH AND RAISE ONE
END OF PIPE TO DRAIN
GROUND LINE

PIPE TUNNEL

SCALE: NOT TO SCALE

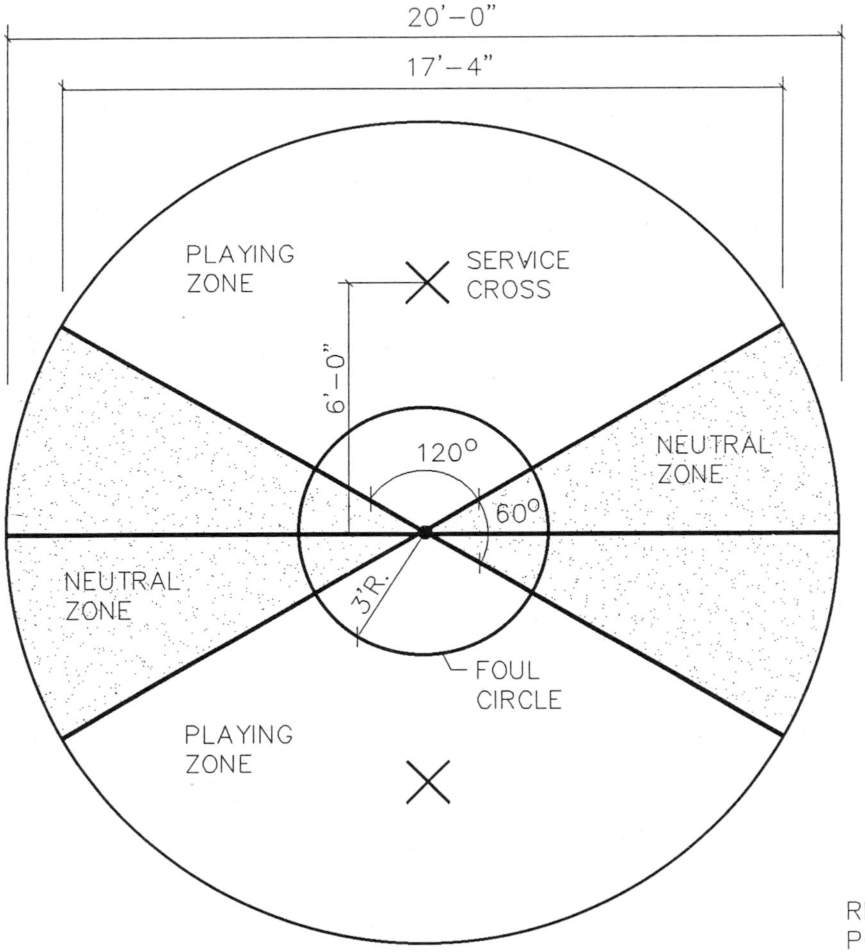

20'–0"
17'–4"
PLAYING ZONE
SERVICE CROSS
6'–0"
120°
60°
NEUTRAL ZONE
NEUTRAL ZONE
3'R.
FOUL CIRCLE
PLAYING ZONE

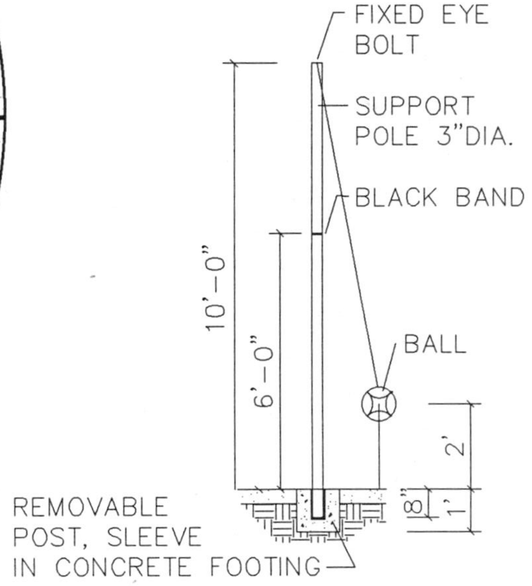

FIXED EYE BOLT
SUPPORT POLE 3"DIA.
BLACK BAND
10'–0"
6'–0"
BALL
2'
8"
1'
REMOVABLE POST, SLEEVE IN CONCRETE FOOTING

TETHERBALL

SCALE: NOT TO SCALE

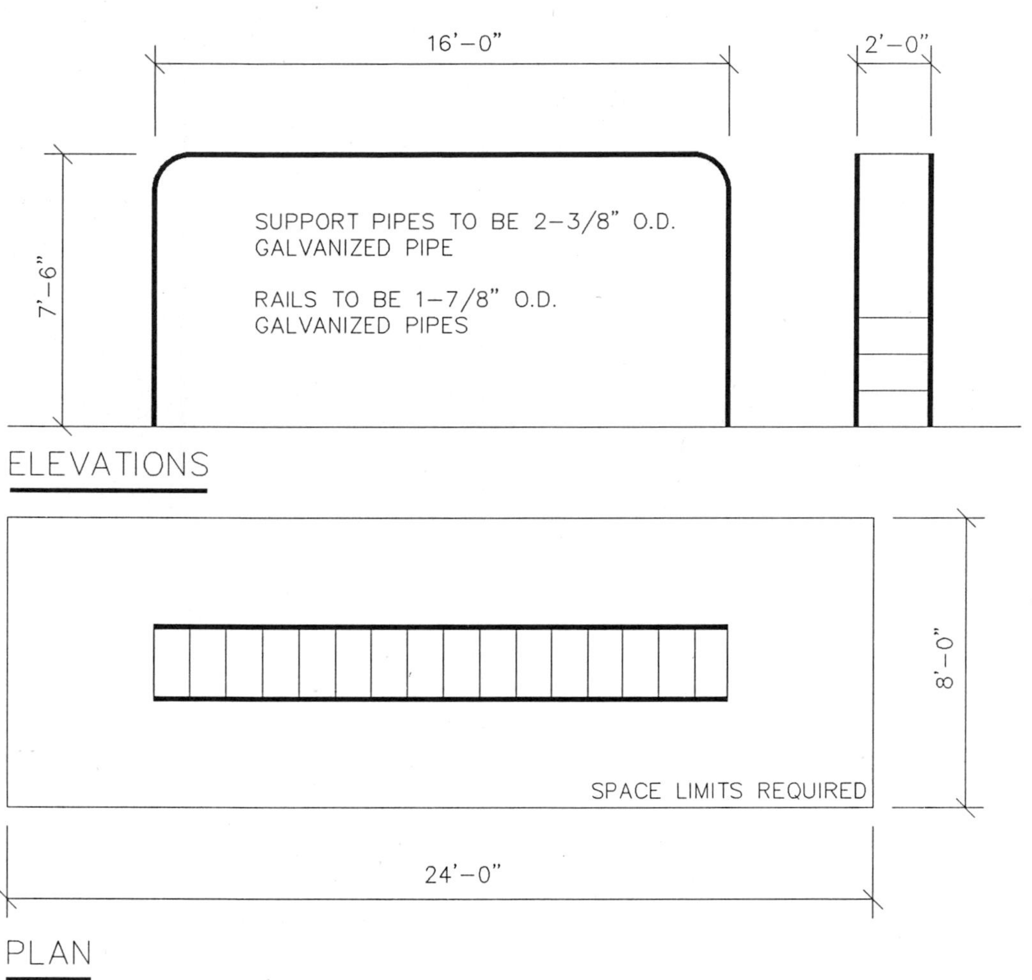
16'–0"
2'–0"
7'–6"
SUPPORT PIPES TO BE 2–3/8" O.D.
GALVANIZED PIPE
RAILS TO BE 1–7/8" O.D.
GALVANIZED PIPES
ELEVATIONS
8'–0"
SPACE LIMITS REQUIRED
24'–0"
PLAN

HORIZONTAL LADDER

SCALE: NOT TO SCALE

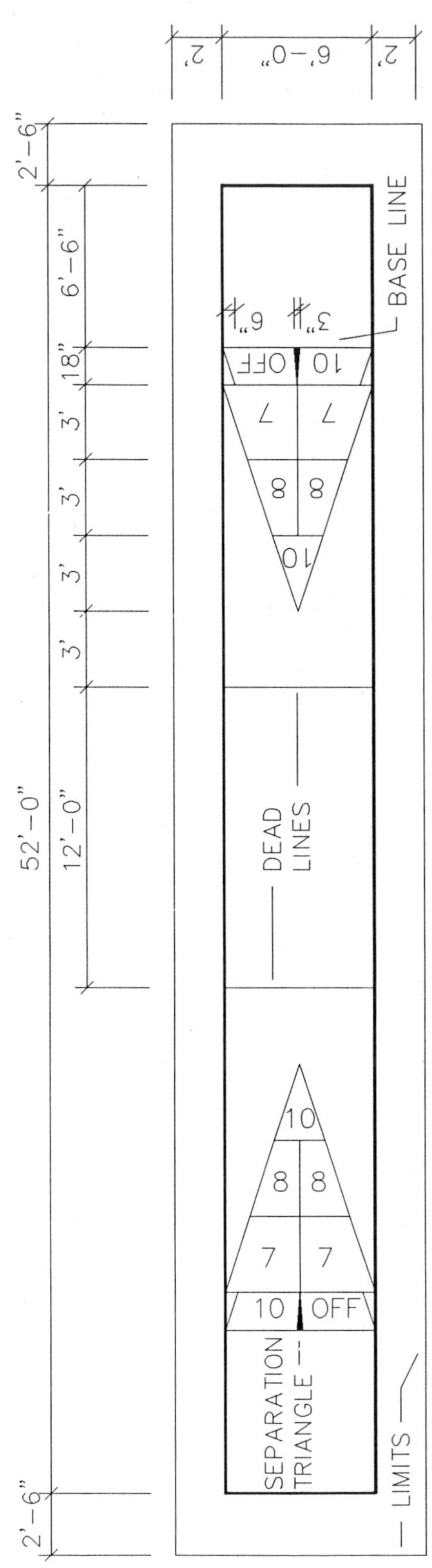
2'-6"
6'-6"
18"
3'
3'
3'
3'
12'-0"
52'-0"
2'-6"
2'
6'-0"
2'
BASE LINE
6"
3"
10
OFF
7
7
8
8
10
DEAD LINES
10
8
8
7
7
10
OFF
SEPARATION TRIANGLE
LIMITS

SHUFFLEBOARD

SCALE: NOT TO SCALE

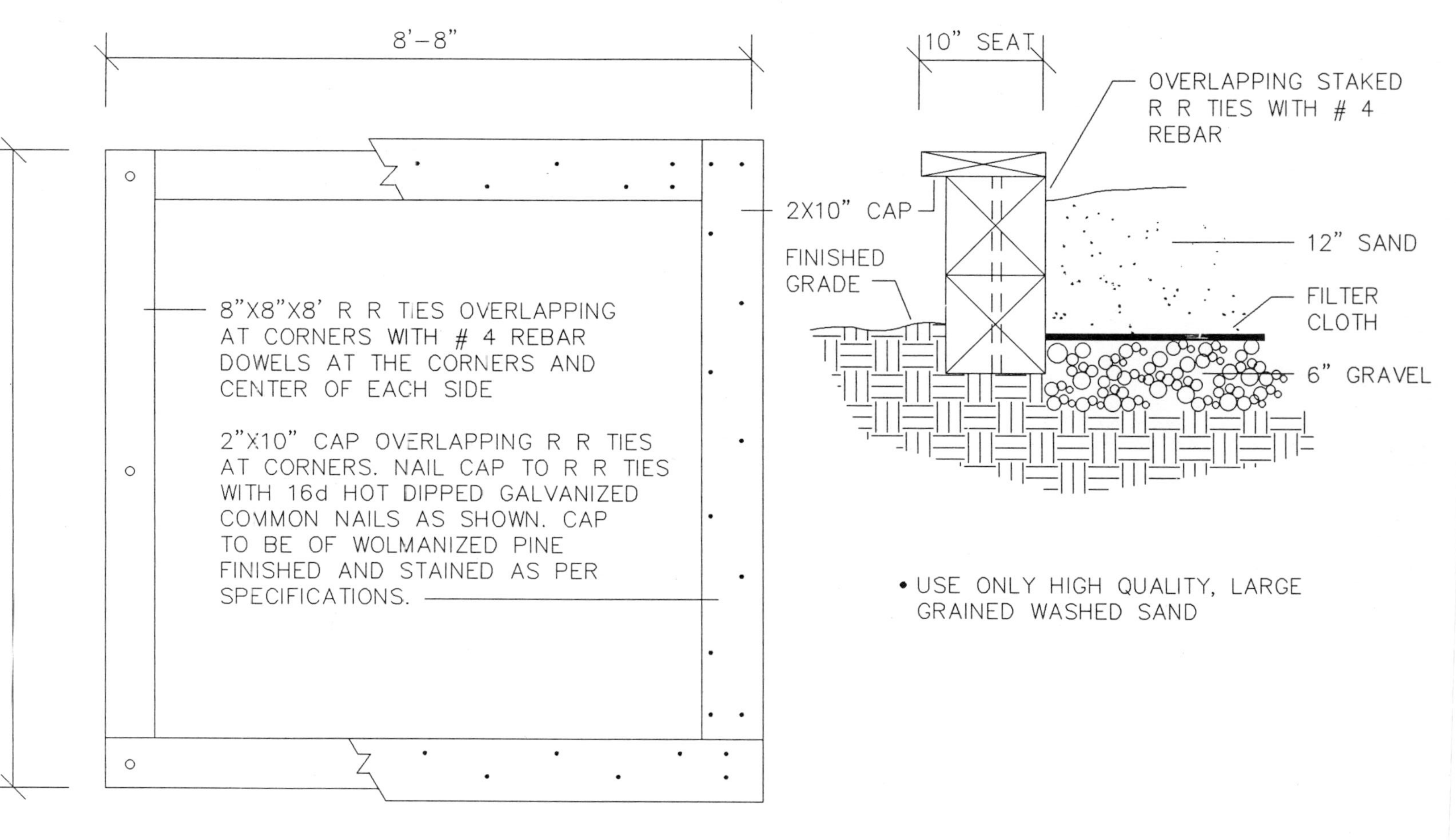
8'–8"
8'–8"
10" SEAT
OVERLAPPING STAKED R R TIES WITH # 4 REBAR
2X10" CAP
FINISHED GRADE
12" SAND
FILTER CLOTH
6" GRAVEL
8"X8"X8' R R TIES OVERLAPPING AT CORNERS WITH # 4 REBAR DOWELS AT THE CORNERS AND CENTER OF EACH SIDE
2"X10" CAP OVERLAPPING R R TIES AT CORNERS. NAIL CAP TO R R TIES WITH 16d HOT DIPPED GALVANIZED COMMON NAILS AS SHOWN. CAP TO BE OF WOLMANIZED PINE FINISHED AND STAINED AS PER SPECIFICATIONS.
• USE ONLY HIGH QUALITY, LARGE GRAINED WASHED SAND

SANDBOX

SCALE: NOT TO SCALE

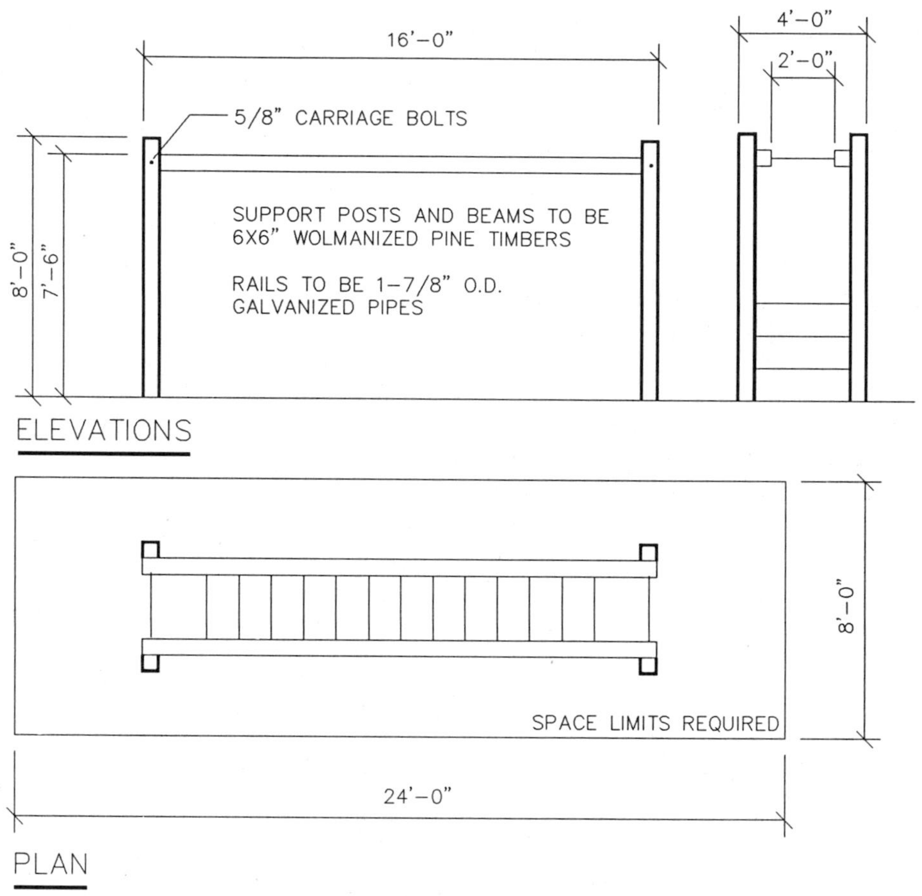

16'-0"
5/8" CARRIAGE BOLTS
SUPPORT POSTS AND BEAMS TO BE 6X6" WOLMANIZED PINE TIMBERS
RAILS TO BE 1-7/8" O.D. GALVANIZED PIPES
8'-0"
7'-6"
4'-0"
2'-0"
ELEVATIONS
8'-0"
SPACE LIMITS REQUIRED
24'-0"
PLAN

HORIZONTAL LADDER W/ WOOD POSTS

SCALE: NOT TO SCALE

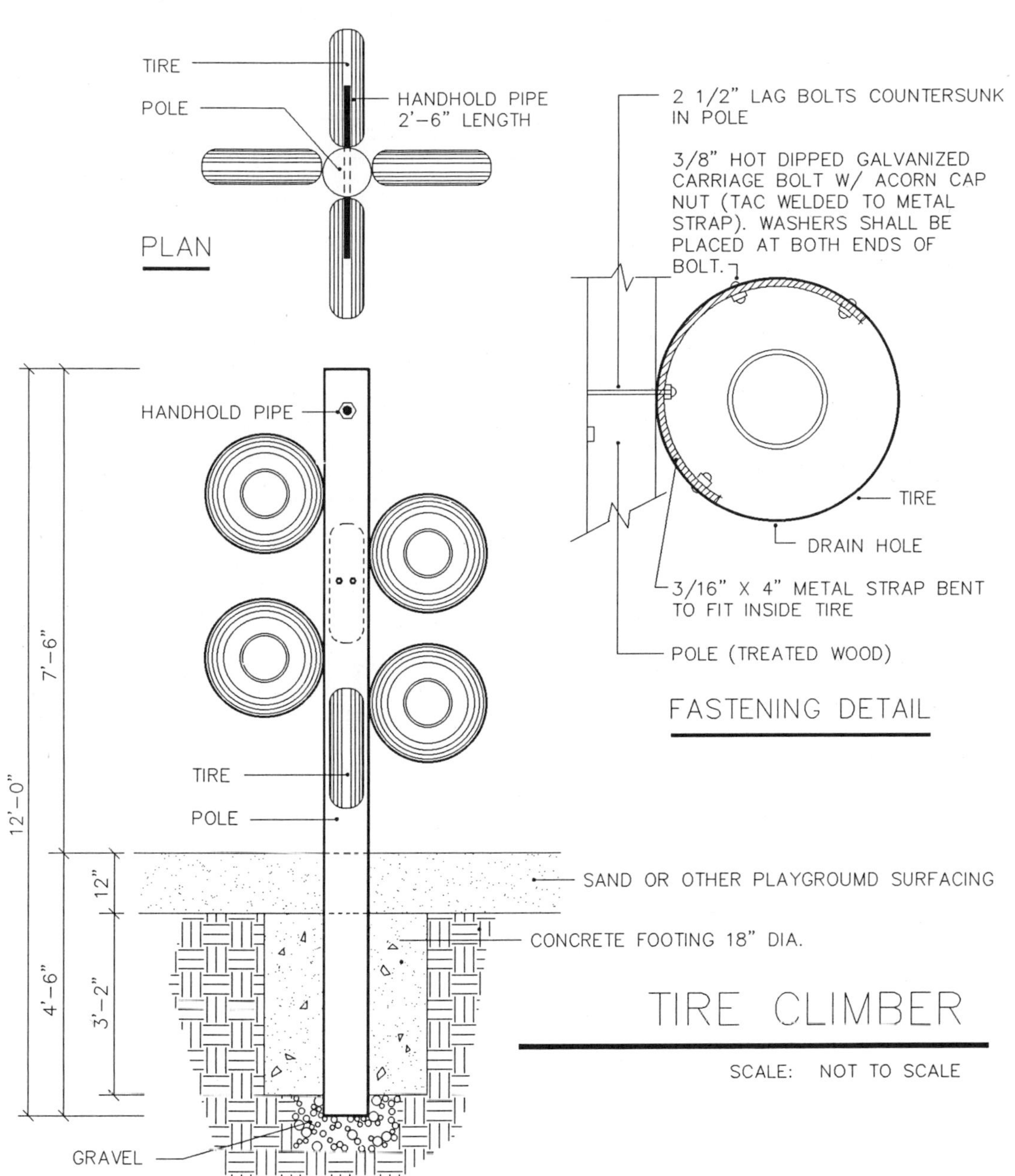
TIRE
POLE
HANDHOLD PIPE
2'–6" LENGTH
PLAN
2 1/2" LAG BOLTS COUNTERSUNK
IN POLE
3/8" HOT DIPPED GALVANIZED
CARRIAGE BOLT W/ ACORN CAP
NUT (TAC WELDED TO METAL
STRAP). WASHERS SHALL BE
PLACED AT BOTH ENDS OF
BOLT.
TIRE
DRAIN HOLE
3/16" X 4" METAL STRAP BENT
TO FIT INSIDE TIRE
POLE (TREATED WOOD)
FASTENING DETAIL
HANDHOLD PIPE
TIRE
POLE
12'–0"
7'–6"
12"
4'–6"
3'–2"
SAND OR OTHER PLAYGROUMD SURFACING
CONCRETE FOOTING 18" DIA.
GRAVEL
TIRE CLIMBER
SCALE: NOT TO SCALE

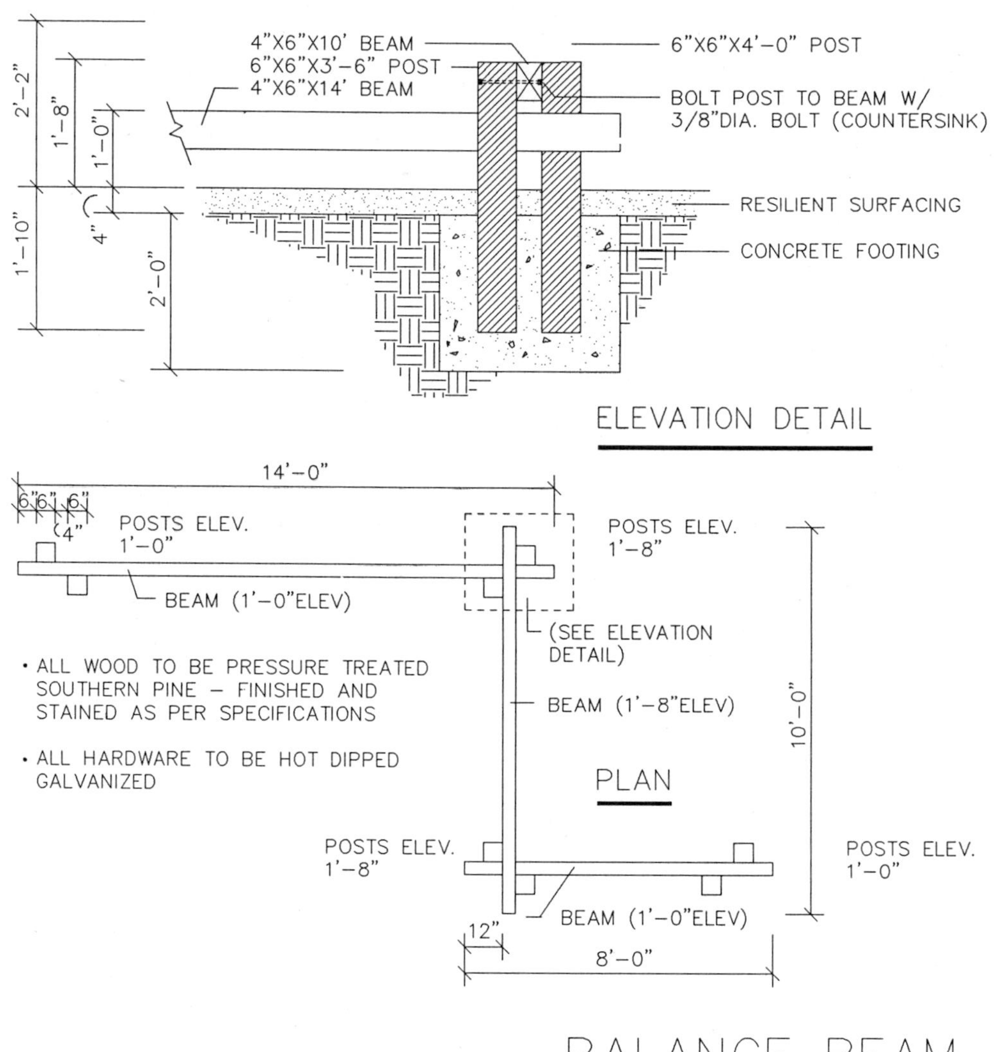
4"X6"X10' BEAM
6"X6"X3'-6" POST
4"X6"X14' BEAM
6"X6"X4'-0" POST
BOLT POST TO BEAM W/ 3/8"DIA. BOLT (COUNTERSINK)
RESILIENT SURFACING
CONCRETE FOOTING
2'-2"
1'-8"
1'-0"
1'-10"
4"
2'-0"
ELEVATION DETAIL
14'-0"
6" 6" 6"
4"
POSTS ELEV. 1'-0"
BEAM (1'-0"ELEV)
POSTS ELEV. 1'-8"
(SEE ELEVATION DETAIL)
• ALL WOOD TO BE PRESSURE TREATED SOUTHERN PINE – FINISHED AND STAINED AS PER SPECIFICATIONS
• ALL HARDWARE TO BE HOT DIPPED GALVANIZED
BEAM (1'-8"ELEV)
10'-0"
PLAN
POSTS ELEV. 1'-8"
POSTS ELEV. 1'-0"
BEAM (1'-0"ELEV)
12"
8'-0"

BALANCE BEAM

SCALE: NOT TO SCALE

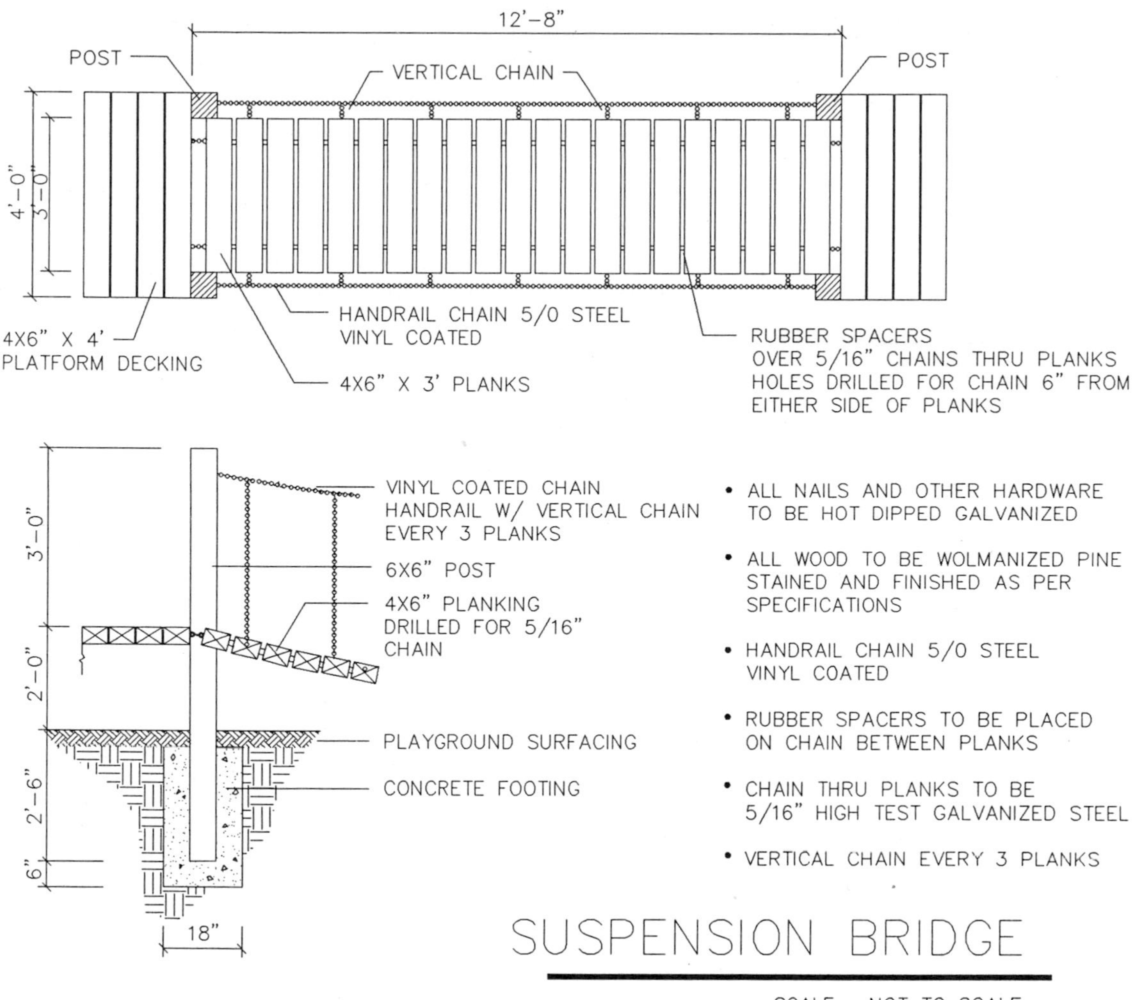
12'-8"
POST
VERTICAL CHAIN
POST
4'-0"
3'-0"
4X6" X 4'
PLATFORM DECKING
HANDRAIL CHAIN 5/0 STEEL
VINYL COATED
4X6" X 3' PLANKS
RUBBER SPACERS
OVER 5/16" CHAINS THRU PLANKS
HOLES DRILLED FOR CHAIN 6" FROM
EITHER SIDE OF PLANKS
3'-0"
2'-0"
2'-6"
6"
18"
VINYL COATED CHAIN
HANDRAIL W/ VERTICAL CHAIN
EVERY 3 PLANKS
6X6" POST
4X6" PLANKING
DRILLED FOR 5/16"
CHAIN
PLAYGROUND SURFACING
CONCRETE FOOTING
• ALL NAILS AND OTHER HARDWARE
TO BE HOT DIPPED GALVANIZED
• ALL WOOD TO BE WOLMANIZED PINE
STAINED AND FINISHED AS PER
SPECIFICATIONS
• HANDRAIL CHAIN 5/0 STEEL
VINYL COATED
• RUBBER SPACERS TO BE PLACED
ON CHAIN BETWEEN PLANKS
• CHAIN THRU PLANKS TO BE
5/16" HIGH TEST GALVANIZED STEEL
• VERTICAL CHAIN EVERY 3 PLANKS
SUSPENSION BRIDGE
SCALE: NOT TO SCALE

- ALL WOOD TO BE WOLMANIZED PINE STAINED AND FINISHED AS PER SPECIFICATIONS
- ALL HARDWARE TO BE HOT DIPPED GALVANIZED
- HANDRAILS AND TIE ROD THRU DECKING AND POSTS TO BE 1–5/16" O.D. HIGH-STRENGTH GALVAINZED STEEL PIPE THREADED AND ATTACHED TO THE POSTS WITH WASHER AND BOLTS (COUNTERSUNK)
- HANDRAIL LOCATIONS AND HEIGHTS OF POSTS AND DECK ELEVATIONS SHALL BE AS INDICATED ON PLANS

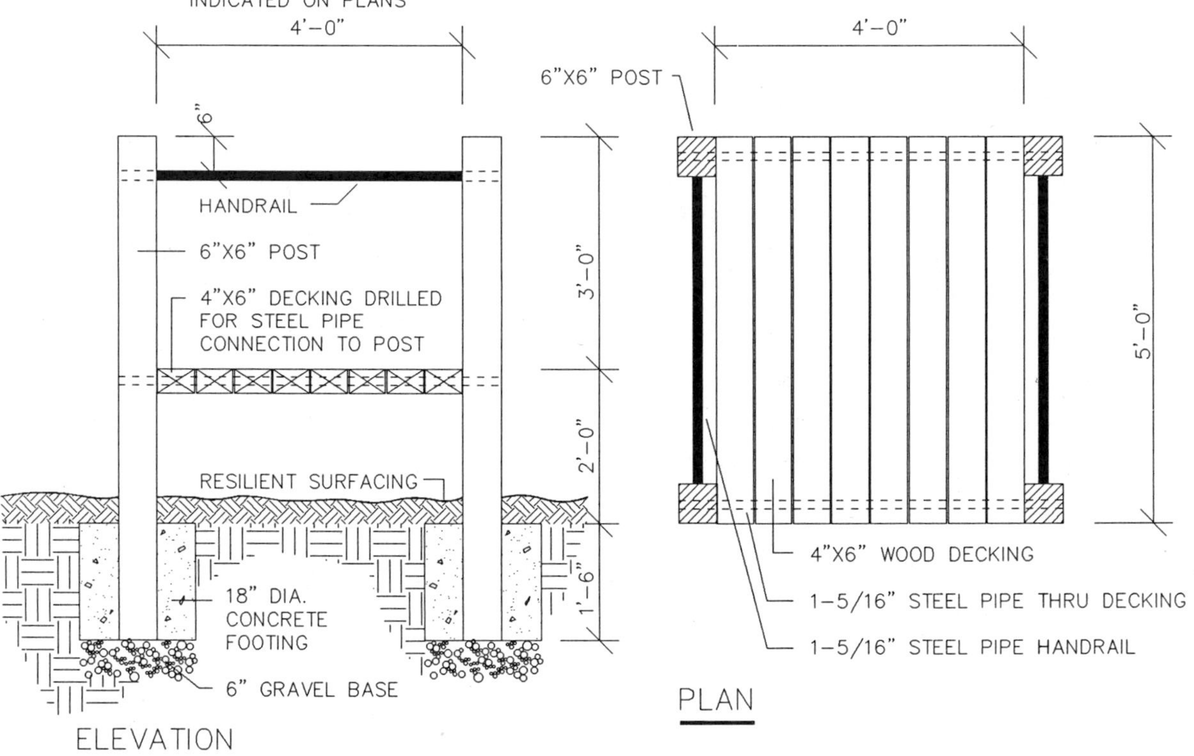
4'–0"
6"
HANDRAIL
6"X6" POST
4"X6" DECKING DRILLED FOR STEEL PIPE CONNECTION TO POST
3'–0"
2'–0"
1'–6"
RESILIENT SURFACING
18" DIA. CONCRETE FOOTING
6" GRAVEL BASE
ELEVATION
4'–0"
6"X6" POST
5'–0"
4"X6" WOOD DECKING
1–5/16" STEEL PIPE THRU DECKING
1–5/16" STEEL PIPE HANDRAIL
PLAN

4' X 5' PLATFORM MODULE

SCALE: NOT TO SCALE

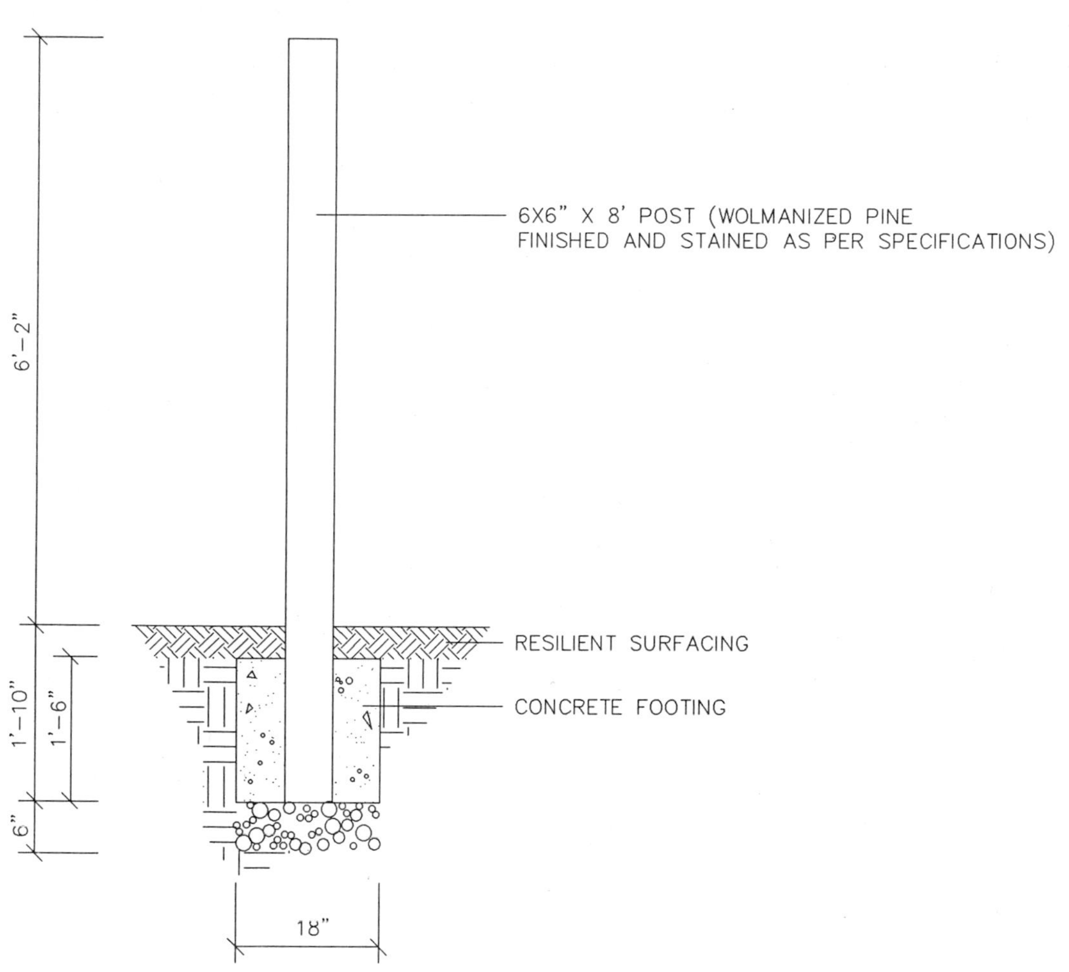

6X6" X 8' POST (WOLMANIZED PINE
FINISHED AND STAINED AS PER SPECIFICATIONS)
RESILIENT SURFACING
CONCRETE FOOTING
6'-2"
1'-10"
1'-6"
6"
18"

STRETCHING POST

SCALE: NOT TO SCALE

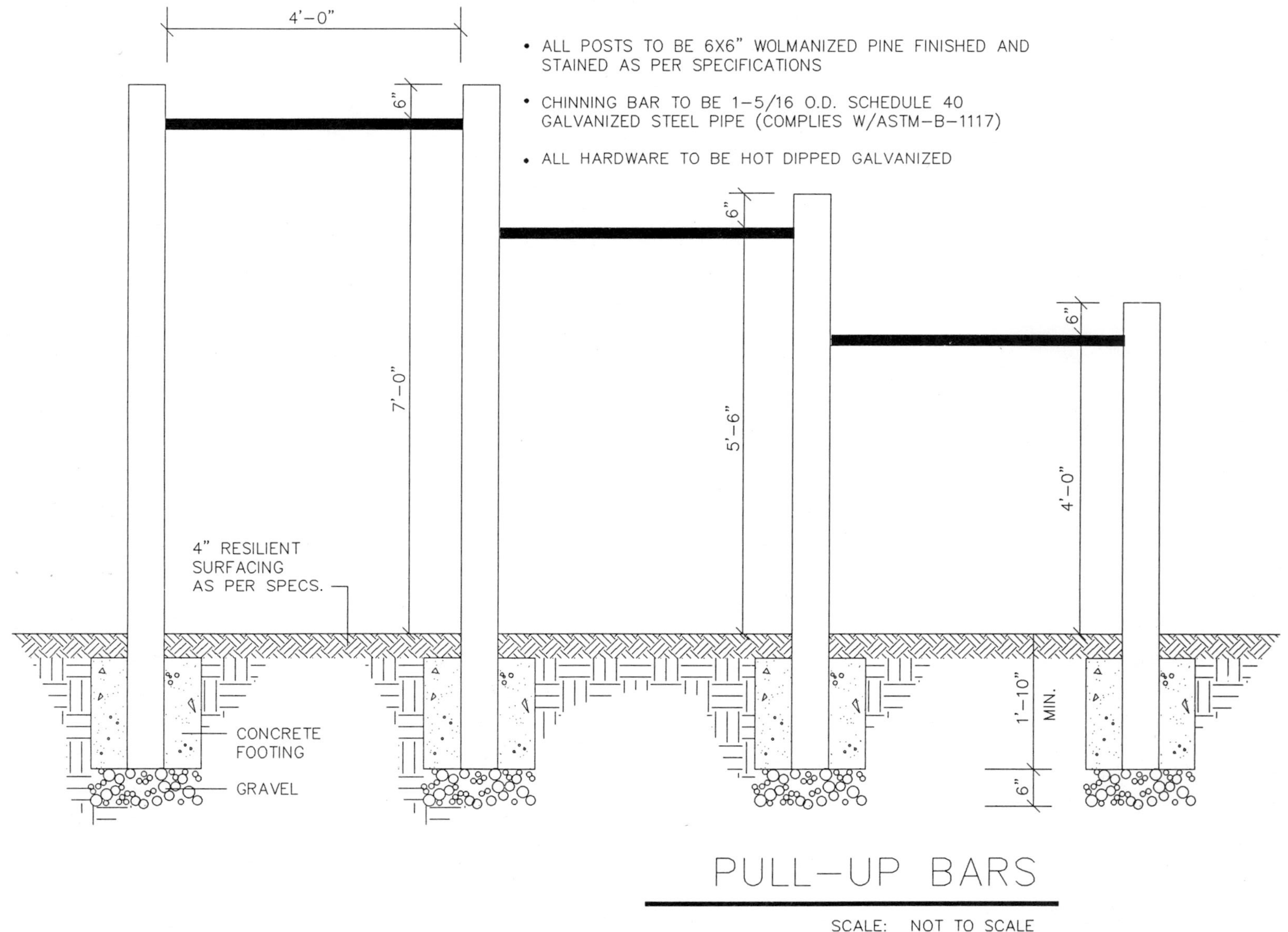
4'-0"
6"
7'-0"
6"
5'-6"
6"
4'-0"
1'-10"
MIN.
6"
4" RESILIENT
SURFACING
AS PER SPECS.
CONCRETE
FOOTING
GRAVEL

- ALL POSTS TO BE 6X6" WOLMANIZED PINE FINISHED AND STAINED AS PER SPECIFICATIONS
- CHINNING BAR TO BE 1-5/16 O.D. SCHEDULE 40 GALVANIZED STEEL PIPE (COMPLIES W/ASTM-B-1117)
- ALL HARDWARE TO BE HOT DIPPED GALVANIZED

PULL-UP BARS

SCALE: NOT TO SCALE

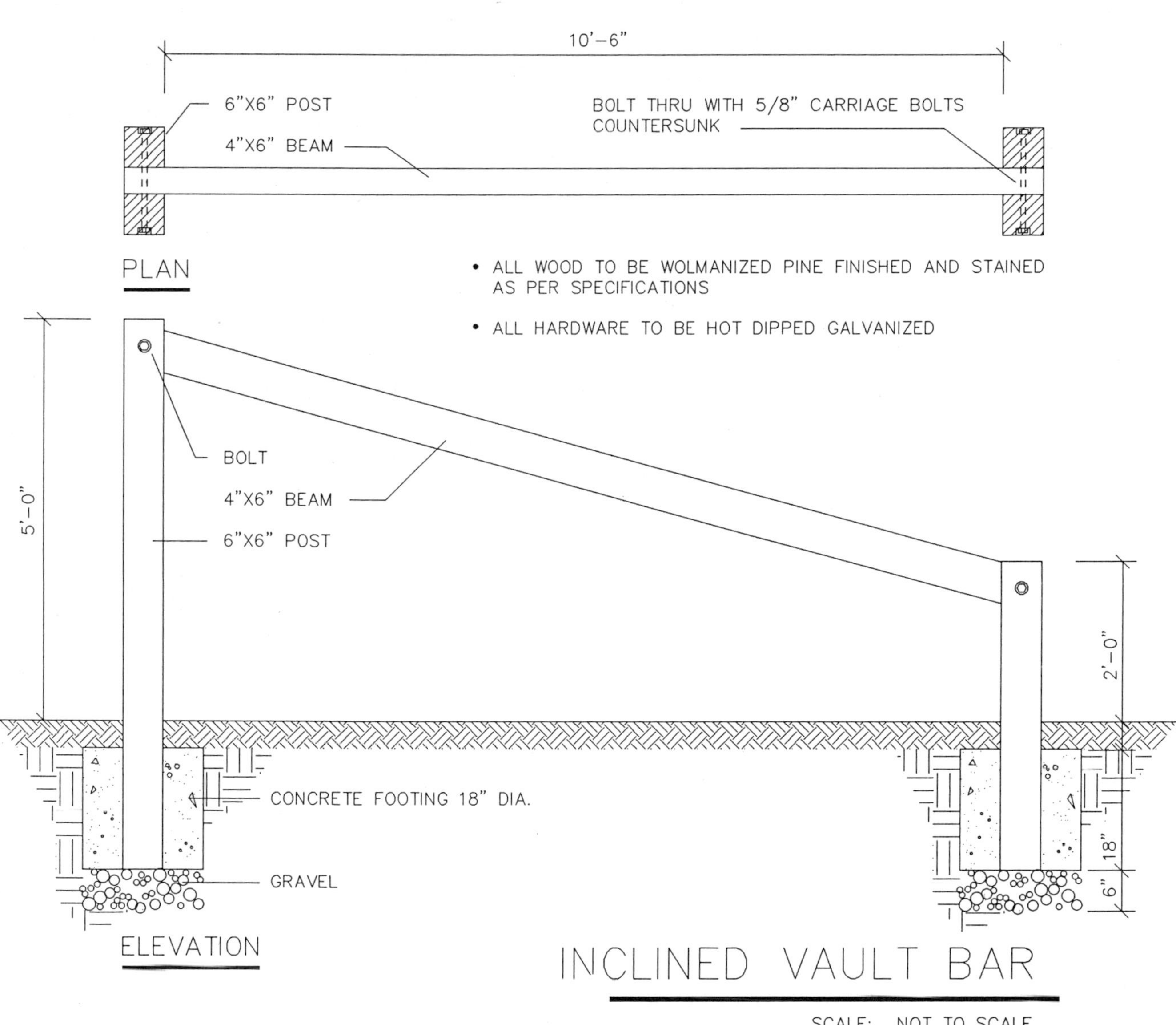
10'–6"
6"X6" POST
4"X6" BEAM
BOLT THRU WITH 5/8" CARRIAGE BOLTS
COUNTERSUNK
PLAN
• ALL WOOD TO BE WOLMANIZED PINE FINISHED AND STAINED AS PER SPECIFICATIONS
• ALL HARDWARE TO BE HOT DIPPED GALVANIZED
5'–0"
BOLT
4"X6" BEAM
6"X6" POST
2'–0"
CONCRETE FOOTING 18" DIA.
GRAVEL
18"
6"
ELEVATION

INCLINED VAULT BAR

SCALE: NOT TO SCALE

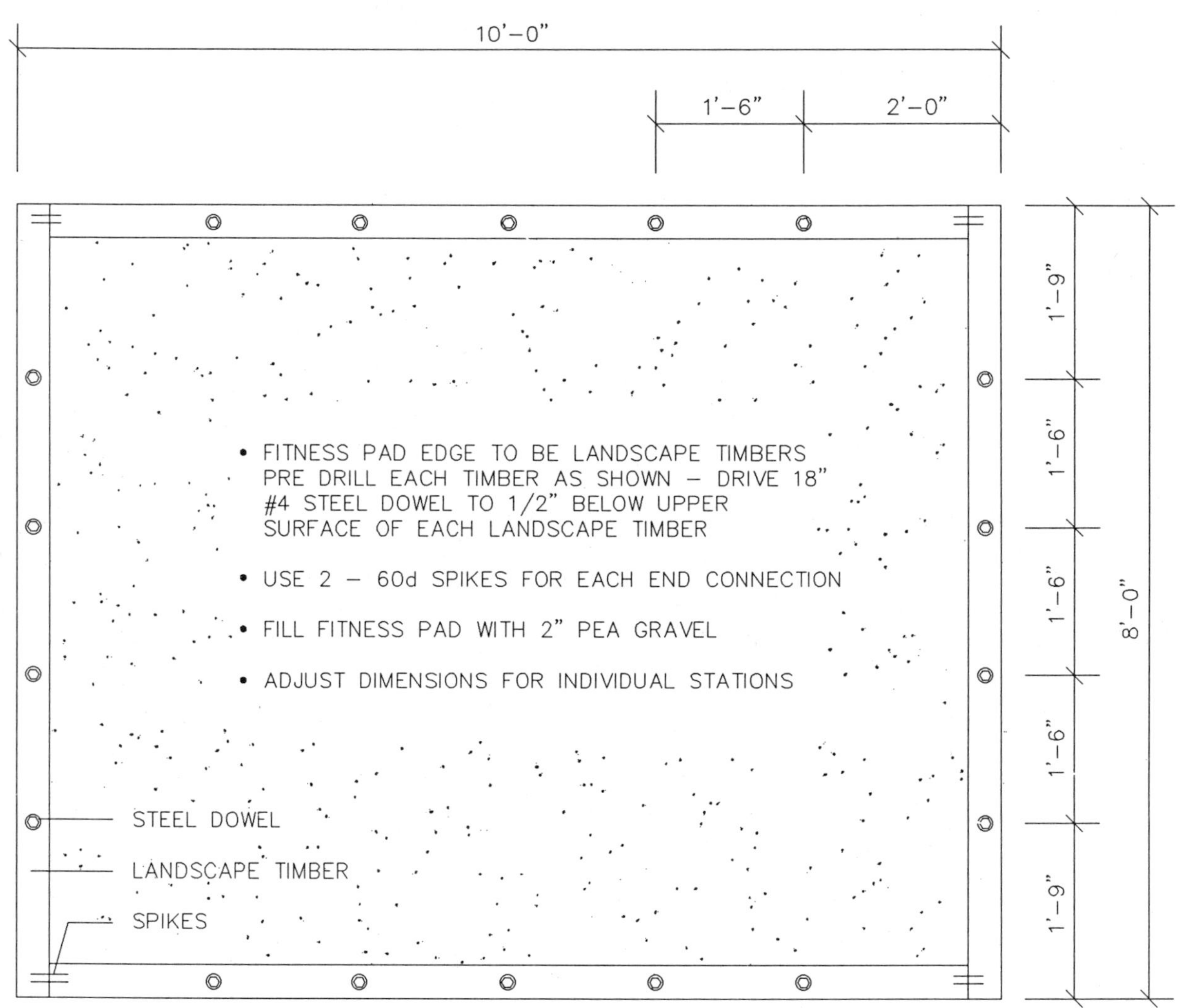
10'–0"
1'–6"
2'–0"
1'–9"
1'–6"
1'–6"
1'–6"
1'–9"
8'–0"
• FITNESS PAD EDGE TO BE LANDSCAPE TIMBERS PRE DRILL EACH TIMBER AS SHOWN – DRIVE 18" #4 STEEL DOWEL TO 1/2" BELOW UPPER SURFACE OF EACH LANDSCAPE TIMBER
• USE 2 – 60d SPIKES FOR EACH END CONNECTION
• FILL FITNESS PAD WITH 2" PEA GRAVEL
• ADJUST DIMENSIONS FOR INDIVIDUAL STATIONS
STEEL DOWEL
LANDSCAPE TIMBER
SPIKES

FITNESS COURSE PAD

SCALE: NOT TO SCALE

- ALL TIMBERS TO BE 6"X6"X5' WOLMANIZED PINE FINISHED AND STAINED AS PER SPECIFICATIONS
- PREDRILL EACH TIMBER AS SHOWN DRIVE 2' #4 STEEL DOWEL TO 1/2" BELOW UPPER SURFACE OF EACH PINE MEMBER
- ALL HARDWARE TO BE HOT DIPPED GALVANIZED

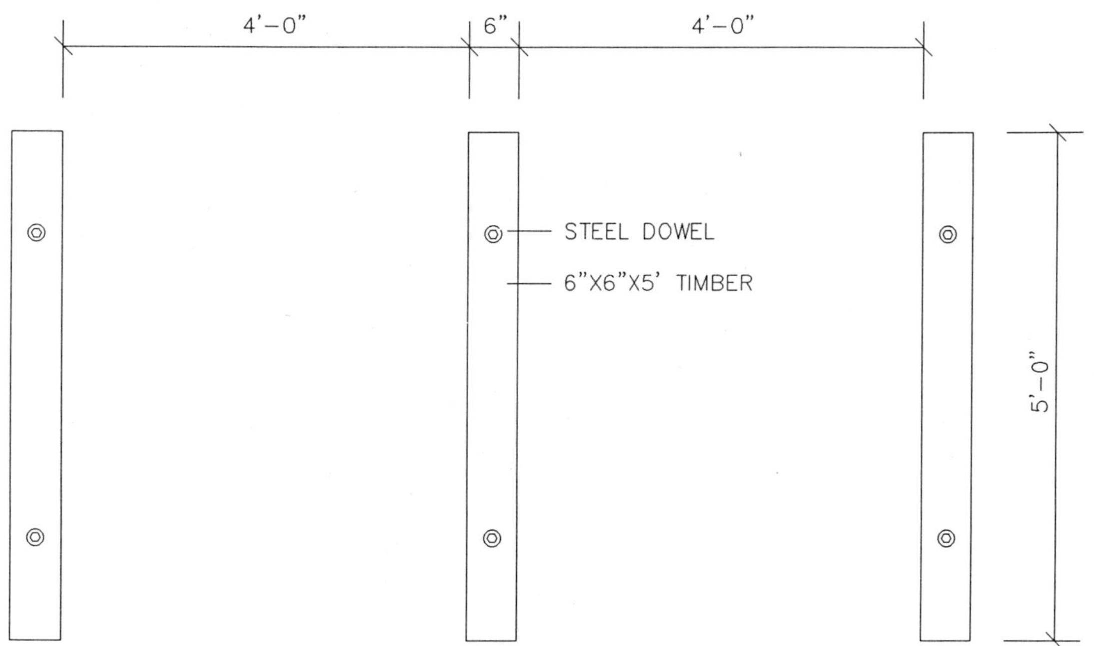

4'–0"
6"
4'–0"
STEEL DOWEL
6"X6"X5' TIMBER
5'–0"

LOG JUMP

SCALE: NOT TO SCALE

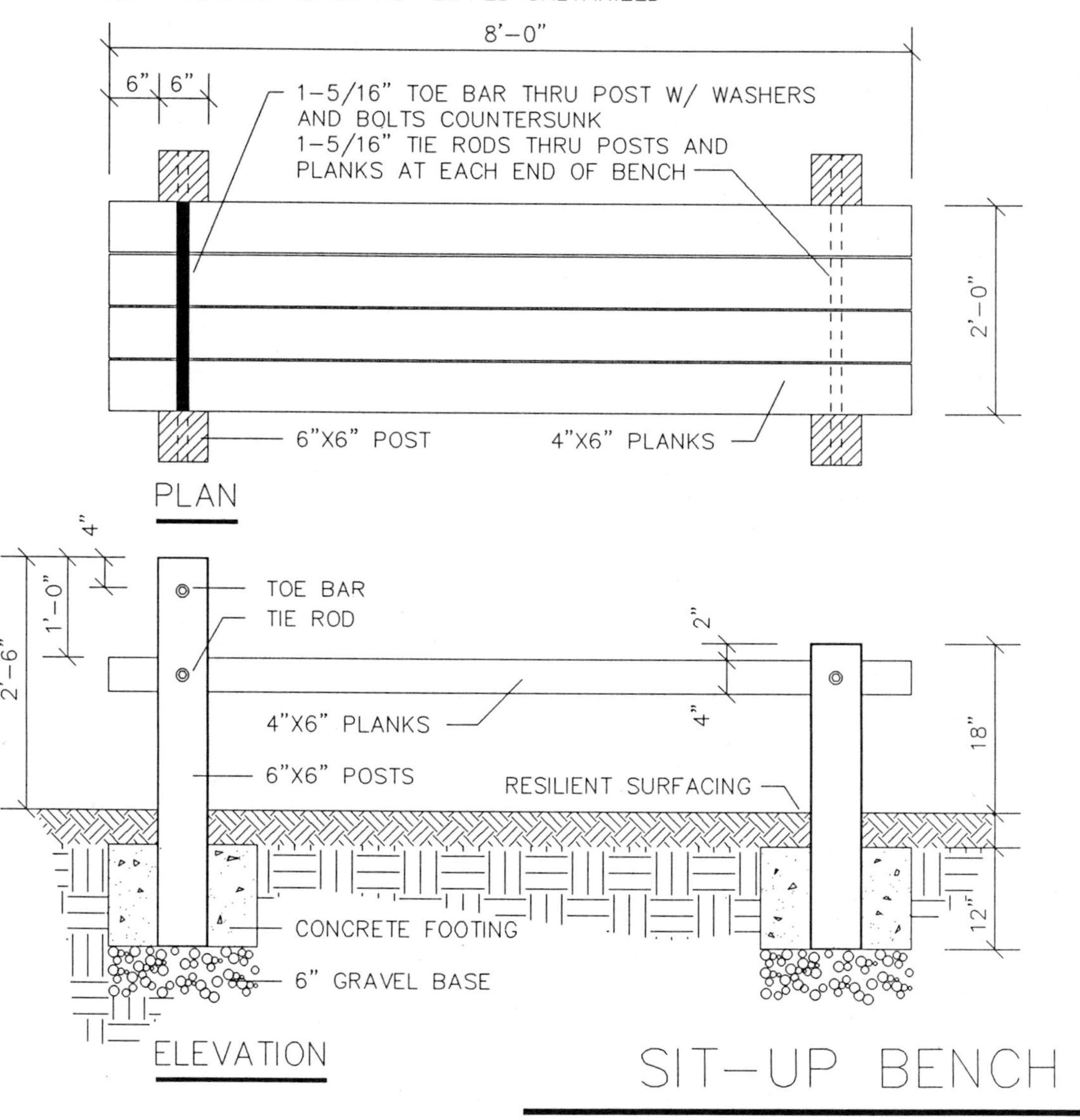
• ALL WOOD TO BE WOLMANIZED PINE FINISHED AND STAINED AS PER SPECIFICATIONS
• ALL HARDWARE TO BE HOT DIPPED GALVANIZED
8'-0"
6"
6"
1-5/16" TOE BAR THRU POST W/ WASHERS AND BOLTS COUNTERSUNK
1-5/16" TIE RODS THRU POSTS AND PLANKS AT EACH END OF BENCH
2'-0"
6"X6" POST
4"X6" PLANKS
PLAN
4"
1'-0"
2'-6"
TOE BAR
TIE ROD
2"
4"
4"X6" PLANKS
6"X6" POSTS
RESILIENT SURFACING
18"
CONCRETE FOOTING
12"
6" GRAVEL BASE
ELEVATION
SIT-UP BENCH
SCALE: NOT TO SCALE

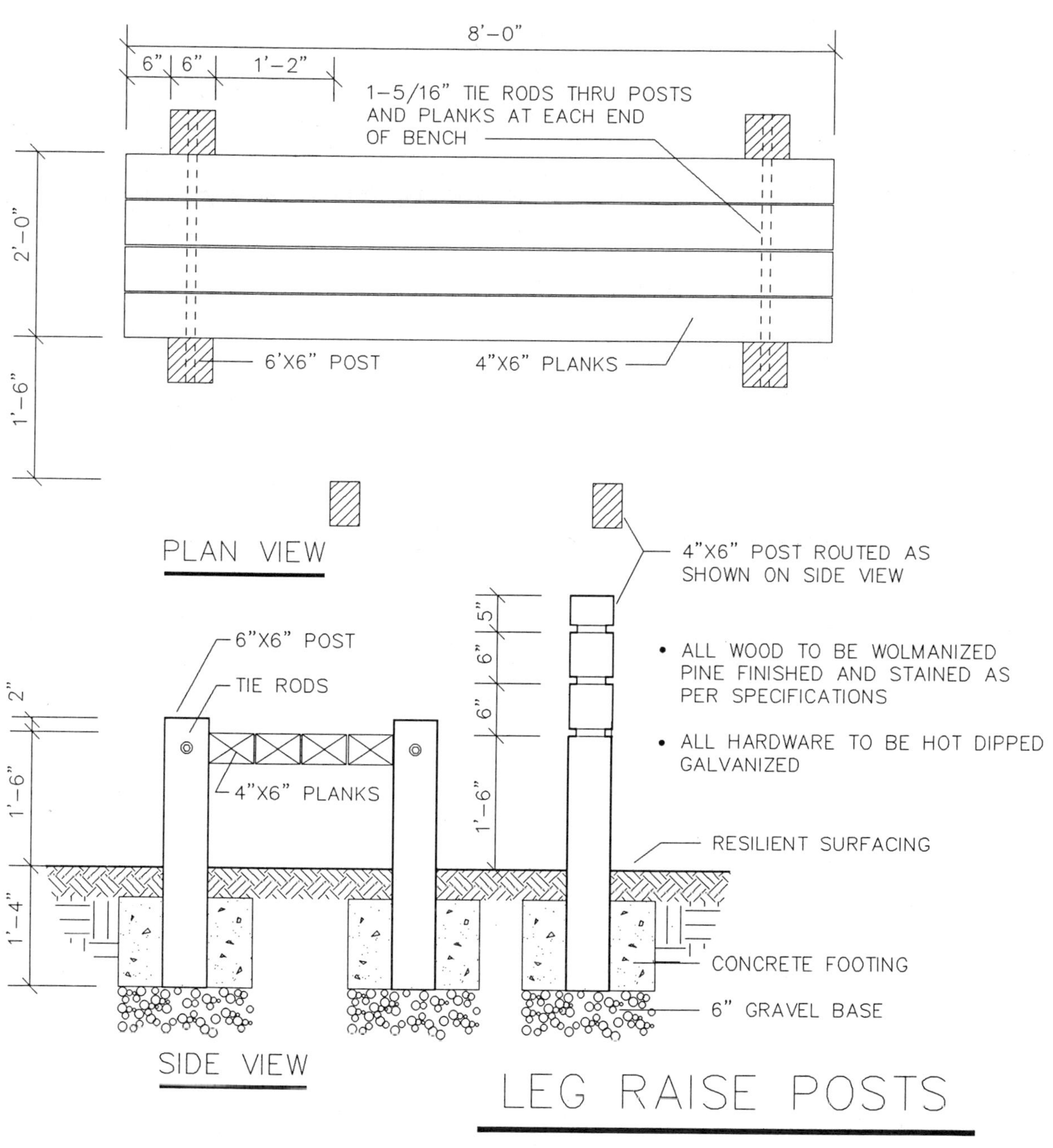
8'–0"
6"
6"
1'–2"
1–5/16" TIE RODS THRU POSTS AND PLANKS AT EACH END OF BENCH
2'–0"
1'–6"
6'X6" POST
4"X6" PLANKS
PLAN VIEW
4"X6" POST ROUTED AS SHOWN ON SIDE VIEW
5"
6"
6"
1'–6"
• ALL WOOD TO BE WOLMANIZED PINE FINISHED AND STAINED AS PER SPECIFICATIONS
• ALL HARDWARE TO BE HOT DIPPED GALVANIZED
6"X6" POST
TIE RODS
2"
1'–6"
4"X6" PLANKS
RESILIENT SURFACING
1'–4"
CONCRETE FOOTING
6" GRAVEL BASE
SIDE VIEW

LEG RAISE POSTS

SCALE: NOT TO SCALE

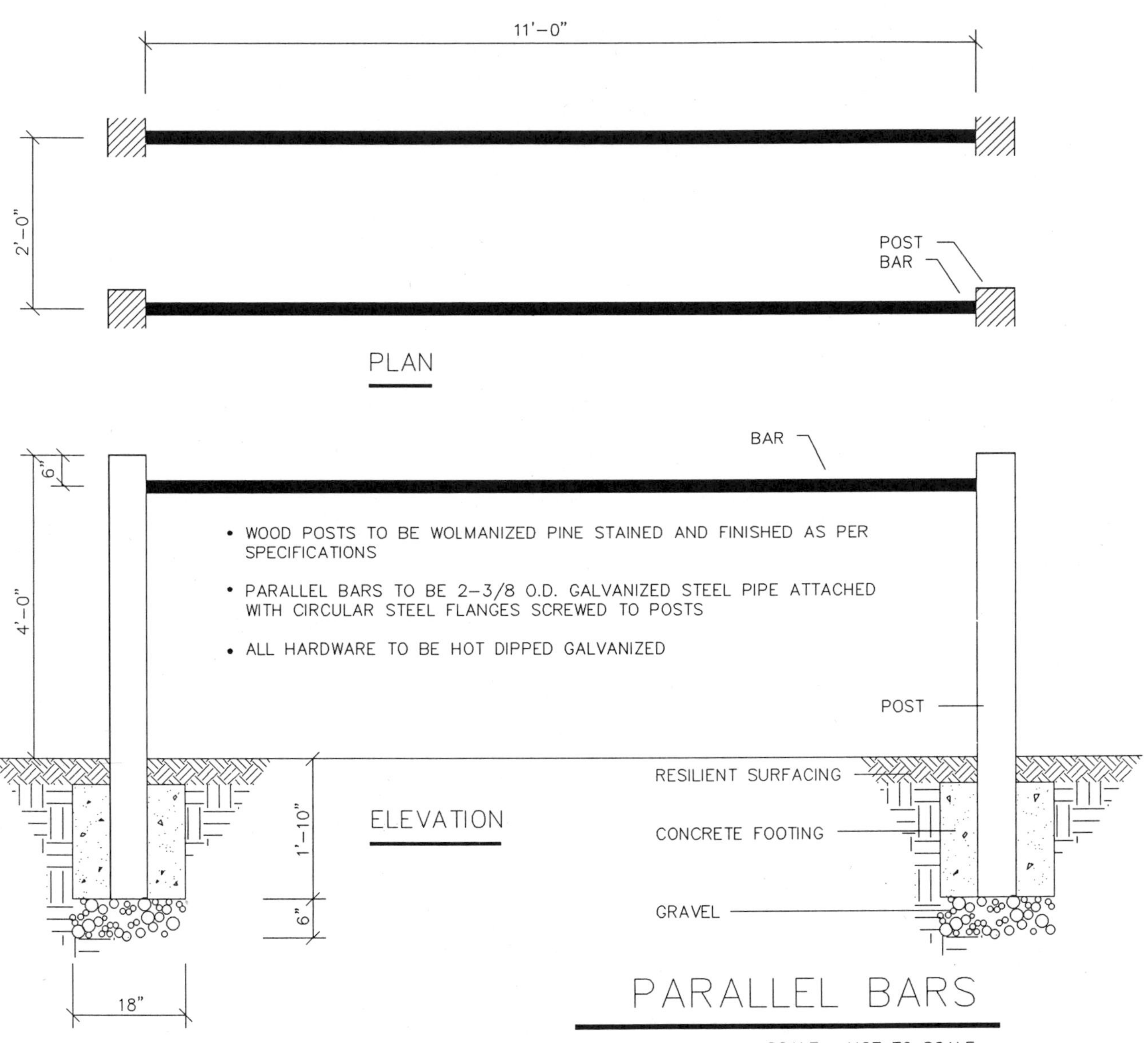
11'-0"
2'-0"
POST
BAR
PLAN
BAR
6"
4'-0"
• WOOD POSTS TO BE WOLMANIZED PINE STAINED AND FINISHED AS PER SPECIFICATIONS
• PARALLEL BARS TO BE 2-3/8 O.D. GALVANIZED STEEL PIPE ATTACHED WITH CIRCULAR STEEL FLANGES SCREWED TO POSTS
• ALL HARDWARE TO BE HOT DIPPED GALVANIZED
POST
RESILIENT SURFACING
1'-10"
ELEVATION
CONCRETE FOOTING
6"
GRAVEL
18"

PARALLEL BARS

SCALE: NOT TO SCALE

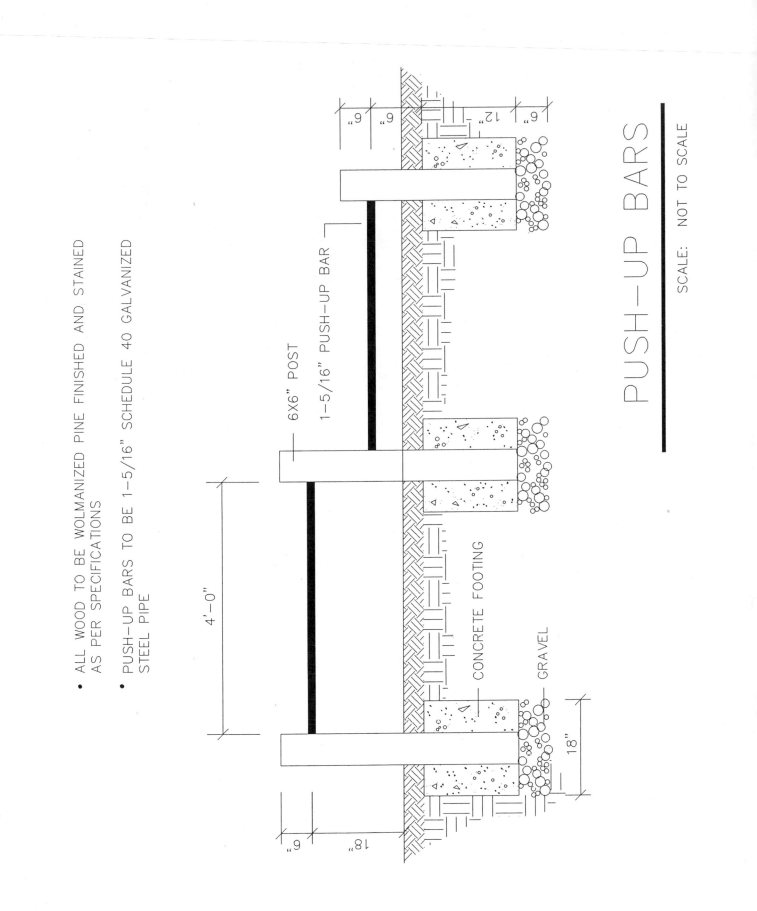

- ALL WOOD TO BE WOLMANIZED PINE FINISHED AND STAINED AS PER SPECIFICATIONS
- PUSH-UP BARS TO BE 1-5/16" SCHEDULE 40 GALVANIZED STEEL PIPE

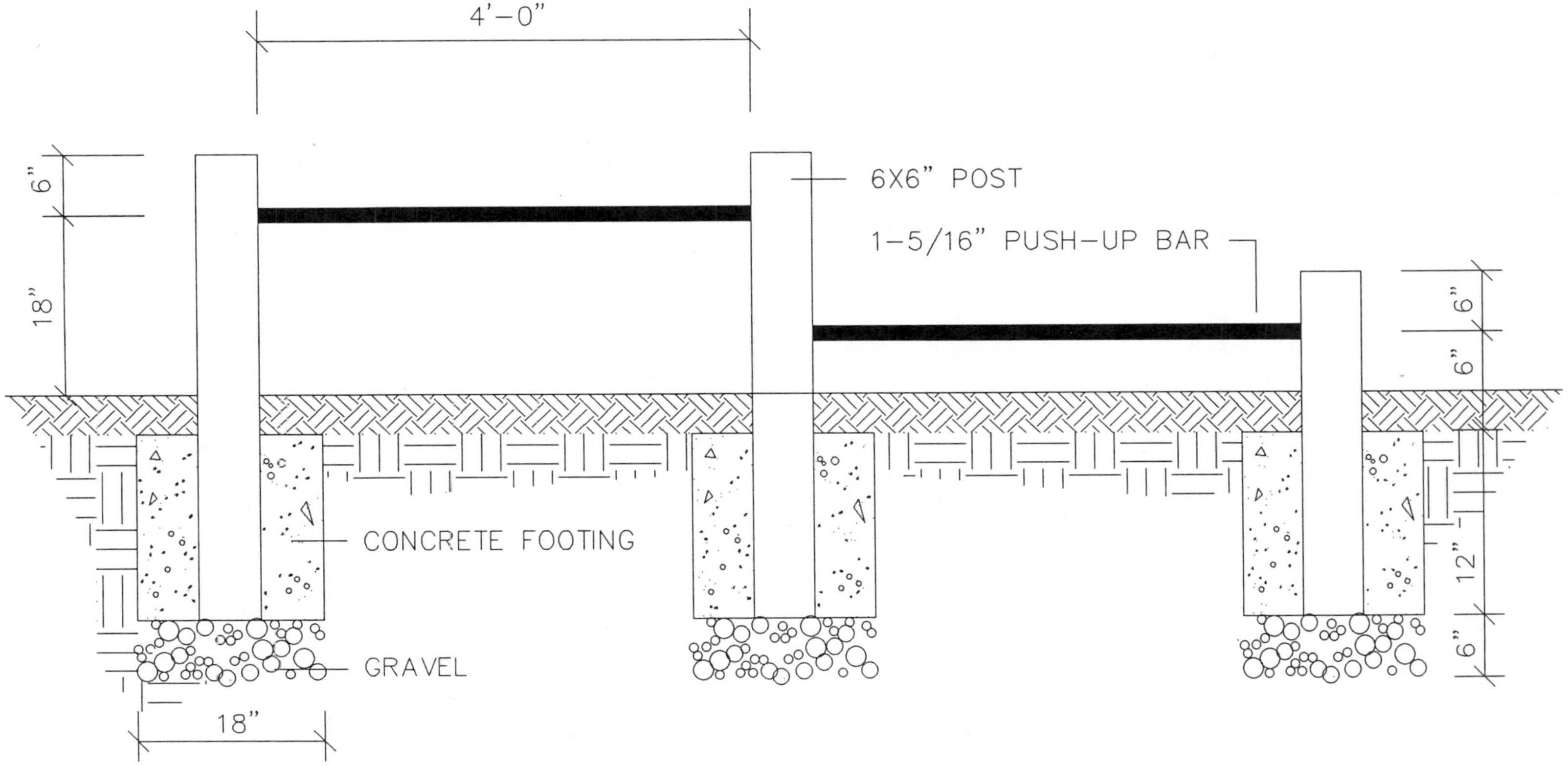

4'-0"

6X6" POST

1-5/16" PUSH-UP BAR

6"

18"

6"

6"

12"

6"

CONCRETE FOOTING

GRAVEL

18"

PUSH-UP BARS

SCALE: NOT TO SCALE

- ALL STEP UP POSTS TO BE 8"X8" WOLMANIZED PINE FINISHED AND STAINED AS PER SPECIFICATIONS

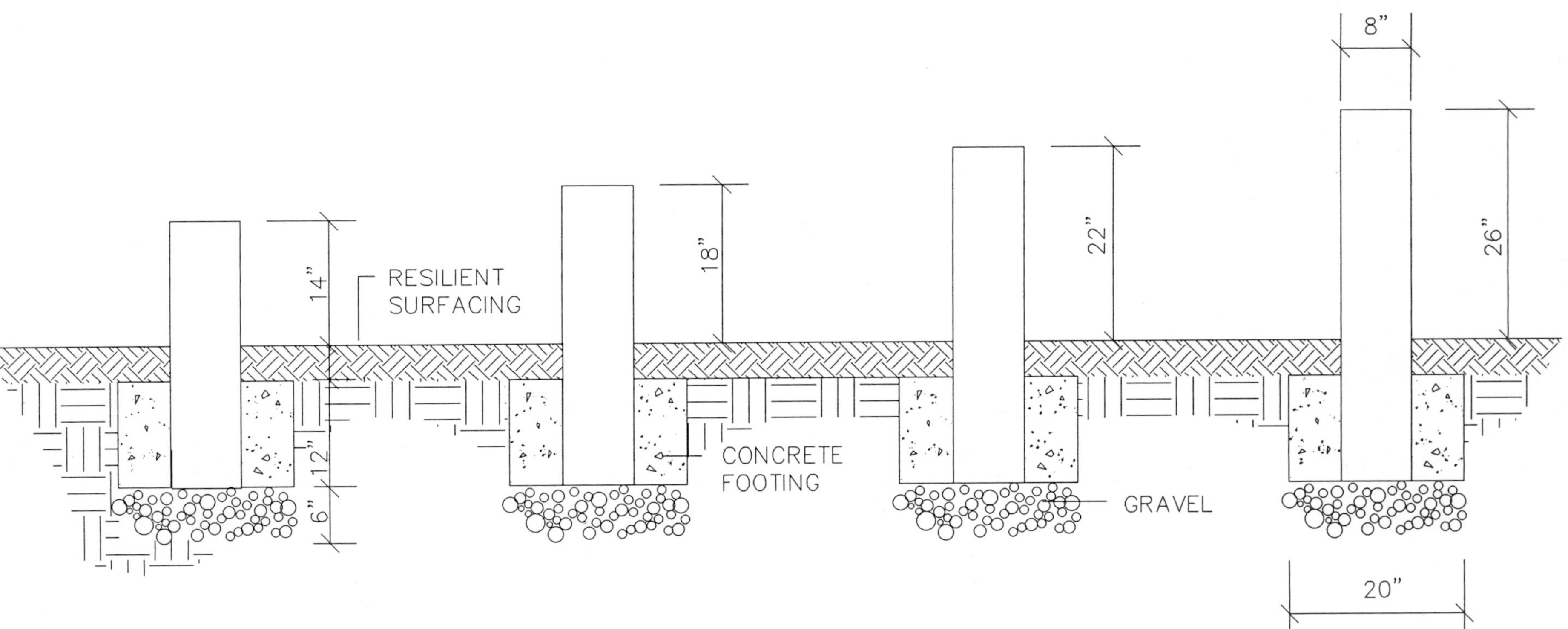

8"
14"
RESILIENT
SURFACING
18"
22"
26"
12"
6"
CONCRETE
FOOTING
GRAVEL
20"

STEP—UP BLOCKS

SCALE: NOT TO SCALE

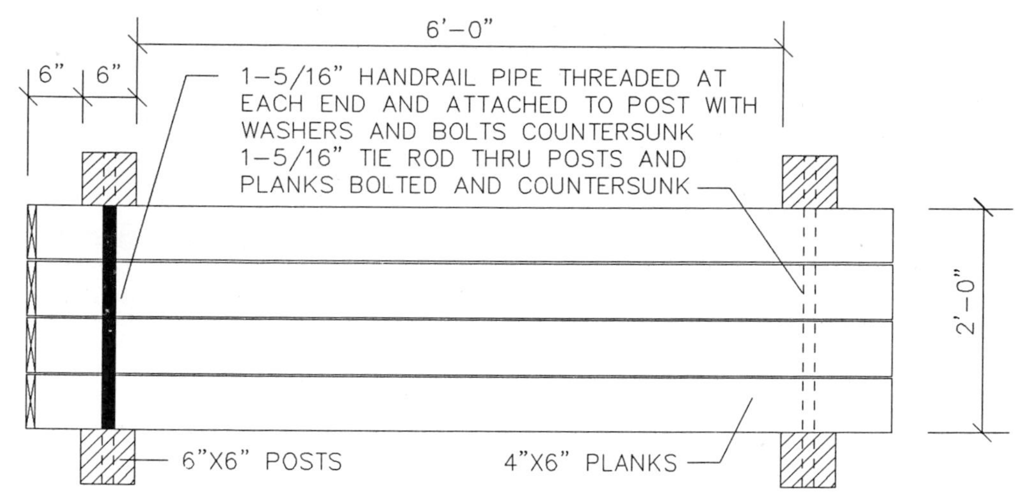
6'–0"
6"
6"
1–5/16" HANDRAIL PIPE THREADED AT EACH END AND ATTACHED TO POST WITH WASHERS AND BOLTS COUNTERSUNK
1–5/16" TIE ROD THRU POSTS AND PLANKS BOLTED AND COUNTERSUNK
2'–0"
6"X6" POSTS
4"X6" PLANKS

PLAN

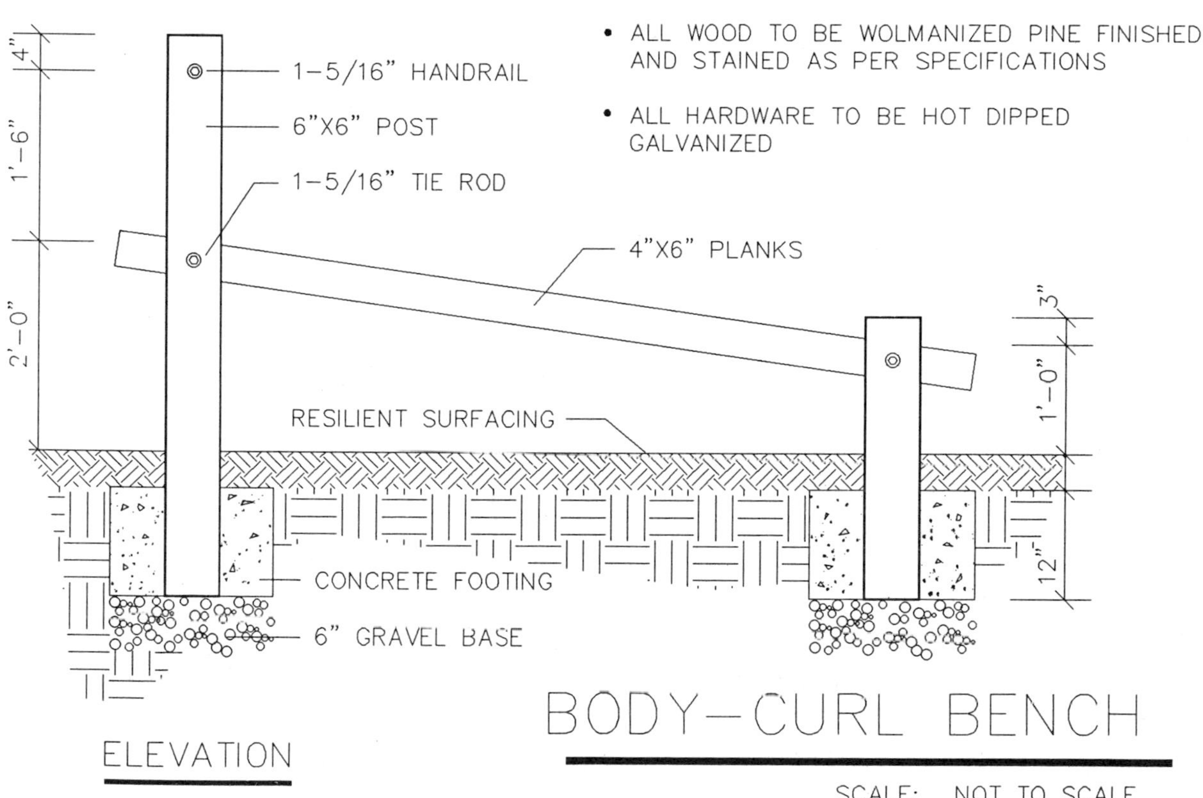
4"
1'–6"
2'–0"
1–5/16" HANDRAIL
6"X6" POST
1–5/16" TIE ROD
4"X6" PLANKS
3"
1'–0"
12"
RESILIENT SURFACING
CONCRETE FOOTING
6" GRAVEL BASE

- ALL WOOD TO BE WOLMANIZED PINE FINISHED AND STAINED AS PER SPECIFICATIONS
- ALL HARDWARE TO BE HOT DIPPED GALVANIZED

ELEVATION

BODY–CURL BENCH

SCALE: NOT TO SCALE

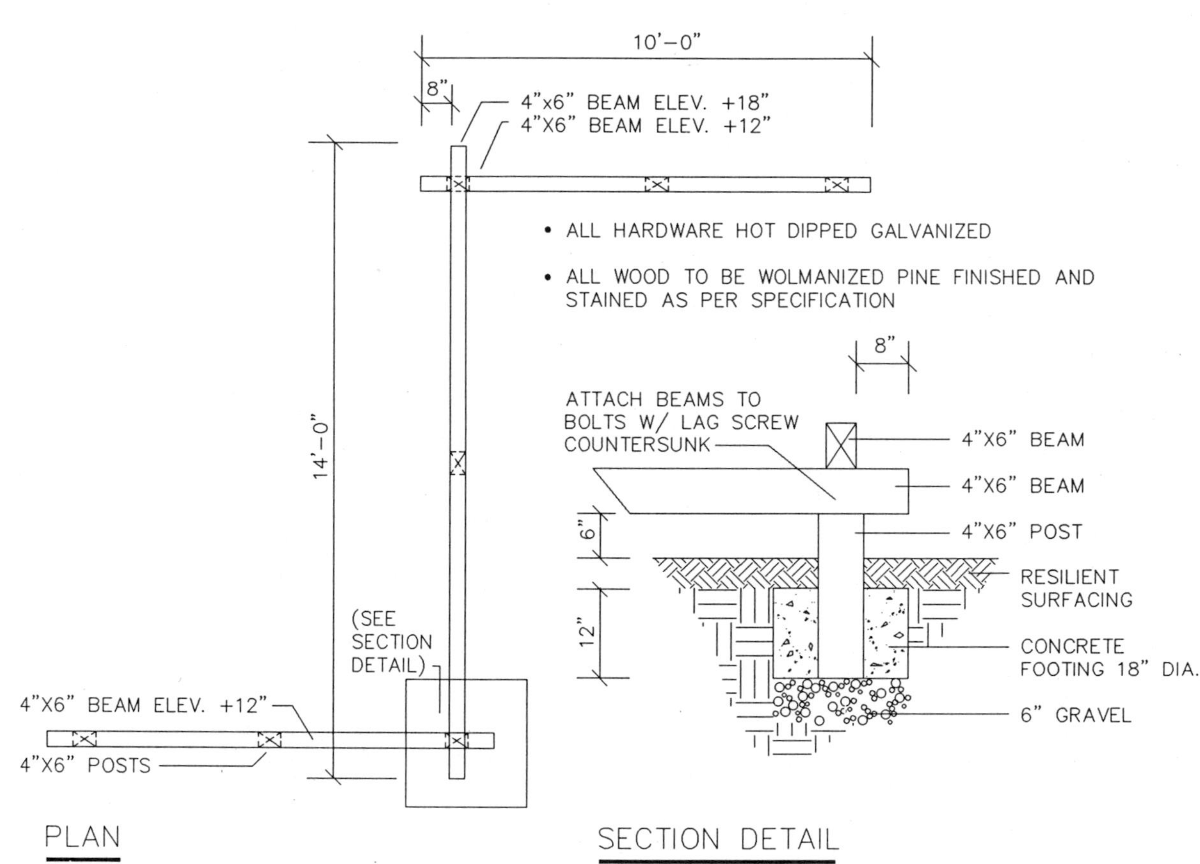
10'–0"
8"
4"x6" BEAM ELEV. +18"
4"X6" BEAM ELEV. +12"
14'–0"
(SEE SECTION DETAIL)
4"X6" BEAM ELEV. +12"
4"X6" POSTS
PLAN
• ALL HARDWARE HOT DIPPED GALVANIZED
• ALL WOOD TO BE WOLMANIZED PINE FINISHED AND STAINED AS PER SPECIFICATION
8"
ATTACH BEAMS TO BOLTS W/ LAG SCREW COUNTERSUNK
4"X6" BEAM
4"X6" BEAM
4"X6" POST
6"
12"
RESILIENT SURFACING
CONCRETE FOOTING 18" DIA.
6" GRAVEL
SECTION DETAIL

BALANCE BEAM

SCALE: NOT TO SCALE

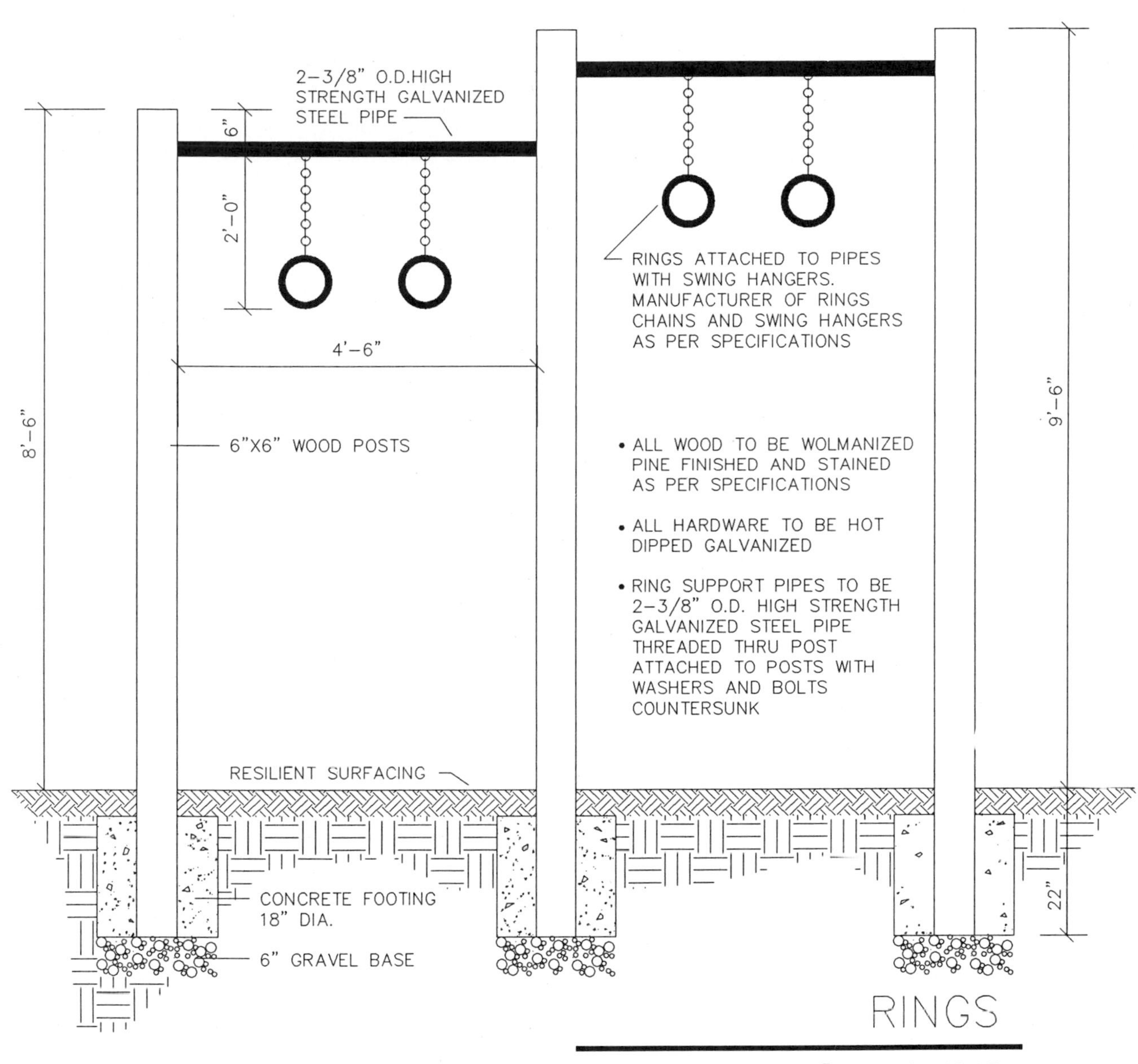

2-3/8" O.D.HIGH
STRENGTH GALVANIZED
STEEL PIPE
6"
2'-0"
4'-6"
8'-6"
9'-6"
RINGS ATTACHED TO PIPES
WITH SWING HANGERS.
MANUFACTURER OF RINGS
CHAINS AND SWING HANGERS
AS PER SPECIFICATIONS
6"X6" WOOD POSTS
• ALL WOOD TO BE WOLMANIZED
PINE FINISHED AND STAINED
AS PER SPECIFICATIONS
• ALL HARDWARE TO BE HOT
DIPPED GALVANIZED
• RING SUPPORT PIPES TO BE
2-3/8" O.D. HIGH STRENGTH
GALVANIZED STEEL PIPE
THREADED THRU POST
ATTACHED TO POSTS WITH
WASHERS AND BOLTS
COUNTERSUNK
RESILIENT SURFACING
CONCRETE FOOTING
18" DIA.
22"
6" GRAVEL BASE
RINGS
SCALE: NOT TO SCALE

Planting

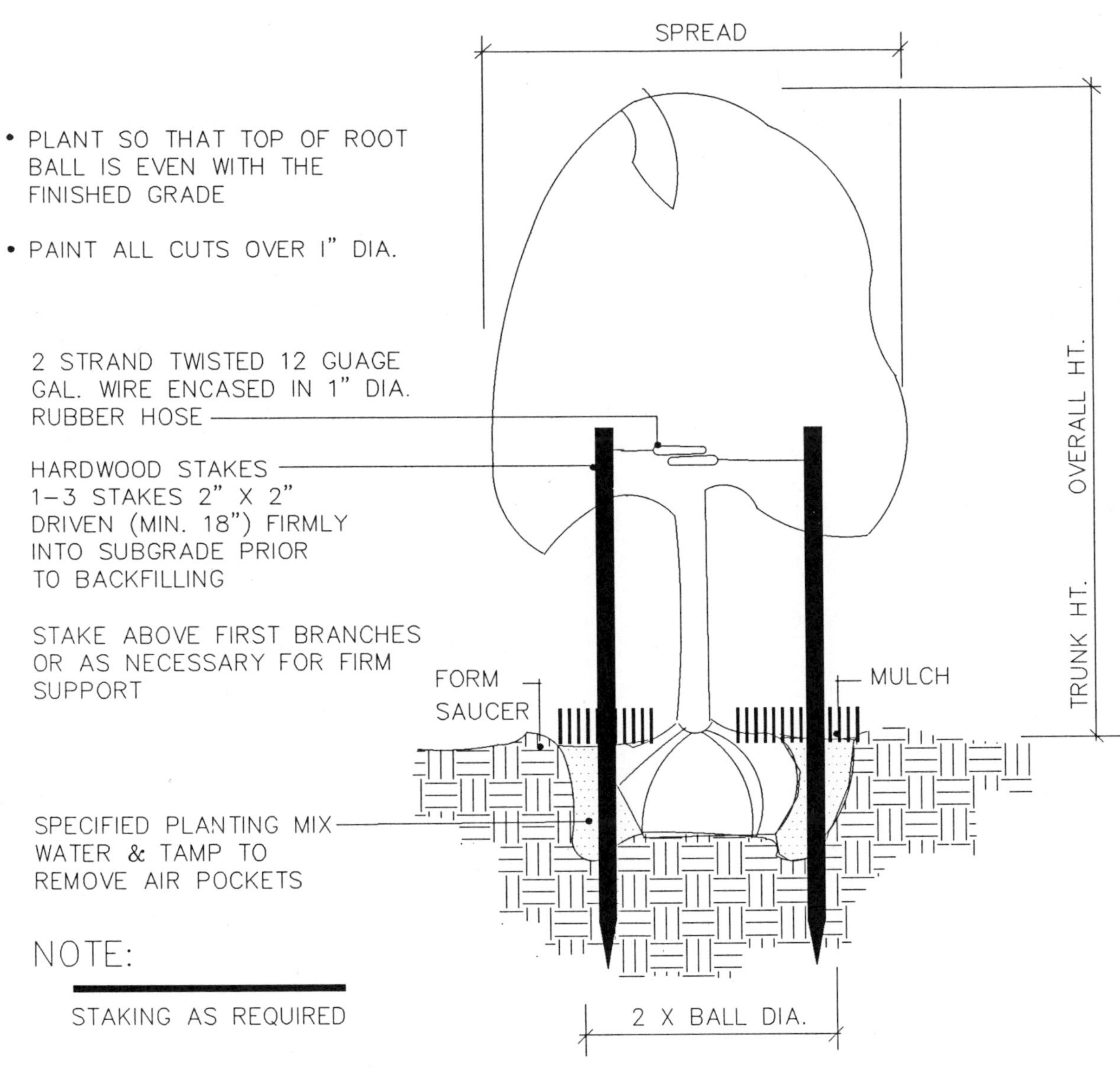
SPREAD
• PLANT SO THAT TOP OF ROOT BALL IS EVEN WITH THE FINISHED GRADE
• PAINT ALL CUTS OVER 1" DIA.
2 STRAND TWISTED 12 GUAGE GAL. WIRE ENCASED IN 1" DIA. RUBBER HOSE
HARDWOOD STAKES 1-3 STAKES 2" X 2" DRIVEN (MIN. 18") FIRMLY INTO SUBGRADE PRIOR TO BACKFILLING
STAKE ABOVE FIRST BRANCHES OR AS NECESSARY FOR FIRM SUPPORT
FORM SAUCER
MULCH
OVERALL HT.
TRUNK HT.
SPECIFIED PLANTING MIX WATER & TAMP TO REMOVE AIR POCKETS
NOTE:
STAKING AS REQUIRED
2 X BALL DIA.

TREE PLANTING — VERTICAL STAKES

SCALE: NOT TO SCALE

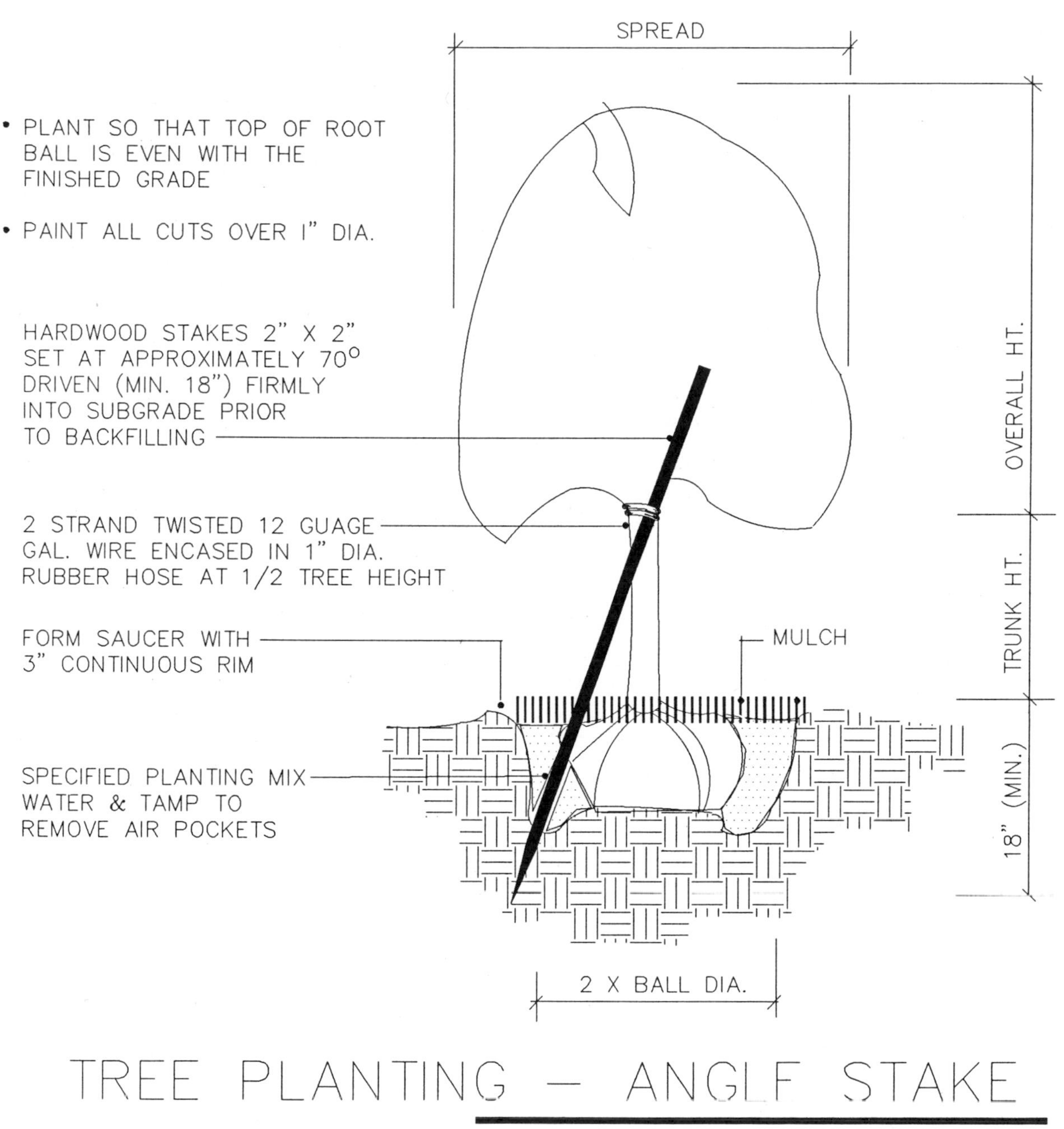
SPREAD
• PLANT SO THAT TOP OF ROOT BALL IS EVEN WITH THE FINISHED GRADE
• PAINT ALL CUTS OVER 1" DIA.
HARDWOOD STAKES 2" X 2" SET AT APPROXIMATELY 70° DRIVEN (MIN. 18") FIRMLY INTO SUBGRADE PRIOR TO BACKFILLING
2 STRAND TWISTED 12 GUAGE GAL. WIRE ENCASED IN 1" DIA. RUBBER HOSE AT 1/2 TREE HEIGHT
FORM SAUCER WITH 3" CONTINUOUS RIM
MULCH
SPECIFIED PLANTING MIX WATER & TAMP TO REMOVE AIR POCKETS
OVERALL HT.
TRUNK HT.
18" (MIN.)
2 X BALL DIA.

TREE PLANTING – ANGLE STAKE

SCALE: NOT TO SCALE

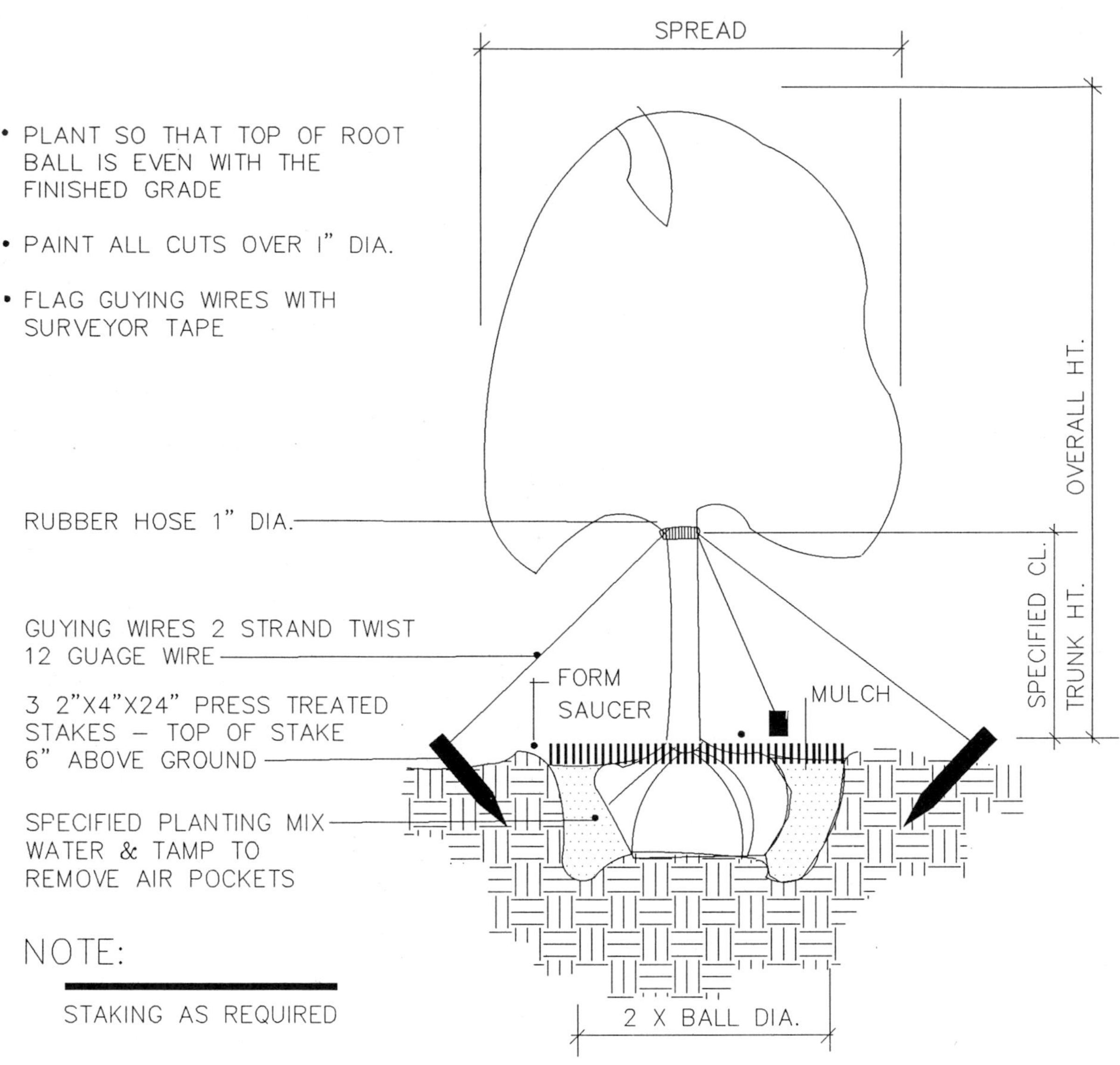

SPREAD
• PLANT SO THAT TOP OF ROOT BALL IS EVEN WITH THE FINISHED GRADE
• PAINT ALL CUTS OVER 1" DIA.
• FLAG GUYING WIRES WITH SURVEYOR TAPE
OVERALL HT.
RUBBER HOSE 1" DIA.
SPECIFIED CL. TRUNK HT.
GUYING WIRES 2 STRAND TWIST 12 GUAGE WIRE
FORM SAUCER
MULCH
3 2"X4"X24" PRESS TREATED STAKES – TOP OF STAKE 6" ABOVE GROUND
SPECIFIED PLANTING MIX WATER & TAMP TO REMOVE AIR POCKETS
NOTE:
STAKING AS REQUIRED
2 X BALL DIA.

TREE PLANTING – GUY WIRES

SCALE: NOT TO SCALE

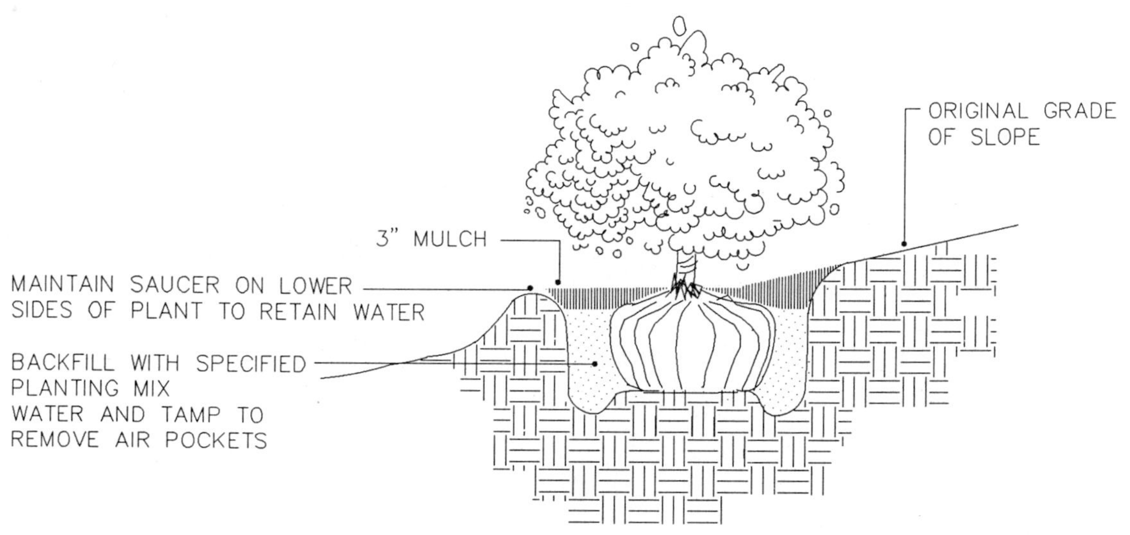
ORIGINAL GRADE
OF SLOPE
3" MULCH
MAINTAIN SAUCER ON LOWER
SIDES OF PLANT TO RETAIN WATER
BACKFILL WITH SPECIFIED
PLANTING MIX
WATER AND TAMP TO
REMOVE AIR POCKETS

SHRUB PLANTING ON SLOPES

SCALE: NOT TO SCALE

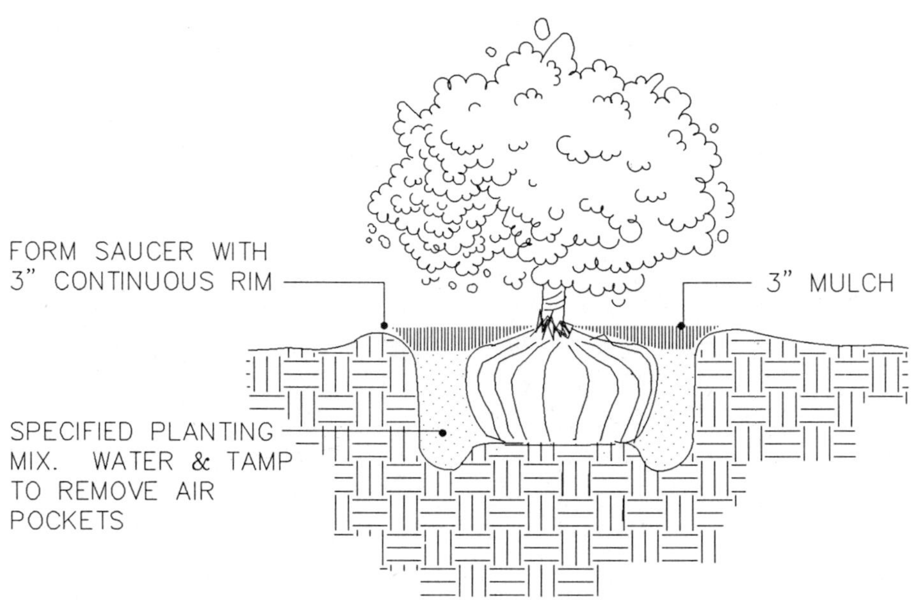
FORM SAUCER WITH
3" CONTINUOUS RIM
3" MULCH
SPECIFIED PLANTING
MIX. WATER & TAMP
TO REMOVE AIR
POCKETS

SHRUB PLANTING

SCALE: NOT TO SCALE

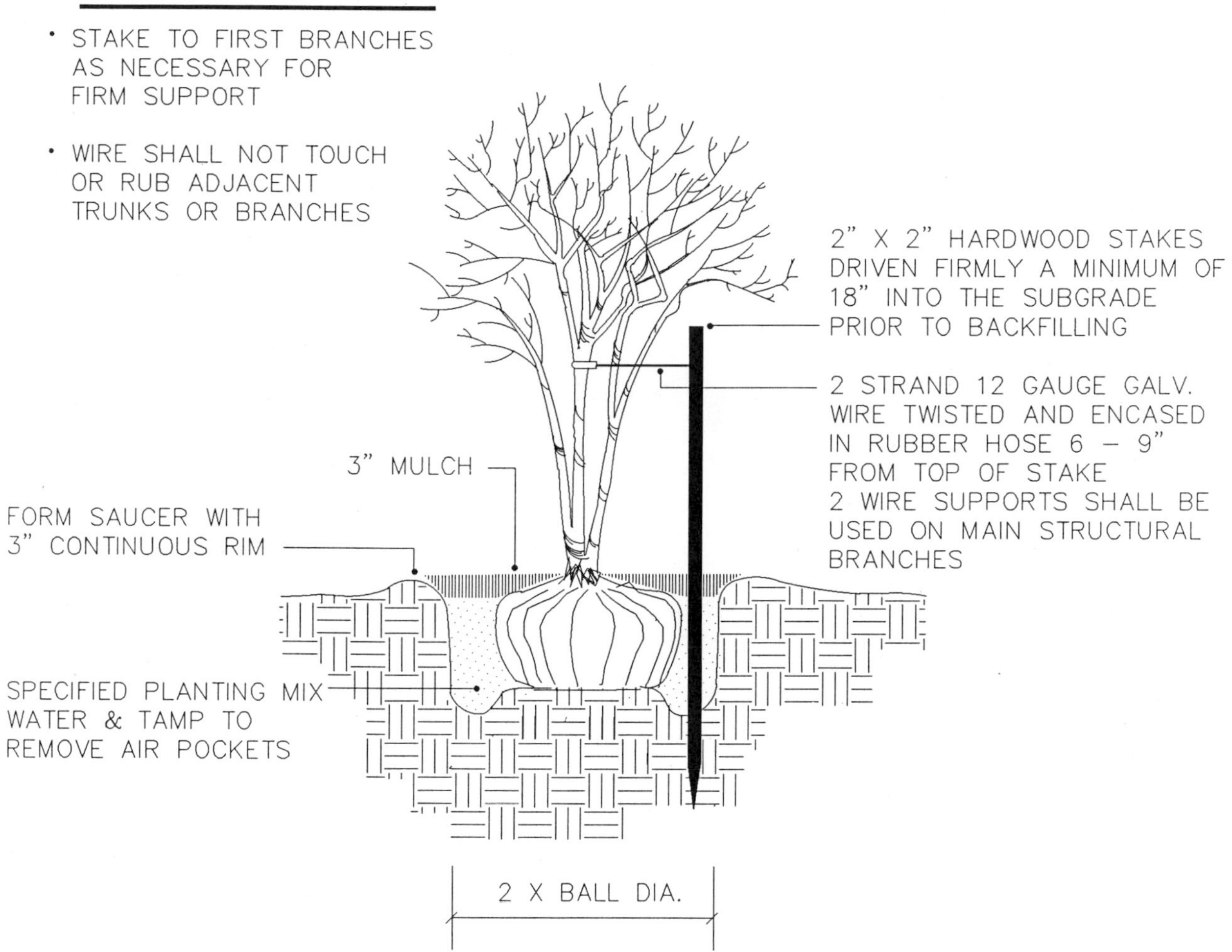
NOTE:
• STAKE TO FIRST BRANCHES AS NECESSARY FOR FIRM SUPPORT
• WIRE SHALL NOT TOUCH OR RUB ADJACENT TRUNKS OR BRANCHES
2" X 2" HARDWOOD STAKES DRIVEN FIRMLY A MINIMUM OF 18" INTO THE SUBGRADE PRIOR TO BACKFILLING
2 STRAND 12 GAUGE GALV. WIRE TWISTED AND ENCASED IN RUBBER HOSE 6 – 9" FROM TOP OF STAKE
2 WIRE SUPPORTS SHALL BE USED ON MAIN STRUCTURAL BRANCHES
3" MULCH
FORM SAUCER WITH 3" CONTINUOUS RIM
SPECIFIED PLANTING MIX WATER & TAMP TO REMOVE AIR POCKETS
2 X BALL DIA.

MULTI–TRUNK TREE STAKING

SCALE: NOT TO SCALE

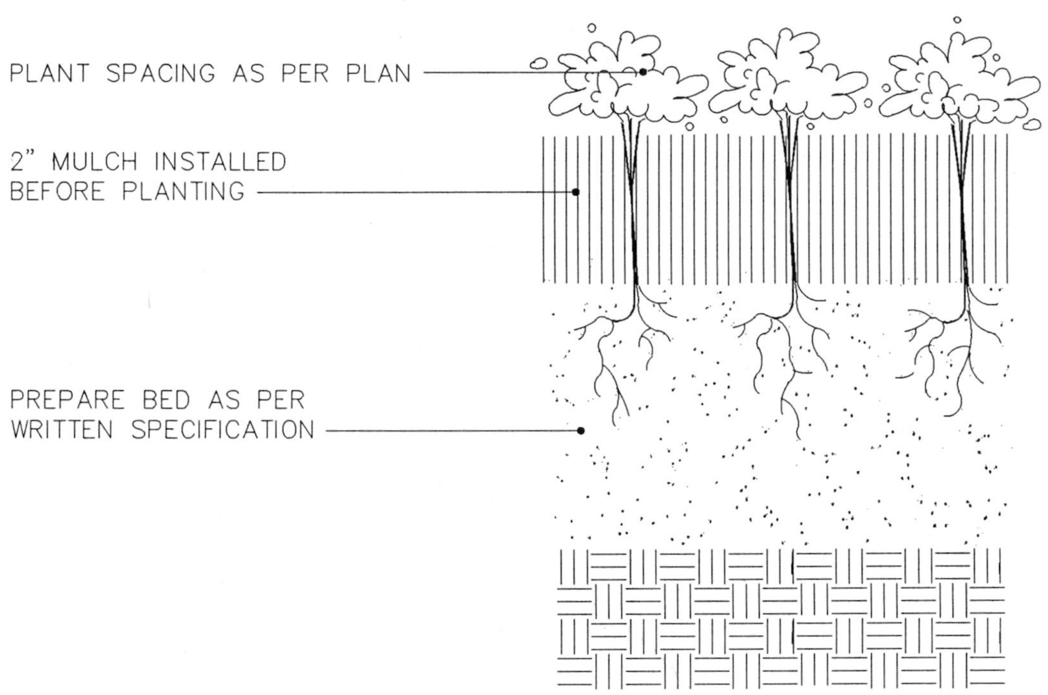
PLANT SPACING AS PER PLAN
2" MULCH INSTALLED
BEFORE PLANTING
PREPARE BED AS PER
WRITTEN SPECIFICATION

GROUNDCOVER PLANTING DETAIL

SCALE: NOT TO SCALE

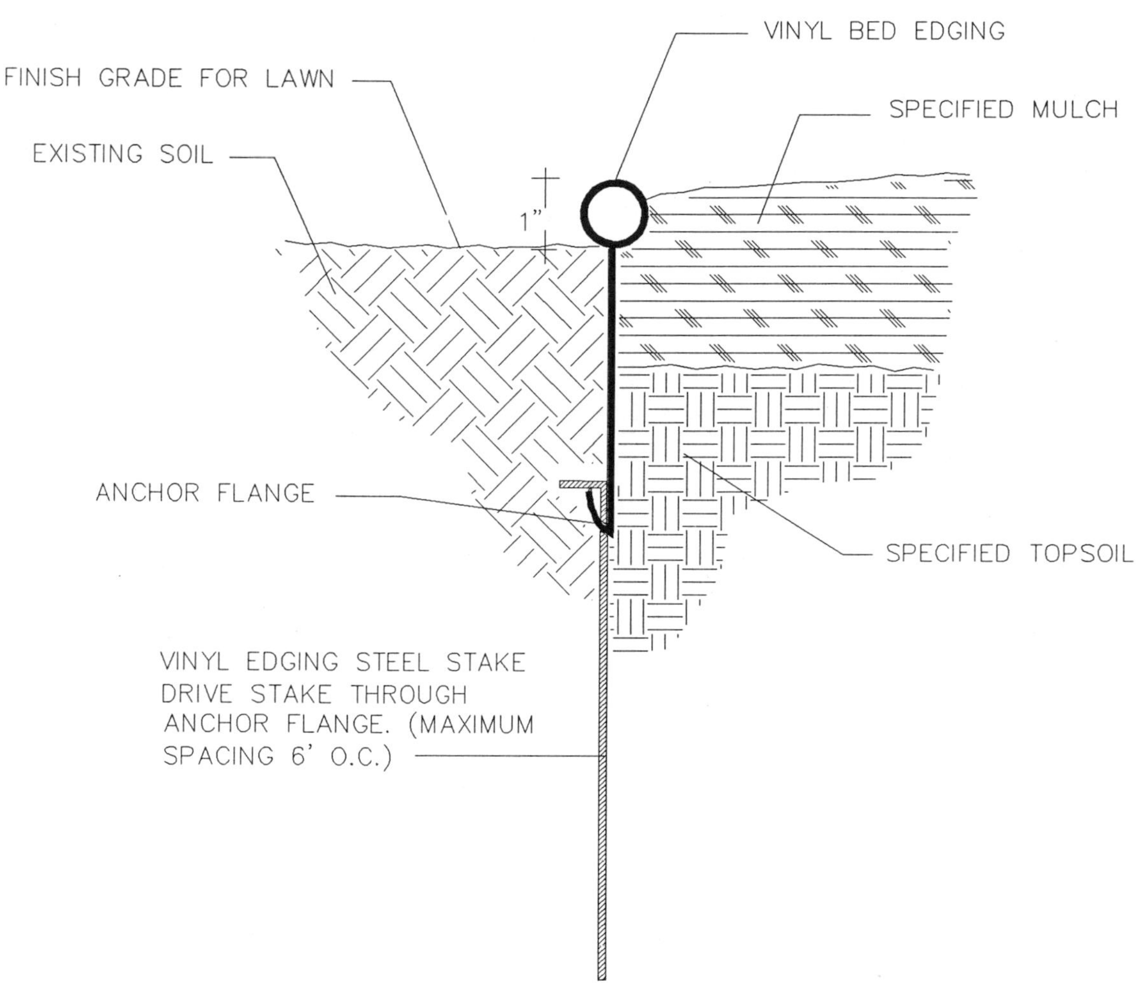
VINYL BED EDGING
FINISH GRADE FOR LAWN
SPECIFIED MULCH
EXISTING SOIL
1"
ANCHOR FLANGE
SPECIFIED TOPSOIL
VINYL EDGING STEEL STAKE
DRIVE STAKE THROUGH
ANCHOR FLANGE. (MAXIMUM
SPACING 6' O.C.)

VINYL BED EDGING DETAIL

SCALE: NOT TO SCALE

Parking

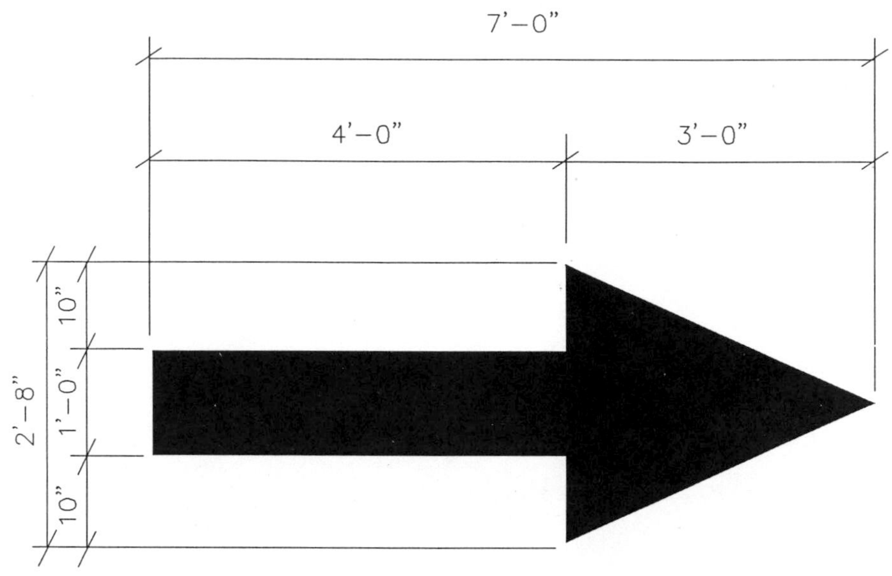
7'–0"
4'–0"
3'–0"
2'–8"
10"
1'–0"
10"

NOTES:

CURVE AS REQUIRED TO PARALLEL CENTERLINE OF ROAD.

USE WHITE REFLECTIVE PAINT. PAINT COLOR– SEE SPECS.

DIRECTIONAL ARROW

SCALE: NOT TO SCALE

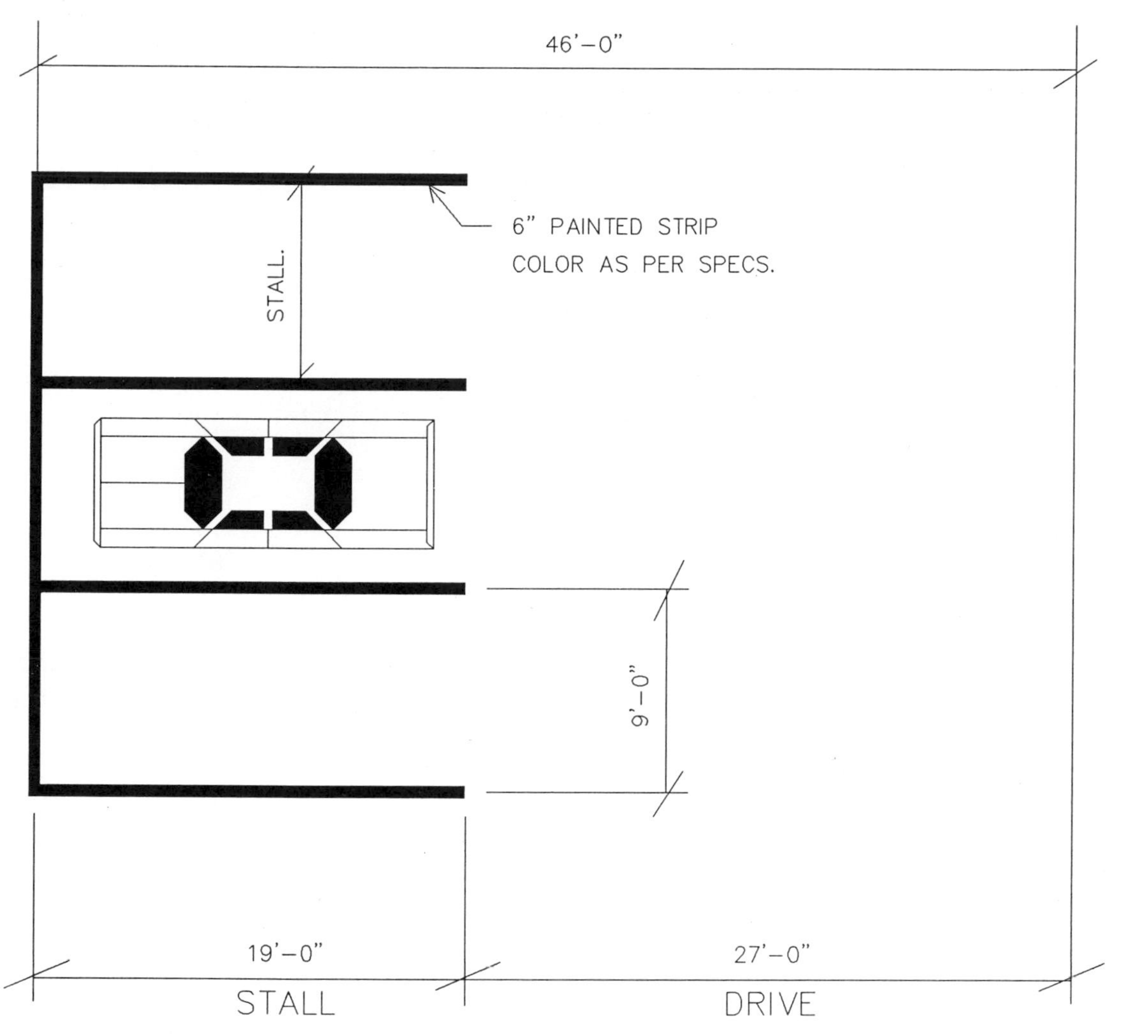
46'–0"
6" PAINTED STRIP
COLOR AS PER SPECS.
STALL.
9'–0"
19'–0"
27'–0"
STALL
DRIVE
ONE ROW – PARKING
SCALE: NOT TO SCALE

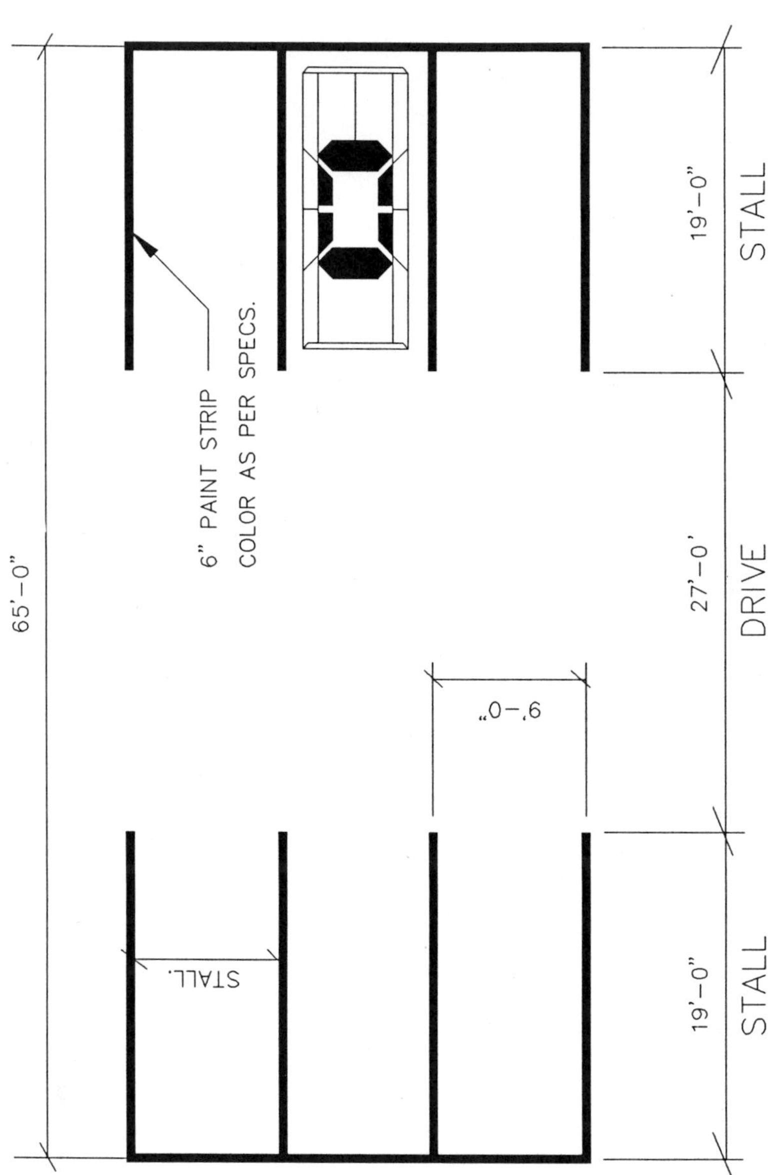
65'–0"
6" PAINT STRIP
COLOR AS PER SPECS.
9'–0"
STALL.
19'–0"
STALL
27'–0'
DRIVE
19'–0"
STALL

TWO ROWS – PARKING

SCALE: NOT TO SCALE

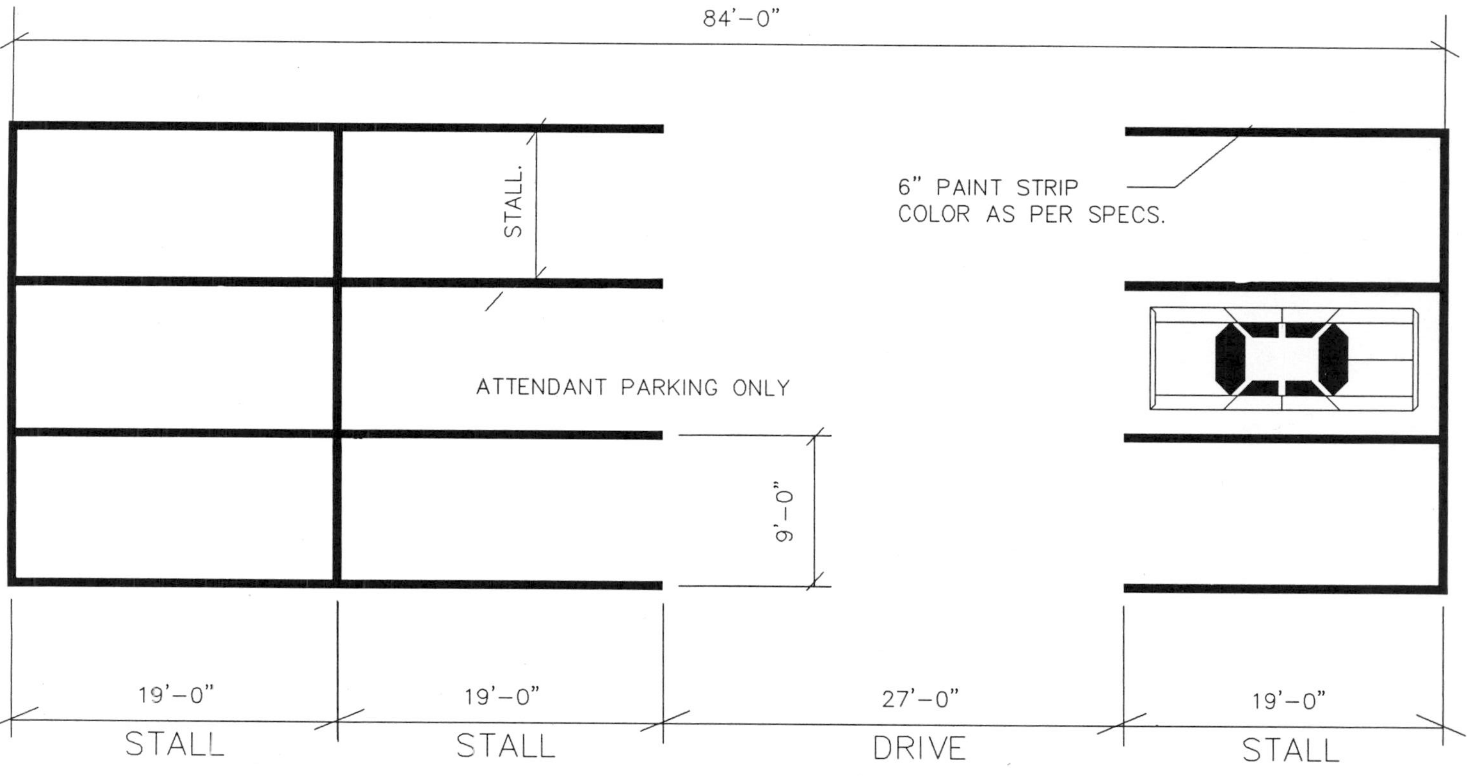
84'-0"
STALL.
6" PAINT STRIP
COLOR AS PER SPECS.
ATTENDANT PARKING ONLY
9'-0"
19'-0"
STALL
19'-0"
STALL
27'-0"
DRIVE
19'-0"
STALL

THREE ROWS — PARKING

SCALE: NOT TO SCALE

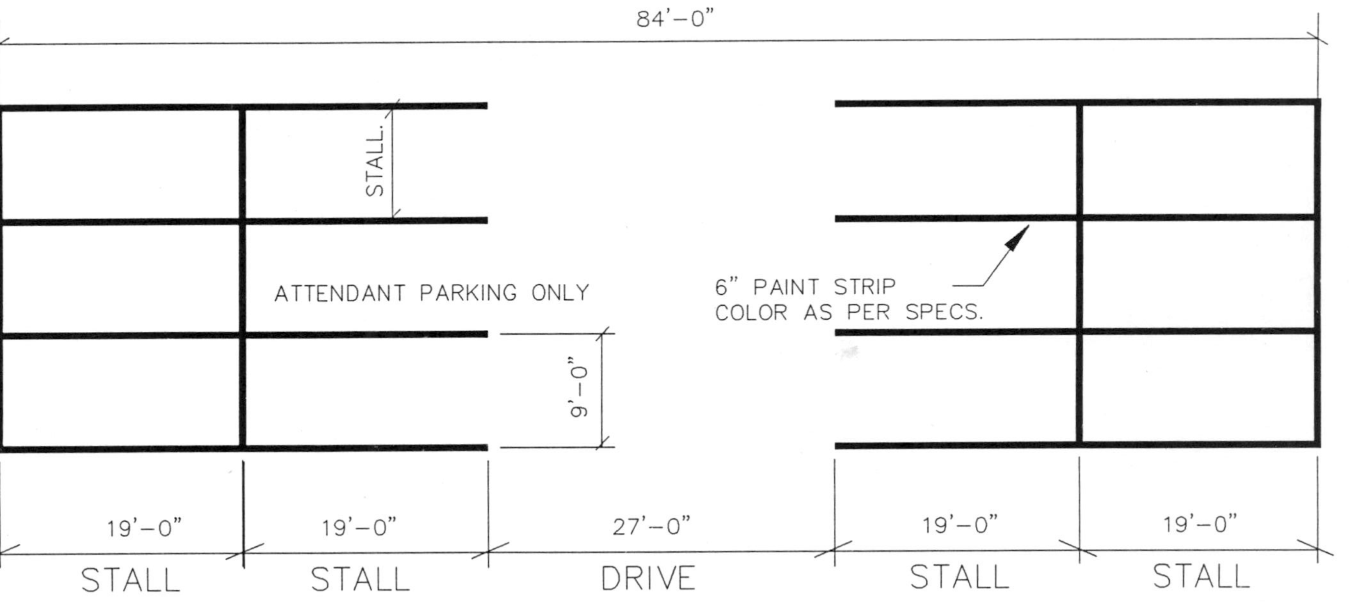
84'–0"
STALL.
ATTENDANT PARKING ONLY
9'–0"
6" PAINT STRIP
COLOR AS PER SPECS.
19'–0"
STALL
19'–0"
STALL
27'–0"
DRIVE
19'–0"
STALL
19'–0"
STALL

FOUR ROWS –PARKING

SCALE: NOT TO SCALE

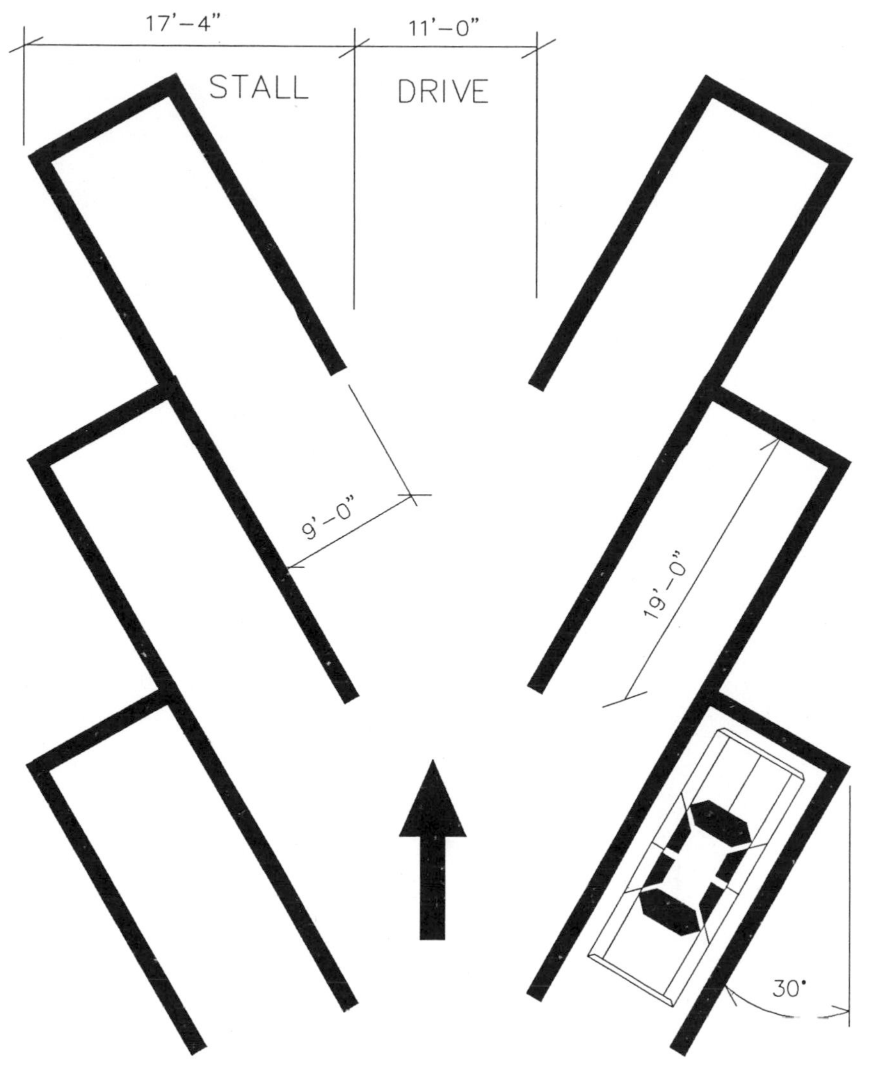
17'–4"
11'–0"
STALL
DRIVE
9'–0"
19'–0"
30°

30° STALL & ONE AISLE PARKING

SCALE: NOT TO SCALE

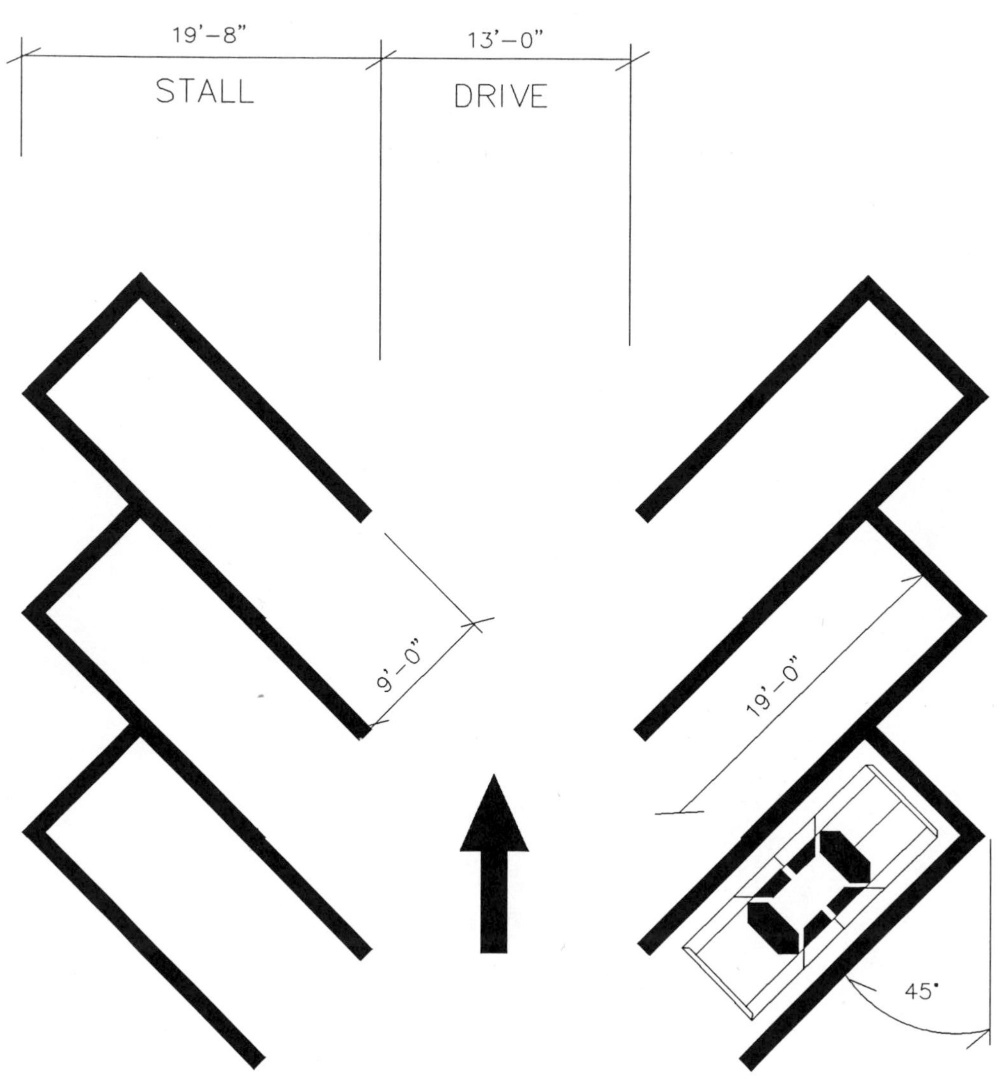

19'–8"
STALL
13'–0"
DRIVE
9'–0"
19'–0"
45°

45° STALL & ONE AISLE PARKING

SCALE: NOT TO SCALE

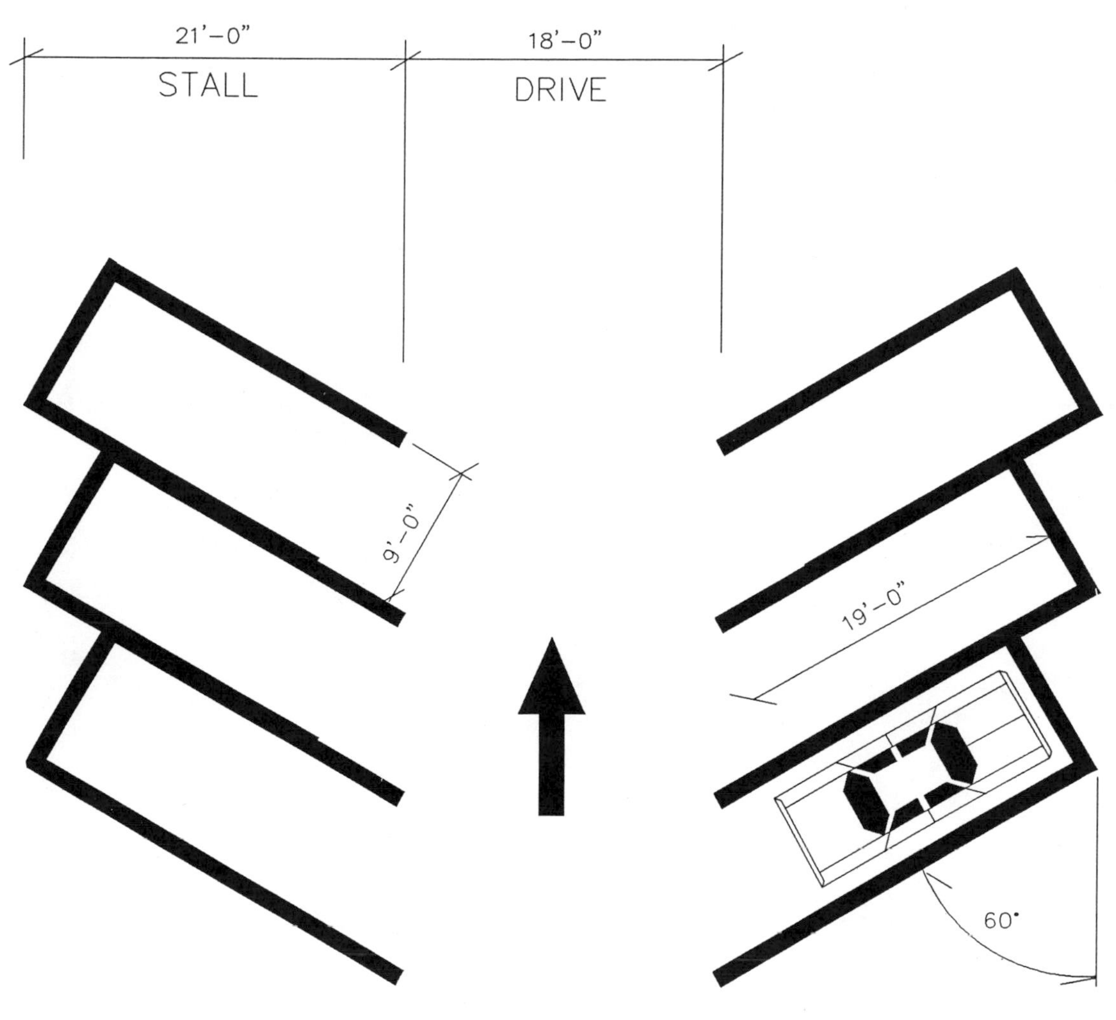
21'–0"
STALL
18'–0"
DRIVE
9'–0"
19'–0"
60°

60° STALL & ONE AISLE PARKING

SCALE: NOT TO SCALE

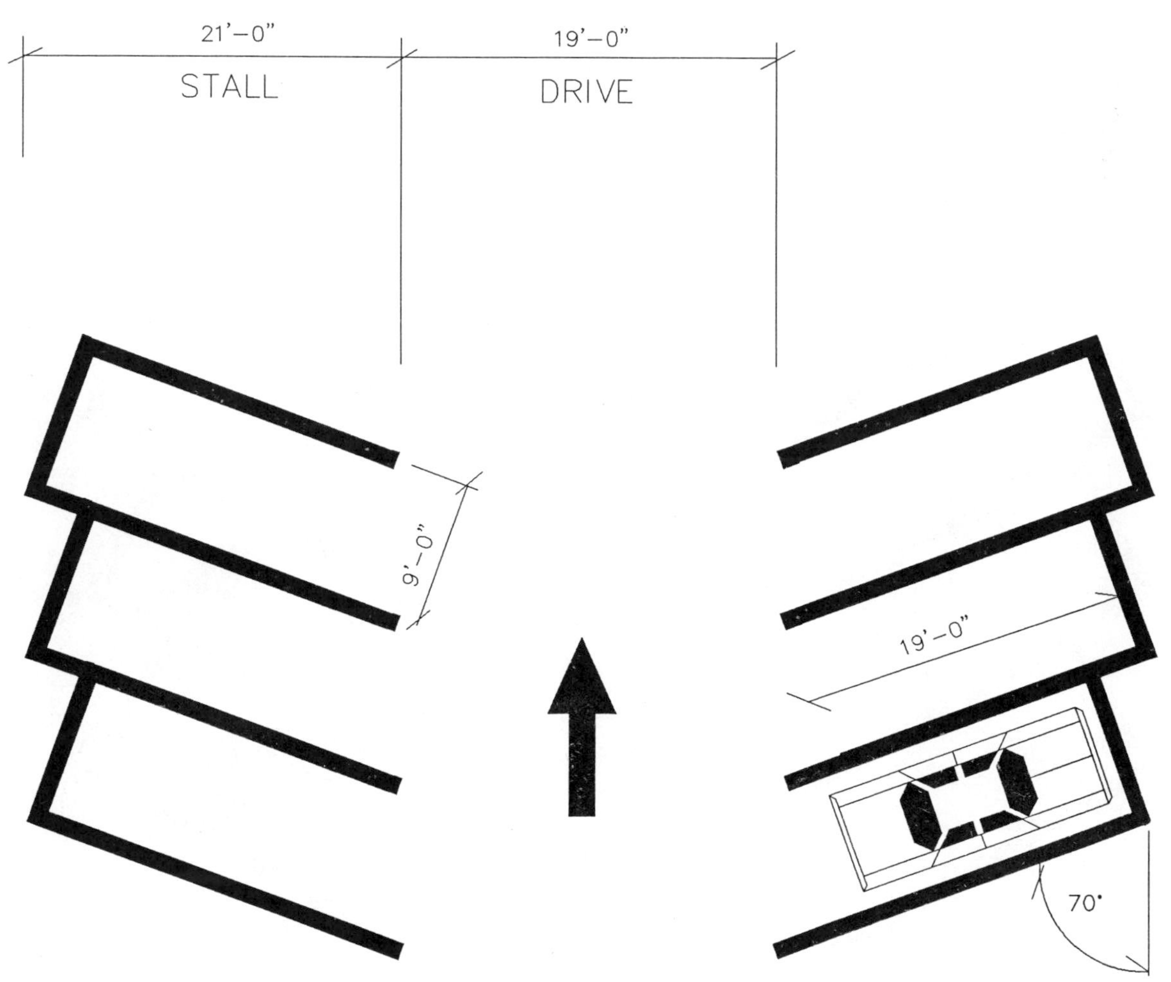
21'–0"
STALL
19'–0"
DRIVE
9'–0"
19'–0"
70°

70° STALL & ONE AISLE PARKING

SCALE: NOT TO SCALE

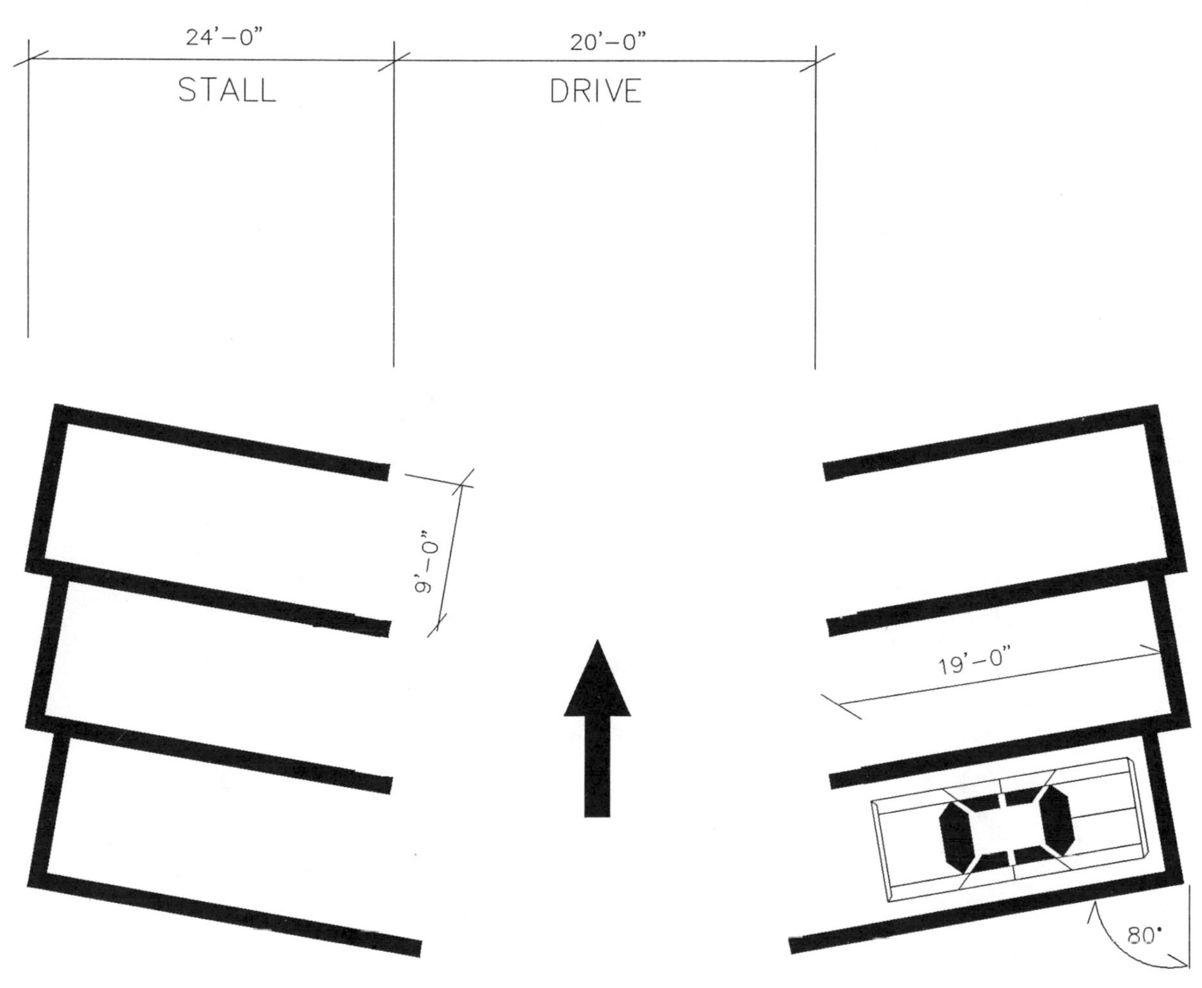
24'–0"
STALL
20'–0"
DRIVE
9'–0"
19'–0"
80°

80° STALL & ONE AISLE PARKING

SCALE: NOT TO SCALE

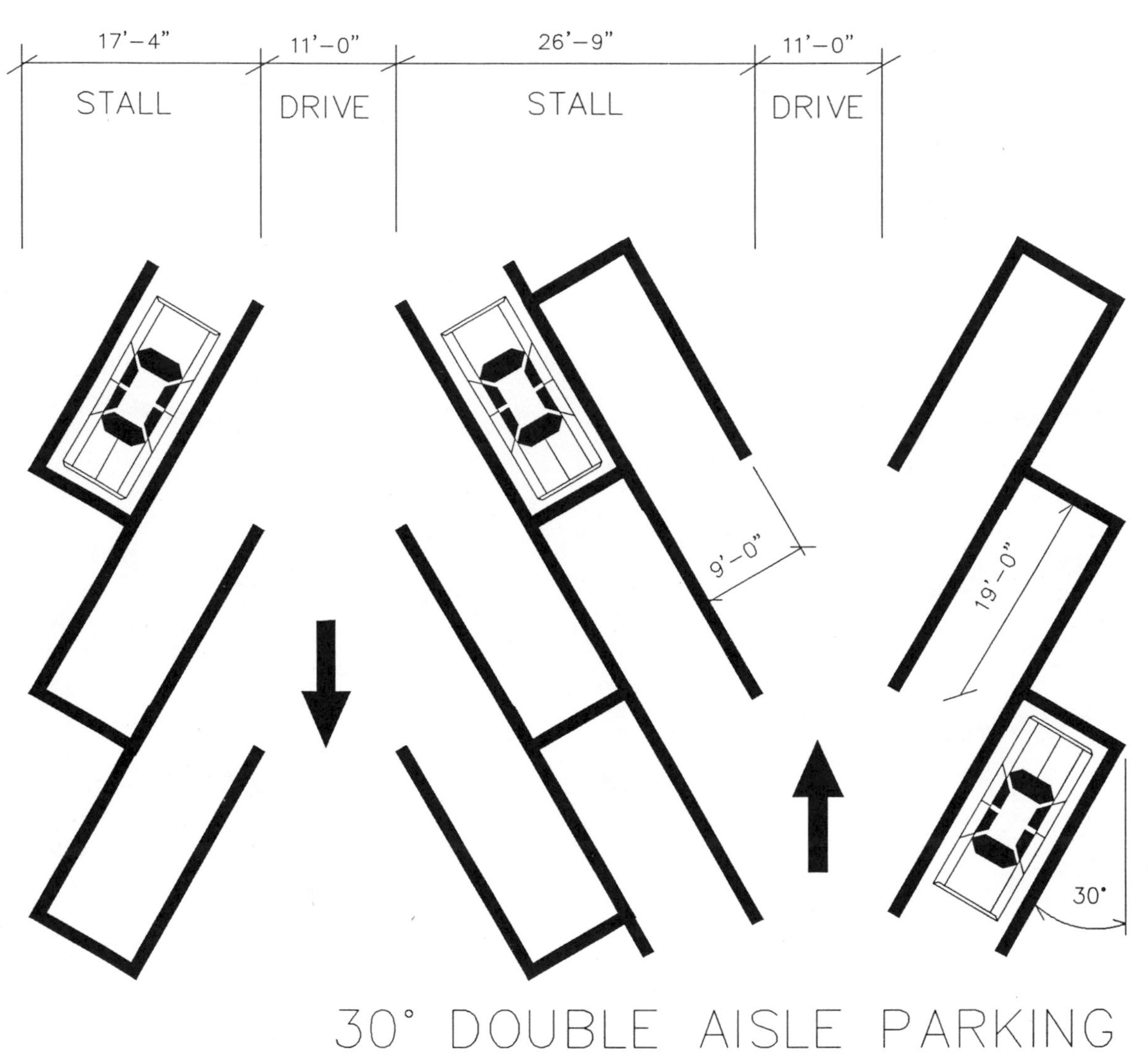

17'–4"
11'–0"
26'–9"
11'–0"
STALL
DRIVE
STALL
DRIVE
9'–0"
19'–0"
30°

30° DOUBLE AISLE PARKING

SCALE: NOT TO SCALE

45° NESTED PARKING

SCALE: NOT TO SCALE

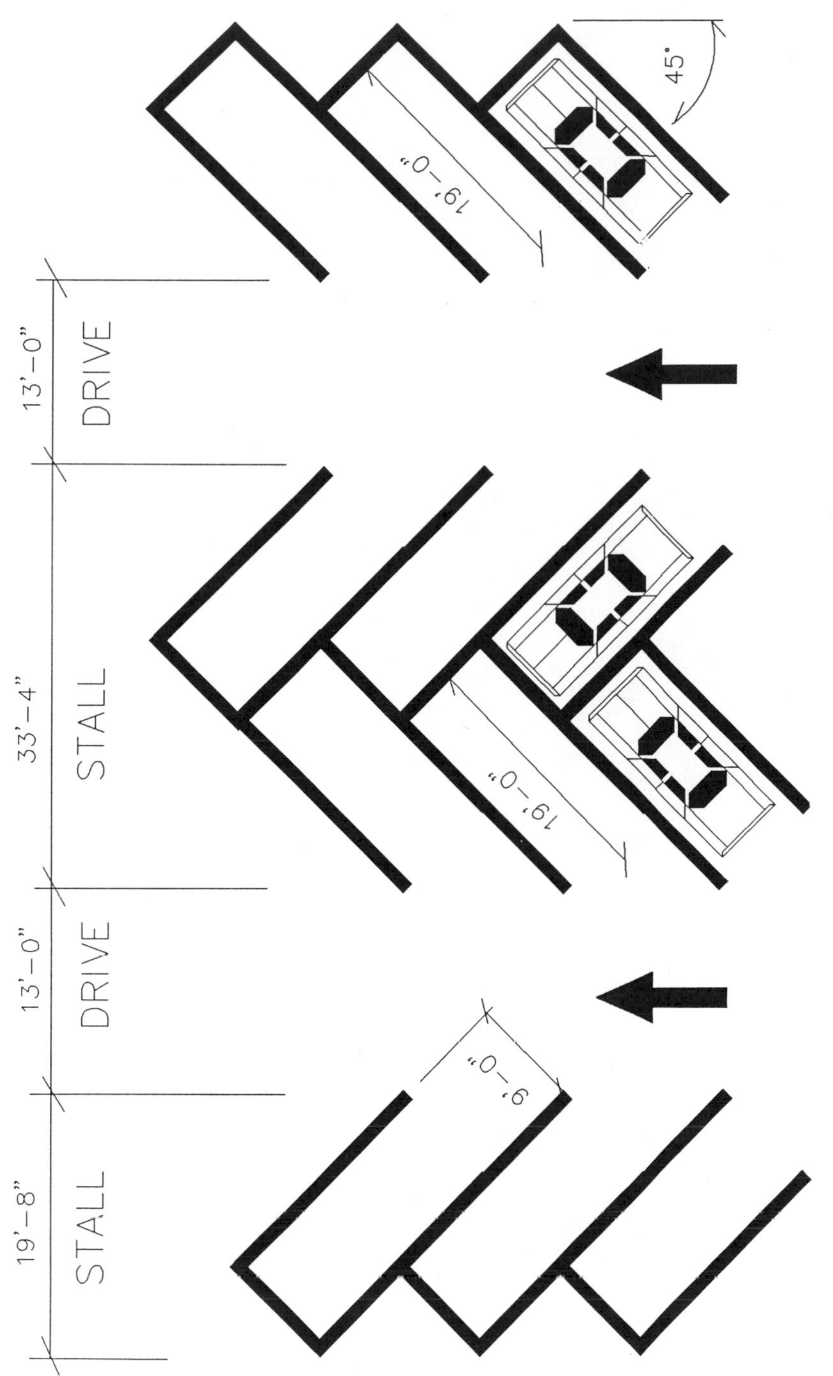

19'–8"
STALL
13'–0"
DRIVE
33'–4"
STALL
13'–0"
DRIVE
9'–0"
19'–0"
19'–0"
45°

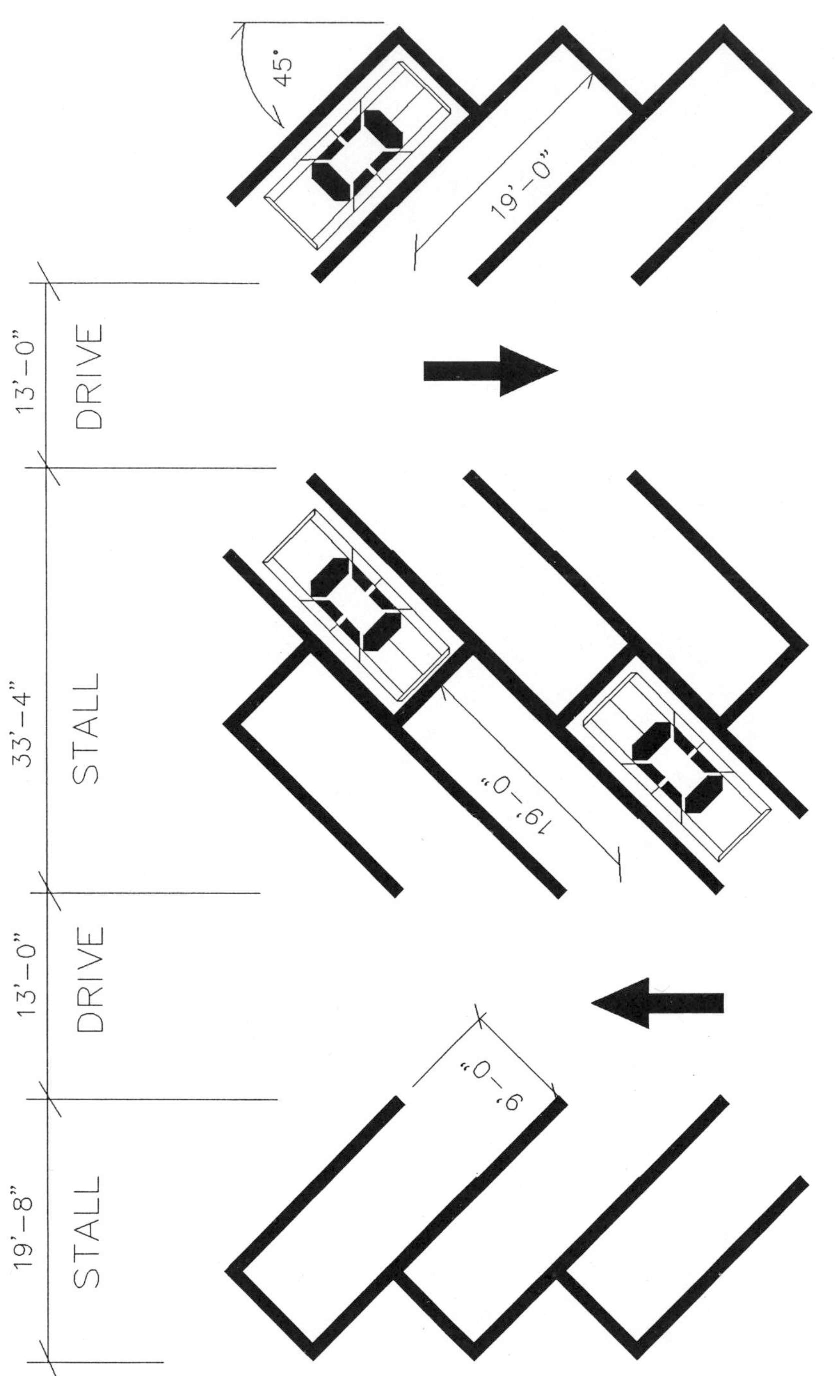

19'–8"
STALL
13'–0"
DRIVE
33'–4"
STALL
13'–0"
DRIVE
9'–0"
19'–0"
19'–0"
45°

45° DOUBLE AISLE PARKING

SCALE: NOT TO SCALE

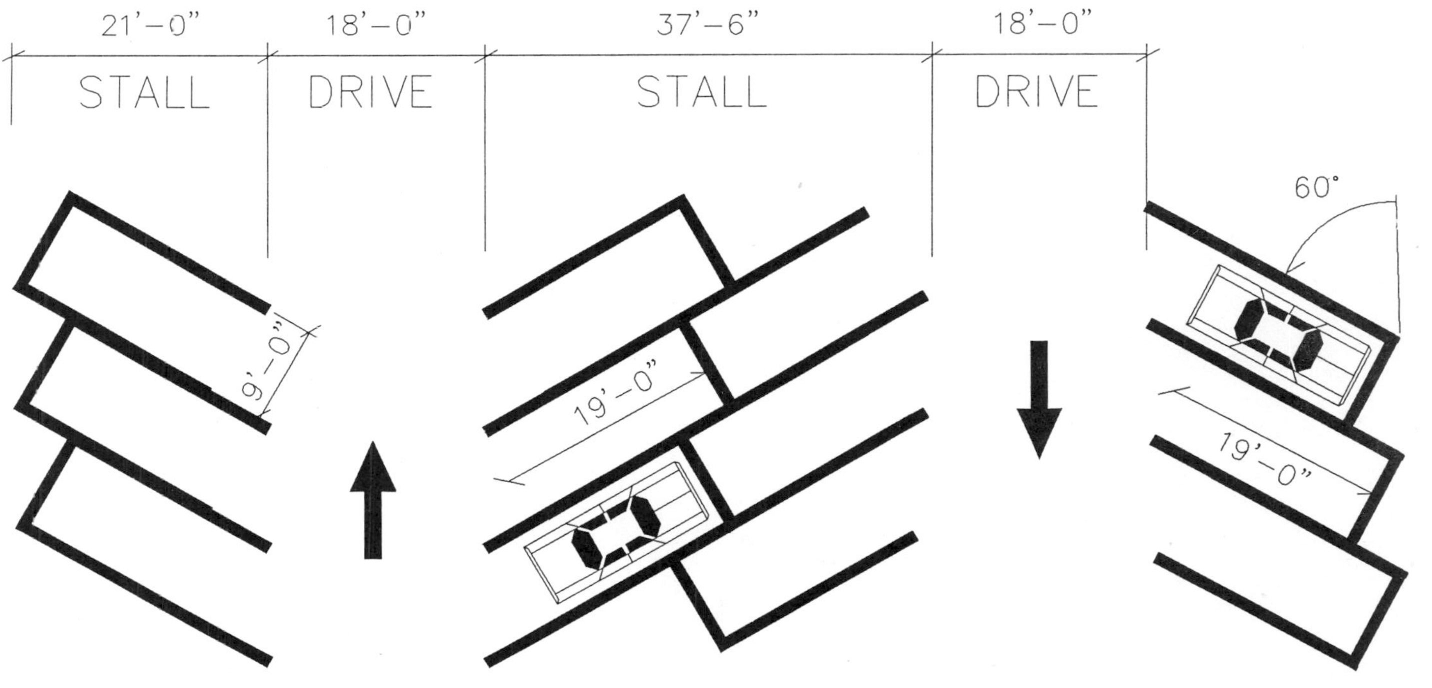
21'–0"
18'–0"
37'–6"
18'–0"
STALL
DRIVE
STALL
DRIVE
60°
9'–0"
19'–0"
19'–0"

60° DOUBLE AISLE PARKING

SCALE: NOT TO SCALE

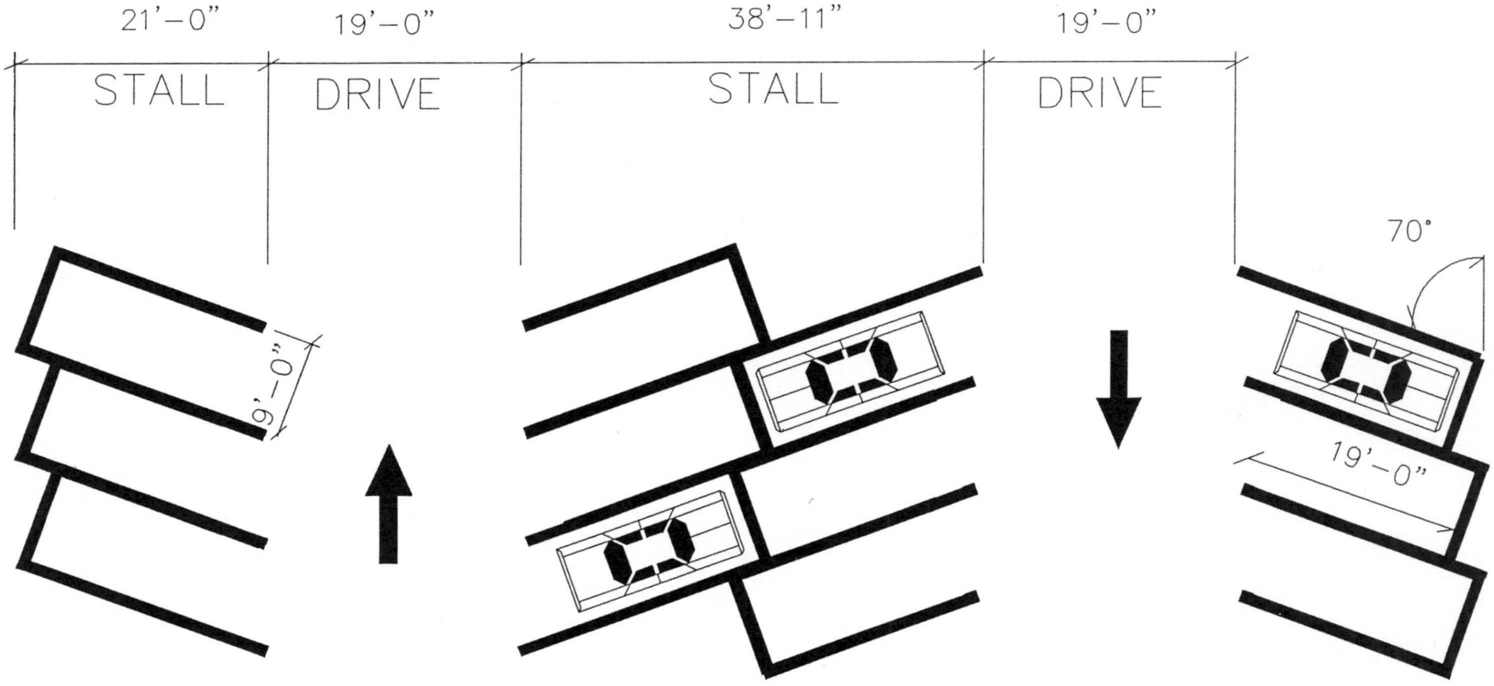

21'–0"
STALL
19'–0"
DRIVE
38'–11"
STALL
19'–0"
DRIVE
9'–0"
70°
19'–0"

70° DOUBLE AISLE PARKING

SCALE: NOT TO SCALE

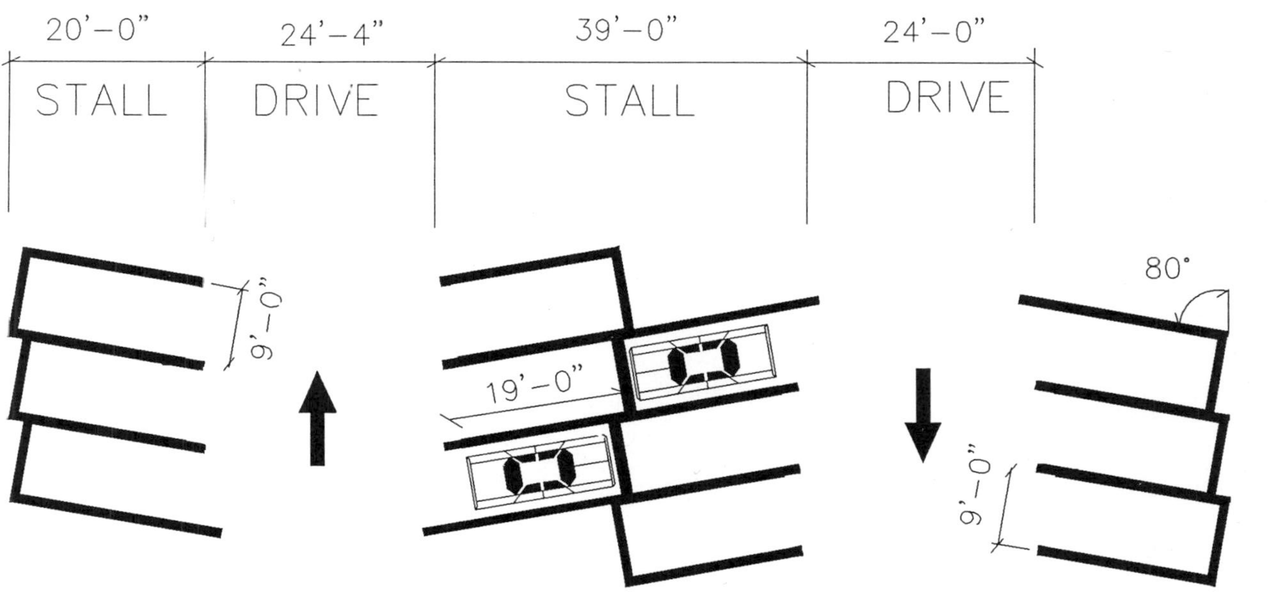
20'–0"
24'–4"
39'–0"
24'–0"
STALL
DRIVE
STALL
DRIVE
9'–0"
19'–0"
80°
9'–0"

80° DOUBLE AISLE PARKING

SCALE: NOT TO SCALE

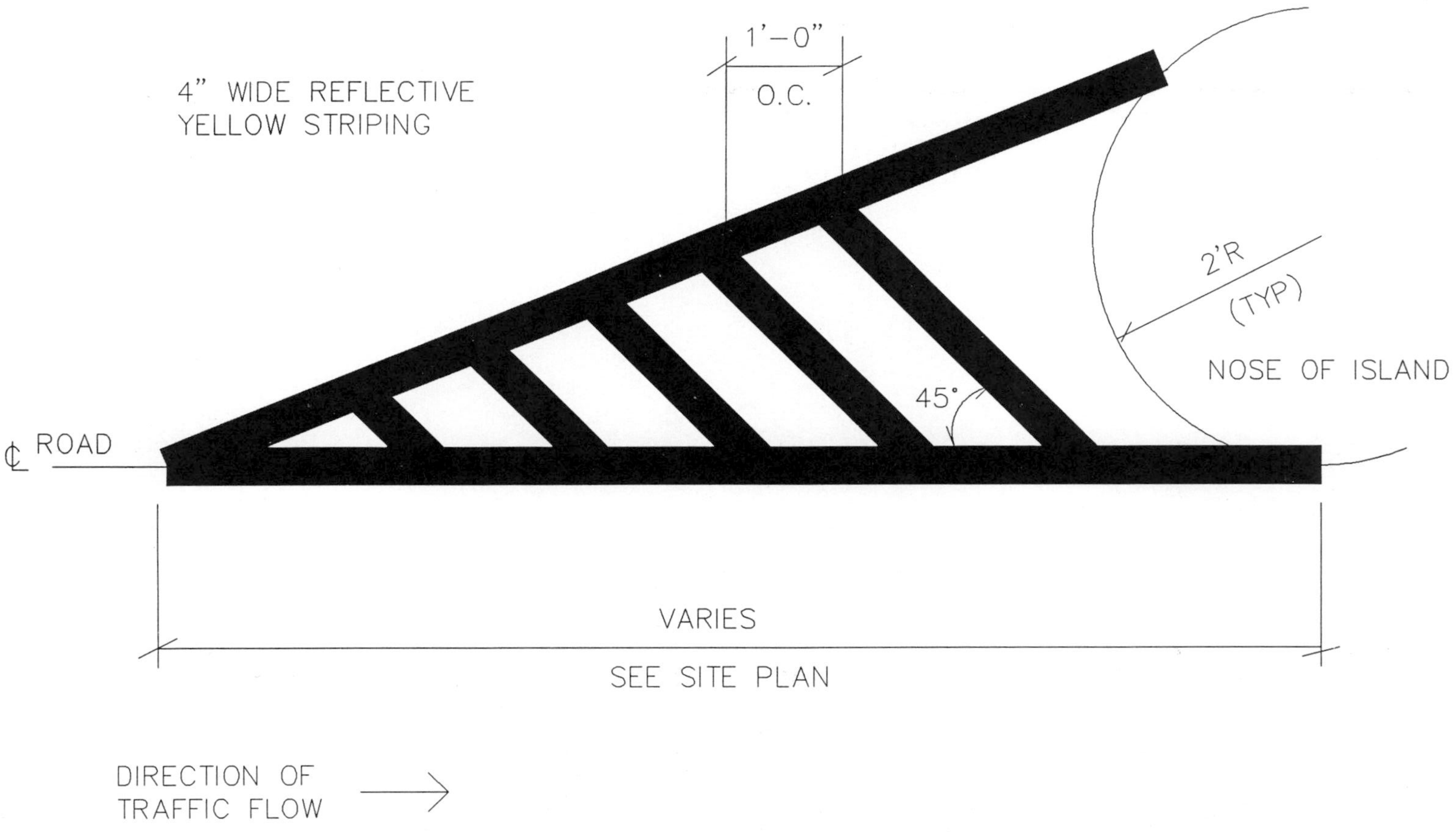

4" WIDE REFLECTIVE
YELLOW STRIPING

1'–0"
O.C.

2'R
(TYP)

NOSE OF ISLAND

45°

℄ ROAD

VARIES

SEE SITE PLAN

DIRECTION OF
TRAFFIC FLOW →

GORE STRIPING DETAIL

SCALE: NOT TO SCALE

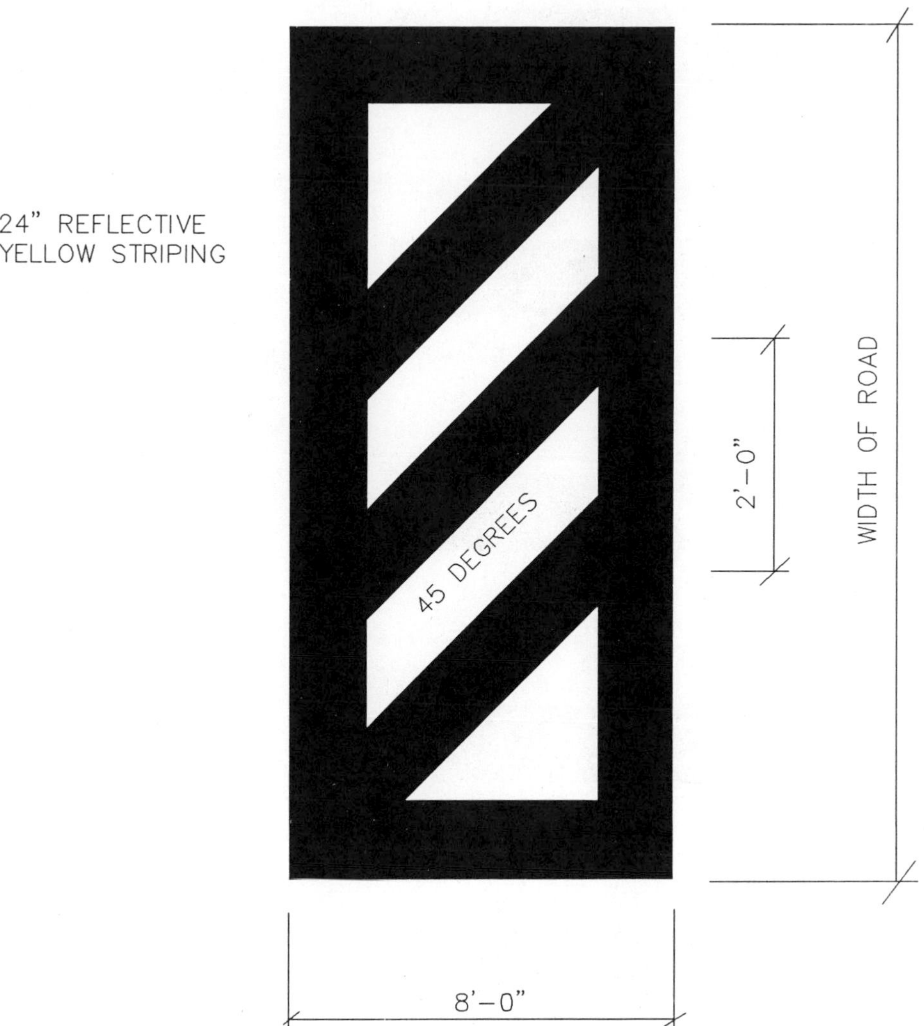
24" REFLECTIVE
YELLOW STRIPING
45 DEGREES
2'–0"
WIDTH OF ROAD
8'–0"

CROSSWALK MARKING DIAGONAL

SCALE: NOT TO SCALE

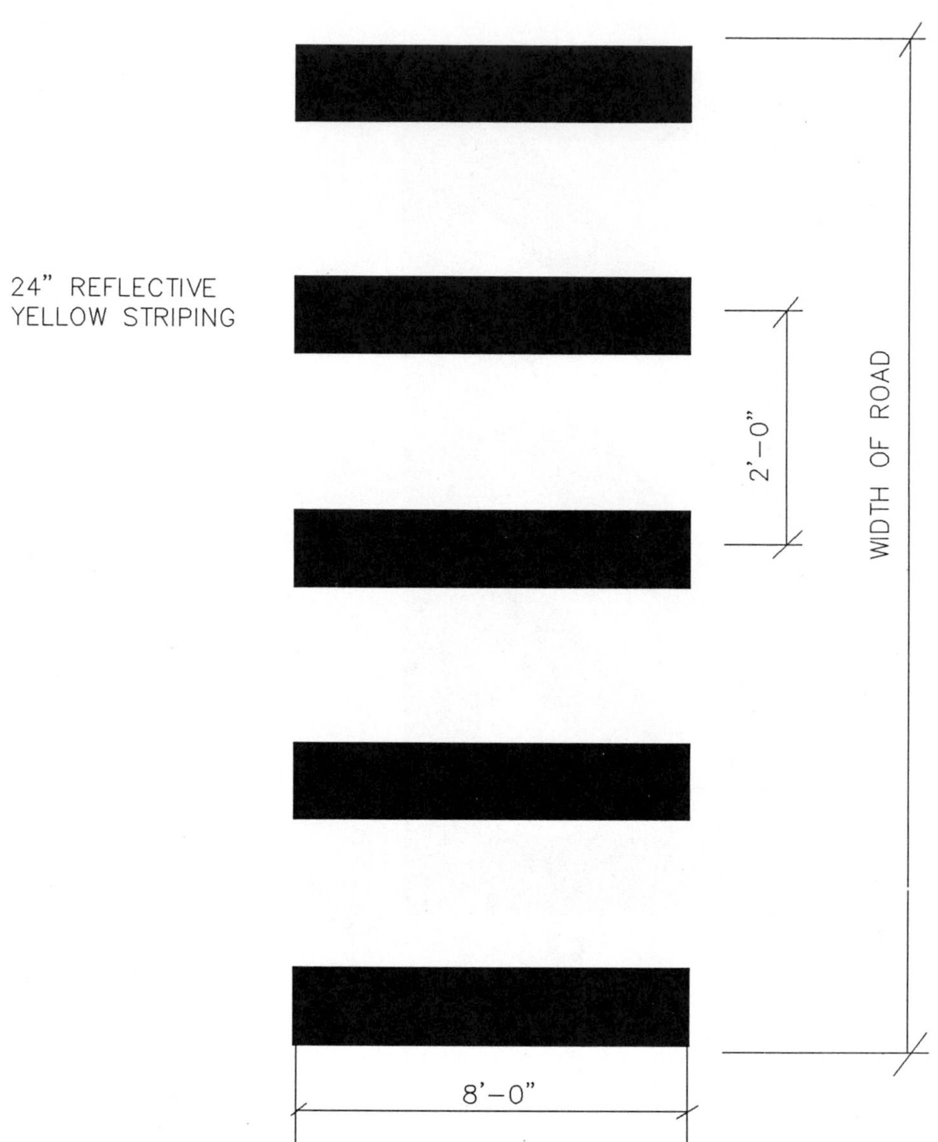
24" REFLECTIVE
YELLOW STRIPING
2'–0"
WIDTH OF ROAD
8'–0"

CROSSWALK MARKING LONGITUDINAL

SCALE: NOT TO SCALE

Railing & Protective Devices

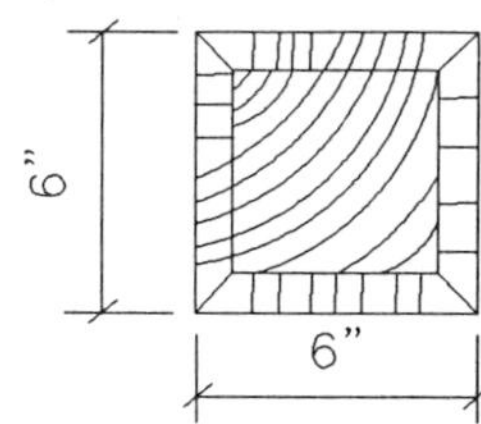
6"
6"

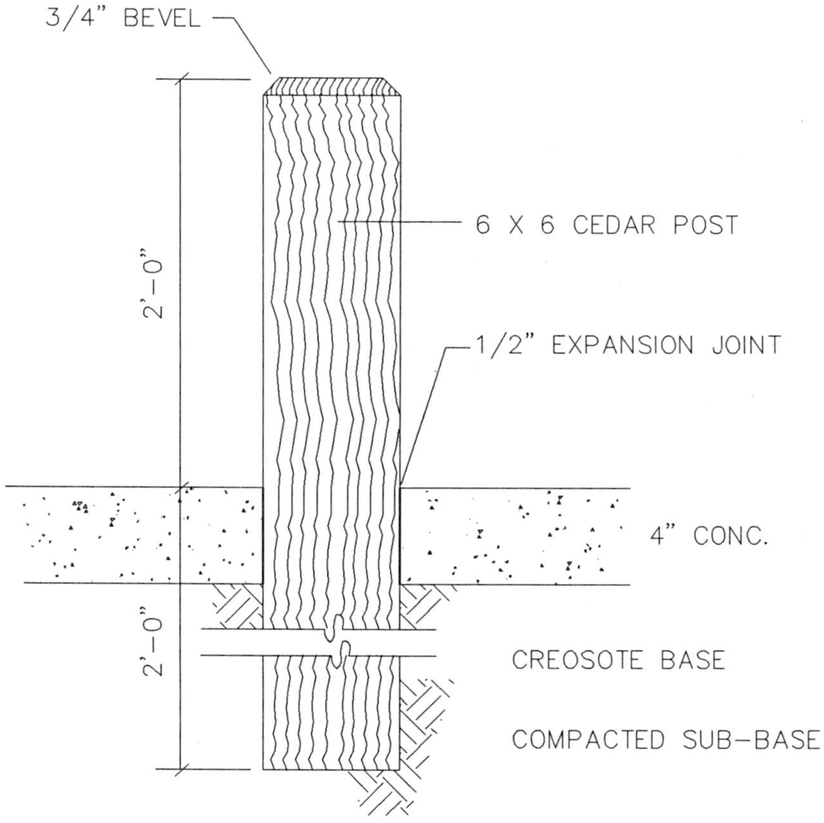
3/4" BEVEL
2'–0"
6 X 6 CEDAR POST
1/2" EXPANSION JOINT
4" CONC.
2'–0"
CREOSOTE BASE
COMPACTED SUB-BASE

WOOD BOLLARD

SCALE: NOT TO SCALE

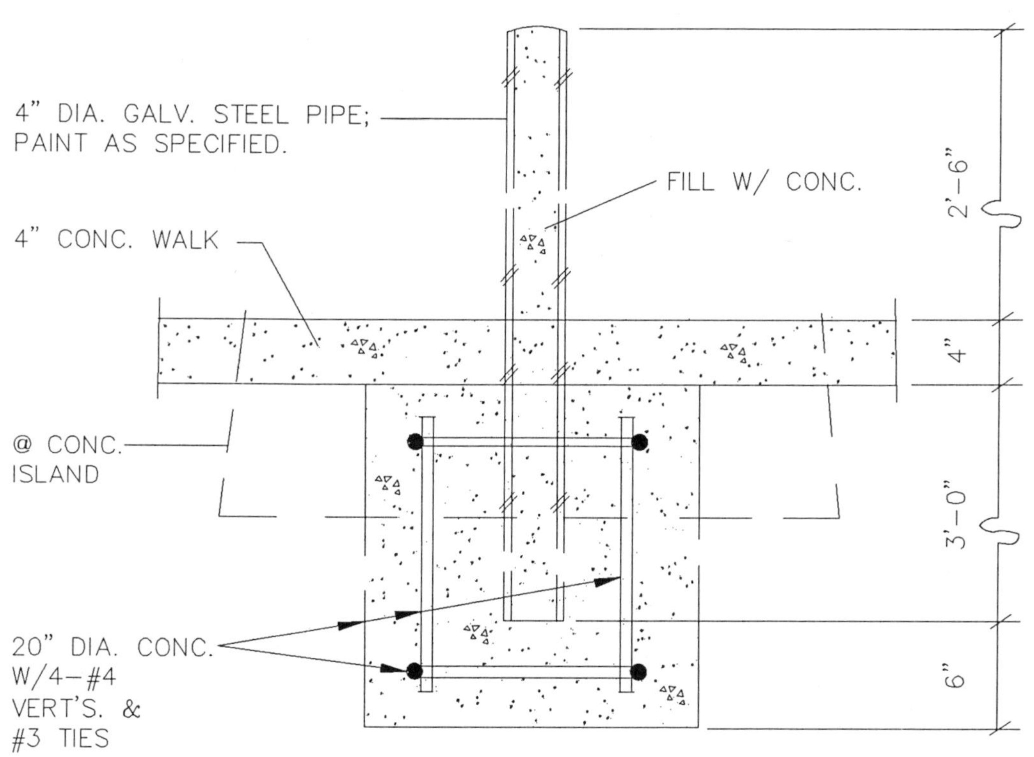
4" DIA. GALV. STEEL PIPE;
PAINT AS SPECIFIED.
FILL W/ CONC.
4" CONC. WALK
@ CONC.
ISLAND
20" DIA. CONC.
W/4–#4
VERT'S. &
#3 TIES
2'–6"
4"
3'–0"
6"

PIPE GUARD BOLLARD

SCALE: NOT TO SCALE

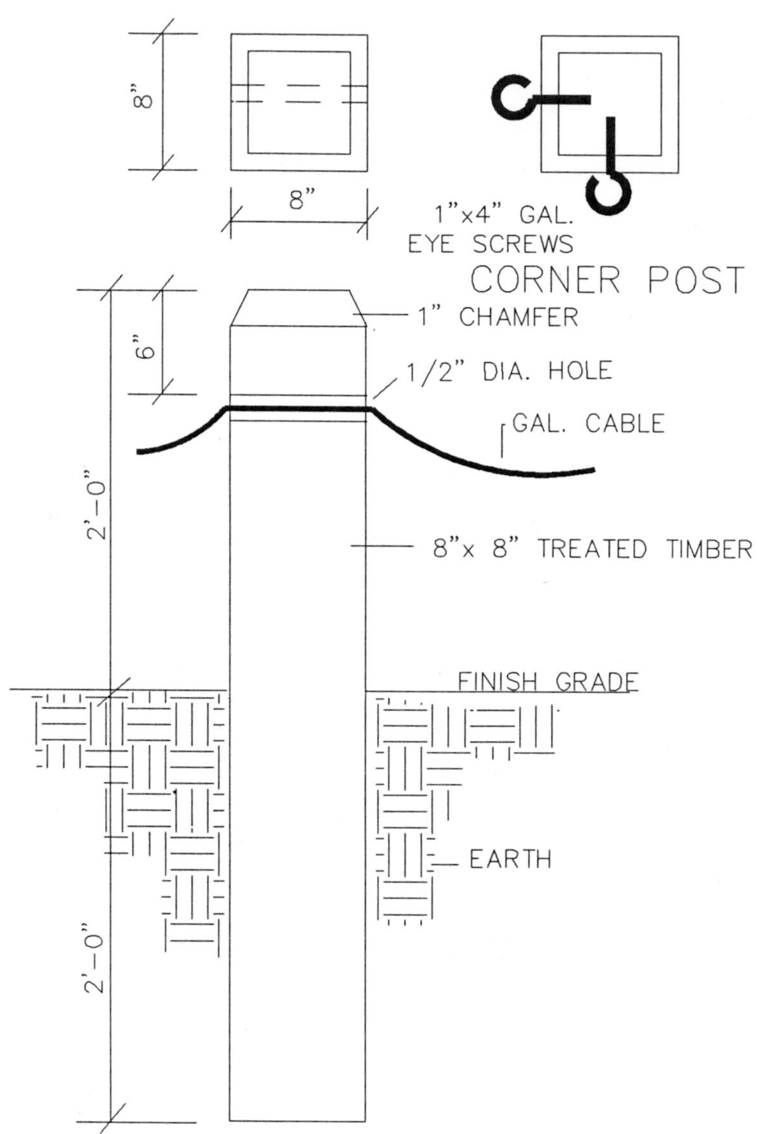

8"
8"
1"x4" GAL.
EYE SCREWS
CORNER POST
6"
1" CHAMFER
1/2" DIA. HOLE
GAL. CABLE
2'-0"
8"x 8" TREATED TIMBER
FINISH GRADE
EARTH
2'-0"

CABLE BOLLARD

SCALE: NOT TO SCALE

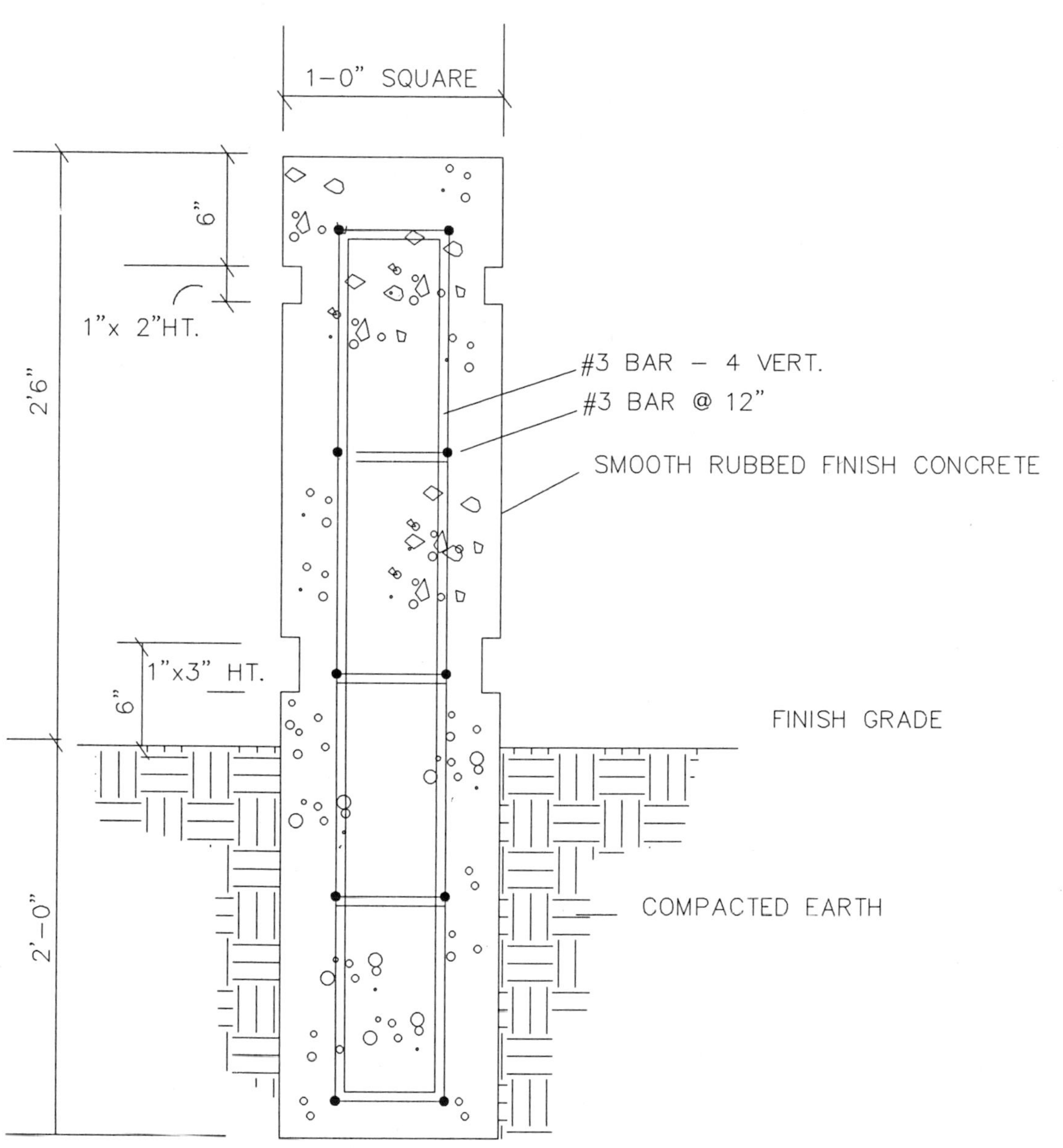
1–0" SQUARE
6"
1"x 2"HT.
2'6"
#3 BAR – 4 VERT.
#3 BAR @ 12"
SMOOTH RUBBED FINISH CONCRETE
1"x3" HT.
6"
FINISH GRADE
COMPACTED EARTH
2'–0"

CONCRETE BOLLARD

SCALE: NOT TO SCALE

Site Furniture

SIZES	12"	18"	24"	30"	36"
24" DIAM.	●	●	●		
30" DIAM.	●	●	●	●	
36" DIAM.	●	●	●	●	●
48" DIAM.		●	●	●	●
60" DIAM.		●	●	●	●
HEIGHTS	12"	18"	24"	30"	36"

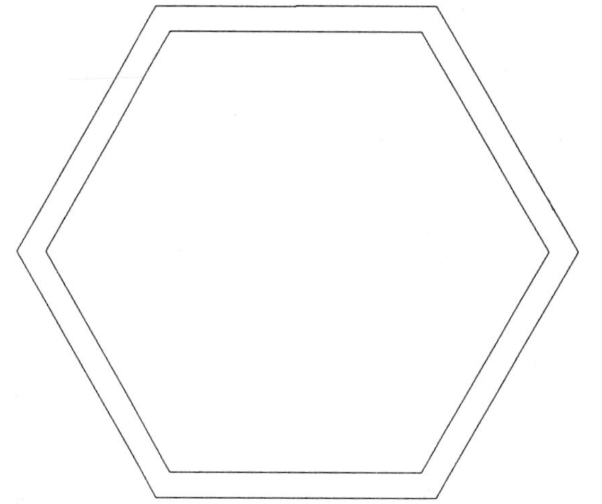

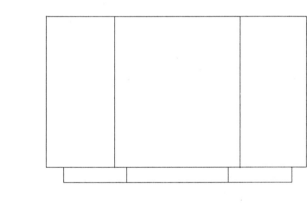

HEXAGONAL PLANTERS \ TYPE FC

SCALE: NOT TO SCALE

SIZE					
18" DIAM.	●	●	●		
24" DIAM.	●	●	●		
30" DIAM.	●	●	●	●	
36" DIAM.		●	●	●	●
48" DIAM.		●	●	●	●
60" DIAM.			●	●	●
72" DIAM.			●	●	●
96" DIAM.			●	●	●
HEIGHTS	12"	18"	24"	30"	36"

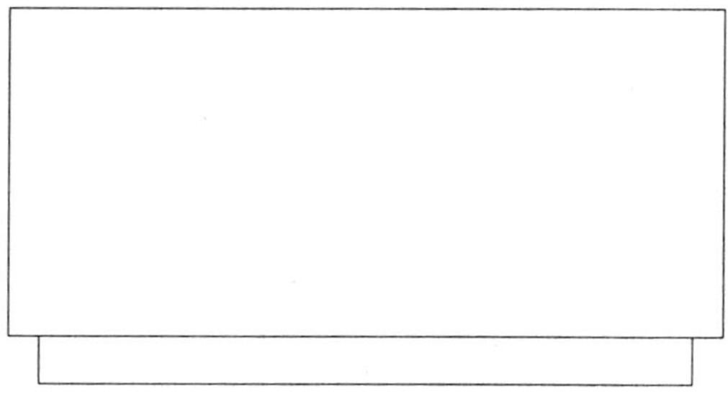

CYLINDRICAL PLANTERS \ TYPE J

SCALE: NOT TO SCALE

SIZES

RECTANGULAR

18" X 36"	●				
24" X 48"		●			
30" X 96"		●	●		
48" X 96"		●	●	●	●
HEIGHTS	18"	24"	30"	36"	48"

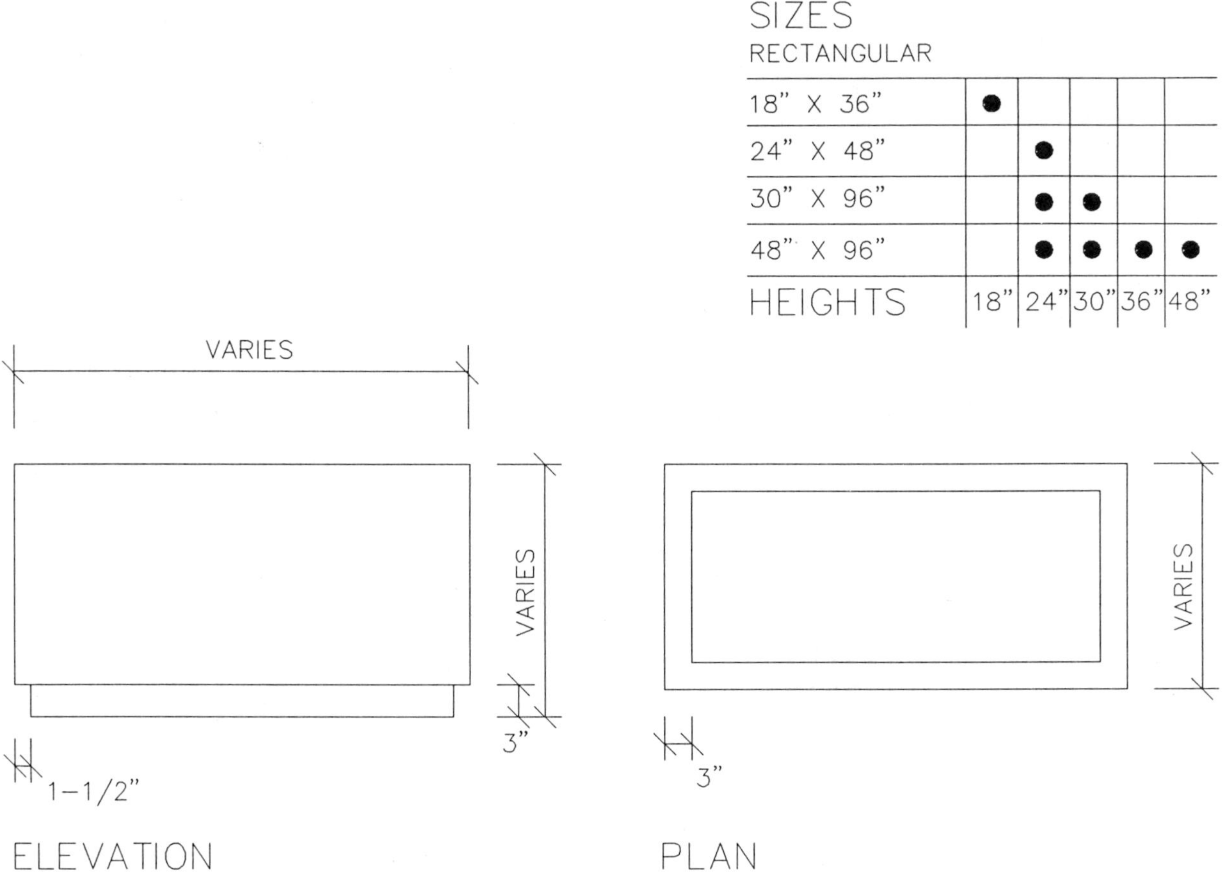
VARIES
VARIES
3"
1-1/2"
ELEVATION
VARIES
3"
PLAN

(SIDEWALK PLANTERS)

RECTANGULAR PLANTERS / TYPE K

SCALE: NOT TO SCALE

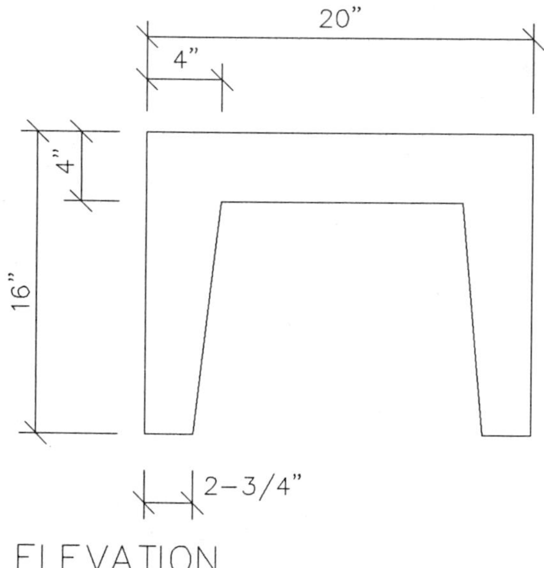
20"
4"
4"
16"
2-3/4"

ELEVATION

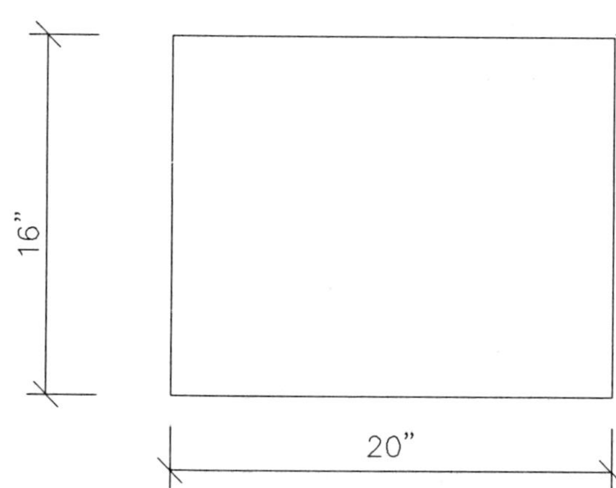
16"
20"

PLAN

LANDSCAPE UNIT / TYPE 71

SCALE: NOT TO SCALE

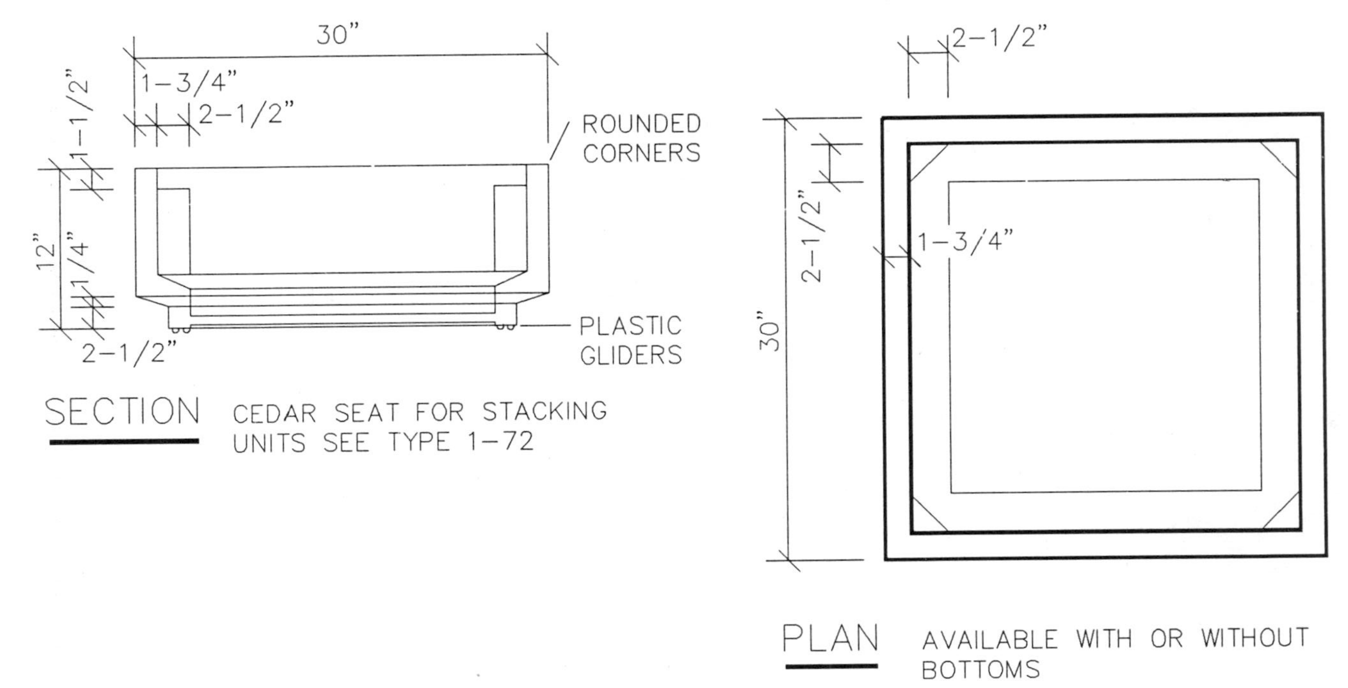
30"
1-3/4"
2-1/2"
1-1/2"
12"
1/4"
2-1/2"
ROUNDED CORNERS
PLASTIC GLIDERS
SECTION
CEDAR SEAT FOR STACKING UNITS SEE TYPE 1-72
2-1/2"
2-1/2"
1-3/4"
30"
PLAN
AVAILABLE WITH OR WITHOUT BOTTOMS

STACKING UNITS / TYPE 1-72

SCALE: NOT TO SCALE

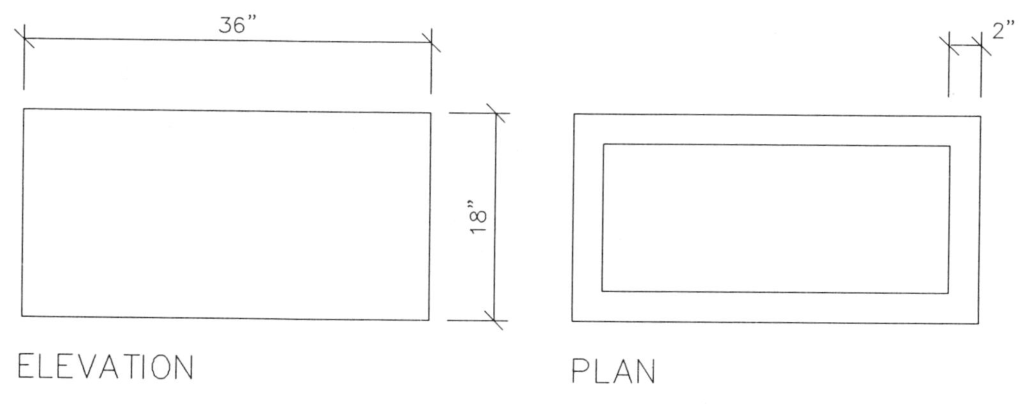
36"
2"
18"
ELEVATION
PLAN

PLANTER / TYPE 1-74

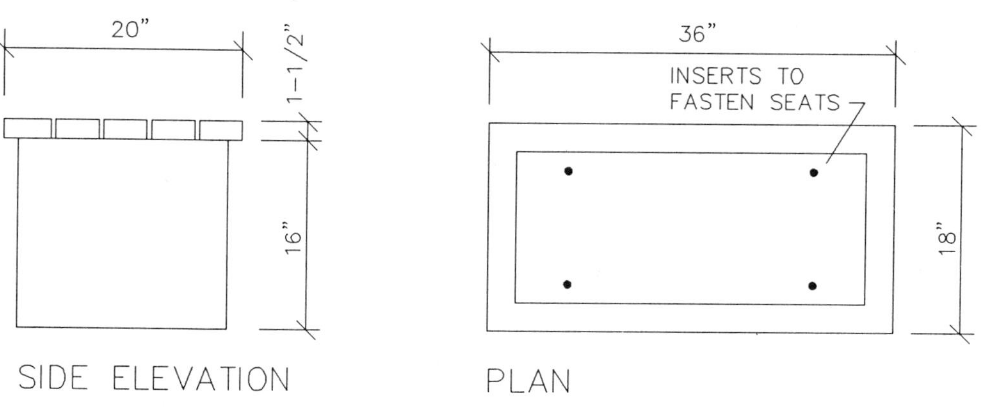
20"
1-1/2"
16"
36"
INSERTS TO
FASTEN SEATS
18"
SIDE ELEVATION
PLAN

BENCH / TYPE 1-74

TYPE 1-74
REVERSIBLE PLANTER AND BENCH UNIT

SCALE: NOT TO SCALE

SIZES						
36" DIAM.	●	●	●	●	●	
48" DIAM.		●	●	●	●	
60" DIAM.		●	●	●	●	
72" DIAM.			●	●	●	
HEIGHTS	12"	18"	24"	30"	36"	

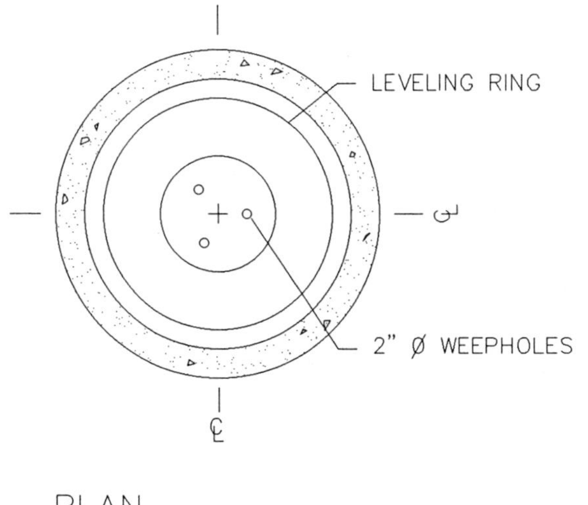
LEVELING RING
2" Ø WEEPHOLES
℄
℄

PLAN

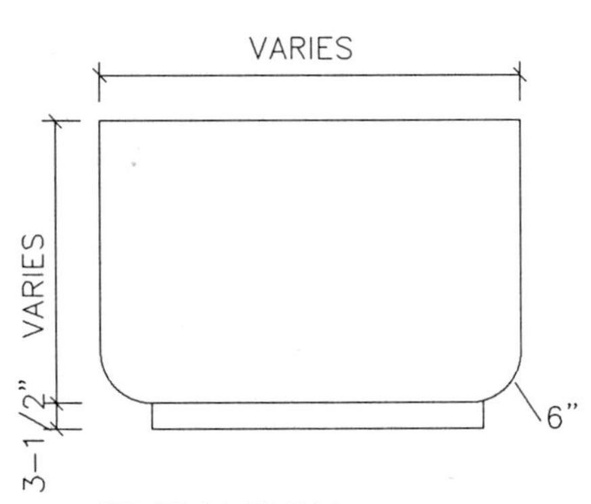
VARIES
VARIES
3-1/2"
6"

ELEVATION

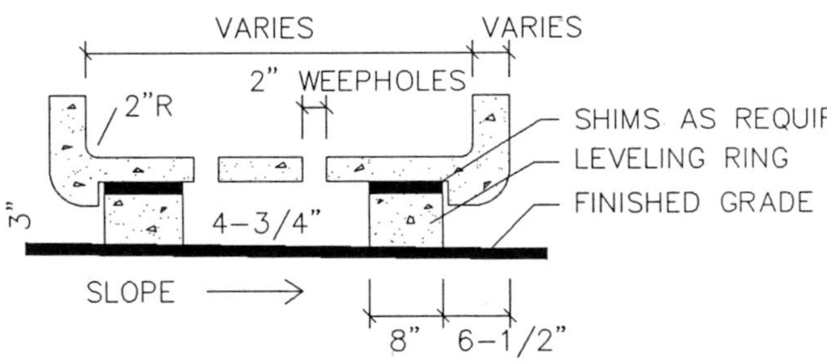
VARIES
VARIES
2" WEEPHOLES
2"R
SHIMS AS REQUIRED
LEVELING RING
FINISHED GRADE
3"
4-3/4"
SLOPE
8"
6-1/2"

SECTION

TYPE JJR
CYLINDRICAL GRADE ADJUSTING PLANTER

SCALE: NOT TO SCALE

SIZES							
12 X 12"	●						
16 X 16"	●						
18 X 18"	●	●	●				
24 X 24"	●	●	●				
30 X 30"	●	●	●	●			
36 X 36"		●	●	●	●		
48 X 48"		●	●	●	●	●	
60 X 60"			●	●	●	●	
72 X 72"				●	●	●	
96 X 96"				●	●	●	
HEIGHTS	12"	18"	24"	30"	36"	48"	

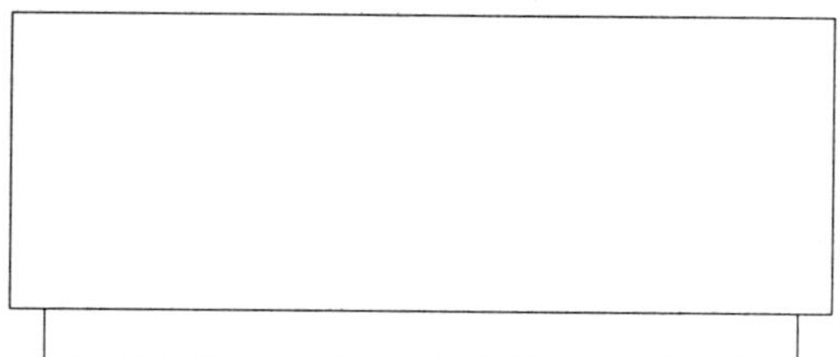

SQUARE PLANTERS / TYPE L

SCALE: NOT TO SCALE

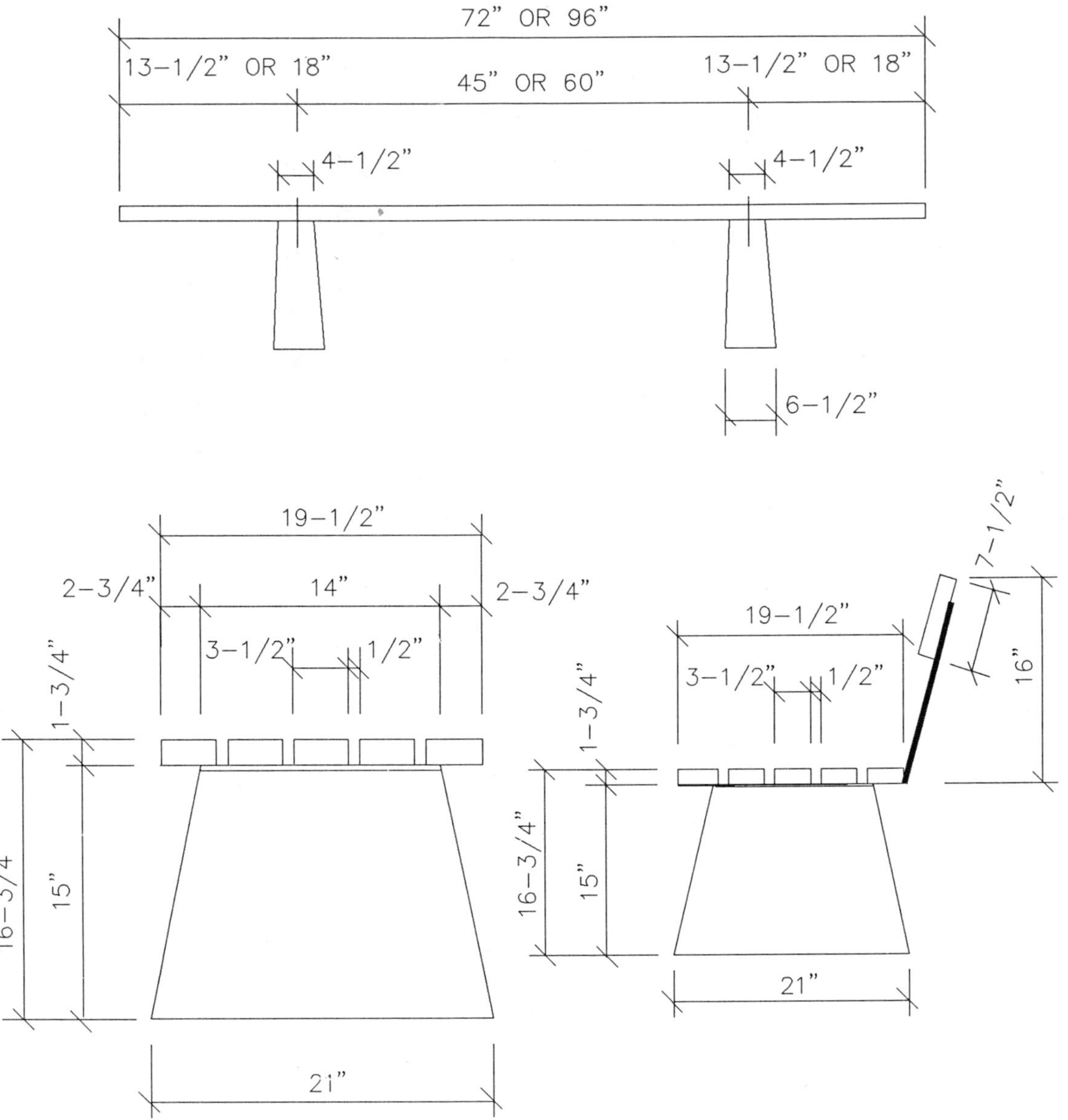
72" OR 96"
13-1/2" OR 18"
45" OR 60"
13-1/2" OR 18"
4-1/2"
4-1/2"
6-1/2"
19-1/2"
2-3/4"
14"
2-3/4"
3-1/2"
1/2"
1-3/4"
16-3/4"
15"
21"
19-1/2"
3-1/2"
1/2"
7-1/2"
16"
1-3/4"
16-3/4"
15"
21"

BENCH / TYPE 264

SCALE: NOT TO SCALE

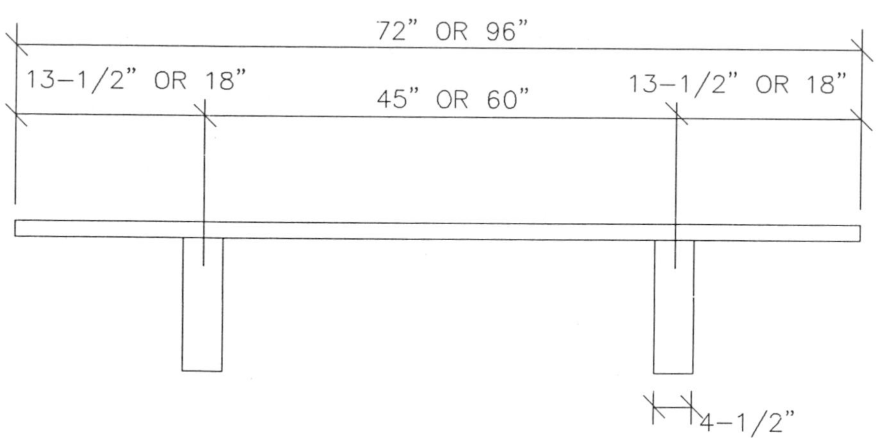
72" OR 96"
13-1/2" OR 18"
45" OR 60"
13-1/2" OR 18"
4-1/2"

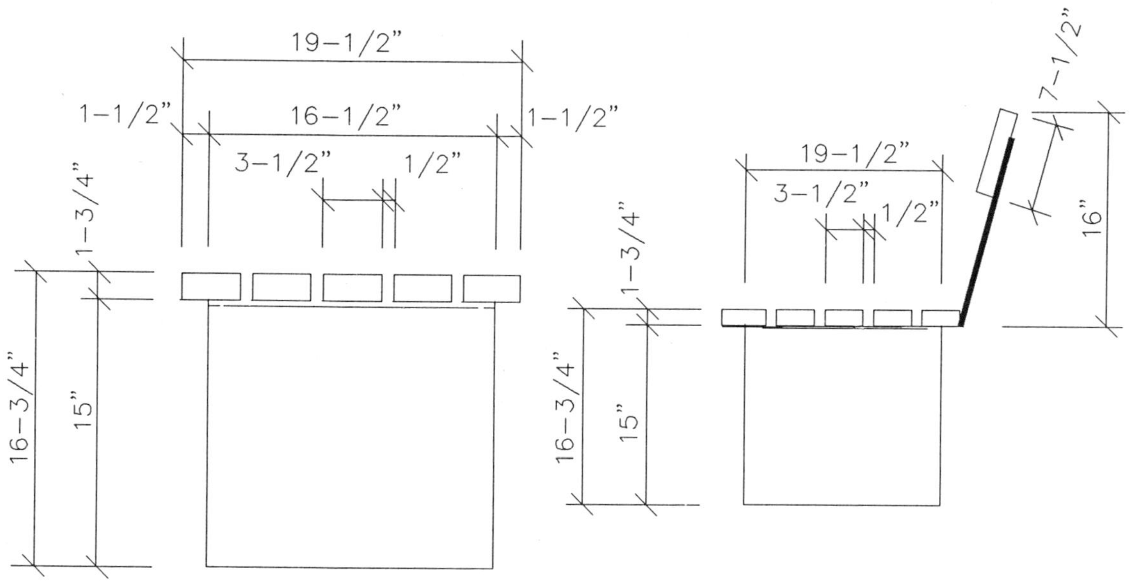
19-1/2"
1-1/2"
16-1/2"
1-1/2"
3-1/2"
1/2"
1-3/4"
16-3/4"
15"
19-1/2"
3-1/2"
1/2"
7-1/2"
16"
1-3/4"
16-3/4"
15"

BENCH / TYPE 364

SCALE: NOT TO SCALE

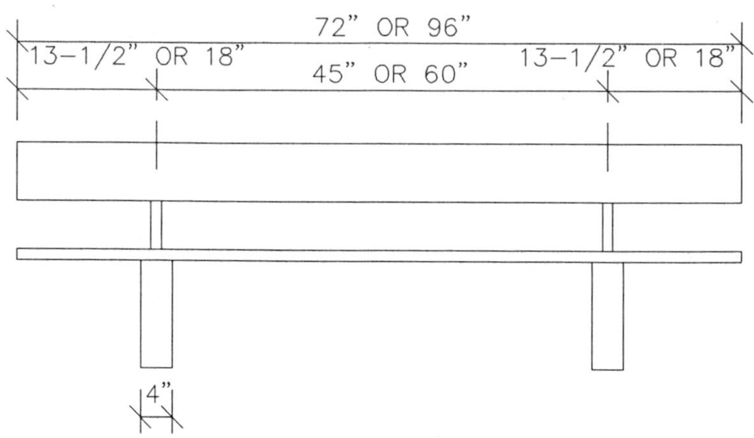
72" OR 96"
13-1/2" OR 18"
45" OR 60"
13-1/2" OR 18"
4"

ELEVATION

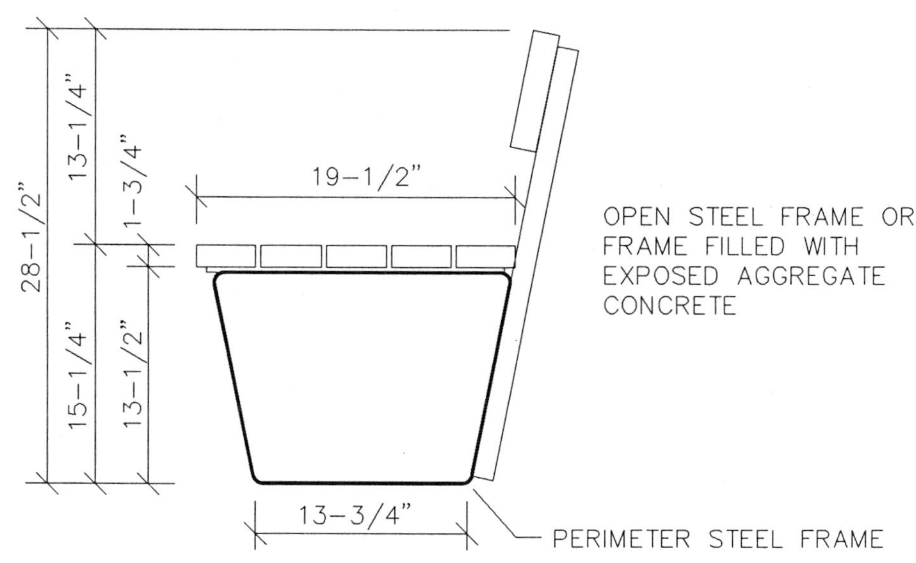
13-1/4"
1-3/4"
28-1/2"
19-1/2"
15-1/4"
13-1/2"
13-3/4"
OPEN STEEL FRAME OR
FRAME FILLED WITH
EXPOSED AGGREGATE
CONCRETE
PERIMETER STEEL FRAME

SECTION

BENCH \ TYPE 167

SCALE: NOT TO SCALE

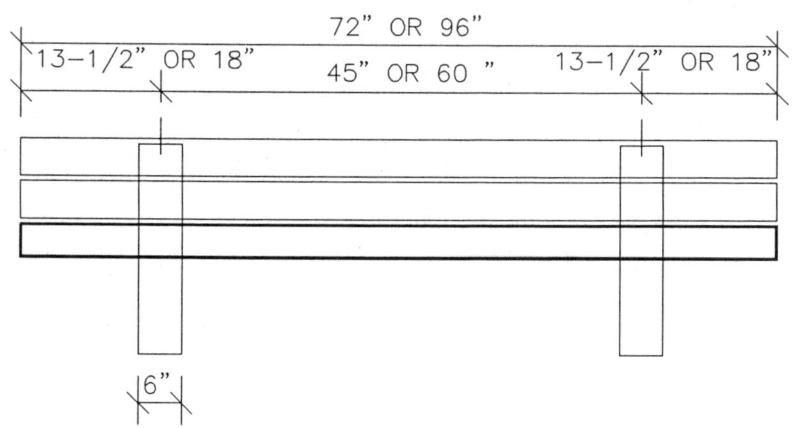
72" OR 96"
13-1/2" OR 18"
45" OR 60 "
13-1/2" OR 18"
6"

ELEVATION

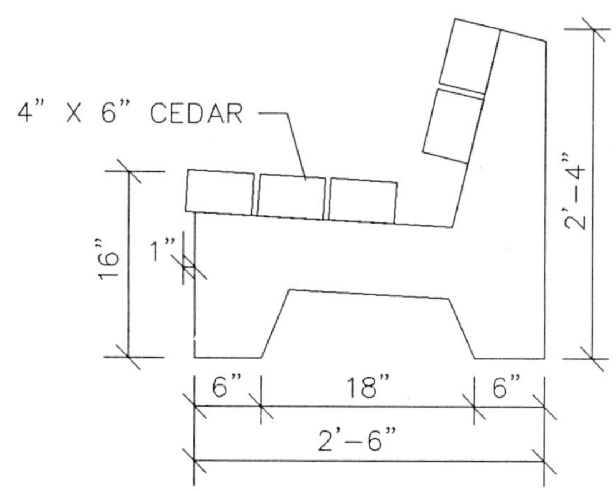
4" X 6" CEDAR
16"
1"
2'-4"
6"
18"
6"
2'-6"

SECTION

BENCH / TYPE 268

SCALE: NOT TO SCALE

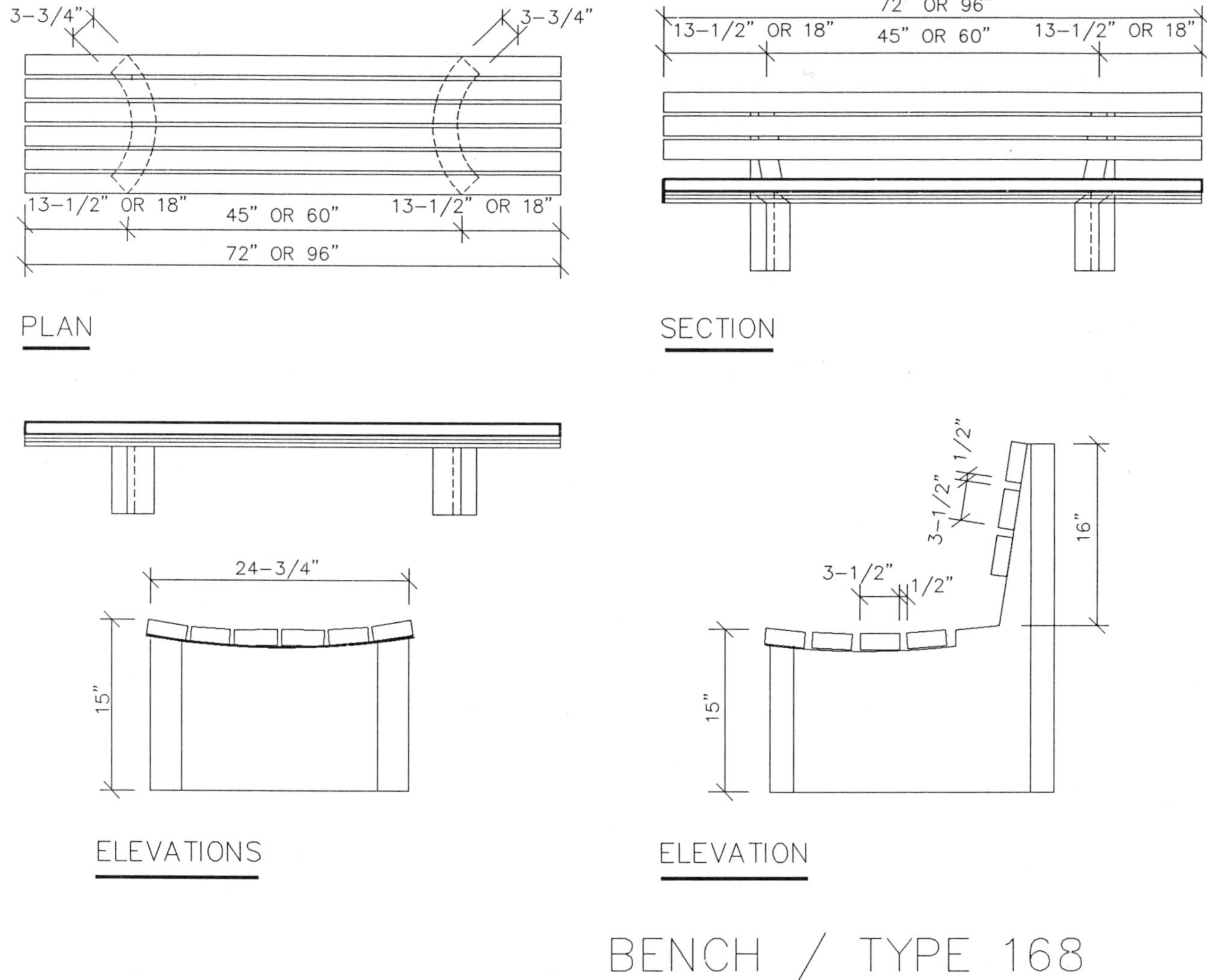
3-3/4"
3-3/4"
13-1/2" OR 18"
45" OR 60"
13-1/2" OR 18"
72" OR 96"
PLAN
72" OR 96"
13-1/2" OR 18"
45" OR 60"
13-1/2" OR 18"
SECTION
24-3/4"
15"
ELEVATIONS
1/2"
3-1/2"
16"
3-1/2"
1/2"
15"
ELEVATION

BENCH / TYPE 168

SCALE: NOT TO SCALE

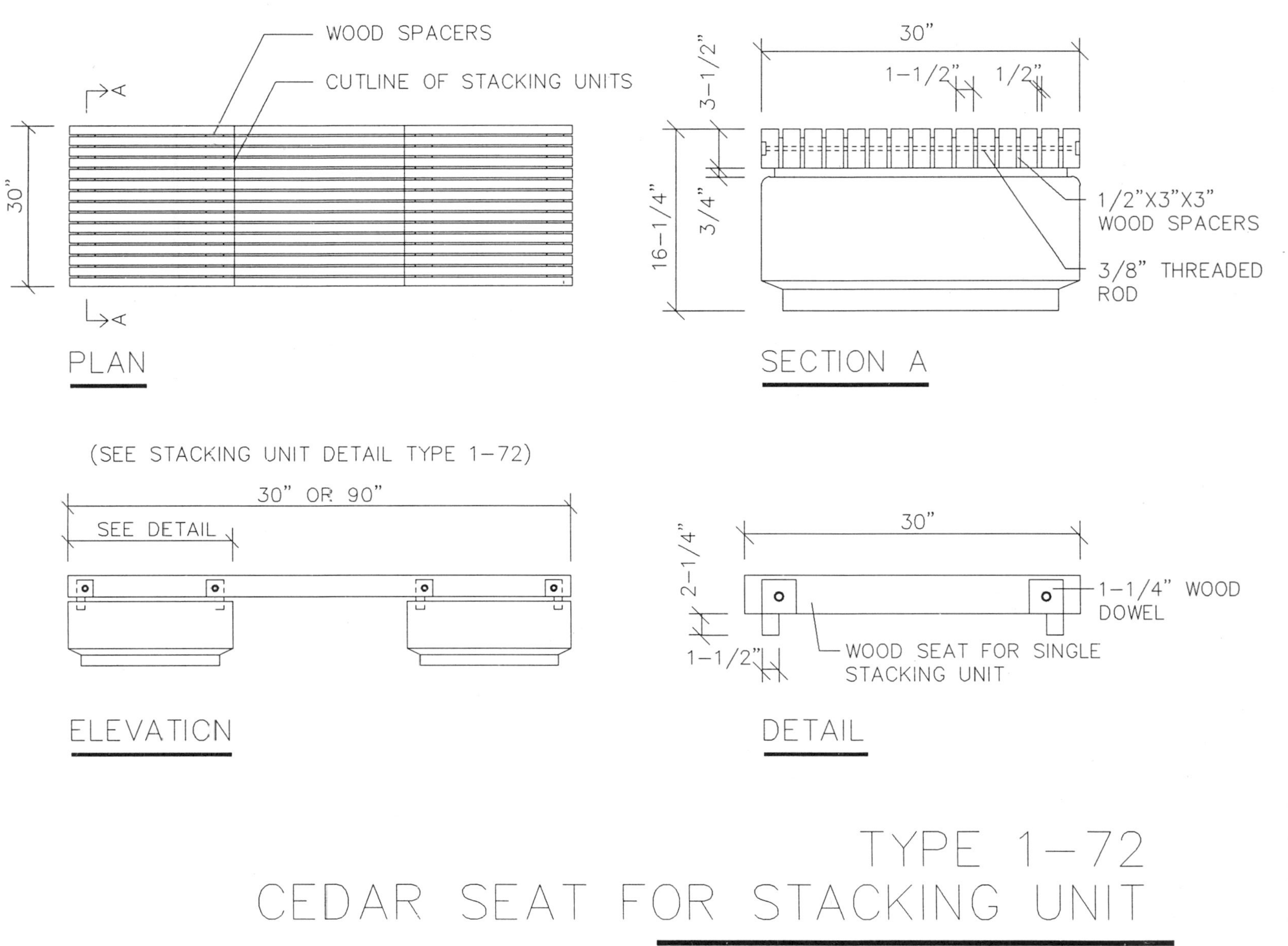
WOOD SPACERS
CUTLINE OF STACKING UNITS
30"
A
A
PLAN
30"
1-1/2"
1/2"
3-1/2"
3/4"
16-1/4"
1/2"X3"X3"
WOOD SPACERS
3/8" THREADED
ROD
SECTION A
(SEE STACKING UNIT DETAIL TYPE 1-72)
30" OR 90"
SEE DETAIL
ELEVATICN
30"
2-1/4"
1-1/2"
1-1/4" WOOD
DOWEL
WOOD SEAT FOR SINGLE
STACKING UNIT
DETAIL
TYPE 1-72
CEDAR SEAT FOR STACKING UNIT
SCALE: NOT TO SCALE

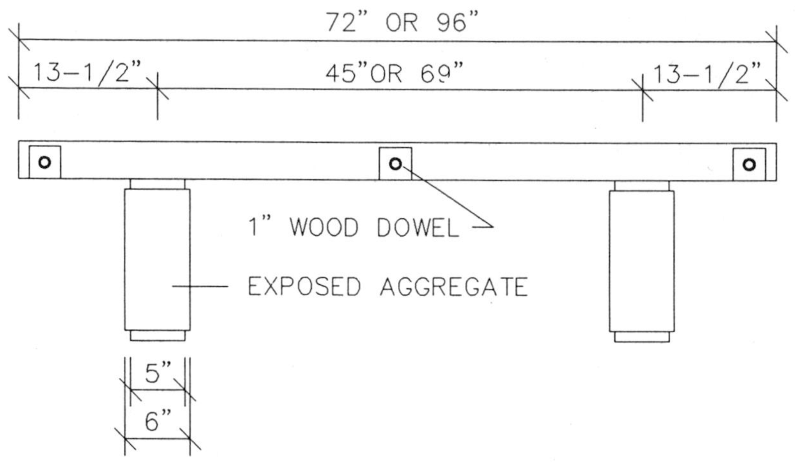
72" OR 96"
13-1/2"
45"OR 69"
13-1/2"
1" WOOD DOWEL
EXPOSED AGGREGATE
5"
6"

ELEVATION

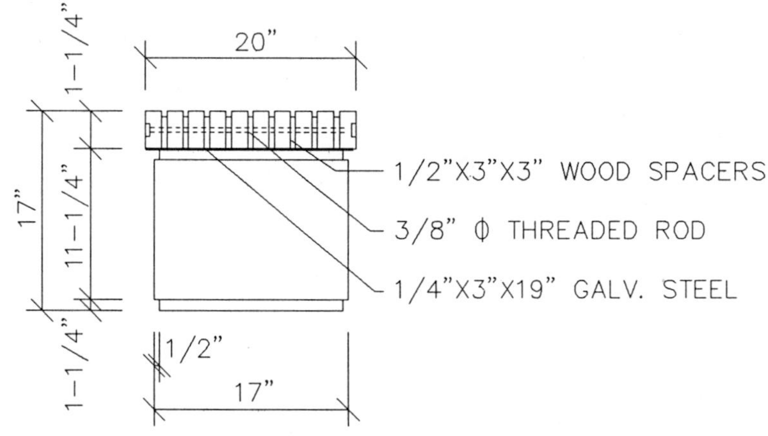
20"
1-1/4"
17"
11-1/4"
1-1/4"
1/2"X3"X3" WOOD SPACERS
3/8" Φ THREADED ROD
1/4"X3"X19" GALV. STEEL
1/2"
17"

SECTION

BENCH / TYPE 272

SCALE: NOT TO SCALE

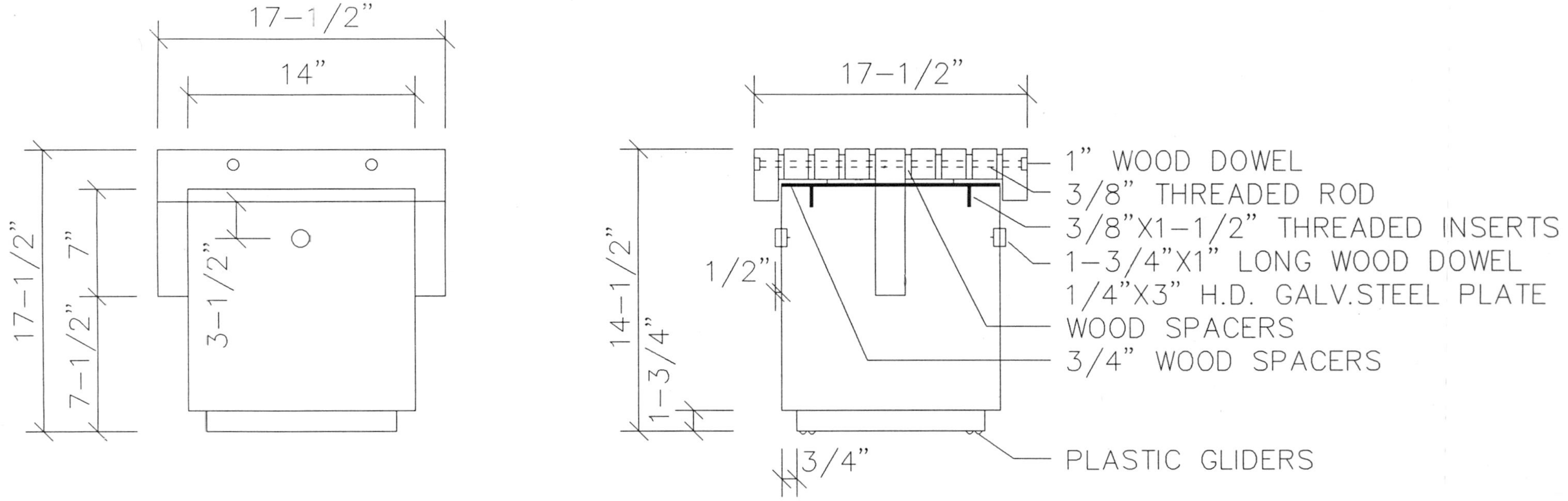

17-1/2"
14"
17-1/2"
7"
7-1/2"
3-1/2"

ELEVATION

17-1/2"
14-1/2"
1-3/4"
1/2"
3/4"

1" WOOD DOWEL
3/8" THREADED ROD
3/8"X1-1/2" THREADED INSERTS
1-3/4"X1" LONG WOOD DOWEL
1/4"X3" H.D. GALV.STEEL PLATE
WOOD SPACERS
3/4" WOOD SPACERS
PLASTIC GLIDERS

SECTION

STOOL / TYPE 273

SCALE: NOT TO SCALE

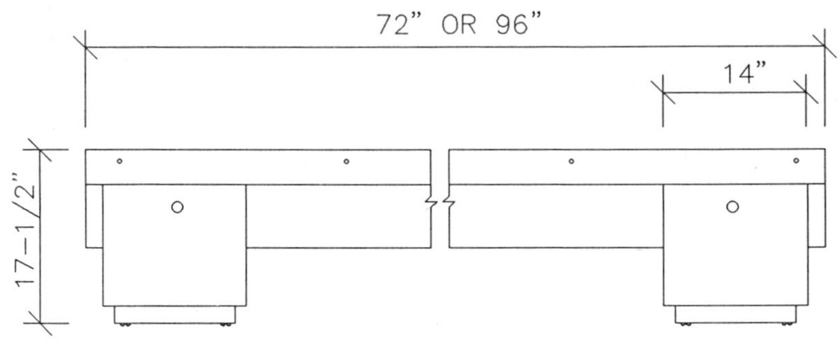
72" OR 96"
14"
17-1/2"

ELEVATION

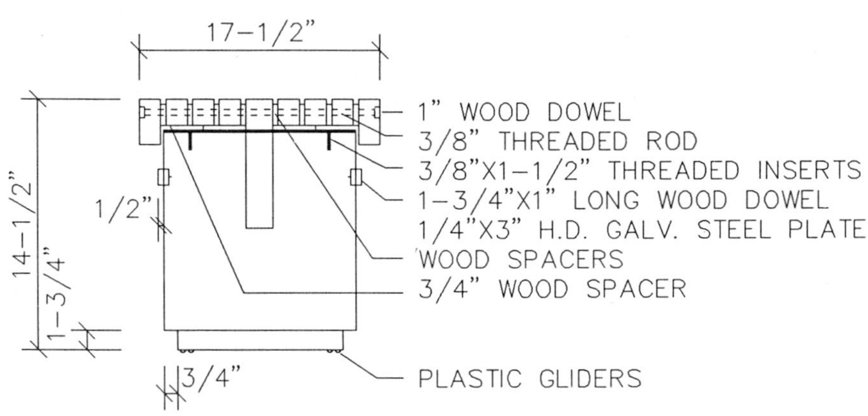
17-1/2"
14-1/2"
1/2"
1-3/4"
3/4"
1" WOOD DOWEL
3/8" THREADED ROD
3/8"X1-1/2" THREADED INSERTS
1-3/4"X1" LONG WOOD DOWEL
1/4"X3" H.D. GALV. STEEL PLATE
WOOD SPACERS
3/4" WOOD SPACER
PLASTIC GLIDERS

SECTION

BENCH \ TYPE 173

SCALE: NOT TO SCALE

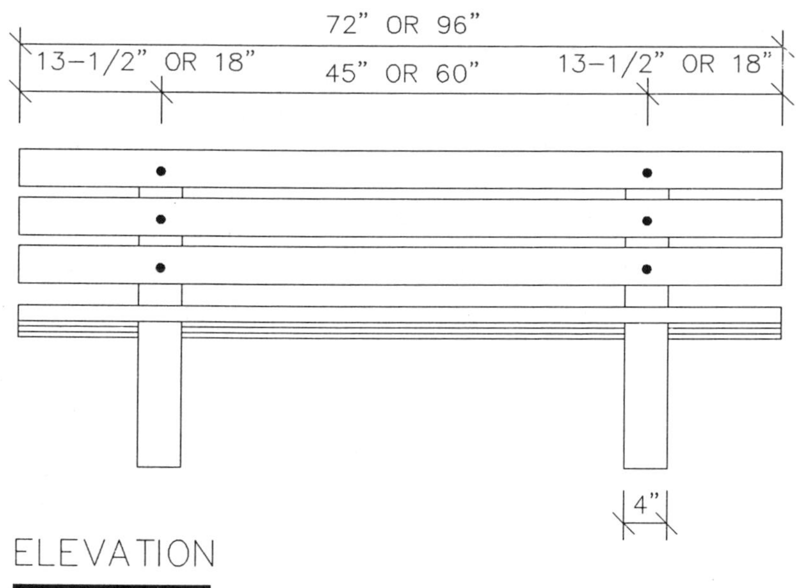
72" OR 96"
13-1/2" OR 18"
45" OR 60"
13-1/2" OR 18"
4"

ELEVATION

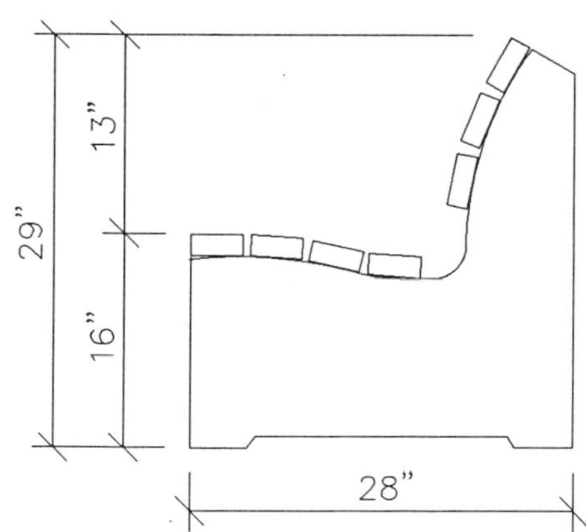
29"
13"
16"
28"

SECTION

BENCH / TYPE 180

SCALE: NOT TO SCALE

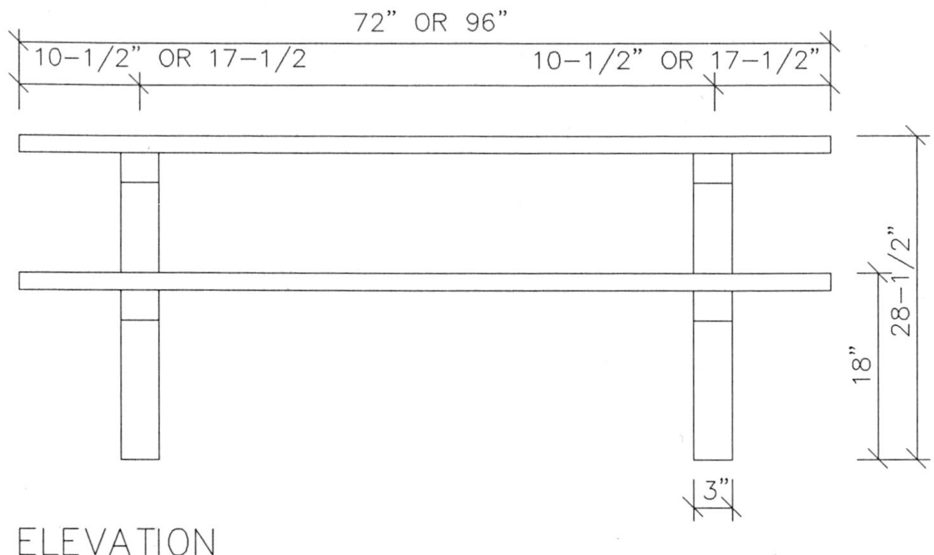
72" OR 96"
10-1/2" OR 17-1/2
10-1/2" OR 17-1/2"
28-1/2"
18"
3"
ELEVATION

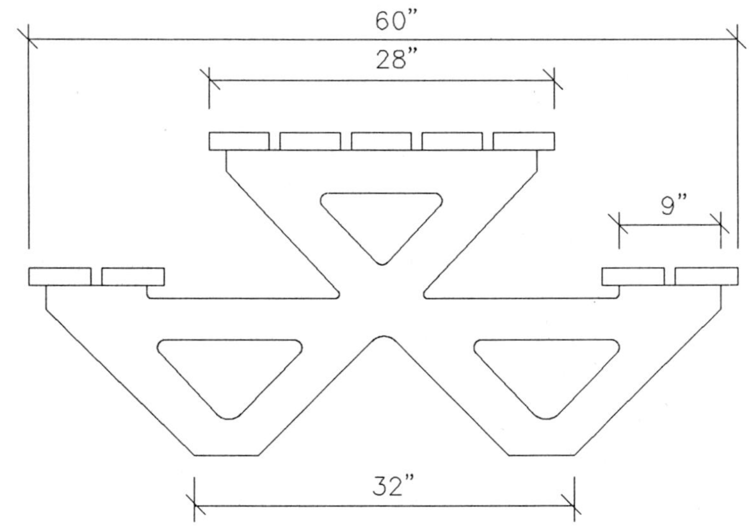
60"
28"
9"
32"
SECTION

PICNIC TABLE/ TYPE 761

SCALE: NOT TO SCALE

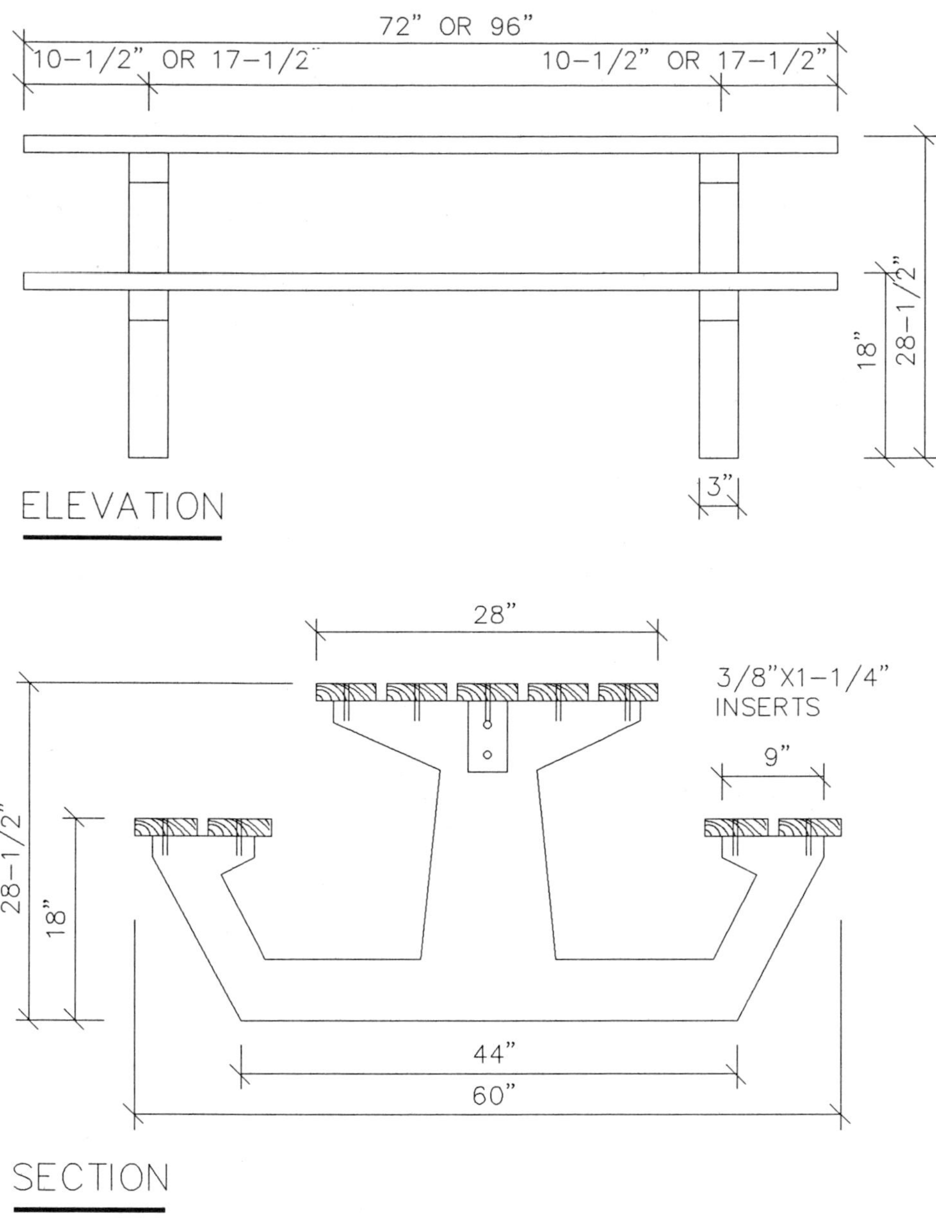
72" OR 96"
10-1/2" OR 17-1/2"
10-1/2" OR 17-1/2"
18"
28-1/2"
3"
ELEVATION
28"
3/8"X1-1/4"
INSERTS
9"
28-1/2"
18"
44"
60"
SECTION

PICNIC TABLE / TYPE 762

SCALE: NOT TO SCALE

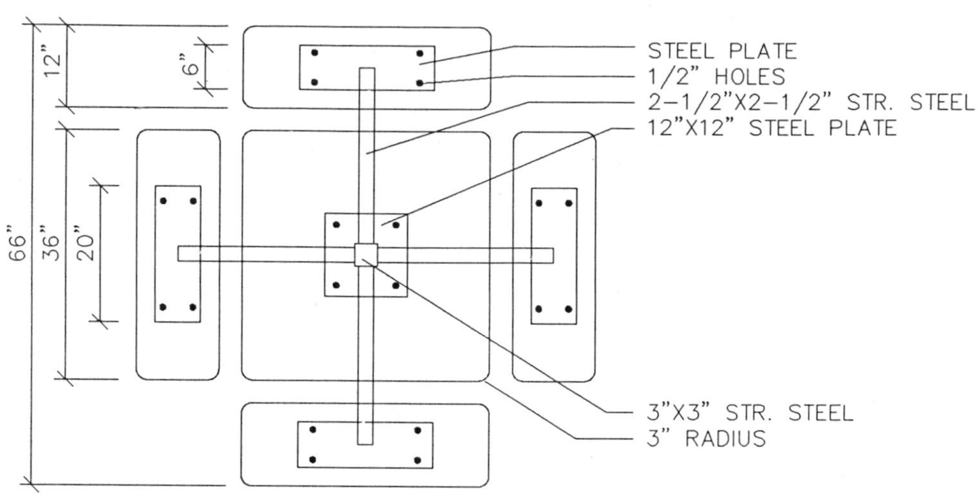
STEEL PLATE
1/2" HOLES
2-1/2"X2-1/2" STR. STEEL
12"X12" STEEL PLATE
3"X3" STR. STEEL
3" RADIUS
66"
36"
20"
12"
6"

PLAN

FINISH: WATERPROOF SMOOTH TERRAZZO, OR AS SPECIFIED

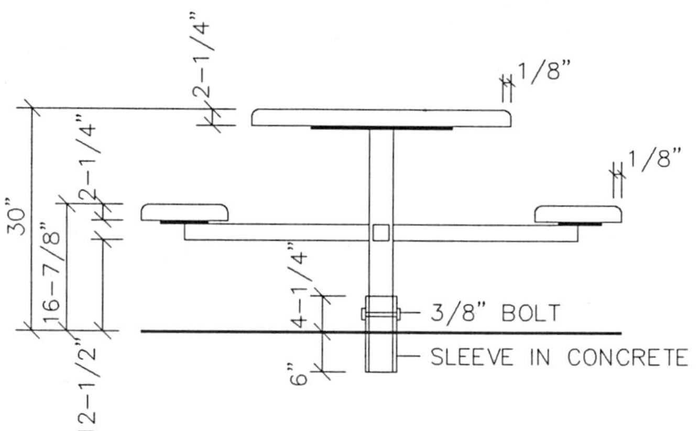
2-1/4"
1/8"
2-1/4"
1/8"
30"
16-7/8"
2-1/4"
4-1/4"
3/8" BOLT
SLEEVE IN CONCRETE
6"
12-1/2"

* "A" DENOTES CENTER COLUMN SUPPORT FOR PERMANENT INSTALLATION. "B" DENOTES SUPPORTS UNDER CENTER OF SEATS FOR PORTABILITY. BOTH TABLE STYLES AVAILABLE WITH OR WITHOUT CENTER UMBRELLA HOLE.

SECTION

TYPE 7702–A, 7702–B *
OUTDOOR TABLE SEATING

SCALE: NOT TO SCALE

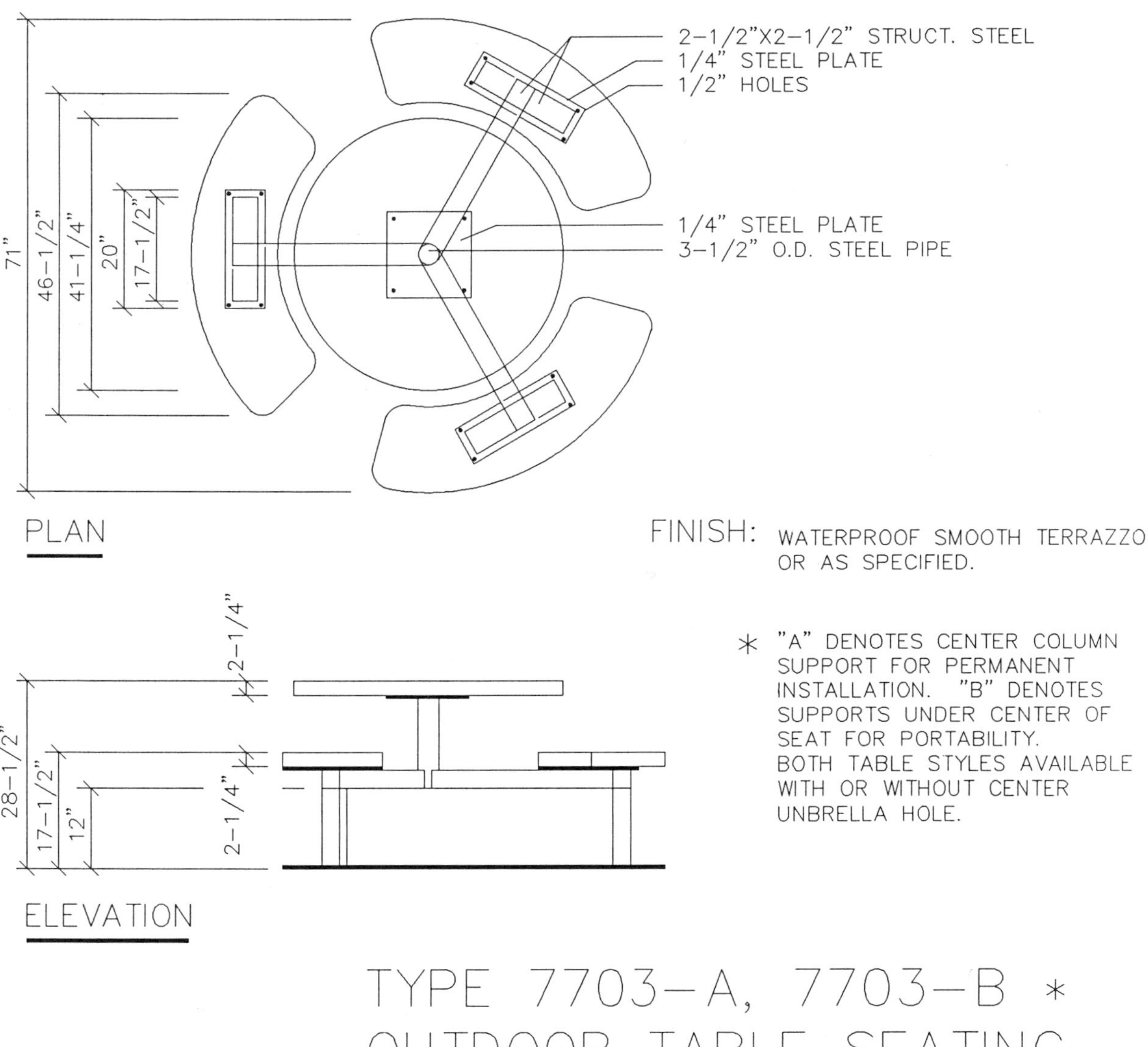
2-1/2"X2-1/2" STRUCT. STEEL
1/4" STEEL PLATE
1/2" HOLES
1/4" STEEL PLATE
3-1/2" O.D. STEEL PIPE
71"
46-1/2"
41-1/4"
20"
17-1/2"
PLAN
2-1/4"
28-1/2"
17-1/2"
12"
2-1/4"
ELEVATION

FINISH: WATERPROOF SMOOTH TERRAZZO OR AS SPECIFIED.

* "A" DENOTES CENTER COLUMN SUPPORT FOR PERMANENT INSTALLATION. "B" DENOTES SUPPORTS UNDER CENTER OF SEAT FOR PORTABILITY. BOTH TABLE STYLES AVAILABLE WITH OR WITHOUT CENTER UNBRELLA HOLE.

TYPE 7703-A, 7703-B *
OUTDOOR TABLE SEATING

SCALE: NOT TO SCALE

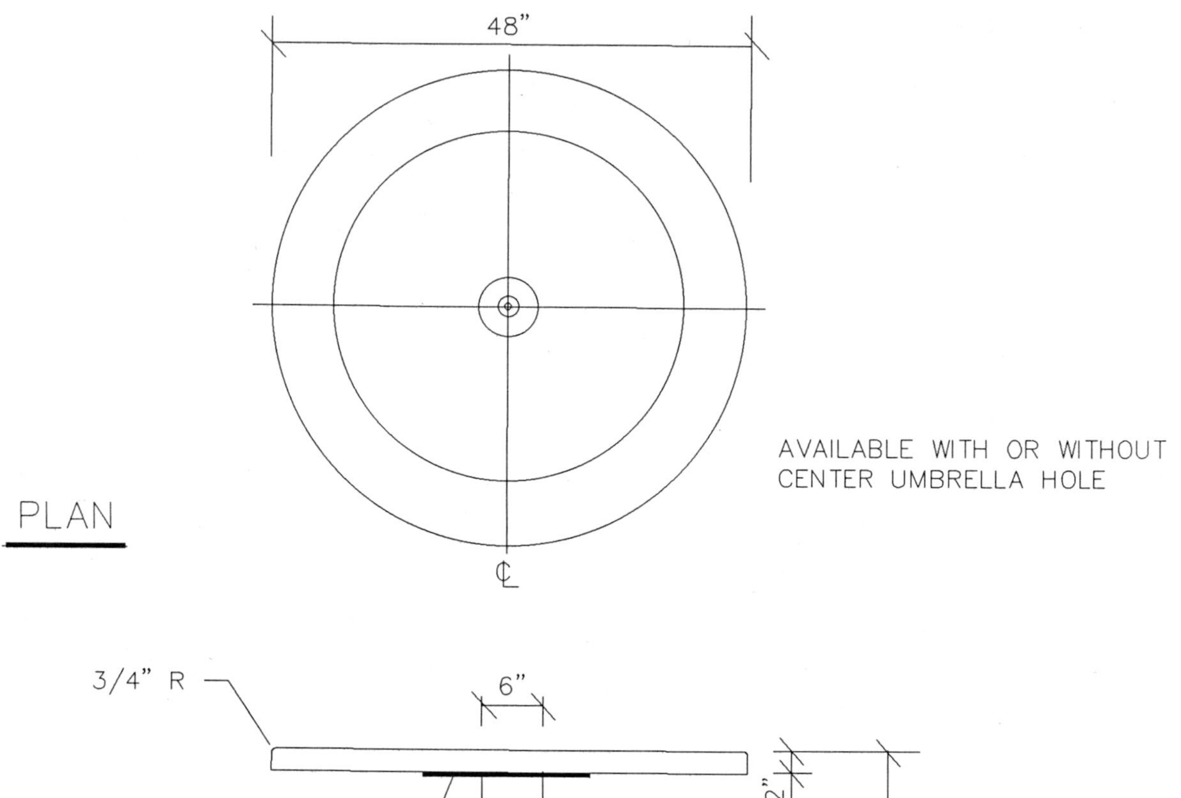
48"
AVAILABLE WITH OR WITHOUT
CENTER UMBRELLA HOLE
PLAN
℄

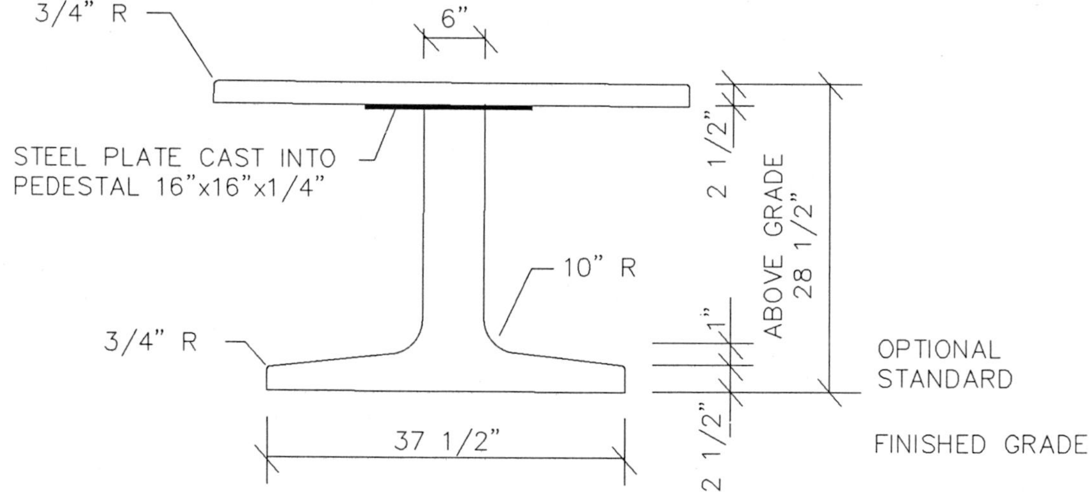
3/4" R
6"
STEEL PLATE CAST INTO
PEDESTAL 16"x16"x1/4"
10" R
3/4" R
37 1/2"
2 1/2"
1"
2 1/2"
ABOVE GRADE
28 1/2"
OPTIONAL
STANDARD
FINISHED GRADE
ELEVATION

PATIO TABLE/PT-1

SCALE: NOT TO SCALE

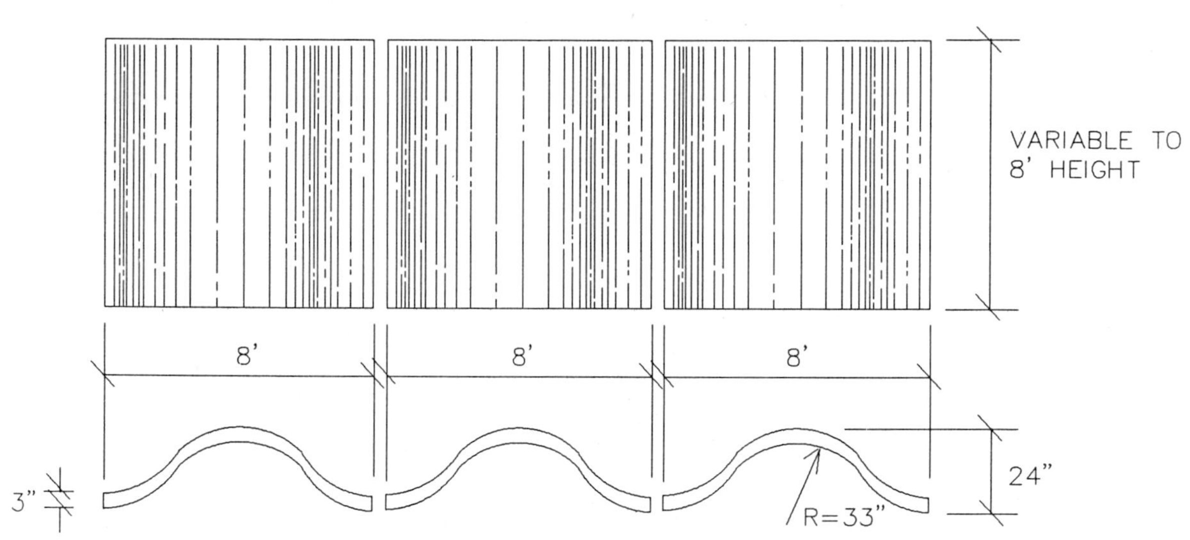
VARIABLE TO
8' HEIGHT
8'
8'
8'
3"
24"
R=33"

INSTALLATION OPTIONS: FROST FREE FOOTING OR PAD,
ANCHORED OR FREE STANDING

FRONT TOP VIEW

SERPENTINE SCREEN WALL

SCALE: NOT TO SCALE

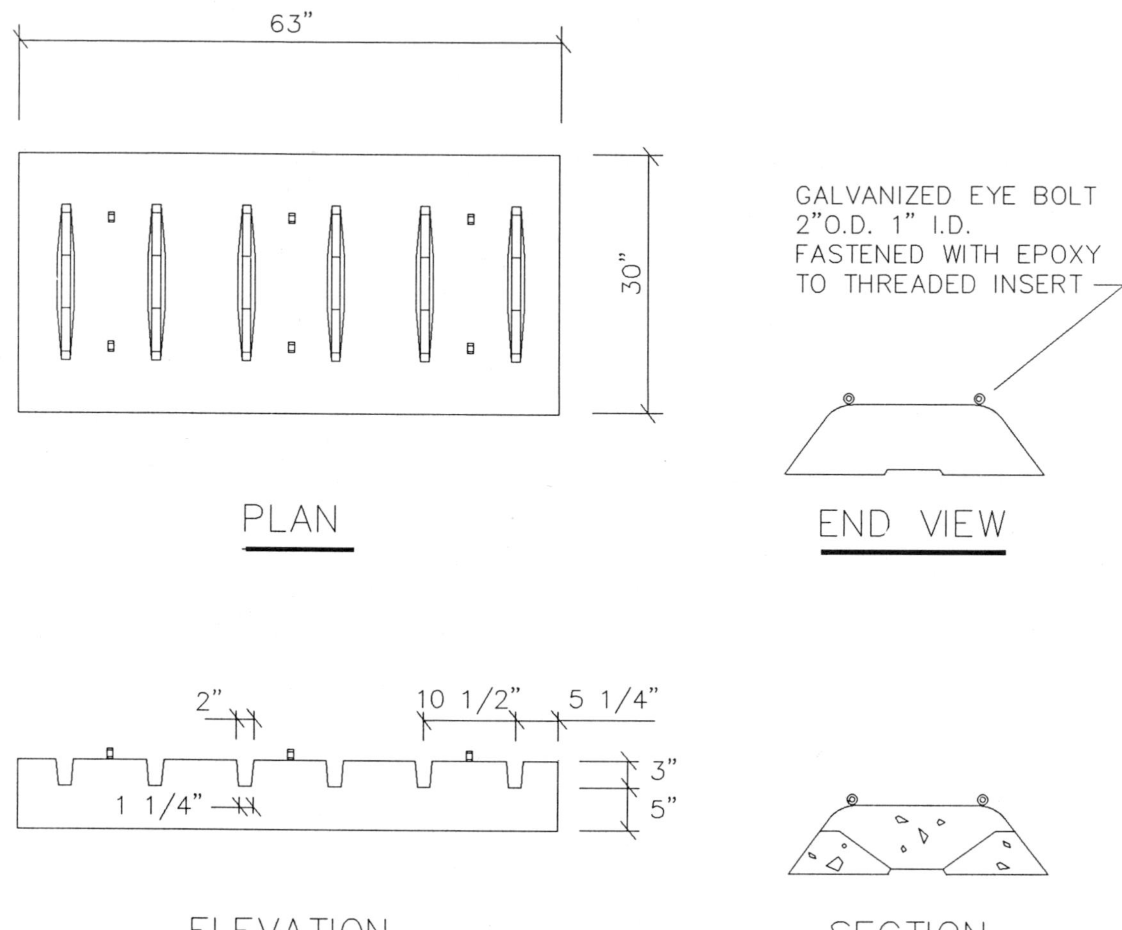
63"
30"
GALVANIZED EYE BOLT
2"O.D. 1" I.D.
FASTENED WITH EPOXY
TO THREADED INSERT
PLAN
END VIEW
2"
10 1/2"
5 1/4"
3"
5"
1 1/4"
ELEVATION
SECTION

BICYCLE BASE

SCALE: NOT TO SCALE

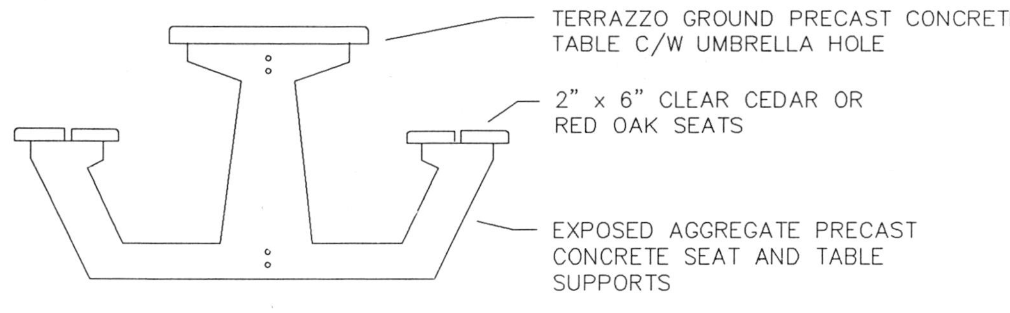
TERRAZZO GROUND PRECAST CONCRETE
TABLE C/W UMBRELLA HOLE
2" x 6" CLEAR CEDAR OR
RED OAK SEATS
EXPOSED AGGREGATE PRECAST
CONCRETE SEAT AND TABLE
SUPPORTS

ELEVATION

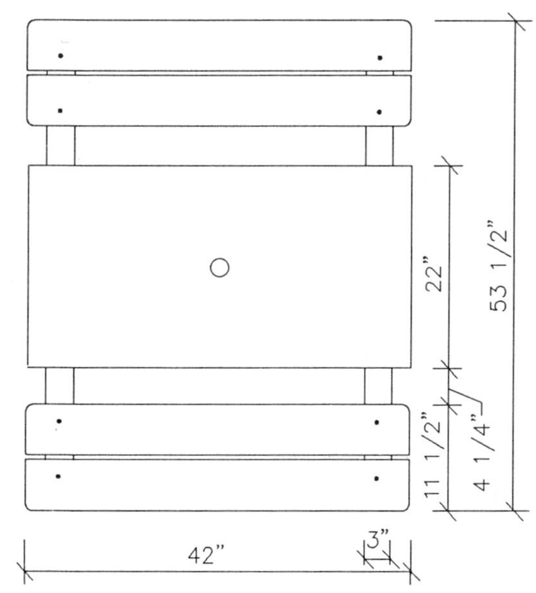
22"
53 1/2"
11 1/2"
4 1/4"
42"
3"

PLAN

FAST FOOD AND BAR PATIO TABLES/TYPE 185

SCALE: NOT TO SCALE

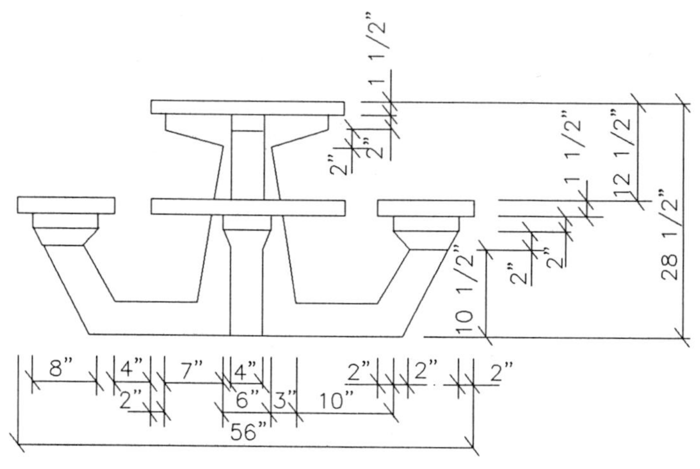

1 1/2"
2"
2"
1 1/2"
12 1/2"
28 1/2"
2"
2"
10 1/2"
8"
4"
2"
7"
4"
6"
3"
10"
2"
2"
2"
56"

ELEVATION

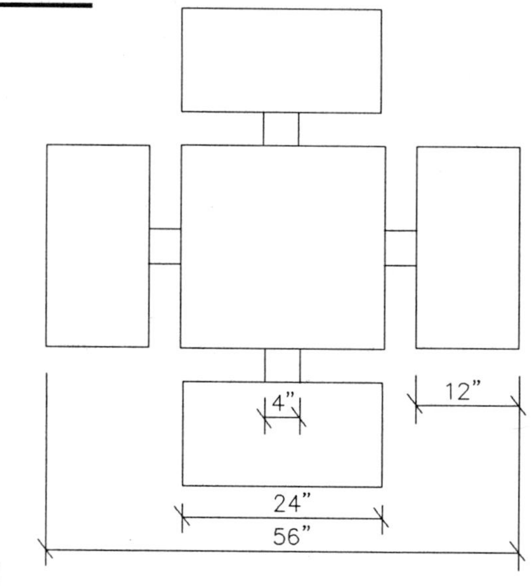

4"
12"
24"
56"

PLAN

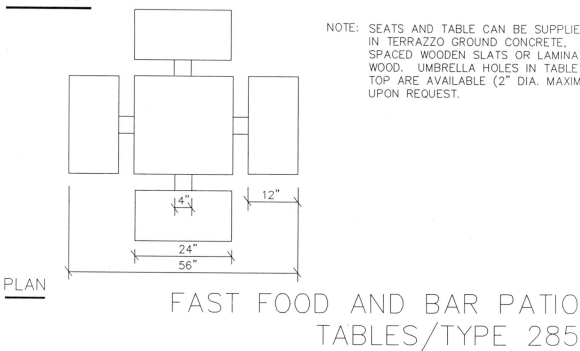

NOTE: SEATS AND TABLE CAN BE SUPPLIED IN TERRAZZO GROUND CONCRETE, SPACED WOODEN SLATS OR LAMINATED WOOD. UMBRELLA HOLES IN TABLE TOP ARE AVAILABLE (2" DIA. MAXIMUM) UPON REQUEST.

FAST FOOD AND BAR PATIO TABLES/TYPE 285

SCALE: NOT TO SCALE

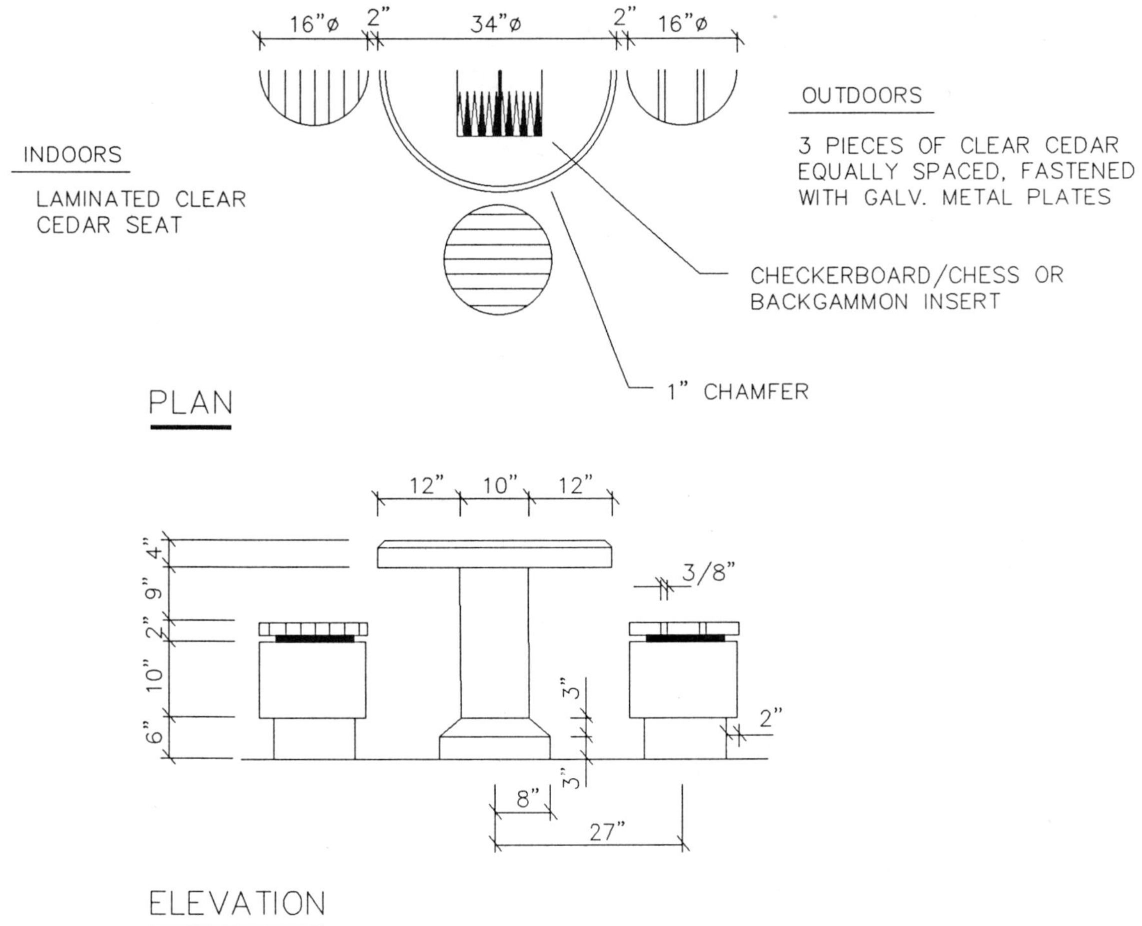
16"ø
2"
34"ø
2"
16"ø
OUTDOORS
3 PIECES OF CLEAR CEDAR EQUALLY SPACED, FASTENED WITH GALV. METAL PLATES
INDOORS
LAMINATED CLEAR CEDAR SEAT
CHECKERBOARD/CHESS OR BACKGAMMON INSERT
1" CHAMFER
PLAN
12"
10"
12"
3/8"
4"
9"
2"
10"
6"
3"
2"
3"
8"
27"
ELEVATION

GAMES TABLES AND STOOLS / TYPE GT-1

SCALE: NOT TO SCALE

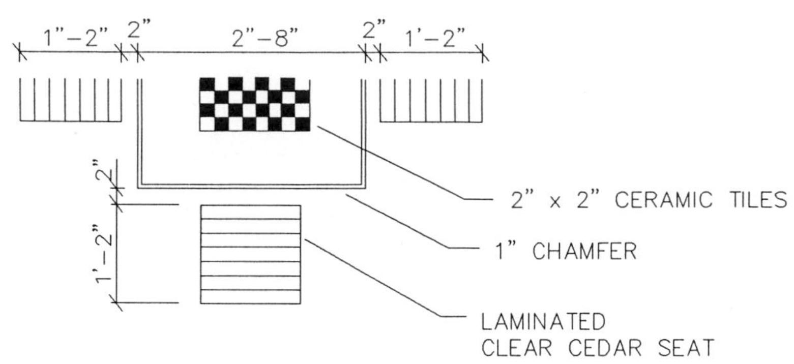
1"−2"
2"
2"−8"
2"
1'−2"
2"
1'−2"
2" x 2" CERAMIC TILES
1" CHAMFER
LAMINATED
CLEAR CEDAR SEAT

PLAN

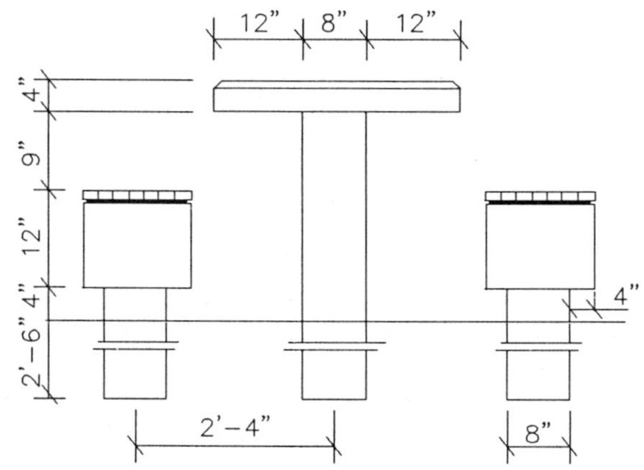
12"
8"
12"
4"
9"
12"
4"
2'−6"
4"
2'−4"
8"

ELEVATION

GAMES TABLE AND STOOLS / TYPE GT−3

SCALE: NOT TO SCALE

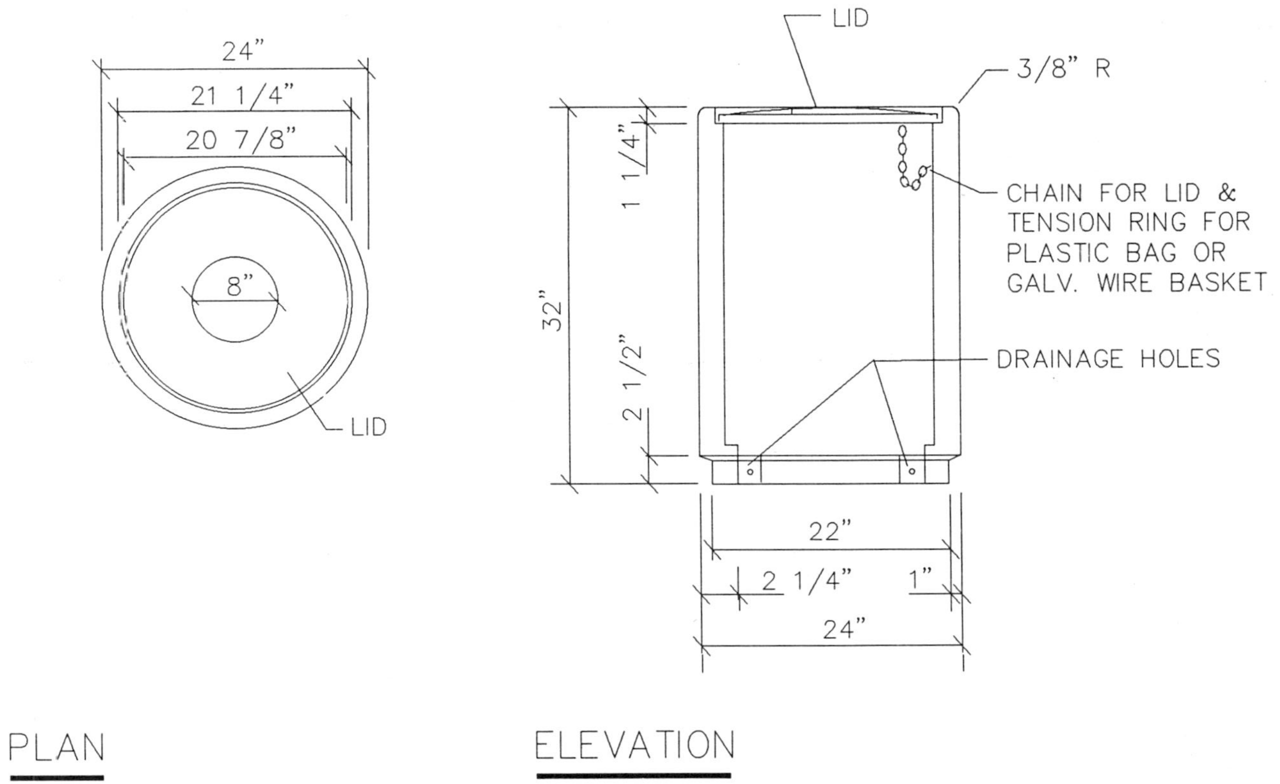

24"
21 1/4"
20 7/8"
8"
LID

PLAN

LID
3/8" R
1 1/4"
32"
2 1/2"
CHAIN FOR LID & TENSION RING FOR PLASTIC BAG OR GALV. WIRE BASKET
DRAINAGE HOLES
22"
2 1/4"
1"
24"

ELEVATION

TYPE TR1
TRASH RECEPTACLE CYLINDRICAL

SCALE: NOT TO SCALE

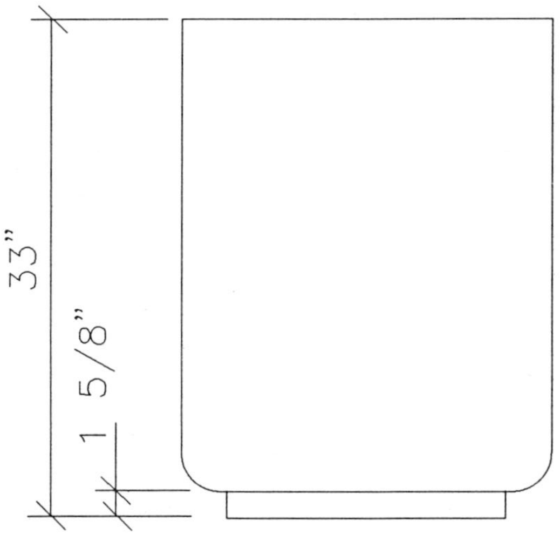

33"
1 5/8"

ELEVATION

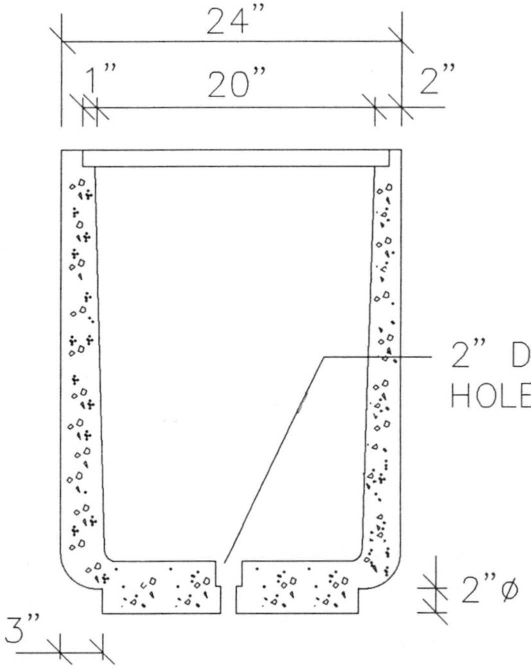

24"
1"
20"
2"
2" DRAINAGE HOLE
2"ø
3"

SECTION

TRASH RECEPTACLE TYPE JJR

SCALE: NOT TO SCALE

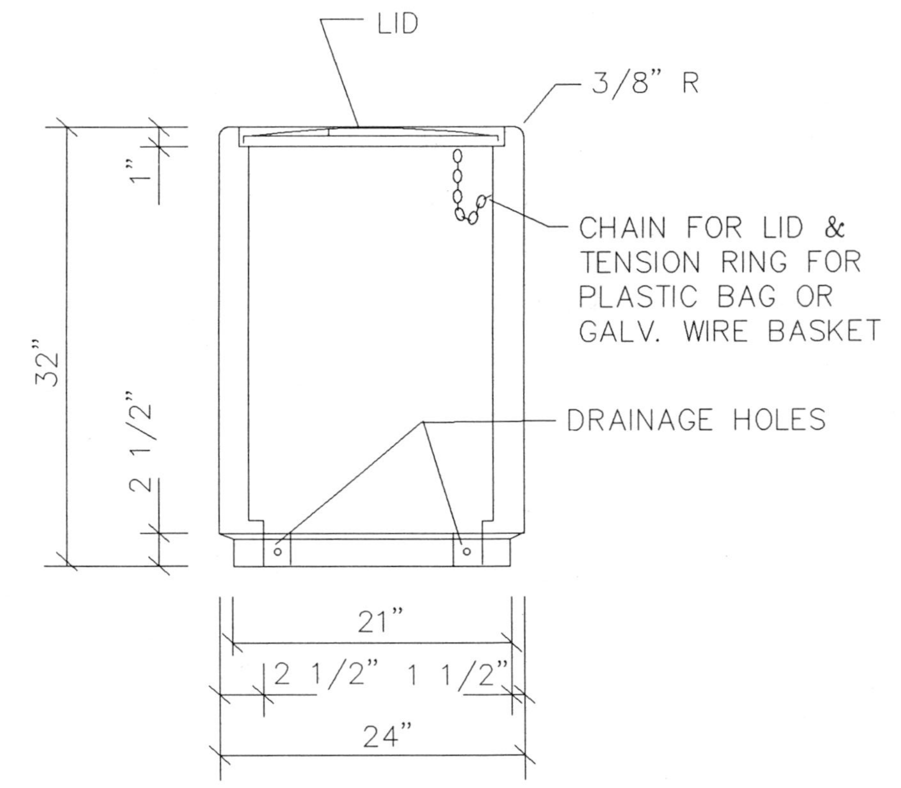
24"
20 3/4"
20 1/2" LID
8"
LID
LID
3/8" R
CHAIN FOR LID & TENSION RING FOR PLASTIC BAG OR GALV. WIRE BASKET
DRAINAGE HOLES
1"
32"
2 1/2"
21"
2 1/2"
1 1/2"
24"

PLAN

ELEVATION

TYPE TR3
TRASH RECEPTACLE SQUARE

SCALE: NOT TO SCALE

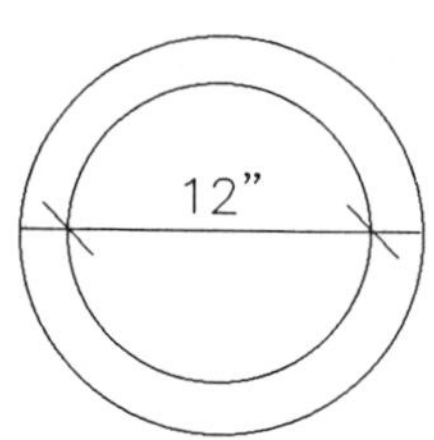
12"

PLAN

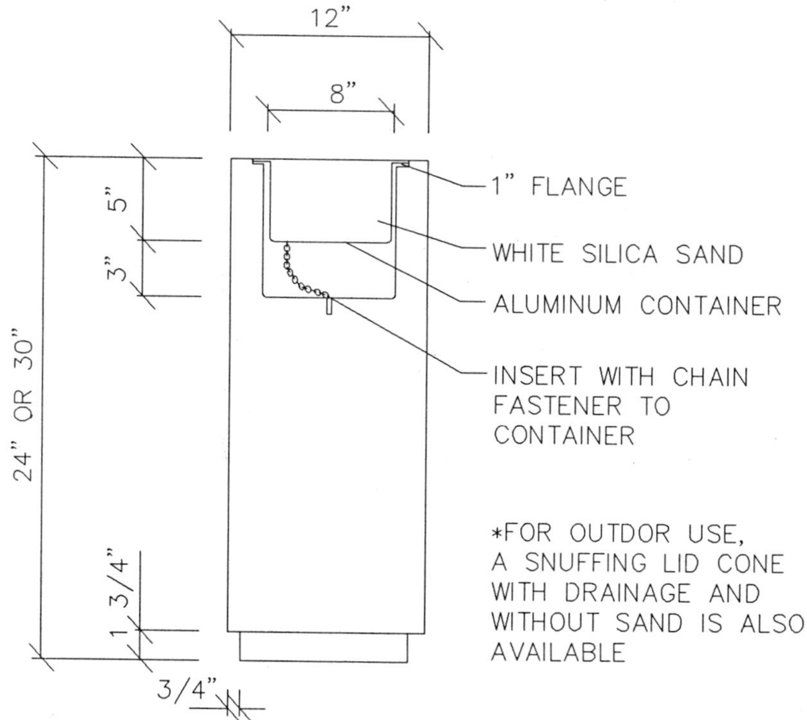
12"
8"
5"
3"
24" OR 30"
1 3/4"
3/4"
1" FLANGE
WHITE SILICA SAND
ALUMINUM CONTAINER
INSERT WITH CHAIN FASTENER TO CONTAINER
*FOR OUTDOR USE, A SNUFFING LID CONE WITH DRAINAGE AND WITHOUT SAND IS ALSO AVAILABLE

ELEVATION

ASH TRAY/TYPE AT1

SCALE: NOT TO SCALE

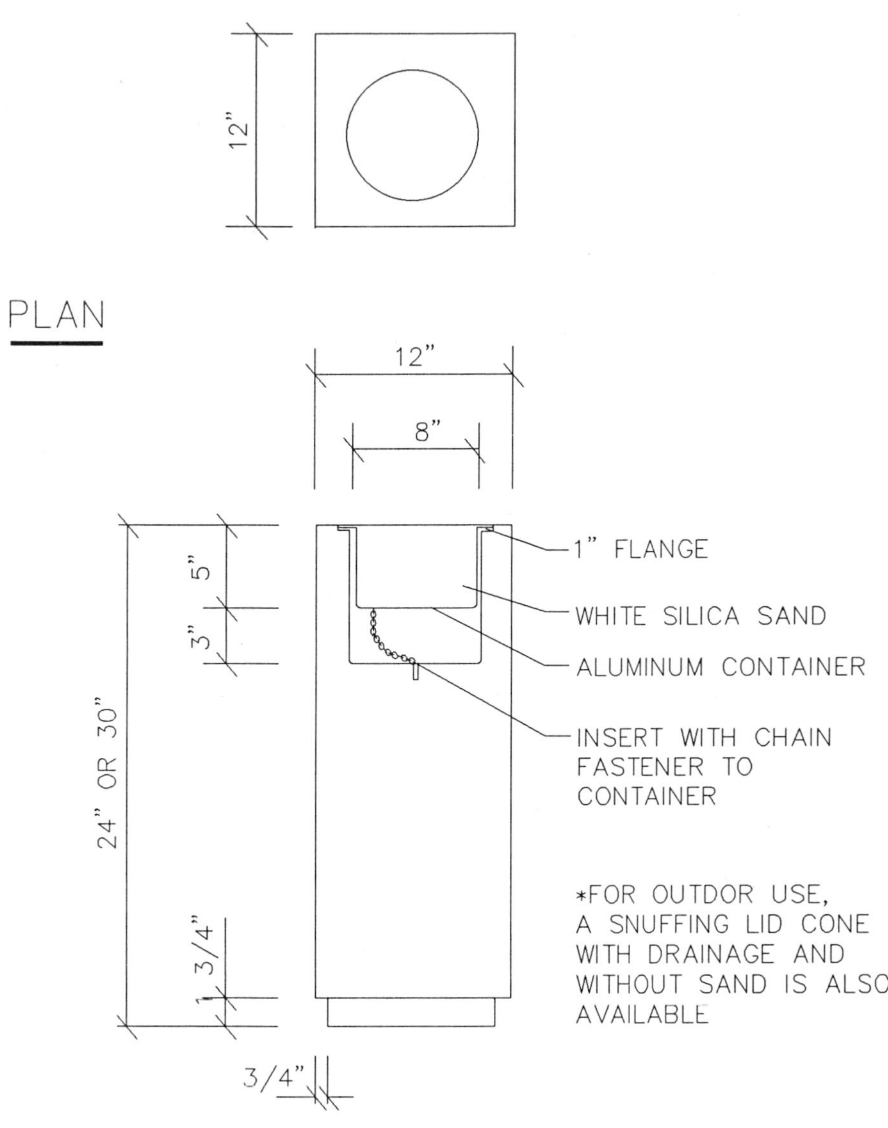

12"
PLAN
12"
8"
5"
3"
24" OR 30"
1 3/4"
3/4"
1" FLANGE
WHITE SILICA SAND
ALUMINUM CONTAINER
INSERT WITH CHAIN
FASTENER TO
CONTAINER
*FOR OUTDOR USE,
A SNUFFING LID CONE
WITH DRAINAGE AND
WITHOUT SAND IS ALSO
AVAILABLE
ELEVATION

ASH TRAY/TYPE AT3

SCALE: NOT TO SCALE

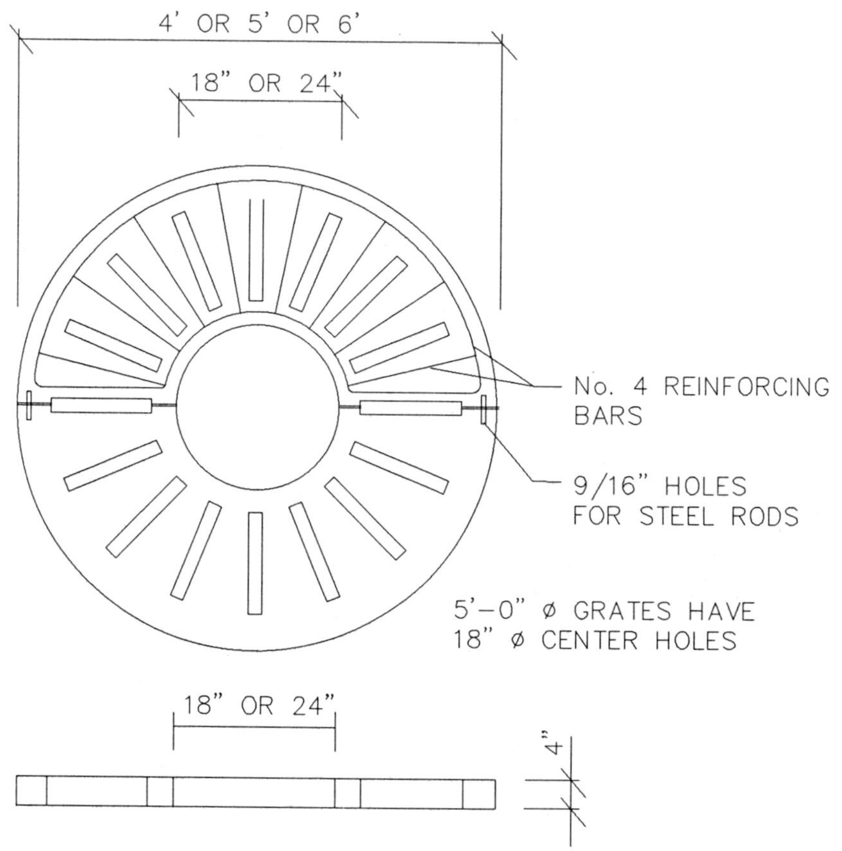
4' OR 5' OR 6'
18" OR 24"
No. 4 REINFORCING BARS
9/16" HOLES FOR STEEL RODS
5'–0" ø GRATES HAVE 18" ø CENTER HOLES
18" OR 24"
4"

CIRCULAR

48"ø x 3 1/2"
60"ø x 4"
72"ø x 4"

TYPE TG1
CIRCULAR TREE GRATES

SCALE: NOT TO SCALE

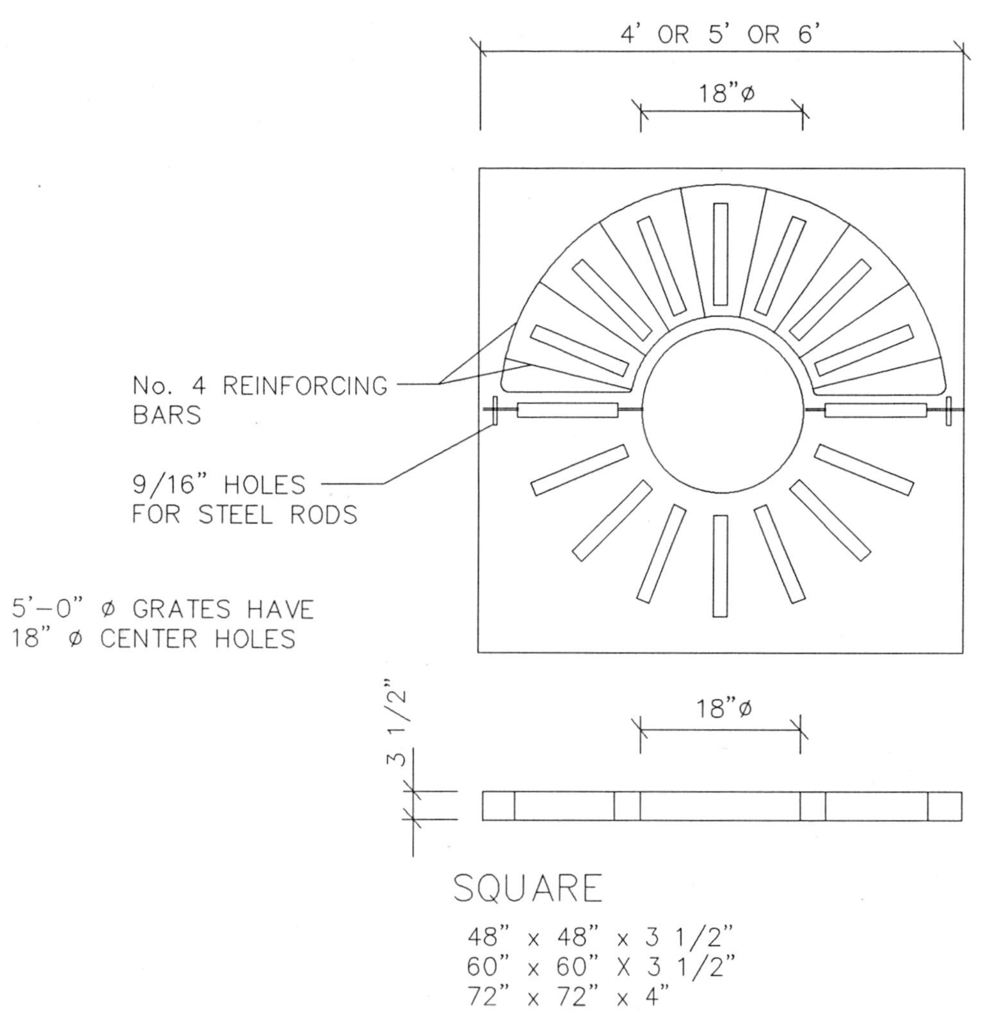
4' OR 5' OR 6'
18"ø
No. 4 REINFORCING BARS
9/16" HOLES FOR STEEL RODS
5'–0" ø GRATES HAVE 18" ø CENTER HOLES
18"ø
3 1/2"
SQUARE
48" x 48" x 3 1/2"
60" x 60" X 3 1/2"
72" x 72" x 4"

TYPE TG1
SQUARE TREE GRATES

SCALE: NOT TO SCALE

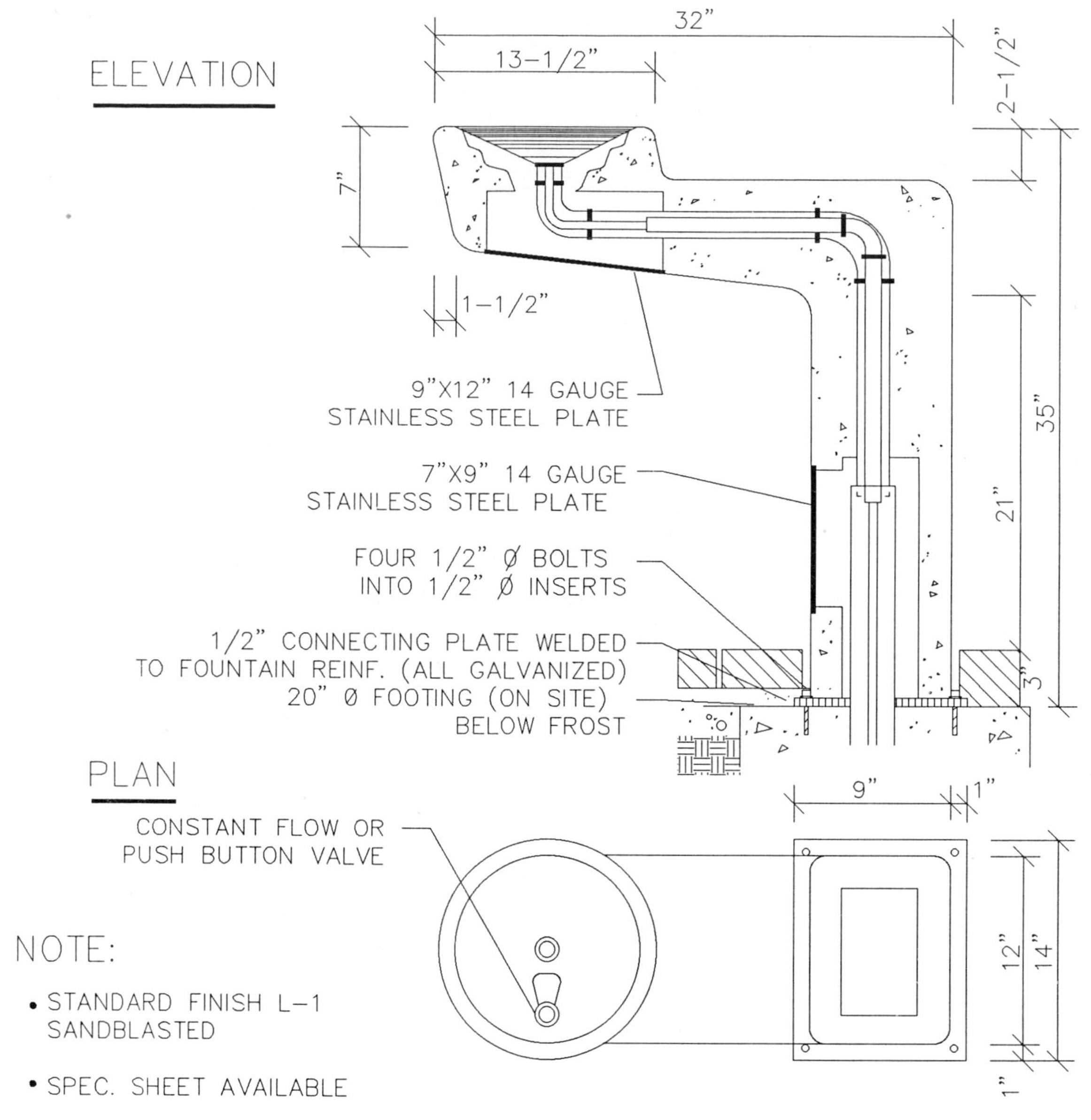
ELEVATION
32"
13-1/2"
2-1/2"
7"
1-1/2"
9"X12" 14 GAUGE
STAINLESS STEEL PLATE
7"X9" 14 GAUGE
STAINLESS STEEL PLATE
FOUR 1/2" Ø BOLTS
INTO 1/2" Ø INSERTS
1/2" CONNECTING PLATE WELDED
TO FOUNTAIN REINF. (ALL GALVANIZED)
20" Ø FOOTING (ON SITE)
BELOW FROST
35"
21"
3"
PLAN
9"
1"
CONSTANT FLOW OR
PUSH BUTTON VALVE
12"
14"
1"
NOTE:
• STANDARD FINISH L-1
SANDBLASTED
• SPEC. SHEET AVAILABLE

DRINKING FOUNTAIN / TYPE 1-82

SCALE: NOT TO SCALE

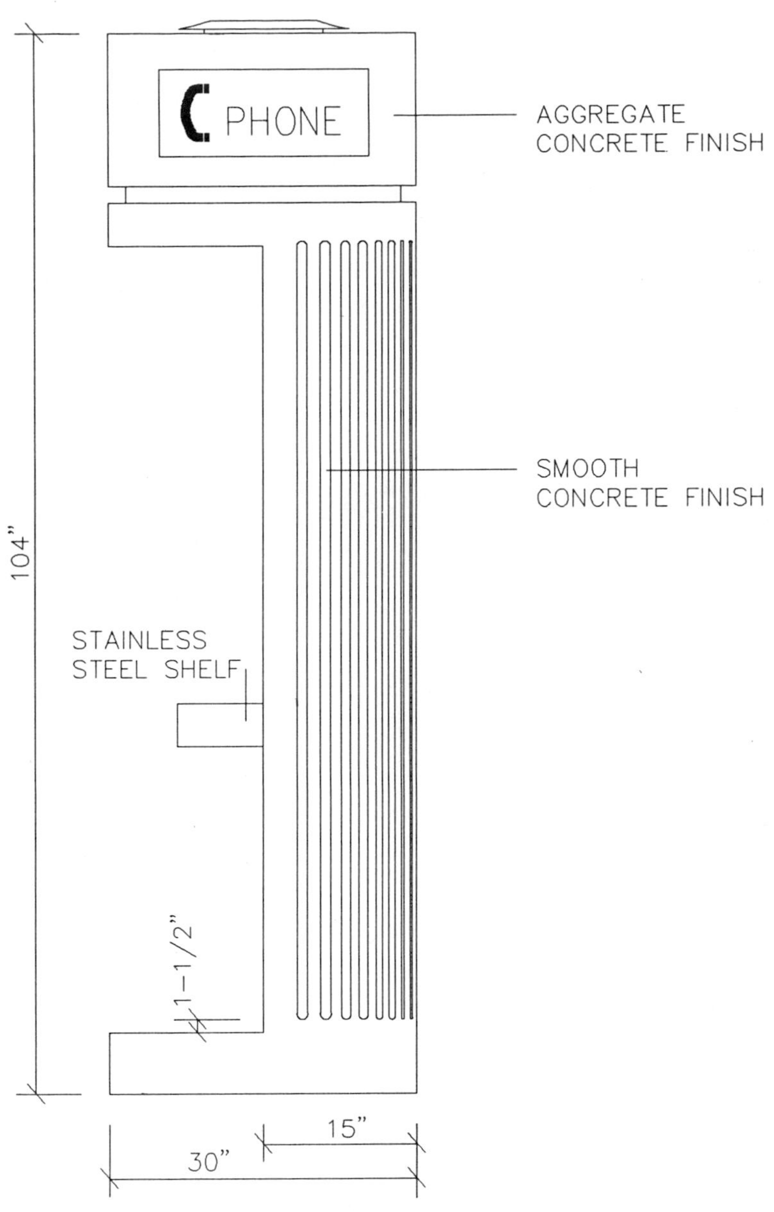
PHONE
AGGREGATE
CONCRETE FINISH
SMOOTH
CONCRETE FINISH
104"
STAINLESS
STEEL SHELF
1-1/2"
15"
30"

TYPE PAC TELEPHONE KIOSK

SCALE: NOT TO SCALE

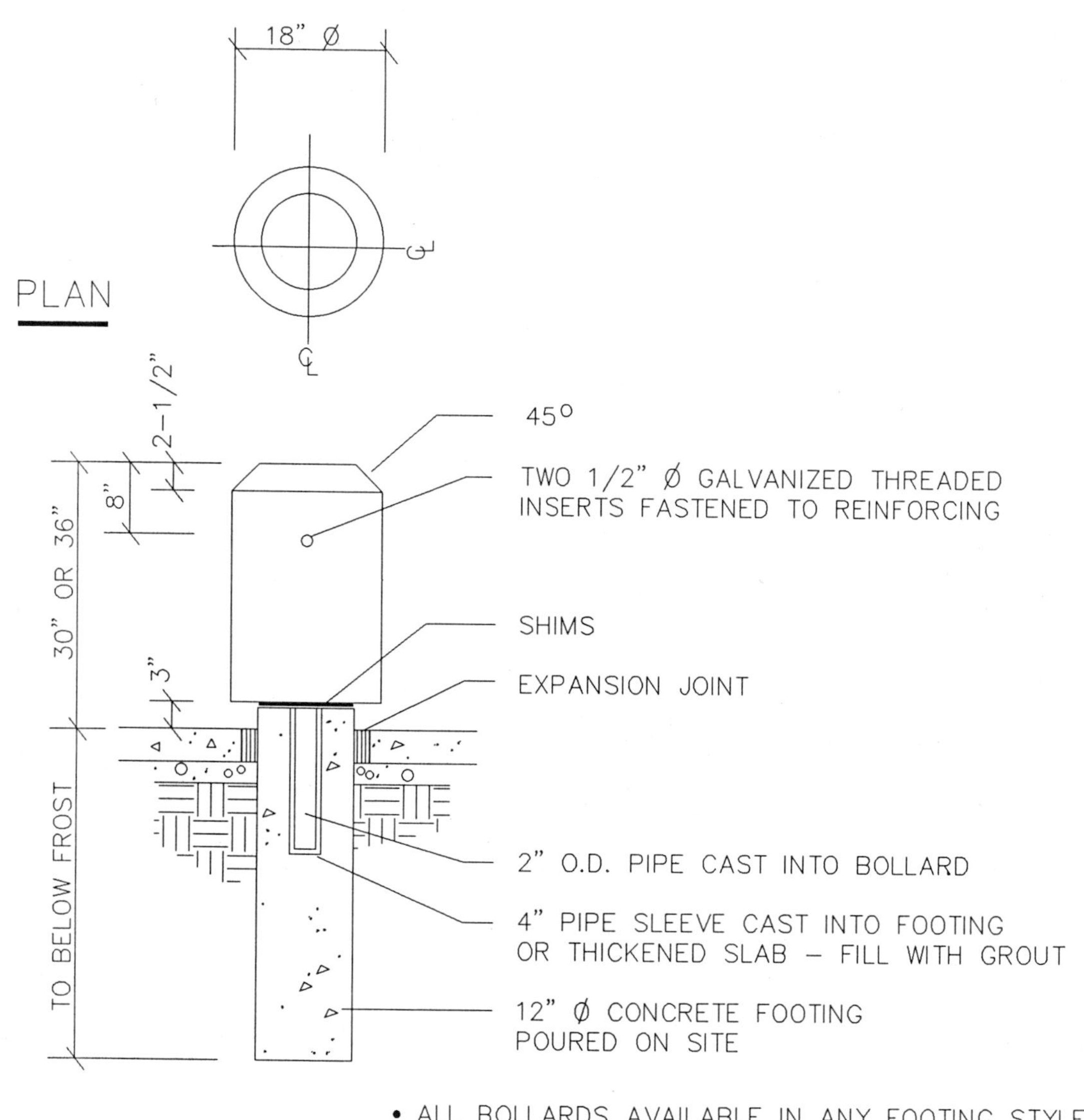
18" Ø
PLAN
℄
℄
2-1/2"
8"
30" OR 36"
3"
TO BELOW FROST
45°
TWO 1/2" Ø GALVANIZED THREADED INSERTS FASTENED TO REINFORCING
SHIMS
EXPANSION JOINT
2" O.D. PIPE CAST INTO BOLLARD
4" PIPE SLEEVE CAST INTO FOOTING OR THICKENED SLAB – FILL WITH GROUT
12" Ø CONCRETE FOOTING POURED ON SITE
ELEVATION

• ALL BOLLARDS AVAILABLE IN ANY FOOTING STYLE

BOLLARD / TYPE 483

SCALE: NOT TO SCALE

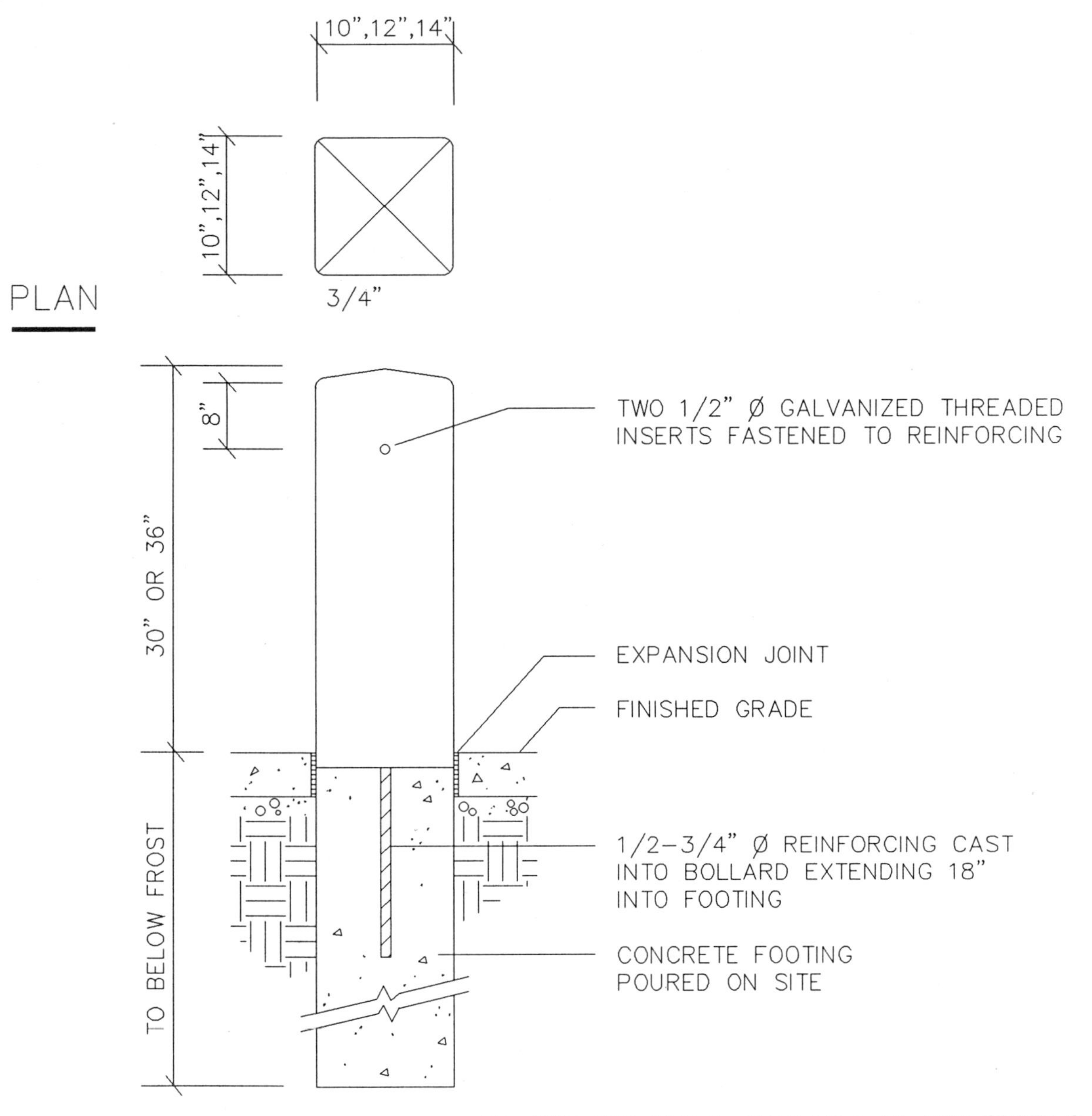
10",12",14"
10",12",14"
3/4"
PLAN
8"
30" OR 36"
TO BELOW FROST
TWO 1/2" Ø GALVANIZED THREADED INSERTS FASTENED TO REINFORCING
EXPANSION JOINT
FINISHED GRADE
1/2–3/4" Ø REINFORCING CAST INTO BOLLARD EXTENDING 18" INTO FOOTING
CONCRETE FOOTING POURED ON SITE

ELEVATION

• ALL BOLLARD TYPES AVAILABLE IN ANY FOOTING STYLE

BOLLARD / TYPE 183

SCALE: NOT TO SCALE

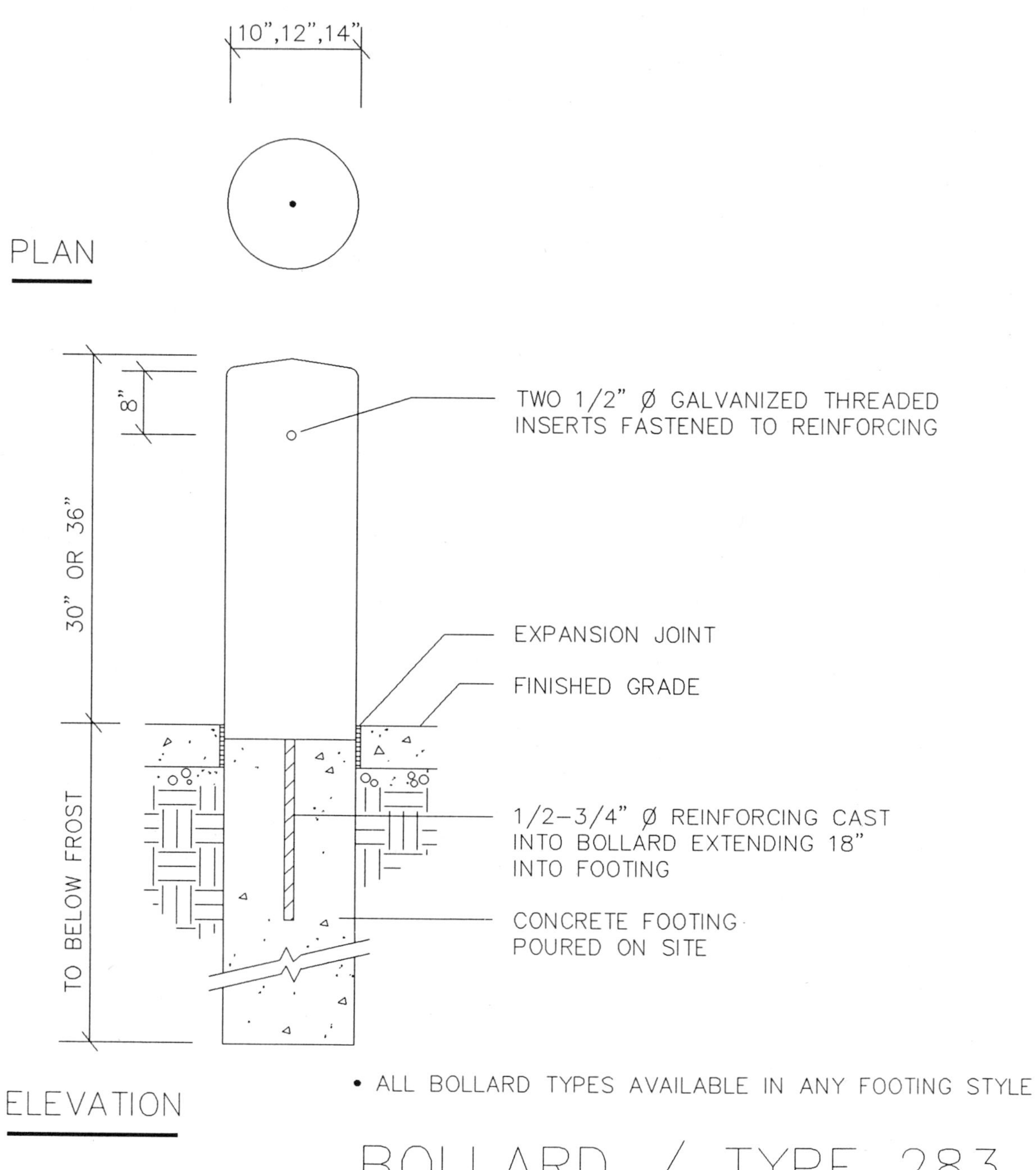
10",12",14"
PLAN
8"
30" OR 36"
TO BELOW FROST
TWO 1/2" Ø GALVANIZED THREADED INSERTS FASTENED TO REINFORCING
EXPANSION JOINT
FINISHED GRADE
1/2–3/4" Ø REINFORCING CAST INTO BOLLARD EXTENDING 18" INTO FOOTING
CONCRETE FOOTING POURED ON SITE
ELEVATION
• ALL BOLLARD TYPES AVAILABLE IN ANY FOOTING STYLE
BOLLARD / TYPE 283
SCALE: NOT TO SCALE

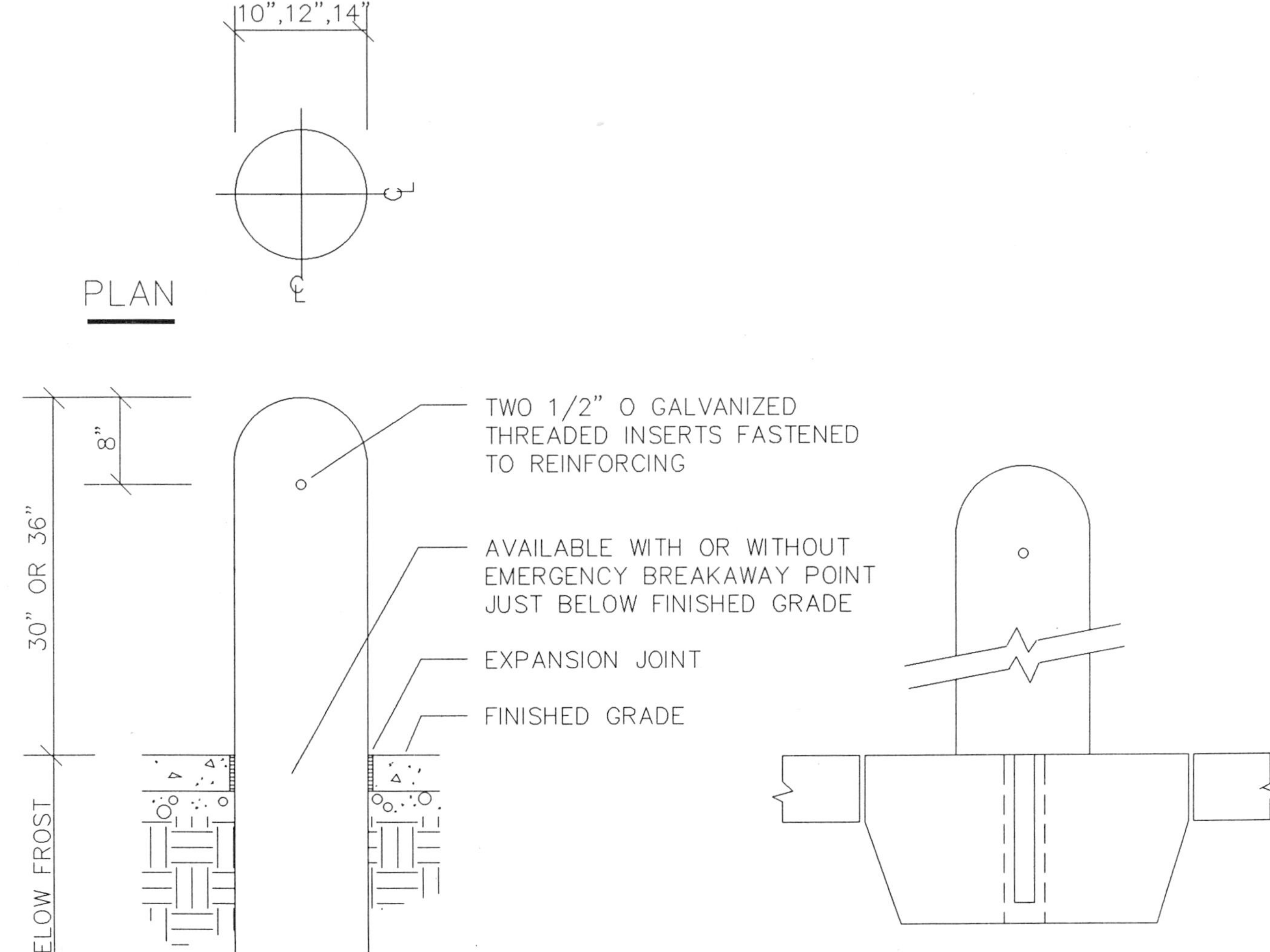
10",12",14"
PLAN
8"
30" OR 36"
TO BELOW FROST
TWO 1/2" O GALVANIZED
THREADED INSERTS FASTENED
TO REINFORCING
AVAILABLE WITH OR WITHOUT
EMERGENCY BREAKAWAY POINT
JUST BELOW FINISHED GRADE
EXPANSION JOINT
FINISHED GRADE
ALT. FOUNDATION
ELEVATION

• ALL BOLLARD TYPES AVAILABLE IN ANY FOOTING STYLE

BOLLARD / TYPE 383

SCALE: NOT TO SCALE

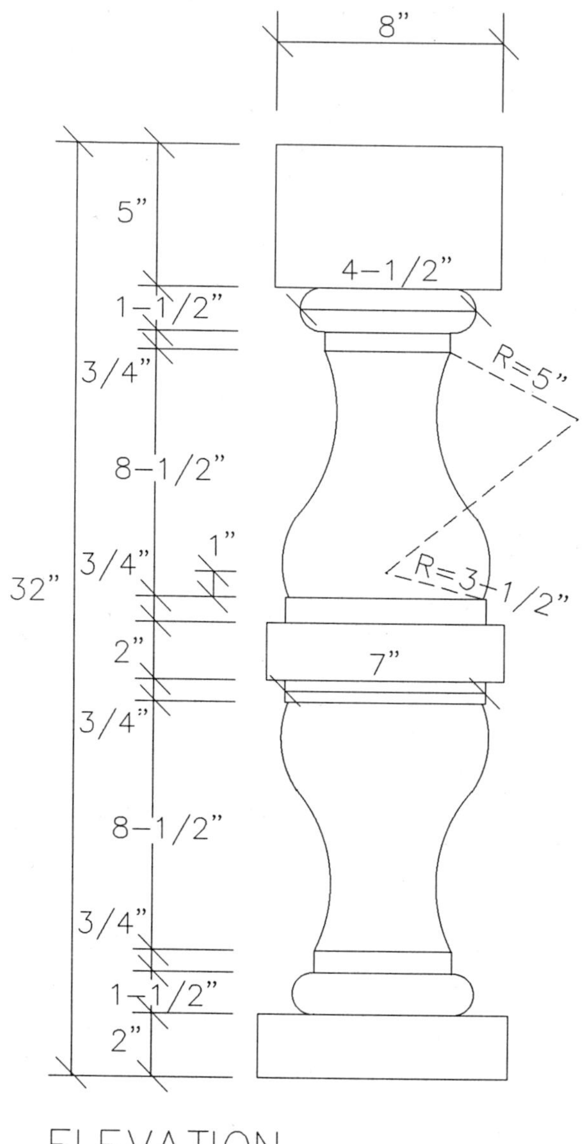
8"
5"
4-1/2"
1-1/2"
3/4"
R=5"
8-1/2"
3/4"
1"
R=3-1/2"
32"
2"
7"
3/4"
8-1/2"
3/4"
1-1/2"
2"
ELEVATION

BALUSTER 184

SCALE: NOT TO SCALE

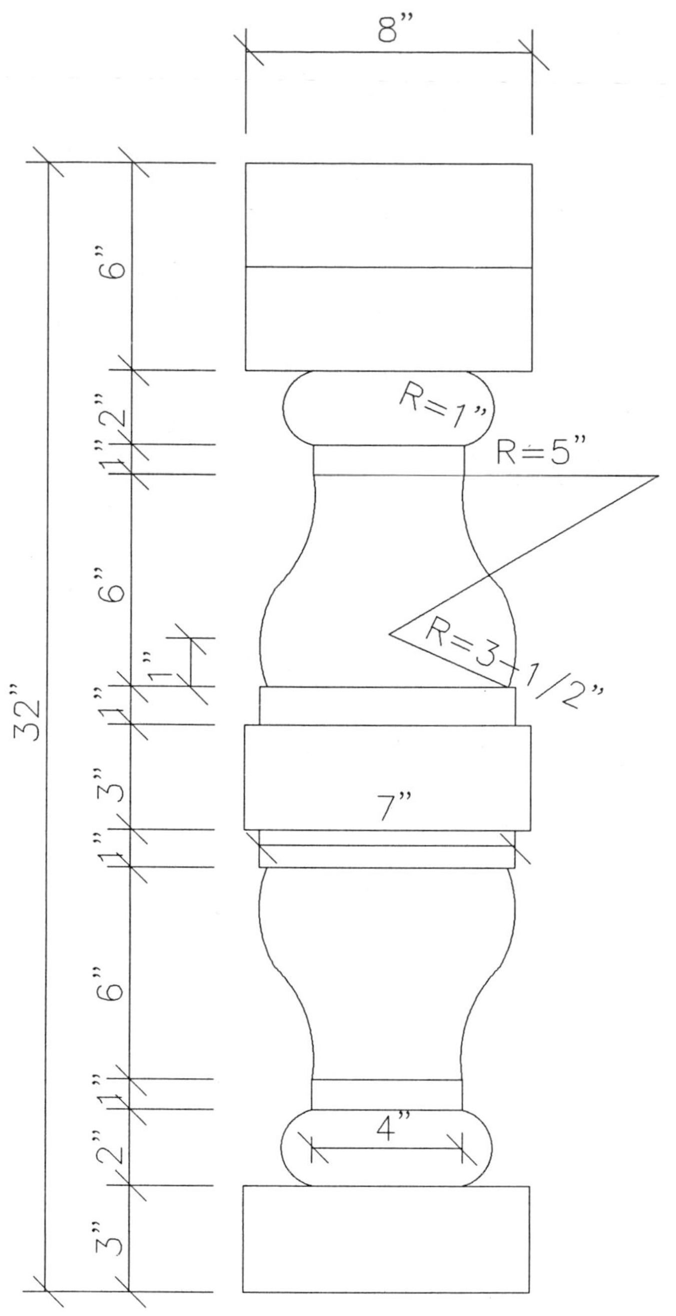
8"
6"
2"
1"
1"
R=1"
R=5"
6"
R=3-1/2"
1"
1"
32"
3"
7"
1"
6"
1"
4"
2"
3"

ELEVATION

BALUSTER 284

SCALE: NOT TO SCALE

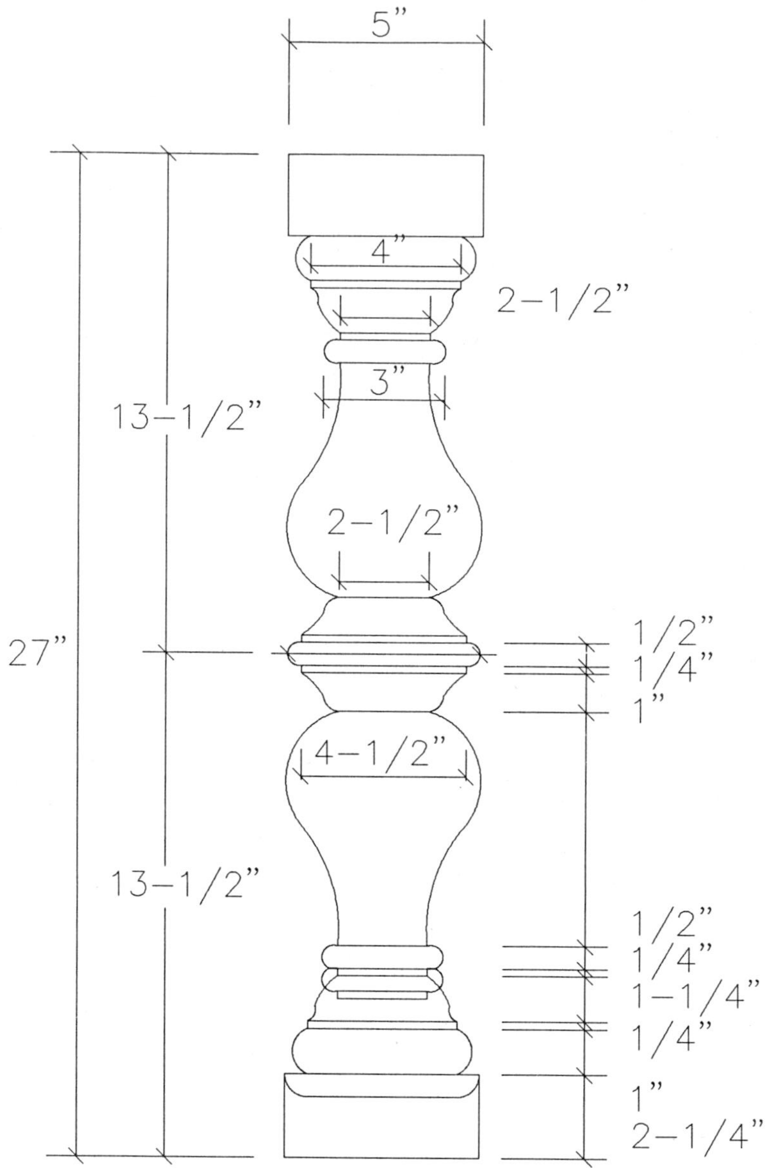
5"
4"
2-1/2"
3"
13-1/2"
2-1/2"
27"
1/2"
1/4"
1"
4-1/2"
13-1/2"
1/2"
1/4"
1-1/4"
1/4"
1"
2-1/4"

ELEVATION

BALUSTER 384

SCALE: NOT TO SCALE

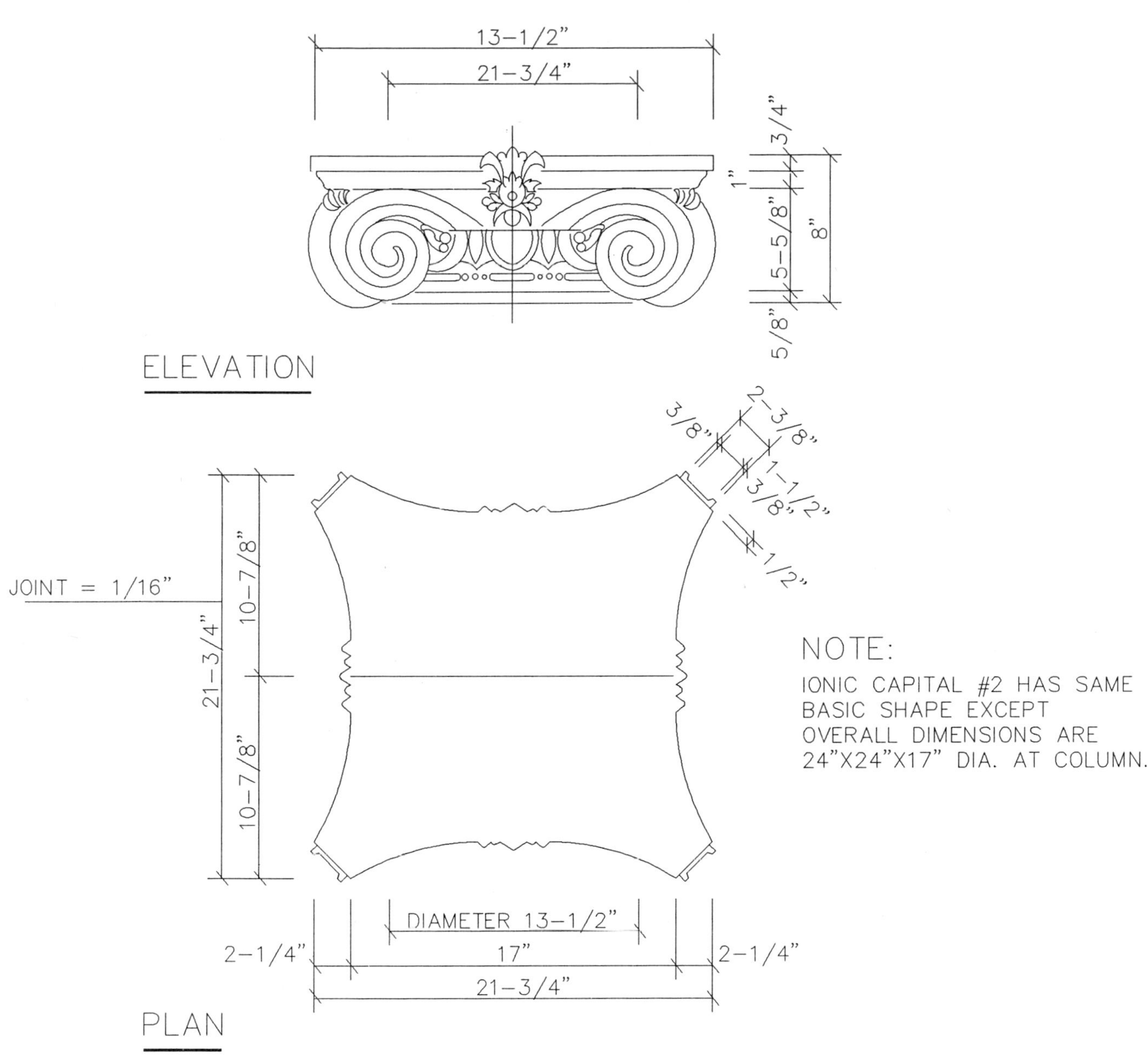
13-1/2"
21-3/4"
3/4"
1"
5-5/8"
8"
5/8"
ELEVATION
3/8"
2-3/8"
1-1/2"
3/8"
1/2"
JOINT = 1/16"
10-7/8"
21-3/4"
10-7/8"
DIAMETER 13-1/2"
2-1/4"
17"
2-1/4"
21-3/4"
PLAN

NOTE:
IONIC CAPITAL #2 HAS SAME BASIC SHAPE EXCEPT OVERALL DIMENSIONS ARE 24"X24"X17" DIA. AT COLUMN.

IONIC CAPITAL # 1

SCALE: NOT TO SCALE

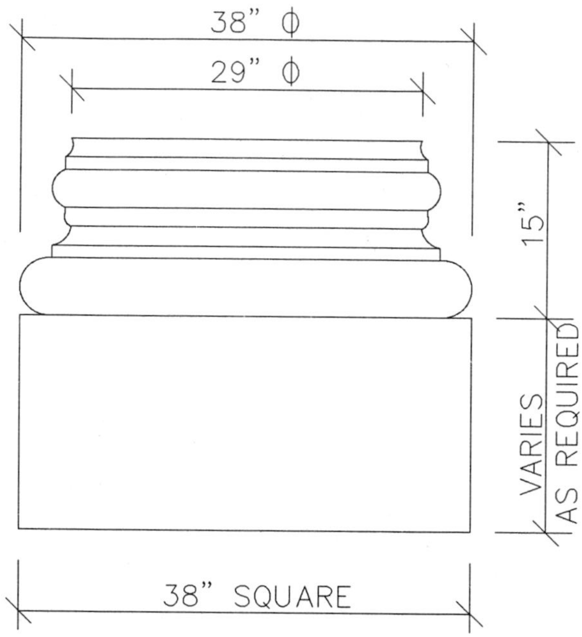
38" Φ
29" Φ
15"
VARIES
AS REQUIRED
38" SQUARE

ELEVATION

CORINTHIAN COLUMN BASE

SCALE: NOT TO SCALE

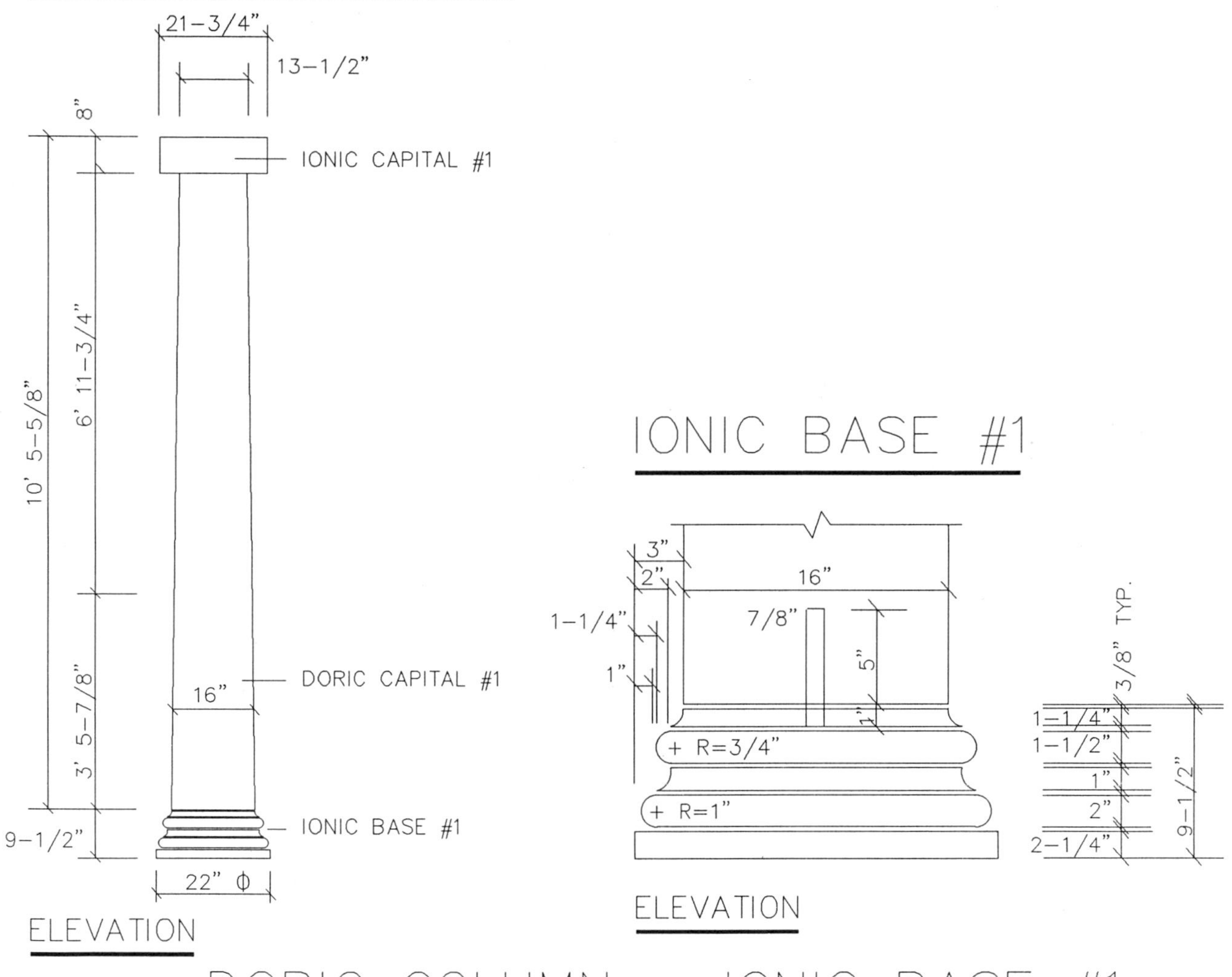
DORIC COLUMN #1
21-3/4"
13-1/2"
8"
IONIC CAPITAL #1
6' 11-3/4"
10' 5-5/8"
DORIC CAPITAL #1
16"
3' 5-7/8"
9-1/2"
IONIC BASE #1
22" Φ
ELEVATION
IONIC BASE #1
3"
2"
16"
7/8"
1-1/4"
5"
1"
1"
3/8" TYP.
+ R=3/4"
+ R=1"
1-1/4"
1-1/2"
1"
2"
2-1/4"
9-1/2"
ELEVATION

DORIC COLUMN – IONIC BASE #1

SCALE: NOT TO SCALE

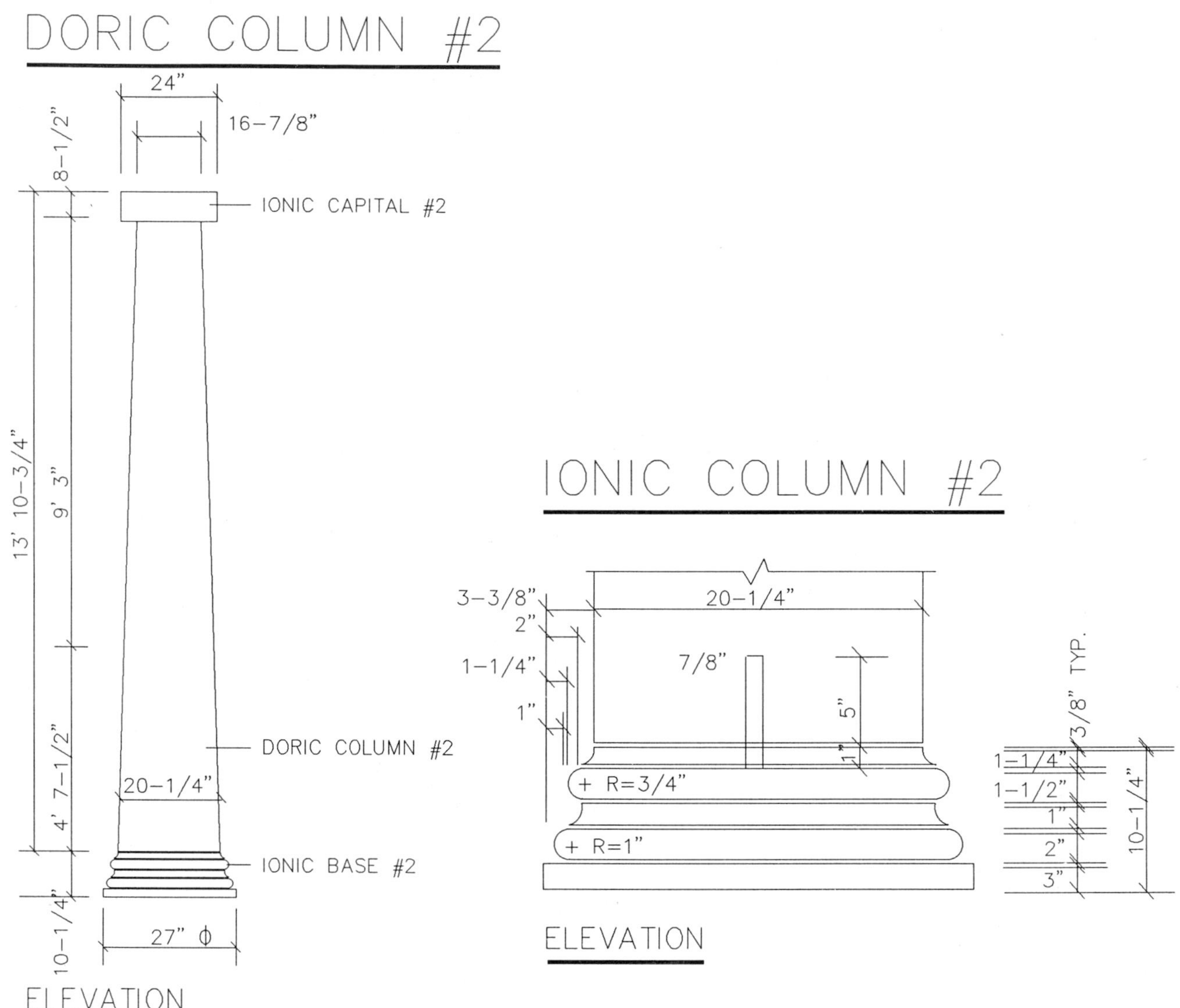
DORIC COLUMN #2
24"
16-7/8"
8-1/2"
IONIC CAPITAL #2
13' 10-3/4"
9' 3"
DORIC COLUMN #2
20-1/4"
4' 7-1/2"
IONIC BASE #2
10-1/4"
27" ϕ
ELEVATION
IONIC COLUMN #2
3-3/8"
2"
1-1/4"
1"
20-1/4"
7/8"
5"
1"
3/8" TYP.
+ R=3/4"
+ R=1"
1-1/4"
1-1/2"
1"
2"
3"
10-1/4"
ELEVATION

DORIC COLUMN – IONIC BASE #2

SCALE: NOT TO SCALE

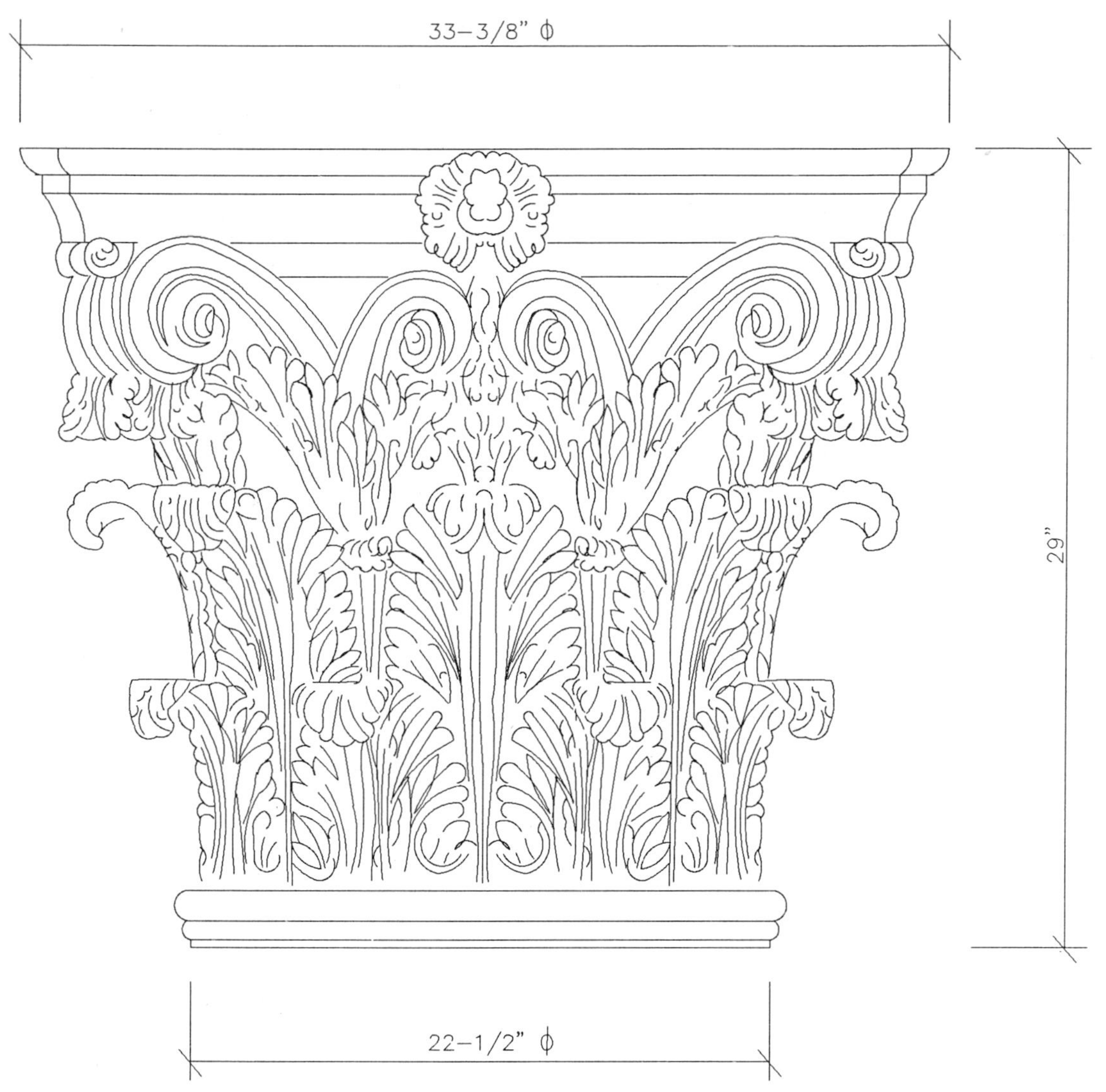
33–3/8" ϕ
29"
22–1/2" ϕ

CORINTHIAN COLUMN

SCALE: NOT TO SCALE

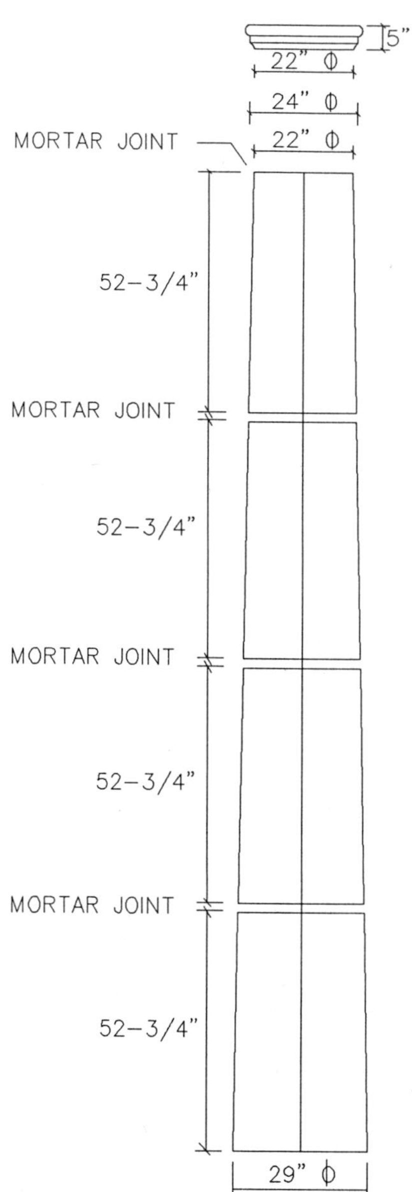
5"
22" ϕ
24" ϕ
MORTAR JOINT
22" ϕ
52-3/4"
MORTAR JOINT
52-3/4"
MORTAR JOINT
52-3/4"
MORTAR JOINT
52-3/4"
29" ϕ

COLUMN AND CAPITAL MOUNTING
BASE ELEVATION

CORINTHIAN COLUMN

SCALE: NOT TO SCALE

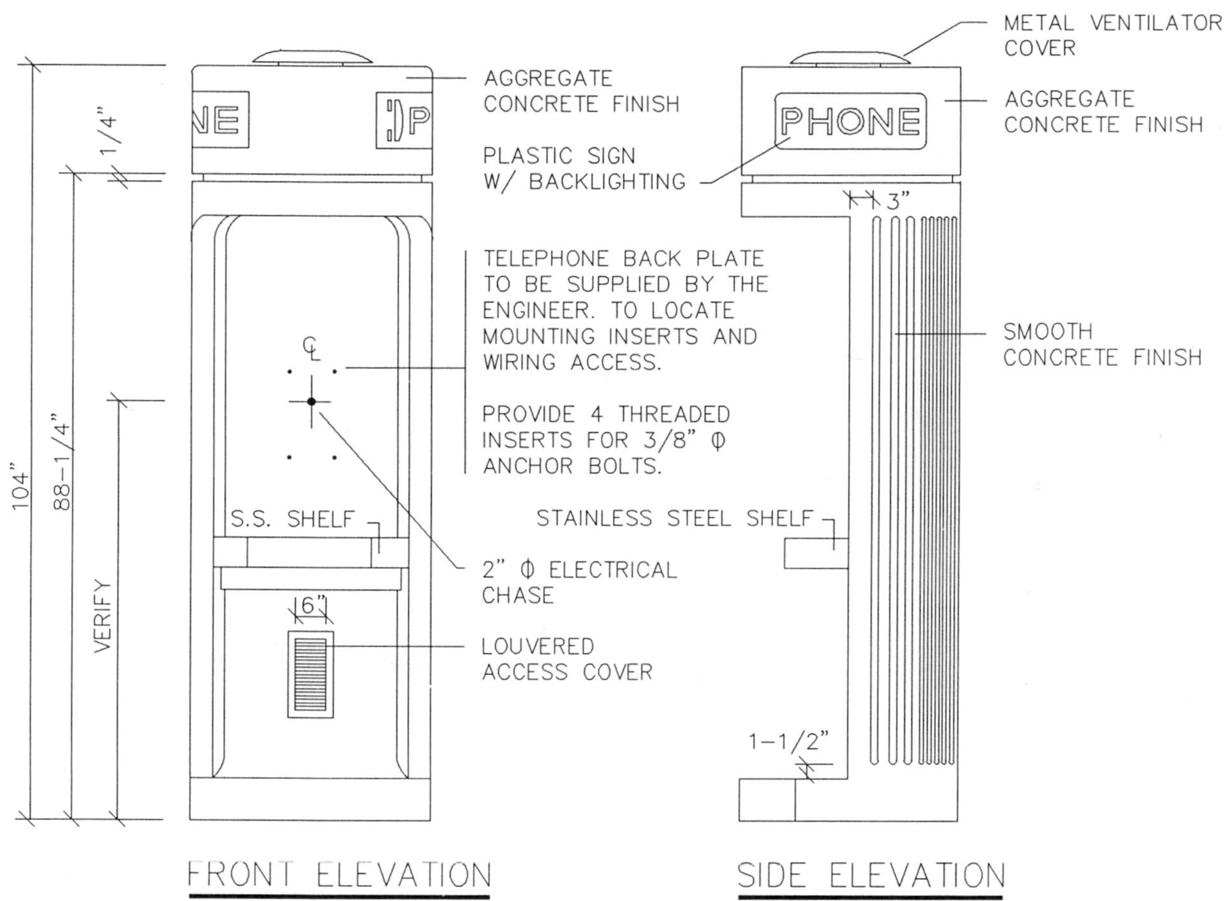
METAL VENTILATOR COVER
AGGREGATE CONCRETE FINISH
PHONE
PLASTIC SIGN W/ BACKLIGHTING
AGGREGATE CONCRETE FINISH
1/4"
3"
TELEPHONE BACK PLATE TO BE SUPPLIED BY THE ENGINEER. TO LOCATE MOUNTING INSERTS AND WIRING ACCESS.
PROVIDE 4 THREADED INSERTS FOR 3/8" Φ ANCHOR BOLTS.
SMOOTH CONCRETE FINISH
104"
88-1/4"
VERIFY
S.S. SHELF
STAINLESS STEEL SHELF
2" Φ ELECTRICAL CHASE
6"
LOUVERED ACCESS COVER
1-1/2"
FRONT ELEVATION
SIDE ELEVATION

NOTE: THIS TELEPHONE KIOSK IS ALSO AVAILABLE AS A DRIVE-UP KIOSK WITHOUT THE STAINLESS STEEL SHELF AND WITH THE PHONE MOUNTED AT SUITABLE HEIGHT.

TELEPHONE KIOSK / PAC-TK

SCALE: NOT TO SCALE

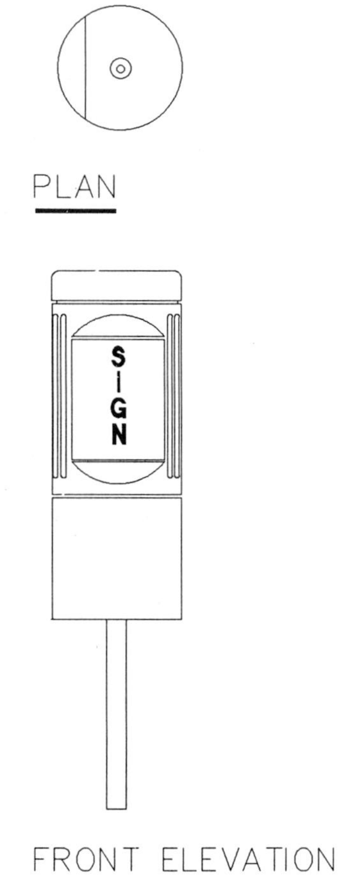

PLAN
SIGN
FRONT ELEVATION

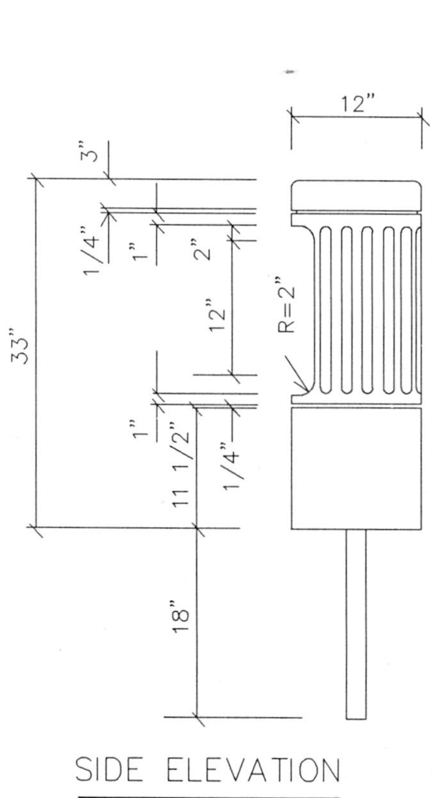

12"
3"
1/4"
1"
2"
33"
12"
R=2"
1"
11 1/2"
1/4"
18"
SIDE ELEVATION

PAC BOL A

SCALE: NOT TO SCALE

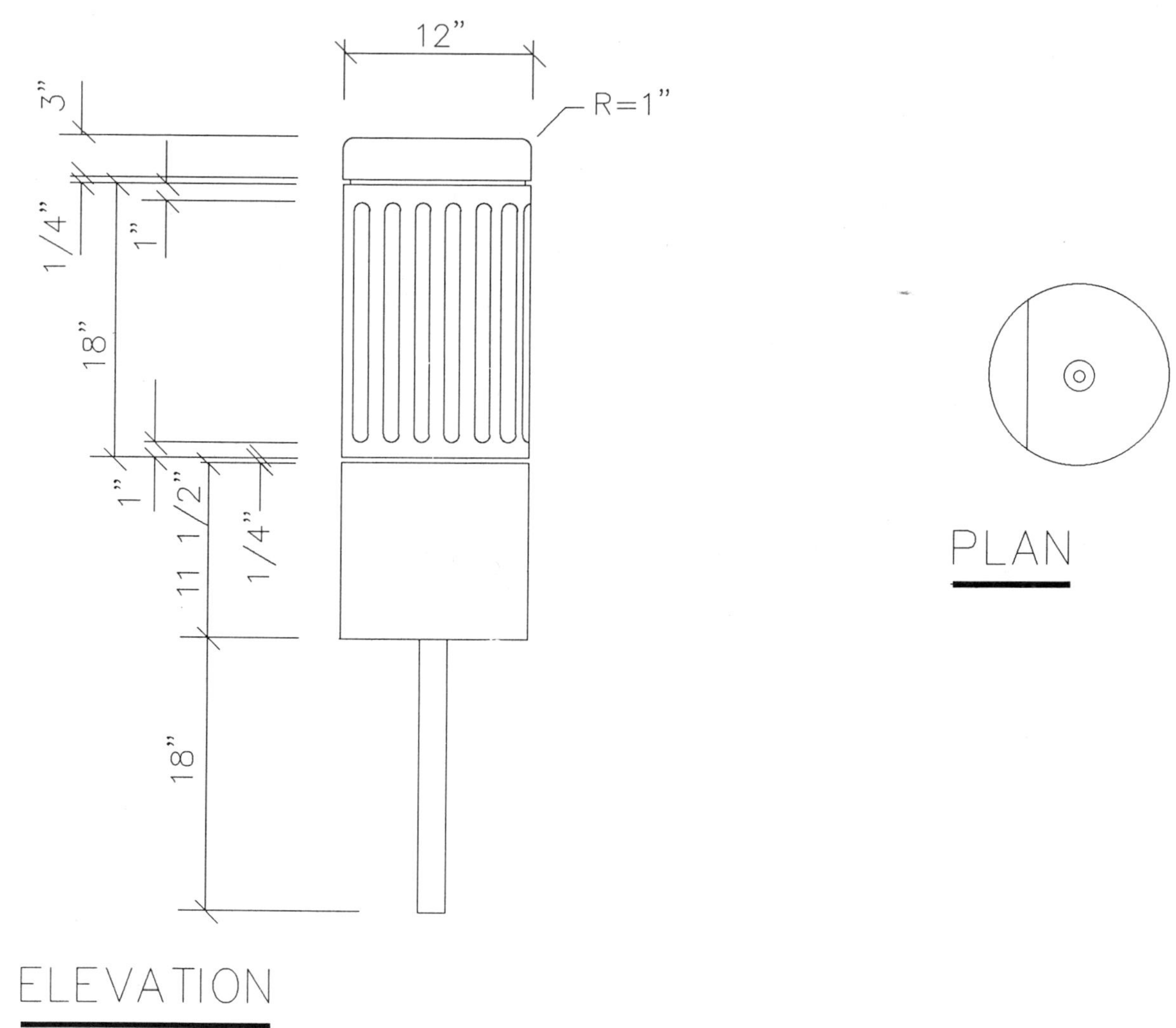
12"
R=1"
3"
1/4"
1"
18"
1"
11 1/2"
1/4"
18"
ELEVATION
PLAN

PAC BOL B

SCALE: NOT TO SCALE

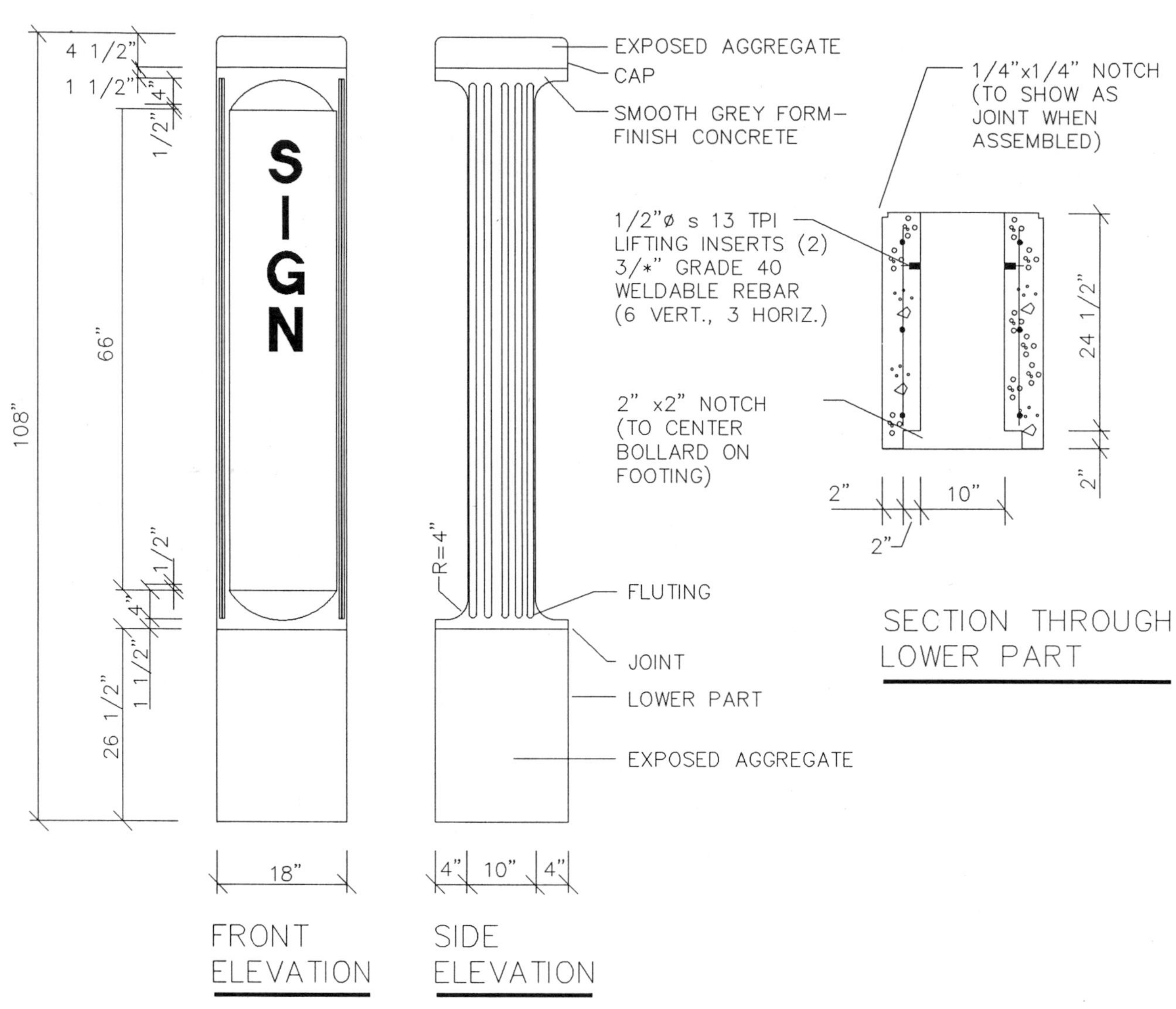

4 1/2"
1 1/2"
4"
1/2"
66"
108"
1/2"
4"
1 1/2"
26 1/2"
SIGN
18"
FRONT ELEVATION
EXPOSED AGGREGATE
CAP
SMOOTH GREY FORM-FINISH CONCRETE
R=4"
FLUTING
JOINT
LOWER PART
EXPOSED AGGREGATE
4"
10"
4"
SIDE ELEVATION
1/4"x1/4" NOTCH (TO SHOW AS JOINT WHEN ASSEMBLED)
1/2"ø s 13 TPI LIFTING INSERTS (2)
3/*" GRADE 40 WELDABLE REBAR (6 VERT., 3 HORIZ.)
2" x2" NOTCH (TO CENTER BOLLARD ON FOOTING)
24 1/2"
2"
2"
10"
2"
SECTION THROUGH LOWER PART

PAC BOL L

SCALE: NOT TO SCALE

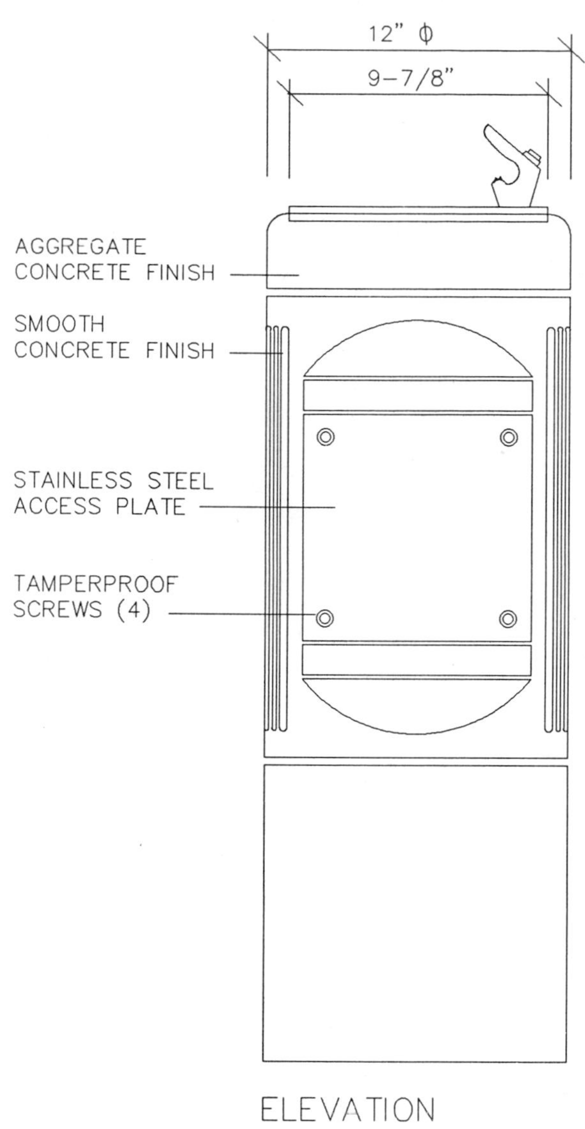
12" Φ
9-7/8"
AGGREGATE
CONCRETE FINISH
SMOOTH
CONCRETE FINISH
STAINLESS STEEL
ACCESS PLATE
TAMPERPROOF
SCREWS (4)

ELEVATION

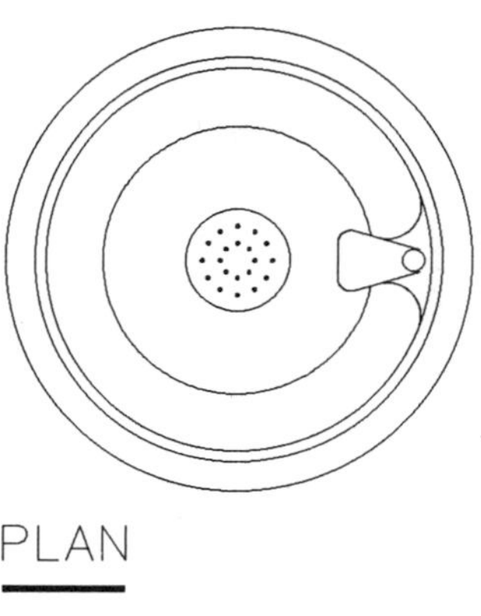

PLAN

DRINKING FOUNTAIN / PAC DF

SCALE: NOT TO SCALE

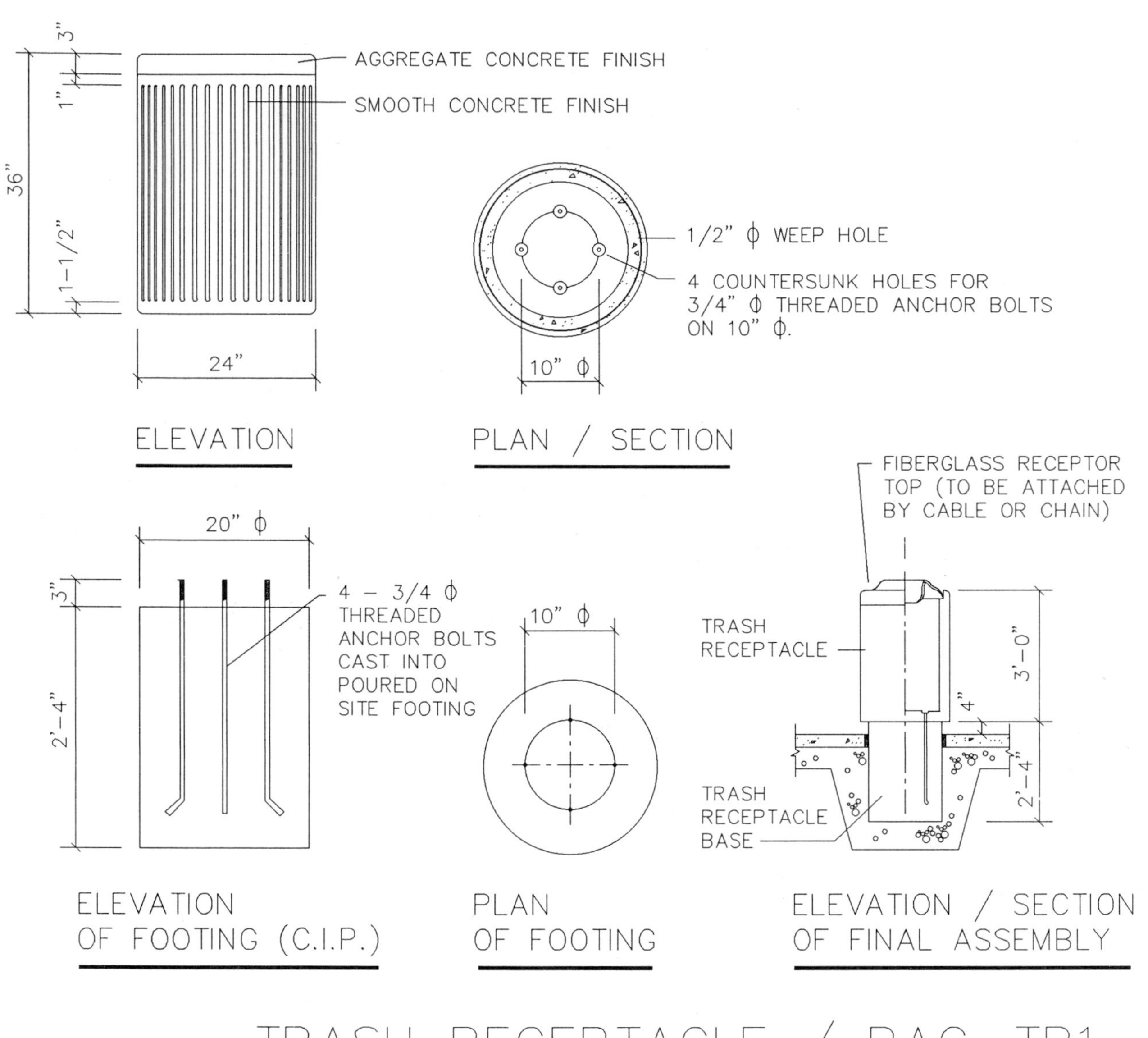

3"
1"
36"
1-1/2"
AGGREGATE CONCRETE FINISH
SMOOTH CONCRETE FINISH
24"
1/2" ϕ WEEP HOLE
4 COUNTERSUNK HOLES FOR
3/4" ϕ THREADED ANCHOR BOLTS
ON 10" ϕ.
10" ϕ
ELEVATION
PLAN / SECTION
FIBERGLASS RECEPTOR
TOP (TO BE ATTACHED
BY CABLE OR CHAIN)
20" ϕ
3"
2'-4"
4 - 3/4 ϕ
THREADED
ANCHOR BOLTS
CAST INTO
POURED ON
SITE FOOTING
10" ϕ
TRASH
RECEPTACLE
TRASH
RECEPTACLE
BASE
4"
3'-0"
2'-4"
ELEVATION
OF FOOTING (C.I.P.)
PLAN
OF FOOTING
ELEVATION / SECTION
OF FINAL ASSEMBLY

TRASH RECEPTACLE / PAC-TR1

SCALE: NOT TO SCALE

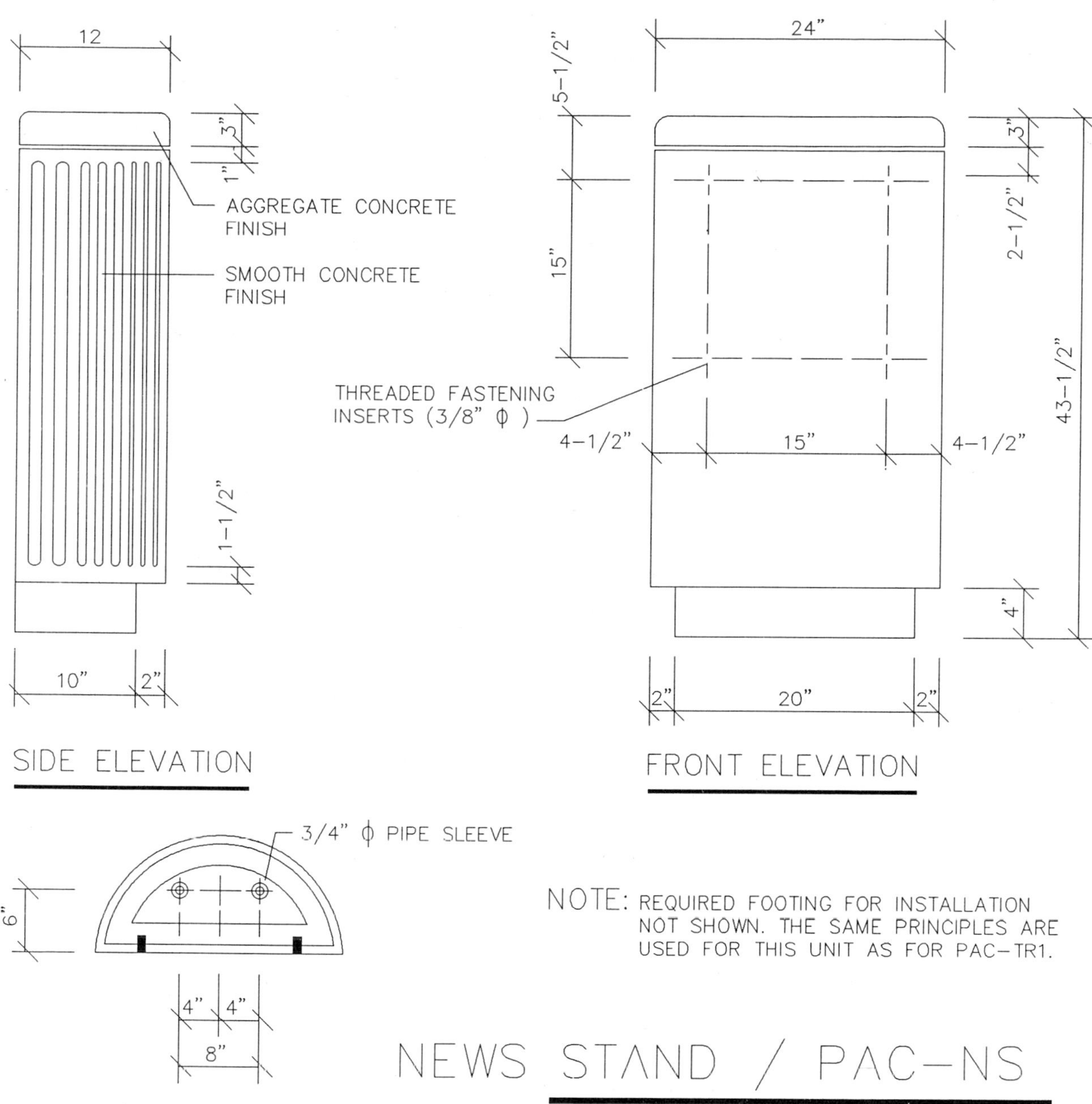
12
3"
1"
AGGREGATE CONCRETE FINISH
SMOOTH CONCRETE FINISH
1-1/2"
10"
2"
SIDE ELEVATION
24"
5-1/2"
15"
3"
2-1/2"
43-1/2"
THREADED FASTENING INSERTS (3/8" ϕ)
4-1/2"
15"
4-1/2"
4"
2"
20"
2"
FRONT ELEVATION
3/4" ϕ PIPE SLEEVE
6"
4"
4"
8"
PLAN / SECTION

NOTE: REQUIRED FOOTING FOR INSTALLATION NOT SHOWN. THE SAME PRINCIPLES ARE USED FOR THIS UNIT AS FOR PAC-TR1.

NEWS STAND / PAC-NS

SCALE: NOT TO SCALE

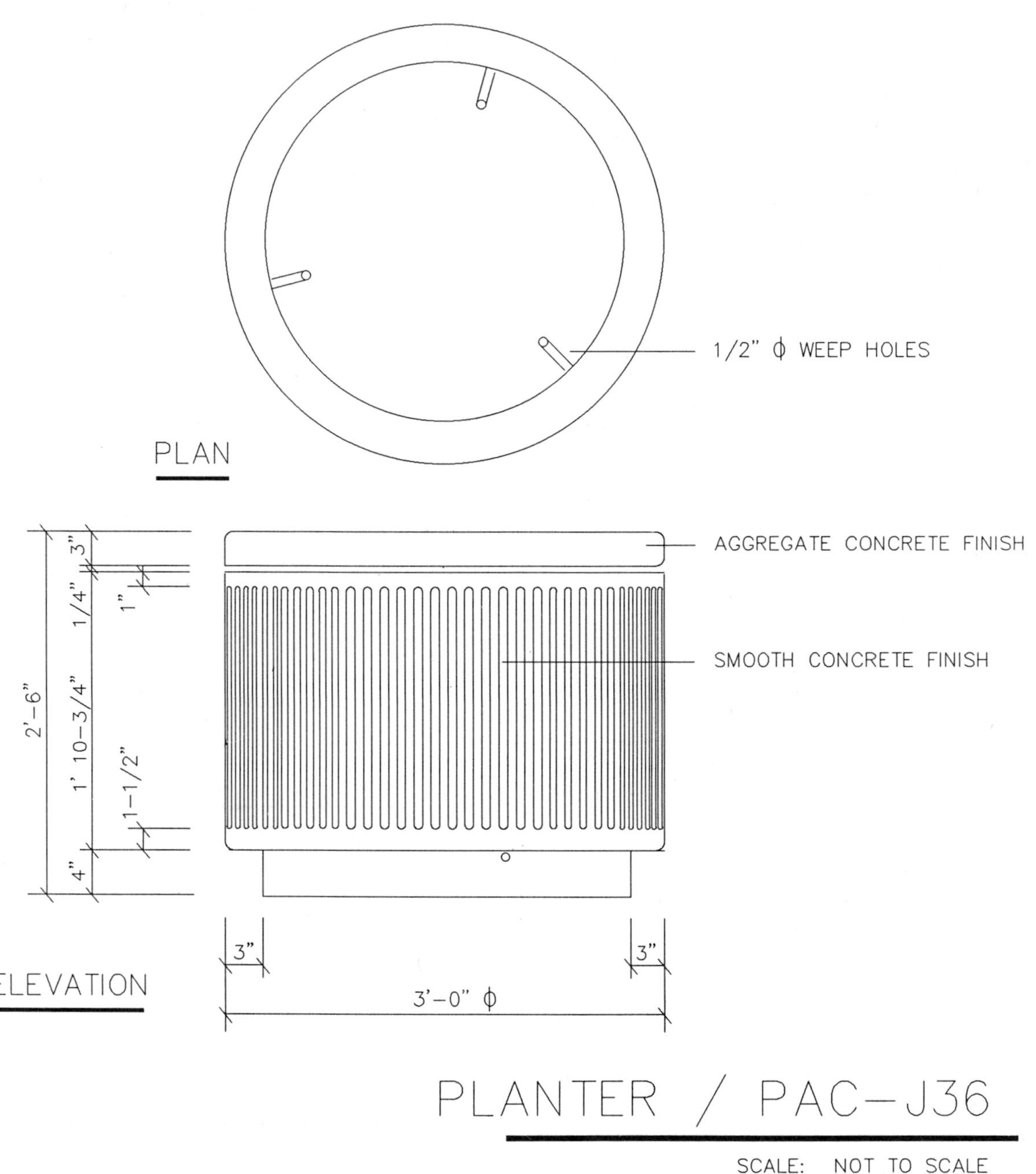
1/2" ϕ WEEP HOLES
PLAN
3"
1/4"
1"
2'-6"
1' 10-3/4"
1-1/2"
4"
AGGREGATE CONCRETE FINISH
SMOOTH CONCRETE FINISH
3"
3"
3'-0" ϕ
ELEVATION

PLANTER / PAC–J36

SCALE: NOT TO SCALE

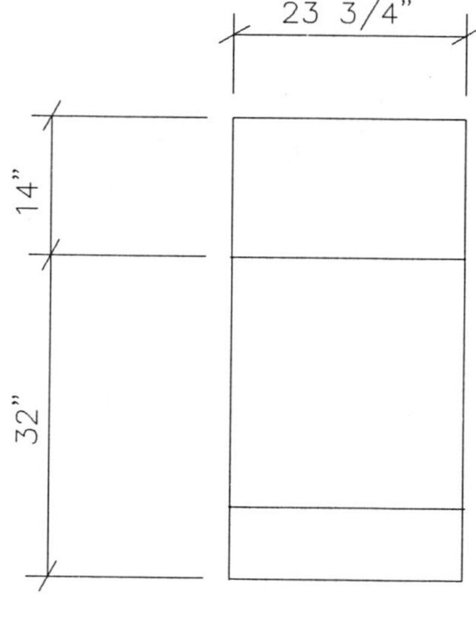
23 3/4"
14"
32"

FRONT ELEVATION

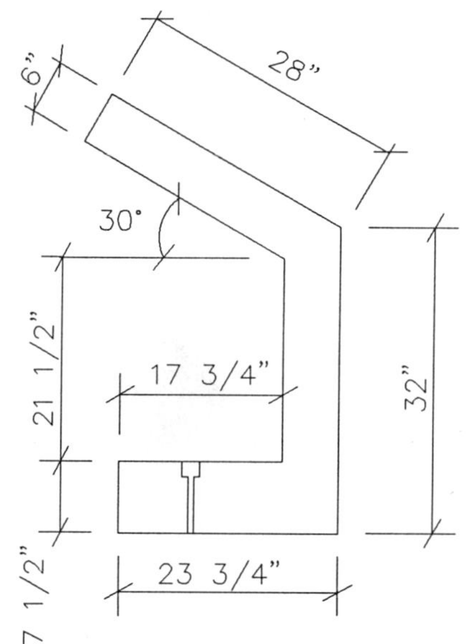
6"
28"
30°
21 1/2"
17 3/4"
32"
7 1/2"
23 3/4"

SIDE ELEVATION

STREET DIRECTORY/MAP STAND

SCALE: NOT TO SCALE

Shelters

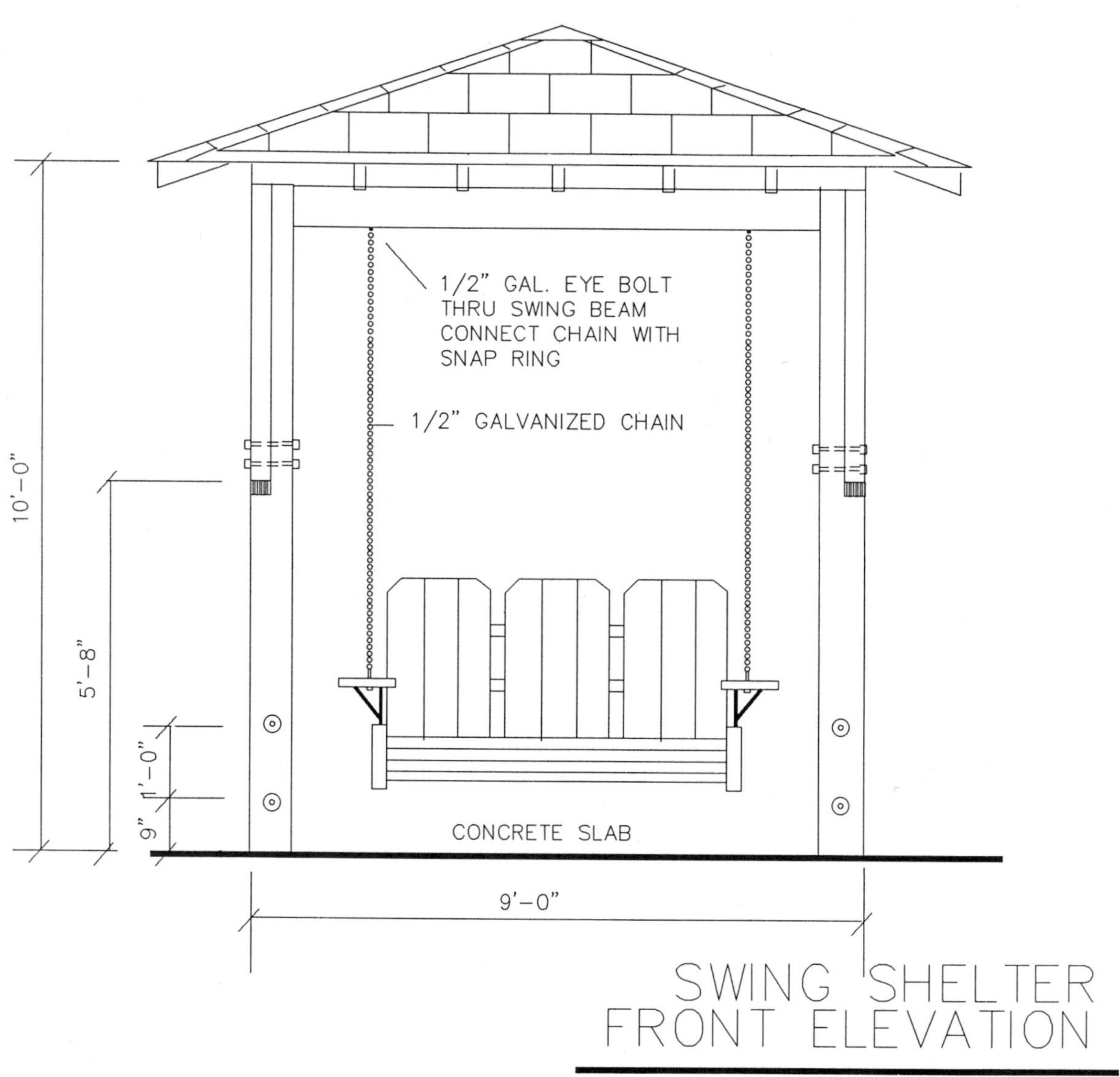
1/2" GAL. EYE BOLT
THRU SWING BEAM
CONNECT CHAIN WITH
SNAP RING
1/2" GALVANIZED CHAIN
10'–0"
5'–8"
1'–0"
9"
CONCRETE SLAB
9'–0"

SWING SHELTER
FRONT ELEVATION

SCALE: NOT TO SCALE

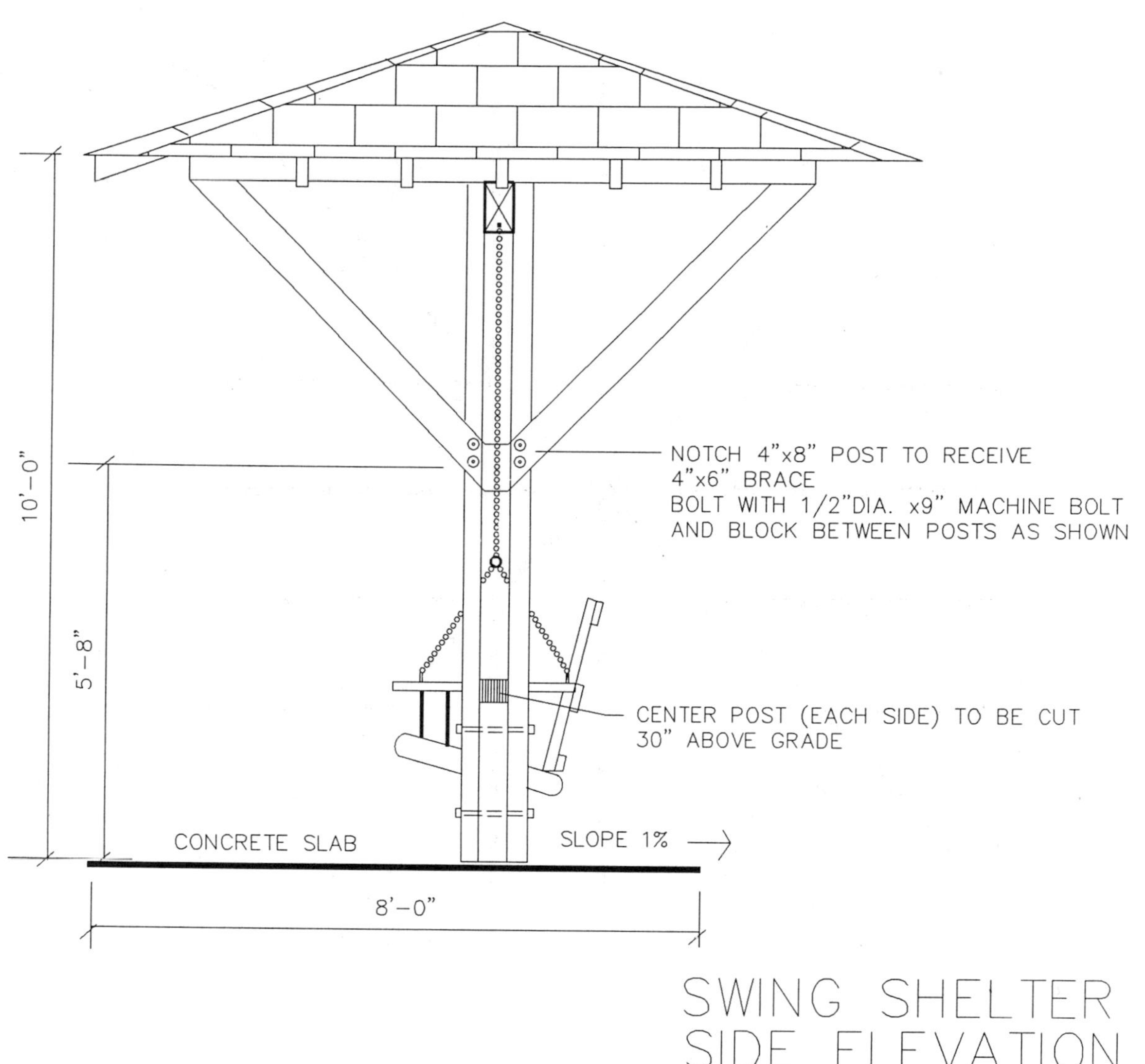

10'–0"
5'–8"
NOTCH 4"x8" POST TO RECEIVE
4"x6" BRACE
BOLT WITH 1/2"DIA. x9" MACHINE BOLT
AND BLOCK BETWEEN POSTS AS SHOWN
CENTER POST (EACH SIDE) TO BE CUT
30" ABOVE GRADE
CONCRETE SLAB
SLOPE 1%
8'–0"

SWING SHELTER SIDE ELEVATION

SCALE: NOT TO SCALE

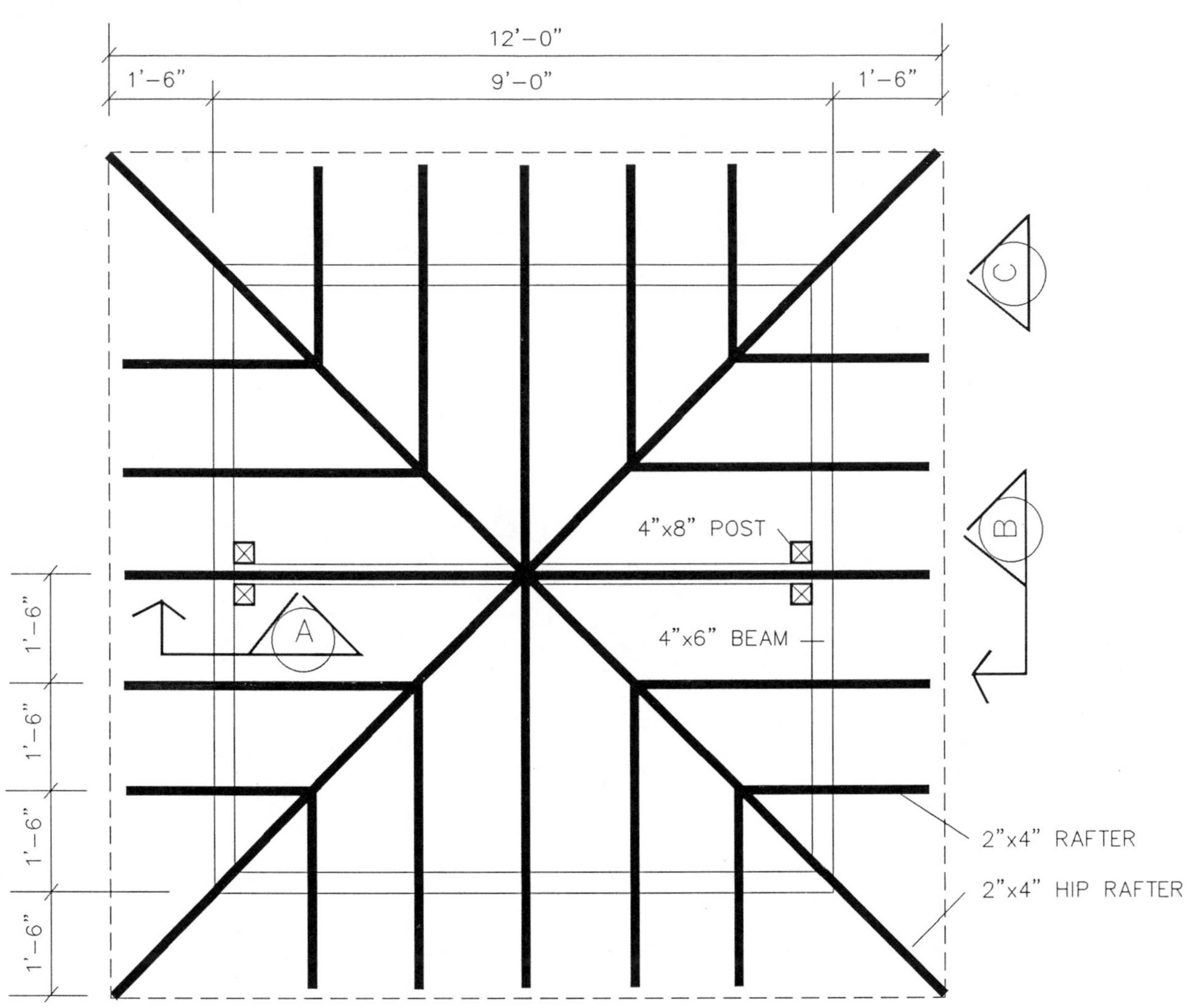

12'–0"
1'–6"
9'–0"
1'–6"
C
B
4"x8" POST
A
4"x6" BEAM
1'–6"
1'–6"
1'–6"
1'–6"
2"x4" RAFTER
2"x4" HIP RAFTER

ROOF FRAMING PLAN

SCALE: NOT TO SCALE

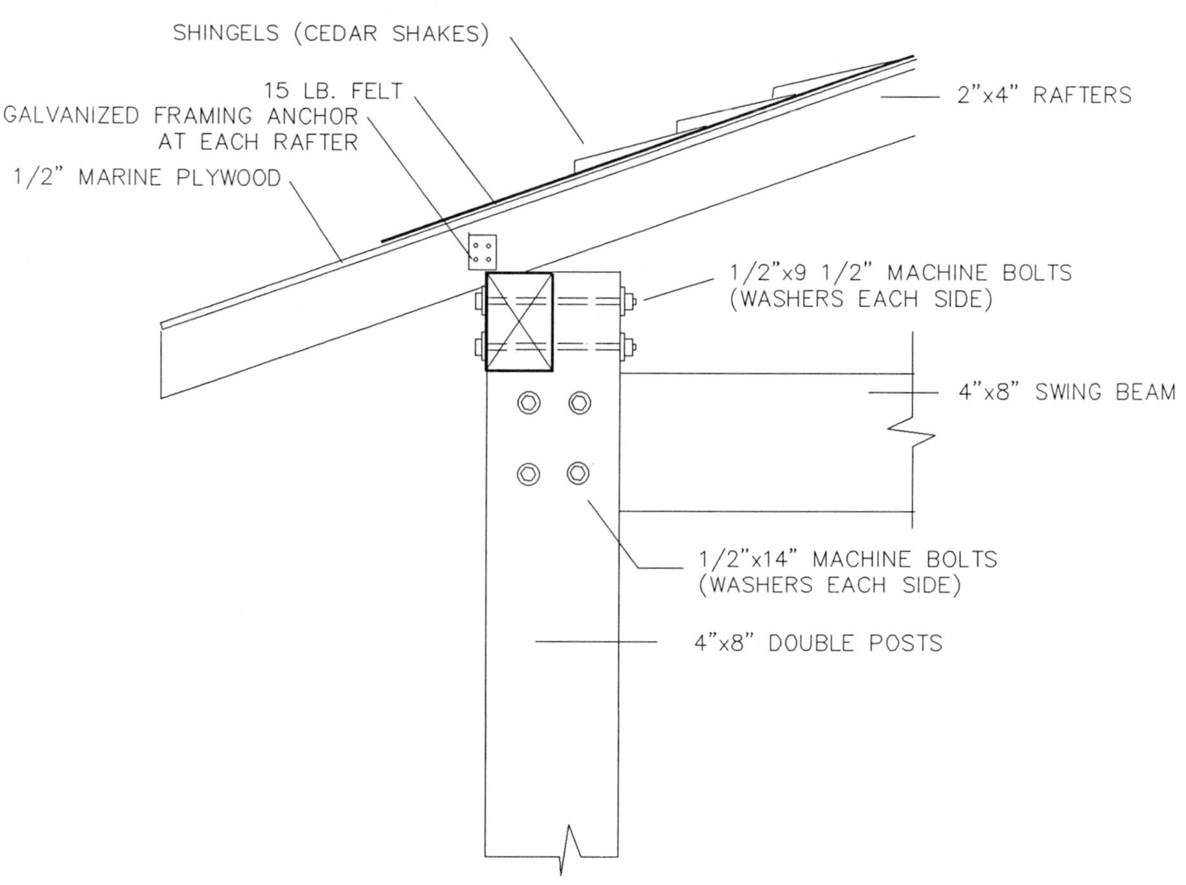
SHINGELS (CEDAR SHAKES)
15 LB. FELT
GALVANIZED FRAMING ANCHOR
AT EACH RAFTER
1/2" MARINE PLYWOOD
2"x4" RAFTERS
1/2"x9 1/2" MACHINE BOLTS
(WASHERS EACH SIDE)
4"x8" SWING BEAM
1/2"x14" MACHINE BOLTS
(WASHERS EACH SIDE)
4"x8" DOUBLE POSTS

DETAIL "A" – POST / BEAM

SCALE: NOT TO SCALE

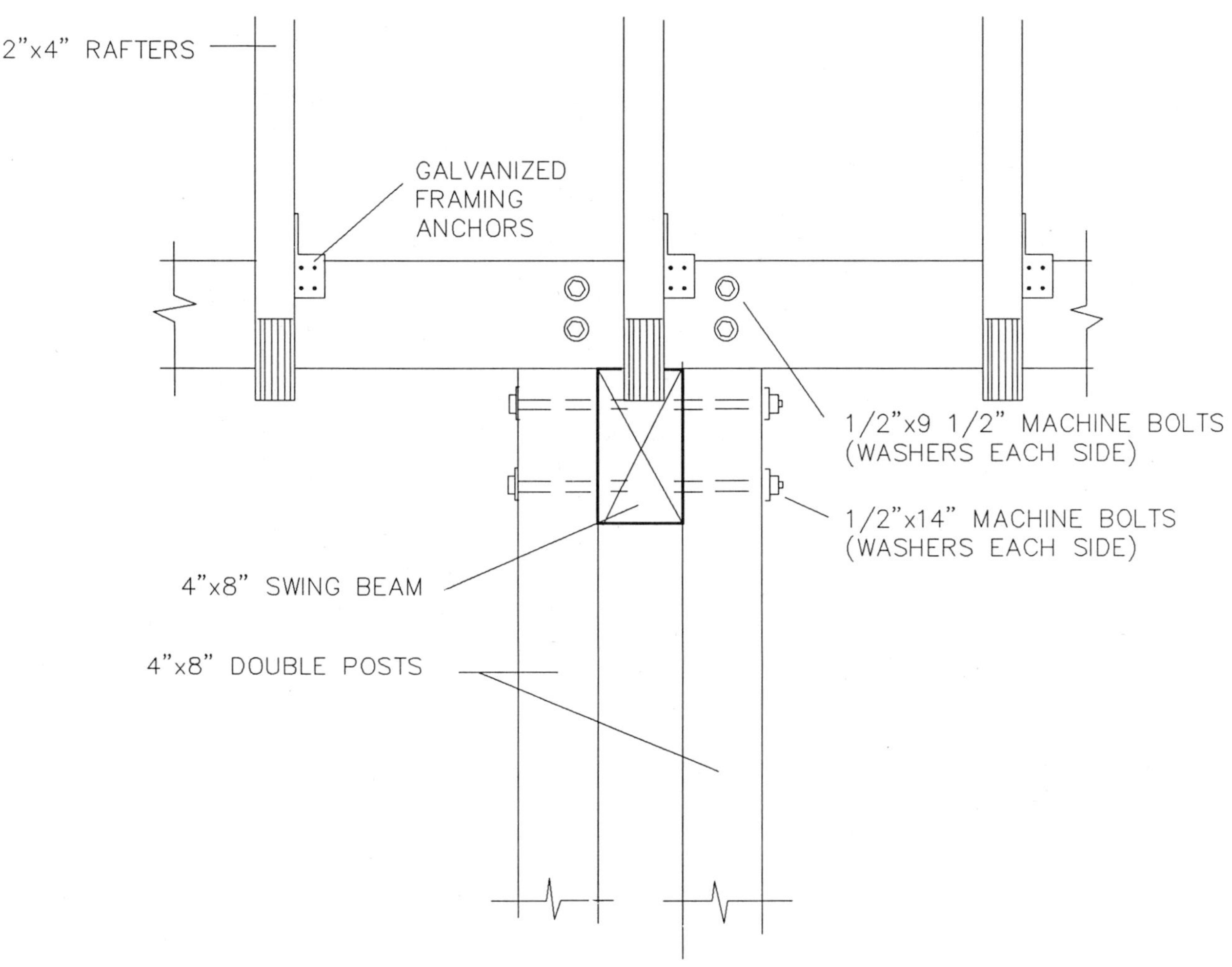
2"x4" RAFTERS
GALVANIZED FRAMING ANCHORS
1/2"x9 1/2" MACHINE BOLTS (WASHERS EACH SIDE)
1/2"x14" MACHINE BOLTS (WASHERS EACH SIDE)
4"x8" SWING BEAM
4"x8" DOUBLE POSTS

DETAIL "B" – POST / BEAM

SCALE: NOT TO SCALE

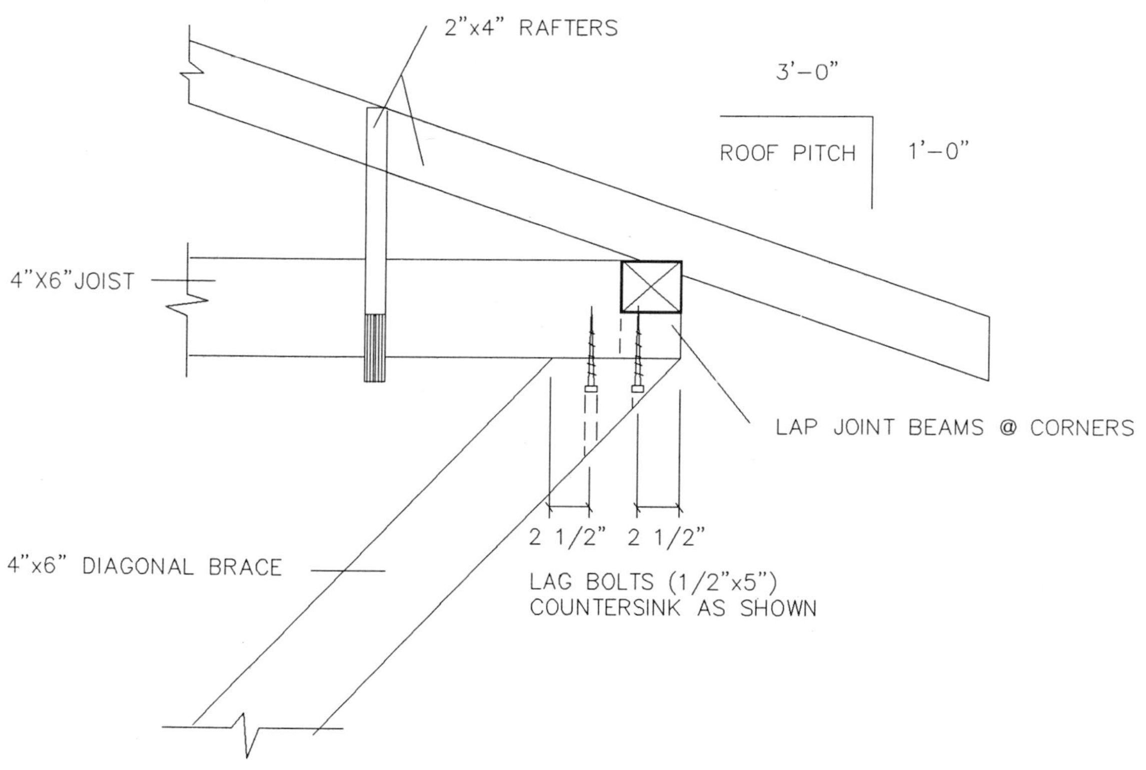
2"x4" RAFTERS
3'–0"
ROOF PITCH
1'–0"
4"X6"JOIST
LAP JOINT BEAMS @ CORNERS
2 1/2" 2 1/2"
4"x6" DIAGONAL BRACE
LAG BOLTS (1/2"x5")
COUNTERSINK AS SHOWN

DETAIL "C" – DIAGONAL BRACE

SCALE: NOT TO SCALE

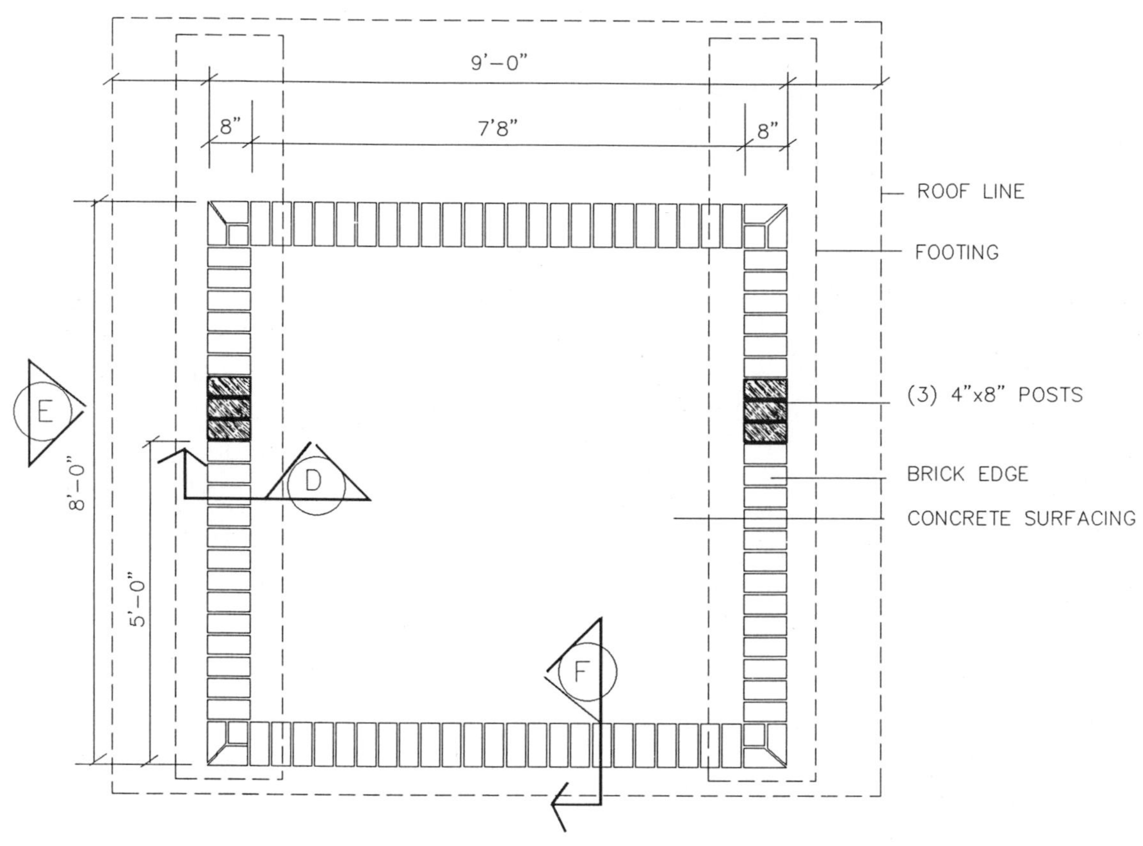

9'–0"
8"
7'8"
8"
ROOF LINE
FOOTING
(3) 4"x8" POSTS
BRICK EDGE
CONCRETE SURFACING
8'–0"
5'–0"
E
D
F

FLOOR PLAN

SCALE: NOT TO SCALE

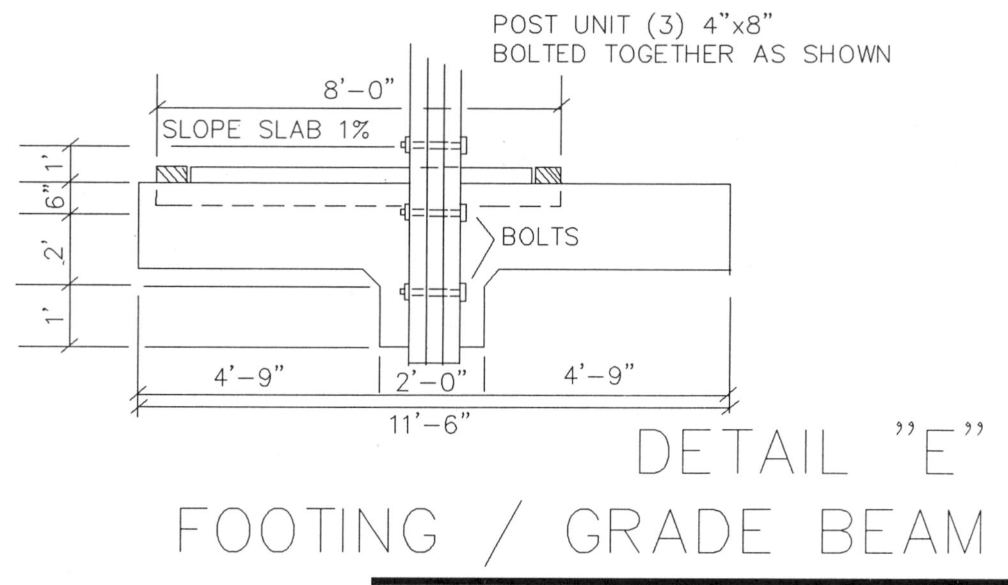
POST UNIT (3) 4"x8"
BOLTED TOGETHER AS SHOWN
8'–0"
SLOPE SLAB 1%
1'
6"
2'
1'
BOLTS
4'–9"
2'–0"
4'–9"
11'–6"

DETAIL "E"
FOOTING / GRADE BEAM

SCALE: NOT TO SCALE

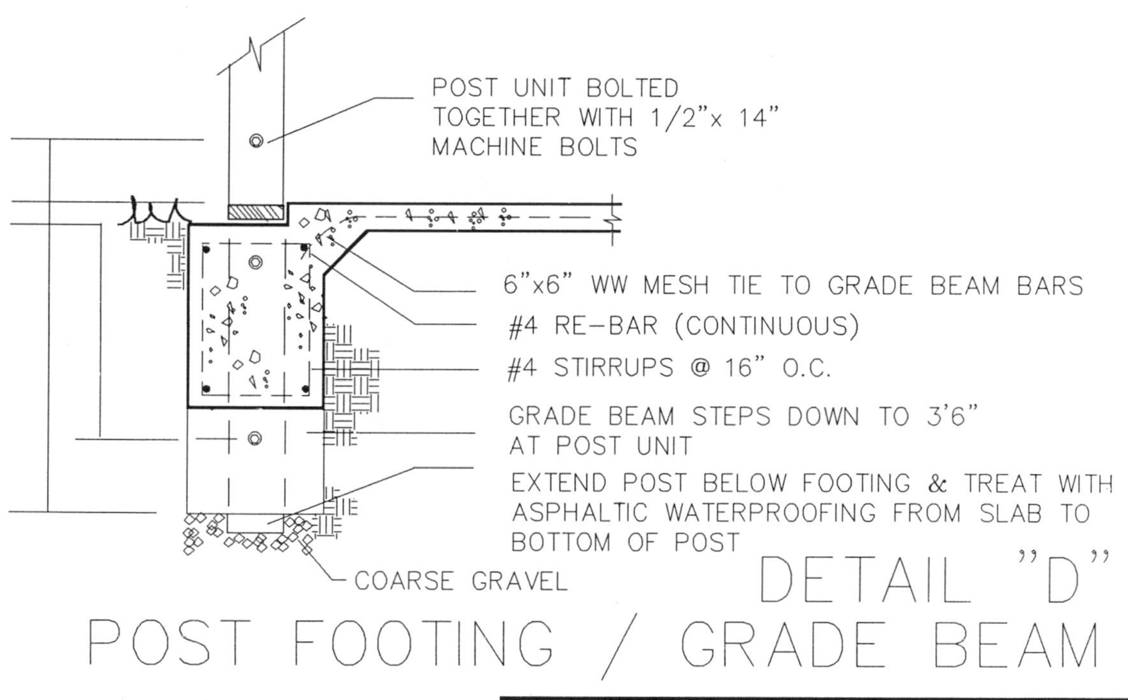
POST UNIT BOLTED
TOGETHER WITH 1/2"x 14"
MACHINE BOLTS
6"x6" WW MESH TIE TO GRADE BEAM BARS
#4 RE-BAR (CONTINUOUS)
#4 STIRRUPS @ 16" O.C.
GRADE BEAM STEPS DOWN TO 3'6"
AT POST UNIT
EXTEND POST BELOW FOOTING & TREAT WITH
ASPHALTIC WATERPROOFING FROM SLAB TO
BOTTOM OF POST
COARSE GRAVEL

DETAIL "D"
POST FOOTING / GRADE BEAM

SCALE: NOT TO SCALE

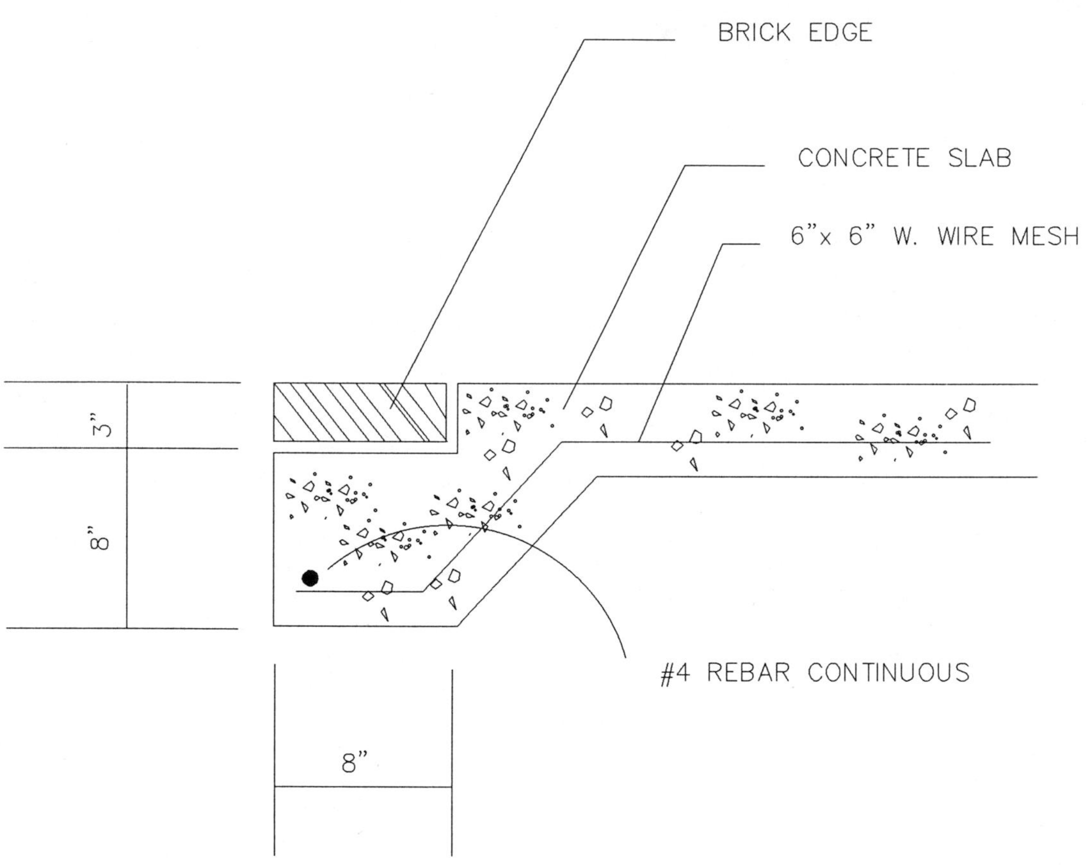
BRICK EDGE
CONCRETE SLAB
6"x 6" W. WIRE MESH
3"
8"
#4 REBAR CONTINUOUS
8"

DETAIL "F" — SLAB AT FOOTING

SCALE: NOT TO SCALE

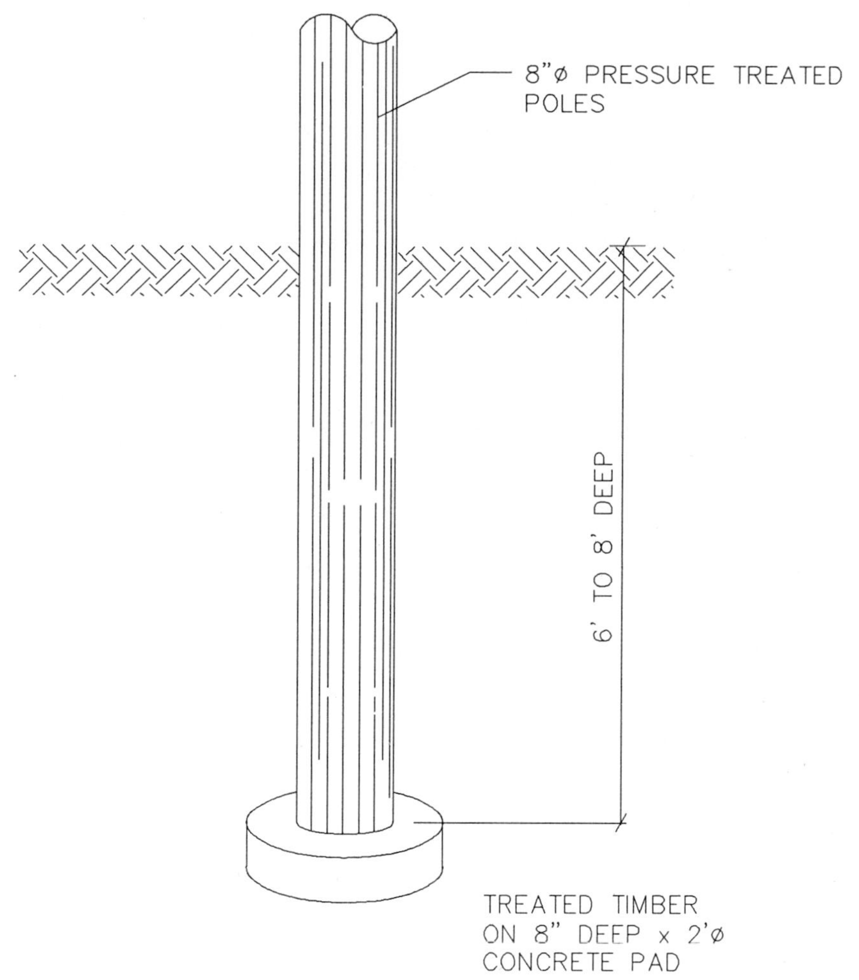
8"ø PRESSURE TREATED
POLES
6' TO 8' DEEP
TREATED TIMBER
ON 8" DEEP x 2'ø
CONCRETE PAD

POLE–FRAME/EMBEDDED

SCALE: NOT TO SCALE

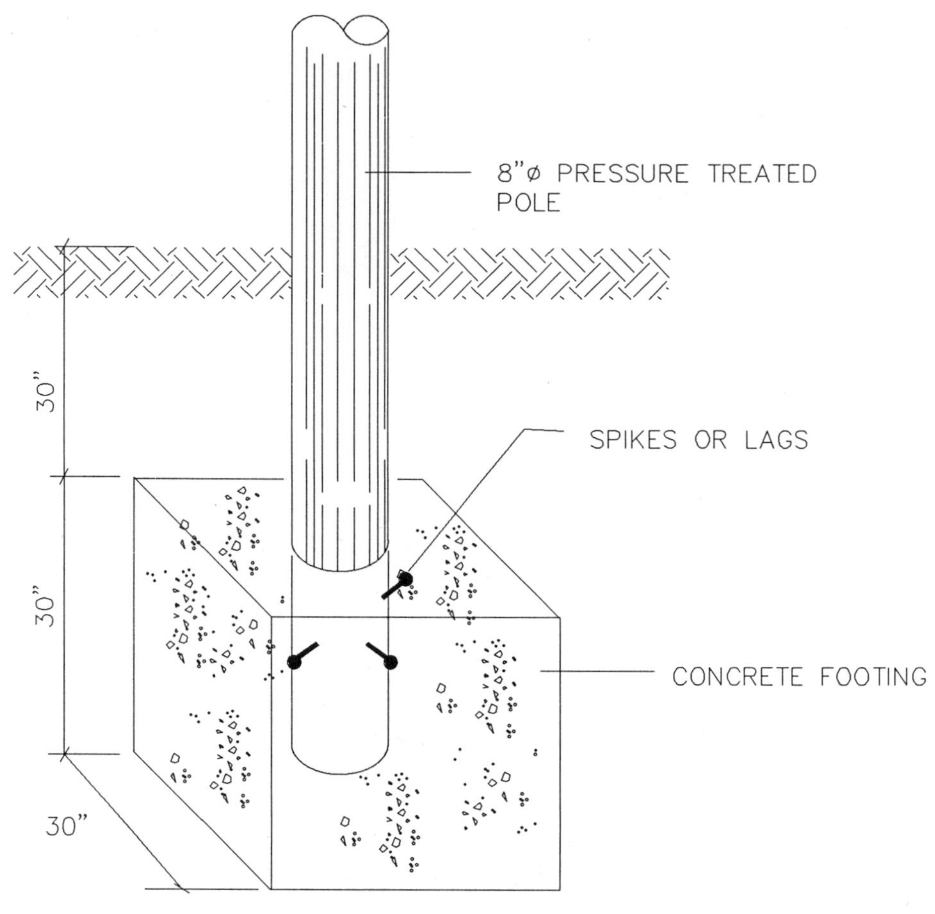
8"ø PRESSURE TREATED
POLE
30"
SPIKES OR LAGS
30"
CONCRETE FOOTING
30"

POLE-FRAME/CONCRETE FOOTING

SCALE: NOT TO SCALE

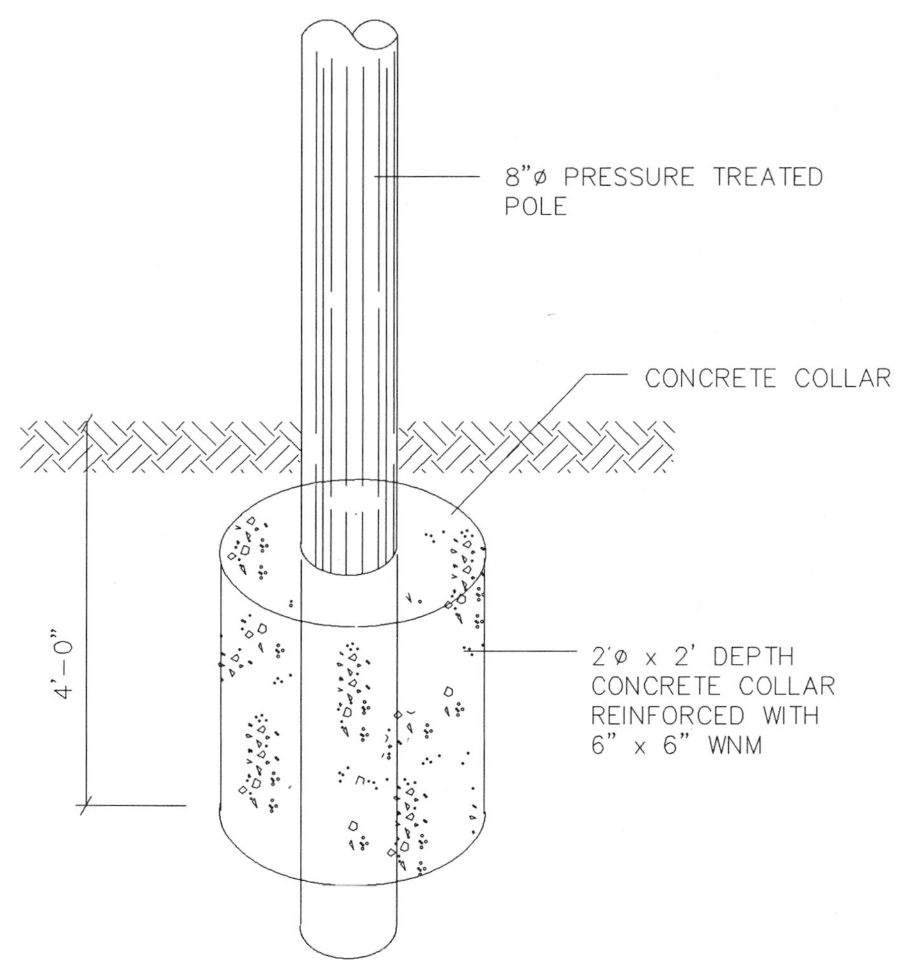
8"ø PRESSURE TREATED
POLE
CONCRETE COLLAR
4'–0"
2'ø x 2' DEPTH
CONCRETE COLLAR
REINFORCED WITH
6" x 6" WNM

POLE–FRAME/CONCRETE COLLAR

SCALE: NOT TO SCALE

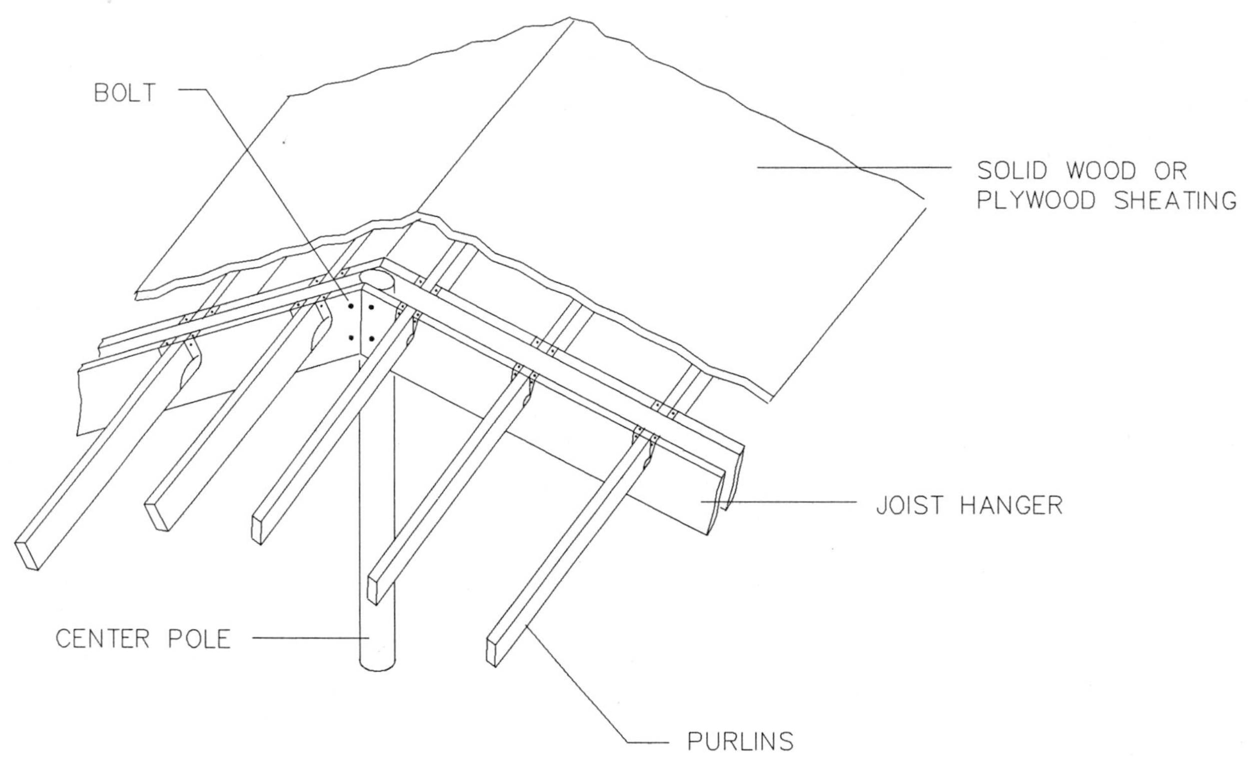
BOLT
SOLID WOOD OR
PLYWOOD SHEATING
JOIST HANGER
CENTER POLE
PURLINS

TYING ROOF TRUSSES, RAFTERS AND CEILINGS JOISTS TO POLES

SCALE: NOT TO SCALE

Signage

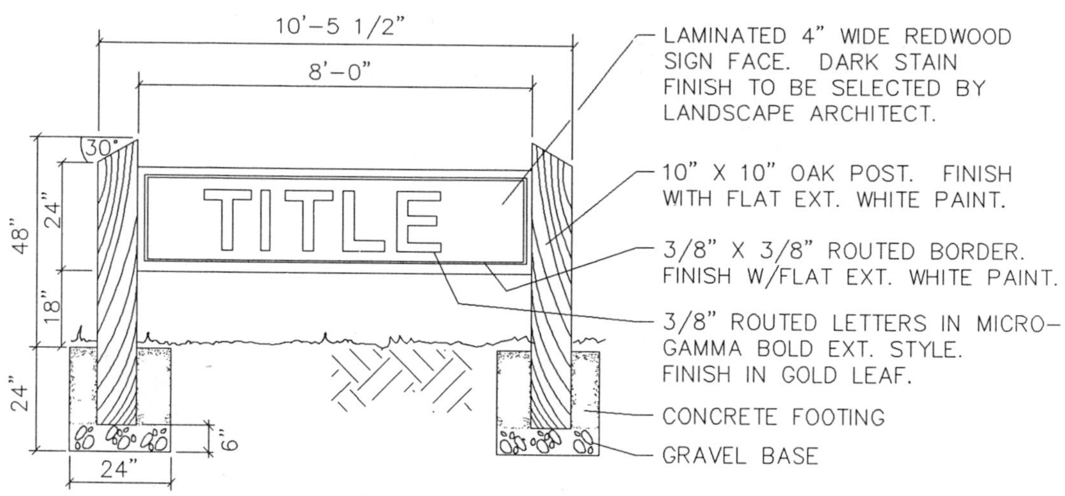
10'-5 1/2"
8'-0"
30°
TITLE
48"
24"
18"
24"
6"
24"
LAMINATED 4" WIDE REDWOOD SIGN FACE. DARK STAIN FINISH TO BE SELECTED BY LANDSCAPE ARCHITECT.
10" X 10" OAK POST. FINISH WITH FLAT EXT. WHITE PAINT.
3/8" X 3/8" ROUTED BORDER. FINISH W/FLAT EXT. WHITE PAINT.
3/8" ROUTED LETTERS IN MICRO-GAMMA BOLD EXT. STYLE. FINISH IN GOLD LEAF.
CONCRETE FOOTING
GRAVEL BASE

FRONT ELEVATION

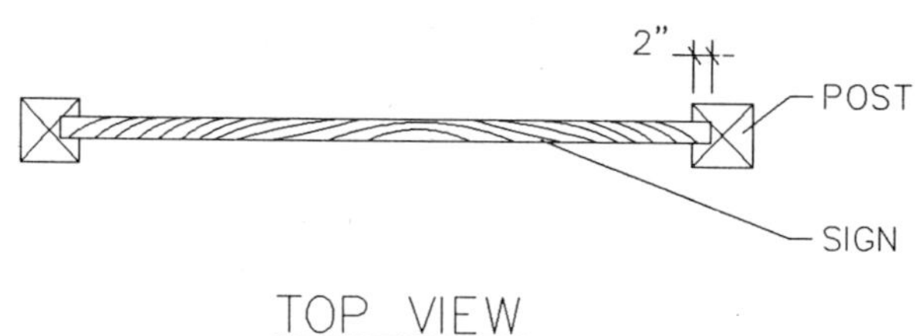
2"
POST
SIGN

TOP VIEW

DOUBLE POST WOOD SIGN-1

SCALE: NOT TO SCALE

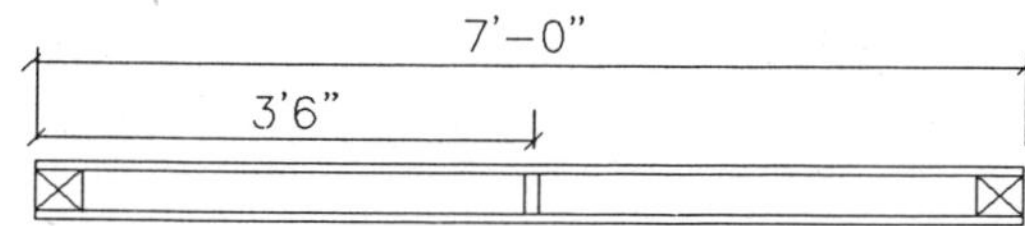
7'–0"
3'6"

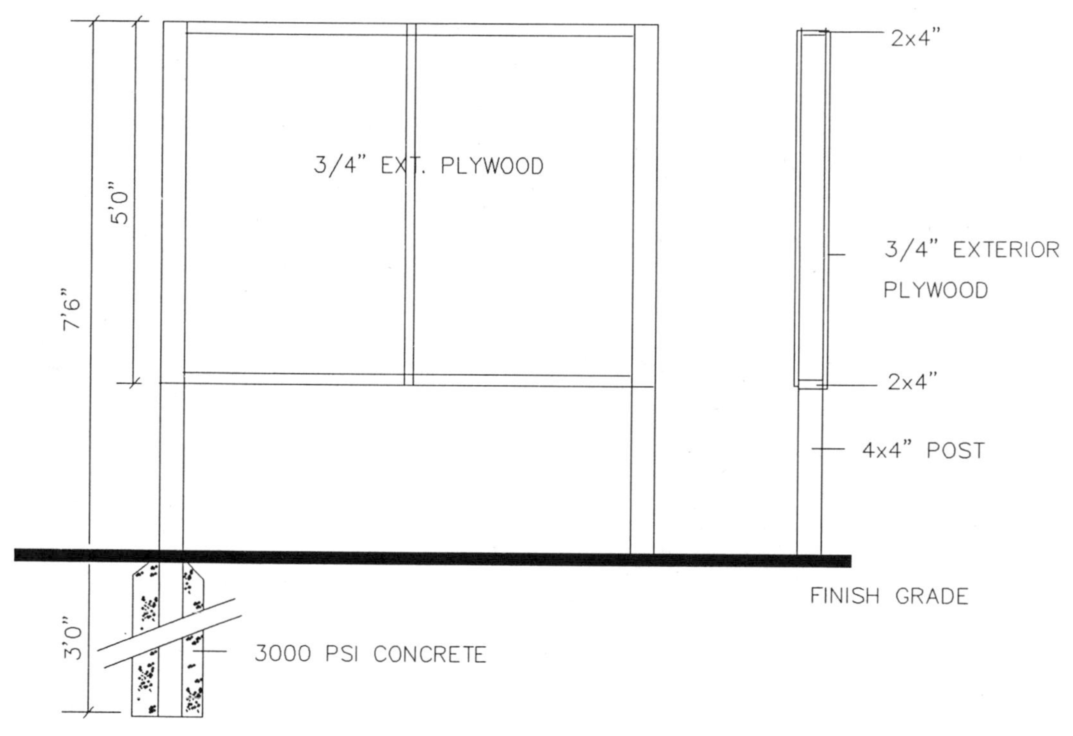
7'6"
5'0"
3/4" EXT. PLYWOOD
2x4"
3/4" EXTERIOR PLYWOOD
2x4"
4x4" POST
FINISH GRADE
3'0"
3000 PSI CONCRETE

JOB SIGN

SCALE: NOT TO SCALE

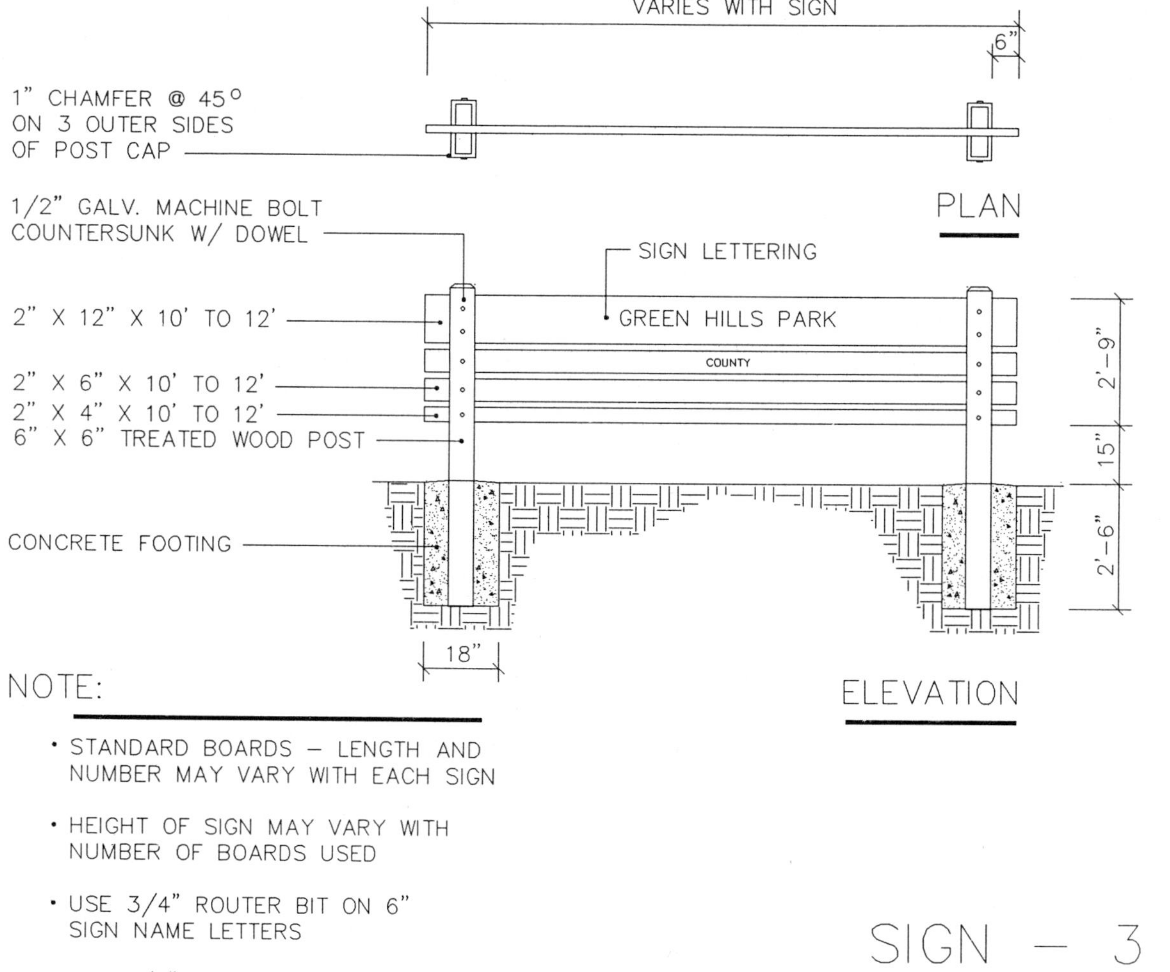
VARIES WITH SIGN
6"
1" CHAMFER @ 45°
ON 3 OUTER SIDES
OF POST CAP
PLAN
1/2" GALV. MACHINE BOLT
COUNTERSUNK W/ DOWEL
SIGN LETTERING
2" X 12" X 10' TO 12'
GREEN HILLS PARK
COUNTY
2" X 6" X 10' TO 12'
2" X 4" X 10' TO 12'
6" X 6" TREATED WOOD POST
2'-9"
15"
2'-6"
CONCRETE FOOTING
18"
ELEVATION

NOTE:

- STANDARD BOARDS – LENGTH AND NUMBER MAY VARY WITH EACH SIGN
- HEIGHT OF SIGN MAY VARY WITH NUMBER OF BOARDS USED
- USE 3/4" ROUTER BIT ON 6" SIGN NAME LETTERS
- USE 1/2" ROUTER BIT ON 3" LOCATION & ETC. LETTERS

SIGN – 3

SCALE: NOT TO SCALE

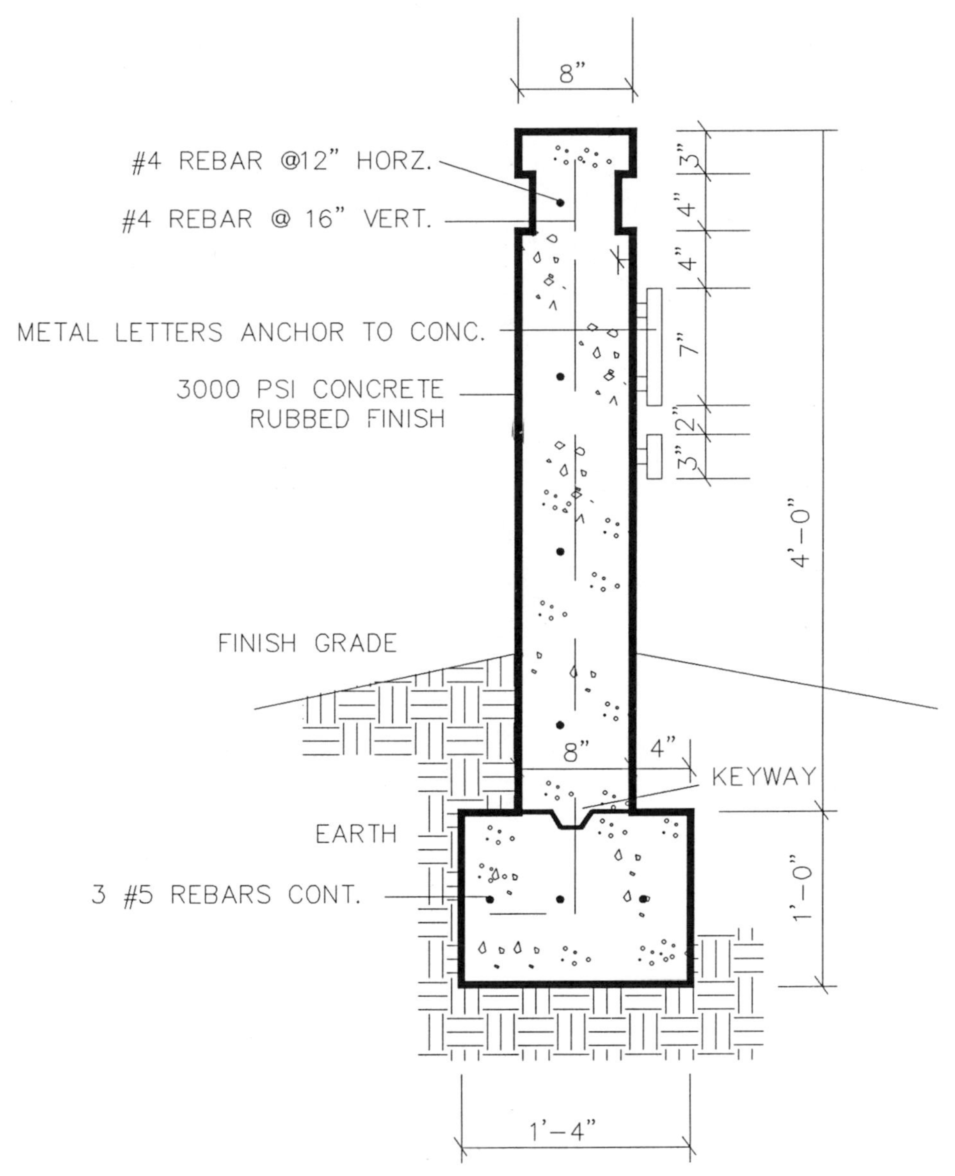
8"
#4 REBAR @12" HORZ.
#4 REBAR @ 16" VERT.
METAL LETTERS ANCHOR TO CONC.
3000 PSI CONCRETE
RUBBED FINISH
3"
4"
4"
7"
2"
3"
4'-0"
FINISH GRADE
8"
4"
KEYWAY
EARTH
3 #5 REBARS CONT.
1'-0"
1'-4"

CONCRETE WALL SIGN

SCALE: NOT TO SCALE

STOP

30" X 30"

STOP SIGN

SCALE: NOT TO SCALE

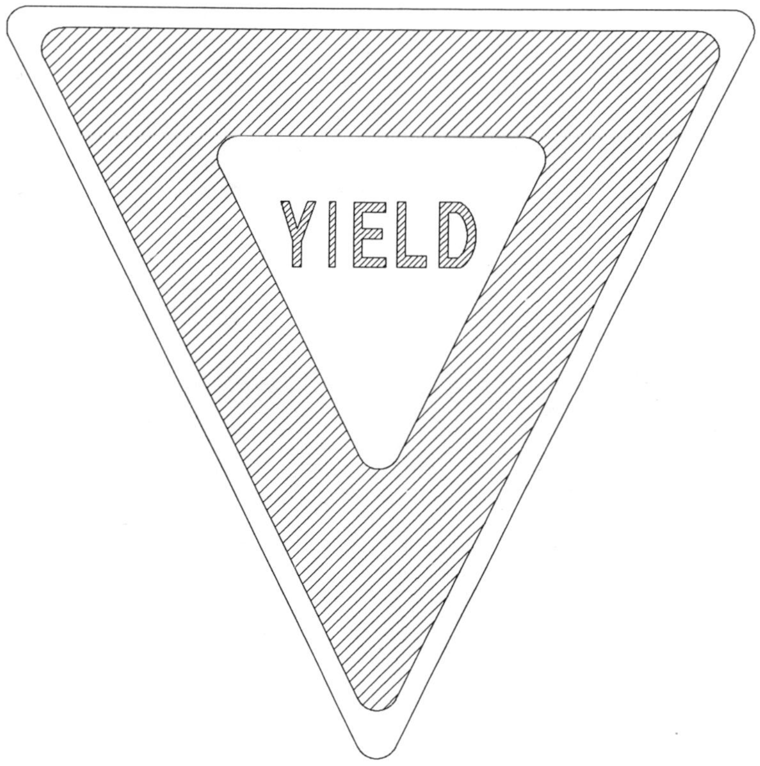
36" X 36" X 36"
YIELD

YIELD SIGN

SCALE: NOT TO SCALE

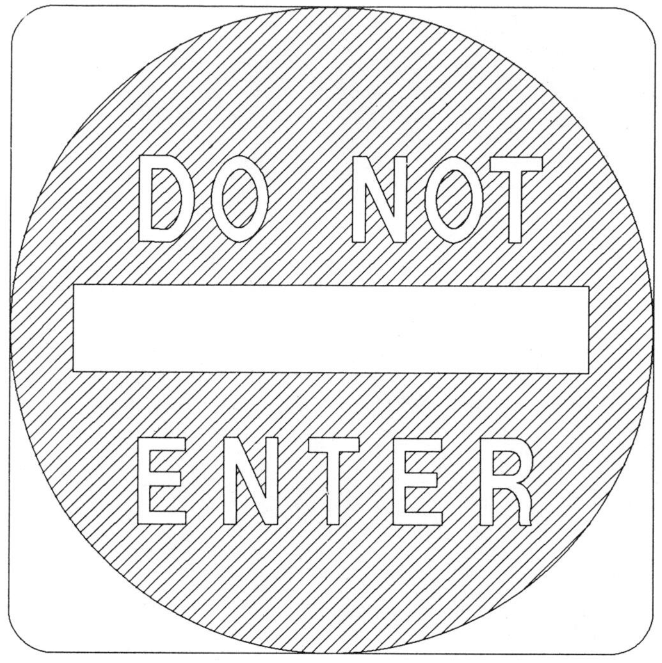
DO NOT
ENTER

30" X 30"

DO NOT ENTER

SCALE: NOT TO SCALE

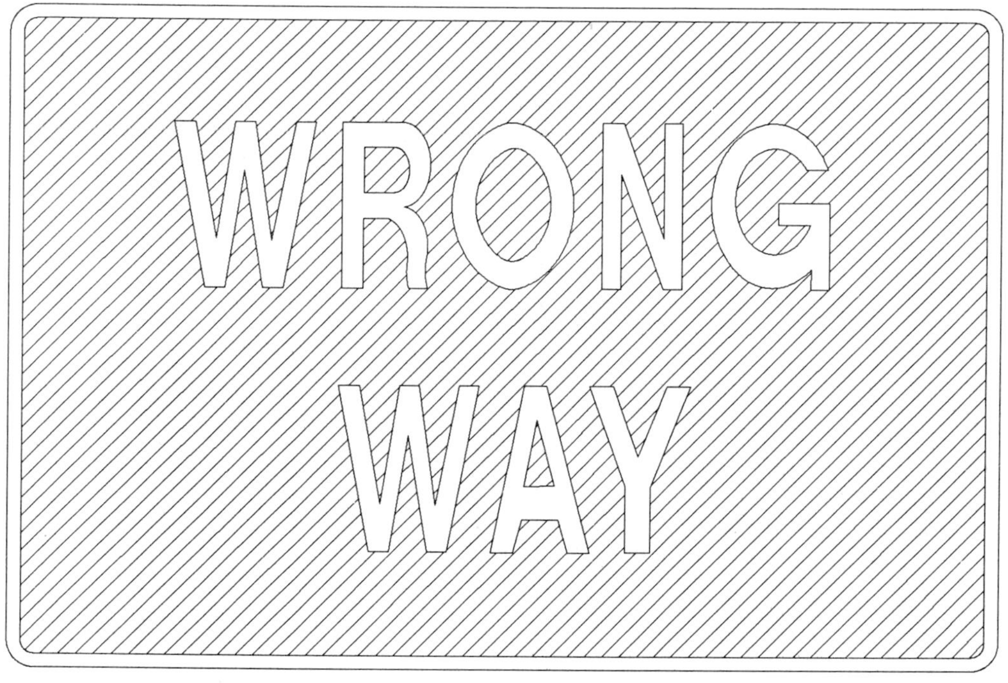
WRONG
WAY

36" X 24"

WRONG WAY

SCALE: NOT TO SCALE

REDUCED
SPEED
AHEAD

24" X 30"

REDUCED SPEED AHEAD

SCALE: NOT TO SCALE

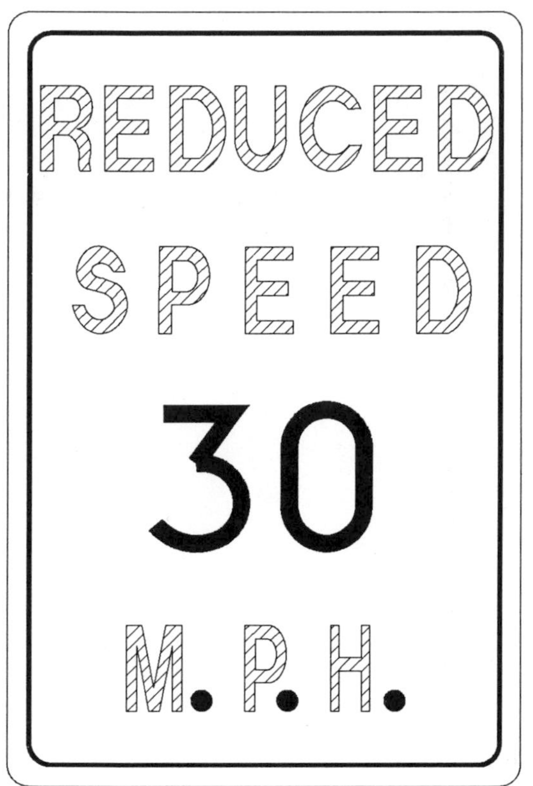
REDUCED
SPEED
30
M.P.H.

24" X 30"

REDUCED SPEED 30 M.P.H.

SCALE: NOT TO SCALE

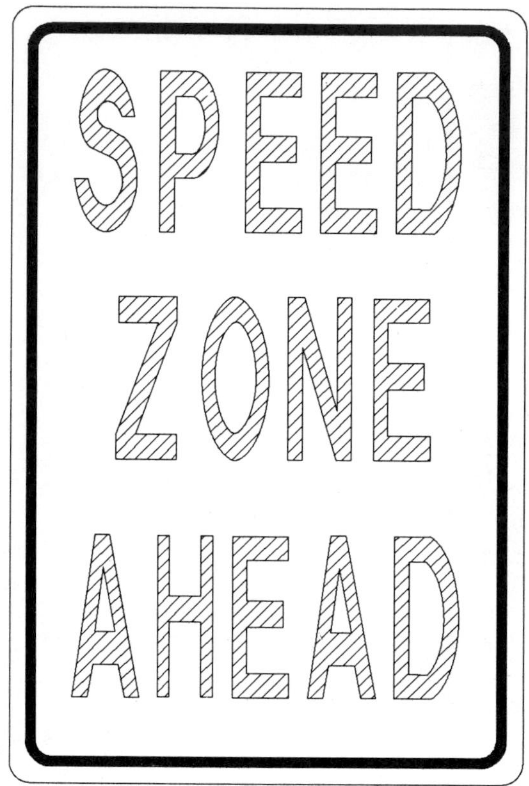
SPEED
ZONE
AHEAD

24" X 30"

SPEED ZONE AHEAD

SCALE: NOT TO SCALE

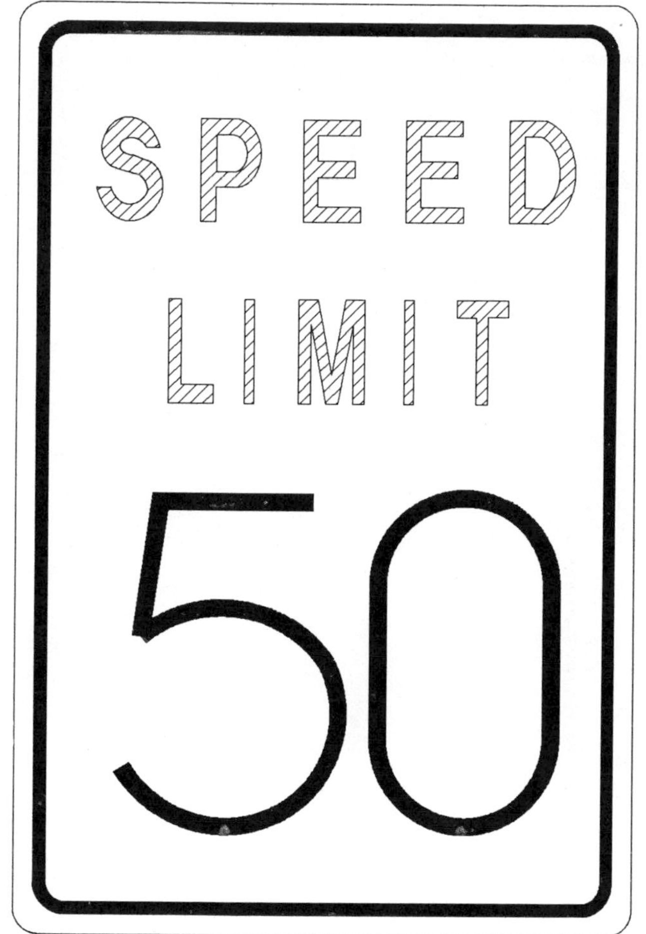
SPEED
LIMIT
50

24" X 30"

SPEED LIMIT

SCALE: NOT TO SCALE

NO
PARKING

24" X 30"

NO PARKING

SCALE: NOT TO SCALE

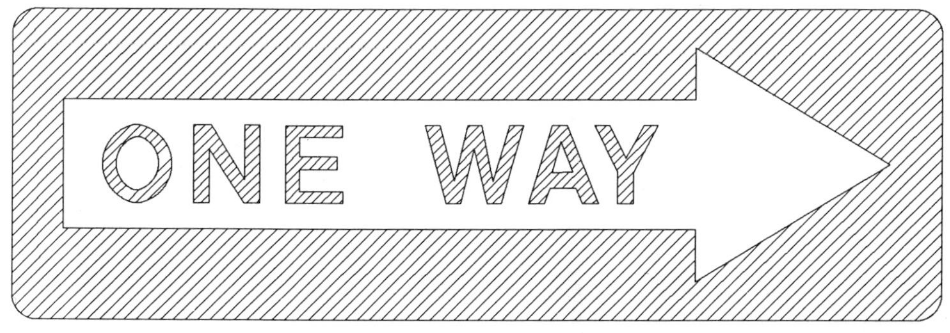
ONE WAY

36" X 12"

ONE WAY

SCALE: NOT TO SCALE

ONE
WAY

18" X 24"

ONE WAY

SCALE: NOT TO SCALE

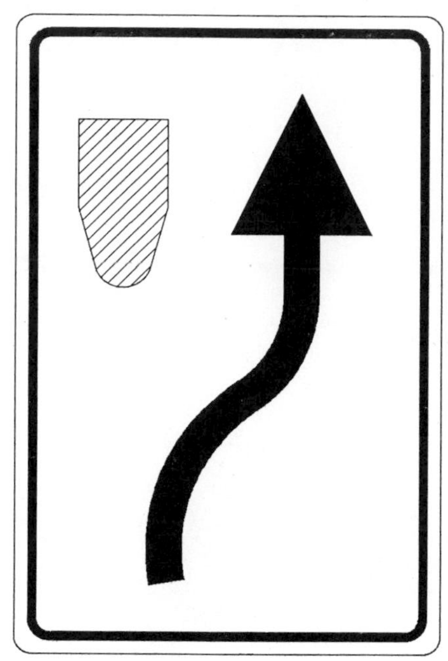

KEEP
RIGHT

24" X 30"
24" X 18"

KEEP RIGHT

SCALE: NOT TO SCALE

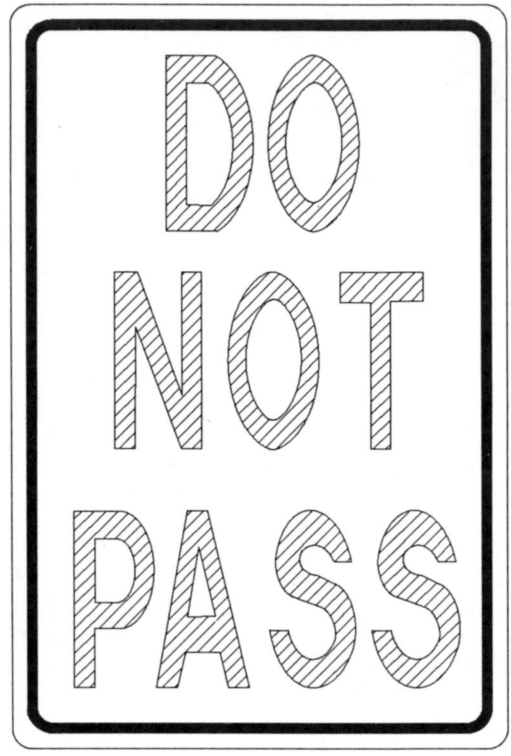
DO
NOT
PASS

24" X 30"

DO NOT PASS

SCALE: NOT TO SCALE

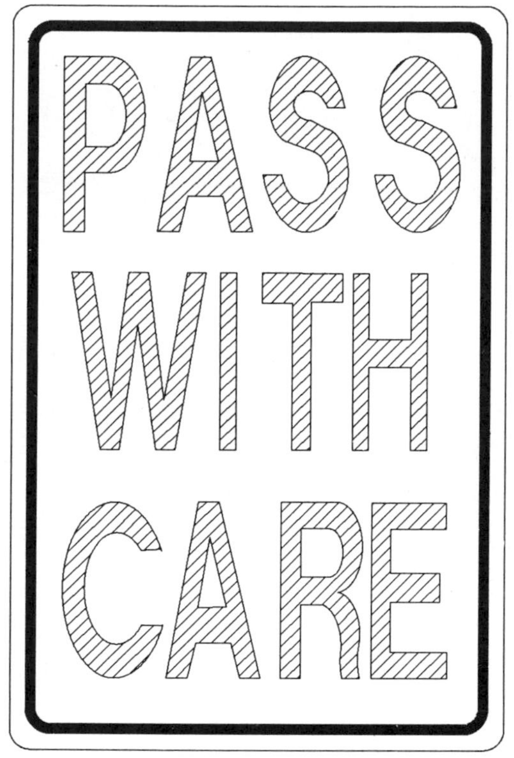
PASS
WITH
CARE

24" X 30"

PASS WITH CARE

SCALE: NOT TO SCALE

Steps & Ramps

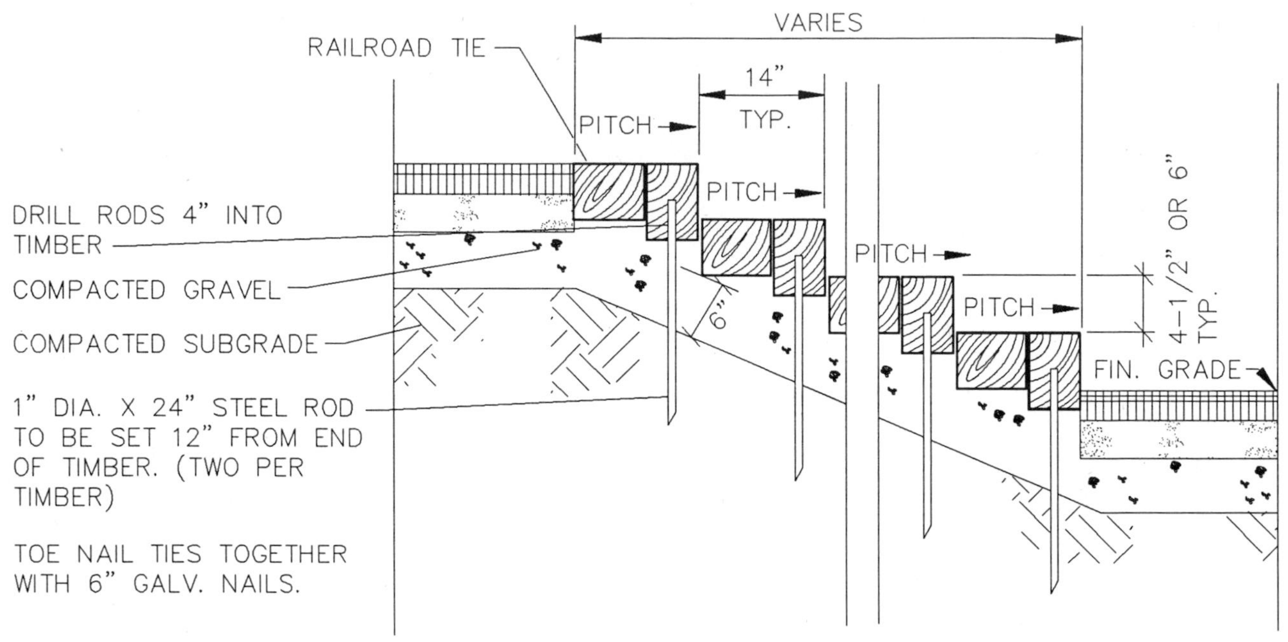
VARIES
RAILROAD TIE
14" TYP.
PITCH
PITCH
PITCH
PITCH
DRILL RODS 4" INTO TIMBER
COMPACTED GRAVEL
COMPACTED SUBGRADE
6"
4-1/2" OR 6" TYP.
FIN. GRADE
1" DIA. X 24" STEEL ROD TO BE SET 12" FROM END OF TIMBER. (TWO PER TIMBER)
TOE NAIL TIES TOGETHER WITH 6" GALV. NAILS.

TIMBER STEPS

SCALE: NOT TO SCALE

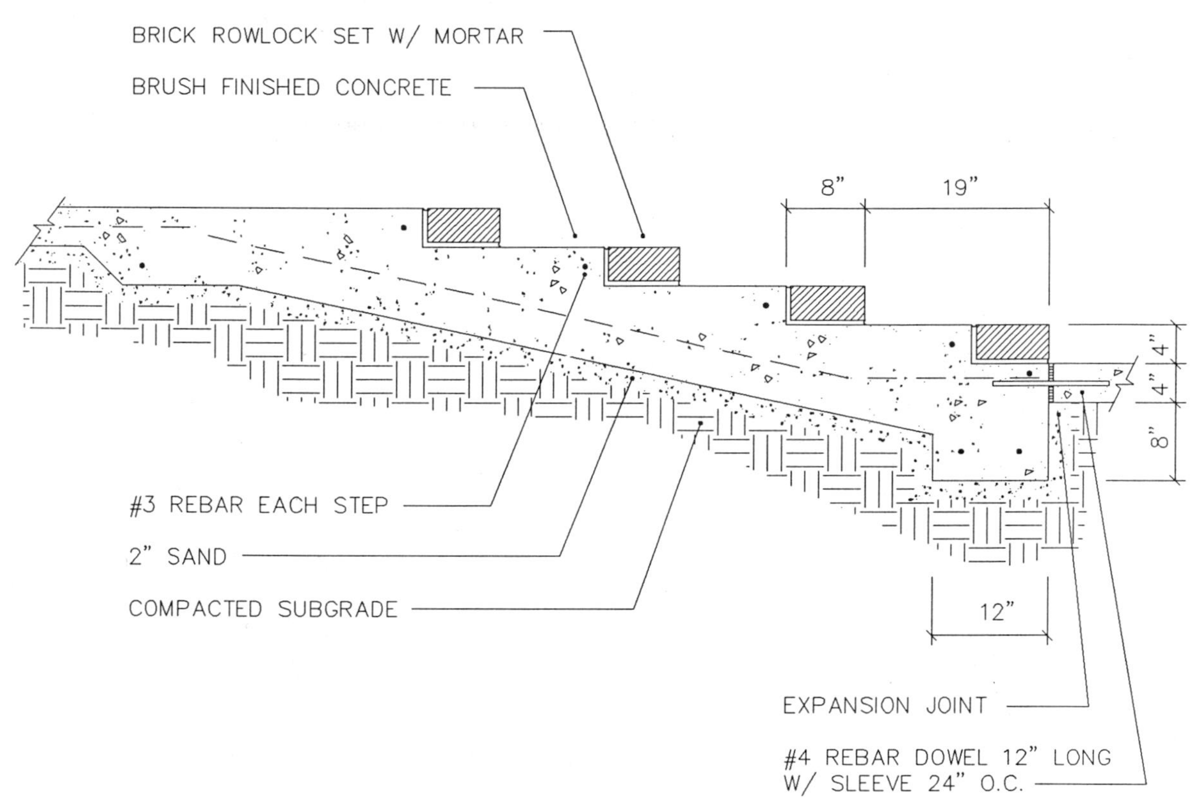
BRICK ROWLOCK SET W/ MORTAR
BRUSH FINISHED CONCRETE
8"
19"
4"
4"
8"
#3 REBAR EACH STEP
2" SAND
COMPACTED SUBGRADE
12"
EXPANSION JOINT
#4 REBAR DOWEL 12" LONG
W/ SLEEVE 24" O.C.

BRICK & CONCRETE STEPS

SCALE: NOT TO SCALE

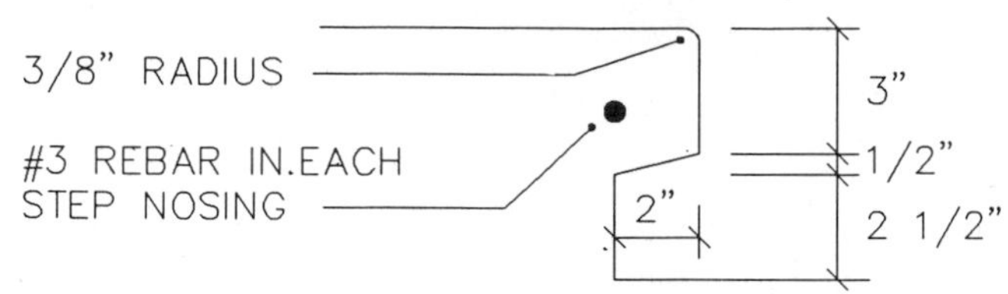
3/8" RADIUS
#3 REBAR IN.EACH
STEP NOSING
3"
1/2"
2"
2 1/2"

STEP NOSING DETAIL

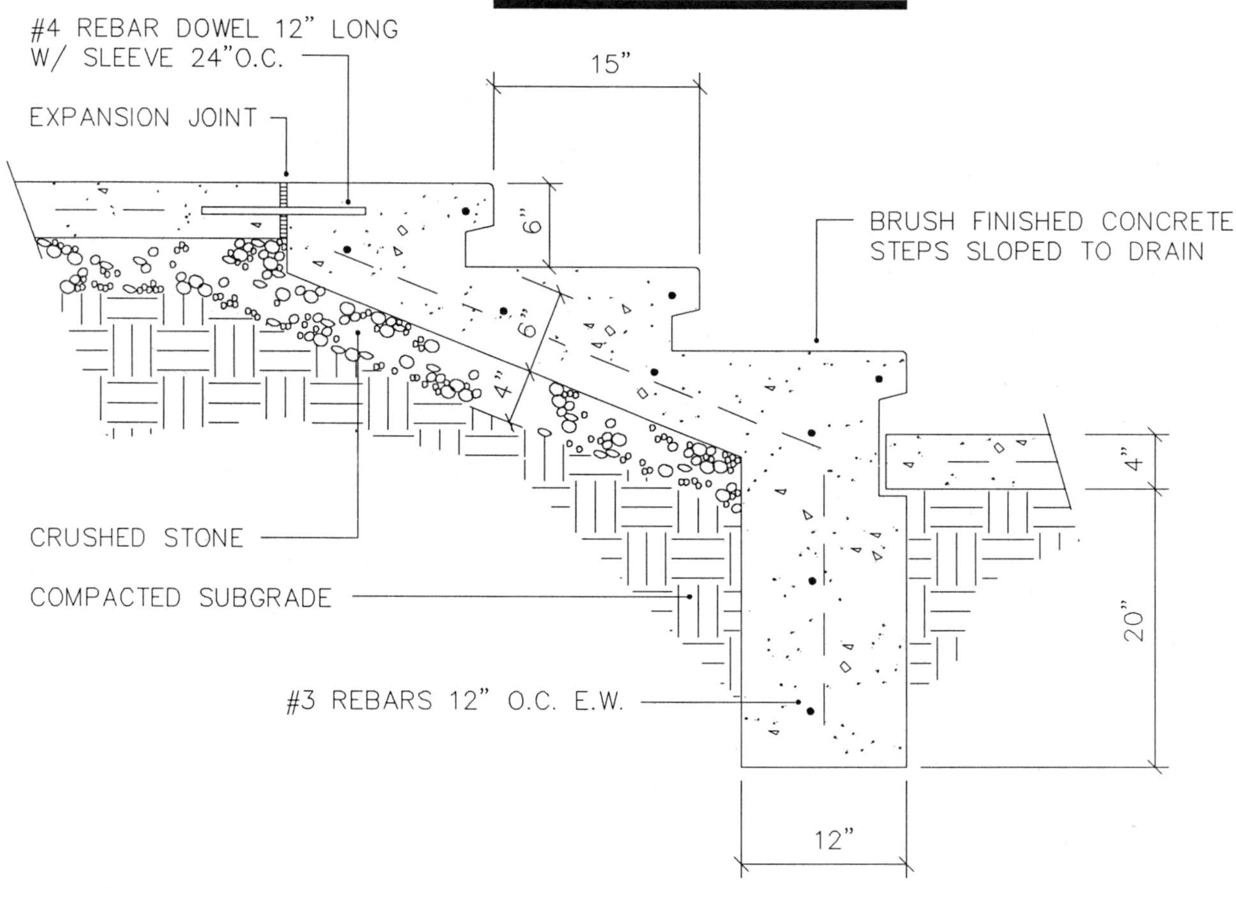
#4 REBAR DOWEL 12" LONG
W/ SLEEVE 24"O.C.
EXPANSION JOINT
15"
6"
6"
4"
BRUSH FINISHED CONCRETE
STEPS SLOPED TO DRAIN
4"
CRUSHED STONE
COMPACTED SUBGRADE
#3 REBARS 12" O.C. E.W.
20"
12"

CONCRETE STEPS

SCALE: NOT TO SCALE

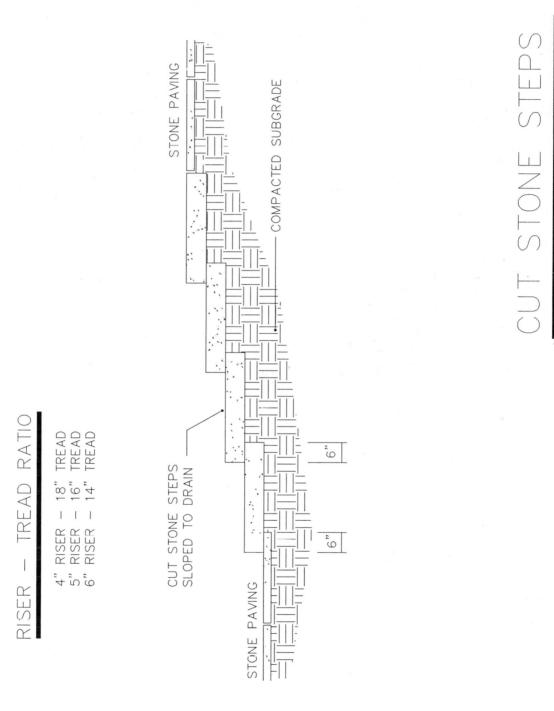

RISER – TREAD RATIO

4" RISER – 18" TREAD
5" RISER – 16" TREAD
6" RISER – 14" TREAD

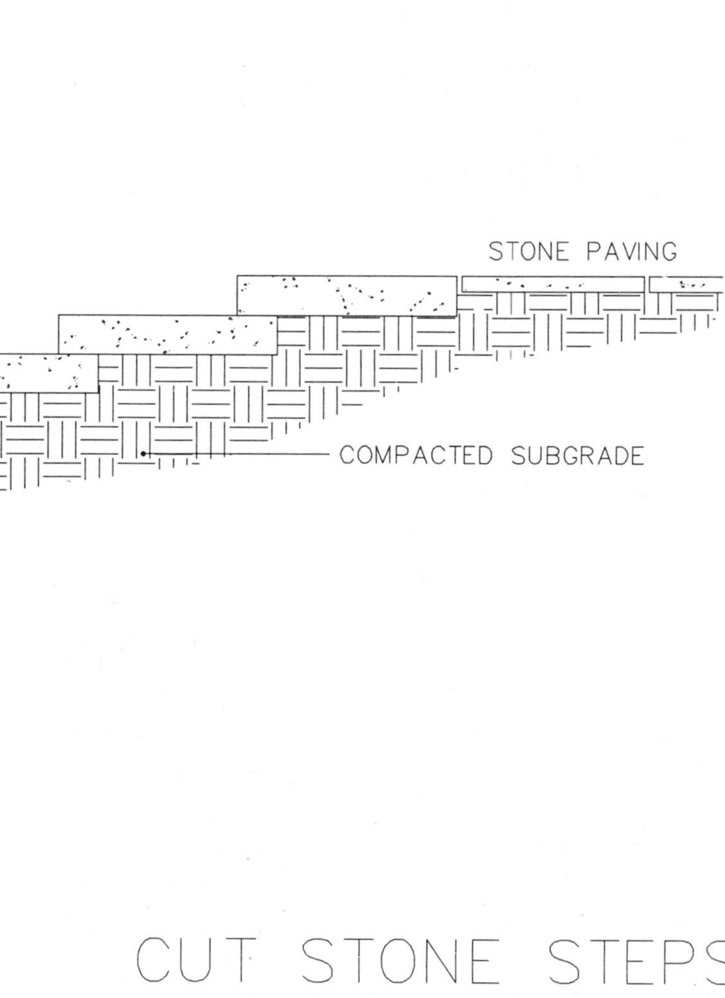
CUT STONE STEPS
SLOPED TO DRAIN
STONE PAVING
STONE PAVING
COMPACTED SUBGRADE
6"
6"

CUT STONE STEPS

SCALE: NOT TO SCALE

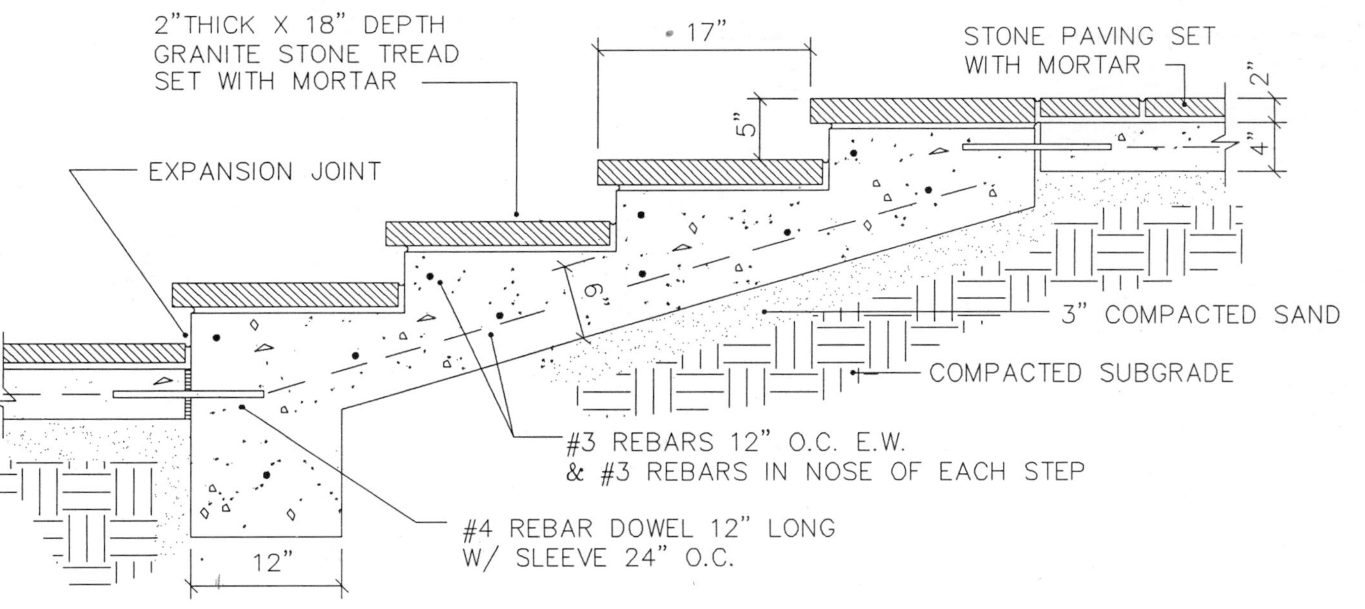
2"THICK X 18" DEPTH
GRANITE STONE TREAD
SET WITH MORTAR
EXPANSION JOINT
17"
5"
STONE PAVING SET
WITH MORTAR
2"
4"
6"
3" COMPACTED SAND
COMPACTED SUBGRADE
#3 REBARS 12" O.C. E.W.
& #3 REBARS IN NOSE OF EACH STEP
#4 REBAR DOWEL 12" LONG
W/ SLEEVE 24" O.C.
12"

STONE CAPPED STEPS

SCALE: NOT TO SCALE

$\frac{3}{4}'' = 1.0'$

Site Utilities

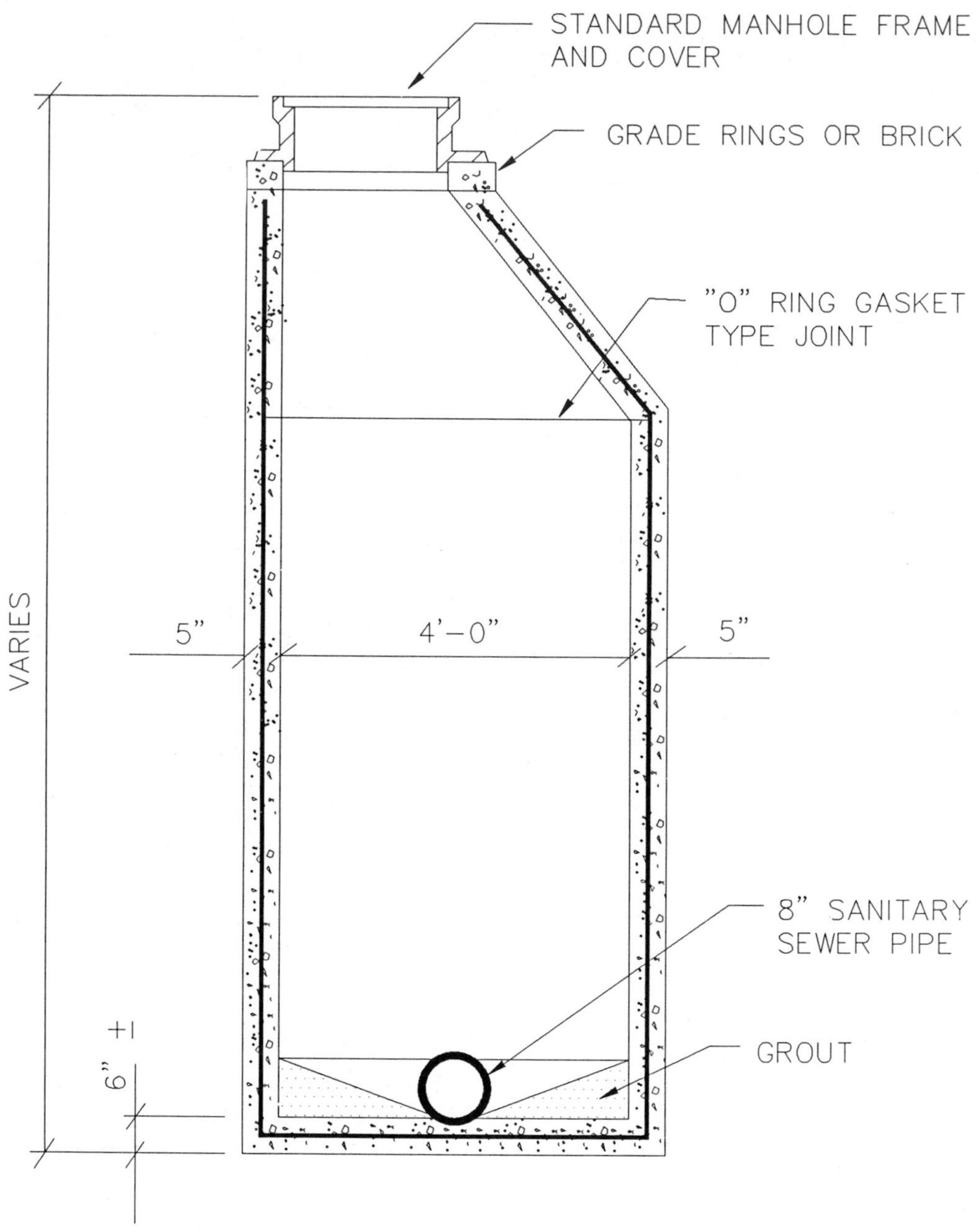
STANDARD MANHOLE FRAME
AND COVER
GRADE RINGS OR BRICK
"O" RING GASKET
TYPE JOINT
VARIES
5"
4'–0"
5"
8" SANITARY
SEWER PIPE
GROUT
6" ±

PRECAST CONCRETE MANHOLE

SCALE: NOT TO SCALE

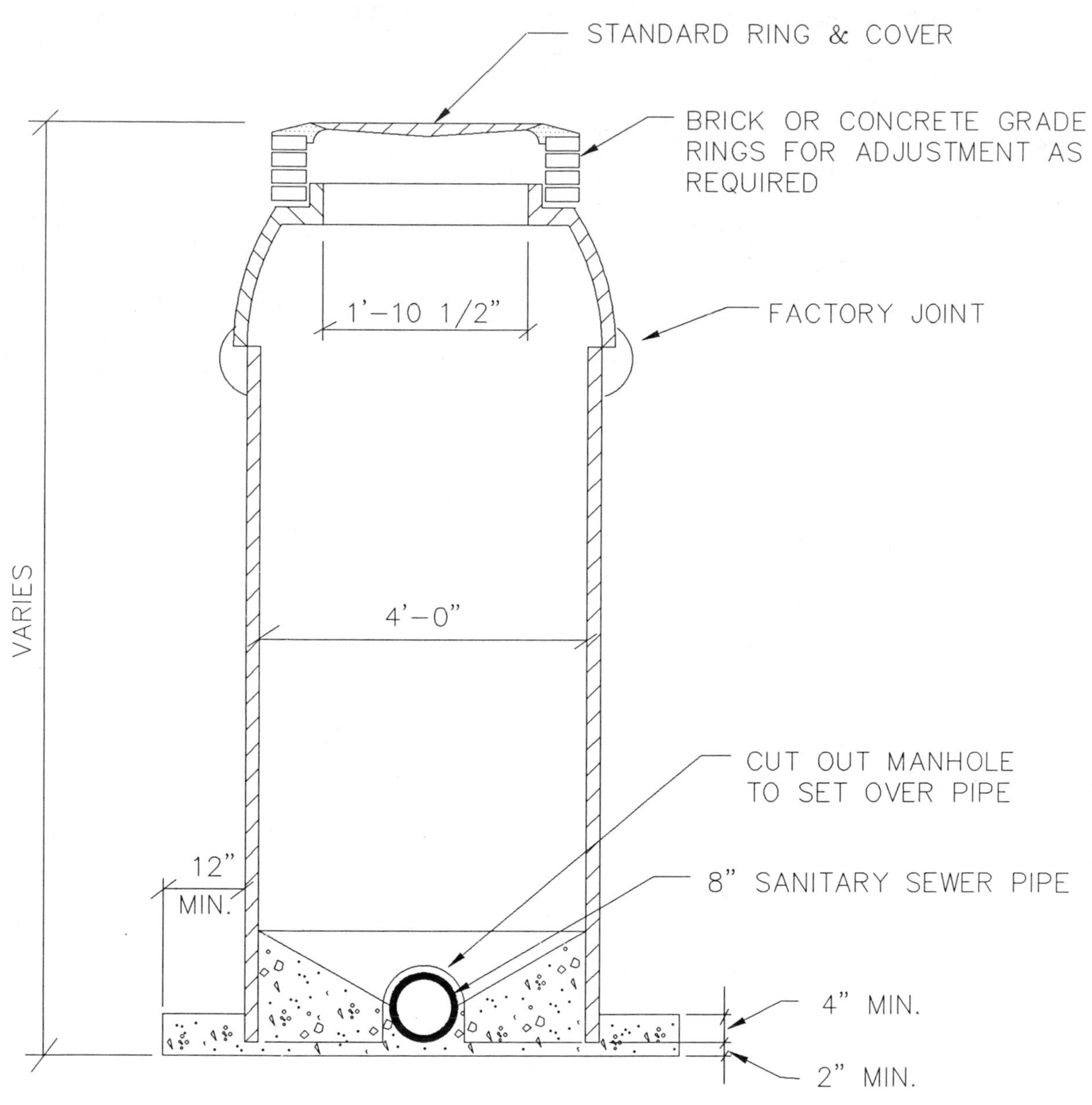
STANDARD RING & COVER
BRICK OR CONCRETE GRADE RINGS FOR ADJUSTMENT AS REQUIRED
1'–10 1/2"
FACTORY JOINT
VARIES
4'–0"
CUT OUT MANHOLE TO SET OVER PIPE
12" MIN.
8" SANITARY SEWER PIPE
4" MIN.
2" MIN.

FIBERGLASS MANHOLE

SCALE: NOT TO SCALE

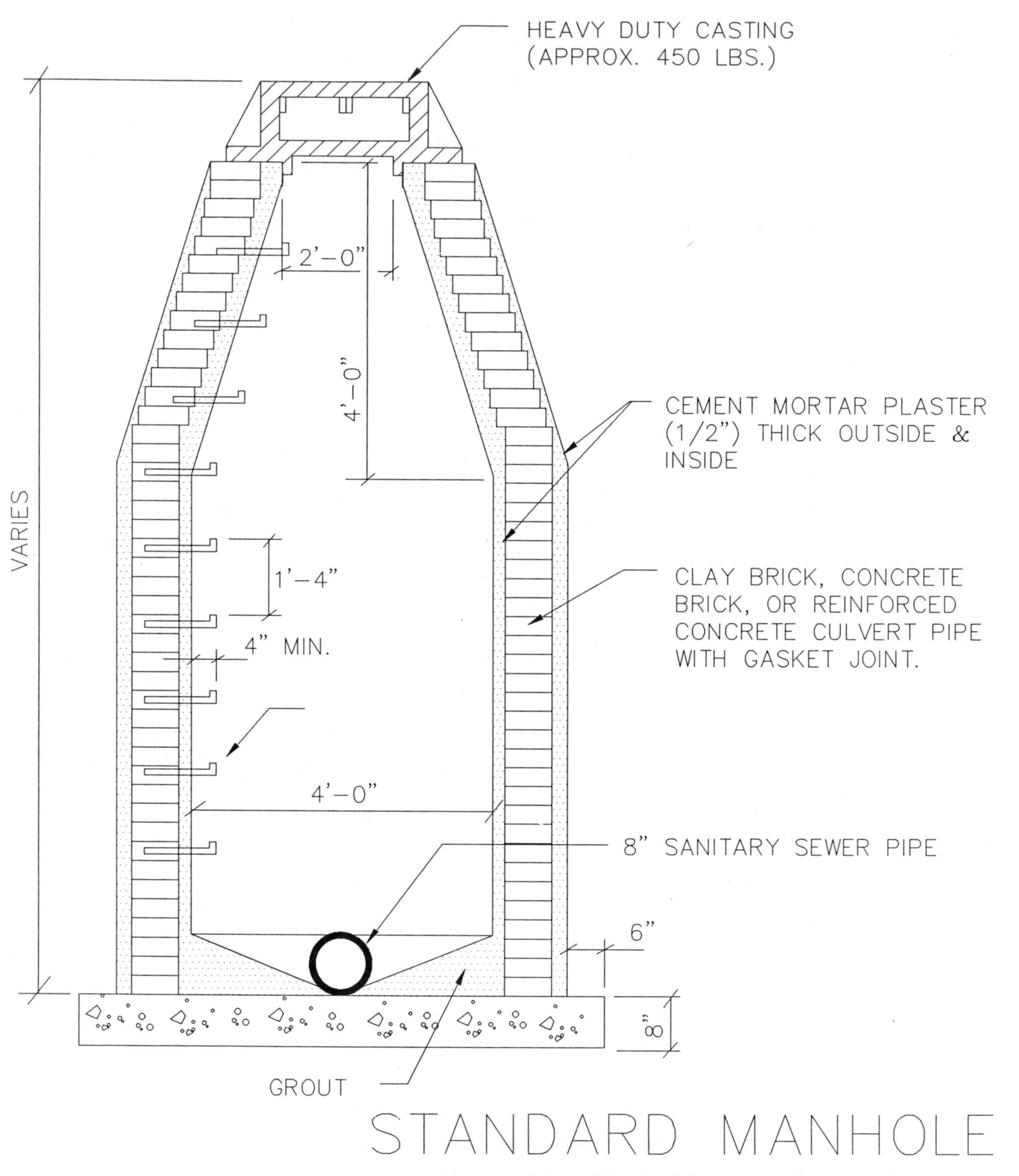
HEAVY DUTY CASTING
(APPROX. 450 LBS.)
2'–0"
4'–0"
CEMENT MORTAR PLASTER
(1/2") THICK OUTSIDE &
INSIDE
VARIES
1'–4"
CLAY BRICK, CONCRETE
BRICK, OR REINFORCED
CONCRETE CULVERT PIPE
WITH GASKET JOINT.
4" MIN.
4'–0"
8" SANITARY SEWER PIPE
6"
8"
GROUT

STANDARD MANHOLE

SCALE: NOT TO SCALE

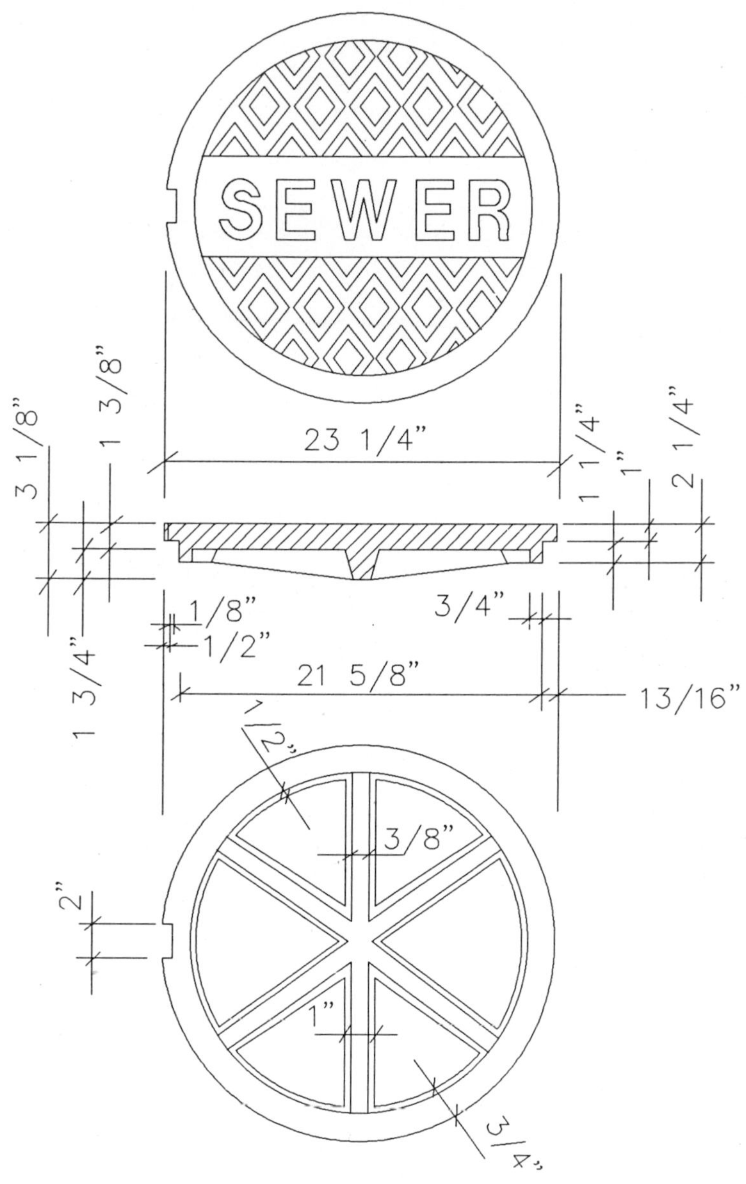
SEWER
23 1/4"
3 1/8"
1 3/8"
1 1/4"
1"
2 1/4"
1/8"
1/2"
3/4"
21 5/8"
13/16"
1 3/4"
1/2"
3/8"
2"
1"
3/4"

STANDARD MANHOLE COVER

SCALE: NOT TO SCALE

Walls

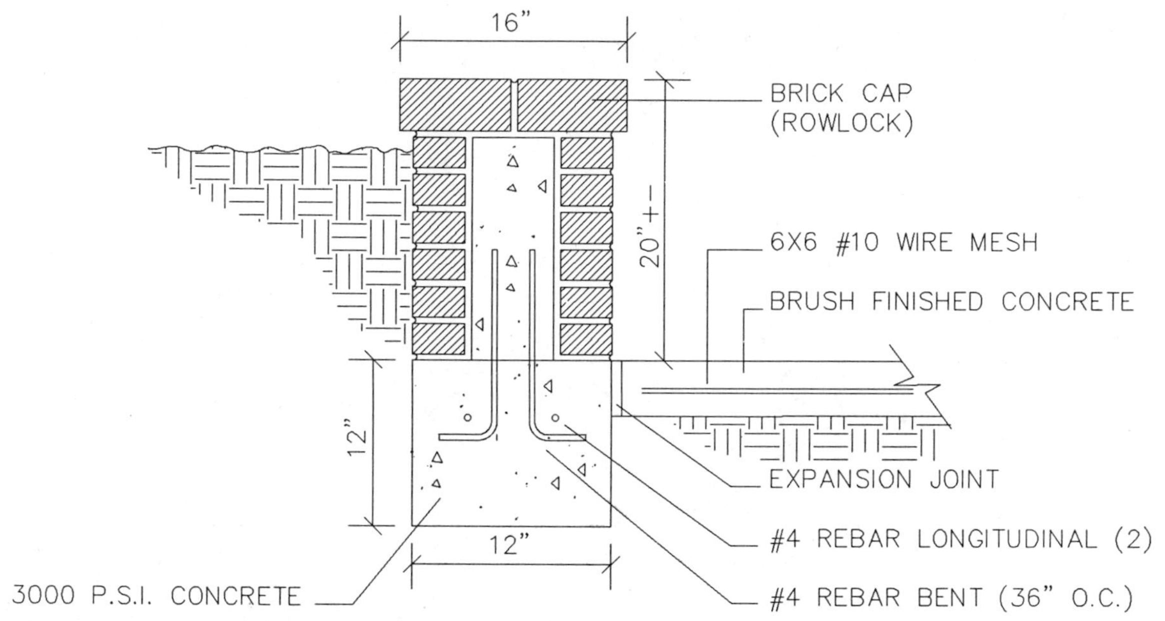
16"
BRICK CAP
(ROWLOCK)
20"+−
6X6 #10 WIRE MESH
BRUSH FINISHED CONCRETE
12"
EXPANSION JOINT
#4 REBAR LONGITUDINAL (2)
12"
3000 P.S.I. CONCRETE
#4 REBAR BENT (36" O.C.)

RAISED BRICK PLANTER

SCALE: NOT TO SCALE

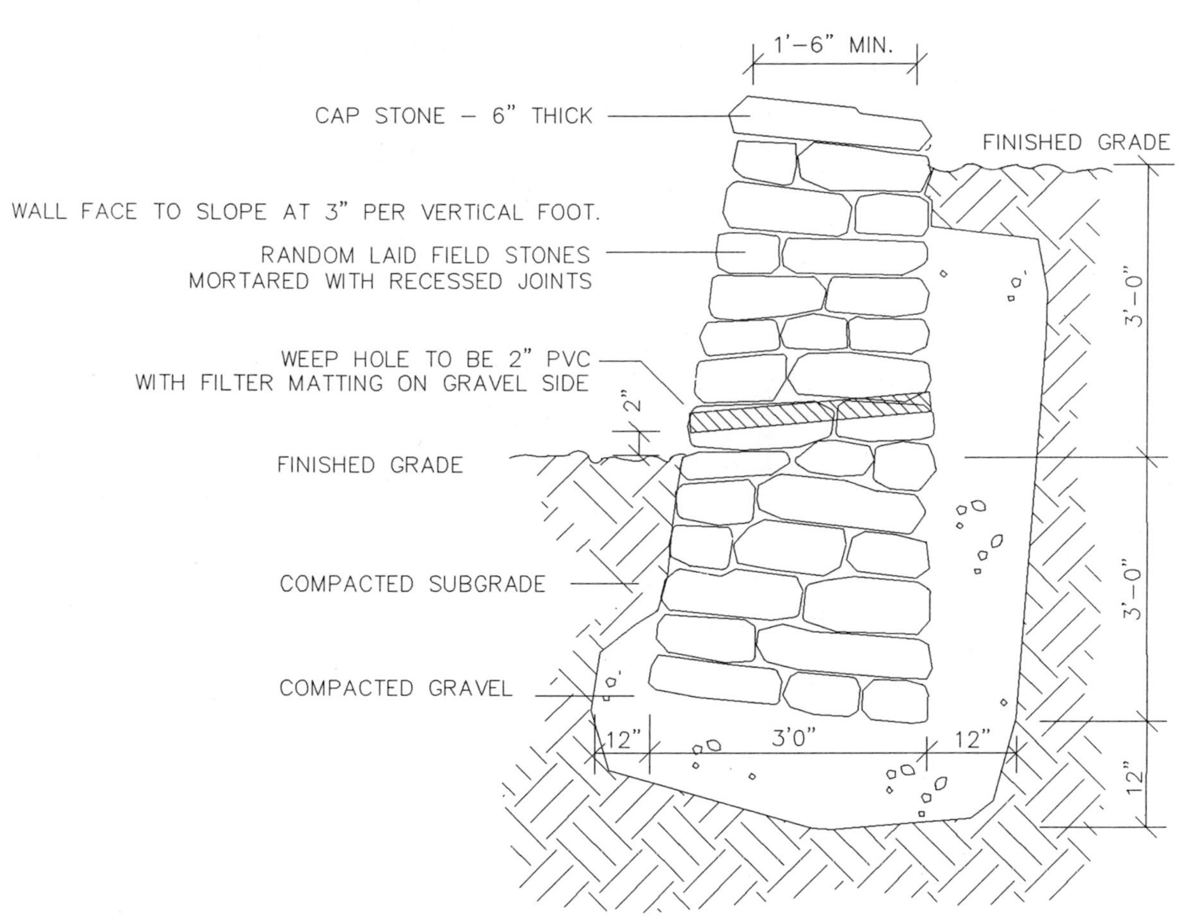
1'–6" MIN.
CAP STONE – 6" THICK
FINISHED GRADE
WALL FACE TO SLOPE AT 3" PER VERTICAL FOOT.
RANDOM LAID FIELD STONES
MORTARED WITH RECESSED JOINTS
3'–0"
WEEP HOLE TO BE 2" PVC
WITH FILTER MATTING ON GRAVEL SIDE
2"
FINISHED GRADE
COMPACTED SUBGRADE
3'–0"
COMPACTED GRAVEL
12"
3'0"
12"
12"

FIELDSTONE RETAINING WALL

SCALE: NOT TO SCALE

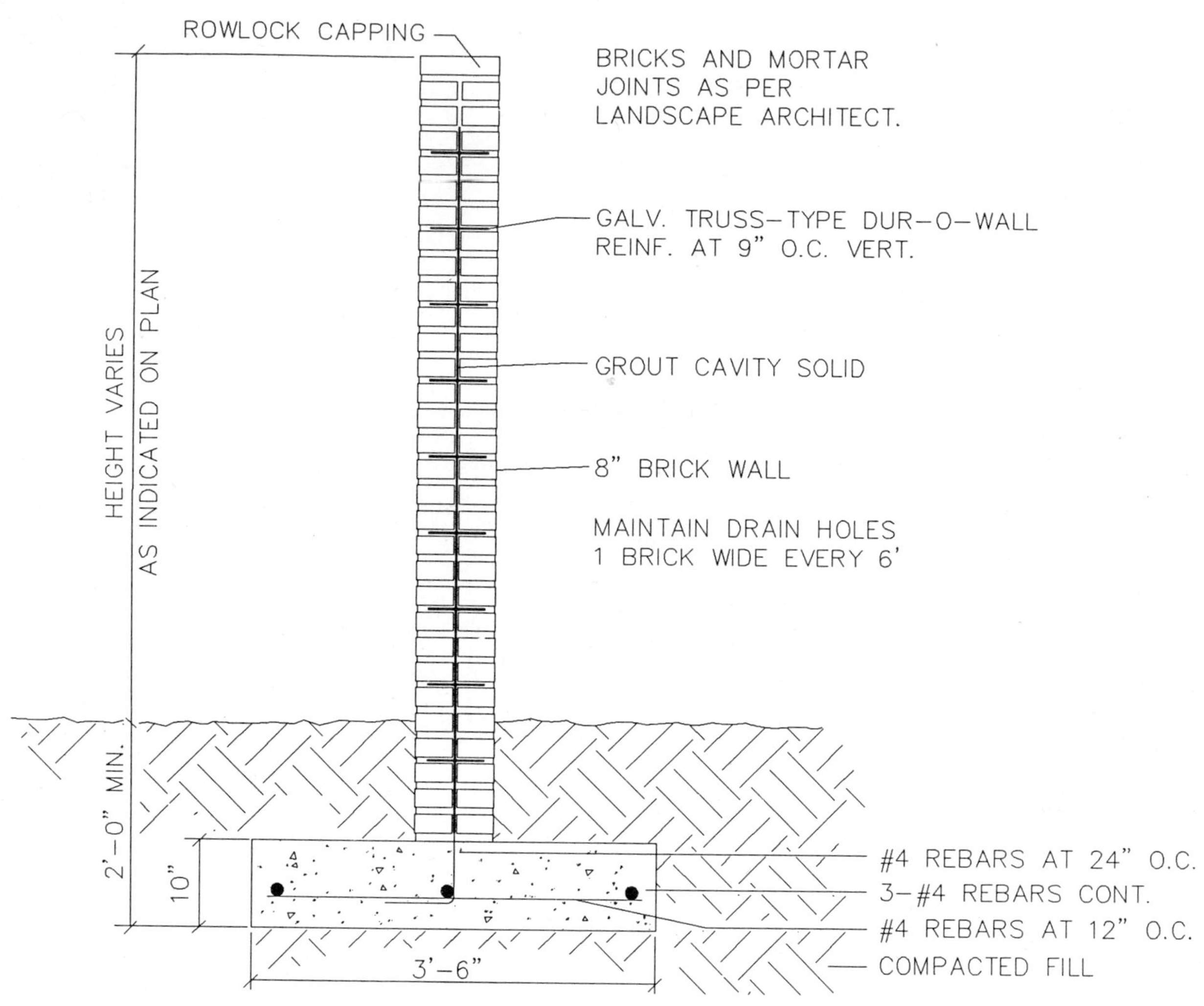
ROWLOCK CAPPING
BRICKS AND MORTAR
JOINTS AS PER
LANDSCAPE ARCHITECT.
GALV. TRUSS-TYPE DUR-O-WALL
REINF. AT 9" O.C. VERT.
GROUT CAVITY SOLID
8" BRICK WALL
MAINTAIN DRAIN HOLES
1 BRICK WIDE EVERY 6'
HEIGHT VARIES
AS INDICATED ON PLAN
2'-0" MIN.
10"
#4 REBARS AT 24" O.C.
3-#4 REBARS CONT.
#4 REBARS AT 12" O.C.
COMPACTED FILL
3'-6"

BRICK WALL SECTION

SCALE: NOT TO SCALE

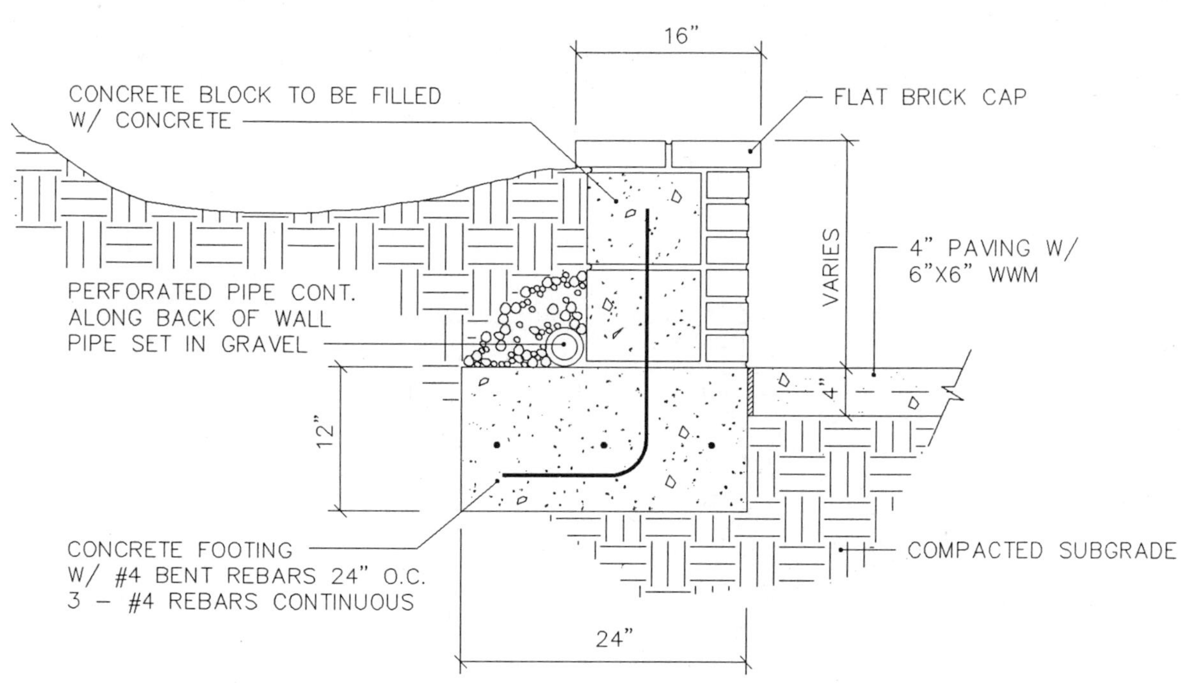
16"
CONCRETE BLOCK TO BE FILLED
W/ CONCRETE
FLAT BRICK CAP
VARIES
4" PAVING W/
6"X6" WWM
PERFORATED PIPE CONT.
ALONG BACK OF WALL
PIPE SET IN GRAVEL
4"
12"
CONCRETE FOOTING
W/ #4 BENT REBARS 24" O.C.
3 – #4 REBARS CONTINUOUS
COMPACTED SUBGRADE
24"

RETAINING / SEAT WALL

SCALE: NOT TO SCALE

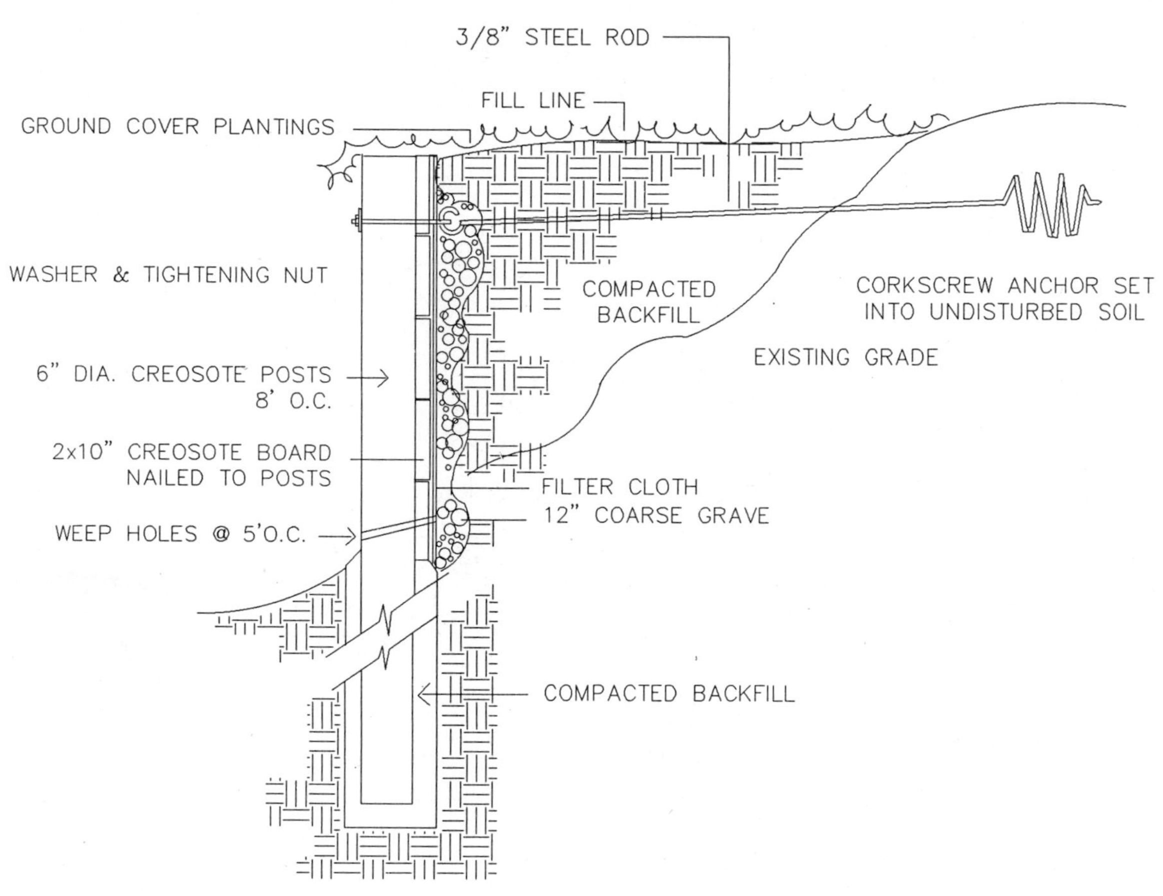
3/8" STEEL ROD
FILL LINE
GROUND COVER PLANTINGS
WASHER & TIGHTENING NUT
COMPACTED BACKFILL
CORKSCREW ANCHOR SET INTO UNDISTURBED SOIL
EXISTING GRADE
6" DIA. CREOSOTE POSTS 8' O.C.
2x10" CREOSOTE BOARD NAILED TO POSTS
FILTER CLOTH
12" COARSE GRAVE
WEEP HOLES @ 5'O.C.
COMPACTED BACKFILL

WOOD RETAINING WALL

SCALE: NOT TO SCALE

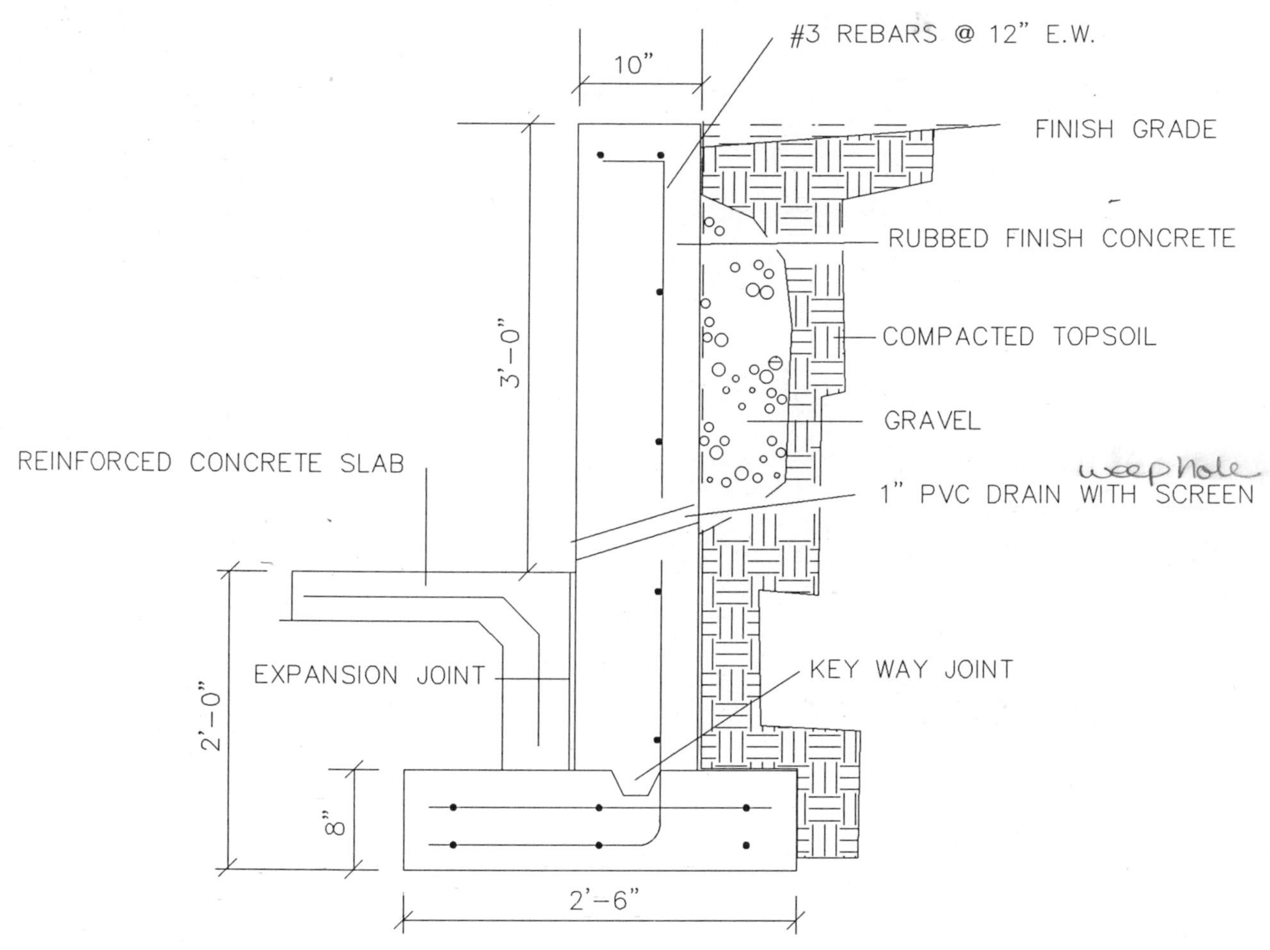

10"
#3 REBARS @ 12" E.W.
FINISH GRADE
RUBBED FINISH CONCRETE
COMPACTED TOPSOIL
3'–0"
GRAVEL
REINFORCED CONCRETE SLAB
1" PVC DRAIN WITH SCREEN
weep hole
EXPANSION JOINT
KEY WAY JOINT
2'–0"
8"
2'–6"

CONCRETE RETAINING WALL

SCALE: NOT TO SCALE

3/4" = 1.0'

RUNNING — BRICK BOND

SCALE: NOT TO SCALE

STACK — BRICK BOND

SCALE: NOT TO SCALE

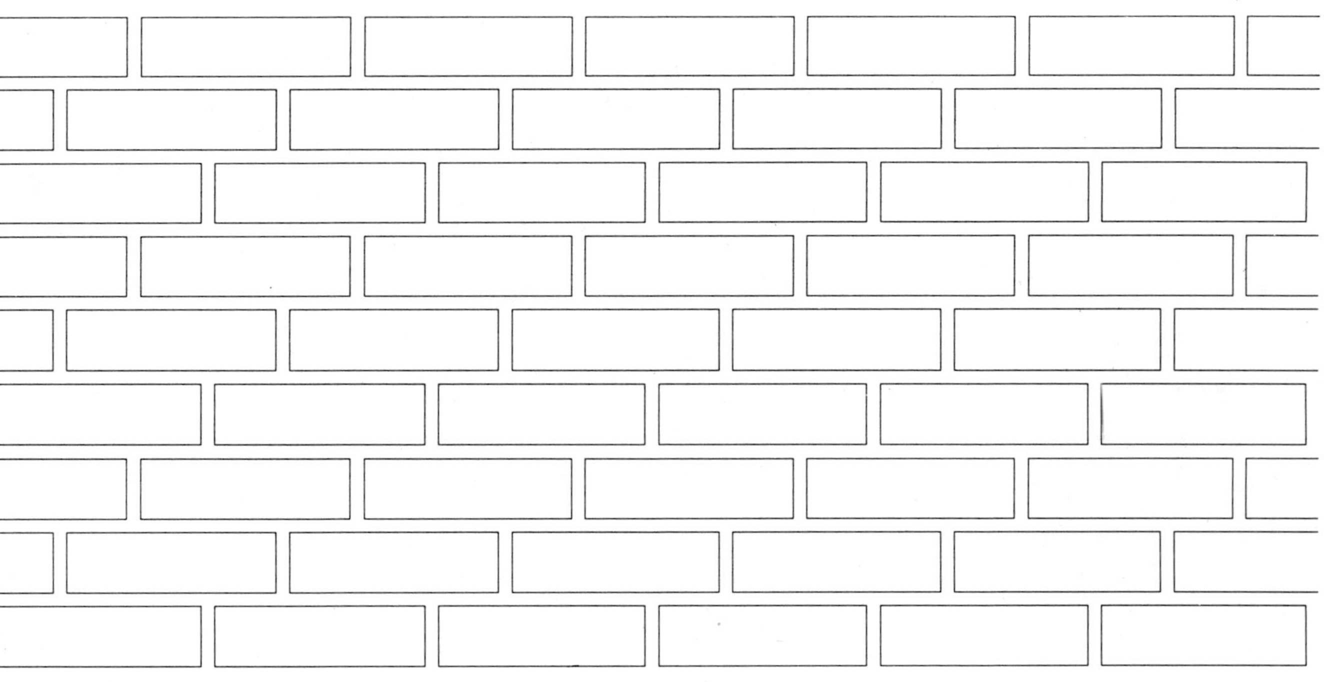

1/3 RUNNING – BRICK BOND

SCALE: NOT TO SCALE

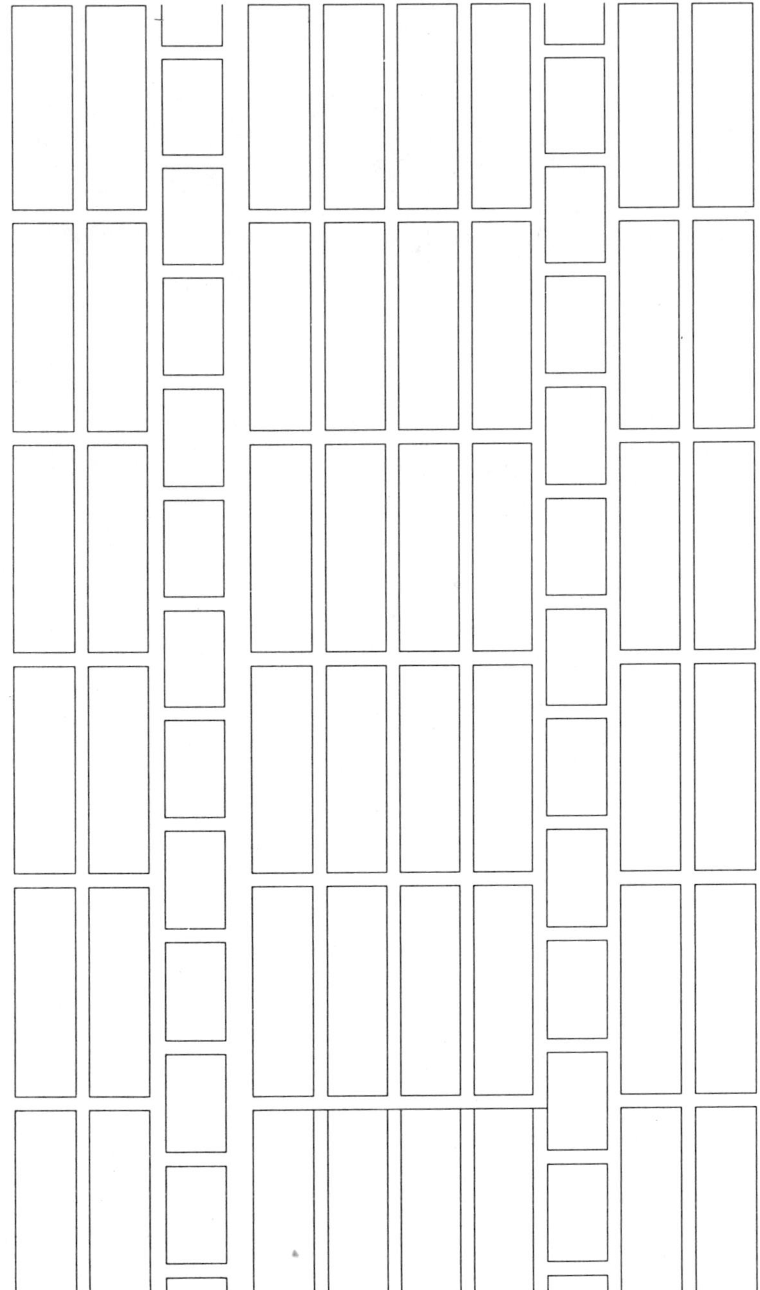

COMMON — BRICK BOND

SCALE: NOT TO SCALE

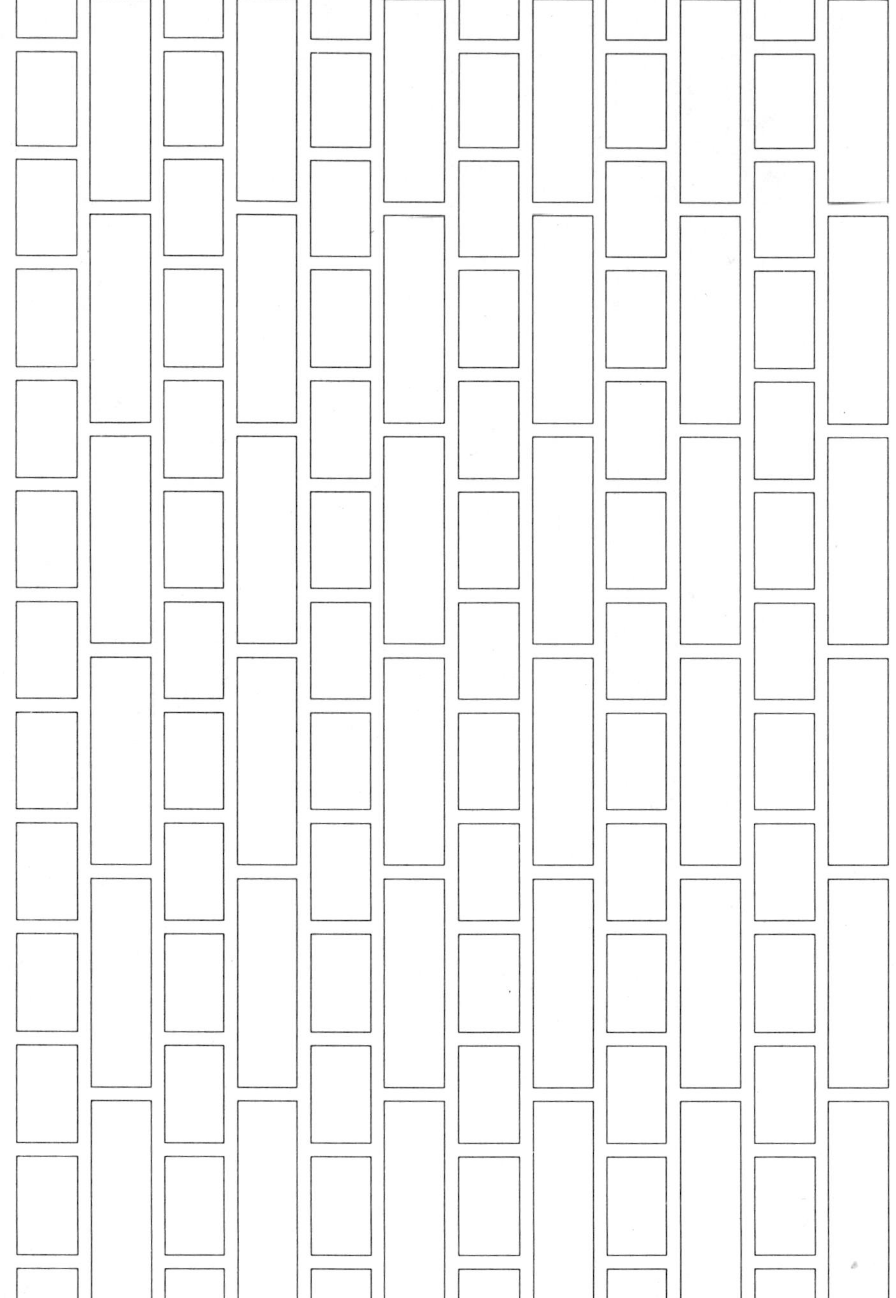

ENGLISH – BRICK BOND

SCALE: NOT TO SCALE

FLEMISH – BRICK BOND

SCALE: NOT TO SCALE

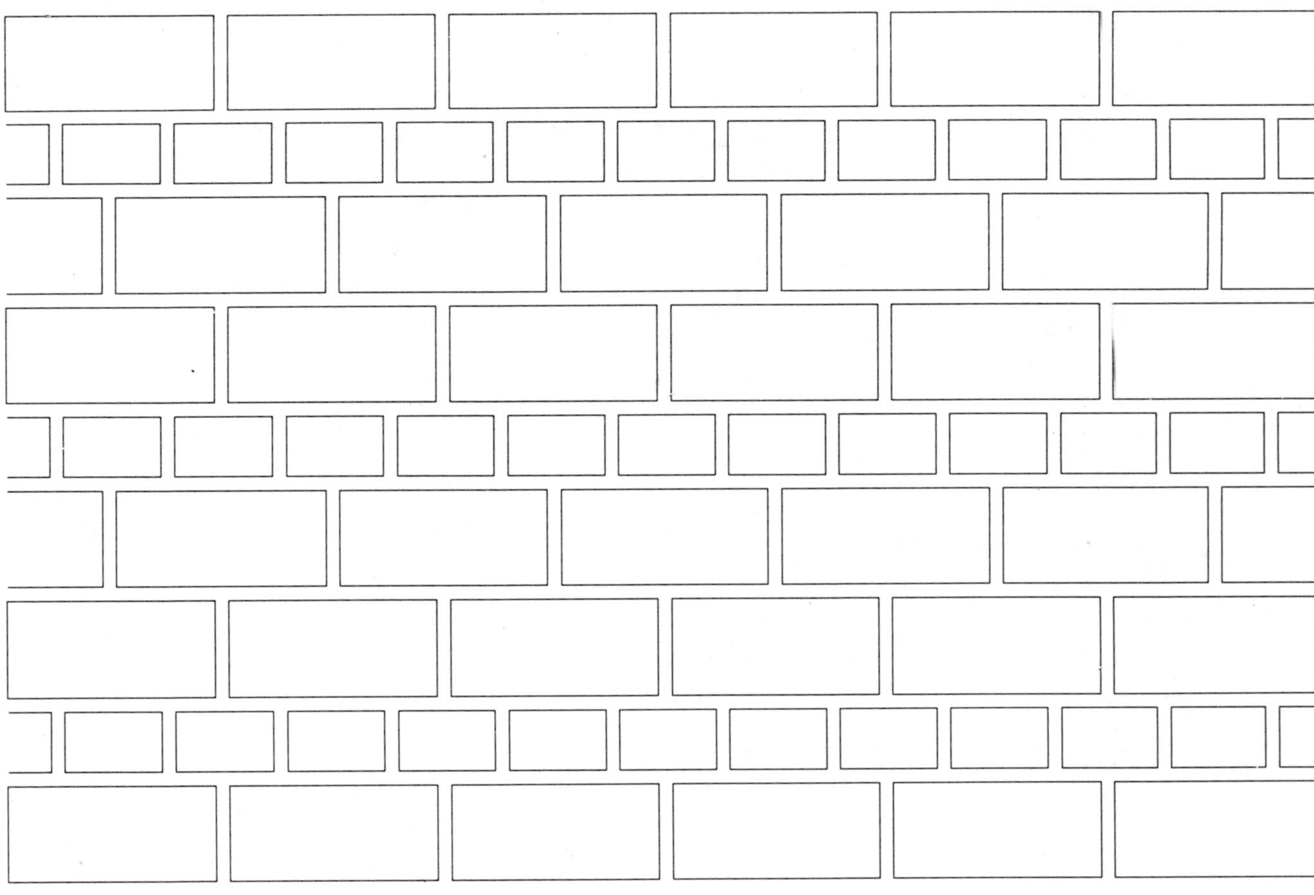

ROLOK — BRICK BOND

SCALE: NOT TO SCALE

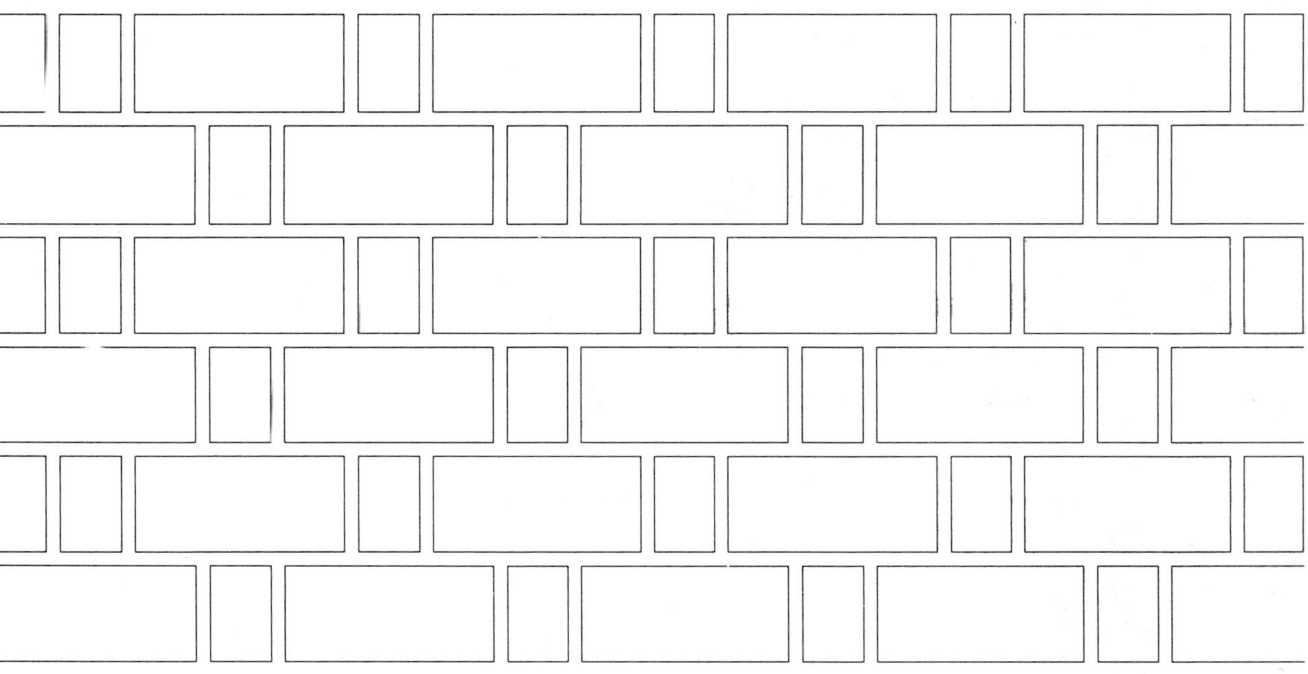

FLEMISH ROWLOCK — BRICK BOND

SCALE: NOT TO SCALE

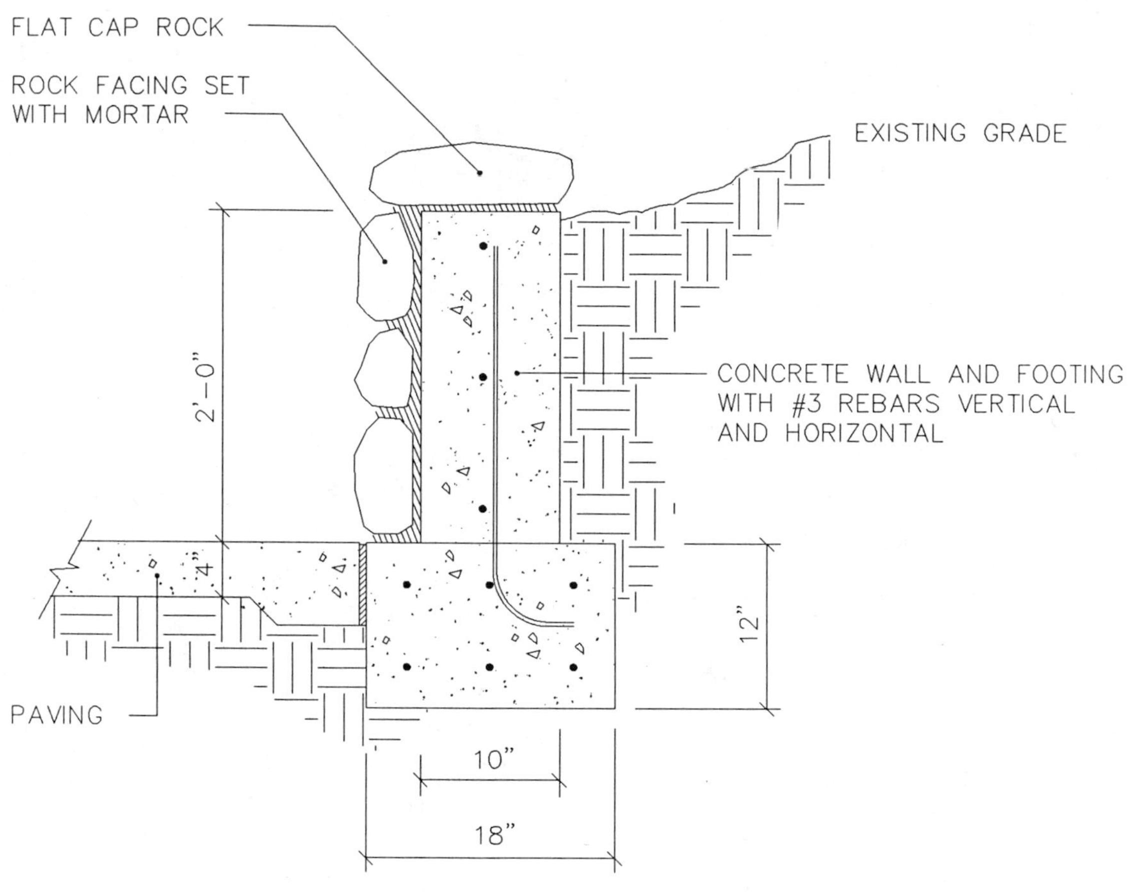

FLAT CAP ROCK
ROCK FACING SET WITH MORTAR
EXISTING GRADE
2'–0"
CONCRETE WALL AND FOOTING WITH #3 REBARS VERTICAL AND HORIZONTAL
4"
12"
PAVING
10"
18"

STONE FACED RETAINING WALL

SCALE: NOT TO SCALE

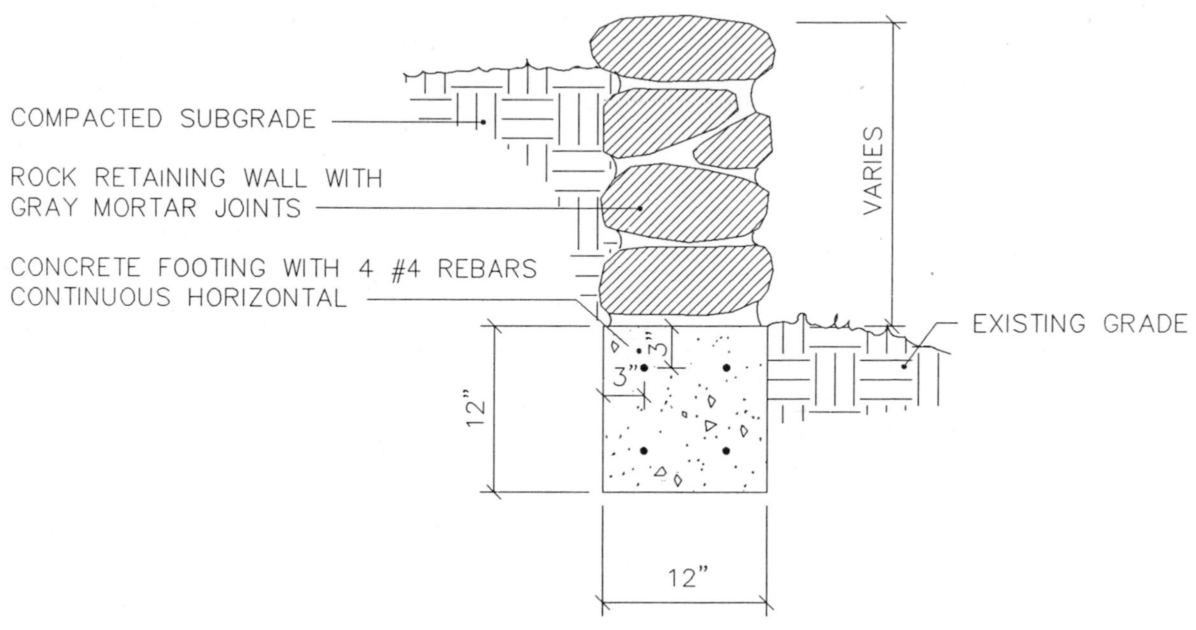
COMPACTED SUBGRADE
ROCK RETAINING WALL WITH
GRAY MORTAR JOINTS
CONCRETE FOOTING WITH 4 #4 REBARS
CONTINUOUS HORIZONTAL
VARIES
EXISTING GRADE
3"
3"
12"
12"

STONE RETAINING WALL

SCALE: NOT TO SCALE

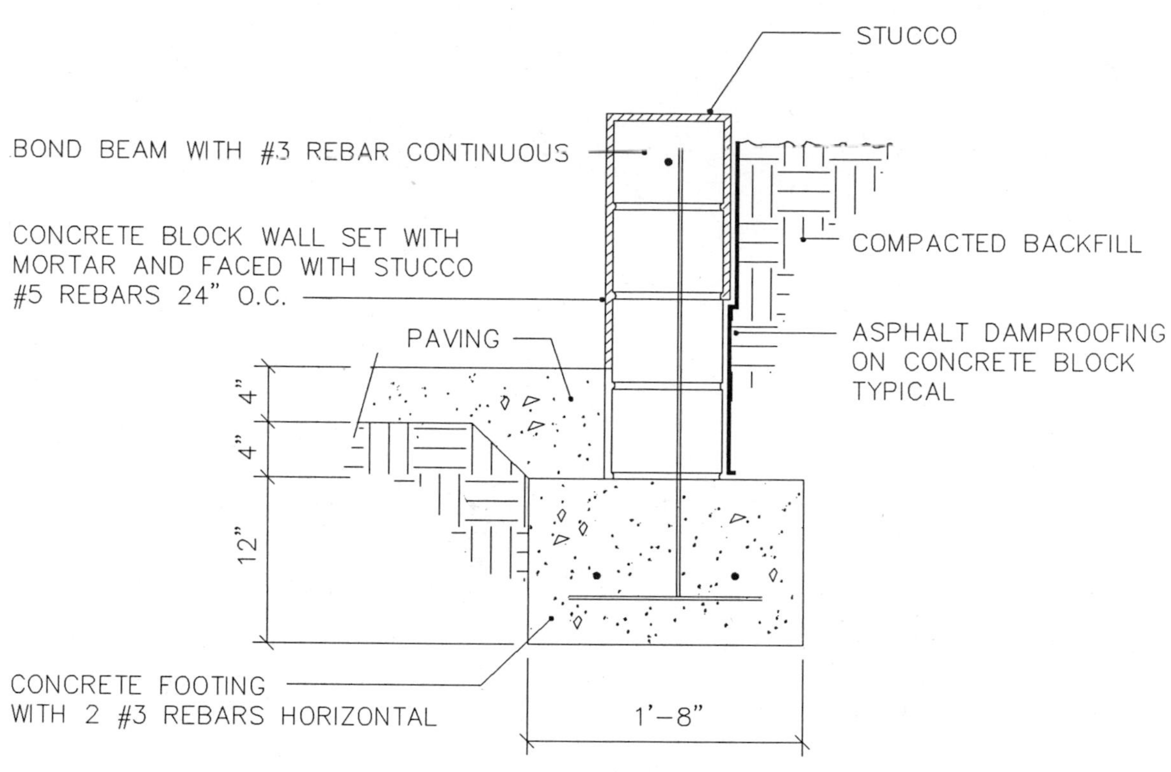
STUCCO
BOND BEAM WITH #3 REBAR CONTINUOUS
CONCRETE BLOCK WALL SET WITH
MORTAR AND FACED WITH STUCCO
#5 REBARS 24" O.C.
COMPACTED BACKFILL
PAVING
ASPHALT DAMPROOFING
ON CONCRETE BLOCK
TYPICAL
4"
4"
12"
CONCRETE FOOTING
WITH 2 #3 REBARS HORIZONTAL
1'–8"

STUCCO RETAINING WALL

SCALE: NOT TO SCALE

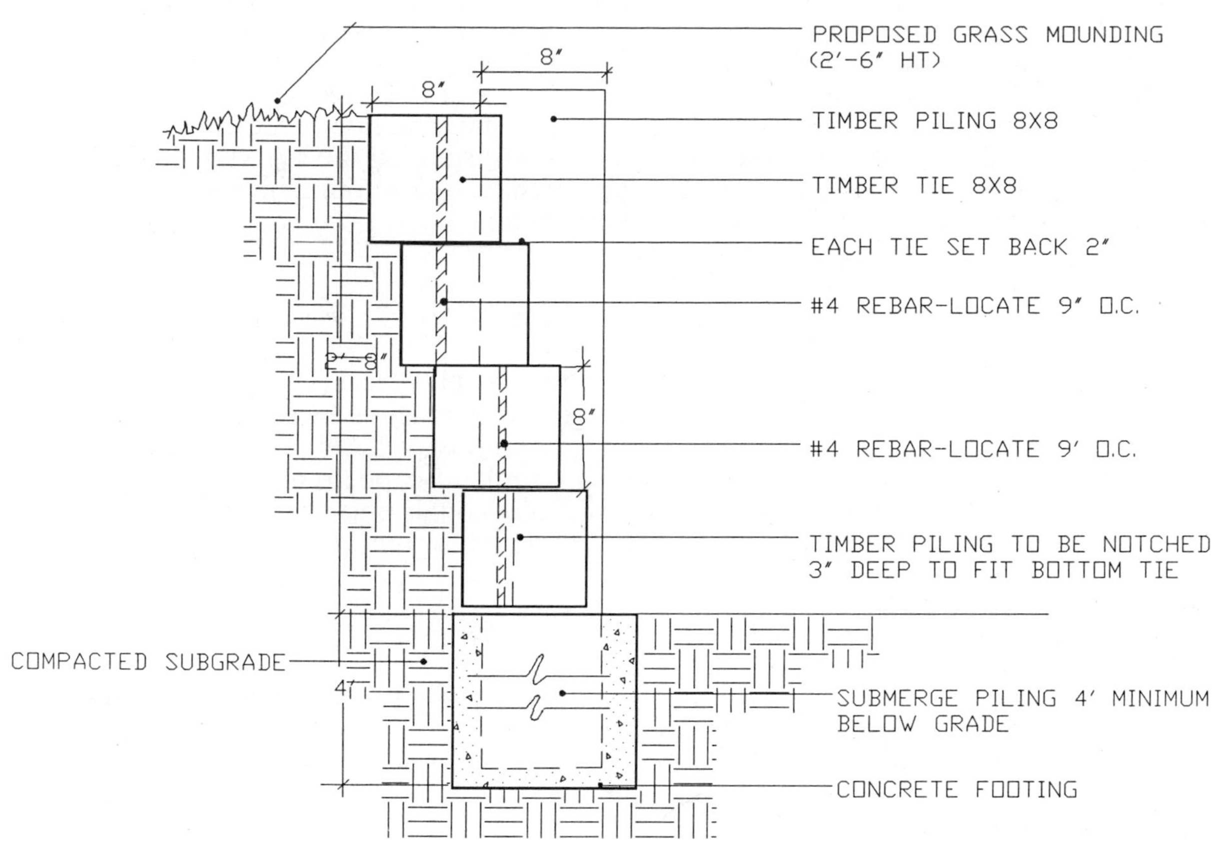
PROPOSED GRASS MOUNDING
(2'-6" HT)
8"
8"
TIMBER PILING 8X8
TIMBER TIE 8X8
EACH TIE SET BACK 2"
#4 REBAR-LOCATE 9" O.C.
2'-8"
8"
#4 REBAR-LOCATE 9' O.C.
TIMBER PILING TO BE NOTCHED
3" DEEP TO FIT BOTTOM TIE
COMPACTED SUBGRADE
4'
SUBMERGE PILING 4' MINIMUM
BELOW GRADE
CONCRETE FOOTING

RETAINING WALL DETAIL

SCALE: NOT TO SCALE

ABOUT THE AUTHORS

Gregory W. Jameson

Gregory W. Jameson, president of LANDCADD, Inc., is a member of the American Society of Landscape Architects and a registered landscape architect in Arizona. He graduated from Colorado State University with a bachelor of science in landscape architecture in 1980, and from the University of Arizona with a master of landscape architecture in 1983. At CSU, Jameson was a winner in the student design competition and was named an outstanding senior. At the University of Arizona, Jameson was selected to the Sigma Lambda Alpha national honor society and received an honor award from ASLA. In addition to running the LANDCADD office, he is an adjunct professor in landscape architecture at the University of Colorado in Denver. He also writes a regular column in *LA Computer News* and has been published in a variety of magazines.

Jameson began programming computers in 1974 and published his first commercially available program in 1975. His studies at both CSU and U of A involved computer applications for landscape architects. His career has been centered around making landscape architects more productive by using emerging technologies such as computer aided design. His company, LANDCADD, Inc., is recognized as the leading developer of software for landscape architects. This book is a further commitment to helping his fellow professionals enjoy the benefits of computer technology, even if they don't have access to a computer.

Michael A. Versen

Michael A. Versen is a principal landscape architect in Kendall-Versen, The Land Design Group of Knoxville, Tennessee, and Versen-Huh, The Land Design Group of Baton Rouge, Louisiana. Versen maintains landscape architectural professional registration in both Tennessee and Louisiana. He is a member of the American Society of Landscape Architects and a past president of the Louisiana Society of Landscape Architects. As a graduate of Louisiana State University's Bachelor of Landscape Architecture program in 1974, he was recognized as a selected member of Phi Beta Kappa Honorary Society. He was the recipient of the AILA National Design Competition Award in 1973 and the 1987 design award of merit winner for the National Parks Service-Women's Rights National Historical Park, Seneca Falls, New York. In addition to his private practice he has been a design instructor in the Department of Landscape Architecture at Louisiana State University.

Versen was one of the first landscape architects in the United States to utilize and convert his landscape architectural practice to a CAD system. His present work focuses on computer applications in a wide range of landscape architectural projects and is involved in training other offices on the use of CAD systems. This book is a natural evolution, integrating CAD into professional practice.

INDEX

T

U

V

W

Y